Dear Helen

Thank you for your fantastic support regarding the wadden book.

Yours John. / Last day of 2020 – and part of the EU

Ribe 700-1050

From Emporium to Civitas in Southern Scandinavia

To the generations of Ribe's antiquaries

Ribe 700-1050

From Emporium to Civitas in Southern Scandinavia

Morten Søvsø

Museum of Southwest Jutland

Jutland Archaeological Society

Ribe 700-1050: From Emporium to Civitas in Southern Scandinavia

RIBE STUDIER 2

© The author and Jutland Archaeological Society 2020

Layout and cover: Ea Rasmussen
Translation: John Hines
Graphics: Lars Foged Thomsen
Cover photo: Jens Karsten Jørgensen

Printed by Narayana Press, Gylling
Type: ITC New Baskerville
Paper: Arctic Volume White FSC
Binding: Buchbinderei Büge

Jutland Archaeological Society Publications 113

ISBN: 978-87-93423-52-7
ISSN: 0107-2854

Published in co-operation with
Museum of Southwest Jutland/Sydvestjyske Museer

Jutland Archaeological Society
Moesgård
DK-8270 Højbjerg

Distribution:
Aarhus University Press

Published with the support of:

Dronning Margrethe II's Arkæologiske Fond

Aage og Johanne Louis-Hansens Fond

VELUX FONDEN

Slots- & Kulturstyrelsen

Contents

Foreword

In 2006, Claus Feveile published *Det ældste Ribe* [The earliest Ribe], launching the publication series *Ribe Studier* [Ribe Studies]. The goal of that series was to make the core archaeological evidence from excavations in the town of Ribe between 1984 and 2000 accessible to the scholarly world and to give an account of Ribe's special status in the archaeological landscape of Denmark and northern Europe.

The present book, *Ribe 700-1050: From Emporium to Civitas in Southern Scandinavia,* is volume 2 in Ribe Studies. The main text here provides a comprehensive presentation and analysis of the archaeology of the town through to the end of the Viking Period. Alongside that, the book has a major topographical section which discusses West Jutland in this period and the connexions between Ribe and the hinterland of the town. In addition, a concluding chapter discusses the origin of towns in southern Scandinavia.

As will become clear in what follows, the earliest Ribe is a unique archaeological site within the borders of present-day Denmark — our only true *emporium* — and that this special status is both a blessing and a challenge when one has the privilege of working on the archaeology of the town.

Archaeologists working here are used to dealing with thousands of finds of glass beads, sherds of glass vessels, moulds and Carolingian pottery; finds of a kind that are exceptionally rare elsewhere in Denmark. How is this massive difference to be understood?

The whole situation is rendered no less complicated by the fact that the closest parallels to Ribe are found in our two neighbouring countries: namely at *Reric*, close to the village of Gross Strömkendorf north of Wismar in Mecklenburg-Vorpommern, and Åhus at the mouth of the Helge River in eastern Skåne. Ribe, Reric and Åhus have inevitably been studied within the frameworks of the legal situation and the research traditions of three different nations, with all of the barriers and differences that those will give rise to.

My hope is that this book about Ribe in the period AD 700-1050 will be able to explain exactly why Ribe is a unique site, and also why the study of the early towns is able not only to provide information about trading patterns but can be part of more general discussions concerning power and economy in those areas of land which were subsequently to become known as Denmark.

A supplementary aspiration, however, is that this book will succeed in crossing contemporary national borders, which impose constraints when one is engaged in research upon the Viking Age and the wide-ranging seaborne mobility that was characteristic of and defines that period.

The text was written in the period 2013-17 and has been updated down to the year 2020. The principal emphasis has been laid upon the archaeological features, rather than upon the artefactual finds. That selection was necessary in consideration of the size of the volume, but it is possible to access the massive collection of finds from Ribe in its entirety in digital form via the museum's on-line collection, accessible at *http://sol.sydvestjyskemuseer.dk*

Research into Ribe continues, and in 2017-18 the research excavation Northern Emporium funded by the Carlsberg Fund and under the leadership of Professor Søren M. Sindbæk from the Centre for Urban Network Evolutions at Aarhus University took place. This exciting project has, amongst other things, produced crucial new evidence about the settlement on the plots of the earliest Ribe. These results will be published separately and have, except for note 20 on page 156 and two sentences on page 169, not led to changes in the present text.

My heartfelt thanks to my colleagues in Sydvestjyske Museer, whose support and constructive criticism has had nothing but a positive effect on the quality of this book. Despite the fact that the museum in Ribe has grown in recent years it has been possible to maintain the excellent working culture which was characteristic of *Den antikvariske Samling* in its day. This sense of responsibility for curating research into Ribe and the history of the town is a constant factor in why the museum has been able to sustain quality in fulfilling its role and to carry out the comprehensive digitisation that has dominated work in recent years.

Finally, warm thanks to the grant-awarding bodies and authorities without whose assistance this book would not have been written. The VELUX FUND has provided support within the project '*1000 års mennesker*' [People over a Thousand Years], while the Castle and Culture Agency granted funds for the production of the manuscript. Translation, completion of illustrations, and the printing of the book are entirely funded by grants from Queen Margrethe II's Archaeological Fund and Aage and Johanne Louis-Hansen's Fund. Thanks to Professor John Hines, Cardiff University, for a particularly competent translation and valuable comments. The illustrations within the book have been completed and reworked by graphic draughtsman Lars Foged Thomsen, while the process of transforming the manuscript into a book has been in the safe hands of editor Jesper Laursen and illustrator Ea Rasmussen of the Jutlandic Archaeological Society.

Ribe, August 2020
Morten Søvsø

1. Introduction

What can Ribe tell us about the early history of the towns of Denmark? Were the earliest towns a product of top-down planning and of decisions taken by those in power at the time, or was the true driving force of this development the essentially uncontrollable hand of the market? What were the first towns like? Who lived there? How many people, and what were they doing? How did the towns change over time? To what extent were such changes the result of royal decrees – for instance in respect of minting, or the establishment of a castle; or consequences of much higher level political factors such as the division of the Frankish Empire after the Treaty of Verdun of AD 843; or reflexes of wide-ranging changes in the flow of goods between the trading networks such as the opening up of trade routes to the Caliphate via the Russian rivers? Could global climatic conditions also have played a part? This series of major questions is central to research into urban history, and they will be discussed in this book using the town of Ribe as the primary case study.

The earliest Scandinavian towns did not appear in a void but were rather buds which grew on an expanding northern European trading network, the nodes of which, the *emporia*, quite literally rose up on the ruins of the Roman urban civilization in the course of the 7th century. In areas where some elements of Roman urban culture had survived, such as the Upper Rhineland, marked continuity between the Roman towns and the emporia is evident (Ellmers 1984), while in other areas only weak connexions, if any, between the older and the newer towns can be seen. The latter situation characterizes the Rhine mouth and the southern coastal regions of the North Sea (Hodges 1989). In Scandinavia, which had not previously had any towns, the appearance of the emporia also represents the introduction of urbanization *per se*.

The boundaries of the study are therefore those of the primary phase of the history of towns in Scandinavia, a period in relation to which scholarly research has struggled to achieve any consensus on the character of its town-like trading sites which, like the later towns, were decisively moulded by trade and craft-production but which appear to a very large extent – in the 8th century at least – to lack the religious and administrative institutions that are typical of the classic medieval towns. The early towns have been labelled *ports of trade, proto-towns, emporia* or *wīcs*, while here and there one encounters the very general German term *Seehandelsplatz* 'marine trading site' or just *trading site*. In this book, which is a product of tradition, the word *town* is preferred – and as the term for both the earlier and the later variants (Skre 2007b). Following the publication of Richard Hodges's book *Dark Age Economics* (1982; 2nd ed. 1989: abbreviated as *DAE*), the early towns experienced a blossoming of research and theoretical study, which the immensely informative evidence from Ribe regrettably played only a relatively peripheral role in. Ribe has rather been discussed first and foremost within the boundaries of the kingdom of Denmark, and was not only a feature of *Projekt Middelalderbyen* "The Medieval Town Project", which did not have any dedicated theoretical strand, but also of the nationally focussed project *Fra Stamme til Stat* "From Tribe to State". The Medieval Town Project was attached to the sub-discipline of Medieval Archaeology and was focussed upon the slightly later, classic medieval town, while From Tribe to State was attached to Prehistoric Archaeology, and town-formation played a minor part in it. For structural reasons, the field of research into early urbanization thus fell between two stools: a problem of approach that has also affected research in the other Nordic countries (Skre 2007a, 47). The Kaupang Project of 2000-2 and the publications it produced, the publication of *Ribe Studier I: Det ældste Ribe* (Feveile ed. 2006), and a new generation of internationally oriented scholars has, however, revitalized this field of research in the last two recent decades (Sindbæk 2007; Kalmring 2010; Arents & Eisenschmidt 2010).

The theoretical discussion in this book forms Chapter 2, *Theory*, which by way of introduction seeks to develop my own epistemological standpoint, after which the focus turns to the emporia and the theoretical discussion that they have been part of. Many other topics – the social structure of the Later Iron Age; the emergence of centralized power; numismatics, and more – are elements of the book, but an exhaustive theoretical discussion of those fields too would burst the banks.

To shed light upon the themes of the book, the focus in the following study lies first and foremost upon the incredibly rich archaeological material from excavations in and around Ribe. The background to the selection is the fact that the archaeological evidence from the town is of wider chronological range than at any other Scandinavian urban site, and also, for the most of the period in question, is of a breadth and density that makes it possible to produce a quite detailed account of the varying topography and economy of the town through time – as shown by the archaeological evidence.

The antiquarian tradition in Ribe is long and extensive, and has, over time, generated a substantial volume of scholarly literature, formally moulded by successive dominant questions or theories – some of which are still current while others have now been set aside. Despite the great quantity of past studies, not until now has a comprehensive history of scholarship been produced. In order to establish a clear view of the shifting paradigms of different ages that have governed the archaeology of the town, this book also presents a relatively comprehensive history of research in Chapter 3.

This book will attempt to answer three key questions:

1. Why and how did Ribe emerge?

A primary requirement for this question to be answered must be knowledge of the society in which Ribe emerged around the year 700. Precisely that period of the Later Germanic Iron Age has traditionally stood as an archaeological gap between a rich body of earlier evidence ranging over graves, settlements, weapon hoards and more which runs into the 6th century AD, and after it the Viking Period's equally rich archaeological evidence supplemented by overseas sources, runestones, etc. (Näsman 1991; 2006).

The explosion in the use of metal-detectors in recent years has, however, radically increased quantities of finds, including material from the Later Germanic Iron Age. Particularly in combination with the cartographic evidence that is now available in the form of cadastral ('matriculation') maps and more, a path has been opened for retrogressive settlement studies, which together with palaeoclimatic research and the so-called Church List in the Ribe Oldemoder (= 'Great-Grandmother') manuscript creates the basis for a topographical analsyis of society and settlement in West Jutland throughout the first millennium AD. This constitutes Chapter 4 of the book, *Topography*.

2. How did Ribe develop in the period AD 700-1050 – in both topographical and economic terms?

The earliest Ribe is known only through excavations, and all of those have been constrained by the fact that there is still a living town above the layers from earlier periods. South of the river, the cathedral itself is the oldest surviving building, founded around 855, while the street plan around it was laid out in the 11th century and has survived pretty much unchanged to the present day, even though the town has, in the intervening centuries, risen up to 5 metres higher because of the deposition of thick culture layers within it. The sequence of culture layers is generally well preserved, and has outstanding potential for tracing the history of the urban zone through stratigraphical excavation. On the other hand, all of the traces of the Viking-period land-surface are hidden below the thick layers, and knowledge of what that landscape looked like has to be gained through excavation.

On the northern side of the river, where the original Ribe was sited, there are no surviving structures, and the area has generally had the character of a suburb ever since the Middle Ages, and been used in a wide variety of ways (Fig. 1). Some parts have been farmed intensively, leading to the complete destruction of the underlying stratigraphy, while others were sealed below culture layers as early as the Middle Ages and so have been extremely well protected from damage. Proximity to the town is thus, for better or worse, the factor which means that the state of preservation of the earliest elements of Ribe varies hugely, in stark contrast to the conditions that are typical of the other Viking-period towns of Scandinavia. An understanding of the taphonomic factors is of fundamental importance for any assessment of what the archaeological evidence tells us.

It will be clear, that Ribe as an entire Ancient Monument is both massively complicated and extremely rich in information which has allowed the town's archaeologists to develop a very intimate grasp of the development of the town and its inhabitants. The most recent overview of the archaeological evidence was published in 2006, but a great deal of new information has come in since then. In connexion with this study, the evidence from Ribe has been reviewed and analysed, and so forms the basis of the most substantial chapter of the book, Chapter 5, *Ribe 700-1050*, in which the development of the town from the *single-street along the river bank plan* of the 8th century to the 10th-century *D-shaped enclosure* to the 11th-century *civitas* is examined against the background of the archaeological excavations.

Through the archaeological discoveries in Ribe it is possible to document unbroken urban development

Fig. 1. Techt's map of Ribe from 1858 was the source for the town plan in the first edition of Trap's Statisk-topographisk Beskrivelse af Danmark. *In addition to the information provided on the map itself, numbers in red mark a series of key components of the town's essential topography. 1: the cathedral, south of the river; 2: the north side of the river; 3: Ribe Østerå (East River); 4: Ribe Vesterå (West River); 5: River Tved; 6: the Stamping Mill Leat; 7: the Dam. After the original held by the national Geodata Agency with additions by the author.*

from around the year 700 onwards. The town changed radically several times over. A church was founded as early as the 9th century, and this provides us with an as yet unique opportunity to observe how the town responded to its presence. As will appear, the town continued to stand, unaffected, where it had been all the time, until some time in the 11th century, and was, amongst other things, at a certain provided with defences where the church had already been located on the other side of the river for a considerable time. Only around the year 1050 did the town relocate towards the church, and so conformed to the civitas-model that is typical of the classic medieval town. That concurrently defines the later chronological limit of this book.

3. Can a model for the development of Ribe be applied to other early towns in southern Scandinavia?

In Chapter 6 of the book, *Urbanization in southern Scandinavia AD 700-1050*, the angle of view is widened to include the other early towns of southern Scandinavia. This section focuses on Denmark, which means that the Swedish emporium of Birka is omitted in what follows, along with other trading places on the southern Baltic shores which can scarcely have been under the control of the Danish kingship: Ralswiek, Wolin, Truso, and more (Kleingärtner 2014).

At a basic level, this study distinguishes between two concepts of the town: the *emporium model* and the *civitas model*. The emporia served as the primary nodal points in the maritime trading network and were from the outset – or very rapidly fell – under royal control. On the merchants' sailing routes there were a number of minor stopping places, landing sites, of varying size and character, the larger of which might also be trading sites, probably controlled by local powers. These provided a basic root for what would later grow into the classic medieval town, and are represented by the towns of:

* Ribe
* Reric/Hedeby/Schleswig
* Åhus
* Kaupang
* Aarhus

The so-called 'central places' of the Iron Age provide another basic stock root for a later group of towns, whose role was to serve as religious and administrative centres for the Christian monarchy. These towns emerged after the Conversion in the decades either side of the year 1000 and are referred to collectively in this book as the *civitas model*, a Christian notion of the urban phenomenon, inspired by an idealized model of the heavenly Jerusalem, *Civitas Jerusalem*, which in the 11th century came also to transform the earlier emporia. The central places appear in some cases to have their origins right back in the Earlier Iron Age, and they share the characteristics of being centrally located in relation to land-traffic; of apparently having been the home sites of a chieftainly dynasty; and of being the sites of religious or political central functions organized around sacrifices and feasts – in other words, a way of life rooted in the pre-Christian religious sphere (L. Jørgensen 2014). They vary greatly in size and presumably also in importance. Gudme, Tissø, Lejre, Uppåkra and Sorte Muld are the largest known sites in historical Denmark. In this book, towns such as:

* Viborg
* Odense
* Roskilde
* Lund

are suggested to be representatives of this model. A number of further towns could have been included in the analysis. Aalborg clearly goes back to the 11th century, but the most recent, important excavations have yet to be published. Næstved too has archaeological features from the Viking Period, but these finds are not adequately published either. Other towns with early finds or mints such as Randers, Horsens, Slagelse and Copenhagen could have been included as well, but it is considered that the towns selected sufficiently illustrate the structural development of urbanization.

References within the volume are given in brackets in the text, and every effort has been made to keep footnotes to a minimum. The bibliography follows the style guide used in Danish Journal of Archaeology. Unless otherwise indicated, the figures and tables have been produced by the author, and the maps are oriented with north to the top. All levels are in meters above sea level following the Danish DNN standard.

The Danish chronology used in the text is as follows:

Neolithic (c. 3900-1700 BC)
Bronze Age (c. 1700-500 BC)
Pre-Roman Iron Age (c. 500-1 BC)
Early Roman Iron Age (c. AD 1-200)
Late Roman Iron Age (c. AD 200-400)
Early Germanic Iron Age (c. AD 400-550)
Late Germanic Iron Age (c. AD 550-800)
Viking Age (c. AD 800-1050)
Early Medieval (c. AD 1050-1250)
High Medieval (c. AD 1250-1400)
Late Medieval (c. AD 1400-1550)
Early Modern (c. AD 1550-1800)
Modern (c. AD 1800-)

2. Aspects of the theoretical discussion of towns and their origins in northern Europe

What has happened will happen again,
and what has been done will be done again,
and there is nothing new under the sun.
(Ecclesiastes 1,9: New English Bible*)*

2.1 Starting point

My own position in respect of archaeological theory is that I do not find it difficult to see inadequacies in all sorts of theoretical approaches, whether or not one can attach the labels of 'culture history', 'processual archaeology' or 'post-processual archaeology' to them. The two latter waves, which particularly emphasize the importance of archaeological theory, are very nearly the worst, having emerged as they did as reform movements, whose primary *modus operandi* would always be to create a platform that is based on attacks on the current state of affairs. Archaeological research that leans very firmly upon a theoretical attitude will all too frequently prove to be the range of literature which most rapidly appears dated. Paraphrasing the Danish author Tom Kristensen, I would say: 'Fear theory and nurture it not, for it is a load upon your back.' And it is also a theory dependent upon my own highly empirical starting point whose utility I hope the following text will demonstrate.

While such a critically negative view of theorizing comes rather naturally to me, it is certainly harder to try to formulate a better or more precise theoretical alternative. This reveals my own existential doubt about how realistic that project is at all, and at the same time my (theoretical) association with the post-modern/post-processual tradition. I cannot refute the proposition that knowledge and theory are social constructs which a critical perspective can reduce to being subjective products of the producer's consciousness – formed by that subject's experiences, desires and cultural background. As a reluctant constructivist, I likewise have no wish to deny that the language spoken and written does to a certain extent shape what we call

'reality', even in respect of Prehistory. But the world is not purely a linguistic or social construct. It exists in reality, where the human body and senses are also found. There is therefore more than language there, but the obscure relationship between language and reality constitutes a real set of problems which lead to relativism and solipsism (Foucault 1966).

As a philosophical movement, this position can be followed down through the ages from the Sophists of Classical Greece onwards. In the second half of the 20th century it has had major influence on sociology and anthropology, with the French philosopher Michel Foucault as a core figure. From there, archaeological theory has been influenced too.

Social constructivism claims that human cognition is a social construct that is tied to the language. In its current incarnation social constructivism was supposed to be a politically left-leaning liberation project that aimed to break down and completely transform the inherited, supposedly bourgeois, conceptual systems concerning sex, power, sexuality, normality, and more. The debate has changed many western societies and sharpened the perception of how language does to an extent form reality, but the deconstruction of scientific conceptual systems has in recent years proved apt to exploitation from different corners of the political playground in order to sow doubt about well-established 'truths' of the natural or social sciences, on the subjects of climate change, social economy, migration, etc. The so-called post-factual society – *perception is reality* – can thus be said to be a product of social constructivism. And here, the revolution has ended up eating its own children.

Motivation-hunters might allege that this position of resignation is born of a contemporary recognition of the fact that the relationship between the research and the object of study is at best suspect (Foucault 1966; Latour 1991), and the current perspective is rather that a range of geopolitical constructs and systems appear ever more uncontrollable, whether that be global financial markets or political structures such as the United States, the European Union, or the Russian Federation. The world, both then and now, does not appear to contain some hidden order, purpose or regularity, but rather a so-far generally growing human population whose past presence in the world is the archaeologist's field of study. This population has always been resourceful, and through the work of hands and spirit turned itself in new directions and away from others.

The frequently criticised 'culture-historical' archaeology formerly developed a series of methods for working with the evidence of the populations of previous ages in the form of typological classification, analogies and distributions. The understanding that lay behind those was that human behaviour is not purely random but rather is meaningfully structured in various ways. Through the interpretation of archaeological remains it was possible to generate knowledge of life in Prehistory. These methodological approaches are still the building blocks of archaeology: inductively, they can be put together and interpreted to produce narratives of the past, and they will continue to serve in that way even while new scientific methods produce new archaeological data.

This book is concerned with the Late Germanic Iron Age (550-800 AD) and the Viking Period (800-1050 AD) in northern Europe: a period of time which scholars connected to different university disciplines and different theoretical traditions have worked on. Prehistoric archaeology swiftly absorbed inspiration from processual archaeology and so from anthropology, and with that orientation came a long series of interesting works concerned with the structure and development of prehistoric societies. As a new concept, a deductive approach was applied as well. Because society was assumed to conform to various laws, these over-riding theories could be applied to the empirical evidence and advance the interpretations beyond what traditionally that evidence had seemed able to provide information on. That the deductive method would be successful, however, is not a given; rather it stands or falls with the quality of the theory applied and the representativity of the archaeological evidence in relation to the specific issue.

The inspiration provided by anthropology meanwhile also introduced the use of various social models that differed greatly from, for instance, historically known conditions in Europe. Access to these marked a clear new break in relation to previous scholarship, and silently and willingly constructed a beguiling prehistoric Otherness, in which social codes reduced prehistoric people to pale shadows, devoid of free will and governed by an alien set of norms. *The past is a foreign country. They do things dif-*

ferently there (Hartley 1953). This social-constructivist narrative is still a powerful one in archaeological theory, and cannot be denied some degree of validity – for instance if the object of study is some form of 'tribe' or a culture group that cannibalistically had its own kind on the menu, or put all of its efforts in to hewing colossal sculptures, as on Easter Island; but if the premiss of Otherness is accepted, it is also necessary to ask, how did it come about, then, that *they* became *us*? Here, we move into disputed ground concerning the relationship between the 'I' and the world, one end-point of which is solipsism: the destructive view that one can only really be certain of one's own existence.

Is the supposition of Otherness valid in the case of northern Europe in the Viking Period too? And if *they* were something different, what are *we* then? This problematization of the relationship between the researcher and the object of study (Latour 1991) or, in terms of phenomenology, the relationship between the Self and the Other,[1] has only been pursued in Danish archaeological theoretical discussions to a limited extent, although it occupies a key place in sociology. In recent years, Bruno Latour in particular has problematized the relationship between the researcher and the object of study, and of the other pairs of opposites which form the building stones of structuralist-influenced research traditions, and pointed out that the analytic division into binary opposites rests upon a non-existent basic premiss of separation. The position is emblematically summed up in the title *We have never been modern*, which thus directs attention to the view that the assumption of contrasts of nature/culture, ideal/reality, language/reality and objectivity/subjectivity, which have been key pillars of the Western philosophical tradition since the Enlightenment, is, according to Latour's reading, an illusion.

The university disciplines of Medieval Archaeology and History have been concerned with rather less distant periods of time, and have been furnished with a corrective in the form of written sources, which are quite profuse for the more recent periods but reduce the further back one goes. From the very nature of the evidence, one is often working retrospectively, and much available information about both society and its individuals has made anthropologically derived models less convincing. The view of people in the distant past has emphasized the similarities between then and now more than the differences. In a more or less pure form, this fundamental and epistemologically based difference in views of the past runs throughout most studies of the Viking Period, and for that reason I shall attempt to clarify the position that I am seeking to work from.

The colossal and continually growing body of archaeological evidence from Denmark (for reasons of preservation, primarily Jutland) clearly shows that the overwhelmingly dominant agrarian society was characterized by a high degree of continuity from at latest the emergence of the villages in the Earlier Iron Age down to the Early Modern Period. There is a strong correlation between the fertility of the land, the level of population, and the relative wealth of the region as it is reflected in the archaeological evidence. At especially favoured places in the landscape chieftain's farms appeared, and/or central places in many cases, and these aristocratic sites can be traced from some time in the Iron Age through to the post-medieval period. Despite changes in climate and in the style of farming, these differences remained, irrespective of whether they were functioning within a heathen or a Christian conceptual world. There is more on this in Chapter 4 of this book, *Topography*.

Throughout the first two millennia AD, far and away the predominant basis of economic production seems to have been the farm, the architecture of which leaves no room to doubt that these were operated by families. Concurrently, the evidence from the cemeteries of various periods, and other archaeological remains, are consistent with this image of an agrarian society structured around family-operated farms, for which natural boundaries in the landscape imposed a framework upon separated, agricultural village communities, which would later be known as village lands (ejerlav). This situation effectively constitutes a long-lived and fully comprehensive social structure, which in turn produced the continuous undertone of southern Scandinavian society. There was no original system of social equality or inequality, but, just as now, some were more successful than others. In contrast to nowadays, kinship apparently meant more for the opportunities for social mobility an individual had. The social and the religious frameworks were closely inter-woven despite the far from insignificant changes in religious practice within the period, both before the Conversion (Fabech 1991) and of course following it. The religious centre at Uppåkra was succeeded by the religious centre at Lund. The discussion about social strata in the Iron Age and Viking Period is a complex one, but the simple models of processualism, involving a social pyramid divided into a certain number of layers, fit ever more poorly with the archaeological evidence, and in Chapter 4, *Topography*, a model is proposed which is inspired to a greater degree by the better known conditions of the (Christian) Middle Ages, when different groups within society – the aristocracy, farmers and craftspeople – are also known each to have been internally highly variegated social units, with great differences even within a given status.

Throughout this book, there runs a sense of history as continuity, in which attempts are made to illuminate earlier situations through retrogressive analyses starting from better understood later conditions. For this 'search for the same' to overlook other crucial elements is a risk, but the method does also reveal a series of slow-moving, coherent structures in the society of western Jutland that it can be proposed will also be discoverable in other regions of Denmark.

Evolutionary biology appears not to question that there is only one human being, irrespective of skin colour, head-shape, place of residence or dates of life. For the same reason, we can also assert at the outset that prehistoric people were like us, and not an Otherness of social constructivism. This does not mean that we can necessarily understand or act our way into the thoughts of the merchants who sailed to Ribe in the 8th century; but the challenge of understanding others is to a high degree also a contemporary problem. Humanity then was just as capable of everything as now, and has never been 'modern' (Latour 1991).

2.2 What is a town?

The question which forms the title of this section is a necessary part of a book on just this subject, and represents a discussion which can expand very widely or be narrowed down considerably. The urban phenomenon appears in different cultures throughout the panorama of Prehistory, and is difficult to understand other than as a form of organization that arises when a certain proportion of a society's agrarian surplus produce is redistributed to other sections of the society which are not primarily engaged in agriculture. The result in such a case will usually be towns or town-like structures, such as emerged independently in various parts of the world: for instance, in different periods, in the Middle East and Central America.

If the view is focussed in upon European contexts, there has also been a long discussion of the definition of what is 'urban' (Hodges 1989, 20ff; Hohenberg & Lees 1995; Kleingärtner 2014). Early on, this discussion was led by historians, geographers, economists and sociologists, and was concerned with the history of the towns as known from existing examples and written sources. The topic was either the Roman towns or the northern European towns from around the year 1000 onwards. The *Dark Ages*, the period AD 500-1000, was regarded as essentially without towns.

With the gradual discovery of Carolingian, Frisian, Anglo-Saxon and Scandinavian trading sites during the 20th century a phenomenon was revealed with an archaeological footprint that did not fit into the established classificational system, and a series of other terms were developed instead, which in their variety reflect a basic consensus that *Dark Age urbanism* was indeed a form of urban life, albeit different from that of later periods. There was, however, no agreement over how those differences should be understood. The early towns were called *ports of trade* (Polanyi 1963), *proto-towns* (Clarke & Simms 1985; Näsman 2000), *emporia* or *wīcs* (Hodges 1989), together with the general expression *Seehandelsplatz* ('marine trading site') or just *trading site*. To complicate matters even more, terms such as *central place* have also been used in the debate over the towns of this period, albeit embracing two different senses of the term: the first the geographical sense deriving from Walter Christaller, and the other as a term for a Scandinavian elite residence (Hodges 1989, 16f; Skre 2007c, 335ff).

Against this slightly confused background, I shall attempt here to explicate the terminology that I shall be using in respect of Ribe and the other southern Scandinavian sites which are the topic of the present book.

2.2.1 Central places

It seems to be agreed that the Germanic 'tribal' areas in north-western Europe had no true towns even though their elite circles were widely familiar with Roman urban civilization. In southern Scandinavia there were, instead, what are known as central places, housing elite residences within which social and religious leadership were closely inter-woven. In the case of Scandinavia, the term 'central place' is synonymous with an elite residence of the Iron Age or the Viking Period, while in cultural geography it is a component within a hierarchical model of (medieval) towns (Høilund Nielsen 2014). These twin senses have, to greater or lesser extents, been merged in several works, but in this book I shall restrict myself to the sense of *an elite residence of the Iron Age or Viking Period*. As a type, these seem to evolve early in the 1st millennium AD, some of them possibly even earlier; amongst the early examples can be noted Uppåkra, Gudme and Dankirke (L. Jørgensen 2014). They must have been nodal points in the aristocratic networks that brought Roman imports and other luxury goods to the North, and were presumably also centres of specialized craft: particularly metalworking in copper alloy and the precious metals. The central places could consist of just one farm, as seems to have been the case at Dankirke, Toftum Næs and Tissø (Jarl Hansen 1990; Fiedler Therkildsen 2015; L. Jørgensen 2014), or to have been larger complexes of farms, as seems to have been the case at Gudme, Lejre and Uppåkra

(Østergaard Sørensen 2010; L. Jørgensen 2014). The central places of West Jutland are examined in more detail in Chapter 4, *Topography*.

The central places have several urban characteristics: not only religious but also political central functions, alongside specialized craftworking and evidence of trade. On the parallelism between central places and a number of the towns that were established by the royal power from the end of the 10th century onwards there is more in Chapter 6, *The urbanization of southern Scandinavia, AD 700-1050*. The majority of the central places, however, appear to have been elite residences, and so to have more in common with the manorial or estate centres of later periods. For that reason, these are not treated as towns in this book. The natural location of the central places on the nodal points of communication routes in the landscape meant that many of them were obvious locations for the centres of, in particular, the Christian monarchy that was established by the Danish king from the end of the 10th century. In Chapter 6, towns of this type are grouped under the term *the civitas model*, and an attempt is made to demonstrate that heathen central places formed the root stock of this type of town.

In the period before the year 700, trade was, of course, not unknown. Considerable quantities of copper alloy must have come to southern Scandinavia for the manufacture of the many brooches which were regularly deposited in graves, sacrificed or lost, and so could not be re-used. Blown glass, glass beads, and presumably other goods as well also came to Denmark in considerable quantity, although the archaeological reflex of this trade in luxury items is limited. Only at Gudme do we know of the landing place at Lundeborg, the impressive size of which reflects the equally high significance of Gudme in the Later Roman and Earlier Germanic Iron Ages, while at many other places minor landing sites with activity from before the year 700 are known, albeit at an apparently low level (Ulriksen 1998; 2014). It would appear that the trading system before the 8th century can be characterized as highly decentralized, and that the system of exchange rooted in the central places carried on long after the appearance of the first proper large trading sites, the *emporia*.

2.2.2 Emporia – the king's trading sites

The emergence of large trading sites in the southern North Sea region at the end of the 7th century represents a marked turning point in relation to the trade and exchange that had gone on before. In a short period, a number of large trading sites adapted to shipping appeared on both sides of the English Channel (Lebecq 1992). Because of their practically explosive growth (and decline), they have been called *mushroom towns* (Theuws 2004; Hodges 2012) or *non-places* in light of their almost complete absence from written sources and manifest lack of religious or administrative central functions (Hodges 2000; 2012 after Augé 1998). Despite these casual and rather dismissive terms, however, they represent a very significant increase in ship-borne exchange of goods in the period c. 650-850. Along with the emergence of these sites there was also a marked growth in monetary activity. A partially monetized economy based upon coins of the *sceatt* type is now a characteristic feature of the emporia.

A fascinating and frequently recurring feature of the emporia is that they seem not to have direct links back to the preceding Roman towns in the area around the English Channel. Anglo-Saxon *Lundenwic* was located immediately west of the then still partly standing Roman town of *Londinium*, while even the most important emporium, Dorestad, appears not to have made use of a nearby Roman frontier fortress. This symbolic rejection of the heritage of the Roman Empire may, however, also be culturally governed, and in the areas further south, where the Roman culture had survived to a greater extent, the slender traces of urban life in the 7th and 8th centuries appear still to be found within the framework of the old Roman towns (Wamers 2007).

The term *emporium* in the sense of a trading place and used of this group of sites appears to have become the conventional one thanks to Richard Hodges's book *Dark Age Economics* (*DAE*: 1982), which is discussed below. It refers to a word which is linked to some of these sites in a few sources of the 9th century, while other sources of that date used the terms *vicus* or *portus*. In DAE the term 'emporium' is used practically synonymously with 'trading site of the period 600-1000', and is applied to a large number of sites in north-western Europe, large and small, with the result that one can scarcely imagine any other scholars to have used the term with any different senses in other contexts. More recent research, however, appears to have reinforced the impression that the trading sites can be ordered hierarchically and underwent various courses of development, determined by their location and political history. Only trading sites in the uppermost stratum of this hierarchy are referred to here as emporia (Sindbæk 2007).

An emporium is, therefore, a large trading site, organized for marine transport, under royal control and often also with a monetized economy. Emporia are not located in the centres of the kingdoms of their time but rather in the border zones against other kingdoms or population groups. In the case of southern Scandinavia, this means that we know of three emporia of the 8th century:

- Ribe from around the year 700, located in the border zone between the Danish and the Frisian areas.

- Reric (Groß Strömkendorf) from around the year 730, in Wismar Bay, located in the border zone between the Danish, Saxon and Slavic areas.

- Åhus in Skåne from the first half of the 8th century, located in the border zones against Blekinge and in a wider perspective Östergötland and the kingdom of the Svear.

An attempt will be made to show that these three sites constitute a meaningful group of royal trading sites controlled by a king of the Danes in Chapter 6.

The variable political history of the lands around the North Sea meant that the emporia too, linked as they were to the central power of the relevant kingdoms, developed very differently. The Frisian-Carolingian and Anglo-Saxon emporia, Dorestad, Quentovic, Domburg, Lundenwic, Hamwic and Ipswich, collapsed entirely on a number of occasions while the Scandinavian sites had a different history, which is also the subject of Chapter 6.

With the relocation of the traders from Reric to Hedeby enforced by the Danish king in 808, a process was initiated which in the course of the 9th century concentrated trade in Hedeby, while the other emporia, Ribe and Åhus, stagnated or declined. Despite their clear lack of both administrative and religious central functions (Hodges 2012, 93) the three emporia noted above are treated as towns in what follows, and they form a second root stock to the later medieval towns which in this book is referred to collectively as *the emporia model*. Because of the relocation of Reric to Hedeby/Schleswig all three can also be said to have had a further life as important towns later in the Middle Ages.

2.2.3 Minor trading sites

All around the coastlines of southern Scandinavia a number of landing or trading sites with evidence of activity back to the Roman and Germanic Iron Ages have been identified. These are the remains of the decentralized and limited trade of that era (Ulriksen 1998; 2014). With the introduction of the royal emporia in the 8th century, transport by ship increased markedly, and along the sailing routes which followed the west coast of Jutland, through the Limfjord and the internal Danish navigable waters leading to the Baltic, a series of stopping points were established at natural landing sites. They are represented by scattered finds from specialized crafts and trade, and often consist of sunken feature buildings (SFBs) or slender traces of light structures, although their extent and organization varies greatly – from well-structured sites with hundreds of SFBs such as Henne or Sebbersund (Ploug et al. 2012; J.N. Nielsen 2004) down to next to nothing. This massive variation could mean that they lay outside the range of the royal power but rather were subject to various local aristocrats or other unions like the large number of 'illicit harbours' which the much stronger monarchy of the Medieval Period sought to deal with with only partial success. This topic too is discussed in respect of a range of details in Chapter 4, *Topography*.

Several of these landing or trading sites lie at favourable places in the landscape, where well-suited natural harbours and roads met: in other words, places which could also become the location for a proper medieval town. The discovery of much older SFBs several centuries older than any other urban features below towns such as Skive and Aalborg (E.F. Christensen et al. 1984; C.V. Jensen & Klinge 2016) is probably evidence of an earlier role for these sites as non-royal trading places.

Aarhus belongs in an intermediary position between the minor trading sites and the emporia. As the archaeological image of the history of town appears at present, it arose around the year 800 as a minor trading site which neither in size nor activity appears any different from many other sites (H. Skov 2008). The brutal fortification of the town in the 10th century sealed in the main street of the town along the river and must be due to a royal order, so that Aarhus from that time on has to be counted as one of the royal emporia. The minor trading sites are not considered as belonging to the category of towns in this book.

2.2.4 Centres of the Christian monarchy from around the year 1000: the civitas model

A typical feature of the emporia is their lack of monumental reflections of a royal presence, while in respect of religion both large heathen cemeteries and early churches show that they functioned as religiously mixed zones where both a range of pagan and Christian traditions and models co-existed. Despite the pervasive coin economy there are no signs of minting, while amongst the many graves excavated both at Reric and Ribe none have yet been found which stand out as being manifestly richer than the others. The demand for royal tolls must have been entrusted to the *comes vici* ('town reeve') who is referred to in the case of Dorestad, Hedeby and Birka. Concrete evidence of this official is still wanting, but it can be assumed to lie somewhere in the vicinity of the emporia (Skre 2007b; Kalmring et al. 2017).

Also despite the huge quantities of finds from the emporia, the absence of high aristocratic finds is a consistent feature around the North Sea. This may indicate that the functions referred to above continued, in the 8th to 10th centuries, to be located elsewhere: plausibly at nearby or more distant central places, understood as elite residences.

After the Conversion of Denmark, a new set of towns was established which in this book are treated as *centres of the Christian monarchy*. These are towns such as Viborg, Odense, Roskilde and Lund, and earlier scholars have also noted their common features. In Swedish research they are referred to as administrative central places (E. Cinthio 1973; Andrén 1985), emphasizing the royal interests; in this book, however, the assumption is that the now Christian monarchy was fully inter-woven with a religious ideology and legitimization of the office, so that royal and ecclesiastical interests went hand-in-hand (Staecker 1999; Gelting 2007). Down to the middle of the 11th century, on the whole we have no finds from this group of towns other than churches and churchyards, and evidence of trade is still concentrated at the emporia. This new group of towns thus housed those features of administrative and religious character which the emporia lacked, and several of them brought about the abandonment of a nearby pre-Christian central place.

In the Danish towns it is only from the middle of the 11th century onwards that one can trace the combination of religious, administrative and trading functions which is reflected, inter alia, in the expansion of the urban spaces in Lund and Viborg and in the relocation of the old emporia of Ribe and Hedeby. The former shifted first across to the church on the other side of the river, while it is suggested that it was the existence of a church on the Schleswig peninsula which drew Hedeby over to that location.

In this way, the classic medieval town was created: a central church building with a nearby royal manor surrounded by a street plan occupied by craftspeople and traders. Towns of this type are collected under the term *the civitas model*, inspired, in fact, by the word which most towns used for themselves on their seals.

2.3 Henri Pirenne and the trade model

The Belgian medieval historian Henri Pirenne has given his name to the Pirenne thesis – which is not in fact a thesis, but rather an attempt to synthesize historical development in western Europe in the period from the fall of the Roman Empire to

Charlemagne: *the Dark Ages*. In contrast to earlier historians, Pirenne emphasized that the fall of the Western Roman Empire in AD 476 was far from bringing about the complete collapse of the existing social structure, but rather, to a greater extent, involved the continuity of a series of organizational structures and institutions with the Church as the source of strength (Hodges & Whitehouse 1983). The Germanic peoples did not destroy Roman civilization but rather appropriated it. Pirenne was of the view that the decisive changes in western Europe came about first in the wake of the expansion of the Umayyad Caliphate in the Mediterranean area during the 7th century and down to the Battle of Poitiers in 732. The Islamic rule over the Mediterranean lands cut the Merovingian courts off from their connexions with the East, and in particular the long-distance trade in luxury items, and brought about a stagnation that was the true end of the Western Roman Empire. From this nadir the Carolingian Empire grew up as a distinct, western European phenomenon. A famous quotation that has become virtually synonymous with the Pirenne thesis is, in English: *It is therefore strictly correct to say that, without Mohammed, Charlemagne is inconceivable* (Pirenne 1939, 234).

Since the 1920s, the archaeological data which shed light upon these matters have grown astronomically, and parts of Pirenne's argument had been superseded both in historical research and by the archaeological evidence already thirty years ago (Lebecq 1992; Hodges & Whitehouse 1983) – but that is the constant risk faced by syntheses of huge amounts of material. The overall approach, and the attempt to understand the structures behind a sequence of historical events, were nonetheless an inspiration for the *Annales* school, and the essential premiss, that trade and exchange can be the driving forces in social change, is still one of the preferred explanatory models of scholarship (Hodges 1989; McCormick 2001). In this way, Pirenne was an exponent of the *trade model*: trade and exchange as the underlying motor of historical development.

2.4 Karl Polanyi and trade in the 'pre-modern' society

The economic historian and anthropologist Karl Polanyi was one of the first to point out that there must have been a significant difference between trade and exchange in what are known as 'pre-modern' societies and their counterparts in 'modern', market-based societies. In the book *The Great Transformation* (1944) on the industrialization of England and the emergence of markets as price-regulating mechanisms, the key idea was that trade in 'the old days' was not regulated by market forces such as supply and demand but was rather governed by social contracts concerning reciprocity and redistribution between those involved in exchange, following the principles of, for instance, gift-giving which were observable through anthropological fieldwork with so-called primitive societies. Polanyi's postulate was that trade in the old days was therefore *embedded* in social relationships and not subject to price-negotiation following the principles of supply and demand. Polanyi himself labelled this view of the economy of earlier societies *substantivism*, in contrast to the traditional understanding of social economy, which he called *formalism*.

The observation that trade and exchange had formerly been extensively governed by social contracts had great impact in archaeological studies of trade and exchange, but in my view contains an erroneous assumption at its core, in that it is silently posited that trade and exchange in modern societies are not also embedded in the social context and to a considerable extent directed by social mechanisms. We are all (also) substantivists. Polanyi forced a view of price-setting mechanisms before and now, and created an image of a radically different past. But even in the past, market forces were operative, and regulated to a considerable extent the basic resources of the society in the form of agricultural production, while other categories of goods, typically those of a more luxury character, were not subject to competition to the same degree. Throughout time, gift-giving has followed its own socially defined laws, and it continues to do so today (Theuws 2004).

2.5 Dark Age Economics

The work which has had an impact beyond any other in research related to the emporia is Richard Hodges's *Dark Age Economics: The Origins of Towns and Trade AD 600-1000* (1982; 2nd ed. 1989; here *DAE*): a textbook specimen of processual archaeology which combined anthropological models with sparse historical sources and sparse archaeological data in an attempt to synthesize the re-emergence of towns and trade in northwestern Europe in the period following the fall of the Roman Empire. *DAE* identifies Henri Pirenne as its key inspiration, and locates itself as a continuation of the *Annales* school's studies of social history and long-term economic developments. A new departure is the combination of this approach with inspiration from another major source, the anthropologist Bronisław Malinowski, whose study of the Trobriand Island group in Papua-New Guinea at the beginning of the 20th century revealed that apparently primitive societies employed an advanced economic practice built upon *Kula*, a system of trade governed by ceremonies and rituals – in other words, *embedded* within social relations as Polanyi would describe it.

Based primarily upon Anglo-Saxon and Carolingian development, Richard Hodges constructed a typological scheme for the emporia which he attempted to apply also to the Scandinavian situations, but which does not sufficiently take account of the very different courses of history in the various regions (Hodges 1989, 47ff; 2012, 91ff). Even a site such as Helgö in Mälaren is classified as an emporium although it should rather, not least in light of the name, be classified as a central place (elite residence) with a core religious component (Herschend 1995). Unfortunately, Hodges's model of the emporia has since been carried further, now with the concept of the central place added in, albeit in the Scandinavian sense of the term which is not the same as Hodges's definition (Skre 2007c). The classification also attaches great importance to whether or not the emporium in question can be identified as a non-permanent or a permanent settlement; in the case of the Scandinavian emporia, however, at the very least their population levels must have fluctuated massively with the seasons and market periods. Neither Hodges's nor Skre's classification incorporates crucial factors concerning the economic systems of the emporia – such as, whether or not the trading site in question used a monetized or a weight-based economy – which are made use of in this study.

With reference to Anglo-Saxon and Carolingian documentary sources, it was pointed out in *DAE* that long-distance trade was a royal privilege, and that the emporia were located in the border zones in order to maximize contact with other regions. This observation does not appear to have been disproved.

With regard to the traded goods themselves, the archaeological evidence has advanced considerably since Hodges undertook his research. The range of goods in the emporia was thought to have been directed towards the aristocracy and to have consisted of 'prestige goods, scarcities, and, on occasions, slave labour' (Hodges 1989, 53). As the following chapters will show, however, really top-level aristocratic finds are absent from the emporia, and the wide-ranging production at these sites was directed towards a broader stratum of society, which metal-detecting in Denmark has shown to be represented in what is thought to be every part of the country. A discussion of the definition of aristocracy and the customers of the emporia consequently follows in Chapters 4 and 5, below.

The style of argument in *DAE* is determined by various models derived from economic theory, anthropology or sociology, which are combined along with the archaeological data available in 1982. To put it summarily: at times this works well, but often not so well, as is typically the case when models are evaluated against a non-representative data-set. Nonetheless this book, like Pirenne's works, is a classic, which managed to grasp the special character of the emporia at an early stage in research and which has to some extent retained its fascination. One important reason for that is that the use of anthropological models gave a mystique to the emporia and turned them into sites at which social codes, defined by various Dark-age aristocrats, reduced the inhabitants of the emporia to actors with very little freedom. This strongly class-structured basic model has a natural background in recent English history, but does not seem to find much support in the very extensive archaeological evidence from Ribe, amongst other sites.

The 'making strange' of the emporia forms its own quite distinct research tradition, which has led to more recent discussions of what some individuals regard as the practically complete separation between the emporia and the agrarian economy of the hinterland (Saunders 2001). However that separation too seems unsustainable when one looks in more detail at the range of goods in Ribe and connexions with the surrounding territory. This discussion is taken further in Chapter 4, *Topography*.

2.6 The Viking Age in Denmark

Klaus Randsborg's book *The Viking Age in Denmark* (1980) was an early and, for its date, a successful attempt to demonstrate the potential of processual archaeology. Its sub-title, *The Formation of a State*, reveals the social perspective, and the principal thesis of the book – that state-formation in Denmark proceeded from a western centre at Jelling, with Kings Gorm, Harald and Svein subordinating the lands that became medieval Denmark – is developed through analyses of documentary sources, runestones, climate and rural settlement, towns and fortifications.

Classic archaeological methods such as distributions in time and space were combined with the models of processualism and deductive approaches. For the same reason, it is interesting to compare the book and its argument with the powerful influx of new archaeological evidence since it was written, in order to test the durability of the hypotheses applied, and so to give processualism a taste of its own medicine.

The section on the chronology and geographical distribution of the runestones draws upon a theory of the stones as symbolic property markers and as testaments to a major redistribution of land in the period, while the 10th-century weapon and equestrian grave horizon draws upon theories of conflict and aristocratic stress rather than the simple marking of status as the background to the militarization of burial practice. Common to both sections is the fact that the empirical evidence has not changed significantly since the book was published, and the interpretation of the material which is used to represent the extent of the embryonic Jelling dynasty still stands as an unopposed proposition concerning 10th-century political history in Denmark. In the case of the rest of the book – climatic studies, rural settlement, towns, fortifications and hoards – one has to note that the archaeological material has now left this book a very long way behind. On this basis, one may conclude that primarily empirical hypotheses formulated on the basis of representative evidence are more durable in face of the processes of erosion than others. Fundamentally, then, not much has changed since the era of Sophus Müller (Müller 1884).

2.7 The Medieval Town Project

The Medieval Town Project (*Projekt Middelalderbyen*), which was initiated in 1977 by the National Humanities Research Council, was a major research project directed by Olaf Olsen, the objective of which was to 'increase our limited knowledge of the age and initial topographical development of the Danish towns through inter-disciplinary work, in which historians and archaeologists will work closely together to define the current status of knowledge of the towns and to look for new methods in urban research' (*Ti byer* 1980). In order to achieve this aim, ten towns were selected for closer examination: Aalborg, Horsens, Køge, Næstved, Odense, Ribe, Roskilde, Svendborg, Viborg and Aarhus, while the National Museum (NM) undertook as part of the project to investigate the abandoned borough of Søborg. In the first phase, an attempt was made to collect all of the documentary, cartographical, archaeological and geological evidence, which are systematized in an ingenious punch-card system, the information in which was plotted in the second phase within a series of uniform maps. The cartographical component was inspired by the report *The Future of London's Past* of 1973, the beautiful, transparent and colourful maps of which were an inspiration to the project participants.[2]

In the third phase, areas were selected in various towns in which minor excavations were undertaken ('postage-stamp trenches'), which in the view of the project were conceived of as pin-point operations that, on the basis of limited field archaeological work, should be able to answer fundamental questions relating to the individual towns. On the excavations of this project in Ribe and the publication *Middelalderbyen Ribe* ('The Medieval Town of Ribe': I. Nielsen 1985), there is more in Chapter 3, *Research History*. More recent experience has shown, however, that small,

scattered trenches in a thick sequence of culture layers often generate more questions than they answer, and this was likewise the outcome of most of the excavations carried out under this project. A number of cases did hit the spot: for instance the trench at Viborg Søndersø which uncovered the well-preserved and waterlogged culture layers from the section of the town on the lake shore (Krongaard Kristensen 1987). But here too it was only the later, major excavations that made it possible to interpret what had been excavated in a more satisfactory manner (Hjermind et al eds. 1998).

Many of the planned monographs on the individual towns were a long time in the making, and some – Horsens, Roskilde and Søborg – have never appeared. Nonetheless, the project left its mark on a whole generation of town archaeologists and brought about major methodological advances in urban archaeology generally: not only in terms of excavation techniques but also in respect of ways of working with source material. The Medieval Town Project involved a plan for some form of final synthesis, and the project was also completely uninfluenced by processual archaeology and could consequently ignore this movement's demands for theorizing and the use of models. Concurrently, there was a comparable project in Sweden, *Medeltidstaden* (The Medieval Town), which was, however, unconnected with the Danish project.

2.8 From Tribe to State

Another major project financed by the National Humanities Research Council was From Tribe to State (*Fra stamme til stat*), which began in 1984, the goal of which was to 'draw a clearer picture of economic, social and political development in Denmark from tribal societies or chieftainships to the kingdom or state' (Mortensen & Rasmussen eds. 1988, vol. 1, 7). Two out of four planned publications have appeared as *Fra stamme til stat* vols. 1 and 2, while the synthesis intended was published by Ulf Näsman (2006). This project, the chronological scope of which was the period from the 3rd century AD to the 10th, had as its aim to understand the society and the structures which conditioned historical development: in other words, processually. As one of many results, the date of the formation of a Danish kingdom could be assigned to the 8th century (Näsman 2006), a perspective which the present study seeks to qualify further by including the archaeological evidence from the emporia. Altogether, however, urbanization played only a minor part in this project, although Stig Jensen discussed the site of Dankirke and its relationships with Ribe within it, and this topic is examined here in detail in Chapter 4, *Topography*.

2.9 The urban stage

Anders Andrén's thesis of 1985, *Den urbana scenen* ('The Urban Stage') remained, until 2016 (Krongaard Kristensen & Poulsen 2016), the only synthetic work on urbanization in Denmark since Hugo Matthiesen's *Middelalderlige Byer* ('Medieval Towns') of 1927. Andrén's background lay in the town archaeology of Lund, and his dissertation was written while both the Swedish and the Danish Medieval Town projects were underway and so was inspired by the discussions going on within both. Unlike the major projects, Andrén did not keep within modern national boundaries but rather worked on urbanization within the whole of the medieval kingdom of Denmark with the aim of discovering, through analysis, the underlying structures of the development. In accordance with the tradition deriving from Pirenne and the *Annales* school the purpose was to write a synthesis which, on the basis of a formalization of the urban source data, could work methodically through to a new understanding of urbanization in Denmark. *Den urbana scenen* was written against the grain of a tradition which emphasized the importance of trade in urbanization and the autonomously evolutionary nature of the towns – in other words, a perspective shaped by continuity; through studies of the parish churches of the towns in particular, however, Andrén tried to show that the towns were rather royal foundations which marked a clear break in the course of historical development in which the king played the absolutely central role.

This discontinuous view of history was a feature of the Marxist-structuralist historiography, and was inspired by the philosophical 'rock star' Michel Foucault, whose works – primarily *Les mots et les choses – une archéologie des sciences humaines* ('The Words and the Things – An Archaeology of the Human Sciences': 1966), published in English translation as *The Order of Things*, shook the foundations of a whole range of human sciences.

According to Andrén, 'the urban churches can thus be seen as a very central ideological expression of medieval town life, and the factors in the town's ecclesiastical structure can therefore reveal how both the concept of the town and the urban context were changed' (Andrén 1985, 18: translated). As an analytical position, the number of churches is used to divide the towns into three classes:

- Plurality: towns with three or more churches
- Duality: towns with two churches
- Unity: towns with a single church

Meanwhile the criterion of whether the town's land included rural settlements or not was used for a bipartite division:

- Open: town land including rural settlements
- Closed: town land without rural settlements

The classificational system was used for a division into six groups which could be seriated against time. From several angles, criticism has since been voiced concerning whether this method really unpacks the evidence or rather confuses discussion by creating a system of classification that is actually uninformative (Nyborg 2004; Krongaard Kristensen & Poulsen 2016, 31). Nonetheless the dissertation has the great quality of being one of the few attempts to *understand* urbanization in Denmark rather than just to describe it.

Since this work is dependent upon the churches, it follows inevitably that pre-Conversion urbanization – in other words the emporia and so trade – are not captured by this method, and this is reflected in the dissertation's starting horizon chronologically, which is around 1050. Furthermore, the number of churches in the oldest towns also seems to be determined by whether the ecclesiastical order was oriented to Hamburg-Bremen or to Canterbury (see Chapter 6) and so not to be a direct reflection of the size or importance of the town in question.

2.10 A theory concerning the emporium of Ribe

Fortunately, archaeological evidence has increased radically since *Dark Age Economics* was published in 1982. If one were to formulate a theory concerning the emergence and development of the emporia in southern Scandinavia on the basis of the present knowledge of Ribe – which will be presented in the next chapter of this book – it might run like this:

In the years following AD 536, northern Europe was gripped by a climatic disaster caused by a series of volcanic eruptions in the years 536, 540 and 547, the effects of which were global and led to a cold period in the northern hemisphere: the Late Antique Little Ice Age (LALIA: Büntgen et al. 2016). This cold period, which lasted for about a century, first brought about a massive horizon of votive offerings in northern Europe followed by a clear fall in population levels (Axboe 2001). It also provided the historical background for the Norse myth of *Fimbulvetrinn*. Only in the course of the 7th century did the population start to recover.

During the 7th century, a growing population in northern Europe and the re-discovery of the ship with a sail led to greater interaction and trade, and the emporia appeared with more or less close links to their Roman predecessors, dependent upon their geographical location. As an outpost of Dorestad, Ribe was established around the year 700 as a result of an agreement between the local elite of south-western Jutland, a king, possibly of the Danes, and maritime merchants. This relationship may have been formed in Dorestad. The first phase of Ribe appears not to have been closely managed, and the range of goods covered a broad range of things which for good reasons were exotic but which were able to find their way to what appears to be every part of Jutland. Only a minor proportion of the trade was in real luxury items. The experiences with Ribe were good, so that after a few years the town came under the control of the Danish king. Following an overseas model, a system of taxation was introduced based on a monopoly coinage, the Wodan/monster sceatt, which remained the only coin that was used in the town down to around 800. A high proportion of the economy was based on barter.

The town's trade flourished, and before the middle of the 8th century the king had founded new emporia in Reric and Åhus, and the stopping places along the routes which the travelling merchants needed emerged inevitably along the tracks of their ships. Some of the landing places grew into minor trading sites in their own right. At both Reric and Åhus the Danish king's Wodan/monster sceattas were used, although apparently only in limited quantities in the case of Åhus. The production of goods in Reric and Åhus was also directed at a broad circle of customers, for the most part residing at farms in the hinterland of the towns.

The population of the towns was both ethnically and culturally mixed, as is the rule in ports, and as free men the traders and craftspeople could try their luck at a new site if they chose to. The population figures have not yet reached the pre-536 level, and there was a need for all hands on the farms. There is little evidence of crowding or conflict over resources, which could explain why a slave trade was of limited significance, even if other emporia in the North Sea network evidently did see dealing in slaves.

With the evacuation of Reric and the growth of Hedeby from AD 808, the trade route across the neck of Jutland grew in importance at the expense of Ribe's trade. New, larger coins were introduced both in Hedeby and in Ribe, but this did not alter the fact that the dramatic growth of Hedeby had serious consequences for Ribe.

In contrast to Hodges's glum Marxist theory of the emporia, this narrative is more liberal and rather a story of continuity, which is of course open to debate – in content, though, it corresponds more precisely with present archaeological facts. A range of issues have virtually undergone 180° turns. The proposition that the emporia must have been the closed network provisioning the elite, providing the courts of western Europe with luxury items through long-distance trade but with no significant contact with the hinterland, lacks support in the Danish archaeological evidence and has now to be rejected. The idea seems to have been inspired by the trading stations of the colonial period such as Danish Trankebar in India, but it cannot be found in the archaeological material from the 8th and 9th centuries.

Likewise, the relationship between the aristocracy and the lower strata of the social pyramid in Hodges's model has been exploded by metal-detecting and rural settlement archaeology, which in Denmark have revealed a very widespread and level 'aristocracy' with what can be quite a number of representatives in practically all of the later ecclesiastical parishes: a society, in other words, in which the differences between rich and poor do not seem to have been anything like as pronounced as Hodges assumed.

The range of goods on offer in the Scandinavian emporia matched what one would expect to find with the widespread jewellery-wearing stratum of society that metal-detecting has uncovered. Here too, it is essentially equivalent products which have more in common with the later classic medieval towns than with the provisioning network of a royal house. Rather than being Suppliers to the Royal Court, Ribe and the other emporia were the *supermarkets* of the age, while in the course of the 9th century Hedeby grew into the kingdom's only *hypermarket*.

✓ T9 — s/Crypto ~~the~~

✓ 21 / Sm Ponts
21
‖

~~(scribble)~~   Thrizt – 1988

Kent
TN1 1HE

3. History of research into Ribe

Previous research into the history of Ribe is presented and analysed in this chapter. This focuses on both the written works and the excavations themselves, as field archaeology – especially from the middle of the 20th century – has been closely inter-twined with the dominant research questions. Works that have contributed crucially to illumination of the history of Ribe in the period AD 700-1500 are included, and particular importance has been attached to explicating the growth of the antiquarian-topographical tradition that in the case of Ribe can be traced back to Peder Terpager's *Ripæ Cimbricæ* of 1736 but which first really emerged following N.L. Høyen's visit to the town in 1830. No comprehensive review of this development has been brought together before, but it can be regarded as useful and informative as the research history in itself contains a narrative not only of the evolution of the decentralized local museums of Denmark but also, perhaps even more significantly, of the paradigms that have been dominant within the period both in archaeology and in urban studies.

The fullest history of research before this is to be found in *Middelalderbyen Ribe* (I. Nielsen 1985), and in the case of the ecclesiastical institutions in the National Museum's *Danmarks Kirker* ('Denmark's Churches': hereafter *DK*). The research history in *Ribe Studier 1: Det ældste Ribe* (Feveile 2006a) focused narrowly on the excavations on the northern side of the Ribe River. The period down to the foundation of Den antikvariske Samling ('The Antiquarian Collection': abbreviated ASR) in 1855 has been thoroughly discussed in the article 'Antikvarer i det gamle Ribe' ('Antiquaries in Old Ribe': Hermansen 1959), but the emphasis in that study lay solidly on objects and monuments.

The following presentation of the research history in respect of Ribe is constructed chronologically and very much related to persons. Significance has been attached to explaining both the educational background of the various scholars and their institutional affiliations, as the academic character and networks of the contributors are essential keys to the dynamics of the history of research. Since the 1970s Ribe has found itself in the zone of overlap between prehistoric and medieval archaeology in Denmark. This has led to much valuable discussion, but has also at times introduced unfortunate boundary lines to research activity.

The chapter concludes with a summary that considers the research history in the perspective of methodological developments.

3.1 The Ribe Episcopal Chronicle

The account of Ribe's history and research into that history has, like the town itself, deep roots. It was the Church which brought a literate culture to Scandinavia and it is from the ecclesiastical quarter that we see the first steps in writing down the history of Ribe. *Vita Ansgarii*, composed by Ansgar's successor as Bishop of Hamburg-Bremen, Rimbert, around AD 870, is the first documentary source to refer to Ribe and the permission granted by the Danish king to raise a church there. The text has remained known ever since, and this information about the existence of the town by the mid-9th century has provided the natural starting point for all discussions of the origins of the town and the background to the fact that that the archaeological hunt for Viking-period Ribe started in the area of the cathedral. This situation did not change until the excavation in the cellar of the Art Museum (*Kunstmuseets kælder*) in 1973.

The *Ribe Episcopal Chronicle* is a short text, whose author must have been one of the cathedral canons. The text is now known only through later copies, but an original core, written around 1230, can be discerned through these (Søgaard 1973). The text contains short biographies of the individual bishops from an account of Liufdag in 948 down to Bishop Tue who died in 1230. The author does not talk about the purpose of the work in the text but it would have been capable of serving both as a practical reference work for the cathedral chapter and concurrently to have reinforced the already long history of the institution by that date.

Since the list of bishops in the Ribe Chronicle differs fundamentally from the information in Adam of Bremen's *History of the Archbishops of Hamburg and Description of the North* of c. 1070, historical scholarship has long regarded the text from Ribe with scepticism. However the most recent analyses of Adam of Bremen's work and its information about the history of the Church in Denmark have been able to reveal an ingenious web of silences and twists which served to mask the very limited success of the archiepiscopal see in the mission to the North (Gelting 2004). As a result, the information in the Ribe Episcopal Chronicle appears more reliable.

3.2 The renaissance historians: Hans Svaning, Anders Sørensen Vedel and Niels Krag

With the Renaissance in Denmark, a new interest in national history was awoken. From the middle of the 16th century there were major efforts by the royal Chancellors, first Johan Friis and then Niels Kaas, to have a new History of Denmark written which would supersede the more than three centuries old *Gesta Danorum* of Saxo. The historian Hans Svaning lived in Ribe from the 1550s, and collected source material with a view to writing a new History of Denmark in Latin. This work continued until 1579 when the task was taken from him by royal command and entrusted instead to Svaning's son-in-law, also resident in Ribe,

Anders Sørensen Vedel, who had previously managed to produce the first complete translation of Saxo. Vedel's work proved time-consuming too, and in 1594 it was passed on to the Ribe man Niels Krag, who died in 1602 without having got much closer to the end. The great majority of the archives and manuscripts of the three historians were destroyed in the fire of Copenhagen in 1728, which left the University Library and much besides in ashes. Various minor fragments of their works were, however, printed or are known from copies. Put into context, this has made outline reconstructions of the now lost sources they had access to possible.

The work of the renaissance historians in Ribe unfortunately has left us no finished historical studies under their names, but their work is nevertheless appreciated as important to note in this context, since it can be considered certain that the documentary sources then known for the earliest history of the town had been examined in an informed manner (S.P. Skov 1937). Although all of these men represent a philological-historical tradition, one can still assume that there cannot have been known runestones then, or conspicuous prehistoric barrows in the town or its close environs, that were not referred to somewhere or other, either in the historical studies or in the otherwise very rich sources from the town of the 16th and 17th centuries. As an example can be cited the fact that the earliest reference to the castle mound of Riber Ulfsborg or *Wlfsborigh*, situated in Østermade 3 km east of Ribe, is from 1530 (I. Nielsen 1985, 73 and n.1).

The prospect of Ribe from Braun & Hogenberg's work *Civitates orbis terrarum*, which the publishers received drafts for in 1586 (Fig. 2), can be regarded as one of the more solid pieces of evidence of the presence of the renaissance historians in the town (Braun & Hogenberg 1572-1617, no page numbers). This de-

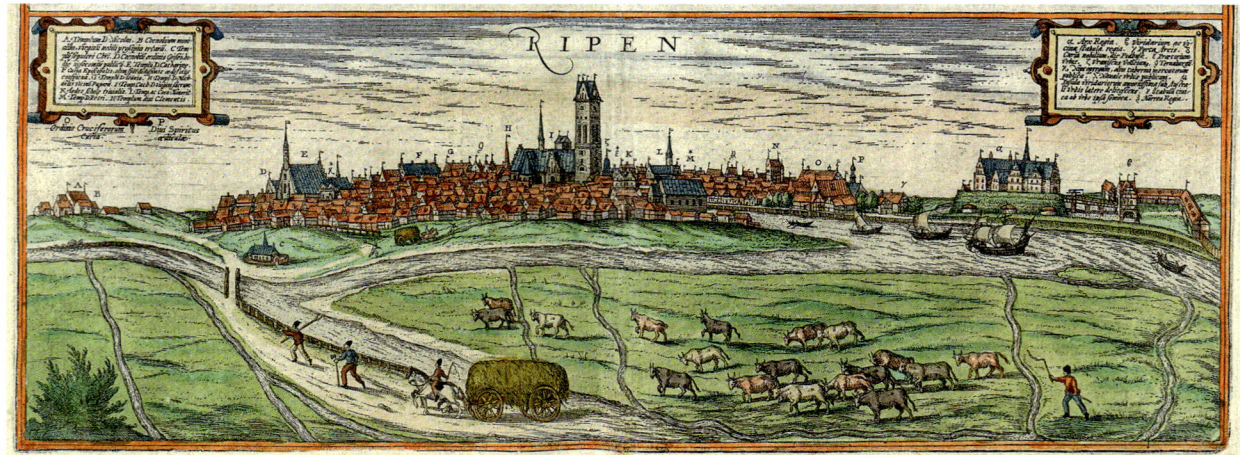

Fig. 2. Prospect of Ribe from the gallows hill north of the town, c. 1585. Published in Braun & Hogenberg's Civitates orbis terrarum. *From an original in the Royal Library.*

tailed and densely packed piece is the most important of the antiquarian-topographical sources from Ribe, depicting the town viewed from the north, probably from a position around the gallows hill. The *skyline* of the town includes the spires and roofs of a large number of ecclesiastical institutions that are correctly placed but which had already disappeared by 1537/8, inter alia because of an aggressive attack from the church-breaker – *den kerken brekker*.[3] Riberhus, by contrast, is reproduced in the Dutch renaissance style and appears in the form the castle mound obtained as a result of Christian III's rebuilding, which in fact made use of materials from the demolished churches (Etting 2010b). Anachronisms evidently were no problem, and the intention appears to have been to present as impressive a town-view as possible. The portrayal of Anders Sørensen Vedel's observatory on Liljebjerget indicates that he must have been one of the sources. The cartographer Johannes Mejer and the historian Peder Hansen Resen also produced maps and drawings of Ribe in the 17th century (Figs. 3-4).

3.3 The ecclesiastical sphere: Peder Terpager and Matthias Galthen

While the 16th and the early 17th centuries were generally good times not only for Ribe but for Denmark as a whole, later in the 17th century Ribe was struck by a series of disasters which impoverished the town and marked the beginning of a long decline which came also to set the key for research into the history of Ribe. The Emperor's War of 1627-9, the storm flood of 11-12 October 1634, the Torstensson War of 1643-5, the Swedish War of 1657-9, the plague of 1659, and finally the introduction of absolute monarchy in 1660, led cumulatively to a massive recession and impoverishment of the formerly rich merchant town. Quite apart from the human suffering, the crises meant that formerly inhabited areas lay waste, and the reduced economy made it ever harder to maintain the built environment of the town, includ-

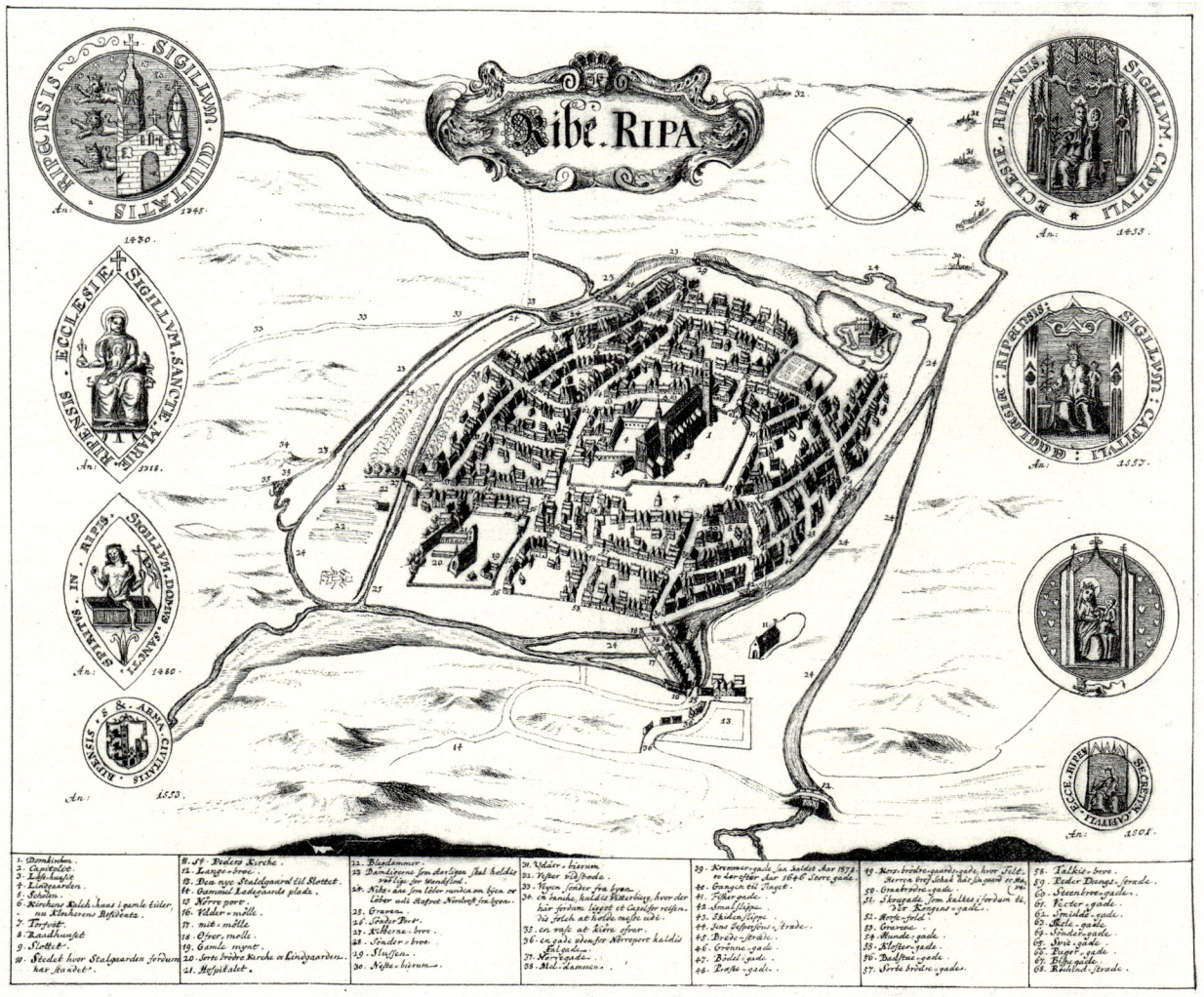

Fig. 3. Pen drawing of Ribe from above. Produced for use in Resen's Atlas Danicus, *c. 1670. From an original in the Royal Library.*

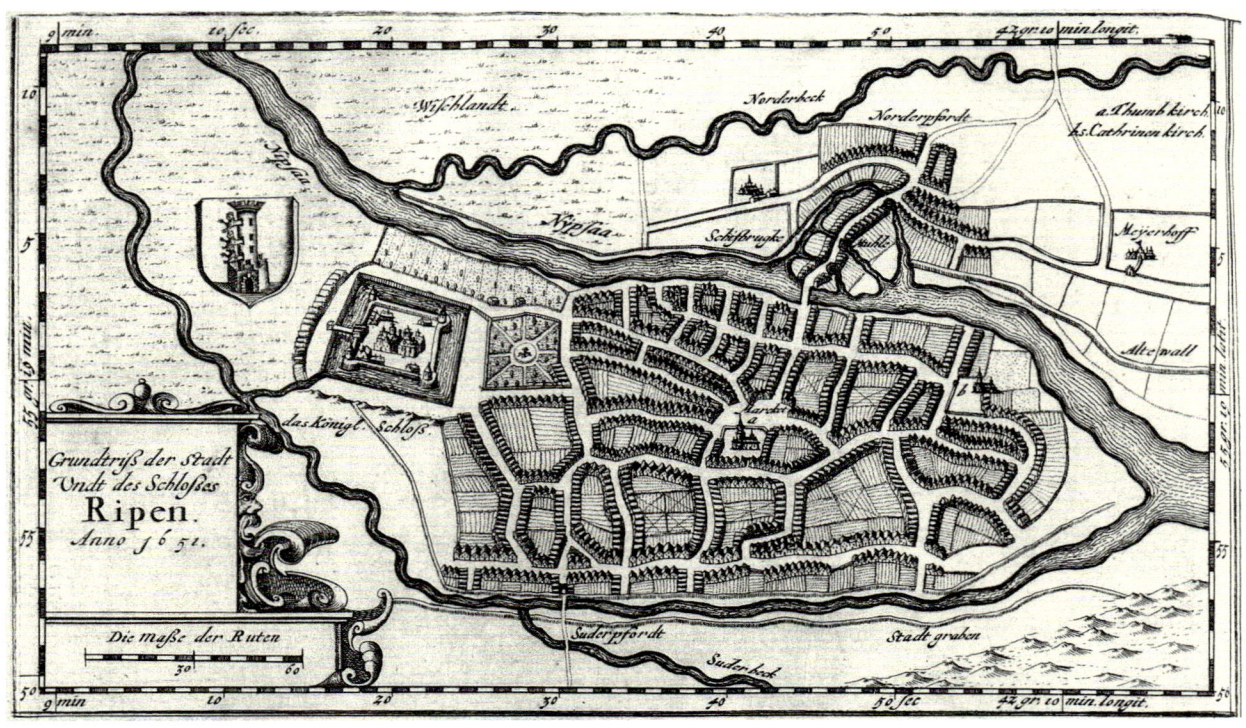

Fig. 4. The cartographer Johannes Mejer's map of Ribe, 1651. From an original in the Royal Library.

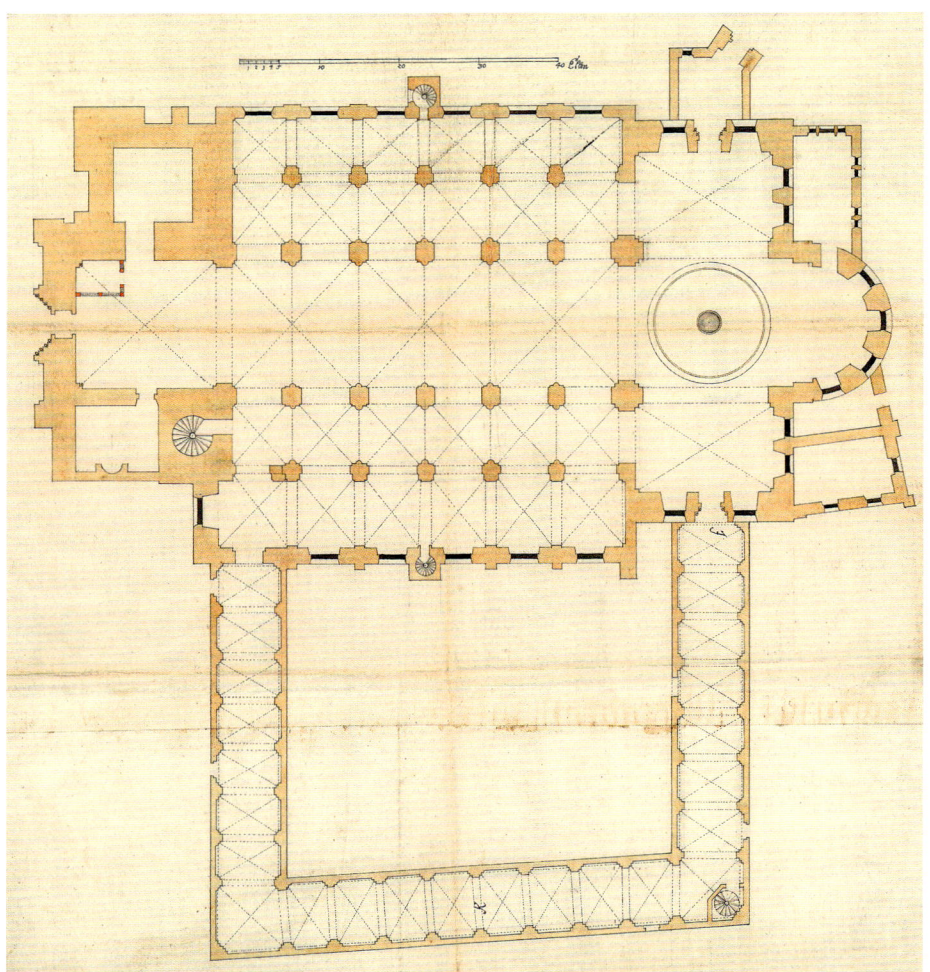

Fig. 5. A plan of the cathedral complex of 1737 produced by K. Stahlknecht immediately before the demolition of the ancillary buildings on the eastern side and most of the cloisters. From an original in The Danish National Archives.

ing the two remaining churches. The great cathedral complex in particular was in a ruinous state.

Amidst this chorus of misery, the priest and *lector theologiæ* – the head of the cathedral school – Peder Terpager (1654-1738) worked on a major work on the history of Ribe. In 1702 *Inscriptiones Ripenses* was published, a conspectus of the preserved inscriptions within the town of both ecclesiastical and secular character, possibly inspired by Peder Hansen Resen's *Inscriptiones Hafniensis* of 1668. Other publications, including the Episcopal Chronicle (1708), subsequently followed. In 1726 the manuscript of the town history was sent to a printer in Copenhagen, but like so much else it fell victim to the flames of the fire of 1728.

The author, then 74 years old, *despite temporary depression* (*Dansk Biografisk Leksikon*), started work on a new manuscript, and the book, *Ripæ Cimbricæ seu vrbis Ripensis in Cimbria sitæ descriptio* – A Description of the Town of Ribe on the Cimbrian Peninsula, or in other words Ribe in Jutland – was finally published in 1736 (Terpager 1736).

Because of his office, Terpager was a member of the still-functioning cathedral chapter, which survived the Reformation in an Evangelical form. Responsibility for the maintenance of the cathedral was in the hands of the two churchwardens, at that time Terpager and the Dean, Søren Serup, both of whom had served for decades. The diocesan prefect (*Stiftamtmand*) Gabel, the royal lieutenant in the town, made a complaint to the king concerning the performance of the duties of the churchwardens in 1734, leading in 1736 to a court case in which the churchwardens were condemned for corruption. Serup died that same year, and Terpager resigned his churchwardenship, following which the chapter, originally established in 1145, was finally dissolved. Terpager himself died on 4 January 1738 and so did not live to see his own exoneration through a subsequent High Court judgement. In 1738 a badly needed restoration of the cathedral complex began, which involved the demolition of the chapter house, several chapels, and much of the cloisters (Fig. 5).

It is this institutional state of decline that forms the essential soundboard in the production of *Ripæ Cimbricæ*. For good reason, the purpose of the book was to describe and to demonstrate the rich history of the town and its former greatness. The presentation is thematically divided with a heavy bias towards the institutions of the town, especially the ecclesiastical ones and in particular the cathedral, which also adorns the title page. Terpager had access to several now lost sources, including the cathedral's later anniversary book which was transcribed along with a series of other documents. Their contents have thus been preserved through Terpager's work. *Ripæ Cimbricæ* also includes a number of quite exceptional engravings for its date (Fig. 6) (Lassen 1981).

In Denmark, the genre of town histories was still a very young one, but Peder Hansen Resen's *Haffnia antiqva et moderna* (Resen 1682) may have been a model. Amongst other early representatives one may cite Christen Eriksen's *Viborg byes beskrivelse* published in 1727 (Degn 1985).

In *Ripæ Cimbricæ* an origin myth was started which subsequently came to be known as the town-relocation hypothesis. On Sønder Farup Hede, barely 4 km south of the town, the place-name *Gammel Ribe* ('Old Ribe') supposedly indicated the original location of the town, *ubi rudera & vestigia veteris urbis abunde satis conspiciuntur* – 'where one can see very many ruins and remains from an old town' (Terpager 1736, 6). Terpager reproduced a local tradition that can be traced back to 1552 (Kinch 1869, 6; Edelberg & Bencard 1962, 22). The location of Gammel Ribe was recorded in the Place-Name Survey of 1921-2, and it is situated immediately west of Tradsborg Plantation (Fig. 67). This site is discussed further in Chapter 4, *Topography*.

In 1792, the resident curate of the cathedral, Matthias Galthen, published *Beskrivelse over Kiøbstaden Ribe fra sin Begyndelse indtil nærværende Tid* ('Description of the Market Town of Ribe from its Beginning up to recent Times'). The book is based primarily on Terpager, and states as the reason for its production:

There is Reason to regret that Some of our Danish Market Towns, which we know were once many, and densely and well inhabited, flourishing in Trade and Wealth, have Time and again turned into small and insignificant Spots, full of poor and wretched Townsmen. But none is more to be lamented in this Regard than Ribe, which in its Time was greater than them all, and, after Roskilde, the leading Town of the Kingdom.

In the patriotic dedication to Crown Prince Frederik (later Frederik VI) typical of its time, it is emphasized that Ribe *was particularly beloved of your Royal Highness's Esteemed Forefathers for its Loyalty and Obedience*. With this, another key foundation stone in the story of Ribe was introduced; the idea of the town as especially *loyal to the king* – a sail that would swell during the period of national romanticism.

3.4 The mapping of Ribe Town and Field

One feature of the Enlightenment in the 18th century was the development of cartography. Denmark and the Dukedoms were mapped to a degree of precision never seen before, and it was also at this time that the first exact survey of Ribe was made. On the order of the royal General Road Commission

Fig. 6. The southern portal of the transept, the so-called cat's head door and Bishop Iver Munk's grave-slab as reproduced in copperplate engraving in Ripæ Cimbricæ. *After Terpager 1736.*

in 1797, Second Lieutenant P.C. van Rönner undertook a survey of Ribe which, despite a few errors of measurement, was the first precise map of the town area (Fig. 7). There must also have been surveys of the town lands, but we have no knowledge of any preserved cadastral map older than the middle of the 19th century. With respect to the extensive town field, there are several such maps drawn from the end of the 18th century onwards which were used, with revisions, in to the second half of the 19th century. Some of these maps have been published in a previous collection (Degn 1983) but only with the digitization of the historical maps from the year 2000 did all of the large amount of information in them become accessible. These are used extensively in the present study.

3.5 National romanticism and J. Kinch's Ribe Bys Historie og Beskrivelse

The Romantic movement saw the introduction to European spiritual life of a cultural critique that has maintained a central position ever since. The Romantics cultivated the sublime: the belief that there was a core of truth behind phenomena present to the senses – the good, the beautiful, and the true/God; but they were also painfully aware of how remote real life was from the ideal. This created a distance between *Sein* ('Being') – the core, the truth, the sublime/diving, that which was represented – and *Schein* ('Appearance'): the perceived world, represen-

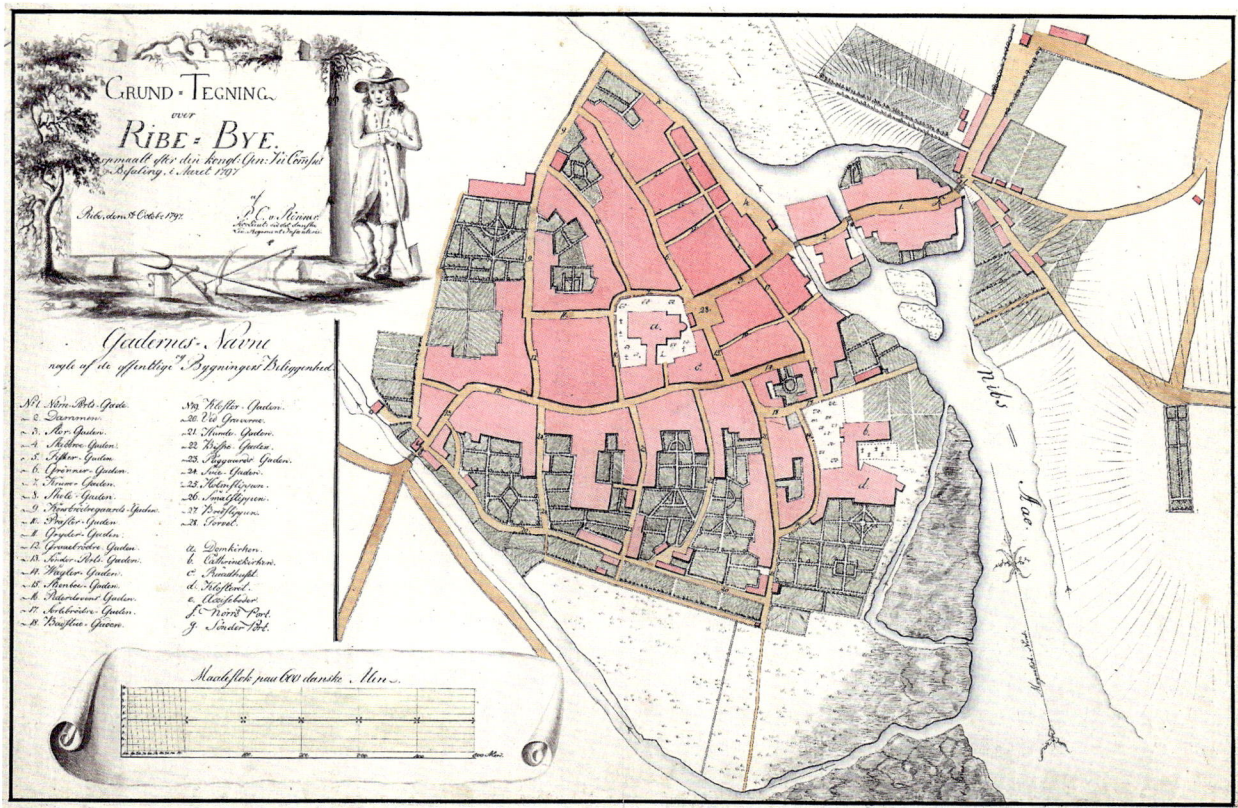

Fig. 7. The Road Commission map of Ribe of 1797 drawn by P.C. van Rönner. From the original with the Geodata Agency.

tations. This understanding was expressed precisely in one of Goethe's aphorisms: *Das Wahre ist gottähnlich; es erscheint nicht unmittelbar, wir müssen es in seinen Manifestationen erraten* (Goethe 1821) – 'The truth is god-like; it is does not appear in person – we have to detect it in its manifestations.'

An idea that was derived from this was the critique of contemporary society. The culture of the urban upper class, their knowledge, order, development and technology, were regarded as having produced an even greater distancing from the genuine. Alternatively, interest was directed towards nature, to the disorderly, the childish, the old, the undeveloped and the innocent: what one could call nostalgia. With the concept of *the noble savage* taken from the French philosopher Jean-Jacques Rousseau, the seed of the social anthropology which was to have great influence on the formation of archaeological theory from the 1960s onwards was planted.

With Romanticism, the perception of the national was also reinforced: the idea that the inhabitants of Europe consisted of distinct peoples with their own distinct character, a cultural core, formulated in Johann Gottfried von Herder's concept of *Volkstum* (literally 'people-dom'). Starting with the cultural critique, interest was turned towards those areas which were thought to be least infected by modernity: typi-

cally peasant culture in remote areas. The principal thesis was that the cultural cores of the peoples, which were often supposed to be the culture of the upper class, would have sunk to the base in these nominally relict areas and have been preserved by the non-innovating underclass, as summarized in the concept of the *gesunkenes Kulturgut* ('the sunken substance of culture'), formulated by the German ethnologist and later leading Nazi Hans Naumann (Naumann 1922).

In the summer of 1830, in the context of the breaking ideas of national romanticism, the art historian N.L. Høyen visited Ribe as part of his comprehensive tour of the monuments of the country. Over three weeks he investigated Ribe Cathedral and could at least roughly determine the architectural history of the church. On the same occasion the tomb in the northern transept of the church was opened. The cavity proved to contain the remains of the three bishops Odinkar (†1043), Nothulf (†1140) and Asser (†1142) (Fig. 8). This can be considered the first recorded antiquarian excavation in Ribe.

Høyen was personally acquainted with Adjunct Peter Adler from the Cathedral School, and Høyen's visit helped to raise interest in Ribe's history within the college of teachers (Fig. 9). This came to fruition in a collection of eleven dissertations which under the general title of *Efterretninger angaaende Byen Ribe* ('Reports

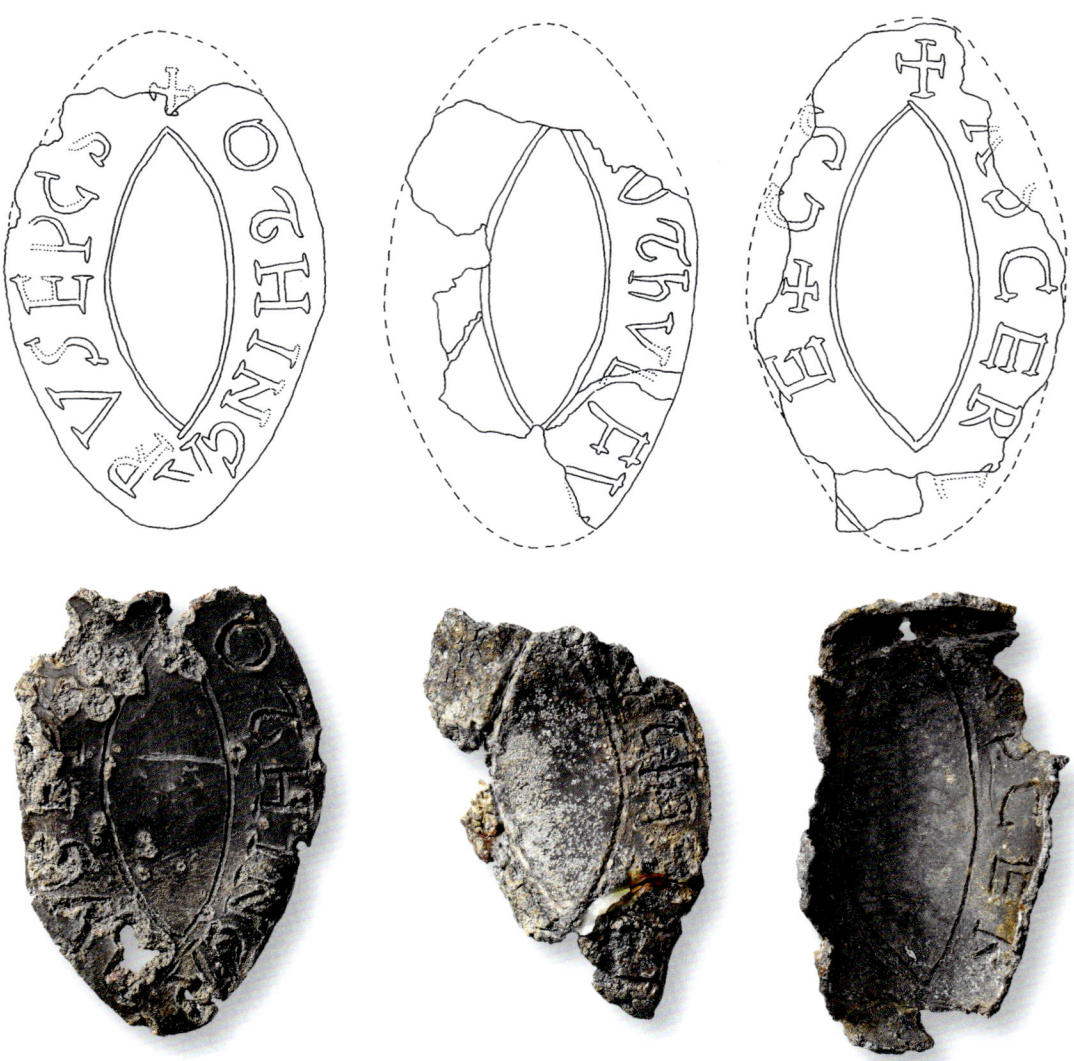

Fig. 8. The uniformity of the three lead seal matrices that were found in 1830 in the tomb in the north transept of the cathedral, of Bishops Odinkar, Nothulf and Asser, must mean that they were made when the bodies were translated to the tomb sometime in the second half of the 12th century. From Danmarks Kirker *and photo in NM.*

concerning the town of Ribe') were printed in the School's prospectuses from 1831 to 1848. Behind the first contributions was Adjunct Peter Tetens Hanssen, and the subject was the changes of Ribe Cathedral in the period following Terpager (Hanssen 1831). Along with this, a drawn plan of the church was printed.

The ten subsequent contributions were written in turn by the Rector of the School, Peter Nicolai Thorup, and Adjunct Adler. The latter focused mainly on the catastrophes of the 17th century while Thorup was interested in the topography of the town and its earlier history. The years 1833, 1835 and 1839 produced a comprehensive topographical account, which in the final contribution was accompanied by a *lithographic ground plan of the Town*, containing a wealth of histori-

cal data (Figs. 10 and 12) (Thorup 1833; 1835; 1839). Thorup's works were a major source of inspiration for Kinch's topographical analyses.

In 1836, the Art Association in Copenhagen announced, on Høyen's encouragement, a prize competition: *Presentation of the Exterior or Interior of the Cathedral in Ribe as one of the most remarkable Buildings in Denmark in architectonic Terms* (Villadsen 1974). The painter Jørgen Roed won the prize with the work *The Interior of Ribe Cathedral* which was was exhibited in Copenhagen at the end of 1836. Høyen presumably was also behind the fact that the young architect Theophilus Hansen arrived in Ribe in 1836, produced drawings and then drew up a major proposal for restoration. The objective of this work was probably that it should form part of a major study

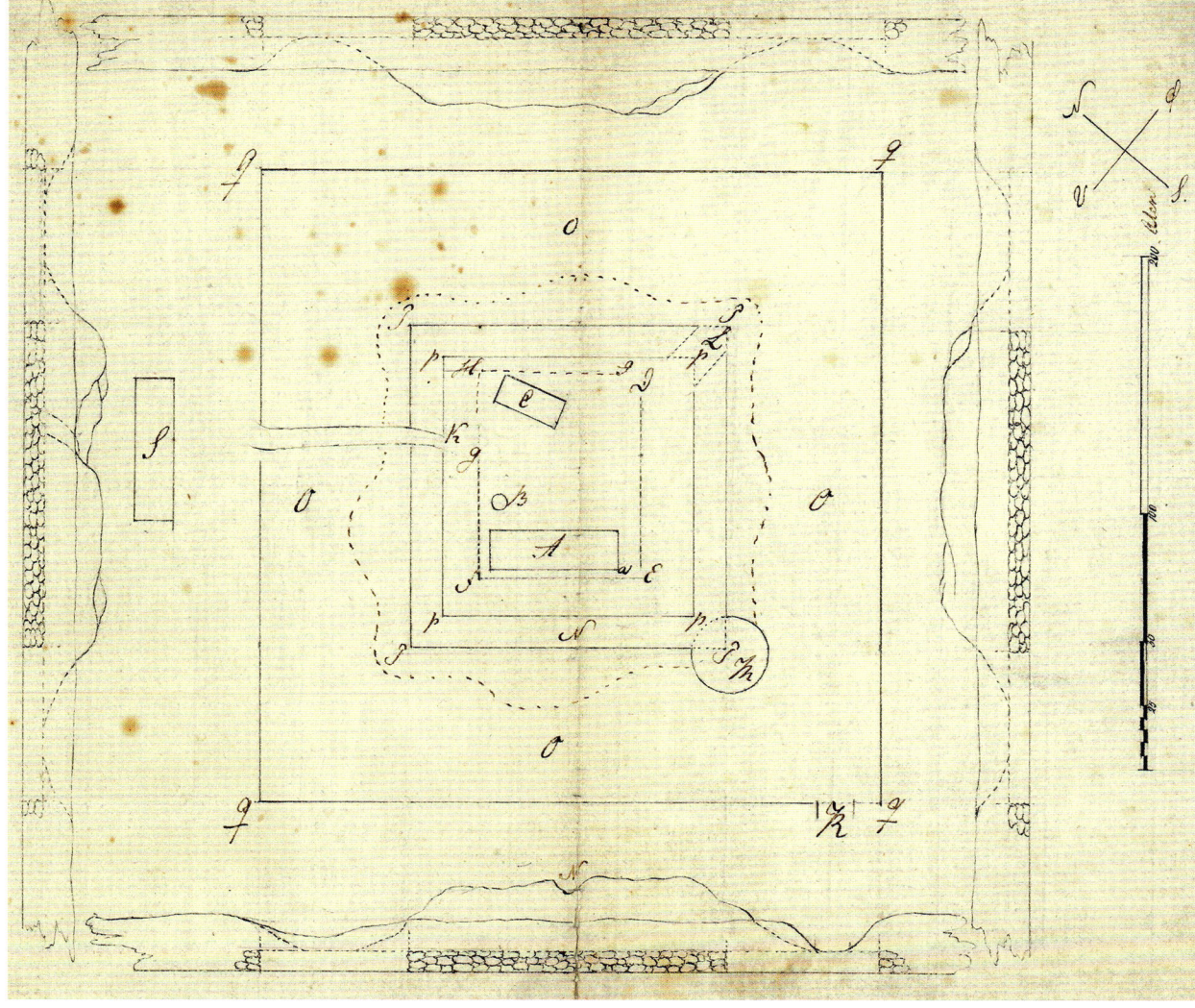

Fig. 9. 'Plan and Elevations of Riberhus Castle' produced by Adjunct P.T. Hanssen of the Ribe Cathedral School following Høyen's visit to the town. From the original in NM.

of Ribe Cathedral like that on Roskilde Cathedral which had been published 1833-5 (Hoffmann, Lund & Hansen 1833-5), but the plans ran aground when Hansen soon afterwards went to Athens and subsequently continued his career in Vienna. Theophilus Hansen's work was also exhibited in Copenhagen, however, and the presence of both in Ribe in 1836 meant that knowledge of this otherwise practically overlooked cathedral, so far from Copenhagen, was raised significantly, which helped to attract funds for the restoration of the tumbledown structure in 1843-5. Roed and Hansen also drew the town's remaining medieval town gate, Nørreport, which was demolished in 1843 (Fig. 11) (Madsen 1991b).

In 1847, the 30-year-old philologist Jacob Frederik Kinch was employed as Adjunct at Ribe Cathedral School. Kinch's capacity for work proved to be formidable, and alongside his teaching duties and several

public posts from the 1850s onwards he published a long series of articles in, amongst others, *Kirkehistoriske Samlinger* (Degn 1985). At the same time he gathered material for a new major town history, the first volume of which appeared in 1869: *Ribe Bys Historie og Beskrivelse indtil Reformationen* ('Ribe Town's History and Description as far as the Reformation') (Fig. 12) (Kinch 1869). The first, historical section is arranged chronologically with useful dates and headings in the margin, and it is still the most complete and thorough presentation of the sources for the history of the town. The second part of the book, *Ribe Bys Beskrivelse* ('Description of the Town of Ribe'), is a topographically organized analysis and review of the quarters of the town followed by descriptive accounts of the most important institutions. That a facsimile of the book was reprinted in 1985 is telling evidence of its quality and continued usefulness.

Fig. 10. Map of Ribe with partial reconstruction of the earlier topographical situation. From Thorup 1839.

Fig. 11. The Nørreport (North Gate) of Ribe, demolished in 1843. Engraving of 1854 after a drawing by Jørgen Roed, 1836. ASR accession no. 29.

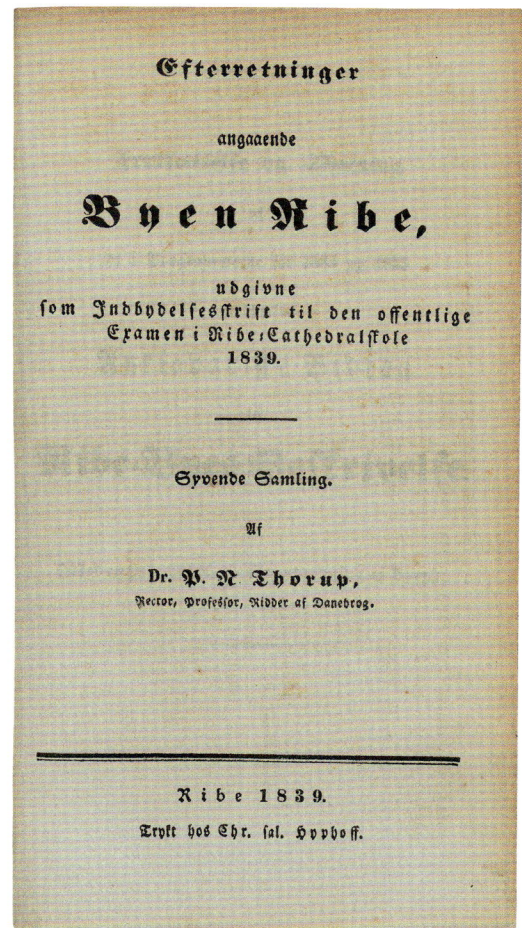
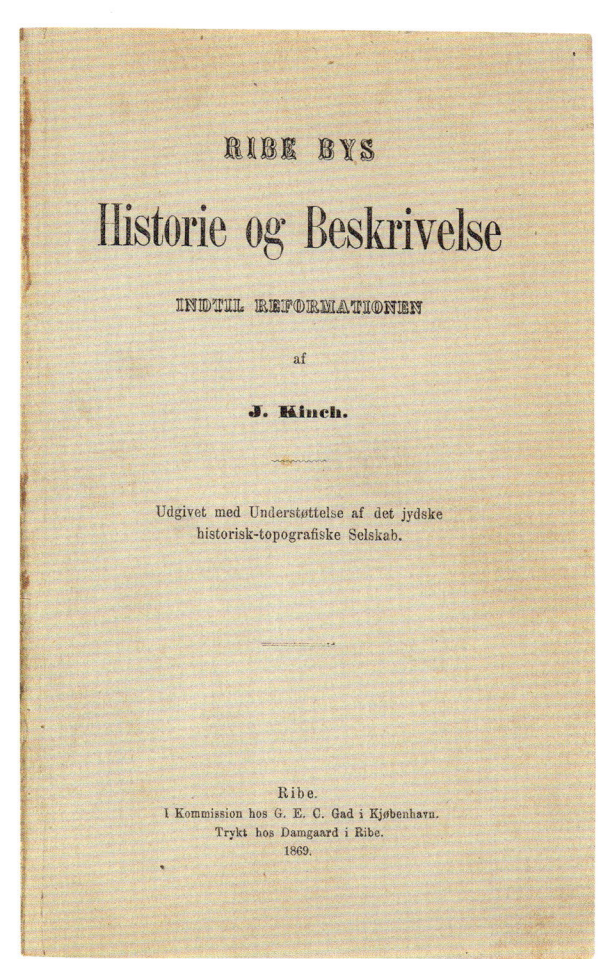

Fig. 12. Title pages from Thorup's Efterretninger angaaende Byen Ribe *(1839) and Kinch's* Ribe Bys Historie og Beskrivelse indtil Reformationen *(1869).*

Based entirely on the evidence of the documentary sources, Kinch drew a comprehensive picture of Ribe's history both chronologically and topographically. His method was a reasoned analysis in which the evidence of the various sources was presented and weighed up comparatively. The quality of this work has in the majority of cases been proven by much later archaeological excavations. As just one example may be noted that Kinch's reconstruction of the town's medieval street plan corresponds very closely to the archaeological results achieved more than a century later (Jantzen, Kieffer-Olsen & Madsen 1994). Equally thought-provoking is the fact that Kinch's work was carried out with practically no knowledge of the rich remains lying in the archaeological strata below the surface. In *Ribe Bys Historie* only two excavations are referred to: the excavation for manufacturer Giørtz's factory in Sønderportsgade in 1850, which uncovered walling from a medieval stone building, and Jacob Helm's plan of the foundations of St Peter's parish church which were lifted in 1855-6. Since the latter work had produced an antiquarian record in the form of a sketch of

the foundations, the clearance of the church site can be regarded as the first precursor of an archaeological excavation in Ribe (Kinch 1869, 32, 508).

In 1884, the second part appeared, *Ribe Bys Historie og Beskrivelse 2den Del. Fra Reformationen indtil Enevoldsmagtens indførelse* ('Ribe Town's History and Description 2nd Part: From the Reformation to the introduction of the Absolute Monarchy') (Kinch 1884), and Kinch's archive came also to form the basis for the treatment of later periods in *Ribe Bys Historie 1660-1730* (Matthiessen, Smith & Hermansen 1929) and *Ribe Bys Historie 1730-1820* (Smith & Hermansen 1929).

In 1855, *Den antikvariske Samling* was founded on the initiative of Adjuncts d'Origny and Kinch from the Cathedral School and the local businessman, founder of Ribe Ironfoundry, Frederik von Stöcken. From the foundation document it was made clear that the objective of the Collection was to preserve finds from Ribe and the surrounding area, both *genuine ancient Artefacts from the heathen Period (...) and Remains from the earlier Periods of the Town, which are either found in the Ground now and again or may be preserved in the Houses* (Busk

Laursen 1981, 276). The background to the founding of the Collection was national romanticism: to provide a reminder of the Fatherland and the ancestral lands. It was a key point, that the focus of the Collection was narrowly directed at the preservation of objects while the recording or drawing of archaeological structures produced during digging was not an issue that was addressed. Until his death in 1861 d'Origny was leader of the Den antikvariske Samling, after which this responsibility was transferred to Kinch who retained it until 1886. In the journal that was maintained by Kinch it is possible to track various excavations in the town, but in these cases too the opportunity for antiquarian recording appears to have been overlooked. It is illuminating that museum recording consisted of an Accessions Register which was maintained until Mogens Bencard took up the post in 1961.

The 1850s' belief in progress and an emergent local industrialization came to abrupt end with the defeat by Prussia and Austria in 1864. Once again Ribe was affected severely, as the town lost its southern hinterland and came to form a dead-end of a truncated Jutland. This defeat came to provide the backdrop to *Ribe Bys Historie*, as the collapse of the cathedral was the background story to *Ripæ Cimbricæ*.

Kinch's meticulous source-based methods had the corollary that those sections of the community which did not produce sources remain rather shadowy in his representation. It is a history dominated by men and the upper strata of society (Degn 1985, 10f.).

3.6 The main restoration of the cathedral and excavations in the churchyard in 1894 and 1930-1

A consequence of the defeat in the Second Schleswig War was that Ribe, and especially the cathedral, became a national symbol. This may have helped to raise the necessary state funding for the essential main restoration of the church which, after long preparation, was carried out from 1883 to 1904 (Fig. 13) (*DK*, Ribe amt, 358). It was preceded by a comprehensive investigation and publication of the building by Jacob Helms (Helms 1870), who had been Adjunct at the Cathedral School since 1850. The text accompanying this folio publication is the most thorough description of the unrestored building and, second to the church itself, the most important single source for the building's history.

Fig. 13. Photograph taken shortly after digging away around the church building in 1894. Thousands of burials were found in the soil removed from around the church, and these were removed with no antiquarian supervision. From a photograph in NM.

Fig. 14. Photograph of the reinforcement of the foundations in 1930. From a photograph in NM.

A history of research must also include what has not been found or has been destroyed without antiquarian record. Alas, the principal monument of the town, Ribe Cathedral, has suffered grievously, and on many occasions without any antiquarian observation. One aspect of the restoration of the cathedral is that there was extensive digging both inside the church and around it.

The reinforcement of the foundations, underpinning the walls, and sinking a heating system, removed burials and building remains both within and around the building, while the removal of the earth surrounding the building that took place in 1894 cleared away thousands of well-preserved burials from the Middle Ages and modern period (Fig. 13). The concurrent restoration of Roskilde Cathedral led to thorough excavations and recording by J.B. Løffler (Løffler 1897) and it is to be lamented that the equally rich potential in and around Ribe Cathedral was simply lost.

In 1930-1 the apse of the cathedral and the eastern transept wall were given new foundations. This extensive digging is testified to in a series of photographs which clearly show the extent of the destruction (Fig. 14). Where the digging of this area in 1894 had removed all the more recent graves, this destruction affected only earlier ones, which were removed in their hundreds with no form of antiquarian supervision whatsoever. A huge opportunity to locate the Viking-period churchyard was lost here; and as just one example it can be noted that in 2012, on the edge of the area dug in 1931, a wagon-body grave of the 10th century containing a silver shield-pendant and a string of beads was found (see section 5.9.8.3). Similarly important burials may have disappeared in considerable numbers in 1931; possibly remains of earlier wooden churches too?

3.7 Treasure finds, 1874 onwards

From Ribe Town and Field from time to time *danefæ* treasure finds have been delivered to the National Museum which have played little if any role in scholarly research. One key reason is that the objects found were neither physically nor conceptually close to the primarily locally active scholars. There are four Viking-period hoards from Ribe Town and Field, found in 1874 and subsequently. All of these appear to have been deposited in the 10th century, and they are discussed in greater detail in section 5.10.5.

3.8 The National Museum's early excavations, 1911-41

In 1902, the owner of plot 281b in Ribe Urban Area stumbled across remains of tufa walling. This was followed by the partial uncovering of the line of the wall, which showed that this must have been from the town's demolished St Clement's parish church. The first investigation was undertaken by the leader of Den antikvariske Samling, the merchant C. N. Termansen, who had the church walls uncovered and a plan of them drawn (Termansen 1905). In 1911 there followed a proper, more detailed excavation under C. M. Smidt from the National Museum, the first archaeological excavation in Ribe, which revealed a range of details about the church building while a number of burials within it were also recorded (Fig. 15). The intention had been for the ruins to form part of a park, but this scheme was halted in the face of public opposition. A fine house now covers some of the remains of the church.

In 1940-1 the National Museum undertook the thorough restoration of Riberhus castle mound. The initiative came from the Ribe Tourist Association, which wanted the castle mound furnished as a site for national celebrations. It was the then 62-year-old Inspector Christian Axel Jensen who was primarily responsible for the work, which was done by directed labour and only occasionally visited by the director (C.A. Jensen 1942). The ham-fisted and partly misguided restoration of the fortification turned it into a form that it had never had and removed the greater part of the archaeological strata that could have told the history of the site. The sides of the Renaissance-period ramparts were walled and had risen much more steeply than they now are, with the result that the surface at the top was once much greater. This is of significance in understanding the excavated building remains, which has never been very successfully achieved (Etting 2010a, 89). The ramparts on the top were also raised at this time although they have nothing to do with any earlier phase. There is a small quantity of finds, 485 pieces in total, from the excavations: a vanishingly small proportion of the thousands of finds that must have been seen. These items are collected under accession number ASR M7727.

Fig. 15. The north wall of the nave, choir and apse of St Clement's church, as it appeared after the NM excavations of 1911. From a photograph in the topographical picture archive of ASR.

3.9 Hugo Matthiessen's *Middelalderlige Byer*

In 1927, *Middelalderlige Byer* ('Medieval Towns'), by Hugo Matthiessen, was published. For Denmark, this marked a radical new direction in terms of research but regrettably it remained in splendid isolation. The book starts with words from Lucien Febvre: *La Terre et l'évolution humaine: introduction géographique à l'histoire* ('The Earth and human evolution: a geographical introduction to history': 1922) and thus declares the author's indebtedness to the embryonic French Annales school. This direction emerged within the discipline of History in reaction to the national romantic, annalistic tradition that Kinch represented amongst others. The two founders of the Annales school, Marc Bloch and Lucien Febvre, had both served in the First World War, and the revolution represented by the Annales school was a consequence of the all-encompassing critical self-reflection that came in the wake of the Treaty of Versailles of 1919.

In *Middelalderlige Byer*, Ribe is discussed in the chapter *Det store Træk over Ribe*, 'The Grand Design of Ribe'. For the first time, the town was positioned within a full northern European trade network, the interaction within which was presented as the motor of historical development. The aim of the book was:

To produce a complete picture, to see our market towns – grouped in time and place – growing up on Danish soil against a background that looms in the changing communication routes; because the towns clung to those, breathed, flourished or sickened in the context of the major movements which from the outside directed their waves towards our coasts. (Matthiessen 1927, 16; translated)

Behind the expressions one can make out a evolutionary, continuity-oriented view of history inspired by Darwin, within which the North was on the periphery of the great history. The mind-set of the book is modernistic, but the lyrically toned and pictorial language gives it a romantic undertow. A similar tension between an old world and a new is typical of a number of Matthiessen's other works, including his many photographs from Danish market towns.

3.10 Mogens Bencard and the Grønnegade excavation of 1953-6

In the years following 1945, clearance work in the northern European town centres that had been the targets of Second World War bombing raids revealed that there could be amazingly well-preserved culture layers, remains of buildings and artefactual finds lying

Fig. 16. The Grønnegade excavation from the west in 1955. In the middle of site is the remains of a High-medieval brick building on sand foundations embedded within organic cultural strata with exceptionally good conditions for the preservation of timber and other organic materials. From a photograph by Hans Stiesdal in the topographical picture archive of ASR.

below the towns. The recognition of this was the starting shot for northern European urban archaeology as a disciplinary field and was the real background to an urban excavation within Ribe started by the National Museum in 1953. This was a research excavation with one over-riding goal: to find Ansgar's Ribe, the Viking-period town, and so to establish an agreement between the written sources and the archaeological finds. For this purpose, with community support, a burnt site lying between Grønnegade and Præstegade was selected, where the Industrial Union's House had stood until it was destroyed by sabotage on 17 December 1943.

The project was initially placed with the First Department of the National Museum, and a trial excavation was carried out under the direction of P.V. Glob and Viggo Nielsen (Bencard 1973, 28). This was followed up by a proper excavation under the direction of Ebbe Lomborg, which came to a halt. In 1955, the project was transferred to the Second Department of the National Musueum under the leadership of the 30-year-old Hans Stiesdal, who had had his first experience in the recently completed excavations at Aggersborg (Sindbæk 2014a). Stiesdal employed as

site supervior the 25-year-old masters student in Art History Mogens Bencard, who undertook the excavation with assistants and workmen in 1955-7.

In terms of excavation methods, the 8x16-m site was divided into 2x2-m squares and the excavation then proceeded in 20-cm spits. This procedure had been used at Aggersborg, but was also employed in foreign town centre excavations and excavations of settlement mounds (terps/Wurten) in the Wadden Sea area (Siegmüller 2010; Sindbæk 2014a). From an early stage, however, it became clear at Grønnegade that the many structures within the ground, in the form of a brick building, wooden buildings and fencing remains, and large quantities of horizontal or standing timbers in the layers, were a challenge to the method selected (Fig. 16). The quantity of features and finds astonished all the participants, and only in 1956, at a depth of nearly 5 m, did the excavation come to the bottom of the human deposits (Fig. 17). The earliest features were dated to around the year 1100.

The afterlife of this investigation can be used as an indication of the challenges that went with the new archaeological discipline of excavation in the medieval

Fig. 17. Photograph from the Grønnegade excavation, 26 May 1956, when the excavation had reached a depth of more than five metres. From a photograph by Mogens Bencard in the topographical picture archive of ASR.

culture layers of towns. The results of this investigation have so far only been published in brief summaries (Stiesdal 1957; 1968). The pottery from the excavation was not processed by the museum and published until 1991 (Madsen 1991a) while the remainder of the comprehensive finds assemblage of 28,893 objects is, with few exceptions, unstudied (Bencard 1972). One exception is the iconic rune-stick – a key source for the medieval mind-set (Fig. 18) (Moltke 1960), the find context of which has never been made any clearer. From the many remains of buildings, which included a series of timber houses and fences overlain by a brick house on sand foundations, only the latter has been acknowledged by scholarship despite its uncertain dating (Bencard 1979a). As the first of its kind, the Grønnegade excavation came to suffer from lack of post-excavation provision and so to identify a critical challenge for urban archaeology: the treatment and study of the masses of data from the highly informative archaeological strata.

After the excavation was completed, Mogens Bencard returned to his studies. Upon completion of his Masters thesis he was appointed to Den antik-

variske Samling with the title of Antiquary. There was a long list of tasks awaiting him, and in light of their quantity it is no wonder that the Grønnegade excavation remained unprocessed (Olsen 1981).

The Museum Act of 1958 was the starting signal for building up the decentralized Danish museum system, with Mogens Bencard's appointment in Ribe as one of the more significant events. Along with the new law came directions for museum work, and from 1958 Den antikvariske Samling adopted the concept of the *museumssag*, which should literally be translated (unfortunately with some ambiguity) as 'museum case' and may also figuratively be referred to as a 'museum file'. The heading could comprise artefacts and other archived items. This concept has constituted the conceptual framework for the museum's professional work ever since.

From the viewpoint of the National Museum, the Grønnegade excavation was the starting point of archaeological excavations in Denmark's medieval towns (Liebgott 1989), but urban archaeology has deeper and more diverse roots. In the most important town of medieval Denmark, Lund, the tradition stretches right back to the founder of the museum *Kulturen* ('The Culture'), Georg Fredrik Johansson Karlin, while actual excavations were introduced by his successor, Ragnar Blomqvist. These pioneering efforts had little influence in Denmark, however (S. Larsson 2000). In Copenhagen, the antiquarian tradition was led by Schoolmaster Hans Nielsen Rosenkjær, who observed the large amount of digging in the archaeological strata of the city in the period around 1900. The military gentleman, Holger Utke Ramsing, later attended to the major digging connected with the defences. In the person of Christian Axel Jensen, the National Museum supported these efforts.

In 1957 an area of 8,000 sq m was cleared southwest of Budolfi church in Aalborg. Around 100 sq m was part-excavated leading to the finding of an interesting metalworking establishment from the 13th century, which was soon published (Riismøller 1960). In 1963-4 the former Hotel Skandinavien site in Aarhus was excavated. Along with much else, the archaeologists came across the Viking Period here, and seven years later three authors with what was then a major institution behind them could publish the results in *Aarhus Søndervold – en byarkæologisk undersøgelse* ('Aarhus Søndervold – an urban archaeological investigation': Andersen, Crabb & Madsen 1971). Of other important early excavations which were published, particular note is due to Store Sct. Pedersstræde in Viborg, excavated by Erik Levin Nielsen in 1966-7 (Levin Nielsen 1969).

3.11 The rescue excavation at St Peder's Church, 1960

In 1960, the National Museum carried out a minor excavation on the site of St Peder's Church in connection with the expansion of Ribe Ironfoundry. This unpublished investigation, *ASR 13/60 St. Peders kirketomt*, was undertaken under the direction of the 24-year-old research assistant at Danmarks Kirker, masters student Else-Marie Boyhus, during a pause in the construction of the factory building that was the reason for the dig. With the assistance of building workers, in the course of one week two trenches each 1 m in width were dug right across the postulated location of the church. At the southern end of both trenches large numbers of burials were found, while further north there were occasional walled graves constructed of both tufa and brick. At the northern end of both trial trenches a layer of fill appeared which was interpreted, apparently correctly, as a robber trench from the south wall of the church. The remainder of the church site must therefore lie further to the north beneath an earlier factory building, while the southern limit of the churchyard should be in the car park south of the building.

This was the first rescue excavation preceding a building development in Ribe: a form of excavation that now forms by far the greatest proportion of fieldwork. The rescue excavation as a form of inves-

Fig. 18. The rune-stick from Grønnegade. A five-sided amulet, 30 cm long, with a 342-graph inscription protecting against disease. From an original in NM.

tigation was then under development in the Danish towns. The construction of a multi-story car park in Næstved in 1957 had led to the excavation of the demolished Franciscan friary church, which was dug over two months by *long-term unemployed* to produce particularly rich although not so very well recorded finds (E. Skov 1959). The excavations in Aarhus and Viborg noted above were elements in the same course of development.

3.12 The slip theory, 1962

The search for Viking-period Ribe continued in the years following the Grønnegade excavation. In 1962, the ethnographer Lennart Edelberg of the Cathedral School, chairman of the council of Den antikvariske Samling and the most important individual in the development of the museum in Ribe from 1958, proposed, along with Mogens Bencard, a composite theory of the origins and development of the town paying particular attention to the position of the earliest settlement and an understanding of the many branches of the Ribe River throughout the

town (Edelberg & Bencard 1962). The legend of Gammel Ribe on Sdr. Farup Hede and a possible early relocation of the town was noted, but attention was otherwise focused on a map of the town of Ribe, which was described as *a spider's web with the cathedral in the middle*. The slip quarter of the town down towards Skibbroen (the Ship Bridge) stands apart from the remainder of the street plan and *to judge by the town plan here, it is the oldest part of the town*. The identification of this difference in street plan was correct, but the chronological relationship was the other way around, as Kinch shows (Kinch 1869, 554). The formation of the slip quarter from reclamation in the 14th century has since been confirmed by archival research (I. Nielsen 1985) and excavations in Fiskergade (excavation ASR 1992).

Empirical evidence from the layers underlying the town remained sparse. In 1958, Hans Stiesdal investigated the culture layers underneath Porsborg's cellar without uncovering *the Viking Period* while in 1962 Mogens Bencard carried out two small trench excavations around Kølholt's Slip in the gardens of Sortebrødregade 7 and Quedens Gård (Fig. 19). *The Viking Period* wasn't there either.

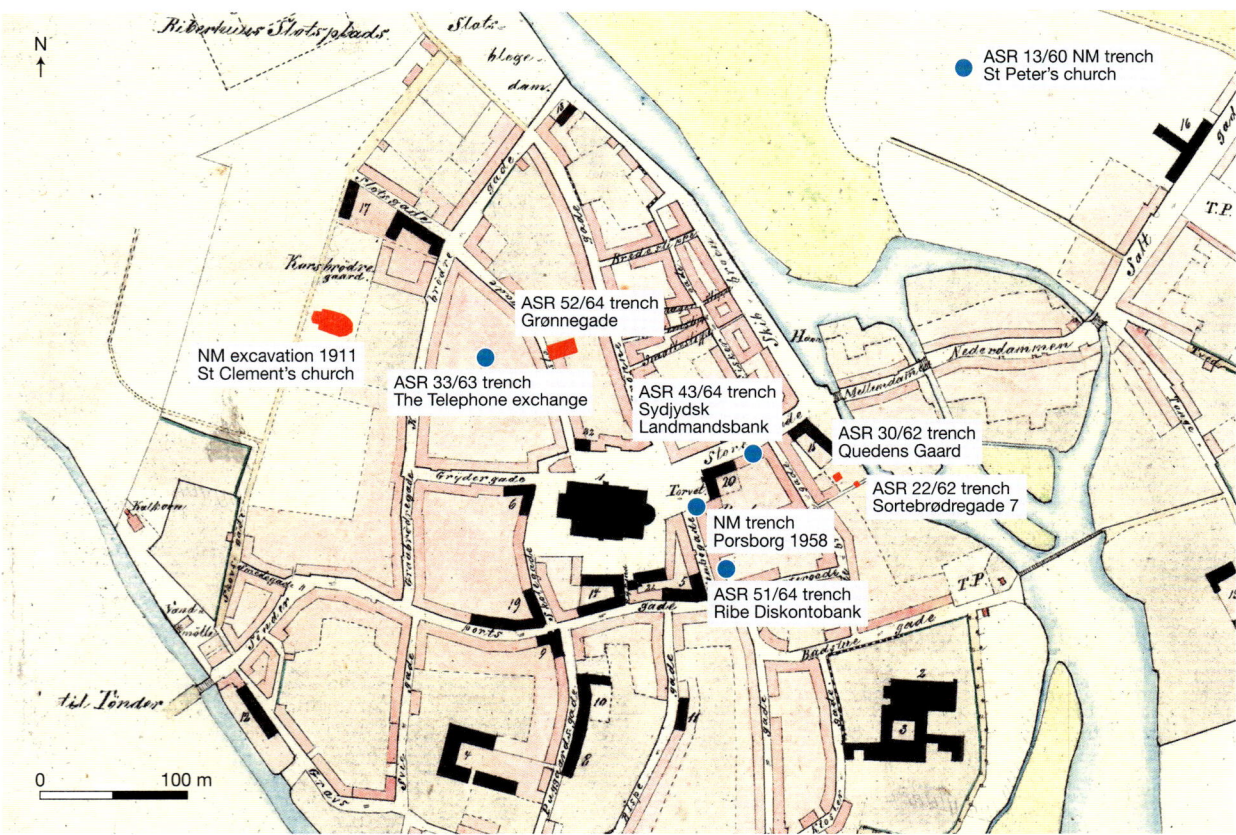

Fig. 19. The location of excavations in the town centre of Ribe down to 1965. Hans Stiesdal and Mogens Bencard's excavations of the 1950s and 60s were the first which reached the bottom of the culture layers in a controlled way, but without succeeding in identifying the missing Viking Period. The base map is Techt's plan of Ribe of 1858 for the first edition of Traps Danmark. From the original with the Geodata Agency with additions by the author.

42

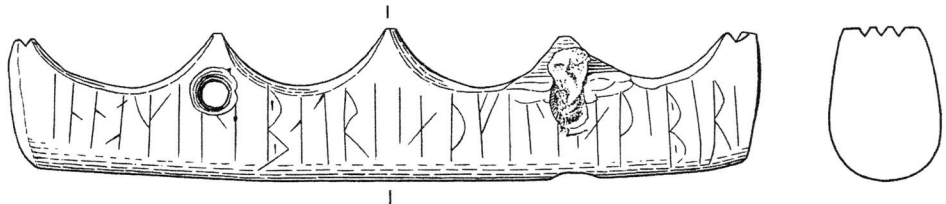

Fig. 20. Wooden handle with runes found in the soil removed during the building of Ribe Diskontobank. Length 10 cm. The inscription reads IN NOMINE PATRIS ÆTH FILII ÆTH SPIRI[TUS SANCTI]. Drawn by Aa. Andersen. ASR MD418.

3.13 New buildings in the town centre, 1959-78

A general lack of economic growth following defeat in the war of 1864 was the most important factor in the preservation of Ribe's old buildings and the town centre down to the enactment of the first Building Protection Act in 1918 and Ribe Kommune Conservation Statement of 1963 (Engqvist 1969). Compared with the other, larger medieval towns of Denmark, building activity has been little, and this has had the happy consequence that both the medieval urban area and the archaeological strata beneath the town have been less subject to interventions than so many other places. All the same, new buildings were put up from time to time, and from the end of the 1950s a number of major building projects took place in the town centre of Ribe which only to a very limited extent were followed by archaeological observations and have slipped out of the story of the archaeology of the town.

In 1959, a new building was put up for Ribe Diskontobank in von Stöckens Plads. The building was to have full-size cellars, and the excavation of those was watched by Mogens Bencard on behalf of the Second Department of the National Museum: investigation ASR 51/64, Ribe Diskontobank (Fig. 19). The laconic report notes that *those observations that could be made ahead of the fast-moving machines were, despite great assistance from all quarters, very limited.* However two E.-W. rows of piles with forked tops were observed. The excavation reached a depth of 3.5 m without coming to the bottom of the culture layers, which after the excavation were carted off to Tangevej, where *young people picked out what they found.*

Another financial institution in the town, Sydjysk Landmandsbank on Overdammen, was substantially extended in 1965. Before the building work, a trial trench excavation was carried out on the site: excavation ASR 43/64, Sydjysk Landmandsbank (Fig. 19). An area of 6 sq m was dug over a fortnight down into the culture layers which revealed well-preserved wooden structures sealed within a brown mass referred to as *culture mud*, which, further down, gave way to a black culture mud with layers of straw and manure. Amongst the 1,857 finds from the excavation may be noted a gold ring with a sapphire inlay from around the year 1200.

The grandest hotel in the town, Hotel Dagmar, was also extended several times in the course of the 1960s, with no significant archaeological recording apart from the collection of finds, the majority of which were from the fill areas in the Tange quarter.

In 1963, a new telephone exchange was built in the block between Præstegade and Korsbrødregade (Fig. 19). This building of some 300 sq m was built upon cast concrete well rings, and the sinking of these was followed by Mogens Bencard, who lifted staves from a barrel well from one of the deep pits.[4] Within the pit was found a broken but largely complete nozzled Pingsdorf jug (Fig. 21): still the only complete vessel of this type from Denmark, although according to Mogens Bencard there was yet another jug in the well which it was not possible to retrieve.[5] The jugs were probably fastened to a cord and used to raise water from the well.

The archaeological losses in connexion with building works in the town centre can only be regretted, but this state of affairs was by no means limited to Ribe. The destructions are a suppressed element in the history of research into the town which in fact produced many of the best artefactual finds in the museum but are practically ignored in the literature (Bencard 1981, 15).

The latest major archaeological loss in Ribe town centre came about in the context of the extension of Ribe Cathedral School in 1978. Here a little under 2,000 sq m was added to the three-sided school complex of 1855-6. Before construction, Den antikvariske

Fig. 21. The nozzled Pingsdorf jug found broken at the base of a well constructed from a French wine cask dated to the period 1146-91. As yet, this is the most complete Pingsdorf vessel known from Denmark. Found in the excavation for the Telephone Exchange of 1963. ASR 33/63 D93.

Samling undertook a major assessment study, the unfortunate result of which was that only in a minor area out by Puggaardsgade were important archaeological remains identified, as a result of which the main area was handed over: investigation ASR 8M75 (Madsen 1978). During the subsequent excavation for cellaring under the new building, however, amongst other things five medieval timber wells were found. In light of more recent discoveries, there are no grounds for doubting that the neglected area was the hindmost part of a series of plots facing on to the main street Sønderportsgade, where rubbish pits and well pits made up a large part of the stratigraphic sequence. This does not, however, change the fact that the area has to be supposed to have been occupied from the 11th century onwards. Some of the erroneous conclusions of the excavation were based upon a newly published geological report to which great weight was attached (Mertz 1977).

Apart from the building in the town centre noted here, there was also active building work going on north of the river, where no one yet realized that Viking-period Ribe was situated. In Sct. Nicolaj Gade both a supermarket (1962) and a new town hall (1963-6) were built, each of which involved a great deal of earth-shifting, without any associated archaeological observations.

3.14 The relocation hypothesis: Dankirke and Okholm, 1962-9

In 1962, an amateur archaeologist, the Rev Knud Høgsbro Østergaard from Aastrup, noticed a circular structure on a military air photograph of the site of Okholm north of Vester Vedsted. At the same time, another amateur archaeologist, Masters student and later famous anthropologist Jan Hjarnø, undertook excavations in Vester Vedsted parish which led to the discovery of several settlement sites and cemeteries of the Iron Age. Together, they carried out a minor excavation in Okholm, which revealed culture layers and a post-hole. The finds were donated to Den antikvariske Samling and a longer programme of excavation was carried out in the years 1963-9 in collaboration between Mogens Bencard and his close colleague Hans Jørgen Madsen of the Museum of Prehistory in Aarhus. The excavations were funded by a grant from the State Scientific Fund. They uncovered a multi-period settlement and huge quantities of blown sand that were a great challenge to recording. Some of this interesting complex of finds has since been published (Bencard 1969; L.C. Nielsen 1998; Høilund Nielsen 1998; Feveile 2001).

While the excavations at Okholm were underway, in 1964 a group of senior school pupils held an excavation in a field called *Dankirke* 2.5 km east of Okholm. Thick, find-rich culture layers from the Iron Age had been recorded at the site as early as 1882, and in 1900 a Roman denarius was found in the field, while very recently, in 1962, Jan Hjarnø had found a spiral-twisted gold finger ring in the neighbouring field. The pupils' shovels broke into a find-rich culture layer, and the museum was contacted. Mogens Bencard was already extremely busy, and the investigation was transferred to the National Museum in the person of Museum Inspector Elise Thorvildsen from the First Section, Prehistory of Denmark. Over six seasons from 1965 to 1970 she excavated a number of building foundations of the Early and Late Iron Age which, along with an exceptionally rich assemblage of finds, constitute the archaeological site of Dankirke, a *locus classicus* as a centre of wealth of the Iron Age (Jarl Hansen 1990) and a foundation stone in the discussion of Iron-age social structure which was particularly dynamic in the 1980s. The finds from both Okholm and Dankirke were of a distinctive character, but the

Fig. 22. Mogens Bencard during the excavation of medieval graves alongside the parish church of St Nikolaj and the nunnery in 1972, with his son on the trench edge. From a press photograph in Den antikvariske Samling's scrapbook.

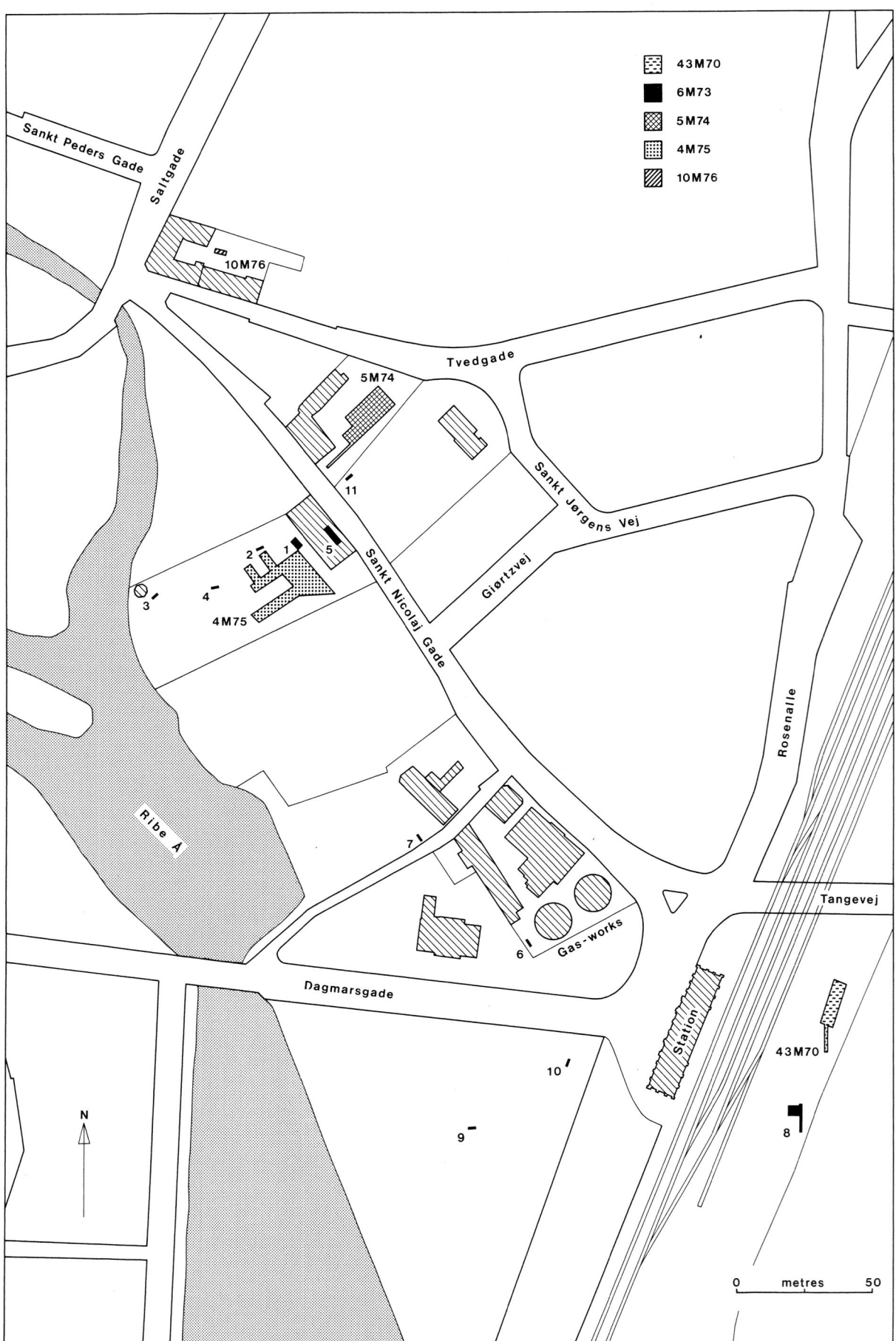

Sankt Peders Gade

Saltgade

43M70
6M73
5M74
4M75
10M76

10M76

Tvedgade

5M74

Sankt Jørgens Vej

11

Sankt Nicolai Gade

2   7
5
4   4M75
3

Giørtzvej

Ribe Å

Rosenalle

7

6   Gas-works

Tangevej

Dagmarsgade

Station

43M70

10

N

9

8

0   metres   50

46

◄ *Fig. 23. General map showing the location of the excavation trenches of the 1970-76 campaign. After the discovery beneath Ribe Art Museum in 1972-3 there was a preliminary programme of excavation in the form of eleven minor trenches scattered around the area surrounding Sct. Nicolaj Gade, ASR 6M73. The best strata were found around the Art Museum, and so the two major excavations in* Dommerhaven *(ASR 5M74) and* Kunstmuseets Have *(ASR 4M75) were deliberately placed as close to the good layers as possible. The map does not show quite a considerable number of modern buildings put up in the area since the 1950s. After Bencard 1981.*

Fig. 24. In layers from the first half of the 8th century beneath the cellar of the Art Museum, a perforated piece of human skull densely covered with runes was found in 1973. The challenging inscription is apparently an amulet to give protection against malice, possibly against a headache, for which the material used would be particularly relevant. ASR 6M73 D13764.

scope for comparison with other sites was still weak in the 1960s, and the question of where the original Ribe was located had to remain open. The problem was, however, about to resolve itself.

3.15 The original Ribe: excavations 1970-76

From 1970 to 1972, Mogens Bencard took up a research fellowship with the aim of writing a dissertation on local and imported medieval pottery. In his absence, Aino Kann Rasmussen, MA in Prehistoric Archaeology, deputized as Antiquary, and under her leadership, in 1970, a research excavation was carried out in the railroad area north of the Ribe River where the town's nunnery and parish church of St Nikolaj had been located (Fig. 23). The objective was to find the nunnery itself and the church. As anticipated, the excavation unearthed a number of burials of the Middle Ages, but beneath them a N.-S. furnished inhumation grave was found. At the waist was a lump of rusted iron, possibly a toilet set, with impressions of the clothing of the deceased in the corroded metal. Around the right wrist, the body had a copper-alloy armring of a type that was datable to the end of the Late Germanic Iron Age. The significance of the find was obvious to the excavation director and it was published immediately (Kann Rasmussen 1971). In 1972, the area of excavation was extended, leading to the finding of several medieval graves and also stray artefacts from the Viking Period (Fig. 22) (Bencard 1973; 1974).

The final breakthrough, however, came at the end of 1972, when work on the foundations was undertaken in the cellar of Ribe Kunstmuseum (Art Museum) in Sct. Nicolaj Gade. It was the long-serving registrar of the museum, the eccentric Mr. Aage Andersen, who walked past the piles of soil dug out and found glass beads, red deer antler and more, which could be dated to *the Viking Period!*

In the site now known as Kunstmuseets kælder the layers were particularly well preserved. There were, amongst other things, intact wooden structures, and in the layers that were very rich in finds were both small coins of the Frisian sceatt type and one iconic find: a piece of human skull with a perforation and densely covered in runes (Fig. 24) (Stoklund 2004). The exceptional results opened the way for two major excavations financed from a number of external sources. The principal grant came from the State Research Council for the Humanities, on which C. J. Becker sat, while Queen Margrethe's and Prince Henrik's Fund gave a significant extra sum, which together with many smaller local contributions secured the completion of the project. The excavations were sited close to the best area from 1973, in respectively the garden of the Judges' Office (excavation *ASR 5M74, Dommerhaven*) and behind the Art Museum (excavation *ASR 4M75, Kunstmuseets Have*) (Fig. 23).

In terms of excavation methodology, the approach, as at Grønnegade, was to divide the trench into squares, which were excavated in pre-determined spits, typically of 10 cm. Unlike the previous excavations, a consistent technique was to work in terms of named perceived units being excavated, using a sequence of combinations of letters – both with respect to individual features within the designated areas and later stratigraphical layers identified from the section drawings.

Things would have been very different if the excavations had been conducted following the stratigraphical method of excavation that was developed and formalized in urban archaeology in England in the course of the 1970s. Winchester and London in particular were important centres of methodological advance (Harris 1989). Ole Schiørring had participated in the Winchester excavation under Martin Biddle's directorship and was familiar with the stratigraphical method of excavation, but the new technique was not fully implemented. Furthermore, for most of 1975 Schiørring was working on excavations at Øm Monastery, and Steen W. Andersen was the site supervisor of the excavation in Kunstmuseets Have.

The stratigraphical method of excavation was introduced in Denmark with the excavations of The Medieval Town Project from 1977 onwards. The method was also implemented in Norway in the 1970s, while its establishment in Sweden was not until considerably later (S. Larsson 2000, 21).

The results of the excavations in Ribe from 1973-5 were sensational, and a *game changer* in the understanding of not only Late Iron-age social structures but also the history of urbanization (Olsen 1975). Mogens Bencard's understanding of the results of the excavations was first published following the excavation of 1973 (Bencard 1973; 1974). *Old Ribe* had now been found. It lay north of the river, and the excavations demonstrated that Ribe was a *vicus*: a trading site which dated back to the 8th century. The trading site was significantly older than Ansgar's church foundation, which was suggested to have been beneath the current cathedral. *In Ribe, the town moved to the church* (Bencard 1974, 15). But the discovery of the roots of the town in the 8th century had not solved the original problem of Viking-period Ribe proper, since no finds or structures appeared to belong to that period. Rather, it was limited to being a lacuna in the history of the town.

After the conclusion of the extensive excavations of 1974-5, a cross-disciplinary project of analysis and publication, the Centre for Historical Archaeology, was established at the University Centre of South Jutland with Mogens Bencard as the project director. In 1979 the first output of the work of this project saw the light of day in the form of the overview article *Wikingerzeitliches Handwerk in Ribe* ('Viking-period craft in Ribe': Bencard et al. 1979), providing an interim account of the rich assemblage of finds comprising 17,688 objects excluding pieces of animal bone. This article also included the first phasing of the stratigraphy. Four principal phases were distinguished:

- Phase 1: a plough-layer with ploughmarks and a thin culture layer above them.

- Phase 2: a midden layer consisting of animal dung.

- Phase 3: a series of thin layers with evidence of craftwork, which is described as an activity horizon.

- Phase 4: a midden layer sealed by layers of the 13th and 14th centuries.

Phases 1-3 were believed to have been formed successively with no significant breaks. The dating of the series of layers was based at this juncture entirely upon artefactual finds, amongst which the coin finds dated Phases 2 and 3 to the period AD 720-825 (Bencard et al. 1979, 120). There was no discussion of the internal organization of the site.

Soon afterwards, the planned series of publications was launched with the multi-disciplinary *Ribe Excavations 1970-76 Volume 1* (1981). At this date Mogens Bencard had taken up a new post as Chief Inspector of the Danish Royal Chronological Collection at Rosenborg. Despite his new position in a quite different part of the Danish museum sphere, the work on the project continued with enthusiasm. The dates of publication of the following volumes, 1984, 1990, 1991, 2004 and 2010, with contributions from historians, numismatists, conservators, geologists and more, is testimony to long-term and committed work, which was well intentioned, but down the line had eventually to see itself overtaken by more recent research discoveries from Ribe, on which more below.

In the course of his 25 years in Ribe, Mogens Bencard – for most of the period the only qualified person at the museum – managed to bring to completion the first urban archaeological excavation, to raise the funds for and carry through the restoration of Quendens Gård, to discover 8th-century Ribe, to undertake a large number of excavations across a large part of the Ribe administrative district, to found and edit the journal *Mark og Montre*, and to publish 57 articles. Of his special achievements particular regard is due to the swift publication, close cooperation with the universities, and the international perspective which, *inter alia*, was reflected in the choice of English as the language in which *Ribe Excavations 1970-76* was published.

3.16 The Medieval Town Project and the dug-away hypothesis

In 1977, the largest urban archaeological project to date within Denmark was launched: The Medieval Town Project, financed by the National Humanities Research Council, with Olaf Olsen as its presiding genius. Ribe was one of ten towns selected for thorough investigation, and the written report was entrusted to a masters student in History and Medieval Archaeology, Ingrid Nielsen, who was in fact the daughter of the previously mentioned Viggo Nielsen. The overall project has been described in Chapter 2, while the local sub-project in Ribe is presented here.

On the basis of thorough examination of the written, cartographic and archaeological evidence, the aim of the project was to formulate key questions concerning the historical and topographical development of the town, and to try to answer those by means of small, targeted excavations. From its start in 1977, two archaeological assistants were linked to the Ribe project in the persons of the recently qualified 29-year-old MA in Medieval Archaeology, Ole Schiørring, and the 23-year-old Masters student in Medieval Archaeology, Per Kristian Madsen. Both had taken part in Mogens Bencard's previous excavations around Sct. Nicolaj Gade and were pupils of Olaf Olsen.

Ribe og omegns jordbundforhold ('The geological context of Ribe and its district') by geologist Ellen Louise Mertz appeared in 1977 (Mertz 1977). This report mapped the geology underlying the culture layers in Ribe town on the basis of cores drilled down through the soft archaeological build-up. This work was highly influential on the members of the project and inspired the drilling of a number of further cores, for instance between Mellemdammen and Nederdammen (the central and lower sections of the street crossing the dam) and in the area east of Saltgade (I. Nielsen 1979; Nørnberg 1979; I. Nielsen 1985, 78f). From the evidence of the cores, a detailed map of the landscape before the town was produced (Fig. 99) (I. Nielsen 1985, fig. 17). The markedly uneven surface relief of this landscape should perhaps have caused the project members rather more concern, but possibly because of the scientific character of the research great significance was attached to the evidence of the cores. These were also used as scientific corrobora-tion of the existence of an area of wetland, Paypyt, referred to in the documentary sources (I. Nielsen 1979; 1985, 81f).

The Medieval Town Project looked first at the development of the built environment and the defences. Then, in the years 1979-81, there followed a large number of minor excavations and coring which were the first to use the stratigraphical method (fig. 25). These excavations led to the formulation of the *dug-away hypothesis* which would govern archaeological research into the town in the years that followed.

In 1979, the first excavation was carried out between Gravsgade and Kirkegårds Allé, where a section was cut through the fill-layers of a previously archaeologically unknown ditch and bank which in 1394 was referred to as *fossura nova*, the town's new ditch: excavation ASR 8M79D (Madsen & Schiørring 1981). The ditch and bank appear to have been constructed in the 13th century and to have filled up in the 16th and 17th centuries. During the summer of 1980 a complex section was dug through Riberhus Castle Mound, the earliest strata of which the excavators found very difficult to interpret (S. Jensen, Madsen & Schiørring 1982), while at the same time there was an excavation in the garden of the Bishop's Palace in Korsbrødregade where the monastery of the Knights of St John had been in the Middle Ages (Madsen ed. 1999, 89ff). All three excavations revealed rich culture layers and each in its own way provided fundamental new information.

In 1981, there was a major campaign of investigation on the northern side of the Ribe River which unfortunately can hardly be described other than as a failure (S. Jensen, Madsen & Schiørring 1982). Under the direction of Ole Schiørring, three or four trial trenches were dug in April between Ribe Ironfoundry and Sct. Peders Gade, where the scanty records indicate that the attention of the excavators was focused primarily on the sections and not the uncovered surface: excavation campaign ASR 141. Later that year Per Kristian Madsen led a series of trial excavations on both sides of the river, and also drilled core samples. North of the river there was an excavation alongside the Ironfoundry, in Hovedengen and in Ribelund, but at none of these sites was there success in identifying significant finds from the Viking Period or the Middle Ages: excavation campaigns ASR 152 and ASR 153.

Put alongside the earlier excavations north of the Ribe River, it now appears clear that there were proper culture layers only in the area east of Saltgade and around Sct. Nicolaj Gade. At the base, layers from the Viking Period were known, and these were overlain by a homogeneous culture layer which the geologists believed to be alluvial silt formed in the water during the Middle Ages. On this basis, a theory was constructed that the culture layers on the northern

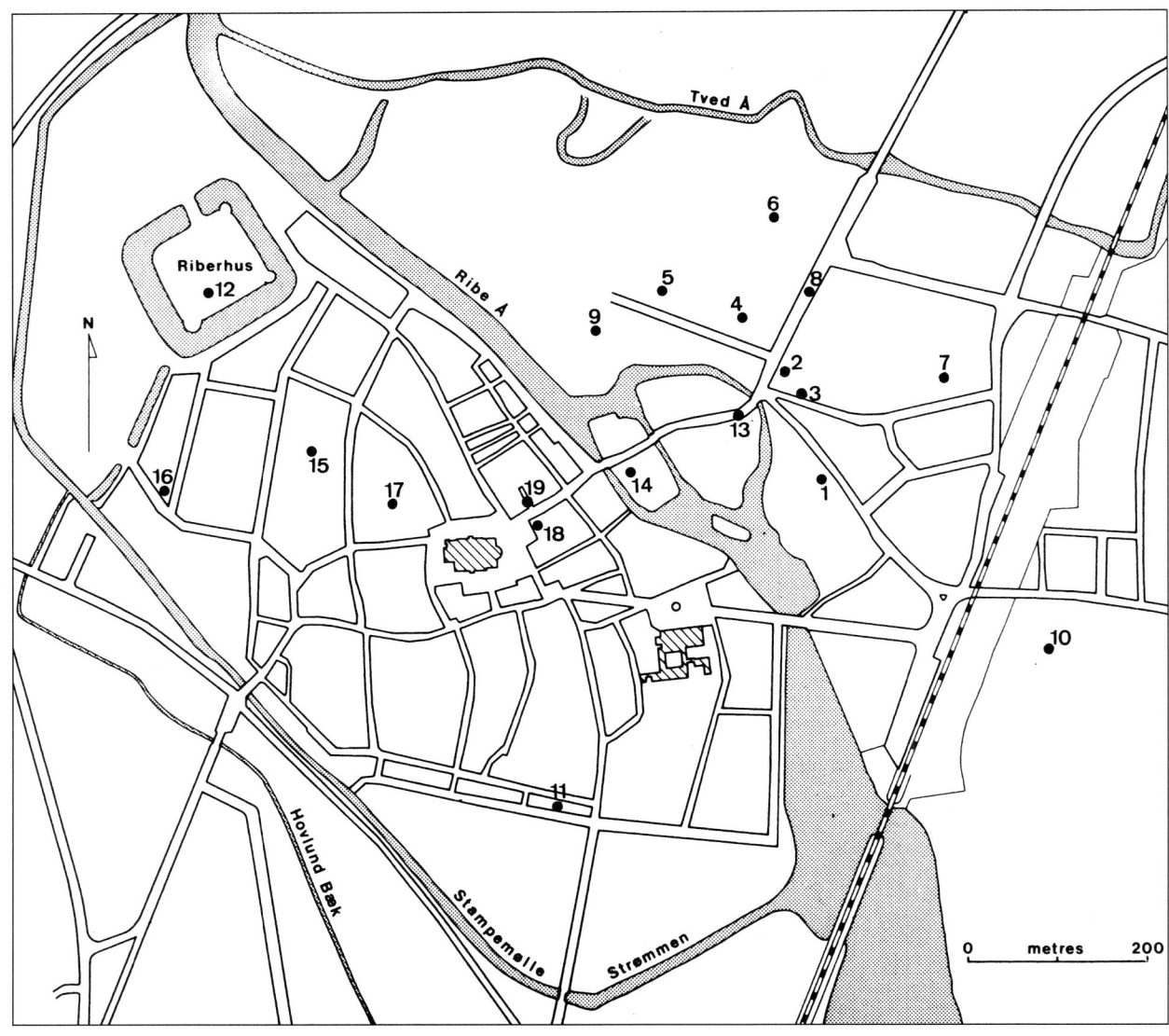

Fig. 25. Map of the many minor excavations and sites of coring undertaken in the period 1979-81. The excavations in the Fossura nova (the new moat) (11) and at Riberhus (12) produced valuable information, but the majority of the other, very small trenches did not reveal much that was new. After S. Jensen, Madsen & Schiørring 1982.

side of the river from the Viking Period and Middle Ages must have been extensively removed by having been dug away in the 13th century with the aim of constructing a pond for the Royal Mill, the building of which around AD 1250 fitted the proposed period of removal very well. In the hollow which this digging away had created the layers of Paypyt subsequently formed. Another version of the development of this area is presented in the chapter on topography.

In *Middelalderbyen Ribe* ('The Medieval Town of Ribe'), the output of the project, the earliest town of Ribe plays a minor part, to some extent sidelined by the failed excavations of this project. The original Ribe was regarded not as a town but as a *centre for trade or exchange of goods in significant quantities*, which emerged on the basis of its favourable location with

respect to both maritime and land traffic (I. Nielsen 1985, 34). The emergence of the site was associated with the expansion of North Sea trade in that period, and agricultural products and raw materials were assumed to be the principal commodities. Exchange of goods was supposed to have taken place in markets, and it was cautiously proposed that peace may have been assured by some central power. A possible connexion between the major rebuilding of the Danevirke in AD 737 and the king of the Danes referred to in connexion with the missionary Willibrord, *Ongendus*, was noted (I. Nielsen 1985, 35).

In the Viking Period proper, AD 800-1050, when the town makes its first appearance in written records, Ribe remained archaeologically completely unknown. Two possible explanations of this paradoxical situation were noted: the dug-away hypothesis for one, or the risk-of-storm-surge hypothesis as an alternative. The latter implied that Viking-period Ribe should be found in the higher areas east of Sct. Nicolaj Gade. The principal focus in *Middelalderbyen Ribe* lay rather on the cathedral side, and it contains many excellent examples of the main objectives of the project: the highly productive combination of the evidence of documentary and archaeological sources alike.

3.17 Danmarks Kirker

In the years 1979-83, the 'Denmark's Churches' project discussion of Ribe Cathedral was published under the editorship of Architect Elna Møller and assistant editor Ebbe Nyborg, MA in History and Archaeology. This publication discussed the questions of the earlier history of the church and town in the sections headed *Vor Frue kirke. Historisk indledning* ('The Church of Our Lady. Historical introduction') written by Busk Laursen MA, who was married first to Hans Stiesdal and from 1972 to Mogens Bencard, and *Domkirken og Byen* ('The Cathedral and the Town'), written by Ingrid Nielsen and Mogens Bencard. These sections also drew upon the work of the Medieval Town Project.

3.18 Stig Jensen and Per Kristian Madsen

The circumstances surrounding the appointment of Mogens Bencard's successor in 1980 were controversial, and came to leave deep marks in the landscape of the museum world of South-West Jutland and Denmark as a whole in the decades that followed. As early as 1976 Mogens Bencard had been asked to leave his post in Ribe and to move to Rosenborg, but the role as leader of the Centre for Historical Archaeology at the South Jutlandic University Centre delayed that scheme for three years. In Bencard's absence, his wife, Bodil Busk Laursen, was appointed Acting Antiquary. When Bencard's change of post became an accomplished fact during 1979, the Museum Board advertised the post of Antiquary. Three of the twelve applicants were called for interview on 20 June 1979, and the appointment committee, consisting of the Museum Board under the chairmanship of Lennart Edelberg, decided to appoint a 30-year-old MA in Prehistoric Archaeology from Aarhus University, Stig Jensen (Fig. 26).

Mogens Bencard, Bodil Busk Laursen, Professor of Medieval Archaeology Olaf Olsen, and Aino Kann Rasmussen, director of Esbjerg Museum from 1973,

Figs. 26 and 27. Stig Jensen excavating a lined well in Gammel Hviding in 1987. The well was subsequently dendrochronologically dated to the beginning of the 12th century. In his hand he has the fine Urnes-style brooch on the right, which had been lying on the bottom. Photograph in case ASR 440 and ASR 440x528. 2:1.

were extremely unhappy at the decision of the management and would have preferred Ole Schiørring as the new leader. One of the reasons was that in the wake of the Museum Act of 1976 with respect to the administration of the regional museum councils efforts were made to coordinate scholarly activity region by region, and those who advocated such specialization were of the view that Den antikvariske Samling should in future focus upon the town of Ribe and should appoint a medieval archaeologist whose expertise would be of benefit to the whole region. This view was not shared by the Museum Board, however.

Ribe amt's Museum Council, on which both Bodil Busk Laursen and Aino Kann Rasmussen sat, subsequently chose, without further discussion with the Board of Den antikvariske Samling, to register a complaint against the management's choice to the State Museum Committee *with the aim of having the decision that has been made changed.*[6] This was a serious challenge, as the State Museum Committee had to agree all academic appointments in local museums. The existence of this objection was also known to the local press.

On 29 August 1979, representatives from the State Museum Committee met with representatives of Ribe amt's Museum Council and the Board of Den antikvariske Samling plus Antiquary Bodil Busk Laursen in the schoolroom of Toldboden in Ribe. There are detailed minutes of the meeting, agreed by the participants, which document the process of appointment and the conflict between the Board's right to appoint whoever they believed to be best qualified and the regional museum council's wish for the new Antiquary's academic profile to reflect the regional needs. The result of the whole wretched business was that on 2 October 1979 the State Museum Committee accepted the appointment of Stig Jensen, who took up his post as Antiquary on 1 August 1980.

Unawares, Stig Jensen, who had been on a digging holiday in Crete during all of the above, was placed in the position of a Uriah, under intense scrutiny both locally and nationally. The new Antiquary proved to be able to exploit this situation with skill in his post over the coming years. Campaigns of advertising for finds, survey work on the ground and from the air, and an extensive use of volunteer workers, set off a sustained scientific quantum leap through the 1980s, the reporting of which was intended for a comprehensive settlement history project, *Marsk, land og bebyggelse* ('Marsh, land and settlement': S. Jensen 1984; S. Jensen ed. 1998). The excavations in Vilslev of 1986-7 and Gammel Hviding of 1986-94 similarly aroused justifiable interest. The idea that Den antikvariske Samling should concentrate upon the medieval town was thoroughly discredited.

In terms of excavation methodology, Stig Jensen's appointment also meant a significant new development, both in itself and in the fact that the so-called 'feature model' was introduced to archaeological fieldwork. A feature of this method of working was that the contexts under excavation were labeled in a series of A-numbers (A1, A2 etc) and that finds which were labeled in a series of X-numbers (X1, X2 etc) could be associated with an A-number, which would typically denote a stratigraphical context. This system has proved to be practical and is still in use. It was accompanied by the introduction of a new Journal Number system in which cases were numbered in succession. Numbers ASR 1-99 were reserved for major cases while the more run-of-the-mill cases were labeled ASR 100 onwards.[7]

In 1982, Per Kristian Madsen, now MA in Medieval Archaeology and Art History, was given a permanent post, and the museum had in its employment two academically strong inspectors who in the following decade would stimulate one another (Fig. 28). The progress of the major project to establish the Museum of Ribe's Vikings (*Museet Ribes Vikinger*) by the 1990s led, however, to ever greater separation between the specialist fields, and to an increasing degree the Ribe River came to be a boundary between the Viking Period north of the river and the Middle Ages to the south. This was the imposition of a boundary that came to be expressed in the permanent exhibition of the Museum of Ribe's Vikings which is divided into two halves, *Viking Period* and *Middle Ages* respectively, each with its own entrance and a partition wall running between them. In practice, this functional division lasted until 2010.

3.19 Excavations in the streets of the town from 1984 and the early damming hypothesis

The Museum Act of 1984 secured access to local government administration for the museums active in archaeology and provided better opportunities for the planning and execution of so-called 'rescue' excavations, which now constitute by far the largest part of archaeological work in Denmark. The Act of 1984 was the starting shot for a campaign of excavations in the streets of Ribe which, in its results and extent, is unparalleled in Danish urban archaeology. Before then, only minor watching had taken place in connexion with pipe-renewal below the street surface; the new law, however, made it possible to incorporate archaeological excavations from the planning stage of street works of that kind. The change in the law coincided with Ribe Kommune launching an ambi-

Fig. 28. Per Kristian Madsen to the left and the long-serving museum Registrar Aage Andersen at lunch in the garden of Quedens Gård early in the 1980s. From a photograph in the ASR archive.

tious, historically oriented restoration of the street area of the town, through which tarmac decks, overhead cables and concrete paving slabs were replaced with cobbles, cast-iron lamps and stone block paving.

All of the pipe trenches that enable a town to function had already been dug into the streets. In Ribe we know of a few wooden sunken drains from the Late Middle Ages and earlier modern period, but these appear to be extremely local phenomena (H. Skov 1993). The first major pipe-system was the gas piping of the 1860s, followed by water pipes in the 1880s and finally the sewage system in the years around 1900. Subsequently centralized heating pipes and various electric and fibre-optic cables have been added. The cumulative effect of this range of trenches on the culture layers of the town has been immense and contrasts incongruously with the small number of archaeological records that the interventions produced. One exception, however, are the observations of regional physician Kiær in connexion with the sinking of water pipes in the streets of the town in 1886 (Kiær 1888). This has given us detailed and usable descriptions of the sequences of layers below particular streets. This was the first time that the appearance and contents of the archaeological strata were described, although this information appears not to have been made use of in a heritage management context before the Medieval Town Project.

The archaeological excavations in the streets began in 1984 in Grønnegade and Torvet ('The Square') (J.E. Petersen 1985). Street by street they have added secure records of both the stratigraphical sequences beneath the surface and, most frequently, the underly-ing natural terrain, (Fig. 29). The typical procedure has been for an existing sewer to be dug up and the pipes removed section by section while the archaeologists record the stratigraphy in the sections and any features that may appear on the surface (Søvsø 2006).

A hypothesis which this series of excavations gave rise to was the idea of an early damming of the Ribe River before the construction of the Royal Mill around the year 1250. This was based upon pollen analyses from the earliest culture layers in Bispegade, from which the excavator drew the wider conclusions that the area had been regularly flooded with river water up to higher than 2.5m above sea-level in the period before the earliest culture layers were formed (H. Skov 1993; Aaby 1993, 25ff). As had been the case with the geological coring, archaeologists attached a great deal of weight to this evidence. It looks rather like a pattern of uncritical respect for interpretations based upon 'scientific' studies. Without being noted in the text, the pollen study was based upon the premiss that the series of layers had formed naturally, but since in fact we are dealing with artificially deposited fill layers this conclusion quite literally does not hold water.

Following on from the idea of an early damming of the river, the hunt now began for the dam itself, which must therefore be deeply hidden in the culture layers. The renovation of Nederdammen in 1994 provided the opportunity to dig a 7-m deep hole in the middle of the line of the street itself, where a 3.2-m thick layer of clay was found. *The thick layer of clay can only be understood as being the core of the dam* (H. Skov 1995, 33: translated). Another interpretation of this clay layer

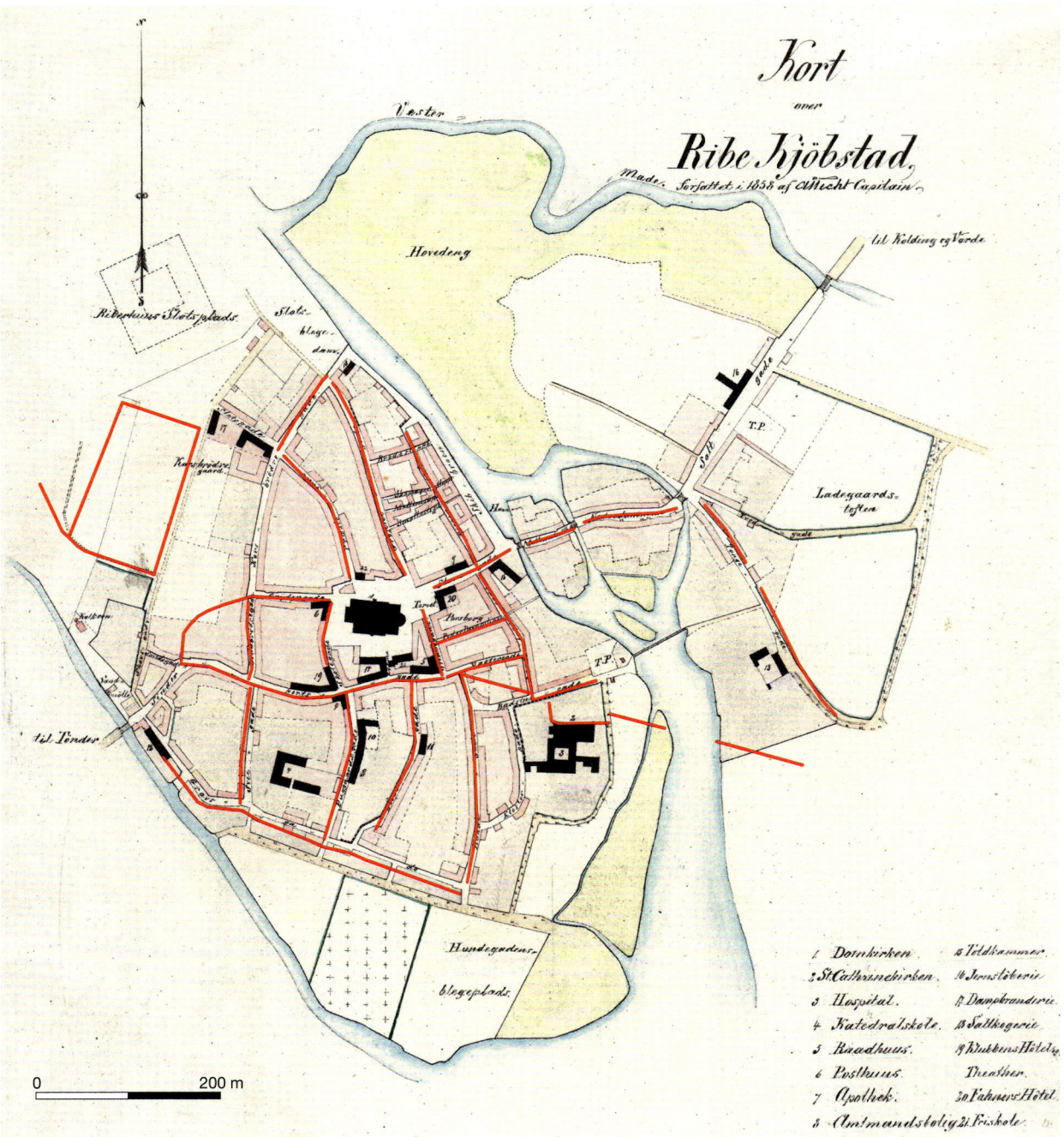

Fig. 29. Marked in red are the street excavations carried out in association with the renovation of pipe trenches and utilities in the streets of the town from 1984 onwards. The base map is Techt's plan of 1858. From the original with the Geodata Agency with additions by the author.

is presented in Chapter 4, *Topography*. The next opportunity to investigate the postulated dam came with the renovation of Overdammen and Mellemdammen in 1996 (L. Andersen 1997). Here too a layer of clay was found beneath the thick, organic, culture layers. That the layer of clay was thinner to the west was interpreted as showing that the hypothesized dam bent towards the south (L. Andersen 1997, 34); that idea can also be interpreted differently (see Section 5.3).

In the majority of the street excavations, the interventions showed that the street plan has been very stable indeed. The excavation in Puggaardsgade in 1989 had already revealed that there had been rows of posts standing in the streets that had carried planked roads. Dendrochronological datings of the posts from the streets excavated produced dates from the end of the 12th century into the first half of the 13th. In the areas where the culture layers were

54

thickest the lines of the sewers rarely reached the bottom so that information on the earliest structures was not accessible.

On the basis of the evidence available, the conclusion was drawn that the area of the town around the cathedral first grew seriously in the period around AD 1200. The thick culture layers of the town were regarded as products of deliberate filling and improvement for building of the lower-lying areas down by the river, influenced by the results of excavations in, for instance, Lübeck (Frandsen et al. 1991).

3.20 The emporium of Ribe, 1984–

Stig Jensen's first excavation in the layers around Sct. Nicolaj Gade was a relatively small site in 1981, excavation ASR 140 (Fig. 30). The first opportunity he had for a larger scale investigation came in advance of the expansion of the residential house Sct. Nicolaj Gade 8 where an extension of just 80 sq m with a full cellar was planned. After a preliminary investigation in 1985, the excavation itself, *ASR 7, Sct. Nicolaj Gade 8*, took place in 1986, with the sequence of layers of

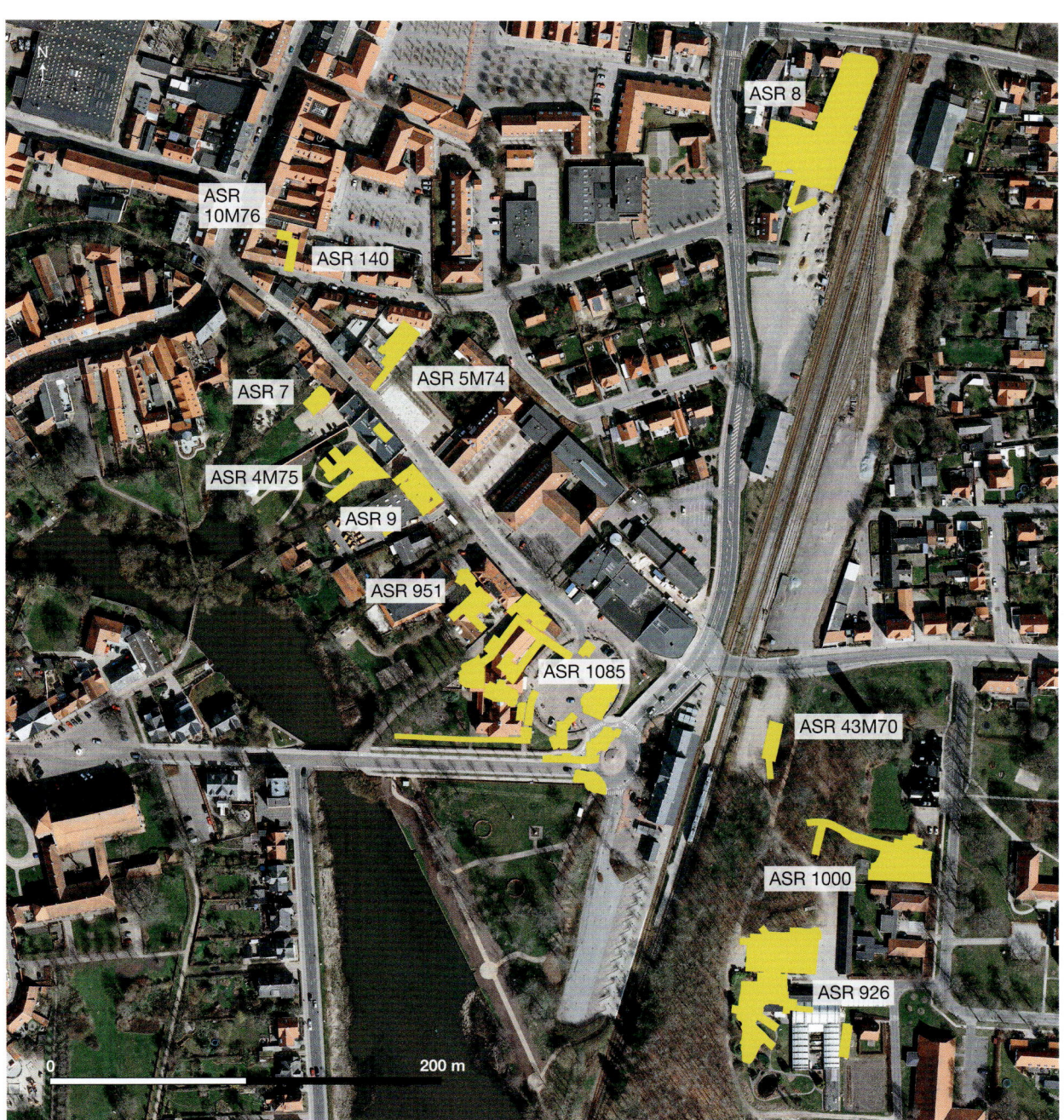

Fig. 30. The location of Mogens Bencard's and subsequently Stig Jensen's most important excavations of the earliest Ribe to the year 1993. The background is an orthophotograph from 2011 and the excavation trenches are shown in yellow.

the earliest settlement of Ribe being excavated stratigraphically for the first time. Those who took part were utterly convinced of the fact that both methodologically and in terms of work it was a breakthrough – and also, therefore, of the implicit criticism of the earlier excavation campaigns (Frandsen & Jensen 1988; 2006). The site director was Stig Jensen, while the 27-year-old MA in Prehistoric Archaeology Lene B. Frandsen was given the role of day-to-day site supervisor. The introduction of stratigraphy as the governing principle of the method of excavation opened up a previously unknown spatial dimension in the form of the well-known plot-tenement structure and made a more detailed phasing possible.

On the basis of this excavation the following image of the foundation and early development of Ribe was generated: The first activity on the site was in the form of a village which could be recognized in what the earliest culture layers contained in terms of pottery, animal bone and loomweights, and the identification of which could hardly have come about were it not for the many ploughmarks recorded underneath the culture layers. Ploughmarks had then already been observed in excavations ASR 6M73, ASR 5M74 and ASR 438 (Fig. 30). This phase was called *the village layer*. It was followed by the foundation of the trading/market site (both terms were used), which is cognitively recognizable in *workshop levels* (VH) or *boundary ditches* (G) (Tab. 1). The workshop levels were clearly stratified,

but that was not the case with the layers of ditch fill. For this reason the workshop levels were understood to be the products of many events while the ditches were seen as products of few actions. The layers in workshop level 2 apparently overlay the boundary lines, but after they had been deposited a new series of boundaries was established on the same lines as before. Excavation ASR 7 also introduced water-sieving as a technique for separating the culture layer as a phenomenon from that of the find.

The series of layers formed in the market site was subsequently cut off by a level that had been dug away; it appeared to cover the period down to the around the year 800 (see the debate in Frandsen & Jensen 1988; 1990; Bencard 1990). The layers from the dug-away horizon and above, around 2 m of culture layers, were removed by machine. For this reason important information on medieval activities in the area and their relationship to the structure of the original Ribe was lost: see section 5.2.

With the excavation *ASR 8, Rosen Allé* of 1989, Den antikvariske Samling started a coup in terms of excavation which over the following four years would revolutionize understanding of the extent and organization of the original Ribe. The Rosen Allé excavation was brought about by a council wish to construct a car park, and in conformity with the terms of the Museum Act the area was assessed archaeologically by Per Kristian Madsen and Stig Jensen, and then excavated under the direction of Stig Jensen, with a 25-year-old masters student in Prehistoric Archaeology on the team, Claus Feveile. He had been linked to Den antikvariske Samling since 1980 first as a volunteer and then as an archaeology student (Fig. 31).

Following the open-area excavation technique of settlement archaeology, the overlying unstratified topsoil was removed, and the excavation came as a result to be concerned entirely with cut features. Complicating the state of affairs even further, it could be seen that the originally slight slope downwards to the north of the area had been leveled out, probably when the railway was built in the 1870s.[8] A result of that was that the ground surface had to varying extents been removed in the southern part of the site but was well preserved on the northern side. The most important discoveries in this complex excavation were as follows:

Digging away	(A)
Cut feature, mixed	(NBLA)
Cut feature, medieval	(NMID)
Cut feature, Viking-period	(NVIK)
Workshop levels 3-6	(VH2a) on the neighbouring plot
Uppermost boundary ditch (G2)	
Workshop level 6	(VH6)
Workshop level 5	(VH5)
Workshop level 4	(VH4)
Workshop level 3	(VH3)
Workshop level 2	(VH2): the phase without ditches
Lowest boundary ditch (G2)	
Workshop level 1	(VH1): on the neighbouring plot (VH1a)
Village layer	(L)
Sub-soil	(U)

Table 1. The phase structure drawn up on the basis of excavation ASR 7 in Sct. Nicolaj Gade 8 introduced a new set of terms to the analysis and interpretation of the oldest Ribe. The earliest culture layers were believed to belong to a preceding village phase called the village layer *while the overlying stratified sequence of layers was divided into* workshop levels *within the newly recognized plot pattern in which the individual tenement areas were divided by* boundary ditches. *After Frandsen & Jensen 2006.*

- *A cemetery* with cremation and inhumation burials, the datable examples of which could be assigned to the 8th or early 9th centuries.

- A slightly curved trench, originally about 2 m wide at ground level and around 0.7 m deep. This trench was labeled *town ditch A* and was also apparently both dug and filled in the course of the 9th century.

- Wheel ruts from a road running E.-W. across the ditch flanked by settlement in the form of sunken feature and post-built buildings. Two of the sunken feature buildings (SFBs) were dated from their finds to *the second half of the 9th century at the earliest*. The connexion between the road and the settlement is based upon horizontal stratigraphical arguments and thus remains open to discussion.

- A fortification in the form of a ditch and bank which at the time would have been around 7 m wide and 1.5 m deep, labeled *ditch and bank B*. The excavation found an opening by which the two lines of ditch and bank lay slightly misaligned with one another.

- Three post-built, N.-S. buildings with associated features in the form of pits and wells that are dendrochronologically dated to c. 1150. The buildings lay alongside a N.-S. roadway represented by wheel ruts which, from horizontal stratigraphical evidence, must be contemporary with the buildings.

Apart from the dendrochronological studies of the medieval wells, no scientific dating has been undertaken, and the chronology of the site is consequently dependent upon comparisons with the well-dated artefactual finds from the stratified plots and the stratigraphy between the individual features of the Rosen Allé excavation. The relationships between town ditch A, the Viking-period settlement and ditch and bank B are problematic, and will be discussed in section 5.10, Ribe in the 9th century.

As early as May 1990 the next major excavation was begun which would eventually expand knowledge of the earliest Ribe and add some new and crucial details to understanding. The nursery garden run by Ribe Amt at Ribelund was to be extended, and the project led to the excavation of c. 1,300 sq m, *ASR 926, Ribelund I* (Feveile 2006d). The director was Stig Jensen and, in terms of method, as at Rosen Allé the topsoil was removed by machine until cut features appeared in the subsoil. This excavation also added significant new information to our understanding of the structure of the original Ribe:

- A multi-phase and densely packed *settlement* comprising both post-built structures and SFBs lying alongside a N.-S. roadway which could be recognized from wheel ruts. Dated from the mid-8th to the mid-9th century from the finds.

- *Town ditch A* ended by this roadway and so respects it.

- A large, previously unknown ditch and bank, called *ditch and bank C*, cuts across the eastern side of the excavation. During the recording of

Fig. 31. A wet and muddy Claus Feveile just after excavating a well on Giørtzvej, ASR 990, in 1991. The well lining was an early 8th century wine barrel from the Mainz region. From a photograph in case ASR 990.

the sections of the excavation trench remains of a turf-built rampart were recognized on the inner side. Later investigations have confirmed the line of this defensive feature.

- The area beneath the rampart had been *ploughed with a mouldboard plough* in the phase between the Viking-period settlement and the construction of the rampart.

- At the western limit of excavation a feature running N.-S. was recorded which was interpreted as an *erosion edge, created by the Ribe River* in the period between the Viking Period and the 12th century. This conclusion, however, cannot be correct: see section 5.3.

As a direct consequence of this, another awesome challenge faced Stig Jensen and Claus Feveile. In Sct. Nicolaj Gade, the museum became aware that there were plans for a major building project, and this led to the largest and most informative excavation so far of the stratified market site plots, *ASR 9 Posthuset*, which took place under Stig Jensen's direction in 1990-91 (Feveile & Jensen 2006b). The occasion was the building of a new Post Office in Sct. Nicolaj Gade which was to be founded upon cast spot foundations connected by concrete girders. The Archaeological Office at the State Antiquary was not prepared to grant funds for excavation in connexion with this project. Stig Jensen threatened the then State Antiquary Olaf Olsen with demonstrations in Ribe if no excavation was carried out. This led to Olaf Olsen turning to an acquaintance, Post and Communications Director-General Israelsen, following which the resources were raised for the excavation which more than any other has drawn the current image of the earliest Ribe to be carried out.

In this excavation, the stratigraphical method was combined with consistent water-sieving. The earliest culture layers of this excavation also contained large quantities of preserved timber which have produced 31 dendrochronological dates (Feveile & Jensen 2006b, 126). With the stratigraphy of the Post Office excavation as a key, a new phasing was worked out, covering the period of c. AD 700-850, which one hopes will not be subject to quite such frequent revisions as its predecessors.[9] The Post Office excavation has produced the best insight to date into the formation and use of the plots, and concurrently introduced a series of new terms to research into the earliest Ribe:

- *The yellow sand layer*, Phase A. Over nearly all of the site there was a yellow sand layer which the excavators understood to have been deposited by human action and which was interpreted as evidence of a master plan preceding the establishment of the plots. An interpretation which was based upon royal command was proposed shortly after the excavation (Jensen 1991b), undoubtedly inspired by the gravel roadways in Hamwic. Since then, however, the sand has proved to be naturally formed driftsand deposited long before the creation of Ribe. Ardmarks were found underneath the sand.

- The village layer from ASR 7 was re-interpreted as a preparatory phase for the first phase of the first town of Ribe preceding the establishment of the regular plot system.

- Stratified deposits on plots from the 9th century too could be identified.

At the same time as the exaction of ASR 9 (!), yet another excavation was carried out slightly to the east, *ASR 951 Plejehjemmet Riberhus* (Riberhus Nursing Home), the results of which now lead one to conclude that the excavators had too much on their plates at one time. A N.-S. roadway of the Middle Ages was found here that had eroded at least a metre down into the ground. In association with the wheel ruts were found a large number of post-holes and trench-like features which were not investigated further. Later activity had destroyed virtually all of the older features but sieving of the machine-dug soil produced a very rich collection of finds (Feveile 2006f).

On what is known as the Water Tower Hill where St Nikolaj's Church and monastery stood in the Middle Ages, coring was carried out which indicated that this was an artificial platform, suggested to have been the location of the *Viking-period royal residence* (S. Jensen 1990). Out of a desire to either refute or confirm this hypothesis, in the autumn of 1991 as a research excavation a trial trench was dug between the standing vegetation, to be followed in 1992 by an area excavation funded by State Antiquary's Archaeological Secretariat as supposedly a site threatened by cultivation. The two sites together form excavation *ASR 1000, Ribelund II* (Feveile 2006h). A total of 625 sq m was excavated. In addition to the identification of the three now known eastern boundaries, town ditch A, ditch and bank B and ditch and bank C, the most important result of the excavation was:

- two cremation graves and fourteen inhumation graves. The latter were unfurnished and possibly Christian. Bones from two of the inhumation graves were radiocarbon-dated and the majority of the calibrated probability falls in the 10th century.

The end of this demanding but productive series of excavations came in 1993, when the Museum of Ribe's Vikings was to be built on a site between the former electricity and gas works of the town. This led to the excavation *ASR 1085 Gasværksgrunden* (The Gas Works Site: Feveile 2006i), which produced two important pieces of information:

- The area had stood relatively high, and in no places were there any preserved culture layers above the ground surface, although finds from the 8th and 9th century of the same character as those from the plots were found within cut features.

- Probably early in the medieval period, a castle was constructed in the area, of which only the moat remained. The inner side of the moat was lined with clay turves. In the fill of the moat deep traffic tracks were visible which had to some extent blurred the limits of the ditch.

There were several more excavations besides those listed above, but these are those which involved the points of interpretation which our understanding of the growth and development of Ribe are founded upon. In the course of four years' intense excavation the perception of the earliest Ribe was revolutionized.

Stig Jensen's untimely death in 1998 meant that responsibility for the publication of this in every way comprehensive evidence passed to his pupil, Claus Feveile, who from 2000 had a permanent job as Museum Inspector at Den antikvariske Samling. The result of this great work appeared in 2006 in the form of *Ribe Studier. Det ældste Ribe. Udgravninger på nordsiden af Ribe Å 1984-2000 Bind 1.1* and *1.2* ('Ribe Studies: The Earliest Ribe. Excavations on the north side of the Ribe River 1984-2000', vols. 1.1 and 1.2: ed. C. Feveile). The principal focus of the publication is *the topographical development of the town and the internal chronology of the site.* By presenting the many excavations in catalogue form, the objective was *to create a foundation so that further analyses can build upon a reliable basis* (Feveile 2006a, p. 10). With his usual modesty, the author stressed the importance of Stig Jensen for the appearance of *Ribe Studier*, but the table of contents tells another story.

3.21 The urban archaeology meeting in Ribe, 1988-

In the spring of 1988, Ole Schiørring and Per Kristian Madsen issued invitations to an *Urban Archaeology Meeting in Ribe* to be held on 9-10 May at Ribe Youth Hostel. The objective was *to discuss practical and shared problems in Danish urban archaeology* and *to produce a sort of overview and indicate where work is needed.* This would prove to be a vital initiative which ended up continuing and developing the networks created by the Medieval Town Project. The following year, the meeting assembled under a general title *Byer før 1200?* (Towns before 1200) and this style of thematic conference with varying titles has been maintained since then. The fifth, fifteenth and twenty-fifth meetings were international conferences.

Per Kristian Madsen was the real driving force and organizer of the conference, and with the help of grants from the National Research Council for the Humanities and later the National Museum Board it was possible to invite international speakers, including a large number of the leading urban archaeologists of the time. Direct written outputs from the 26 meetings so far have been limited, but as a forum for the dissemination of experience and forming networks the importance of the initiative in Danish town archaeology has been considerable.

3.22 The periodical By, marsk og geest, 1989-

In 1965, Mogens Bencard was one of the driving forces behind the establishment of the periodical *Mark og Montre* ('Field and Showcase'), which – within the bounds of Ribe Amt – published articles on cultural history representing both archaeology and more recent times (Fig. 32). In 1988, Ribe Amts Museum Council introduced a new layout in a larger format and concurrently redirected the editorial focus of the periodical more towards the presentation of exhibitions and topics in museum politics. Behind that lay a desire to offer a general platform for a growing and more diverse museum landscape in South-West Jutland. The result, however, was rather a draining away of contents, and after the reorganization of 2007 *Mark og Montre* came to share the same fate as the old amt-system.

Den antikvariske Samling wanted to be able to carry on with more traditional scholarly publication which had found a place in *Mark og Montre* down to 1988. In order to create a place for this, the periodical *By, marsk og geest* ('Town, marsh and geest') was founded, the first annual issue of which, with the sub-title 'Annual Report 1988' was published in 1990 (Fig. 32). A couple of key directions were specified in the Foreword: *This is an annual report which emphasizes scholarly content* with articles *ideally written by authors from outside the museum's own sphere.* This line has been maintained since then. *By, marsk og geest* included English summaries from the start and also includes, when appropriate, articles in English or German.

The founding of *By, marsk og geest* was a brave and key decision on the part of Stig Jensen and Per Kristian Madsen. Over the years it has supported the museum's ambitions in respect of weighty research publication and the very existence of this periodical has helped many articles across the final barrier of prioritization between writing up and the many other duties of the staff. In its early years in particular, the layout and format of the publication were unimpressive, but that reflected far more than the contents did that it was a relatively small institution that was responsible for the publication.

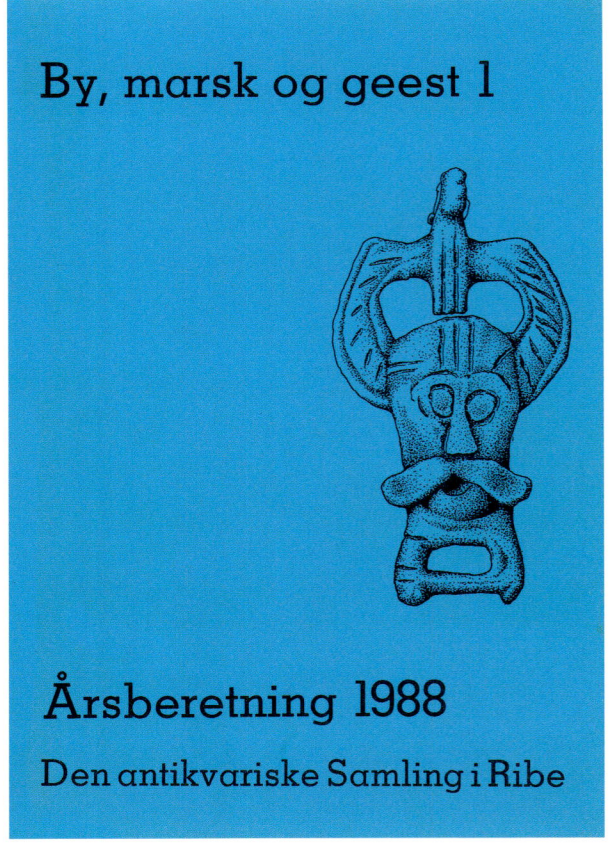

Fig. 32. From its launch in 1965, Mark og Montre *was the preferred local channel of publication for the staff of the museum, but editorial changes with the periodical led to Den antikvariske Samling launching its own periodical,* By, marsk og geest, *in 1988, which has appeared annually ever since and is now on the endorsed list of the Ministry of Education and Research. The last issue of* Mark og Montre *appeared in 2007.*

3.23 Major excavations in the western suburbs of Ribe, 1987-2000

In 1983, in the search for the still absent later Viking Period, a series of minor excavations were carried out in the western part of Ribe with support from various funds. These did not discover the Viking Period but did reveal that that there were really substantial culture layers from the Middle Ages in this part of the town as well (Madsen ed. 1999). The first larger open-area excavation in the area was caused by the Ribe Diocese's extension of its administrative building at Korsbrødregård; in 1987 an area of c. 200 sq m was dug: excavation *ASR 565 Korsbrødregård* (Fig. 33). The excavation was now conducted following the stratigraphy here south of the river too, and in the publication of the work the characteristic phrase *strictly stratigraphical* appears again and again – possible an unconscious expression of the excavator's experience of this record-heavy but informative technique

(Madsen ed. 1999, p. 90). The majority of the finds and features from this excavation were dated to the High and Late Middle Ages, the period in which the Monastery of the Knights of St John stood here, while the earliest culture layers and the original ground surface had been extensively removed by later pits.

It is well known that the western part of Ribe was settled in the medieval period and that amongst other things it housed a number of ecclesiastical foundations. However the wealth and complexity of the archaeological remains were first seriously revealed in 1993 through excavation *ASR 1015 Dagmargården*. In connexion with the extension of the Dagmargården Nursing Home around 800 sq m were excavated, an area which proved to contain well-preserved remains of the Franciscan friary of the town: some of the church, the claustral buildings and the churchyard with a total of 583 burials. Beneath the cloister an earlier settlement horizon was discovered. Sections of two roadways known from documentary sources were also excavated, the course of which had not changed from their establishment early in the medieval period

Fig. 33. A plan showing the major excavations in the western part of Ribe of the 1980s and 1990s. The base plan is an orthophotograph of 2011, and the areas of excavation are in yellow.

until they were abandoned in the post-medieval period (Jantzen, Kieffer-Olsen & Madsen 1994). The site supervisor was 39-year-old Jakob Kieffer-Olsen, with a PhD in Medieval Archaeology, who completed the severely under-funded excavation in five months from April to September 1993 (Fig. 34). Funding for the report was equally meagre, and proper post-excavation began only in 2013. In 1995 Per Kristian Madsen left Den antikvariske Samling to take up a post as leader of Vejle Museum. Jakob Kieffer-Olsen was appointed as the new Medieval Inspector, and after Stig Jensen's death in 1998 he moved to the position of Antiquary.

In 1997-8, the old Bakelite factory of the town – an interesting early industrial building from 1855 – had to pass on in order to make room for housing. This project led to the complete excavation, in 1997-8, of the c. 1,400-sq m site, *ASR 1200 Bakelitten,* with 33-year-old MA in Medieval Archaeology Lis Andersen as site supervisor. She and Jakob Kieffer-Olsen were at that time a couple (Fig. 34). The overall stratigraphy was like at Dagmargården: at the top were the archaeological remains of an ecclesiastical foundation, in this case the Monastery of the Knights of St John, *Korsbrødregård.* Below those were found the remains of an earlier settlement horizon. The density of settlement at the Bakelite site was, however, less than that at Dagmargården, and the picture of the settlement preceding the religious house was particularly diffuse. After the excavation was finished the results of dendrochronological datings from timbers from the wells that it revealed came in. The earliest of these gave a date that was surprisingly early for the excavators: AD 1077, at that stage the earliest securely dated evidence of settlement on the cathedral side (L. Andersen 1999).

On the site where another of the old enterprises of the town had been located – Danielsen's Timber

Fig. 34. Jakob Kieffer-Olsen with timber from well A 1855, later dendro-dated to AD 1077, in the excavation at the Bakelite Factory, ASR 1200, in 1998. The site supervisor Lis Andersen is seen left. The picture also includes the medieval archaeologists Lars Christian Bentsen and Susanne Nissen Gram in the background. From a photograph in case ASR 1200.

Fig. 35. From the excavation of Danielsen's Timber Yard in Nygade. The light strips are sand foundations for the south wing of the Franciscan Friary from around the year 1300, which had been dug down through thick culture layers of earlier in the Middle Ages produced by the preceding settlement in the area. Culture layers covering more than 2,000 sq m and up to 3.5 m thick were excavated in the course of one year in 1999-2000.

Yard in Nygade – a private builder made plans in 1998 for a substantial housing development with underground parking. This led to the complete excavation of around 2,000 sq m with culture layers up to 3.5 m thick: to date, the largest excavation in Ribe, *ASR 11 Danielsen's Timber Yard* (Fig. 35). As what was called a P-case (P = 'private'), the excavation was financed by the State Antiquary with the aid of a special grant under the Finance Act, and this extra grant of 10.5 million kroner was the particular case which led to the introduction of the 'developer pays' principle in the Museum Act of 2002.[10] The period of excavation ran from April 1999 for a year under the direction of Lis Andersen, who fell seriously ill during that time.

This excavation had the same basic sequence of strata as its two major predecessors: a monastery overlying settlement. The extent of this excavation, however, made a more precise reconstruction of the settlement of the early medieval period possible, but remains to be carried through. Lis Andersen's premature death in 2003 is one of the reasons why few of the excavation results have been published (L. Andersen 2003). This excavation was in fact the present author's first encounter with the archaeology of Ribe.

There are two observations which are particularly interesting in respect of an understanding of the earliest contexts:

- The area had been ploughed by ard in prehistory. At a later time, but before the settlement was established, the area was ploughed using a mouldboard plough.

- When the settlement was established, around the year 1100, the area was laid out in large plots. One of these was effectively completely excavated and measured 35 m x 20. On this site there had stood a substantial, post-built house with fine finds. This house remained on that site until the Francisan friary took over the area in 1232.

The three major excavations in the western town all posed massive logistical challenges for the museum, which were met in a professionally competent manner within the constraints of the available budget. This does not alter the fact, though, that the information potential of these excavations is still largely unrealized and needs time-consuming work of digitalization and analysis.

Table 2. The quantities of finds from a range of street excavations.

Journal number	Site	Year	Water-sieved?	Number of finds	Finds per sq m
ASR 366	Grønnegade I	1984		257	3.4
ASR 1070	Grønnegade II	1993		1278	8.8
ASR 1152	Gråbrødregade	1995		89	2.1
ASR 1174	Over- og Mellemdammen	1996		442	2.8
ASR 1219	Peder Dovns Slippe	1997		24	0.3
ASR 1275	Præstegade	1998		364	2.4
ASR 1843	Sønderportsgade	2004	x	9053	32.7
ASR 2089	Dagmarsgade	2005	x	6238	67.8
ASR 2162	Hundegade	2006	x	2774	13.1
ASR 2163	Grydergade	2006	x	1519	19

3.24 The use of metal-detectors and water-sieving in excavations in Ribe

From the end of the 1980s, Stig Jensen and Claus Feveile employed metal-detectors on excavations north of the Ribe River. In general, though, the conditions are difficult for detecting, as the long history of the town has left a comparably large number of metal objects in the upper soil layers. From 2004 onwards metal-detectors were also introduced to excavations south of the river, and the soil removed from street excavations has proved to be especially rich in finds.

It was the immense quantities of finds from the workshop layers of the oldest Ribe that led to the use of water-sieving as a method for separating the finds form the culture layers, first employed on a large scale in the excavation of ASR 7 in 1986. After that, water-sieving was used on a large scale in excavations north of the Ribe River. From 2004 it was introduced for the culture layers on the southern side of the river. The dramatic impact on the quantities of finds

is shown by the tables below, which have the figures from a number of excavations in respect of which the precise finds data are available (Tabs. 2-3).

The plot compares widely different excavations but the trend is clear. In the case of the street excavations water-sieving has produced 17 times more finds, and in the case of the open-area excavations 4.5 times more finds.

3.25 Excavations at Ribe Cathedral, 2008-12

The antiquarian tradition in Ribe emerged, as noted, around the cathedral as a monument in the wake of Høyen's visit in 1830. It may seem strange that 178 years would pass before this focal point itself would be the object of a major archaeological investigation. A consciousness of the failure of the antiquarian authorities both during the principal restoration of the 1890s and the underpinning of the foundations in the 1930s may have put a damper on any enthusiasm for excavation at the National Museum, but it does not

Journal number	Site	Year	Area of excavation in sq m	Thickness of excavated culture layer in m	Cubic meters excavated	Number of finds	Amount of pottery amongst the finds	Water-sieved?	Finds per cu m
ASR 52/64	Grønnegade	1955-56	157	4	628	**28917**	24566		**46**
ASR 5M74	Dommerhaven	1974	205	1	205	**10071**	5496		**49**
ASR 4M75	Kunstmuseets have	1975	335	1	335	**16198**	7577		**48**
ASR 7	Sct. Nicolaj Gade 8	1986	78	1	78	**13344**	3844	x	**171**
ASR 9	Posthuset	1990-91	167	2	334	**67176**	17015	x	**201**
ASR 1015	Dagmargården	1993	839	2.5	2097.5	**25085**	15855		**11**
ASR 11	Danielsen's Timber Yard	1999-2000	2312	3	6936	**71146**	58228		**10**
ASR 13	Lindegården	2008-9, 2011-12	509	3	1527	**106225**	77066	x	**70**

Table 3. The quantities of finds from a range of open-area excavations.

explain why attempts to uncover the earlier history of the church, at the heart of the process of conversion in Denmark as it had been, were so sparse and half-hearted as they were. In association with *Danmarks Kirker*'s discussion of Ribe Cathedral (see section 3.17) a small excavation was undertaken within the Borgertårn (Citizen's Tower) with the aim of finding the foundation of the northern tower that collapsed in 1283: from any perspective, a research question of limited significance (E. Møller 1971).

In 1986, the National Museum and Den antikvariske Samling undertook an excavation in the crossing of the church beneath King Christoffer I's tomb of 1259. This went down to a layer of graves, the alignment of which differed from that of the standing building, at which point the excavation was halted. Den antik-variske Samling's participant, Per Kristian Madsen, went on paternity leave. The National Museum's participant, Knud J. Krogh, returned home.

In 2000 a major property south of the cathedral was destroyed by fire. The building was owned by the cathedral and the chapter wanted to build a significant new structure on the site.

In 2008, funds were raised for the excavation of some of the site, and the excavation, *ASR 13 Lindegården*, was again one of the crucial turning points in the study of the history of the town of Ribe (Fig. 36) (Søvsø 2011). The site director was the present author, then 36 years old and an MA in Medieval and Prehistoric Archaeology. The results helped to clear the way to gain funds for a full excavation of the site, which took place in 2011-12 (Fig. 37). The most important results concerning the earlier history of the town were:

- The discovery of a large Christian cemetery from the Viking Period. The excavated segment was sealed by culture layers around the year 1050 which it therefore pre-dates. In agreement with the stratigraphical dating, radiocarbon dates have assigned the graves to the 9th to 11th centuries.

- An urban settlement along the main artery Sønderportsgade appeared around the year 1050.

- *Spolia* and building material from the present cathedral's predecessor, Bishop Thure's stone church, were found.

- The canons' cloister referred to in documentary sources was found in the form of a brick build-ing from the 12th century: probably the house's refectory.

At the same time, plans were being worked on for a thorough renovation of the cathedral square in Ribe, the form of which was the product of the clearance of fill in the 1890s. The successful project required only limited excavations in the later culture layers at the site to be undertaken, which helped to clarify the shifting but intense exploitation of the zone from the High Middle Ages onwards. In small trenches of varying shape the earliest deposits on the site could also be examined, shedding light on the extent and boundaries of the earliest churchyard. These inves-tigations are combined in the case *ASR 2391 Ribe Domkirkeplads*. The most important results are:

- The eastern end of the current cathedral is built on a blown-sand dune, the top of which is about

Fig. 37. Alongside Ribe Cathedral, the years 2008-12 saw an area of altogether 500 sq m with culture layers 4 m thick excavated, with a complex sequence of burials together with both secular and ecclesiastical occupation covering a period of a thousand years from the middle of the 9th century to the middle of the 19th century. Photograph in case ASR 13.

4 m above sea-level, which, with the rest of the terrain, forms a natural terrace standing around 1.5 m above the principal roadway Sønderportsgade.

- The Viking-period churchyard was roughly circular and about 9,000 sq m in area.

- The churchyard was surrounded by several phases of ditches and fences.

- The number of those buried before 1050 can be estimated as two to three thousand.

3.26 Summary: research history and the conceptual framework of town archaeology

As the present chapter shows, the antiquarian tradition in Ribe is a long and diverse one. Both Terpager's *Ripæ Cimbricæ* (1736) and Kinch's *Ribe Bys Historie og Beskrivelse* (1869) were key works in their time, produced by local forces. Although the first archaeological investigations, initially recorded to a quite different level, can be traced right back to 1830, archaeological involvement in the 19th and the first half of the 20th century was sporadic in the extreme. A crucial reason for this was the distance from the National Museum in Copenhagen, and we can be happy that the buildings works and the consequent destruction of archaeological remains in Ribe were nevertheless very limited in extent compared with other larger towns of medieval Denmark. The earliest excavations were concentrated around the monuments of the town, both the surviving leading monument, the cathedral, and the many demolished churches and monasteries together with Riberhus castle. In this first phase there was no, or very little, focus upon the archaeological strata themselves: those were a fill that was to be removed so that the ruins could appear. Occasionally some exciting find which could be added to the museum collection might be made in the soil. The archaeology of the town was based upon the account of the textual sources.

The National Museum's excavation in Grønnegade of 1955-7 was a massive step forward that revealed the richness of the medieval culture layer but also the associated problems in recording the stratigraphical sequence and in handling the large quantities of finds and other data. The results from Grønnegade were also crucial in the appointment of a permanent archaeologist at the museum in Ribe, and they came to determine the direction of investment in archaeology which has shaped the museum ever since.

A stratigraphical understanding of the layers beneath the town inspired by geology can first traced in Ribe from the Grønnegade excavation. Even the fundamental premiss that Viking-period Ribe should be detectable through excavations down into the culture layers shows that what the layers contained in the way of finds was regarded as able to date the individual strata and the features associated with them. Both Stiesdal and Bencard consistently described the culture layers on the southern side of the river as 'culture mud' (*kulturgytje*) which was not defined in more detail although 'midden' and 'waste layers' are other terms that appear in the

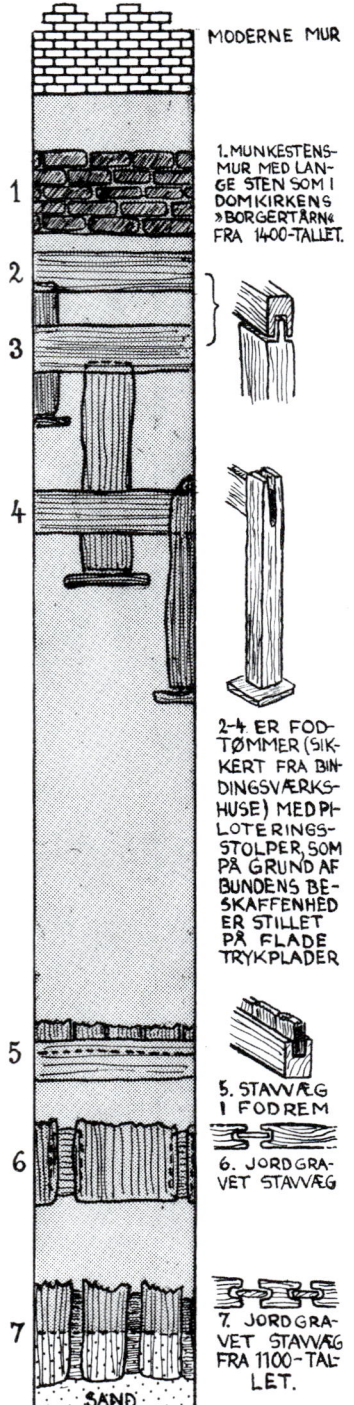

MODERNE MUR

1. MUNKESTENS-
MUR MED LAN-
GE STEN SOM I
DOMKIRKENS
»BORGERTÅRN«
FRA 1400-TALLET.

2-4 ER FOD-
TØMMER (SIK-
KERT FRA BIN-
DINGSVÆRKS-
HUSE) MED PI-
LOTERINGS-
STOLPER, SOM
PÅ GRUND AF
BUNDENS BE-
SKAFFENHED
ER STILLET
PÅ FLADE
TRYKPLADER

5. STAVVÆG
I FODREM

6. JORDGRA-
VET STAVVÆG

7. JORDGRA-
VET STAVVÆG
FRA 1100-TAL-
LET.

SAND

summary descriptions. In the Grønnegade excavation it was observed that the oldest building plot was placed upon the surface of a soil layer and that above was a sequence of remains of buildings and fencing which were successively renewed on the same spot (Edelberg & Bencard 1962). The culture layers that the features were embedded within were perceived as a product of settlement – in other words, the waste and midden material of the town that was levelled out in the context of new building and thus led to the town slowly growing higher (Fig. 38). The dating of the pace of formation of the culture mud was still undetailed, but a relatively steady growth throughout the Middle Ages was a basic assumption behind this evolutionary model.

The next big step in the history of research into Ribe was the discovery of 8th-century Ribe in 1972. In contrast to the medieval layers' contents in the form of remains of buildings and fencing which had clear parallels in other medieval towns and thus did not pose any difficulties of interpretation, for very good reasons it was not at that time possible to turn to any clear parallels to the strata of the 8th century and their fine stratigraphy. The layers were presented as *waste deposits* completely dominated by trade and craft, and the absence of unambiguous buildings was seen as an indication that the layers must represent a seasonal market site with flimsy structures: tents, windbreaks and the like. This discovery also brought about an ambitious and internationally oriented approach to publication (Bencard et al. eds. 1981-2010).

After a careful approach through the excavations in Dommerhaven and Kunstmuseets Have, the stratigraphical method of excavation and the associated model of representation were introduced by Ole Schiørring and Per Kristian Madsen through

Fig. 38. To the left, a diagrammatic profile of the sequence of strata found in the excavation between Præstegade and Grønnegade. Below, a diagrammatic section through the culture layers of the town and the watercourses that surround it. After Bencard and Edelberg 1962.

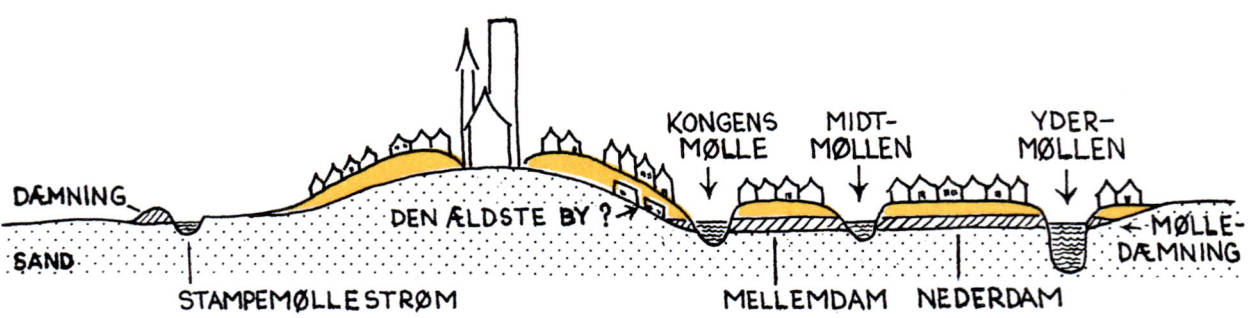

DÆMNING

SAND

STAMPEMØLLESTRØM

DEN ÆLDSTE BY ?

KONGENS
MØLLE

MIDT-
MØLLEN

YDER-
MØLLEN

MØLLE-
DÆMNING

MELLEMDAM NEDERDAM

the Medieval Town Project's excavations of 1979-81. A layer is an interpretative context distinguished on the basis of visual and material characteristics, and what the layer contains in the way of finds is the source for determining the date and function of the layer. Sequences of superimposed layers and their relationships can be represented diagrammatically in *Harris matrices* (Harris 1989). The Medieval Town Project's excavations were grounded on the understanding that that crucial topographical information could be obtained even through very small excavations, but the meagre results of these constraints, especially compared with the results produced later in the same areas, has shown that these very small excavations often raise more questions than they answer.

Stig Jensen's first achievement was to consolidate the links between the archaeology of the town and that in the open country – work which found expression in the settlement project *Marsk, land og bebyggelse* ('Marsh, land and settlement': Jensen ed. 1998). The revelation of the plot structure in the market place followed later, and finally the excavations at Rosen Allé and Ribelund which revealed cemeteries, settlement and fortification and added a considerable number of new components to the picture of Ribe in the 8th and 9th centuries. Another important but rarely noted feature is that Stig Jensen thought in new methodological ways and was logical and systematic in his work. Shortly after his appointment, both a new journal number system and a model of registration of excavations were introduced, together with, already in the 1980s, the first database for the recording of archaeological finds which has since been developed into the system SJM SYS which is still in use. In respect of systematic aerial surveying and the use of metal-detectors the museum was going ahead at full speed in the 1980s.

The open-area excavation technique of prehistoric archaeology and the emphasis on the high informative value of the uncovered sub-soil surface that went with it were introduced with great success on larger areas on the northern side of the river. The open-area method of excavation also had the great advantage of being economically practical, although a budgetary prerequisite for this position is that the topsoil which covers the surface of the sub-soil must be removed by machine with some loss of archaeological information as a consequence; dependent upon the immediate formation processes, that may be greater or lesser.

Stig Jensen never got to present a complete scholarly publication of his revolutionary excavations in Ribe, but the key ideas were presented in the article *Dankirke-Ribe: Fra handelsgård til handelsplads* ('Dankirke-Ribe: from trading farmstead to trading site': S. Jensen 1991a) and in the more broadly targeted book *Ribes Vikinger* ('Ribe's Vikings': S. Jensen 1991b).

In Stig Jensen's view of Ribe, before the appearance of the market site there was *a small village, or perhaps just a couple of farmsteads on the northern bank of the Ribe River*, which *must have given way to something different and greater – a market site*. The preceding settlement was supposed to have produced the so-called village layer from ASR 7. The foundation of the market site is described as a planned *event* which can be dated to between AD 704 and 710. Behind this foundation is assumed to stand some powerful chieftain or really *a royal power* (S. Jensen 1991b, 10). The foundation of Ribe is perceived as an important element in a concurrent process of state-formation and the concentration of power in the hands of a Danish king at the beginning of the 8th century, under inspiration from processual archaeology and the trains of thought of the From Tribe to State Project (see Ch. 2).

In the case of the cathedral side, Per Kristian Madsen's view, based upon the geological report, was that the cathedral stood upon *an artificially constructed higher point in the terrain*. This erroneous idea was decisive in the later development of the model. Reconstruction of the landscape, again based primarily upon coring, had shown that under much of the later town areas there would have been low-lying wet areas which could not be settled until after extensive filling. A guiding hand was seen behind such a colossal level of earth-shifting: again, one can detect an emphasis on dark impalpable 'power' as the motor of history typical of the age.

A constant feature of the archaeology of Ribe has been that the museum has never been closely linked to any larger institution in the form of either the National Museum or a university. Collaborative work has, over time, been diverse and generally of high quality, although it is also typical that, since the 1960s, this relatively small museum has been responsible for, carried out and published the far from insignificant excavation tasks which through time have produced an archaeological collection that comprises more than a million objects (Tab. 4).

In this way, Ribe differs sharply from the other early towns of Scandinavia. Research into Hedeby/Schleswig, Birka, Kaupang and Lund has in every case been characterized by projects based in central museums or universities. While it was the central position of Ribe in the trading networks of the Viking and Medieval Periods that created the town's rich archaeological remains, it has in contrast been the peripheral position of Ribe in 20th-century Denmark which marked out the framing lines of archaeological research into the town.

Year	Journal number	Site	Institution	Site director
1911		St. Klemens church site	NM	C.M. Smidt
1940–41		Riberhus	NM	Chr. Axel Jensen
1953–57	ASR 52/64	Grønnegade	NM	Mogens Bencard
1958		Porsborgs kælder	NM	Hans Stiesdal
1960	ASR 13/60	St. Peder's church site	NM	Else-Marie Boyhus
1962	ASR 22/62+30/62	Quedens gård/Sortebrg. 7	ASR	Mogens Bencard
1965	ASR 43/64	Sydjysk Landmandsbank	ASR	Mogens Bencard
1963–69	ASR 30M70	Okholm	ASR/FHM	Mogens Bencard/Hans Jørgen Madsen
1965–70	ASR 57/64	Dankirke	NM	Elise Thorvildsen
1970	ASR 43M70	St. Nikolaj church and cloister	ASR	Aino Kann Rasmussen
1973	ASR 6M73	Kunstmuseets Kælder	ASR	Mogens Bencard
1974	ASR 5M74	Dommerhaven	ASR	Mogens Bencard
1975	ASR 4M75	Kunstmuseets Have	ASR	Mogens Bencard
1979–81	Several numbers	The Medieval Town Project	ASR	Ole Schiørring/Per Kristian Madsen
1980	ASR 19M80C	Andersminde	ASR	Steffen Stummann Hansen
1982	ASR 270	Nr. Farup	ASR	Per Kristian Madsen
1985	ASR 565	Korsbrødregård	ASR	Per Kristian Madsen
1986	ASR 7	Sct. Nicolaj Gade 8	ASR	Stig Jensen
1984–94	ASR 440	Gl. Hviding	ASR	Stig Jensen
1986–87	ASR 491	Vilslev	ASR	Stig Jensen
1989	ASR 8	Rosen Allé	ASR	Stig Jensen
1990	ASR 926	Ribelund I	ASR	Stig Jensen
1990–91	ASR 9	Posthuset /The Post Office	ASR	Stig Jensen
1991	ASR 1000	Ribelund II	ASR	Stig Jensen
1993	ASR 1015	Dagmargården	ASR	Jakob Kieffer-Olsen
1995–96	ASR 583	Okholm	ASR	Claus Feveile
1998	ASR 1200	Bakelitten	ASR	Lis Andersen
1999–2000	ASR 11	Danielsen's Timber Yard	ASR	Lis Andersen
2000	ASR 1357	Giørtzvej	ASR	Claus Feveile
2008–09	ASR 13	Lindegården I	ASR	Morten Søvsø
2010–11	ASR 2360	Sct. Nicolaj Gade	ASR	Sarah Qvistgaard/Michael Alrø Jensen
2011–12	ASR 13	Lindegården II	ASR	Morten Søvsø/Troels Bo Jensen
2012	ASR 2391	Ribe Domkirksplads/ Cathedral Square	ASR	Morten Søvsø/Michael Alrø Jensen

Table 4. The most important archaeological excavations in Ribe and the surrounding area through time.

4. Topography – the coastal zone of West Jutland in the Iron Age, the Viking Period and the Middle Ages

4.1 Introduction

This chapter contains a description and analysis of the cultural landscape of West Jutland from the Tønder Marsh to the south to the mouth of the Limfjord in the north, a geographical area that corresponds approximately to the medieval Ribe Diocese. The main focus of attention will be placed upon the period c. AD 500-1500, corresponding to the *Medieval Period* (*Middle Ages*) in the European chronological framework. This section of the book gives an account of the key features of the formation of the landscape with a view to reaching a position from which a more thorough description can be given of the situations in the Late Iron Age, Viking Period and Scandinavian Middle Ages, which have changed hugely through to the present.

The primary topic of this book is the town of Ribe from its foundation around the year 700 through to around the year 1050. In order to locate that phenomenon better in its historical, social and geographical contexts, and to be in a position to offer some answer, however qualified, to the question of the links between the town and the society of the surrounding hinterland, it is also recognized to be important to draw a picture of the agrarian population of western Jutland in the Late Germanic Iron Age. Was this community similar to the other areas of the territory which subsequently became Denmark? What opportunities does the evidence offer for us to form a view of social organization at that time? What was the organization of the villages like, their farms and systems of cultivation, and what links were there between the various settlements?

A general methodological approach is that in many cases we shall start from later, better known sources on both social structure and principles of spatial organization in the villages which can be found in documentary sources and maps. From this starting point, inferences can be drawn moving retrospectively towards earlier situations. This way of working is a logical consequence of my own scholarly starting point in the discipline of Medieval Archaeology, and a position which also is intended to impose something of a limit upon other approaches which have attempted rather to extrapolate from other groups of sources. In the case of the Iron Age, grave finds, votive hoards of weaponry, and settlement archaeology represented most prominently in the Roman Iron Age (AD 1-400), have became the foundation stones of the reconstruction of communal organization at this time, strongly influenced by models of processual archaeology (Näsman 2006; Ethelberg 2014).

The premiss underlying the preferred approach is that there were many fundamental similarities between the agricultural society of the Iron Age and that of later periods, and that these long lines run throughout the pre-industrial agrarian subsistence economy with few changes (Søvsø 2020). The landscape and its agrarian potential set out the framework for human life all through the period. As will be shown, climatic changes have limited the potential for living in parts of the West Jutlandic coastal zone markedly, but through a range of sources, including the list of churches in the source *Ribe Oldemoder* ('Ribe Great-Grandmother') it is possible, with reservations, to suggest what the preceding situation was. With corrections made for these factors, a picture emerges in which the essential agrarian structures that supported the population all the way through this period are characterized by a high degree of continuity.

4.1.1 The representativity of the archaeological evidence

In the absence of documentary sources, the archaeological data-set provides the core components for most discussions of types of community and social structures in the period of the Late Iron Age and the Viking Period. It is therefore crucial, in order to work with the archaeological evidence, to make a range of assessments of how representative that evidence is. What formation processes have shaped the data from which conclusions are drawn? What regional differences in the soil, conditions for preservation or museum traditions may have influenced the production of the archaeological data?

The phenomenon which is often described using the teleologically loaded term *the state-formation process* occupies a core place in the discussion of Late Iron-age society (Mortensen & Rasmussen eds. 1988; 1991), and usually builds upon analysis of regional differences or similarities between excavated settlements and collections of finds in respect of which

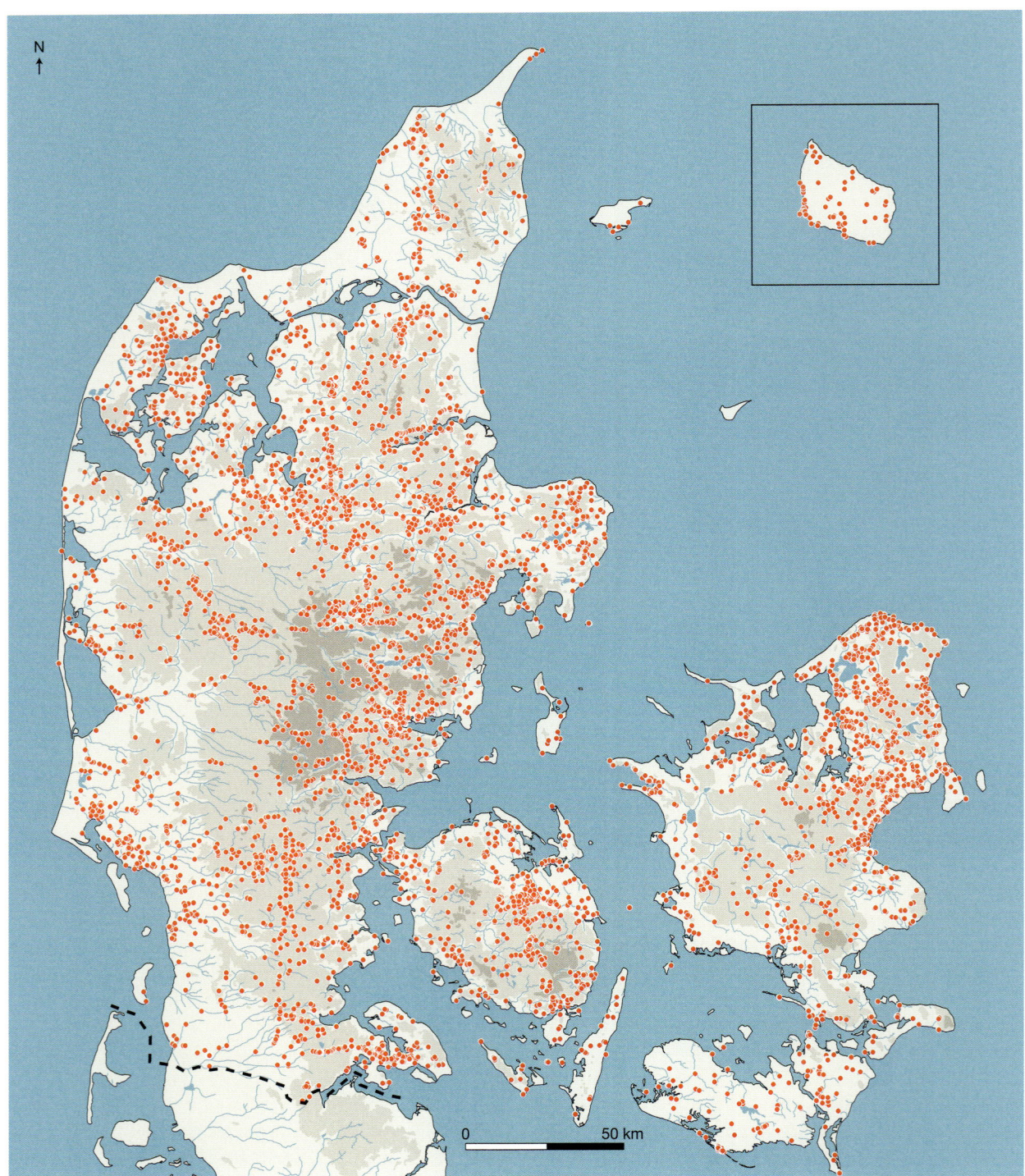

Fig. 39. Map of event type 'Museum excavation' (MUG) since 2001 (n = 7,768). Some dots cover more than one event. Data-pull from the Castle and Culture Agency's database Finds and Ancient Monuments 5 November 2019.

such differences or similarities can be taken as supporting one view or another. In the archaeology of the Late Iron Age there are indeed a number of conspicuous regional differences which can be used to argue for a series of basic cultural differences between eastern and western Denmark (Holst 2014). Before drawing this conclusion, a series of evaluations have to be made concerning the factors which, in combination, form the archaeological evidence, be that excavation activity, the use of metal-detectors, or different museum traditions and institutional conditions.

4.1.2 Excavation in Denmark

The quantity of archaeological evidence in Denmark has grown enormously just in the last fifteen years. The most relevant cause of this has been the introduction of the developer-pays principle in the Museum Act of 2001, which together with the economic boom before 2007/8 led to a hitherto unseen level of rescue excavation in the context of new building, roadworks, extraction of aggregates, etc. The excavations were not evenly distributed across Denmark but rather concentrated in the areas of growth around the larger towns and the corridors which the major infrastructure projects, such as new motorways, affected.

Figure 39 shows the entries for *Museum-based Excavation* (MUG) from the Castle and Culture Management's database of Finds and Ancient Monuments, *Fund og Fortidsminder*, with the year of the event being 'greater than 2001' (*n* = 7,768). Despite possible inconsistencies within these register-generated data, the map should nevertheless present a relatively true picture of the general situation. The map combines two principal factors: for one, economic development in Denmark in the years 2002-14, and the other, the level of activity of the museums responsible and their thoroughness in processing the entries.

It is immediately evident that excavation activity is not evenly distributed across the country, and that the number of excavations in the coastal zone of West Jutland has to be considered relatively low. The 7,768 excavations in the period 2002-19 have generated a colossal body of the data which has been worked through and/or published from a research perspective only to a very limited extent. The situation is often that only a limited group of those employed at any one museum have anything more than superficial knowledge of what are key excavations in terms of research. The post-excavation analysis and publication of these excavations is going to be one the major tasks for Danish archaeology in the coming years.

4.1.3 The use of metal-detectors

A second key circumstance relating to the period under discussion is the huge growth in the number of metal-detectorists, who in recent decades have enriched the collections of the National Museum and the local museums with thousands of metal finds, not least from the Late Germanic Iron Age, Viking Period and Middle Ages (Stidsing et al. eds. 2014; Hilberg & Lemm eds. 2018). The majority of the finds are items of jewellery in copper alloy, often with additional adornment in a precious metal. For the earlier half of the period, this set of finds is the best preserved and by far the principal source of evidence for the aesthetics, styles, and cultural and religious conceptions and alignment. Often emphasized is the importance of the metal finds that is due to the function of the jewellery as what carries and announces identity, in terms of sex, social status and ethnicity (P.V. Petersen 1991).

The use of metal-detectors is even less evenly distributed across Denmark than archaeological excavations are (Fig. 40). The data source here is a combined data-pull from Finds and Ancient Monuments of the event type *Private Detector Use* (PME) and *Museum Detector Use* (MME). Although there is no uniform administrative approach behind the criteria and interests employed by the individual museums in opening detector cases, there is no reason whatsoever to doubt the main trend of the map: most cases are on Bornholm, many on Sjælland, the islands and Fyn, and fewer in Jutland.

The conditions for the preservation of metals in the ground also vary significantly. In general, metals are better preserved in chalky clay soil than in the slightly acidic sandy soil of West Jutland. In the case of the latter area we also have to reckon with the fact that both the conditions for preservation and the low level of searching lead to the fact that as of yet a lower proportion of the metal finds have reached the museums.

The growth in new finds over the last decade has been of such magnitude that no one has a full overview of it any more; the following example serves to illustrate the explosion in finds. In 1966 Mogens Ørsnes counted a total of 72 known specimens of the brooch-type 'beak brooch' from the Late Germanic Iron Age in Denmark (Ørsnes 1966, 120ff). From 1967 to 1988 a further 69 examples were found, bringing the total known up to 141 (P.V. Petersen 1991). There is no published score for the increase since then, but on the web-site *http://detectingpeople.dk*, for the period 2005-14, in other words a period of just ten years, images of 322 beak brooches were uploaded, which represent only part of the total number of finds. The National Museum has no figure for the whole amount.[11]

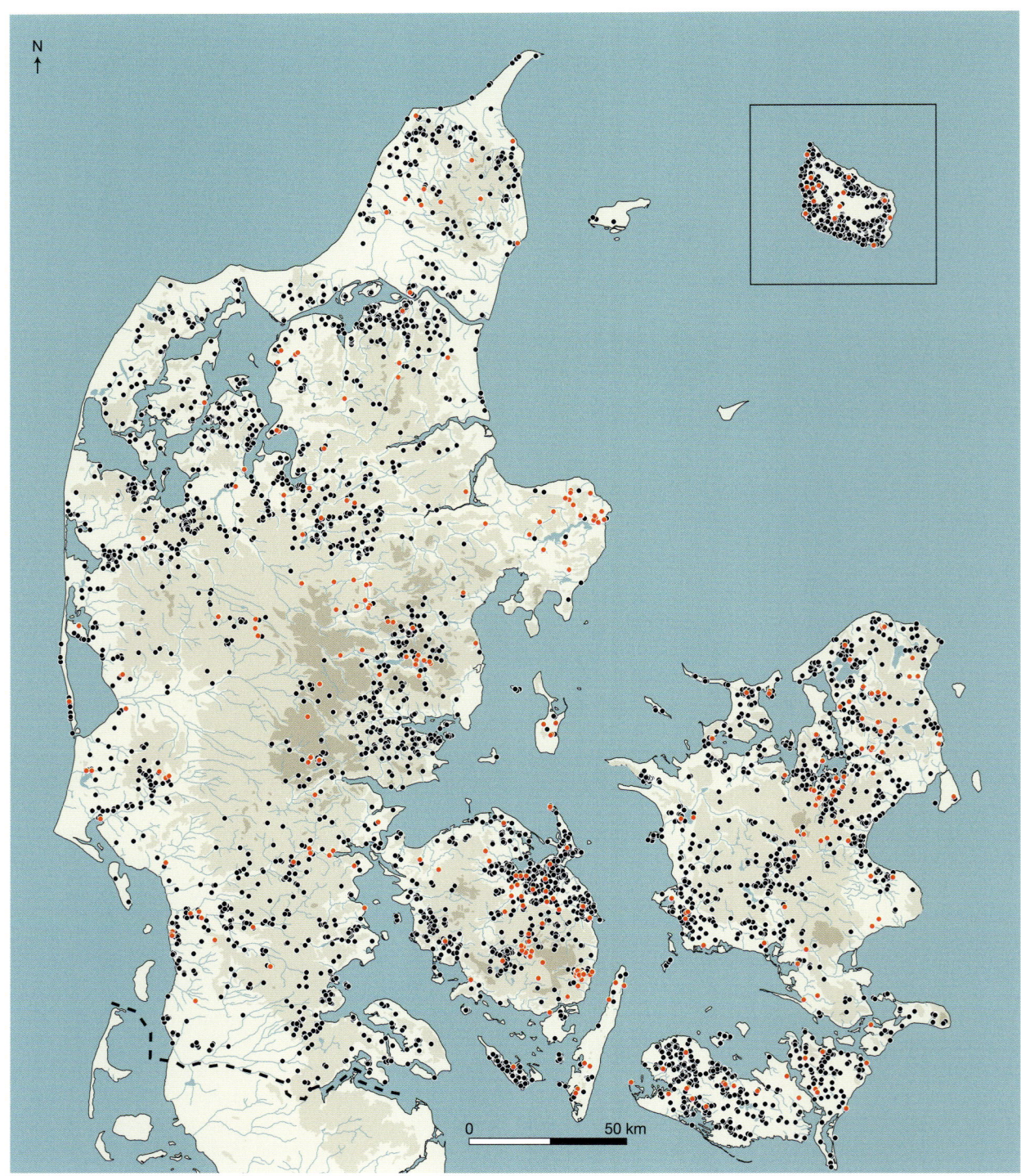

Fig. 40. Map of event type 'Private detector use' (PME) (black, n = 7,619) and 'Museum detector use' (MME) (red, n = 390). Some dots cover more than one event. Data-pull from the Castle and Culture Agency's database Finds and Ancient Monuments 5 November 2019.

Similar exponential growth curves could be produced for all other types of detector find, and the situation is reminiscent of that with the rescue excavations: in other words, we have a large and vital body of evidence which is unprocessed and only accessible to some degree or another via web-fora or in overviews produced by individual museums. It is immediately apparent that this evidence holds the potential for the generation of a range of radical modifications to the models proposed concerning exchange, trade and settlement, especially in the Iron Age. Just two points will be noted here:

- The brooch-finds from the Iron Age, Viking Period and Middle Ages show that families were resident in what would appear to be all of the villages in what is now the area of Denmark whose womenfolk wore brooches, often finely manufactured and gilded.

- The 7th century, which is so elusive in settlement archaeology, is remarkably clearly evident in detector finds through numerous finds of small equal-armed brooches, beak brooches, bird brooches, plate brooches, and more. This striking discrepancy between settlement archaeology and detector archaeology is not yet fully explained (Näsman 1991).

4.1.4 Aerial photography as a survey method

From the 1950s onwards, it became more and more common for an archaeologist to take a flight in a light aircraft and to be able to observe the landscape from above. From earlier military and geodetic aerial photographs it was well known that certain types of ancient monument could appear clearly from the air, either in colour variation in the soil of ploughed fields or as crop-marks produced by differences in growth produced by the fact that the underlying archaeological features may provide either better or worse conditions for growth immediately above them. From the 1980s a regular search from archaeological sites was introduced, particularly in West Jutland, where the conditions for observation had proved to be most favourable, and where most flying archaeologists were working (Helles Olesen & Schlosser Mouritsen 2015). This has unquestionably affected some of the emphatic skewedness that is apparent in Figure 41.

A nationwide set of aerial photographs has been accessible on line since just after the year 2000 and is currently accessible from Danmarks Miljøportal (The Environment of Denmark Portal) with the web-address *http://arealinformation.miljoeportal.dk/distribution/*. Dependent upon the date at which the particular set of photographs was taken, it is more or less possible to search for ancient monuments sitting at one's computer screen at home, and this tool is intermittently used by both archaeologists and metal-detectorists, albeit without having managed to change the striking concentration of ancient monuments in the coastal zone of West Jutland very much. The most significant reason for the clear skewedness of the map is the difference in soil-types. In the sandy soil of West Jutland cut features below the top-soil are simply easier to see. Other parts of Denmark have sandy areas too, where the state of preservation should be similar, but with no matching clusters of ancient monuments recognized so far. Other sources of evidence, however, reveal dense settlement in those areas too, and the mapping of ancient monuments from the air thus cannot really say much about differences between western and eastern Denmark: it can, however, be assumed to present a relatively comprehensive picture of the relative population density in West Jutland, with a clear concentration towards the coastal zone and much more diffuse settlement on the wide heathlands in the interior.

4.1.5 Summary: the representativity question

As the mapping presented above shows, both excavation and the density of metal-detecting are at a much lower level in West Jutland than in other parts of Denmark. This inevitably means that fewer data from this zone have entered the overall archaeological data-set. Another method of prospecting, archaeological aerial photography, conversely shows that in the coastal zone of West Jutland there is almost a surfeit of archaeological sites. This state of affairs is due both to the favourable soil conditions in West Jutland and a local research tradition, but that cannot be the whole explanation: the number of ancient monuments seen from the air has to reflect a correspondingly dense population in prehistory, typically the period from the Iron Age onwards, which appears much more clearly from the air than do earlier periods. The West Jutlandic coastal zone thus emerges as a densely populated landscape in the period under discussion here – which we know proportionally less about than in the other areas of Denmark.

4.2 The landscape of West Jutland in the Iron Age, the Viking Period and the Middle Ages

4.2.1 The evolution of the landscape

The geographical area that is discussed in this chapter – the coastal zone of West Jutland from the Tønder Marsh in the south to the mouth of the Limfjord in the north – was last completely covered in ice during the Saale Ice Age around 130,000 years ago (J.T. Møller 2000). The melting of the ice left a moraine landscape which was decisively changed again during the following and to date the last glaciation, the Weichsel Ice Age, which lasted from around 115,000 to 11,700 years ago. During the Weichsel Ice Age West Jutland was largely ice-free, but the later melting of the enormous masses of ice created melt-water floods

Fig. 41. Ancient monuments discovered from the air. Data-pull of event type 'Observation from aircraft' (MFL) (black, n = 1347) and 'Private Observation from aircraft' (PFL) (red, n = 662). from the Castle and Culture Agency's database Finds and Ancient Monuments 5 November 2019.

which leveled the landscape and deposited sediments both in and along the rivers. The moraine outcrops of the Saale Ice Age that were leveled by the melt-waters are called hill-islands while the old courses of the rivers of melt-water are called heath-plains. The geological composition of the hill-islands is mixed, varying between sand, gravel and clay, while the heath-plains are formed of sand and gravel. These are the basic forms of the overwhelmingly flat West Jutlandic landscape. The northern part of the area around the Limfjord was under ice during the Weichsel Ice Age and this younger moraine landscape is hillier and the soil more clayey than in the areas south and west of the limit of glaciation.

In the following inter-glacial, the period in which we now live, geological and climatic changes, in combination with the flora and fauna present and human farming, have continuously modified the landscape.

4.2.2 Changes in sea-level

Changes in the relationship between sea and land can be due to changes in overall sea-level as a consequence of global circumstances, typically matters of temperature. With low temperatures, proportionally more ice will be locked up as ice at the poles of the globe, leading to a relatively lower amount of water in the world's oceans than is the case when temperatures are higher. The relationship is termed *eustasy*, and accounts for the general rise in sea-level during the Stone Age that was caused by rising temperatures and which largely determined the current bounds between land and water in southern Scandinavia. Another circumstance,

equally decisive in the case of the Danish coasts, is the more local land-rise that has taken place in those areas that were covered in ice during the last glaciation. The weight of the ice-cap pressed the earth's crust down and since the thaw it has moved back towards a point of equilibrium termed *isostasy*. In the case of the only partially ice-covered Jutland this has the consequence that the northern part of the peninsula is rising while the southern part is sinking (J.T. Møller 2000, 41f). Behind this general context more local geological factors can also play a part, so that the contour line around isobase 0 is only a guideline (Fig. 42).

The relationship between land and sea, and how it has changed over time, are determined by geological investigation and shed light on the development of the landscape in outline terms. If one wants more detailed information to illuminate the period in question here, the Late Iron Age, the Viking Period and the Middle Ages, the sources are sparse.

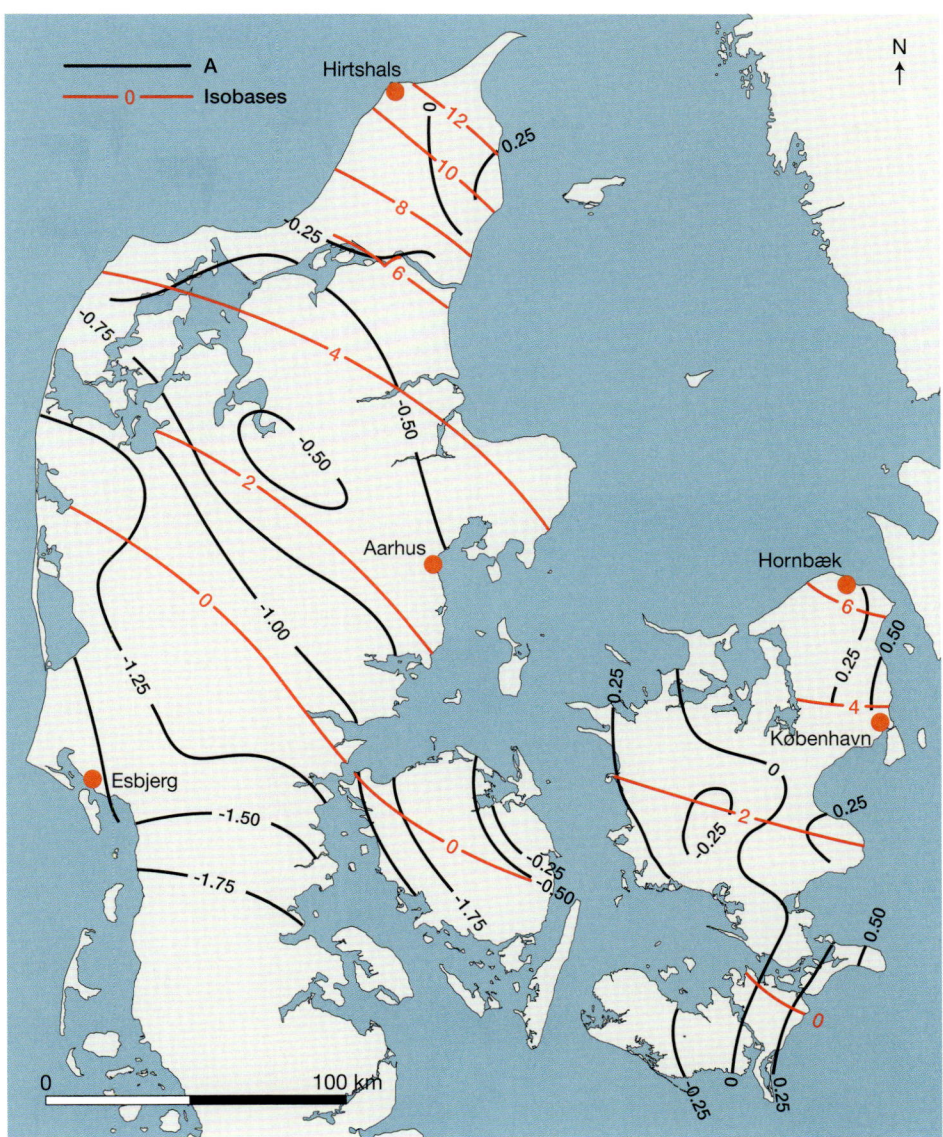

Fig. 42. The red contour lines are isobases which show the inferred rise in land-level since the Stone Age in metres. The black lines show measured changes in level in millimetres per year over the last 100 years. 1 millimeter per year will give 1 metre over a millennium. From Møller 2000.

4.2.3 The Wadden Sea and the formation of the marsh

The Wadden Sea now extends from Horns Rev in the north to Den Helder in present-day North Holland (Fig. 43) (Behre 2008). It is a recent geological formation created as a result of rises in sea-level reinforced by more local sinking of the land. These two factors together have meant that at high water the sea covered the shorelands, the flats around the rivers and coastal bogs, and consequently deposited fine clay and sand which over time came to form the fertile marshland pastures, ideally suited to grazing. These grass-covered flats could support large animal populations and the conditions gradually improved as the marsh zone grew in extent through the Bronze Age and the Iron Age (Thamdrup 1998).

A key feature of the Wadden Sea are the so-called barrier islands, with Fanø now as the northernmost of a string of islands which extends in the south to Texel north of Den Helder. Geological studies on, for instance, Rømø show that the formation of the barrier islands, of the lagoons behind them, and of the marsh, was an interlinked process set off by the rise in sea-level of the Stone Age (Pejrup et al. 2009).

As the rise in sea-level slowed, in the Late Neolithic and the Bronze Age the coastal zone became more stable and the marsh landscape that we know today was slowly formed by the repeated sea flooding. Radiocarbon datings from buried growth surfaces beneath marsh formations show that the emergence of the marsh began in the Early Bronze Age and that marsh-formation is a later phenomenon the

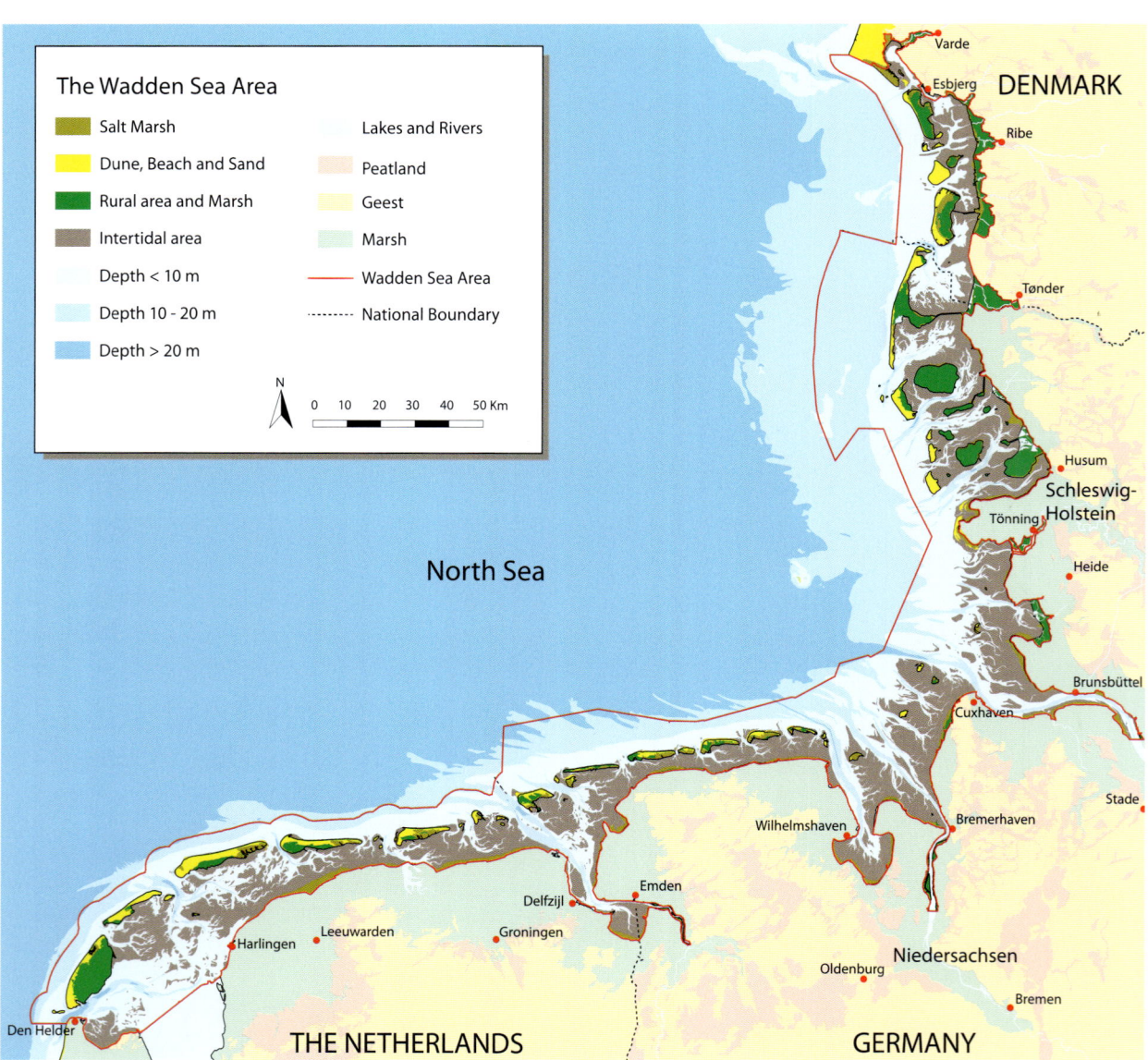

Fig. 43. Map of the Jutlandic west coast and the Wadden Sea. Produced by the Common Wadden Sea Secretariat. http://www.waddensea-secretariat.org/about-us *(30 October 2017).*

further north one goes: a natural consequence of the fact that the sinking of the land also reduces as one moves north.

The relationship between land and water thus was not constant in prehistory, but rather fluctuated between periods with rising water-levels, known as 'transgressions', and periods with falling water-levels, known as 'regressions' (J.T. Møller 2000; Behre 2008). These eustatic factors have to be combined with the sinking of the land in the Wadden Sea area, an isostatic variable, which together with the climatic circumstances generates the complicated equation behind the evolution of the coastal landscape. A consequence of all this is that the formation of the marsh – the deposition of sediments in the coastal zone – is not a linear process but rather one that has primarily taken place during transgressions while the state of affairs during regressions may have been more placid and less insecure for the population of the coastal zone. South of Ribe the marsh extends down to Ballum hill-island, which marks the boundary to the Tønder Marsh. South of there the marshland flats extend unbroken all the way to present day North-Holland.

4.2.4 The Late Antique Little Ice Age – Fimbulvetrinn?

It has already been suggested that the context of the massive votive deposition of gold in the period c. AD 500-550 was an environmental catastrophe caused by a volcanic eruption in the year 536 that had world-wide consequences and was described in Late Antique sources (Axboe 2001). A recently published global climate study has strongly supported this theory (Büntgen et al. 2016). Rather than just one event, however, it was a case of truly major eruptions in the three different locations in 536, 540 and 547 which emitted so much ash into the atmosphere that it seriously reduced the effect of the sun on the surface of the Earth. That solar activity in this period was also historically low served to reinforce the effect. The thoroughly based climatic reconstruction of that study shows that the period from AD 536 to c. AD 660 was, without rival, the coldest period of the 1st millennium, called the *Late Antique Little Ice Age* (*LALIA*). The impact of the cold period was not equally distributed, but could have been ameliorated or reinforced by tides or regional metereological conditions. The Gulf Stream may have had a softening effect in the case of western Europe. This does not change the fact that the theory of climate change as a cause of both the Scandinavian gold hoard horizon and the small number of settlements from the 7th century has been strongly corroborated. The view of this study is that the deterioration of the climate caused a marked reduction in population, as is also indicated by the conspectus of dendrochronological dates (Fig. 55). A memory of this cold period could have turned into Norse mythology's narrative of *Fimbulvetrinn*, 'the Fimbul-winter' (Gräslund 2007).

4.2.5 The Little Ice Age

Nowadays, Skallingen and Horns Rev form the northern limit of the Wadden Sea, north of which the west coast evolves into an even linear coastline with strong movement of material parallel to the shore and dune-formation. From around Nymindegab northwards coastal erosion is taking place, now countered by protection measures. The natural conditions in the coastal zone were previously very different. Below and behind the rows of dunes of the coastal zone there was extensive marsh-formation, which shows that the fjord landscape of the west coast was previously open to the sea and so formed a zone similar to the Wadden Sea which reached as far as Nissum Fjord. Through documentary sources and maps of the 17th to 19th centuries one can trace the gradual transformation of the coastal zone into a cohesive, balanced coast, with the land alongside seriously plagued with driftsand (P. Eriksen et al. 2009, 17ff).

The reasons for this environmental disaster are associated with the phenomenon of the *Little Ice Age*, a cold period which lasted from the Late Middle Ages to around 1850. While there appears to be agreement over the existence of this cold period, why it happened is still debated. As well as poorer harvests and general failure of growth, more frequent storms were another consequence, and from 1362 onwards we have reports of storm floods along the west coast of Jutland.

The slow reduction in land-level in the Wadden Sea area meant that marsh, tidal flats and barrier islands were able to keep pace with the changing sea-level thanks to the alluvial deposition of sediment and dunes. In the extensive marshlands to the south there was an early wave of reclamation, but in the Tønder Marsh and further north deliberate initiatives of that kind seem to have taken place only from the Late Middle Ages onwards (Porskrog Rasmussen 2013, 17ff).

On the night of 16 January 1362 a storm flood struck East and North Frisia. This was subsequently called the *Grote Mandrenke*, 'the Great Drowning of Men', and it decisively changed Uthland, a rich archipelago which incorporated, amongst other things, a settlement with a legendary reputation, Rungholt (Poulsen 2003). The absence of detailed sources, and later storm floods in the area, mean that it is barely possible to reveal the extent of this catastrophe with any great certainty, but the disaster is the first recorded example of the destructive storm floods which in the following centuries would shape life on the west coast of Jutland. The list of later storm floods is a long one, but the super-storm that struck on the night of 11 October 1634 is reckoned to have been the worst in the post-medieval period (Fruergaard et al. 2013).

Increased storm activity is considered to be a direct product of the Little Ice Age (Clemmensen 2005). There is very little information about the strength of storms in earlier times, but both studies of drifting sand in West Jutland and the location of a series of archaeological sites in relation to the coast indicate that either there were no violent storms or storm floods or that they were very uncommon events. At risk of presenting the preceding medieval warm period as a positively paradisical state of affairs, it could indeed appear that the Little Ice Age with its lower temperatures, storms, storm floods and drifting sand changed and reduced the opportunities for human life along Jutland's west coast to a marked degree. On the basis of a combination of various sources, ranging from ice-core samples to accounts of famine in Europe, the deterioration of the climate is dated as a process with an onset in the mid-13th century while the drifting sand of West Jutland appears to have reached a peak in the period c. 1500-1800 (Clemmensen 2005). The drifting sand was anything but limited to the coastal zone; indeed it caused problems over much of sandy West Jutland (Dalsgaard et al. 2000; Breuning-Madsen et al. 2013).

4.2.6 Vegetational development

The development of vegetation and the human exploitation of the landscape that was linked with it have usually been studied through pollen diagrams derived from lakes or bogs. While there are a number of analysed pollen sequences from West Jutland, that is not the case in the south-west (Odgaard 2000; P. Eriksen et al. 2009, 17ff). The method also has one intrinsic weakness, in that the likelihood of retrieving undisturbed pollen sequences from bogs in intensively exploited landscapes is lower because peat-cutting has been continuous up to the 20th century. At the extreme this may mean that the few undisturbed pollen sequences have that quality precisely because relatively few people lived in the area they represent, and this evaluation has to be put in the context of the frequency and distribution pattern of the individual pollen-types, which varies significantly from species to species.

One can also note, in the West Jutlandic pollen range, that woodland is weakly represented, although archaeological excavations show that for most of prehistory there was no shortage of timber for building in the large number of settlements in the area, unlike the situation in Thy for example (P. Eriksen et al. 2009, 27). The place-name evidence from West Jutland also contains numerous names which relate to woodland.

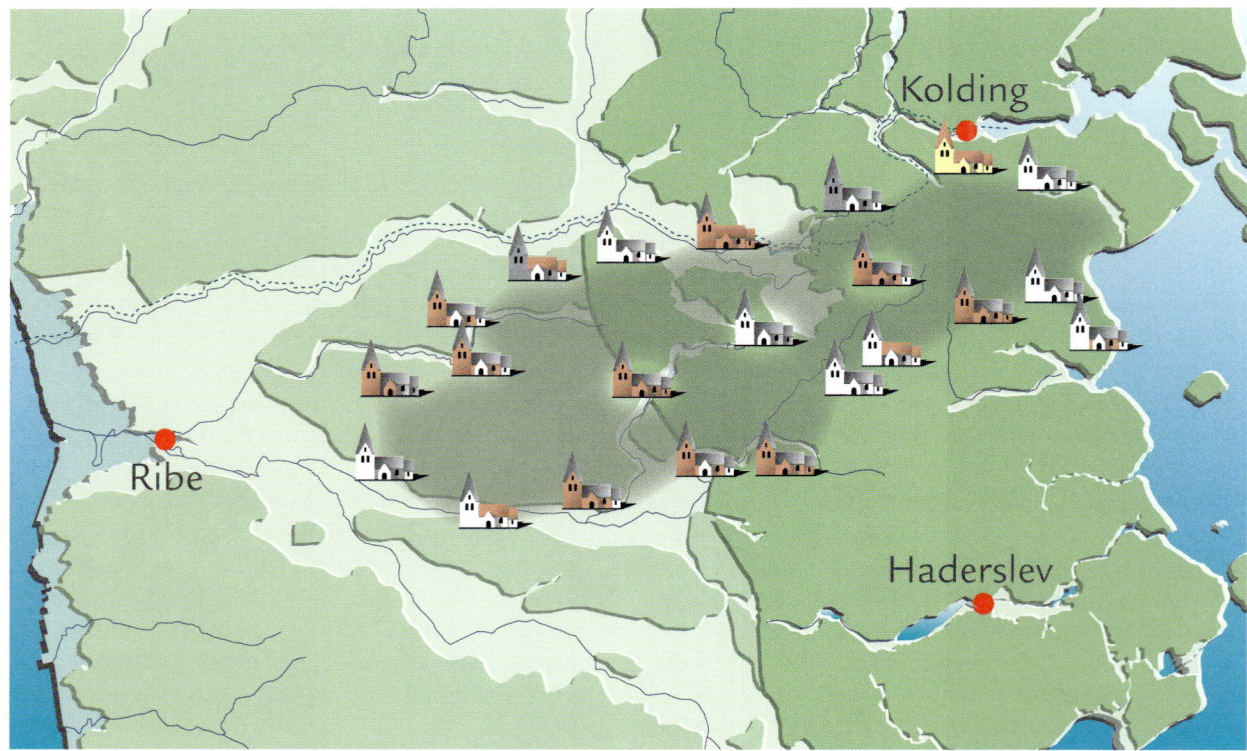

Fig. 44. The Farris Forest spread out around the course of the Ribe River. This reconstruction of the former extent of the forest is based upon the density of churches and place-names. After Poulsen 2003.

4.2.7 The Farris Forest

The extent of this area of woodland has been debated, but on the basis of the most recent examination of the place-name evidence and the distribution of Romanesque parish churches the outline of a particularly large forest emerges which basically ran from coast to coast in the boundary zone between the Dukedom of Schleswig and Northern Jutland (*Nørrejylland*) (Fig. 44) (Pilgaard 2009). The place-name record in Hviding and Vester Vedsted parishes south of Ribe includes a variety of woodland-related names, and they become denser towards the east between the parishes of Roager and Spandet that form the boundary of the historically known forest-area (Aa. Andersen 1998).

The presence of this forest can be regarded as having been one of the constitutive elements of the border line between Schleswig and Northern Jutland, just as the Jernved ('Iron wood') forest was spread across the borderlands south of the Danevirke (Poulsen 2008, 44f). The distribution of ancient monuments in the former Farris Forest shows that in parts of prehistory this wooded area had been more or less felled while the distribution of woodland-related place-names conversely shows that it was real presence when these locations were named in the period from the Iron Age to the Middle Ages. From the present picture of settlement in South and Southern Jutland in the Late Germanic Iron Age, the Viking Period and the Middle Ages, there is much to suggest that following the environmental catastrophe of 536 the Farris Forest grew to a maximal extent and so can be regarded as an absolutely central factor in the overall landscape picture (Matthiessen 1930).

4.2.8 The Church List in Ribe Great-Grandmother

As a consequence of climate change which came about in context of the Little Ice Age, it has been argued, above, that there were drastic landscape-related changes in the West Jutland coastal zone. In the Wadden Sea huge areas of marsh and whole settlements disappeared into the sea. Between Horns Rev and Nymindegab wave-action and drifting sand have reshaped the coastline and covered large, fertile pasturelands with sand. From Nymindegab up to the mouth of the Limfjord the sea is eroding the land, and the 8th-century shoreline is now far out to sea. Inland there are now large areas impacted by dune-formation and wind-stripped surfaces.

What things were like before that is a question that has occupied the historians of earlier eras, and an early example is the cartographer Johannes Mejer, who produced several different maps which were meant to portray the earlier state of affairs in the Wadden Sea (Fig. 45). The maps were drawn up while the storm flood of 1634 was fresh in the memory. They show a large number of settlements and churches which by implication had been drowned, including some that gave rise to tenacious local legends, such as that of St Anna's Church on Fanø, identified by local tradition as the first church on the island even though Johannes Mejer's unreliable map is the principal source for this information (*DK*, Ribe amt, 2107ff).

The manuscript which is now called *Ribe Oldemoder* but which must originally have been called *Træbogen* ('The wooden book') is a collection of copied documents relating to the espiscopal see in Ribe (O. Nielsen 1869; Severinsen 1921; Skyum-Nielsen 1949; Aakjær 1952). It was begun in 1291 and continued down to c. 1323 by the same hand, the canon Aastred. Amongst the later additions to the book is a list of the churches of the diocese and of tolls given in English shillings graduated on a scale from one shilling to ten (Fig. 46). One shilling corresponded to twelve pence – in other words twelve English long-cross pennies, which, together with other foreign silver coins, primarily French and German, constituted the hard currency of the time, in contrast to the contemporary local coins with their high copper content (Fig. 47). The bottom of the list is occupied by Lemvig, the only parish that was worth just one shilling. Most of the inland parishes on the poor heathlands were worth just two shillings, while the churches of the coastal zone generally had higher valuations, often as high as eight shillings. The church in Tønder, which probably refers to Møgeltønder, was the only parish valued at ten shillings.

The individual churches were responsible for an annual payment of between 12 and 120 English sterling pence to the episcopal see in Ribe. What this toll covered exactly has been a subject of lively discussion, but the best suggestion is that it is a tax for the rural dean, the supervisory dean, who was a member of the chapter in Ribe. The sum was presumably paid on the occasion of the annual visitation (Severinsen 1921). There is consensus that the sum was realistically correlated with the productivity of the parish and thus reflects the economic potential of the individual parishes at the relevant date. The list is undated, but from the structure of the rural deaneries its compilation can be assigned to c. 1325 while the copy in the manuscript was added c. 1380-1410.

The churches in the list are grouped rural deanery by rural deanery (syssel) and then by *herred* ('district'), except for the deanery of Jelling. There are added notes alongside some of the churches. Anflod church near Tønder is annotated *submersa*, while alongside a number of other churches stands *desolata*. These additions must pre-date the last entry in the manu-

Fig. 45. Extract from Johannes Mejer's map of the western part of Haderslev amt in 1649. On the tidal flats between the islands a large number of presumably lost churches and villages are marked which do not appear in other, otherwise well-informed sources, such as the Church List in 'Ribe Great-Grandmother' – for instance the supposed church of St Anna east of Fanø. From the original in the Royal Library.

script of 1518 and are believed to come from the 15th century. The list has been made use of in many historical studies, and investigations have shown that the register of churches is accurate and represents the parishes that existed around 1325. The only definite lacuna in the list is the churches on Holmsland, called Gammel and Ny (Old and New) parishes, but their absence can be explained in that they belonged to the dean *ex officio* and so of course were not subject to these dues (Severinsen 1921). The annotations can be treated as reliable too. The churches marked *desolata* are all gone now, except for Vejrup in Gørding district, where building archaeological investigations have confirmed that this Romanesque structure was probably in ruins before it was thoroughly renovated at the end of the Middle Ages; consequently the annotation in the Church List can indeed be accepted as reflecting the situation at the date in question (*DK*, Ribe amt. 3003-22).

There are solid grounds to argue, as a result, that the level of payments stands in a practical and direct relationship to the agrarian economy of the individual parishes and reflects the conditions before both the

Black Death of 1350 and the great storm flood of 1362. Local conditions, such as, for instance, the existence of the abbeys of Tvis and Løgum, produced minor local inconsistencies, but again not of such a magnitude as to affect the overall trends. As Ribe Diocese includes a number of parishes in the moraine landscapes of East Jutland, it becomes possible to undertake direct comparisons of the conditions in East and West respectively.

Nearly all of the churches in the list still survive, and by mapping the information it is possible to reconstruct a precise economic map of Ribe Diocese in the first half of the 14th century, and then, on the basis of this information, to undertake a series of assessments of subsequent changes. In the maps in Figures 48 and 49 an attempt has been to reconstruct the parish structure of the churches though retrogressive cartographic study, re-establishing the parishes of the abandoned churches as they can be determined on the basis of historical information and natural divisions in the landscape. The starting point has been the digitized parish maps of the Culture

80

Cantoria.
  frøshæreth.
hygyngh viij solidi.
foorlæ v.
røthing iiij.
lynwy iiij.
skragh iiij.
manø iiij.

  kalfslwndhæreth.
kalfslwnd iiij.
hyortlwnd iiij.
dowerth ij. desolata.
linthorp vj.
faarthorp viij.
hyrtingh ij.

almyndsysæl.
  anstethhæreth.
bekky iiij.
ersteth iiij.
gesten iiij.
wamthorp v.
hyarthorp iiij.
ansteth v.
jorthorp iiij.
wyrsteth ij.
skanthorp v.
karbyergh ij. desolata.

  broskoghæreth.
wæthælby iiij.
bramthorp iiij.
wigøth iiij.
hersløf iiij.
vghælthorp iiij. desolata.
brestorp iiij.
ærexhøgh iiij.

taflygh iiij.
wylsthorp ij.
ælmætungh vj.
kungesteth iiij.
hartæ iiij.
nybæl ij.
stathorp iiij.
almind iiij.
smiszthorp v.

  holmbomoothæreth.
garzløøf iiij.
gauærlwnd vj.
skyepthorp iiij.
winningh iiij.
petæsteth iiij.

  jærløfhæreth.
ekthyuf v.
øøthsteth iiij.
kaldingh iiij.
jærløf iiij.
hinghælswi ij.
almstok ij. desolata.
worbas ij.
ødingh ij.
karbyergh ij. desolata.
høthærn iiij.

jællinghsysæl.
wæthlæ iiij.
skipwith iiij.
breethsteen iiij.
nythorp iiij.
randæbøøl ij.
grenæ ij.
griinsteth iiij.

Fig. 46. An extract of the information in the Church List transcribed by Oluf Nielsen. The churches are listed by deanery (herred) and parish. By each church is given the payment due in roman numerals. At a later date, by some of the churches the word desolata *was added, 'waste'. After O. Nielsen 1869.*

Fig. 47. The obverse and reverse of two English long-cross pennies of the 13th and 14th centuries, found by metal-detecting at Damhus in Ribe' medieval town-field. Coins such as these were the currency units referred to in 'Ribe Great-Grandmother'. ASR 2327x367 and x380. 2:1.

Agency (*Kulturstyrelsen*), with the coastline corrected according to Society of Scientists' (*Videnskabernes Selskabs*) maps from around the year 1800. For the inland parishes, the task of reconstruction is relatively uncomplicated, even though it presumably will be possible to discover minor errors, but it is believed that possible revisions of the parish limits which are not currently known to me will scarcely affect what the mapping shows in general terms.

In the coastal zone the situation is rather different. One parish, Anflod, which is thought to have been located south-east of Højer, has disappeared

completely (*DK*, Tønder amt, 1336). The church is known to have survived the storm flood of 1362 but the parish finally succumbed after a storm flood in 1436. The churches included in the list on both Mandø and Fanø, and possibly also on Rømø, are no longer there, and their parishes must likewise have been radically changed by storm floods. Furthermore, in the Tønder Marsh, deliberate reclamation has been undertaken since the Late Middle Ages, which recurrent storm floods have nonetheless succeeded to greater or lesser extents in wresting back from the farmers for a while.

The further north in the coastal zone one goes, the reconstruction of the precise boundaries of the parishes becomes impossible because of the all-encompassing sand-drifting. Nonetheless, the list shows that neither parishes nor churches have been lost since that time. The location of the churches in the landscape reveals that the loss of land to coastal erosion is significant only north of Nissum Fjord, where, however, from the position of the churches, it must be inferred to have taken more than a kilometre in the parishes of Ferring, Trans and Fjaltring in Vandfuld district.

The large number of changes in the coastal zone are the reason why no attempt has been made to determine the coastline in the map but rather to keep to what is presented in Videnskabernes Selskab's map. In Figure 48 the returns paid by the individual churches are shown on a reconstructed parish map, coloured in relation to the level of payment. This introductory exercise shows a clear concentration of the more important churches in the coastal zone while the poor heath parishes inland were typically responsible for low payments. Since both the land-conditions and the sizes of the parishes vary markedly across the extensive diocese of Ribe, a more solid expression of the taxable potential/wealth of the

individual parishes would combine the level of return with the size of the parish. This is shown in Figure 49 on a graduated scale.

These maps present a clear economic image of Ribe Diocese around 1325. The West Jutlandic coastal zone produced returns on the same level as the fat morainic soils of East Jutland, while the extensive heathland parishes of the interior must with few exceptions be characterized as poor. The mapping must also reflect the distribution of population to some degree.

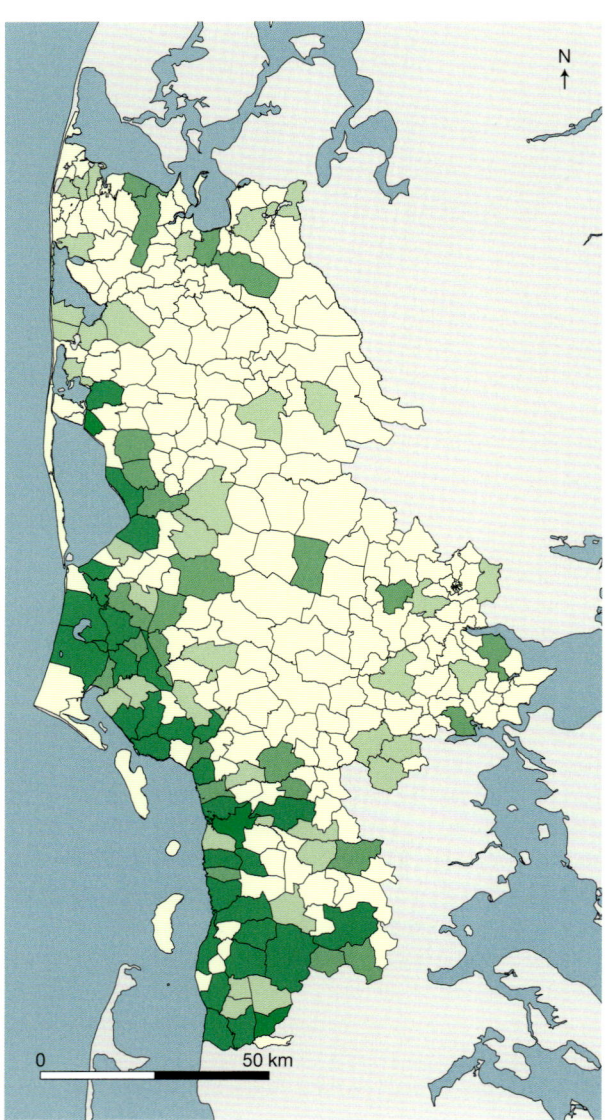

Fig. 48. Reconstructed parish map of Ribe Diocese based on the information in 'Ribe Great-Grandmother' from c. 1325. The coastline is as given in Videnskabernes Selskab's map of c. 1800, and it would have been somewhat different in the Middle Ages. The payments due from the individual parishes are shown in a graduated scale, with the lowest in light yellow and the highest in dark green.

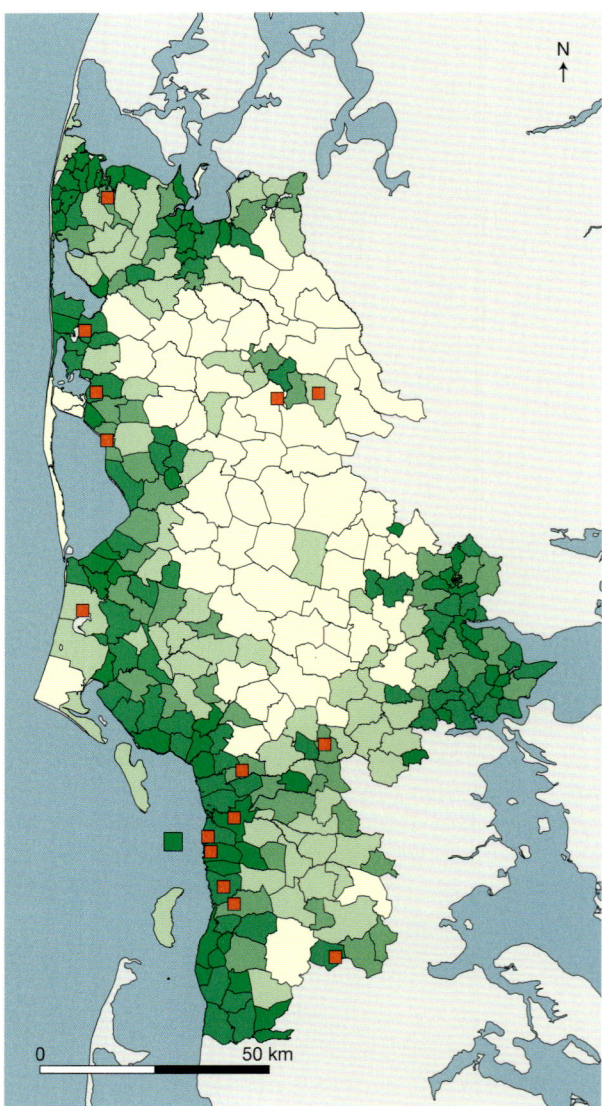

Fig. 49. Map showing the dues of the individual parishes adjusted according to the size of the parish. The light yellow zones show the lowest proportional yield while the dark green ones show the highest. As is shown, the whole of the coastal zone of West Jutland was responsible for returns at the same level as the moraine landscapes of East Jutland, presumably reflecting a similar density of population. The red dots mark the known Romanesque church towers.

Also marked in the map in Figure 49 are the churches which had a tower in the Romanesque period. The motives for raising a tower could be diverse but typically a prestige-related, aristocratic motivation can be detected behind early tower building (Larsen 2010). The Romanesque towers also cluster in the coastal zone, and this image will only be reinforced if other qualitative elements of the churches' Romanesque architecture are included such as the materials and quality of the buildings themselves, sculpture, wall paintings etc – which altogether would confirm that the relative wealth of the coastal zone can also be traced back to the period in which the churches were built in the 12th and 13th centuries.

The Church List and its levels of dues help to document the fact that both the Tønder Marsh and even more the islands of Rømø, Mandø and Fanø were decisively impacted by storm floods. What they were like before then cannot be stated with any certainty, but since Mandø was due for the same level of payment as the other islands, four shillings, it must have been more or less the same size, a glaring contrast to the situation now. From Skallingen northwards there does not appear to have been any significant loss of land since the 14th century but rather a high level of impact from drifting sand and dune-formation, which has completely changed and reduced the scope for farming in the coastal zone. From Nissum Fjord north to the mouth of the Limfjord extensive coastal erosion can be demonstrated which can be determined to have removed more than a kilometre's width of land since the churches in Ferring, Trans and Fjaltring were founded.

The economic image of the diocese of Ribe that the Church List yields was produced at a juncture when the climatic deterioration of the Little Ice Age had probably begun, and the probability is that conditions had been even more favourable in the preceding medieval warm period.

4.3 Landscape and people

4.3.1 Communication, transport and trade

The form of transport for long-distance contact was the ship, and the comfortable sailing conditions in the Wadden Sea provided optimal scope for communication with a network that covered the whole of the North Sea, the Channel lands and the river systems connected with them. The west coast north of Horns Rev was also presumably part of the same range of navigable water which could have extended as far as Harboøre, from where the Limfjord offered sailors calm water across to the Baltic Sea as well, at least until the opening to the North Sea was sanded up early in the Middle Ages, cutting off this core transport artery.

The growth of the emporia in the southern North Sea zone during the 7th century was driven by trading ships under sail and the long-distance trade which they made possible. From around the year 700 they reached Ribe, and later in the same century sailed through the Limfjord and deep into the Baltic where the trading sites of Reric/Groß Strömkendorf in Wismar Bay, Åhus in eastern Skåne, and Truso in eastern Poland, were buds in a then expanding network (Sindbæk 2007).

This coastal traffic required a system of minor anchorages along the routes, landing places at which the travelling merchants could stop for the night, seek shelter from adverse weather, and obtain drinking water and other supplies (Ulriksen 1998). As meeting points between local and foreign traders, the landing places were natural fora for trade and exchange.

Whatever factors controlled the trade will have divided up the waters. From a Marxist-substantivist viewpoint, the trade was controlled by *the power*, in the form of the king or the aristocracy, and it took place in accordance with fixed social norms that directed the valuation of goods and trading regulations – such is the tradition from Karl Polanyi and Richard Hodges (Hodges 1982; 1989). Other more liberally oriented lines of thought have emphasized that free agents would also have been able to make their own choices based on market forces and personal preferences (Sindbæk 2007; Skre 2007c).

In the Middle Ages, in respect of which our knowledge of trade is much greater than for the preceding period, we know that trading sites, nearly always towns, could be under royal, ecclesiastical or aristocratic control. Lund, Odense, Viborg and many more towns were royal. For a long time Copenhagen belonged to the Bishop of Roskilde, Næstved was owned by the Benedictines at Skovkloster, and Kalundborg was founded around 1170 by the nobleman Esbern Snare, while the king and the bishop shared power and income from Ribe until 1234. Contemporary with these major trading sites there was a large number of minor sites which the royal authority called *illicit harbours* where trading also took place. Behind these might be local leaders, or maybe just a group of local farmers who were trying to secure income from trade for themselves. The largest and most important harbours were far more likely than the small and less significant ones to be referred to in the documentary record and so to be known today. Some eventually became towns; others disappeared. Unsurprisingly, the king waged an ongoing campaign to monopolise and regulate trade, but the many struggles over this issue show just as clearly that there were continuous and successful attempts to avoid tolls by trading outside the law.

This model, with a differentiated system of trading sites subject to the control of various agents, might in fact also describe the conditions in the preceding period. There is agreement that the leading Viking-period trading sites in the North were under royal control while the extent and character of the other stopping sites is subject to more debate. With this model in mind one could suggest that the well-structured site at Henne, the small tofts at which are conspicuously different from a purely agrarian settlement, should be regarded as a trading site that may have been controlled by a Viking-period aristocrat resident at a predecessor of the nearby Hennegård (Ploug, Jepsen & Frandsen 2012, 28ff).

Traffic overland on the public highways accounted for the majority of regional communication and for all of those travelling who did not have access to a ship (Matthiessen 1927; 1930). Rows of long barrows and burial mounds from the Funnel Beaker Culture, the Single Grave Culture or the Bronze Age reflect the prehistoric network of routes, and in some cases correspond to surviving road-lines – in others, not (Johansen, Laursen & Holst 2004).

A newly collated map of the preserved hollow-ways in Denmark paints an astonishingly clear picture of the overall communication routes in Jutland in pre-history and the Middle Ages (Fig. 50) (Bang 2013; cf. M.S. Jørgensen 1988). Surviving but undated traces of hollow-way lie scattered throughout the peninsula, on a wide range of soil-types, and must be assumed to have been formed primarily by wagon transport. The heavier the wagon the deeper and therefore the better preserved the wheel tracks. Taking a long view, the overall map of the hollow-ways must express a diachronic cross-section of prehistoric and medieval wagon transport which, considering the 6,000-year time-depth, stands out extraordinarily clearly.

If we add to this barrows, cemeteries, pit-strips (representing post barriers: sometimes referred to as 'wolf-pits' or *trous du loup*) (Rindel & Eriksen 2018), ramparts and other ancient monuments which are positioned in relation to traffic, two well-defined and primary routeways up through the Jutlandic peninsula stand out. Along the East Jutlandic watershed ran the Hærvej (Matthiessen 1930; M.S. Jørgensen 1988; Andresen et al. 2008). The most heavily travelled route in Jutland, to judge by the wheel-ruts and prob-ably rightly so, this seems to have been a permanent feature of the post-glacial landscape.

In West Jutland, *Ravvejen* (The Amber Way), or *Drivvejen* (The Droveway) as the route is known in this context, also stands out very clearly, although the traces of the road-line lie in a rather wider tract through the landscape (Gammeltoft 2005). This is probably due to the fact that the course was not tied to a watershed but rather had to cross a variety of watercourses and major wetlands along its line. Sedimentation and peat-growth in lakes and rivers could lead to a general rise in the water table, while gradual erosion could reduce the water table cor-respondingly. These counteracting forces will have been operative at the same time, and have not least affected the flat terrain of West Jutland where even small changes in the water table can have marked con-sequences. These conditions are significant especially where routes cross wetlands, so that, for instance, even a beaver dam somewhere in the West Jutlandic river system could have been sufficient to force the traffic to find a new crossing point. Drifting sand could also have forced the traffic to find a new route.

The remains of hollow-ways reveal parts of the courses of the main communication arteries of the Iron Age, Viking Period and Middle Ages. Where such remains do not survive for one reason or another, routes can still be reconstructed from other ancient monuments, burial mounds, cemeteries, pit-strips, ramparts etc, and generally there is a close corre-spondence with the principal routes that appear on the earliest land maps of the 17th century onwards (Matthiessen 1927, 74ff; 1930).

In recent years, archaeological excavations have been able to contribute a number of crucial observations concerning the principal land route of West Jutland in the period under discussion here. North of Varde the finding of road-bridge structures at Nybro shows that there was investment in the construction of N.-S., post-built causeways in order to facilitate transport across wet areas as early as the 8th century (Ravn 1999). In the town of Varde itself parts of an extensive N.-S. hollow-way route that can be traced back to the Viking Period although it could have even earlier roots have been examined. In this case, this appears to have been the preferred passage across the voluminous Varde River, and the routeway is directed down towards the castle of Vardehus (Bentsen 2008). If the river itself was crossed by bridge or ford we do not know. At Henne on the north side of Lake Fil (Filsø) an extensive Viking-period settlement has been discovered characterized by sunken feature buildings which belonged to relatively small farmsteads. This could be because the settlement was not solely based upon agriculture. The main period of the site was in the 9th to 11th centuries, and its core element is a N.-S. routeway (Ploug, Jepsen & Frandsen 2012, 28ff). Immediately to the west is Hennegård, where in 1145 Bishop Elias of Ribe signed the letter establishing the diocesan chapter in Ribe.

By the Skjern River, the river with the greatest flow in Denmark, remains of bridge structures have been examined, the earliest components of which could be dendro-dated to AD 1105: telling evidence of the energy which even then was being invested in the infrastructure of West Jutland (Egeberg 2004).

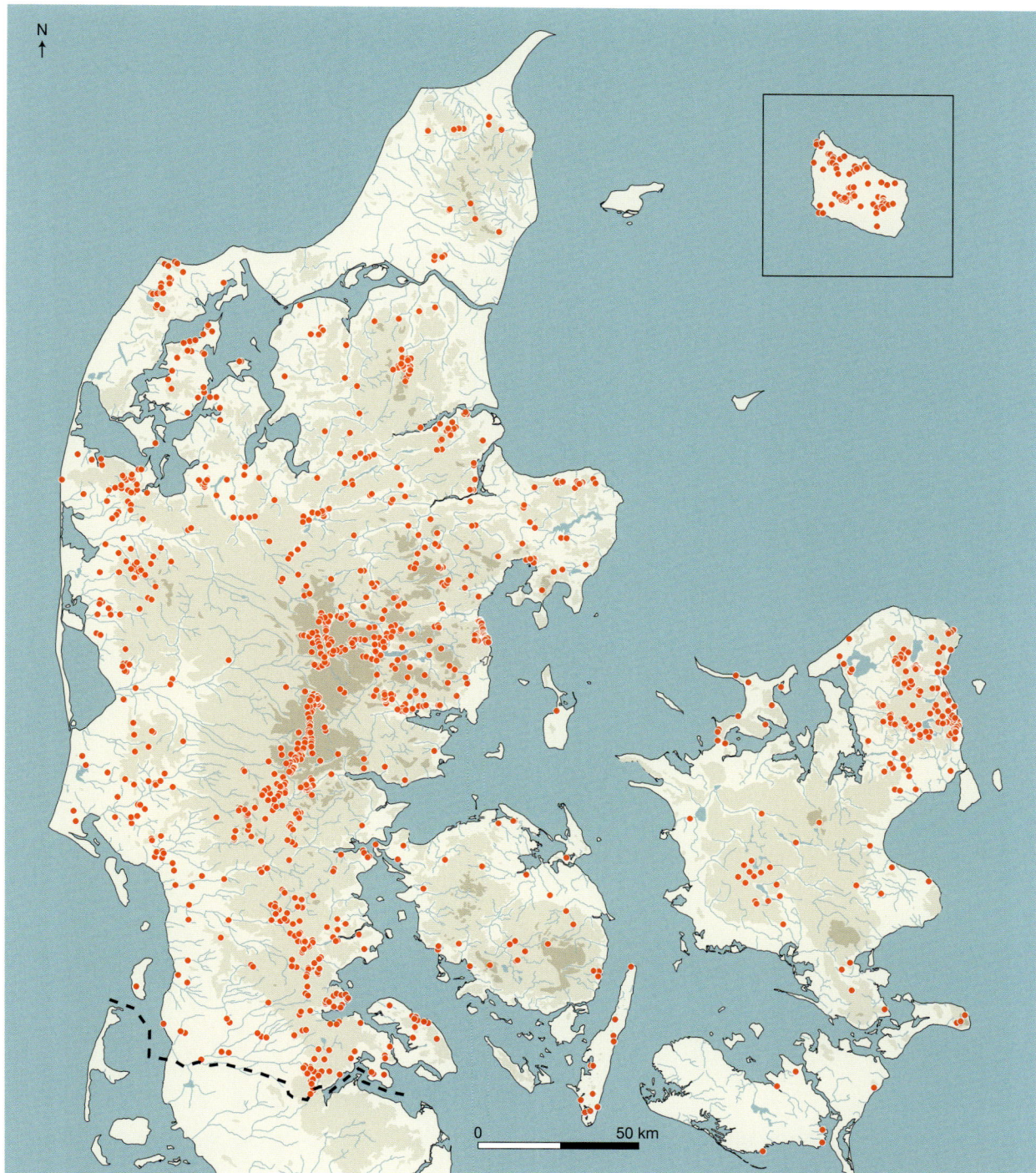

Fig. 50. Map of hollow-ways and tracks in Denmark. The Hærvej *('Military Way') along the ridge of Jutland and the Droveway in the West Jutlandic coastal zone stand out as the two principal routeways in Jutland. Data-pull of feature type 'Road Tracks' (XVS) (n = 1334) from the Castle and Culture Agency's database Finds and Ancient Monuments 5 November 2019.*

No investigations have yet been carried out in the course of the river itself within the town of Ribe to look for the bridges which must have carried traffic across the water before the current road dam was built around 1250. However the identification of particularly heavy timber-paved roads in Badstuegade

which lead down toward the river is perhaps what most strongly suggests the presence of a bridge (Søvsø 2007a). On the other side of the river both planked roads and hollow-ways have been found which run up across the steep river bank in the form of a fan. The 12th-century castle that was found in

Fig. 51. Undated wheel tracks from an early course of the land route between Ribe and Kolding recorded during a trial excavation north of Ribe. On the right the present Ribe-Kolding road can be seen. Excavation ASR 2167.

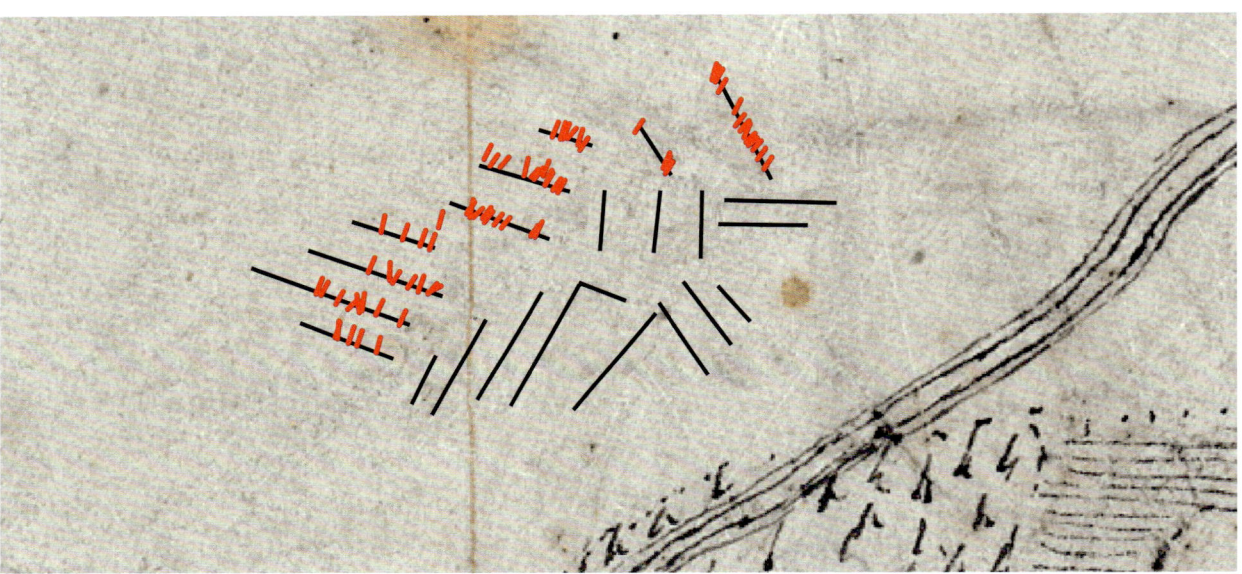

Fig. 52. Predecessors to the road between Ribe and Kolding in the form of wheel tracks (red) found in trial trenches (black). The direction is marked in thick red strokes. The base map is Videnskabernes Selskab's map of 1794, and the Ribe-Kolding road is the road line to the south. Excavation ASR 2167.

1993 may have been meant to guard this strategically important passage (Søvsø 2010b).

Immediately north and south of Ribe, remains of old land routes have been found in the form of innumerable wheel tracks that follow the course of the main routes towards Varde, Kolding and Haderslev in broad corridors (Figs. 51-53). At Kalvsund, remains of the Viking-period Kolding road have been excavated: this can be traced back at least to the year

1000 and continued along the same line until the 17th century (Fig. 54) (Søvsø 2013).

The diffuse range of observations over a wide geographical area could be added to with further examples without forming a comprehensive picture but rather to display the more or less random surviving traces of a practical road-network that had deep roots. Especially the main land route running N.-S., the later Droveway, stands out very clearly, and must

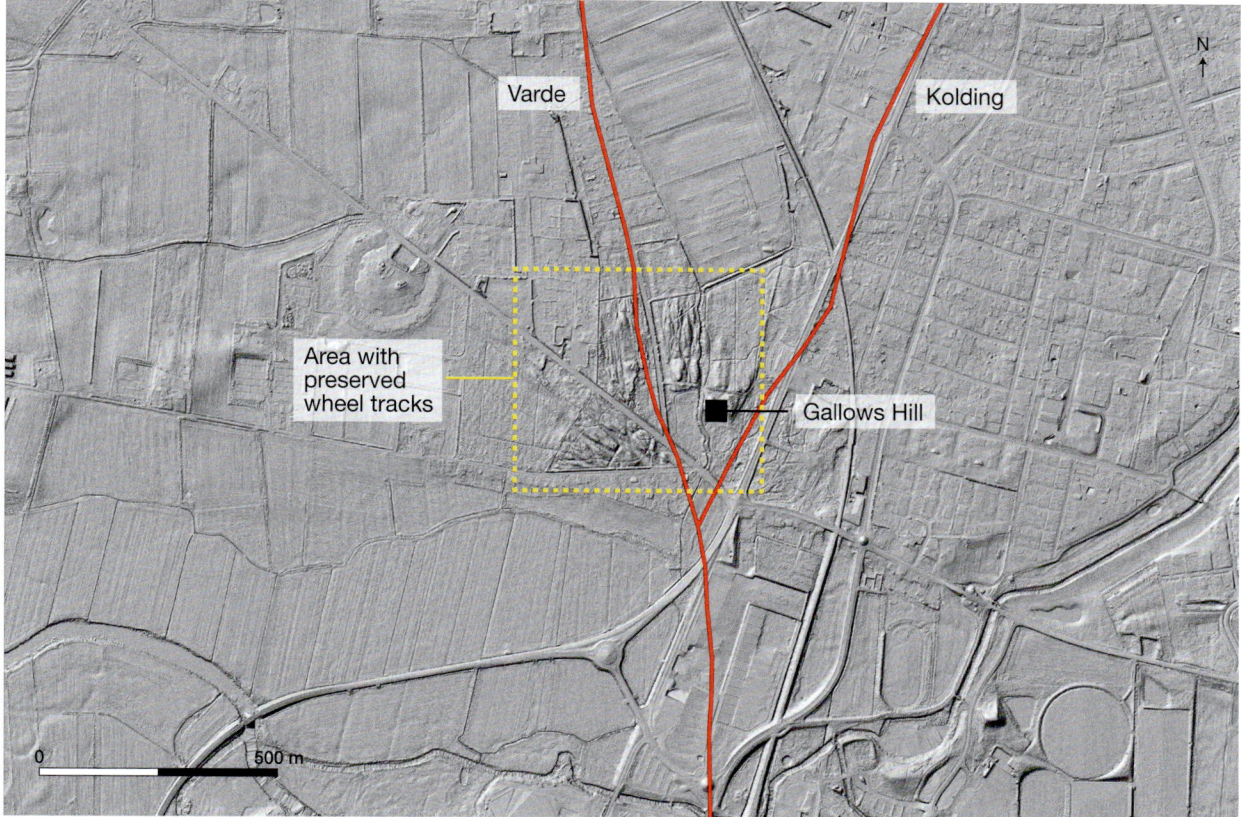

Fig. 53. In the plantation immediately north of Ribe LIDAR scanning has revealed the existence of many wheel tracks from earlier courses of the land road to the north. The red lines show the course of the land route from Videnskabernes Selskab*'s map of 1794.*

be supposed to have joined up the whole of the coastal tract of West Jutland. But the land routes from Ribe towards Kolding, Haderslev and Urnehoved also emerge in the archaeological evidence, and can in some cases be shown to have existed in the Viking Period.

The investigation of the roads available serves to show that in terms of land traffic Ribe lay at a central node from which routes radiated out in every direction (I. Nielsen 1985, 44; Matthiessen 1930). The roads towards Kolding, Haderslev and Urnehoved all joined up with the Hærvej and so the whole network connected with that. Thus the geographical location of Ribe conjoins two factors: a navigable river and easy access to the overall infrastructure of Jutland. While there is no doubt that both the Hærvej and the Droveway were there before Ribe emerged, it is not so easy to produce equivalent evidence for the crossing roads towards the Hærvej, although a clear clustering of cemeteries along all of the present Kolding, Haderslev and Toftlund roads strongly suggests it. In a wider view, the utterly central position of the town in relation to the general infrastructure of Jutland shows that the connections between Ribe and the hinterland were of critical importance.

4.3.2 Settlement in West Jutland in the Iron Age, Viking Period and Middle Ages

In the past decade, the number of archaeological excavations in Denmark has risen markedly. Along with detector finds, the large number of excavations clearly shows that from the pre-Roman Iron Age onwards settlement was concentrated in the coastal zone of West Jutland. In the northern zone of the Wadden Sea the marsh areas formed a relatively narrow zone that could be exploited by farmers living on the edge of the drier land: the geest edge. From the Tønder Marsh southwards the marsh reached an extent which meant that the farmers were actually living on the low marshland flats. Over time these settlement sites turned into what are known as *værfter* or terps, artificial mounds formed by the accumulation of clay and turf in which the remains of earlier farmsteads on the site can be exceptionally well preserved, as the excavations at Feddersen Wierde and many other sites have demonstrated (Haarnagel 1979; Siegmüller 2010). The date of foundation of the terps varies from place to place dependent upon the local history of marsh-formation, but the general tendency appears to be that when the marsh grew to

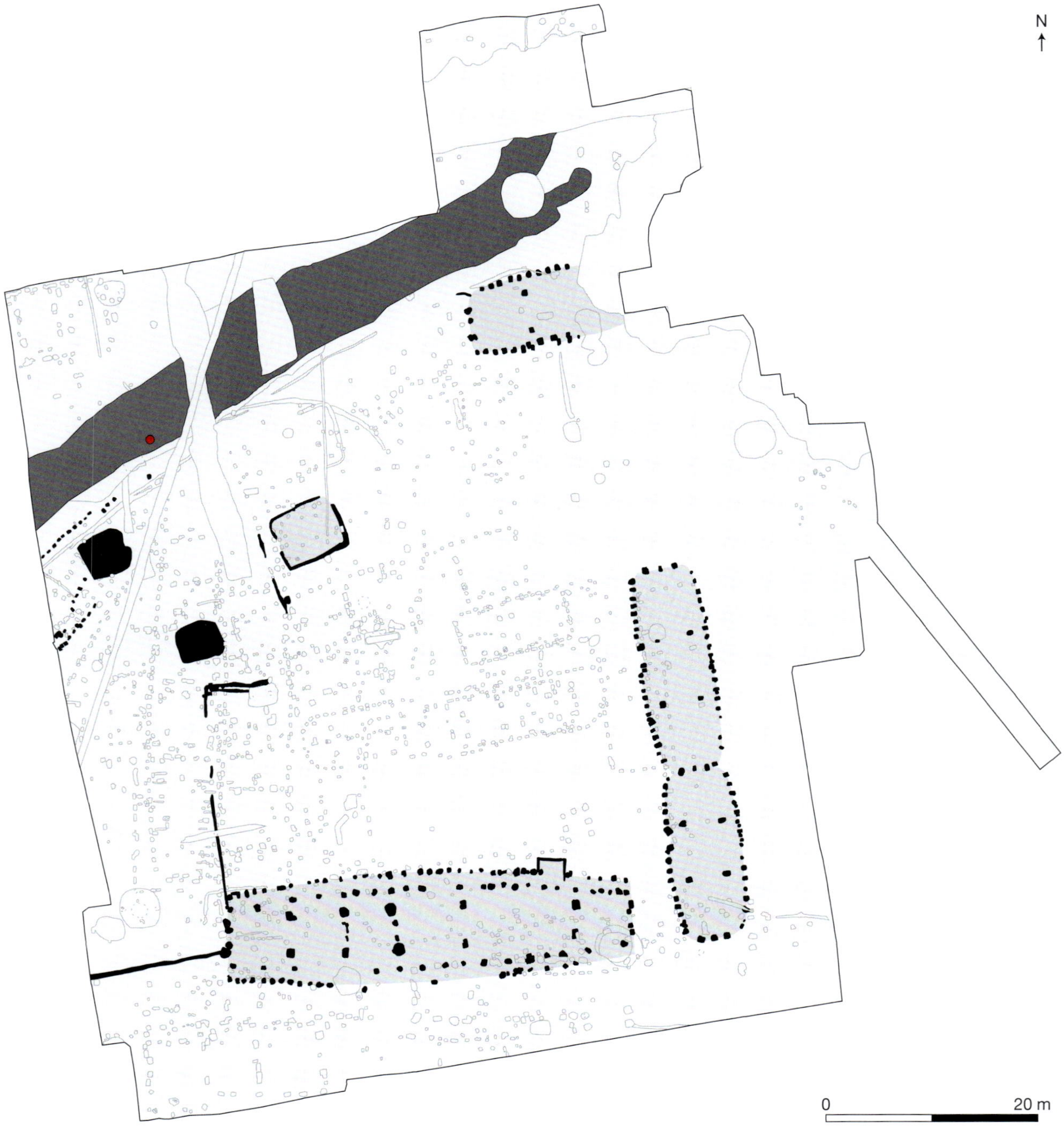

Fig. 54. South of Kalvslund church a single farmstead has been excavated which was probably located here from the 7th century right through to the 11th. This plan shows a phase dated to around the year 1000, when the land route (dark grey) just north of the farmstead was in the same position as is shown on Johannes Mejer's map from the middle of the 17th century. In the fill of the road was found a German coin struck in Hildesheim in the period 1022-38. Excavation ASR 1906, coin: ASR 1906x6.

an extent that it was no longer possible to exploit it from the edge of the geest, people moved out into it.

In the old Ribe Diocese it was only the Ballum and Tønder Marshes which reached a size that caused the farmers to move out off the geest and settle on artificial mounds. The few excavations that have been carried out in these northern terps indicate that they were established only in the late Viking Period or early Middle Ages (L. Madsen 2000). The northernmost group of terps, *Misthusum* near Skærbæk, was abandoned after the storm flood of 1634 (Poulsen 2003).

The undrained landscape from the period around 1800 that is shown on the earliest cadastral maps can be reconstructed, village land by village land, in GIS systems. In areas which have not undergone major changes in the form of storm floods, drifting sand or erosion, the basic form of this undrained landscape is the same as it was a thousand years ago.

There is no easy way of generating clear ideas of the level of population in prehistory, but ultimately the climate and the agrarian productivity dependent upon that, together with outbreaks of sickness and war, must have been the all-controlling factors which regulated numbers. Famine, crop failure and epidemics were regular events in the Roman Empire and there is no conceivable reason to suppose that the peoples of northern Europe had fundamentally better strate-

gies to counter the consequences of a failed harvest, the onset of disease, or war. The level of population could have fluctuated considerably, and the greater its density the greater the risk of epidemics striking. One must therefore presuppose both general and local fluctuations in the number of people.

Excavations in Denmark often retrieve wood, typically from wells, although other waterlogged contexts may also have preserved timber. In contrast to the wooden posts in the village buildings, the wells cannot be ploughed away, and the datings they produce can thus serve as a source for the history of settlement that only to a limited degree is distorted by modern land-use, which has in fact largely ploughed away most remains of settlement on the clay soil of eastern Denmark.

The dendro-laboratory *dendro.dk* has plotted all of the datings they have produced and presented the result as a function of the date of felling and the range of annual growth-rings (Fig. 55). This diagram includes all the datings undertaken by Aoife Daly during her employment at NNU from 1995-2002 and from 2002 onwards as director of *dendro.dk* . In the diagram where the individual datings are plotted according to the latest preserved growth-ring, and so will often be placed somewhat earlier than their felling date, a significant cluster of results can be seen which in some way or another must represent human exploitation of oak as a resource. If this exploitation

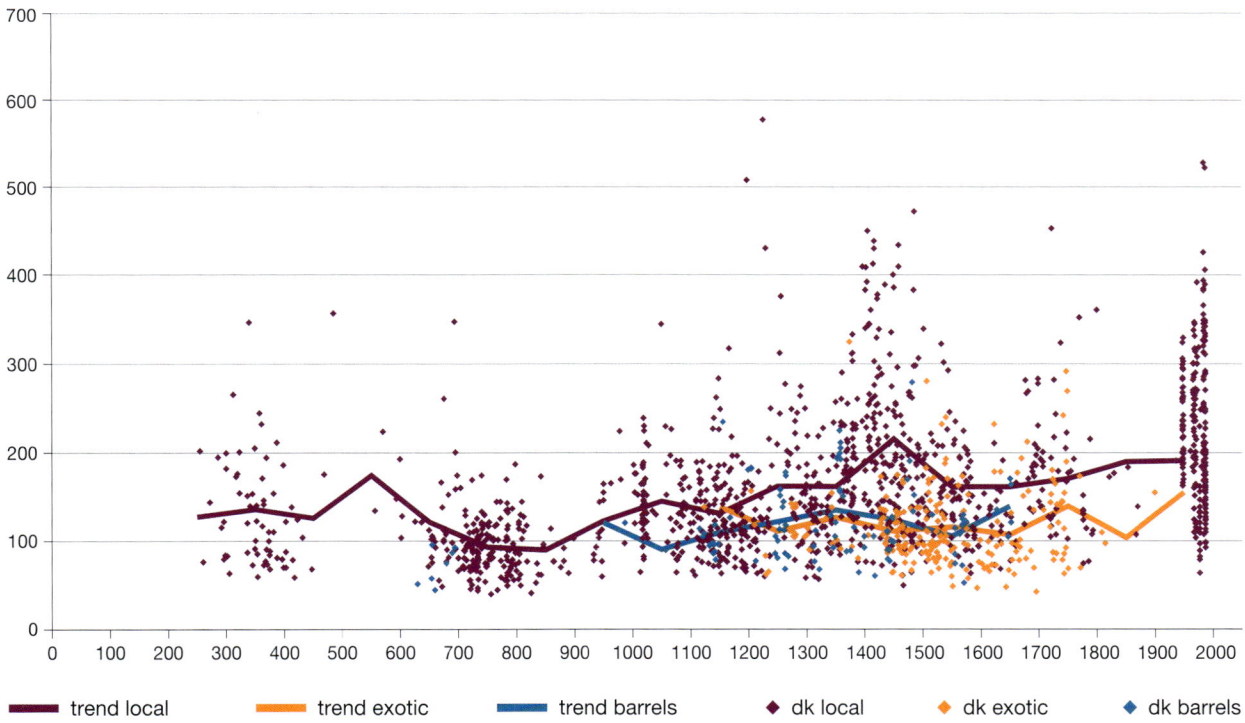

Fig. 55. A large random sample *of dendrochronological datings from Denmark produced in the years 1995-2002. The individual samples are plotted with reference to their latest surviving growth-ring, which is often close to the felling date. Note the almost complete absence of datings in the period after AD 536. After Daly 2017.*

can be described as a direct function also of the level of human population, an overall plot of all dendro-chronological dates from Denmark should also be a relative graph of the fluctuations in population levels. The plot shows a low point in the 6th century, which it seems obvious to connect to the volcanic eruptions of AD 536-47 and the environmental catastrophe that followed them (Axboe 2001; Büntgen et al. 2016), and another low point in the 10th century, after which the well-known expansion and growth of population of the earlier Middle Ages appears clearly.

Studies of settlement on Fyn also show the 7th century to have been a sharp break in the settlement pattern (Fig. 56) (J. Hansen 2015).

Depending upon the systems of cultivation and the climate, a resource area would have been able to support a fixed number of people. If the population grew, it was necessary to establish new settlements, and the rise in population and inheritance rules must have been the most significant driving forces behind relocation to what are very often more limited and in some cases less favourable areas of settlement.

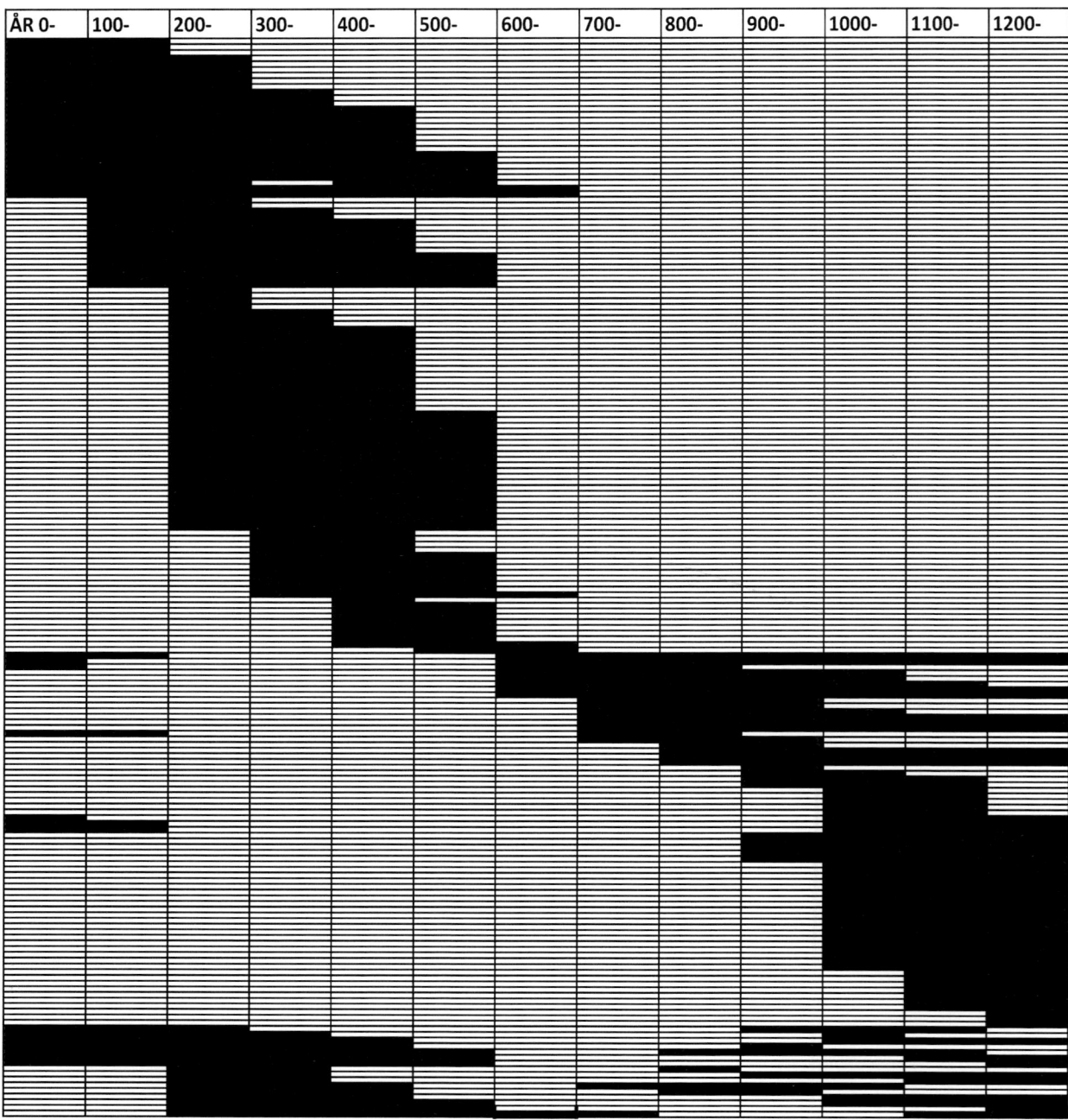

Fig. 56. Seriated diagram showing the functional date-ranges of settlements on Fyn. Each line represents a settlement. In this area too, the 6th-7th centuries stand out as a marked break. After J. Hansen 2015, 73.

4.3.3 The village: main villages and thorps, single farms

The village and the farming community associated with it is understood to have emerged during the pre-Roman Iron Age and was, for the period under discussion here, the overwhelmingly typical type of settlement and form of social organization in West Jutland (Hvass 1988; Ethelberg 2003). The size of each village was governed by the accessible resource areas and with boundaries between villages determined by natural divisions in the landscape, usually wet areas.

In the Early Iron Age, the field-systems were what is known as *digevoldinger*, 'Celtic field'-style banked oblong enclosures, ploughed using the ard. Many remains of such systems of cultivation have survived and can be found on aerial photographs as colour changes in the soil or preserved in heath- or woodlands; in recent years they have been discovered in great quantity through digital contour modelling. Already, probably, in the course of the Roman and at the latest in the Germanic Iron Age, the ard was superseded by the mouldboard plough on the light West Jutlandic soils, and this must have led to a re-structuring of the field-systems into longer and narrower fields, possibly formed as ridge-and-furrow (Agersnap Larsen 2015). In relation to the many known fossil field-systems from the Early Iron Age there are remarkably few known fossil field-systems of the following period, and those that are known have nearly always been preserved under sand drifts. This must be taken as strong evidence that the earliest field-systems cultivated using the mouldboard plough were to a very large extent the same as the fields of later periods.

A digitized map of land-use and landscape-types, such as are shown by the earliest cadastral maps, the so-called 'Original 1' map, will in many cases be a precise mapping of the Iron-age settlement potential too. That varied quite strongly from area to area according to naturally imposed constraints, as the examples in Figures 57-59 show. The digitization of the old cadastral maps has been undertaken by the author.

The medieval landscape laws distinguish between *main villages* (*adelbyer*) and *thorps* (*torper*), with the former designating some form of principal villages recognizable through names ending in *-inge*, *-lev*, *-løse* or *-sted*, while the thorps were a later stratum, similarly distinguished by name-endings: *-rup*, *-rop*, *-rød*. That the facts are more complex will not come as a surprise to many archaeologists, but all the same the dichotomy works as an operational description of the situation in many cases (Porsmose 1987).

If we consider a West Jutlandic – or indeed any – landscape, the agrarian and settlement potential are not uniformly distributed. Soil, infrastructure, access to resources and presumably also a range of phenomenological circumstances involved in the experience of the landscape and whatever meaning one or another circumstance is associated with, will render some areas preferred over others. The continual investment of labour in these areas in producing field-systems, pasturelands, coppices and more will function as centralizing dynamics which eventually create and maintain the phenomenon that can be called a main village, and its resource area, the village lands (ejerlav). These favoured locations in the landscape with particularly positive living conditions, and perhaps literally with control over those, may also have been a key motor driving the creation of greater social differentiation and the emergence of the so-called central places.

Vorbasse, lying in Jerlev district in the Middle Ages, the settlement history of which is well known through the comprehensive excavations of 1974-87, can be picked out as an example of a main village (Fig. 60). Its location close to the Hærvej has to be regarded as central.

Although Early Iron-age Vorbasse has not been excavated, the cemeteries to the east show that the village of that period was probably sited in that area. The excavations both north of and within present-day Vorbasse demonstrate that there has been continuity of settlement from the Roman Iron Age down to today, and it is hardly coincidental either that Vorbasse became a church-site and later a site of pilgrimage which developed into a local market site. The demise of the parish during the Swedish wars and under the driftsands of the Little Ice Age is also well described (O. Nielsen 1868).

Another example of a main village that can be noted is Tjæreborg in Skast district (Fig. 61). Extensive excavations here around the present village have also been able to reveal the main lines of the settlement history. The Early Iron-age village lay a little further inland and can be traced through the pre-Roman and Early Roman Iron Ages. Comprehensive excavations south of the present village have revealed the location of the village during the Late Iron Age and down to the current settlement. Tjæreborg also became a church-site.

The thorps were formerly regarded as having essentially been a product of population growth and a general expansion in the earlier Middle Ages, which was also linked to the introduction of the mouldboard plough. Excavations in many thorp settlements have subsequently shown that their history can go much further back, although often only in the form of intermittent occupation and periodical settlements which were located on the site for a while. It may be possible to infer that

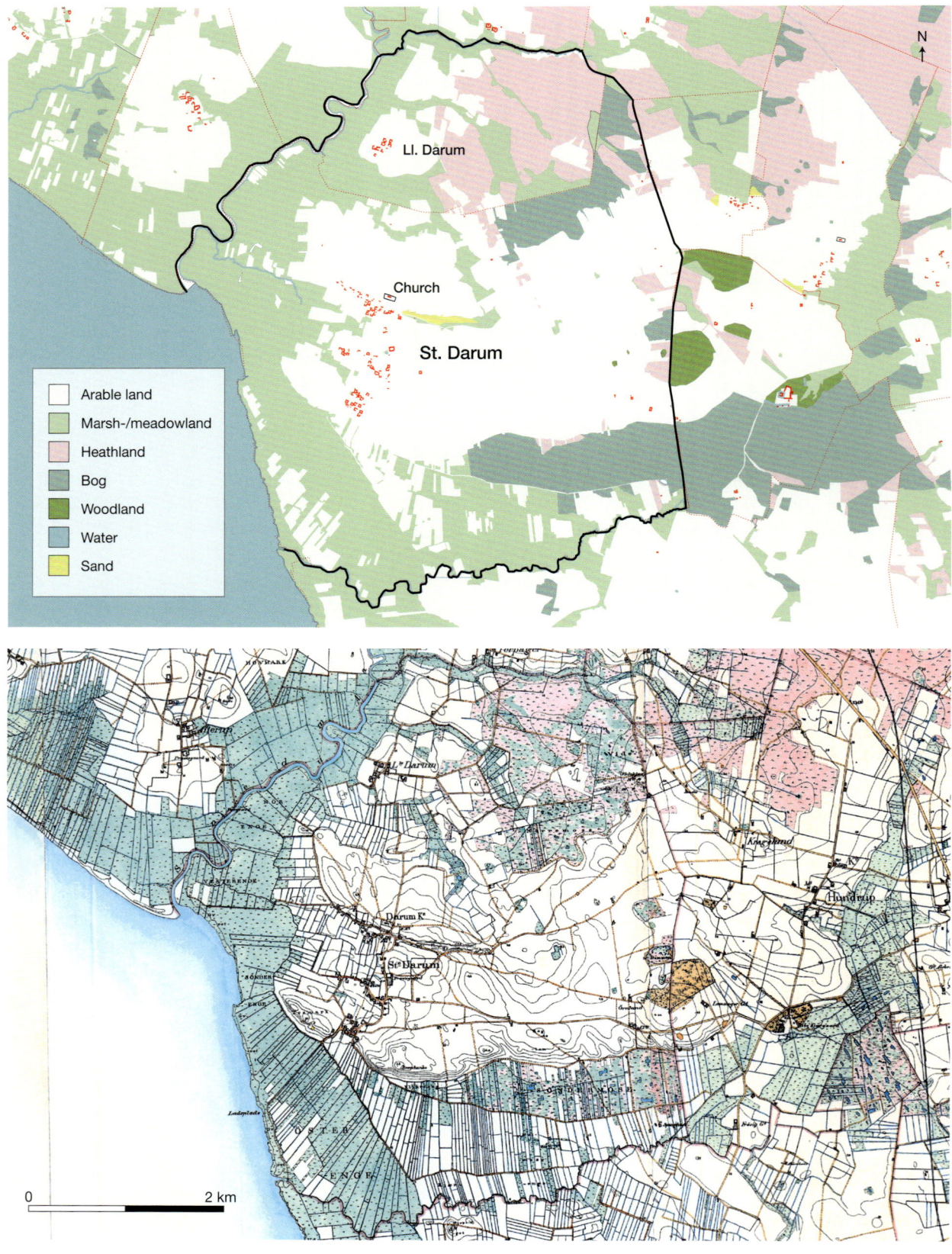

Arable land
Marsh-/meadowland
Heathland
Bog
Woodland
Water
Sand

Ll. Darum

Church

St. Darum

N

0   2 km

Fig. 57. Store Darum parish, as shown on the digitized Original 1 cadastral map from the beginning of the 19th century (above) and on the High Topographical Map sheet of the 1860s (below). In this marsh parish a Saalian moraine hill forms a large, coherent settlement area, the marshy meadowlands of which and extensive cultivated area could support a large number of farms. In the Middle Ages and modern period here there were many farms, and a particularly large number of settlements of the Iron Age is known from a series of minor excavations and aerial observations.

92

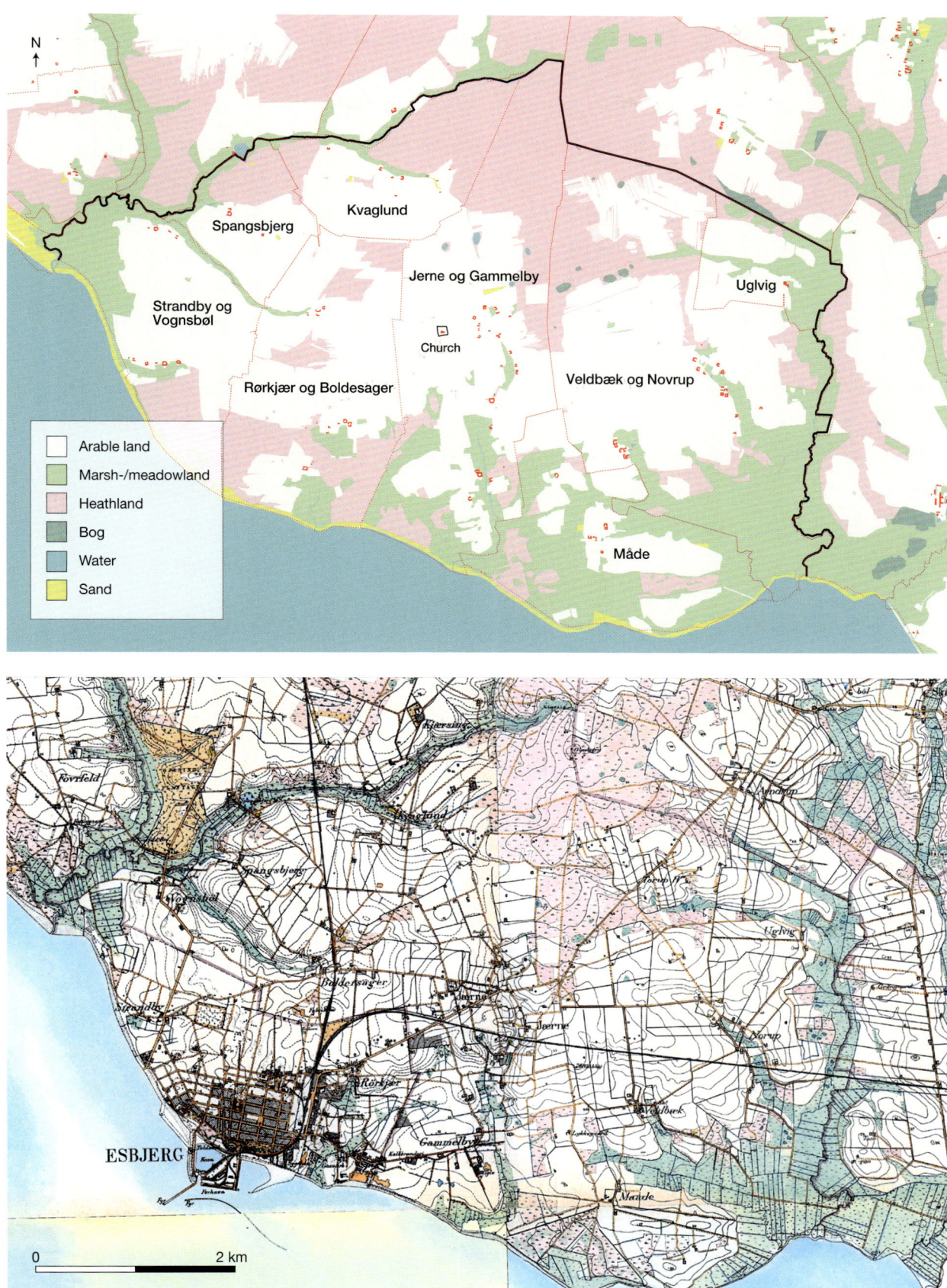

Fig. 58. In Jerne parish the clayey and slightly undulating Saalian moraine hill created many minor settlement areas divided by small watercourses and heathlands. Correspondingly, settlement in the area was divided up into a large number of small village lands (red lines). A series of excavations has shown that this state of affairs goes back to the Iron Age.

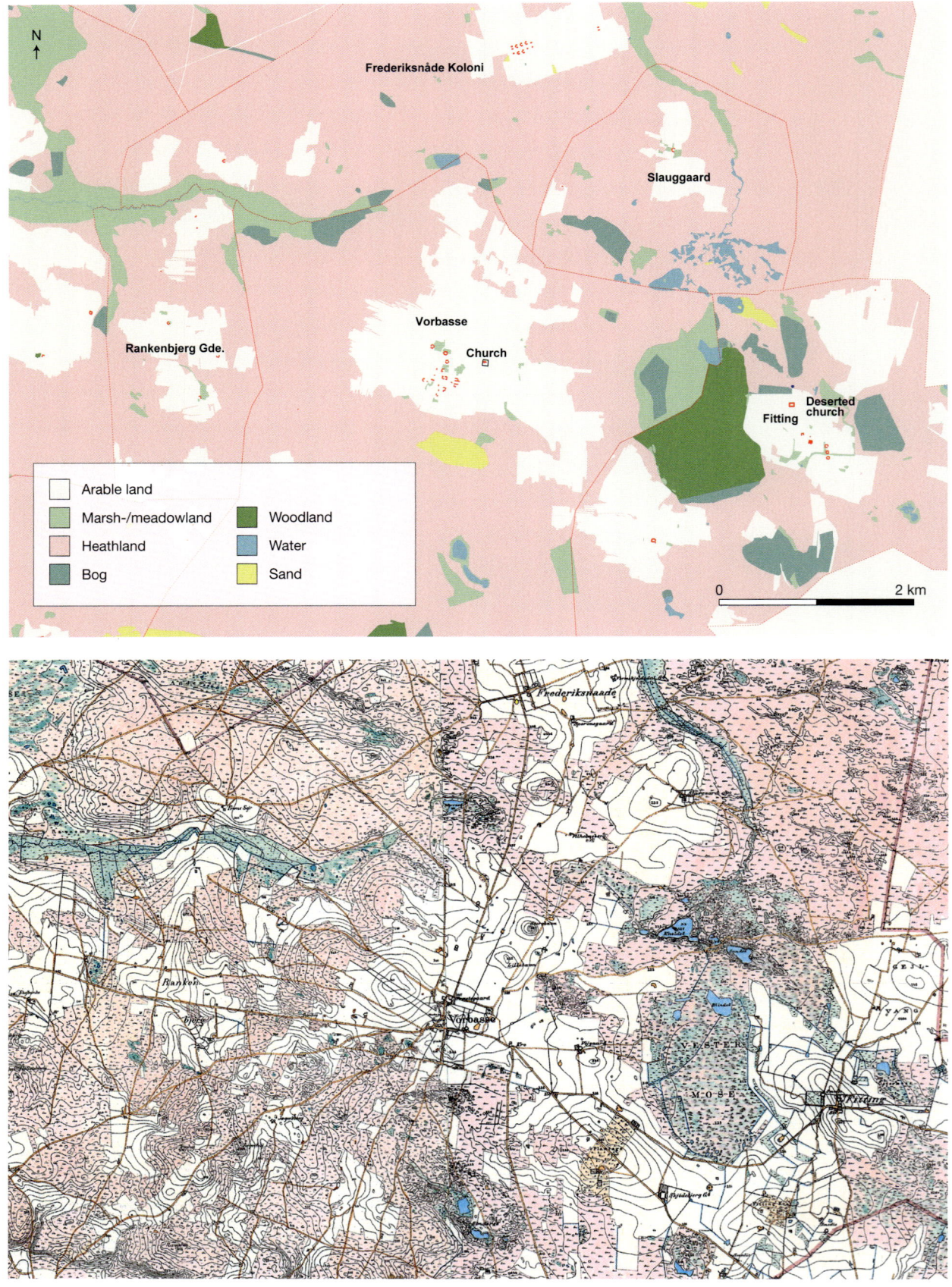

Fig. 59. Vorbasse in Mid-Jutland was formerly a small village, whose fields formed a small island in the wide heath-lands. The excavations at Vorbasse of 1974-87 have shown that this small main village can be traced on the site far back into the Iron Age.

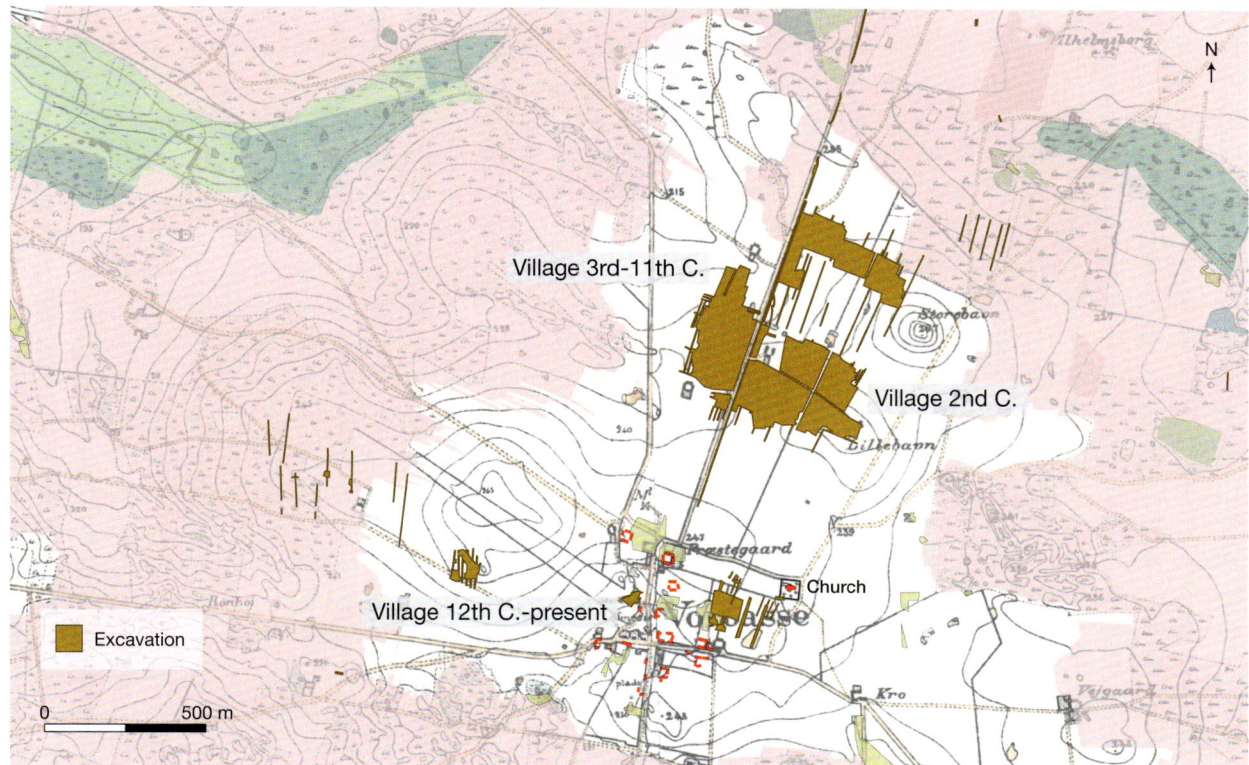

Fig. 60. The main village Vorbasse can be traced through excavations from the Early Iron Age down to the present day. The base map is the High Topographical Map sheet.

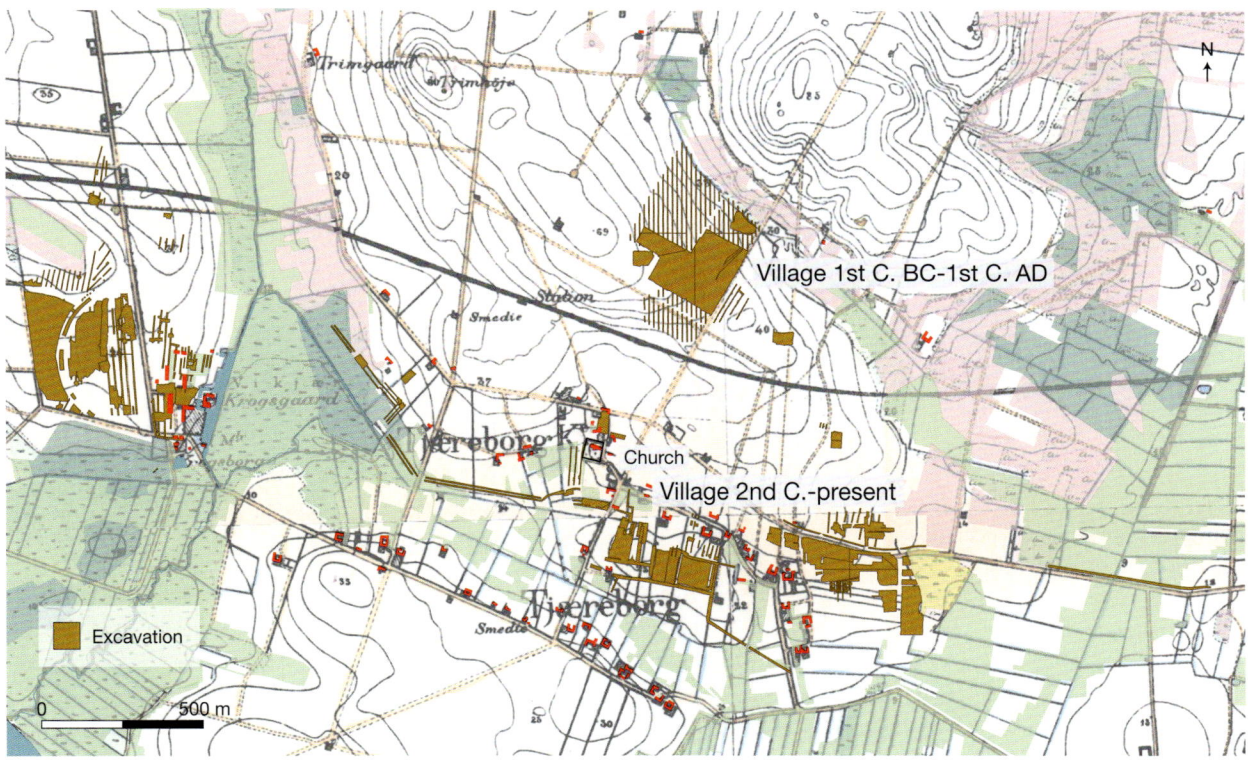

Fig. 61. The main village Tjæreborg close to Esbjerg. Here too, the unbroken existence of the village since the Early Iron Age has been proved by excavation. North of the present church village parts of a larger earlier village of the Early Iron Age have been excavated. The large number of farms of the modern period reflect a correspondingly dense settlement which can be traced back to the emergence of the village in the Early Iron Age. The base map is the High Topographical Map sheet.

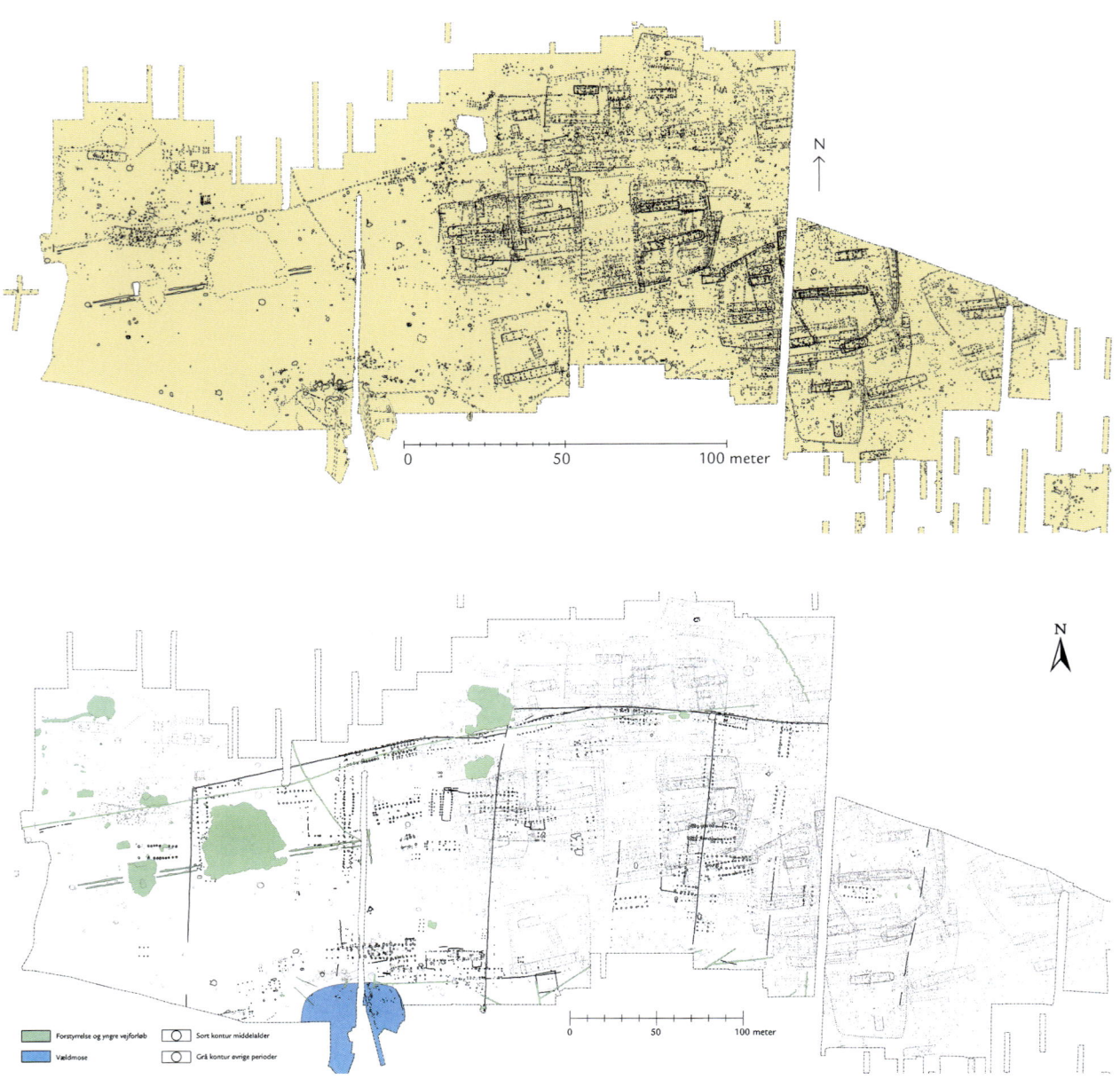

Fig. 62. The thorp settlement of Hyrup, the site known as Østergaard, in Nørre Rangstrup district, has been practically fully excavated. Here discontinuous settlement of the 3rd and 4th centuries AD (upper), of the 8th century, and from around the year 1000 onwards (lower) was found. After Ethelberg 2003 and Sørensen 2011.

those periods will also in many cases mark local population peaks.

Some resource areas may be so small that they could only support one or two farms, a pattern which is particularly in evidence on the poor heathlands and is therefore governed by the natural environment. But there can also be social or religious factors behind the fact that a farm stands quite alone or isolated in relation to settlement otherwise. This state of affairs is seen on a large scale in the central places and was probably the situation for some, although not all, of the farmsteads of the aristocracy: the chieftain's farms.

The farmstead at Dankirke, which will be presented below, conforms to this pattern.

This distinction between main villages and thorps thus appears to be a settlement pattern that can be traced back to the origins of the village as an organizational feature. The distinction is intended primarily to be an analytical term, which will describe the circumstances quite precisely in some territories, while in others – entirely dependent upon the character of the landscape which housed the farms – there will be greater problems in categorizing the individual village lands and their settlements as either main villages or thorps.

4.3.4 The internal organization of the villages, including inheritance practices

When we look at the settlement structure of villages that had not relocated around the year 1800, as it is shown on the Original 1 maps, and compare that with the historical sources that describe the ownership of the farms, their methods of farming and the fire evaluations of that date, a series of points are immediately obvious. The villages themselves had a highly varied overall structure. In some cases the farmsteads were located side by side; in others they were dispersed over large areas. In some cases that was dictated by the face of the landscape or in relation to a road, but in others one cannot instantly point to clear reasons for the great differences in density of settlement. The buildings that made up the farmstead and which collectively made up the village were similarly often highly varied, in terms of lengths, plan and the cumulative number of spaces (Vensild 2004; Porskrog Rasmussen 2013).

Social differences amongst the residents of the village are sometimes clearly expressed: the priests' farmsteads are, for instance, often markedly larger than the others, and smallholders' homes markedly smaller; in other cases, though, farmsteads of around the same economic level may have very different buildings in the toft. A social analysis of a village based upon the architecture of the farmsteads would thus, for example, put a priest's farm and the smallholders' dwelling at the top and bottom of a social hierarchy, while it would be possible to produce many different results for the large group in between which in most cases would be the great majority of the farmsteads.

The weak connexion between architecture and social structure must be based upon the fact that the villages were living organisms with deep roots, in which the farmsteads had continually changed hands, buildings were replaced and added, farmsteads were relocated, some were abandoned and others newly founded, but all in all without the physical outline of the farmsteads having been subject to strict regulation. The structure of the villages around 1800 was, therefore, a complex product of their earlier settlement history and the field-systems around them, and which was forged in the inter-zone between the observance of local traditions, the law, and the wishes and means of the builder (Porskrog Rasmussen 2013).

Similarly complex processes must have shaped the villages of the Iron Age, Viking Period and Middle Ages (Holst 2010). The villages of the Late Roman Iron Age and Early Germanic Iron Age have produced the best data on village structures here, as the fences of the farmsteads are often also preserved. Despite traditionally-dictated similarities in both the structure of the buildings and the fences, an innumerable range of very different sizes of farmstead and farmyard can be seen across Jutland in this period, along with non-stop rebuilding, extension and reduction of both individual buildings and farmyards which must mean that the connexion between architecture, farmyard-size and social structure in this period also has to be seen in broad-brush terms and not interpreted too categorically (Fig. 63). In the same way, the development of farmyard sizes is only a rough rule of thumb, with much local variation (Hvass 1988; Holst 2014).

If, starting from the documented periods of agricultural history in Denmark, typically the period from 1500 onwards, one forms a view of the many local developments, reforms, models of organization and vicissitudes that the region experienced, one has to recognize that there seems to be some link between a weak central authority and a diversity of local developments promoted by a local elite (Porskrog Rasmussen 2013, 529f).

In the Iron Age, Viking Period and Middle Ages, the central power was either weak or non-existent in comparison with later periods, and this can only raise the question of whether there are any good arguments for claiming that the agrarian communities of those periods were not also regulated by a flood of different local laws, rules and traditions rather than one simple and consistent system. Such arguments are few, in my judgement, and the discouraging part-conclusion has to be that the possibility of ever being able to reconstruct rules of entitlement and inheritance in the Iron Age and Viking Period must be limited to utterly general aspects, and that any further level of detail will inevitably be subject to great uncertainty (Wickham 2005, 370; Holst 2010).

4.3.5 Elite farmsteads, aristocrats and central places along the west coast of Jutland

It was the excavations at Helgö in the Mälar region, followed by the excavations at Dankirke of 1965-70, which first unearthed remains of a particular type of farmstead of the Iron Age and Viking Period that has since played an ever more significant role in research in the history and social structure of the Late Iron Age – while further sites and steadily richer finds have been forthcoming too (L. Jørgensen 2014). In the current context, a short resumé of the phenomenon in relation to the area under discussion here will be given.

In the Middle Ages, the nobility came to constitute a well-defined class of society that enjoyed a range of privileges, including exemption from tax, in return for service in war. Behind the overall group-designation stands a group of people of very different social and economic ranks, ranging from exceptionally wealthy,

Fig. 63. Two farm-steads shown at the same scale, both from the Early Germanic Iron Age but of very different sizes. Upper one from Store Darum, ASR 2253, and the lower one from Andrup by Esbjerg, ESM 2676. Both of these villages had farmsteads of equal size and finds including copper-alloy brooches from Store Darum show that the occupants were of a certain social rank. Cases ASR 2253 and ESM 2676.

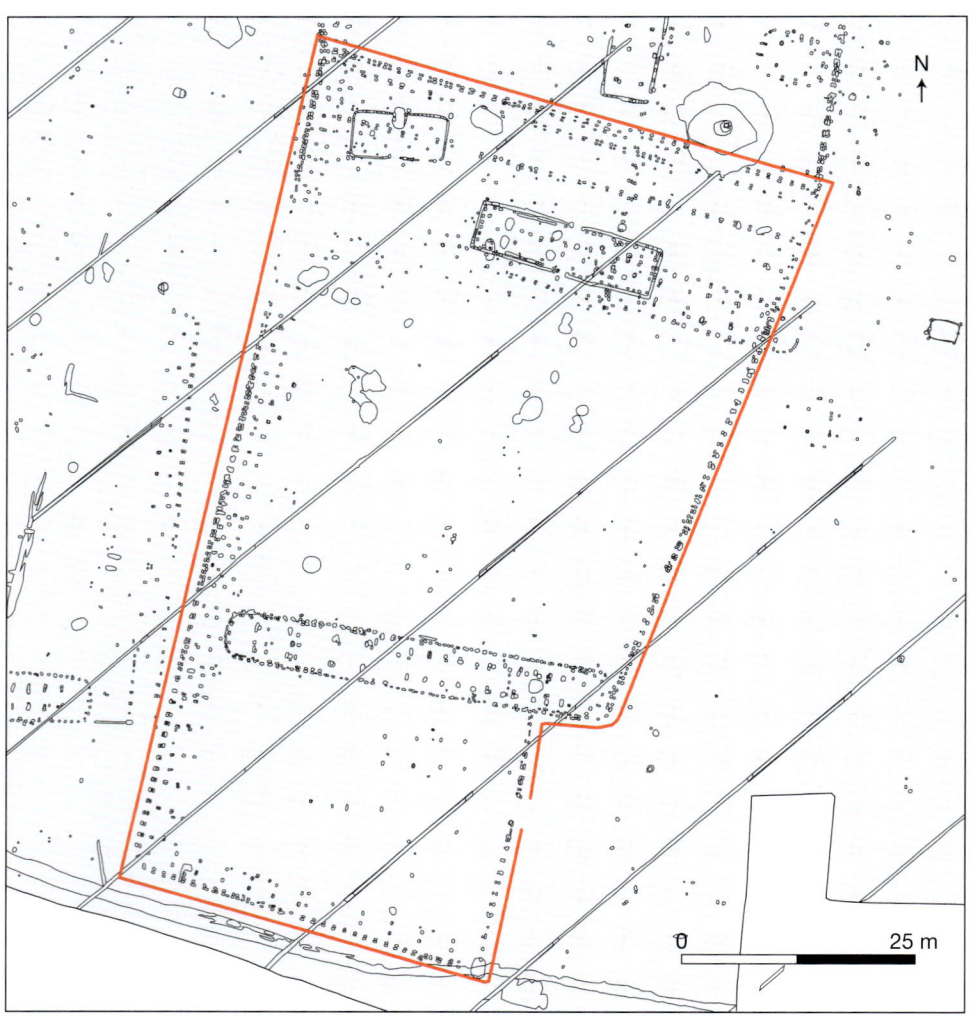

pre-eminent aristocrats to bankrupt soldiers with less in their coffers than many farmers. The group was not static, and history provides many examples of social mobility in the form of individuals or families who won or lost wealth and privileges as a result of their own or others' actions, deliberate or accidental. Other families had the good fortune to hold their position at the summit of society for centuries. The nobility thus is no homogeneous group, but is rather a term which can apply over a social group of highly varied social and economic positions. The power of the aristocracy was also unevenly distributed in medieval Denmark. The eastern part of the kingdom was more marked by the aristocracy, as came to be seen in the phenomenon of the Hvide ('White') dynasty, a large number of Romanesque church towers, excavated elite farmsteads, and more (Søvsø 2011a).

The aristocracy of the Iron Age is often represented through simple models as being hierarchically positioned within a social pyramid based upon grave finds in which the right to wear snake-head rings or access to imported Roman goods are seen as associations with artefacts which define class (Ethelberg 2014). Another approach starts from the votive hoards of military equipment and works through to a system of hierarchically placed officers within a warrior aristocracy (Ethelberg 2003, 272ff). Down to and including the Early Germanic Iron Age we have a large amount of evidence, but after that both grave finds and weapon hoards become few or non-existent in the archaeological material.

There is a discrepancy between most of the simple, stratified models of Iron-age society and the relatively well-described but complicated state of affairs in the Middle Ages. In relation to the steadily growing volume of archaeological evidence from the period in question, I am inclined to believe that there are also steadily better and better reasons to argue that the aristocrats of the Iron Age and the Viking Period also formed a differentiated and composite group, with regional differences too, and that their differences may have been like those of the Middle Ages as described above.

In the agrarian-based medieval society, values were primarily dependent upon income from possession of land, while trade, and to a lesser degree craftwork, were other ways of making a living which, having played a generally subordinate role in the Iron Age and Viking Period, gradually came to be of greater and greater importance. As described above, the landscape is no uniform land-mass but both locally and regionally has varying agricultural potential – which means, in simple terms, that the working of a farm will produce a greater surplus in a favourable location than for a humble bog-trotter. Apart from the agricultural potential the landscape may contain many other phenomena of religious, symbolic, aesthetic and communicative character, which can animate areas or terrain with peculiar value. Control of and rights to these special places, and the charisma they endow those who control them with, must be one of the most important driving forces.

The large number of detector-finds, which are made in West Jutland too, show that there was a very high level of continuity in settlement throughout the 1st millennium AD (Stidsing et al. eds. 2014; Hilberg & Lemm eds. 2018). This continuity is inevitably most strongly reflected in the main villages, which in many cases subsequently became parish centres. Especially in the case of the Late Germanic Iron Age, which is still weakly represented in settlement archaeology, the detector-finds do not of themselves show any detectable radical reduction in the quantity of finds from this period. The detector-finds also appear to show that in all of the villages of West Jutland (and all over Denmark) there were women who wore copper-alloy brooches, often gilded and of high craft quality, as part of their costume. This brooch-wearing class of society, which is also known to varying degrees in the grave finds, must have occupied the large middle range of fairly uniform farmsteads that is known from settlement archaeology (Fig. 64).

Amongst the Iron-age graves in West Jutland there is a small group which stands out very markedly from all the others because of their wealth. In a very few cases these graves can also be associated with excavated settlements, as is the case at Tjørring, north of Herning. An elite farmstead of the Early Iron Age has been excavated here and connected to it has been found, amongst other things, an unparalleled grave containing a gold brooch. Altogether these put the complex in a category on its own for this period (Møller-Jensen 2010).

Looking at the map in the Figure 49 it can be seen that more than a thousand years later the Tjørring area still stood out by being responsible for much higher returns than the places around it. This terrain therefore had some special potential and so provided the foundation for an exceptionally rich and powerful family or families. It is to be stressed once again that this potential cannot be reduced to the matter of land quality alone but was completely inter-woven with phenomenological factors too. What significance did the place in question hold for the prehistoric farmers in both religious and infrastructural terms?

In other cases only isolated components of such elite milieux are known, in the form of either graves, settlements, hoards or detector-finds, as the following tour of the elite locales of the west coast as they appear in the archaeological evidence at present will show, moving from south to north.

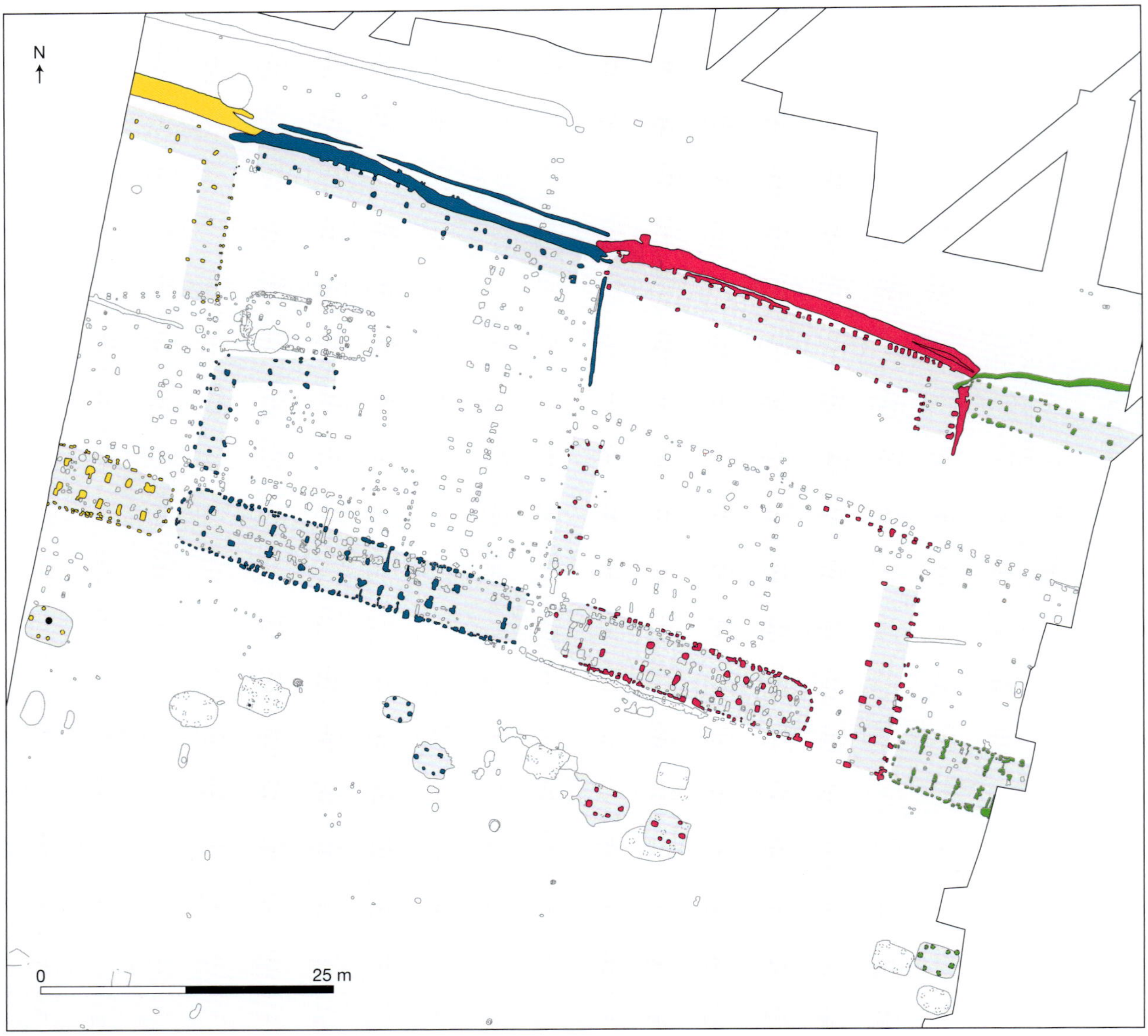

Fig. 64. A row of farmsteads built together from around the year 500 excavated at Store Darum. In the sunken feature building to the left (black dot) two brooches (bottom, 2:1) were found that were probably lost by women who were weaving in the hut. After Søvsø 2010c and S. Jensen 1985.

4.3.5.1 The Tønder Marsh and the Vid River, the islands in the Wadden Sea

The Tønder Marsh around the major watercourse of the Vid River (Vidåen) cuts deep into the land, and once offered extensive pasturelands for the farmers of the marsh. Out towards the coast and in the Wadden Sea around the North Frisian islands of Sylt, Amrum and Föhr, the changes caused by storm floods have fundamentally changed the landscape, and what the situation was in the Late Iron Age is largely uncertain. On the edge of the geest, with a view out over the

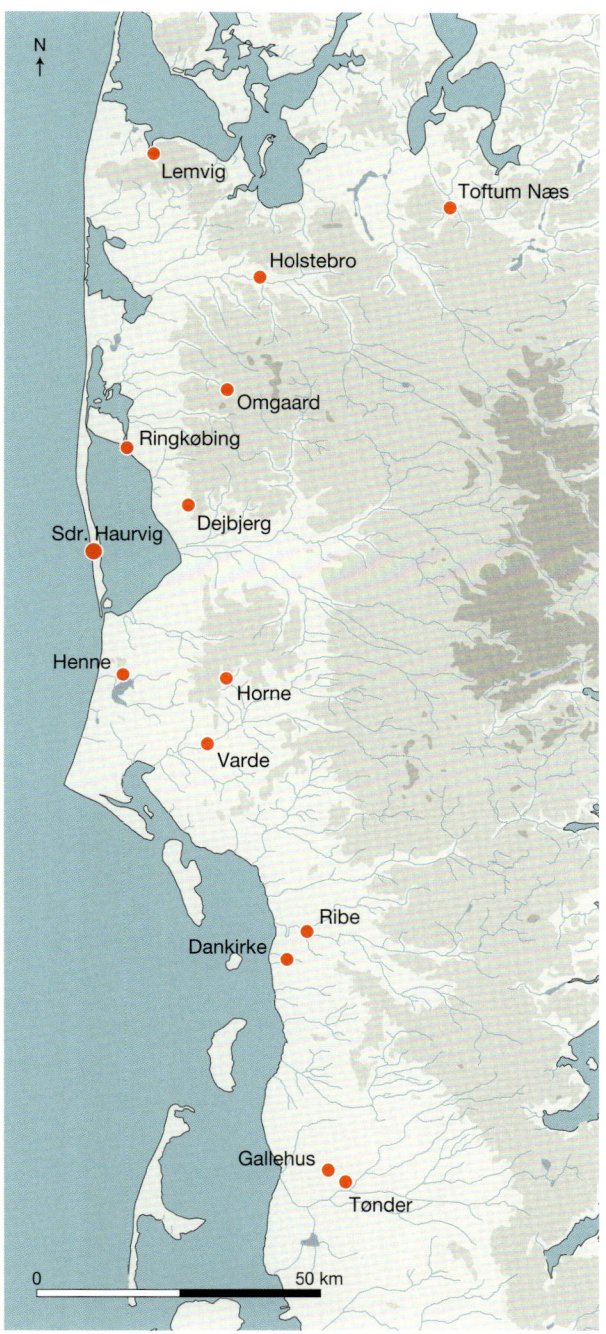

Fig. 65. Map of the sites referred to in the following section.

wide marsh flats and in the immediate vicinity of the Droveway along its course down to the crossing of the Vid River, the Gallehus gold horns were found (barely 2 km from Møgeltønder and Schackenborg) in 1639 and 1734 respectively. These two horns, made in the 5th century, weighed a total of 6.8 kg and constitute the largest gold find from Danish prehistory (Fig. 66). To date it has not been possible to locate traces of the settlement that sacrificed these horns, but there is little doubt that it would belong to the topmost layer of the society.

As early as 1233 the Bishop of Ribe had major holdings around Møgeltønder, the later Schackenborg, and this state of affairs might go back to Bishop Odinkar (†1043) who endowed the see with large areas of land (Gelting 2004, 184). The town of Tønder and the Cistercian monastery in Løgum may both have sprung from this estate complex. This cluster of estates subsequently became part of the so-called Royal Enclave in the Dukedom of Schleswig, securing a long historical later life for it. That the historical roots may also be deep is suggested by the gold horns, but unfortunately both the number of archaeological projects and the use of the metal-detector in this area have been very limited. It is considered probable, notwithstanding, that there is a connexion between the gold horns and the concentration of leading aristocratic estates in the area from the late Viking Period onwards, which evolved into a town in the Middle Ages. Structurally, this is parallel to the Dankirke-Ribe relationship. Storm floods have subsequently changed the situation in the Wadden Sea and on the North Frisian islands irreversibly, but it is suggested that the settlement which sacrificed the gold horns could have functioned in the Germanic Iron age as a central place serving also the North Frisian islands in a regional system (Segschneider 2014). Further up the coast, the hill-island of Toftlund stretches right out to the Wadden Sea and the marshlands are small. This could be why no sites of aristocratic character are known in this area.

4.3.5.2 Dankirke, Hviding, Vester Vedsted, Okholm, Ribe and the Ribe River

South of Ribe lie the parishes of Vester Vedsted and Hviding, the marsh flats of which spread out towards the navigable mouth of the Ribe River (Fig. 67). These two parishes contain a large number of archaeological sites and since the 1960s have been studied intensively by Den antikvariske Samling in Ribe and the National Museum. From 1963-9 Mogens Bencard, together with Hans Jørgen Madsen of Moesgaard Museum, led excavations at Okholm. The museum's interest in the area led to a school class, on the initiative of its teacher, excavating in

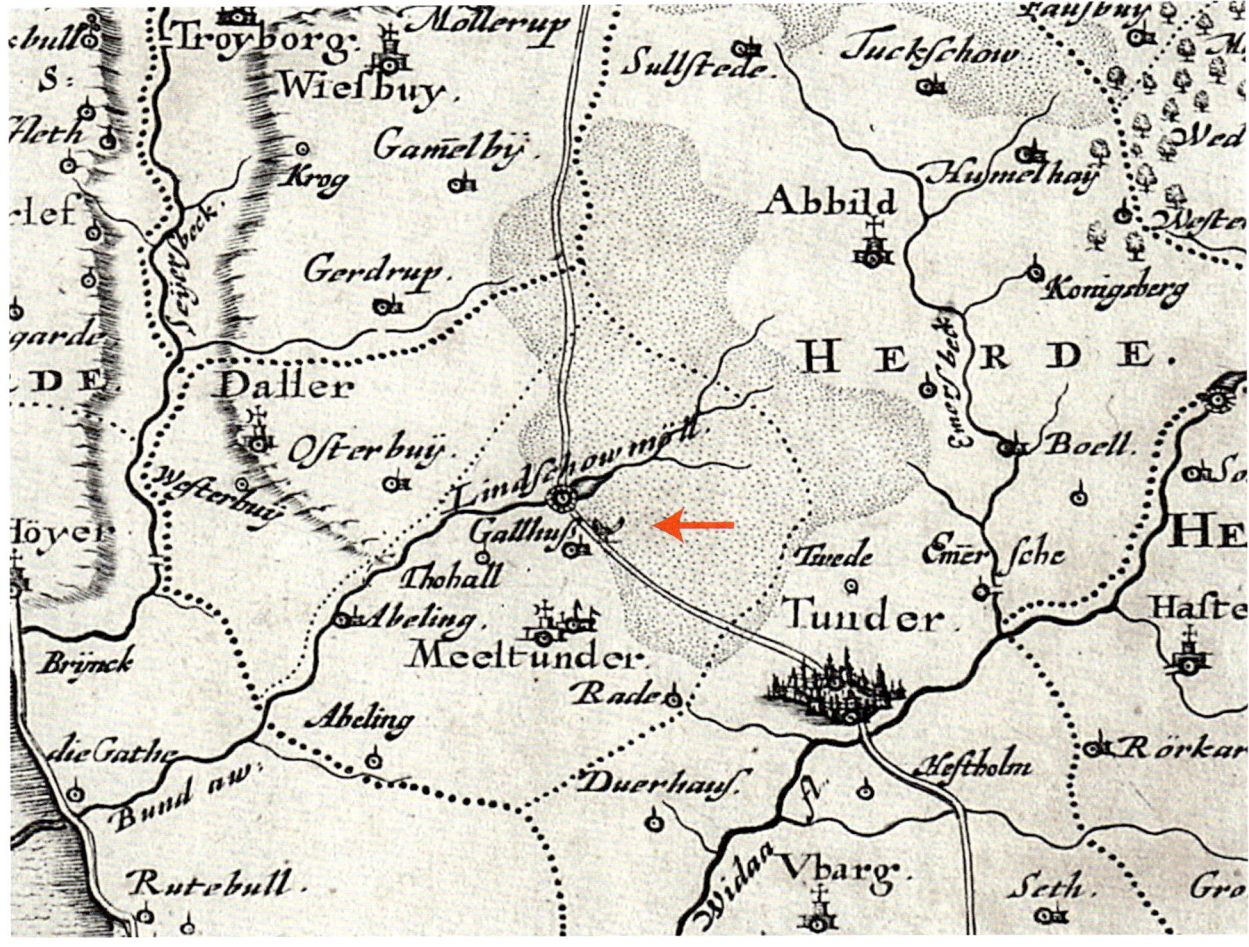

Fig. 66. The find-spot of the large gold horn was marked with a horn (alongside the red arrow) on Johannes Mejer's map of 1649. The caption of the map reads 'Place where the golden horn found'. The spot lies out alongside the line of the Droveway, and future investigations must determine whether the connexion between the richest votive deposit of the 5th-6th centuries and the concentration of estates and urbanization of the earlier Middle Ages is simply coincidental. From the original in the Royal Library.

the field of Dankirke, a site in Vester Vedsted parish that was already known, and immediately striking a roof-bearing post-hole from one of the halls of the site, with many finds to follow (see below).

The discoveries of the earliest Ribe inside the town itself in 1972 brought the excavations at Vester Vedsted to an end, and the research only began again when Stig Jensen flew over the area and undertook hedgerow surveys in the 1980s, followed by excavations in Gammel Hviding from 1986-94 and metal-detecting. Contrary to the situation in many other places, the Museum Act of 2001 onwards has not led to many new excavations in the area, as on the whole it sees little building activity. One may say of the archaeology of the parish in general that the extent of excavation has been very limited, but from aerial surveys, hedgerow studies and metal-detecting we know of very extensive settlements of the Iron Age, the Viking Period and the Middle Ages.

The spectacular results from the excavations at Dankirke remained on their own for some time, and occasioned lively discussion. This really took off when the Gudme investigations revealed much larger halls contemporary with the later phases of Dankirke. Together with the rich cemeteries and hoards from the Gudme area it became possible to draw a much fuller picture of an even wealthier elite milieu of the Late Roman and Germanic Iron Age (Østergaard Sørensen 2010). The evidence from Dankirke is as yet only published in summary articles (Thorvildsen 1972; Jarl Hansen 1990). The building remains found are accessible, but regrettably that is not the case with the massive finds assemblage, only small parts of which have been made available.

Subsequently, however, a number of minor excavations have been undertaken around Dankirke, in connexion with afforestation projects, and these have produced a range of important information

Fig. 67. Map of settlement and landscape use in the area south of Ribe around 1800, produced from the Original 1 cadastral maps and Prussian maps. The settlements and their names are also shown. The Droveway is in grey. On the map is also shown the location of the place-names Gammel Ribe (Rief) and Dankirke.

helping in the understanding of the area excavated. The large quantity of finds, which are registered in the National Museum's database GenReg, have been downloaded as part of the current project and converted to Museum of Southwest Jutland's find database SJM SYS. This has made it possible to quantify a range of categories of finds. This research produces the interpretation of Dankirke that follows.

4.3.5.2.1 Dankirke

The first investigations in the field of Dankirke took place as early as 1882, when the site was a ploughed field and stood out as a slight, elongated rise, the soil of which stood out clearly from that around it because of its conspicuous contents of charcoal, burnt clay and pottery (Fig. 69). Similar circumstances must have produced the name of the site of Sorte Muld

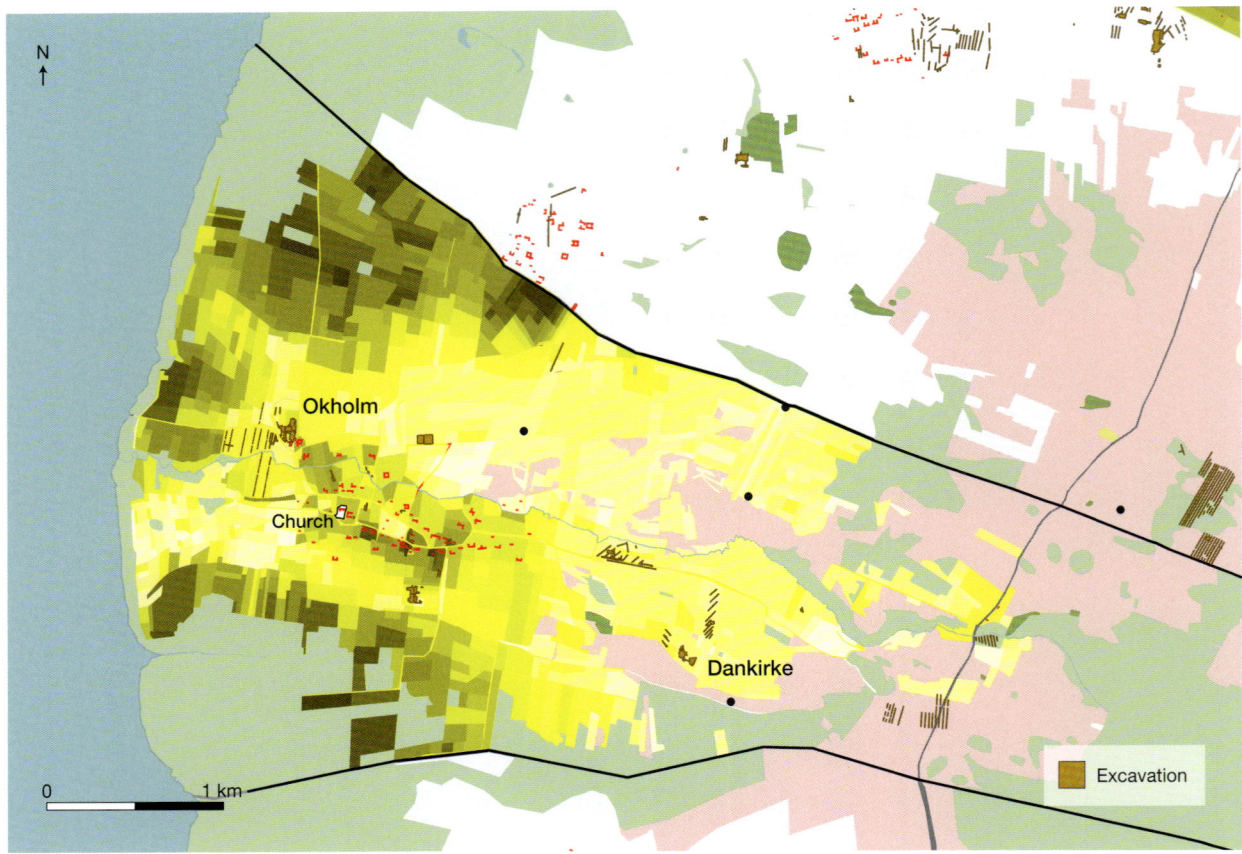

Fig. 68. Diagrammatic map of the assessment of quality of agricultural land in the village lands of Vester Vedsted based on the older cadastral maps. Darker colours represent higher assessment. Unlike the situation on clayland, the quality of the soil does not serve as a strong indicator of earlier settlements. Neither Dankirke nor a series of other known sites have left any footprint in the form of soil quality. What is seen instead is that the highest valued land is that very closely adjacent to the village and the cultivated saltmarshes.

(Black Earth) on Bornholm. Excavation at Dankirke in 1882 were able to show that there was a layer of earth here up to 3 feet (c. 1 m) thick, which was also very different from the soil-layer of just 6-8 inches (15-20 cm) in the fields around it. The area of the site was determined as 3 *tønder* or c. 1.65 hectares (ha).

The excavations of 1965-70 showed that the thick layer of earth is a culture layer formed during the Early Roman Iron Age and on into the Early Germanic Iron Age. 0.3 ha, corresponding to 18% of the area, has been excavated (Fig. 70). The very thorough method of excavation, with extensive sieving of the soil, secured a large collection of finds, some of them from more recent periods in the form of clay pipes, post-medieval pottery, window glass and more, and it is clear that the finds do not show any trace of settlement later than the Early Germanic Iron Age which thus marks the end-point of the site in terms of settlement (Feveile 2006k). The abandonment of the site has been debated, principally because of the interesting coin finds from the 7th and 8th centuries that are discussed below, but neither the pottery nor the many

brooches give the slightest indication of activity after the Early Germanic Iron Age. The building foundations excavated and their dating, plus the boundaries of the culture layer, show beyond any real doubt that the buildings are from a single farmstead which had stood here from, at the latest, the Early Roman Iron Age down to the end of the Early Germanic Iron Age: a period of around 500 years.

To the south, the area has a natural boundary in the form of an area of wetland, and to the east and north subsequent trial excavations have shown that there are no signs of settlement present (Fig. 69). To the north-west the situation is different, as here a settlement of the Early Germanic Iron Age has been found, called Dankirke North, known from aerial photographs and a couple of minor excavations. There appears to be an unoccupied area of at least 200 m between these two sites, which cannot have been conjoined. Detector surveys and excavations do not suggest that Dankirke North differs from a typical village of the period (S. Jensen 1991a). A well from Dankirke North has been dendro-dated to

Fig. 69. Shown on this map are the fields as they appeared on the earliest cadastral map, the five-foot contour lines from the High Topographical Map sheet, and the excavations carried out to date. It can be seen that the direction of ploughing in more modern times has been N.-S. and that in the 1800s the actual site of Dankirke stood out as a well-defined prominence formed of culture layers which has since been largely ploughed down. Neither preliminary excavations ASR 1753 or ASR 1830 contained features from the functional period of Dankirke, showing that the elite farmstead apparently stood alone.

the 5th century and thus shows that in the immediate vicinity of the Dankirke farm there was an Early Germanic Iron-age village. As the area has been flown over frequently, one can suppose that the usually clear roof-bearing post-holes of Early Roman Iron-age farmhouses would have been seen if they were there. On the basis of current knowledge we have to conclude, then, that the Dankirke farmstead stood on its own, and that the activities at the site produced a stratified accumulation of culture layers with a very rich finds assemblage.

The excavations of 1965-70 also provided detailed information on the local topography. The basis of the settlement was slightly undulating terrain, where the earliest buildings were raised on natural rises separated by dips up to a metre deep. The accumulation of culture layers, however, must very soon have evened these variations out, and after the abandonment of the settlement the decomposition of organic material and its ploughing up have gradually modified the conditions so that the sequence of layers found in the excavations of 1965-70 was primarily preserved in the hollows. Enormous quantities of finds from the ploughsoil around the higher building foundations and the distribution of finds in the plough layer

show, meanwhile, that building foundations were also sealed within a sequence of culture layers that has subsequently eroded and been ploughed out. The coin finds show that there was a clear scattering of objects in the plough layer before the excavation (Feveile 2006k; Bjerg 2007). The oldest traces of settlement on the site are from the pre-Roman Iron Age, but not enough has been uncovered to assess the architecture of those building foundations or the character of the settlement in any way. The four supposed wells of that period, which were found in the southern end of the western trench, nevertheless constitute an unusual feature in comparison with other excavated settlements and so might conceivably be remains of votive activities.

The most complete farm buildings excavated were buildings VII and III, of the Early Roman Iron Age: the 1st century AD to judge by the finds (Fig. 71, left). Both buildings have many phases and must have replaced on the same spot several times. Their functioning period must have been considerable – perhaps a century?

From many structural similarities between these two buildings and their structural similarity with other farmsteads of the period which consist of one main

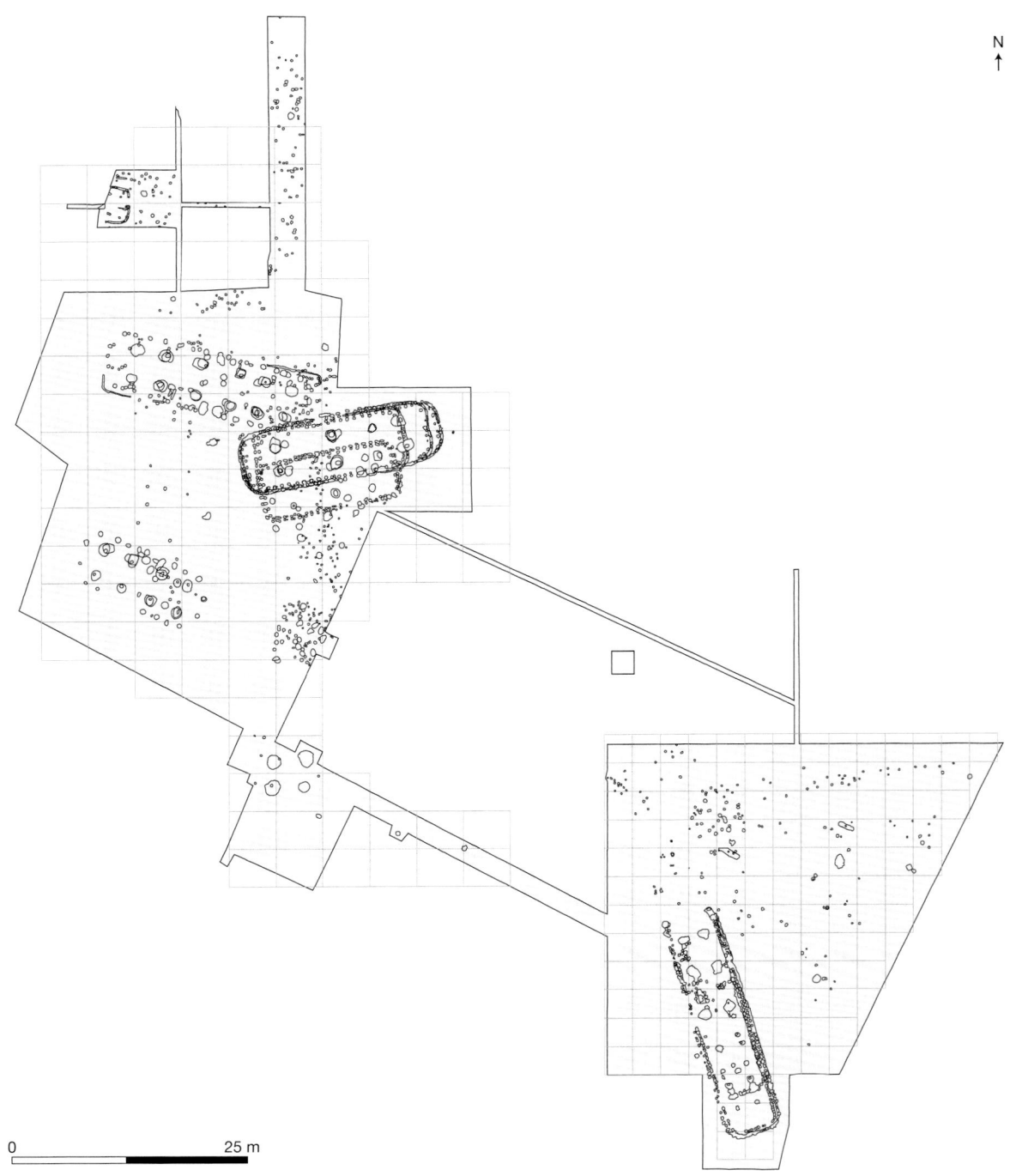

N
↑

0   25 m

Fig. 70. General plan of the excavation trenches of 1965-70. The eastern area was excavated over three seasons from 1965-7 in a grid of 3 x 3 m squares and the western area was excavated from 1968-70 in a grid of 5 x 4 m rectangles.

building and one or more outhouses, buildings VII and III are regarded as a contemporary unit. This is supported or confirmed by the eight radiocarbon dates, four from each building, which assign both to an extended functioning period throughout the 1st century (Jarl Hansen 1985). If we compare this farmstead with other excavated examples it is clear, however, that both the size of the buildings – particu-larly their width – and the distance between them puts them in a category on their own in relation to contemporary building, which is otherwise very uniform (Ethelberg 2003, 196ff). It is noted to begin with that the farmstead was apparently not enclosed with a fence, contrary to the norms of the time, and perhaps a marker of the fact that this was an isolated farmstead (Søvsø 2013).

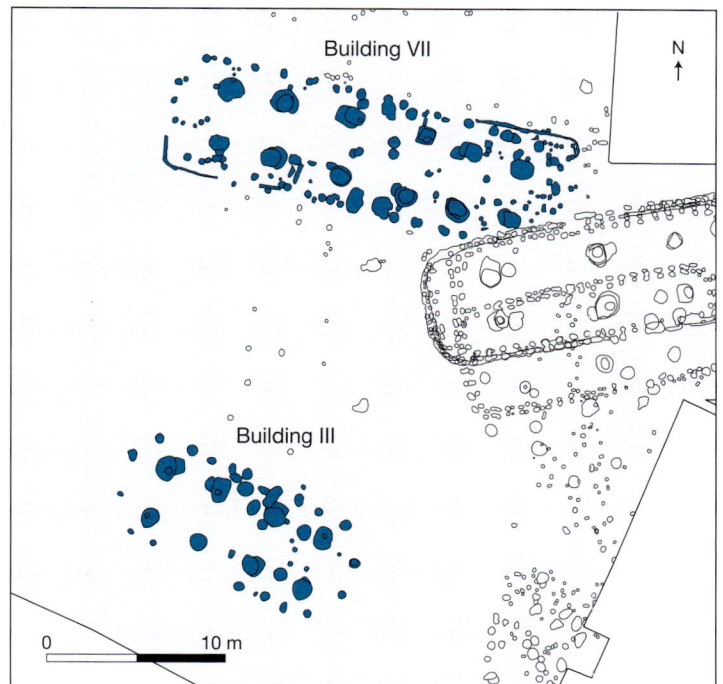
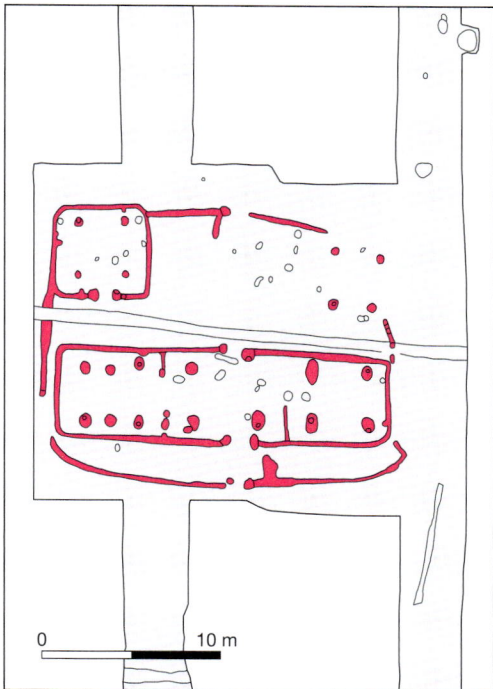

Fig. 71. The Dankirke buildings from the Early Roman Iron Age, building VII above and building III below, compared with a typical farmstead in South-West Jutland excavated near Esbjerg (ESM 1903 Vestergård). Shown at a common scale.

Especially in building VII, and to a lesser degree in building III, burnt remains of a wagon of the Dejbjerg type were found. It is difficult to explain these in any other way than that this wagon must have been standing in one of the buildings, which was destroyed by fire, which could have been what killed off this farmstead (Jarl Hansen 1985). The finding of the wagon must also mean that one of the buildings had at least one wide door opening, as apparently might have been the case at both gable ends of building III.

What can be regarded as probably the successor to the unit comprising buildings VII and III is the NNW.-SSE.-aligned building I, which was excavated in the eastern trench (Fig. 72). This too was an unusual building, both in respect of its width, at 6.5 m, and its alignment, neither of which has any clear parallels in the large amount of comparable evidence from excavations in West Jutland. It was a multi-phase building, and the artefactual finds from it allow us to assign it to an extended functioning period in the Late Roman Iron Age. Its northern gable end was open, and it is noted that this unusual feature was preserved throughout its long life. One explanation could be that there was also a cultic vehicle in this building too. It is to be assumed, too, that other buildings were associated with this farmstead but stood outside the area excavated.

The final building sequence at Dankirke comprised successive and partially overlapping buildings, build-ings Va and Vb, the former of which appears to have had just one phase while its successor was rebuilt and extended on the same spot twice, before the fire which destroyed the building and its rich finds assemblage around the year 500: an assemblage to which much of the fame of the site is due (Fig. 73). This sequence appears, then, to involve four full building phases, and a functional period of over a century does not seem unrealistic. In width, these buildings too stand clearly apart from many other buildings of the same type that are found on contemporary farmsteads. The large and deep post-holes could indicate that this building also stood significantly higher than its ordinary counterparts.

From the ploughsoil above the halls and in the features below it, amongst many other things over a thousand beads were recovered and more than 1,200 sherds of imported blown glass (Fig. 74); some scholars have seen this as a warehouse and thus evidence of trade (Jensen 1991a). Others view the inventory of artefacts as a reflection of the building being a typical hall furnished for hospitality and *conspicuous consumption* (Herschend 1995). Excavations of halls in more recent years decisively favour the latter interpretation (L. Jørgensen 2014, with refs.). There must have been other buildings associated with this sequence of halls too, which also lie outside the area of excavation.

In addition to the excavated and identified build-ing foundations, several rows of post-holes and other

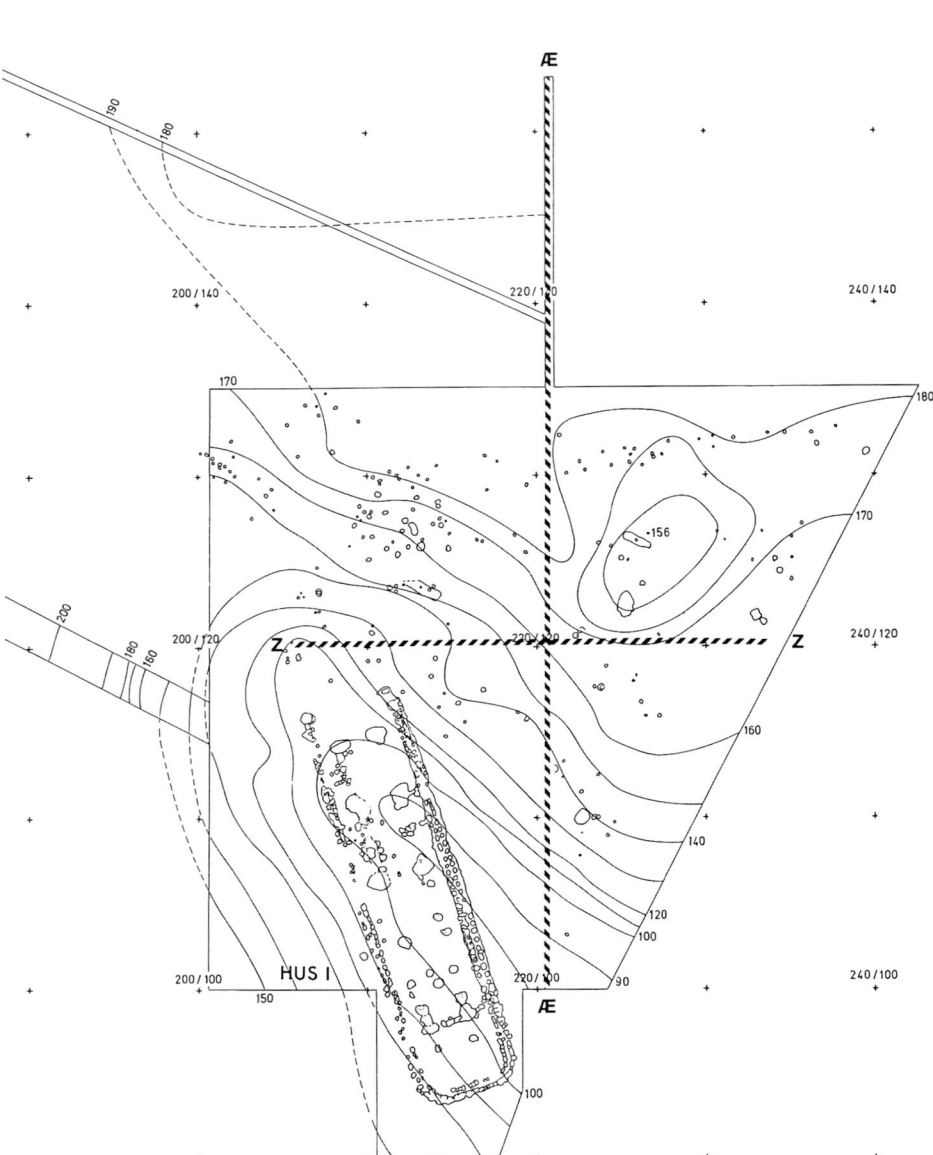

features were found which presumably formed fences or the like, but the accumulation of the culture layer could mean that many structures have left no trace in the natural subsoil and were unrecorded as a result. In comparison with other elite farmsteads the absence of fences and other evidence of an overall pattern of enclosure of individual farmsteads together with further sub-divisions of the area is striking. It is most unlikely that this is due in some way to the methods of excavation, but not impossible. It may also be due to the fact that the small excavation trenches were all located within the as yet undiscovered farmyard boundaries. The aristocratic farmstead at Tjørring had an enclosed area of around 5,000 sq m which might not have been discovered if only 3,000 sq m were opened up, as is the case at Dankirke (Møller-Jensen 2010).

In addition to the exceptional sequence of buildings there is a colossal assemblage of finds from the excavations which both qualitatively and quantitatively is in a class of its own, especially when one remembers that there was only one farmstead at this site (Tab. 5). The finds, their distribution and implications in connexion with the buildings excavated, have only been made use of to a very limited degree (Feveile 2006k; Bjerg 2007). The majority of the finds were planned in against the overall grid system that was used for the excavations, which thus allows slightly coarse but probably very practical distributional analyses of the many categories of find. That task, however, is considered to fall outside the limits of the present study.

All of these many finds of complete objects, which were made not only in the building remains but also

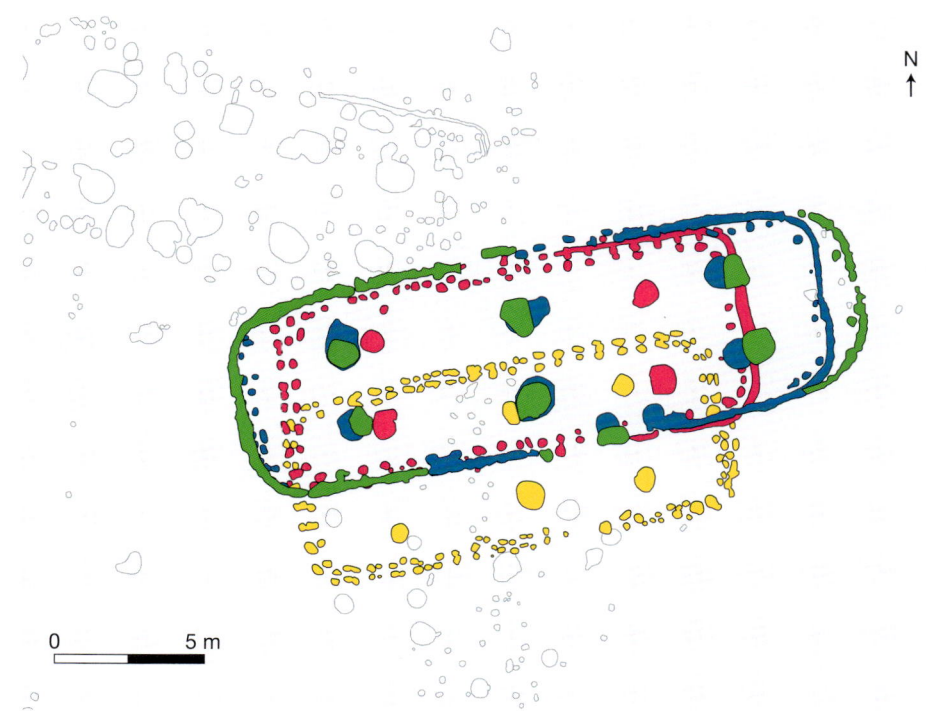

Fig. 73. The sequence of halls from the Late Roman and Early Germanic Iron Ages, building V, had four phases, each of which also involved the replacement of the roof-bearing posts. The majority of the rich finds that make Dankirke so famous come from the overlying plough layer and the buildings' post-holes. All of these building phases appear to have had a single entrance-way from the south in the eastern segment. The smallest and earliest hall (yellow) measured 6.5 x 15.0 m while the latest and largest (green) measured 7.2 x 22.0 m. Interpreted by the author.

0   5 m

in the ploughsoil and enclosed within the culture layers, were unquestionably not day-to-day features at the many other excavated sites in West Jutland, and they cannot merely represent haphazard loss or be the result of disastrous fires: they must be regarded as for the most part votive offerings, in keeping with a pattern that is known from other, mostly slightly later cult sites: Gudme, Sorte Muld, Helgö, Lunda, Tissø, Uppåkra, and more (L. Jørgensen 2014).

In addition to the rich finds from the Roman and Early Germanic Iron Ages, the Dankirke excavations are also well known for the finding of 13 coins of the 7th and 8th centuries. These too caused a sensation when found, as hitherto only four coins of this period were known from the entire historic area of Denmark (Bendixen 1972; 1985). From an analysis of the find spots that draws on experience from other ploughed-out hoards, it has most recently been proposed that these represent two separate hoards: one deposited to the east from the period AD 650-720 and one to the west from AD 720-750 (Feveile 2006k). Two Madelinus *tremisses* from Dorestad to the east are die-identical,

Fig. 74. From the more than 1,300 blown glass fragments in the halls one vessel could be reconstructed, the blue coloration of which stood clearly out. Other sherds of blue glass have also been found, however, which are not from this beaker. By far the majority of the blown glass fragments are of a light yellow-green glass of various forms. In the National Museum.

Selected groups of finds from Dankirke	
Brooches	52
Denarii	37
Glass beads	1032
Blown glass sherds	1257
Arrowheads	9
Spearheads	10
Knives	47

Table 5. Selected groups of finds from Dankirke. The assemblage differs sharply from other sites. The counts are based on the records of the National Museum, including record photographs, and not on a review of the material itself.

which suggests that they were deposited together, while five Wodan/monster sceattas to the west all have the same test mark from a knife – otherwise an unusual way of treating coins at that date – and these five coins must also have been deposited together. On at least two occasions in the period 650-750 then, long after the abandonment of the settlement, coins were deposited at the site. The features which characterize Dankirke are thus the following:

- Site continuity

- Monumental building

- Burnt halls

- Cult vehicles of the Early and Late Roman Iron Ages

- The accumulation of the culture layer

- Votive offerings

  - Weaponry

  - Copper-alloy jewellery

  - Glass beads

  - Precious metals in the form of gold and silver, and Roman denarii

  - Drinking horns (rim-mounts)

  - Pottery

  - Foodstuffs

  - A ritual afterlife in the form of later coin deposits

From this interpretation, the farm at Dankirke can be viewed as an elite farmstead which stood on its own, the function of which was predominantly religious: to provide a setting for religious ceremonies which must have involved cult vehicles and very probably ostentatious votive or sacrificial feasts that may have been the context of the accumulation of the find-rich culture layers. Similar features are characteristic of a series of other religious centres in southern Scandinavia, and Dankirke must be assigned to that group. Even though Gudme, Tissø, Lejre, Uppåkra and Lunda are all, in particular, much larger sites, the structural features are identical to an extent that must reflect an essentially uniform religious cult and how it developed over time from the Early Roman Iron Age through to the Conversion to Christianity (L. Jørgensen 2014).

The first element of the place-name *Dankirke*, the earliest known form of which is *Dankierk* in the 1683 fieldbook, is thought to mean 'low-lying meadowland'. Depending upon the pronunciation, though, which is not recorded, it could in fact derive from the same word as the first element of *Dejbjerg* with the sense of 'those who are killed'.[12] There is, meanwhile, no doubt that the second element is the word for 'church' in the familiar sense of that word. That most certainly cannot have been the name of the site in the Iron Age, although the hoards from the 7th and 8th centuries could indicate that the memory of the site and of its former role remained alive for some time, and the suffix -*kirke* could then refer to the originally religious character of the site. A series of other cult sites also have specifically religious names: Helgö, Lunda, Gudme and Lund/Uppåkra.

From this viewpoint, Dankirke must have been a religious centre for a major area and to have been occupied by a chieftain and cult leader. What relationship he may have had to the chieftains and elite womenfolk who were buried at Brokær, Sneum, Veldbæk and Billum during the functioning life of the Dankirke farmstead (see below) is beyond the scope of this work, and must remain an unanswered question for now.

From the emphasis on continuity in historical development which is at the heart of the present study, one should be able to find a centre of a similar level in the Tønder Marsh, very likely around Gallehus/Møgeltønder, while from present knowledge we have to go all the way to Dejbjerg to find any comparable structure further up the west coast.

The recently discovered complex in Harreby, Sdr. Hygum parish, just over 10 km east of Ribe also seems to belong to this group of aristocratic sites with a continuity spanning most of the first millenium AD.

4.3.5.2.2 Other sites in Vester Vedsted and Hviding parishes

Besides Dankirke, several other aristocratically toned sites are known from these two parishes (Fig. 67) (Feveile 2014). They are known principally from hoards or detector-finds, in some cases backed up with observations from the air and only to a small extent by actual excavation.

Fig. 75. The Høgsbrogaard hoard is composed principally of Late-Roman hacksilver, dress-accessories, a number of siliqua *coins (upper left), and a small amount of gold. The hoard was deposited in the 5th century and was found by metal-detecting a small distance to the north of Høgsbrogaard in 2009. Photograph: John Lee, NM.*

North-west of Høgsbrogaard in 2009 one of the rare hacksilver hoards of the Early Germanic Iron Age was found, the Høgsbrogaard hoard, consisting of 493 g of silver and 42 g of gold, apparently buried in the 5th century (Fig. 75) (Feveile 2014). A small excavation immediately around the find-spot revealed that it had been buried in a small hollow just north of a poorly preserved, 32 m-long building in which the owner of the hoard may have lived, with a stall at the eastern end; it is also possible, however, that wider excavations around the find-spot would produce a different result.

West of Gammel Hviding church a large farmstead with its roots in the 9th century and which can be traced through to around the year 1200 has been excavated (Fig. 76) (Søvsø 2011a; 2018a). This farmstead is one of the largest to have been excavated in Denmark, and a large quantity of detector-finds from the fields around it show that the settlement also spread out over that area. In an area of around 75 ha west of the church, at a conservative estimate around 1,500 to 2,000 hours of detecting have been carried out, and that has inevitably led to many superb finds (Feveile 2014). Amongst the detector-finds from Gammel Hviding up to now 165 more or less fragmentary brooches or pendants of copper alloy from the Iron Age and Medieval Periods have been recorded.

For comparison with Dankirke, above, these come from an area that is 250 times greater and covers more than twice the length of time. Pushing the figures to an extreme, one should therefore expect around 500 times more brooches from Gammel Hviding than from Dankirke and not just the multiplier of 3 which is what we have. This strikingly emphasizes the exceptional character of Dankirke. Amongst the 165 brooches from Gammel Hviding there are 154 which from form and type can be dated more precisely within the whole period of use, and distributed by phase the evidence appears as shown in Figure 77.

On one of the brooches from the Early Roman Iron Age, signs of melting show that it has come from a cremation grave. In the case of the remainder of the material it is not possible to determine for certain whether the dress-accessories ended up in the ground as a result of casual loss, deliberate placement, or in graves. It must, however, be most likely that the majority of the material from this area represents casual losses.

The brooches of the Iron Age show that the area was occupied throughout that period, and yet neither in quality nor in quantity do these finds seem to stand out from what one could find at many other main villages of this date in south-western Jutland. That changes,

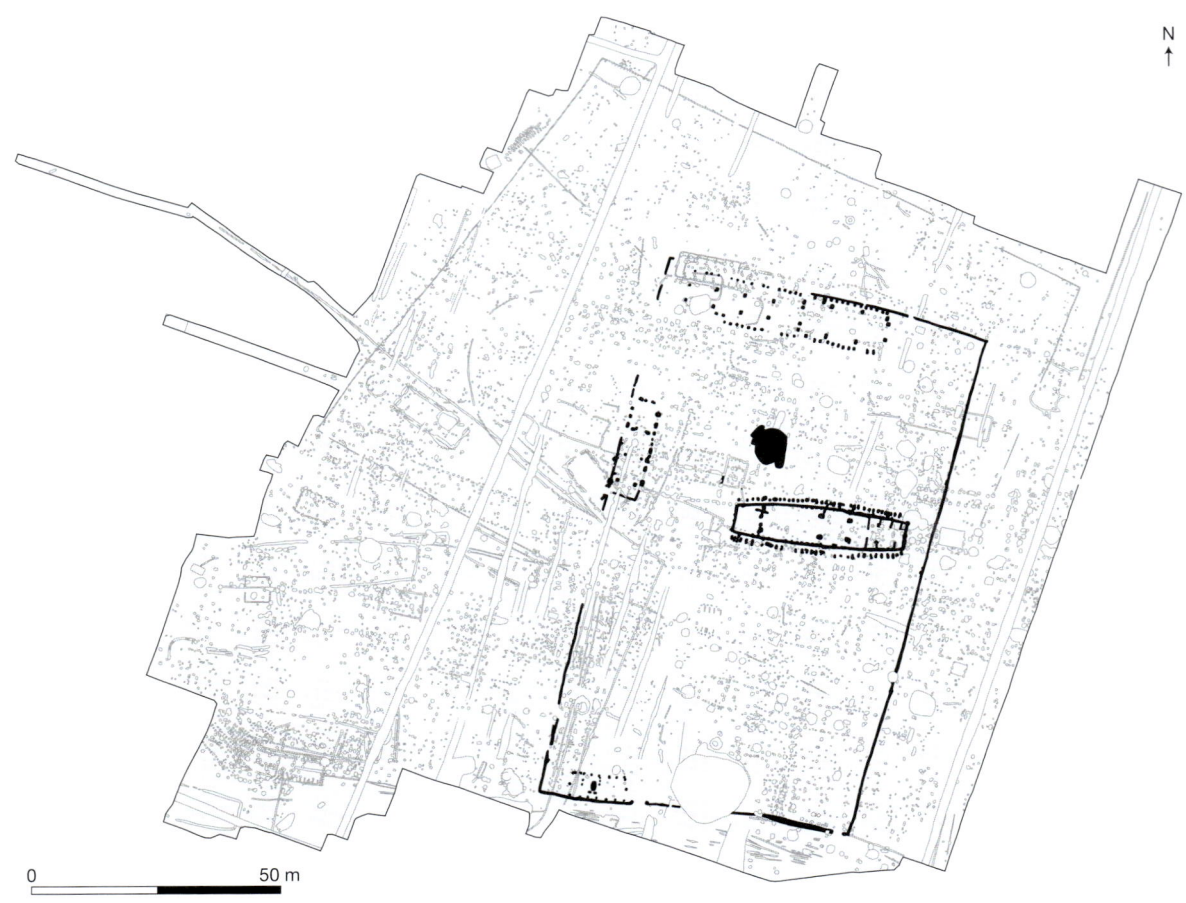

Fig. 76. Top: Settlement of many periods was found in excavations in Gammel Hviding. Particularly clear was a large farmstead of around the year 1000. Bottom: The 75-ha area which has produced a large number of detector-finds is surrounded by a black line. The excavation trenches in yellow. After Søvsø 2018a.

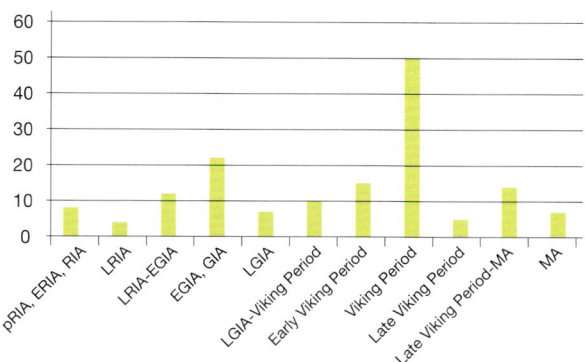

Fig. 77 Diagrammatic distribution of a total of 154 brooches and pendants from excavations and detector-surveys at Gammel Hviding, journal numbers ASR 440, 1265, 1375, 1425 and 1689. Note the partially overlapping phase-designations. (After Søvsø 2018a).

Gammel Hviding, Viking-period brooch-types	
Carolingian-Ottonian enamel brooch	34
Carolingian pseudo-coin brooch	2
Carolingian cross brooch	1
Disc brooch for suspension or with a pin, local	7
Cross-shaped brooch of the Råhede type, local	3
Equal-armed brooch, local	7
Trefoil brooch, local	3
Lozenge brooch with animal heads, local	3
Oval brooch, local	3
Hilt-shaped brooch, local	1
Valkyrie pendant, local	1
Total	**65**

Table 6. Amongst the 70 items of jewellery from the Viking Period, 65 are sufficiently well-preserved for more precise typological classification.

Fig. 78 Examples of imported jewellery found by metal-detecting at Gammel Hviding. From the top can be seen four variants of Carolingian-Ottonian enamel brooches. At the bottom, a so-called pseudo-coin brooch. ASR 1265x30, x58, x82; ASR 1375x38, x90. 2:1. Photograph: ASR.

however, when we get to the Viking Period. The majority of the finds of that date are of jewellery imported from the Carolingian-Ottonian Empire, principally in the form of what are known as enamel brooches of various shapes or pseudo-coin brooches (Table 6; Fig. 78).

The large quantity of foreign brooches from the Viking Period must indirectly be a consequence of the emergence of Ribe and the close contacts with the Carolingian-Ottonian Empires which followed (Baastrup 2007). That can hardly come as a surprise in view of the location of Gammel Hviding at the old entrance to the Ribe River. Only one of the brooches stands out qualitatively, a large hilt-shaped brooch with whitemetal inlays, ASR 1375x37 (Klæsøe 2005). It is also notable that the Scandinavian world of ideas is represented in the material in pendants formed as a coiled snake and a valkyrie while the Christian cross

appears both on imported items and the presumably locally manufactured cross-shaped brooches of the Råhede type that are dated to the 9th century (Feveile 2011). Even in the Early Viking Period, contacts with Christian lands appear to have influenced the fashion of local dress-accessories, and thus also quite probably the religious notions of their wearers.

In 1963-9, 1995-6 and 2015-16 a series of excavations have been carried out at Okholm (Fig. 79). A settlement of the Late Germanic Iron Age and the Viking Period has been found here, characterized by sunken feature buildings and small longhouses and thus conspicuously different from a farming village. A well at the site excavated in 2015 has been dendro-dated as constructed around the year 600 and to have remained in use down to the middle of the 8th century. The finds assemblage from the excavations is unusual, and dem-

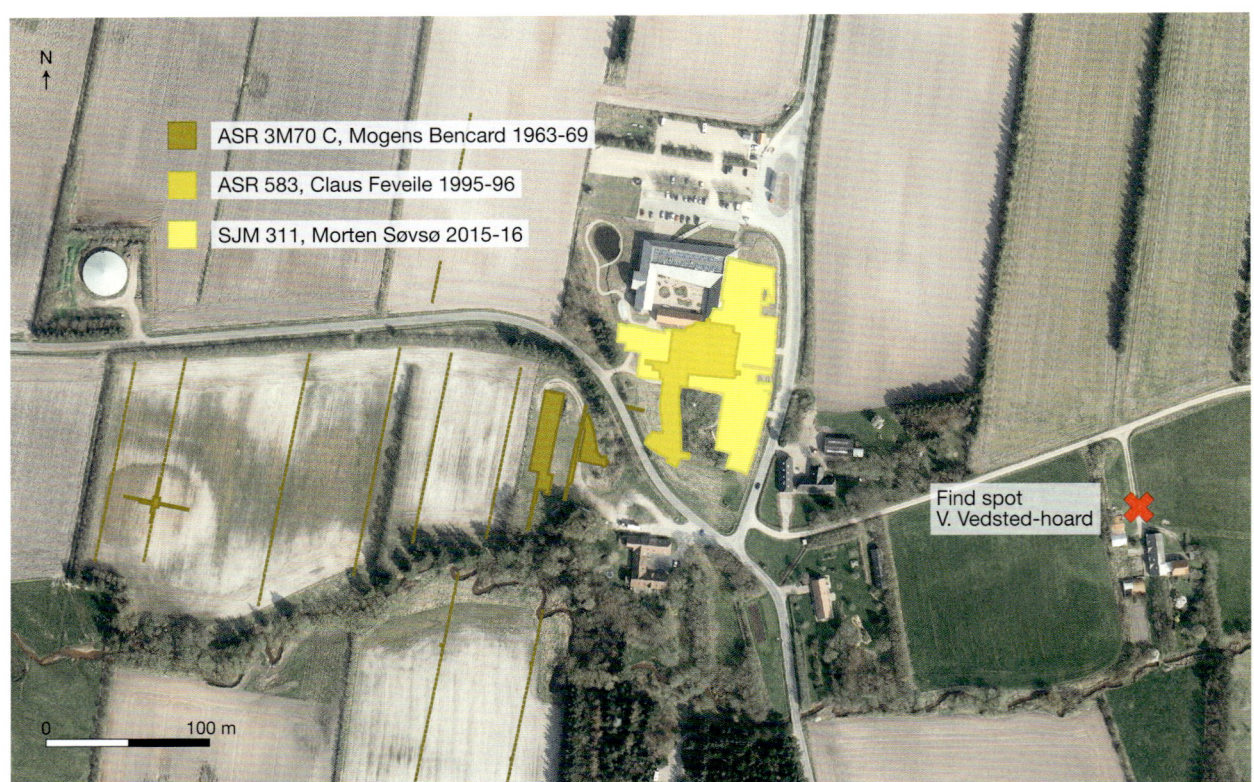

▲◄ *Fig. 79. Top: Plot of the excavations at Okholm and the find-spot of the Vester Vedsted hoard in 1859. The hoard is shown to the left. The base of the plot is an aerial photograph of 2011 with additions by the author. Photograph: NM.*

ASR 3M70 C, Mogens Bencard 1963-69

ASR 583, Claus Feveile 1995-96

SJM 311, Morten Søvsø 2015-16

Find spot
V. Vedsted-hoard

0   100 m

N

Fig. 80. Sword pommel from Gammel Hviding found by metal-detecting in 2014. The object, shown unconserved in the photograph, is of Jan Petersen's type O and dated to the 10th century. ASR 872x289. 2:1.

onstrates the presence of specialized craftsmen such as are also known in early Ribe: both beadmakers and bronzecasters (Feveile 2001). The finds assemblage is thus what one would expect from an emporium, and this is underlined by the finding of several sceattas and early Danish pennies. The sceattas could date pre-700, and this may therefore be a landing place which then could also be older than Ribe but in any case was in existence at the same time as the town in the 8th and 9th centuries. Specialist craftsmen were therefore working outside the town too.

In 1859, 250 m east of Okholm, what is called the Vester Vedsted hoard of the Late Viking Period was found (Fig. 79). This splendid hoard must have belonged to a member of the high aristocracy, and Okholm must be the most likely candidate for where the chieftain of Dankirke moved to in the 6th century (Fig. 67). Both the specialized craftsmen and the hoard point to the presence of an elite farmstead in this area.

Also known at Råhede is a large building of the Trelleborg type with a number of associated sunken feature buildings which were discovered from the air. Amongst other finds from this site there is a cross penny of Harald Bluetooth (Moesgaard 2015, 30) and the coin hoard from Danelund which consisted of 72 pennies from the end of the 11th century which were deposited in a large farmstead that is also partially visible in aerial photographs (Moesgaard 2007). We can add to these finds and observations a relatively large number of farmsteads of the Iron Age, Viking Period and Middle Ages discovered by flying.

This fractured image is anything but complete, and relies upon a range of different forms of prospection; nonetheless it shows that over long periods this area must have housed not just one but a series of rich settlements. Amongst these, Dankirke must have provided a religious centre down to the 6th century, and one may anticipate that somewhere else in the area there was a successor site which has not yet been securely identified. As things stand, Okholm, where the Vester Vedsted hoard was find, must be considered the most likely candidate.

4.3.5.3 Skanet Bro, Øster Vedsted

Immediately west of the modern village of Øster Vedsted a settlement of the Roman Iron Age is known from aerial photographs, surface finds and metal-detecting. Denarii have been found in the area on several occasions, and in 1975 a large gold ring with an internal diameter of 2.3 cm and weighing 18 g, case ASR 15M75C, was a surface find. This ring is much bigger and heavier than its counterparts in the graves at Brokær and Sneum described below, and thus is another example of an aristocratic presence in the area.

4.3.5.4 The Konge River, the Brokær graves, Store Darum

At Brokær, where the Droveway crosses the Konge River, in the Early and Late Roman Iron Ages there was a cemetery in which a number of individuals from the highest rank of society were laid to rest (Rasmussen 1995). In the 1st century AD the cremated remains of the so-called Brokær chieftain were buried there in a Roman cauldron along with rich armament, a gold ring and more (Fig. 81). More spectacular still was a boat grave with a clinker-built boat at least 12 m long about which, regrettably, very little can be said. The dating of that grave is also rather uncertain, although it is probably of the Late Roman Iron Age. The excavation of the site was undertaken by Conrad Engelhardt in 1877, and much of the cemetery has since been destroyed or built over with no further investigations. The Brokær graves continue to be surrounded by many unanswered questions.

The recent identification of a major settlement of the Late Roman/Germanic Iron Age beneath the modern railway town of Gredstedbro just on the other side of the Konge River must be assumed to represent another segment of the milieu that the individuals buried came from: excavations ASR 1932 Kjærmarken and ASR 2137 Gredstedbro Kirkegård. The place-name that is now Gredsted was *Grithæstath* in 1291, meaning 'a place of sanctuary' (Gammeltoft 2005), which might indicate an earlier sacral or political central role. Since Gredsted

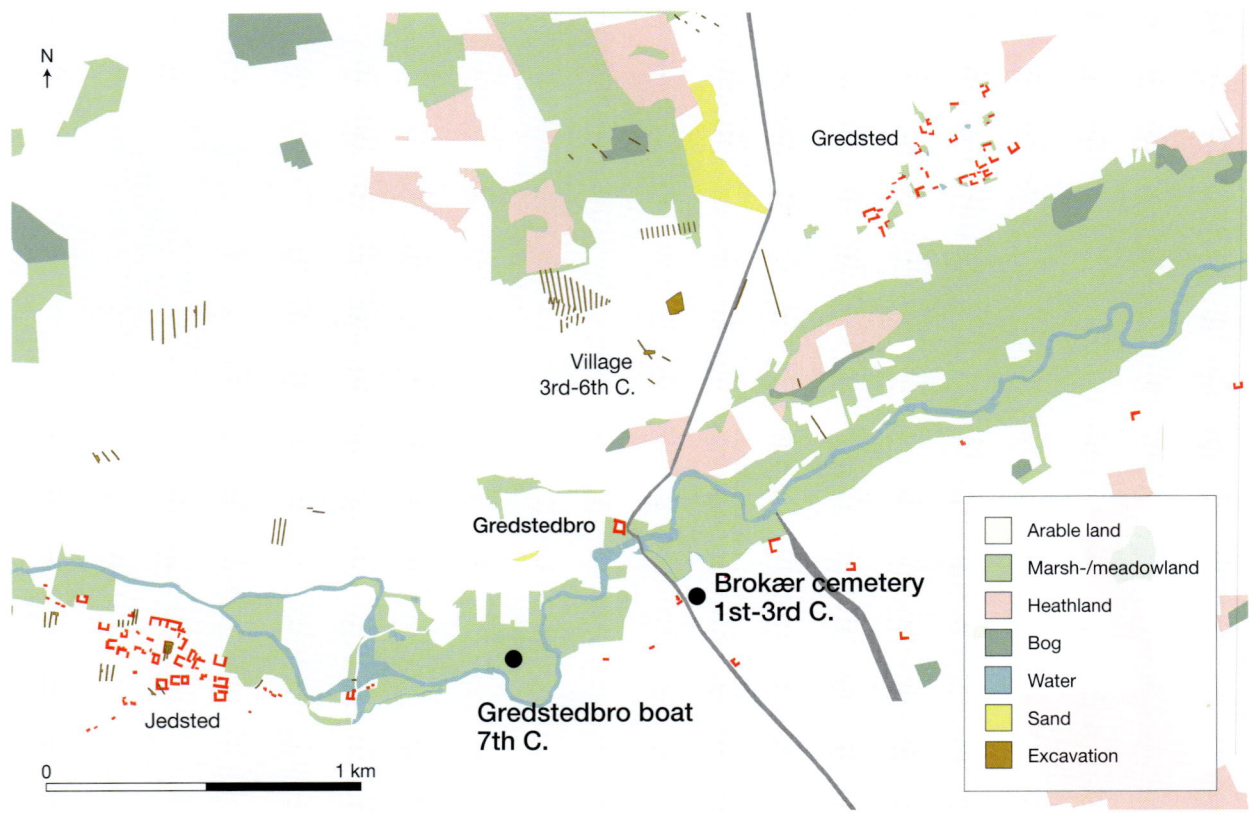

Fig. 81. Brokær and Gredstedbro by the Konge River. The terrain as it was surveyed around 1800 with the addition of selected archaeological sites and excavation trenches. The line of the Droveway is shown in grey.

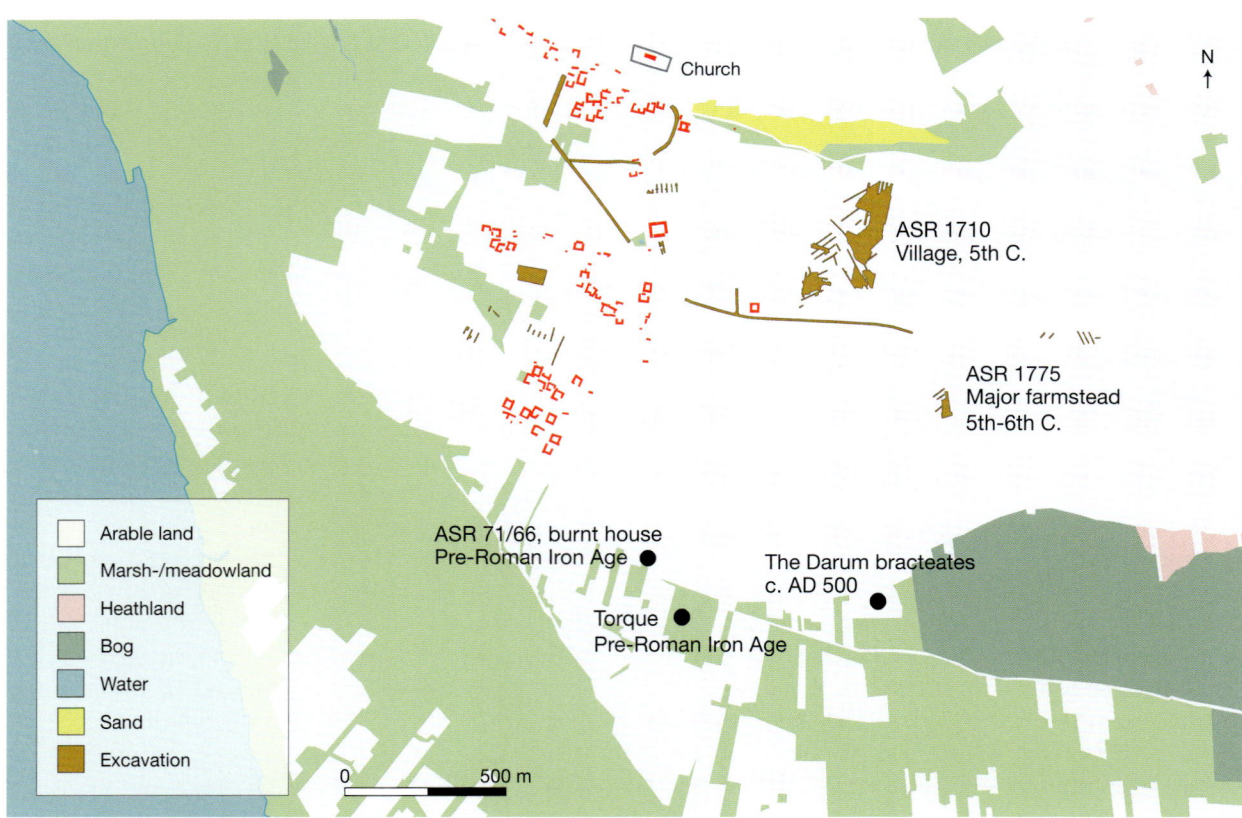

Fig. 82. Sites in Store Darum plotted on the digitalized Original 1 map.

did not develop into a parish, this implied main village may have disappeared at an early date for what otherwise are unknown reasons. Down to the Late Roman Iron Age, however, there must have been a significant centre around the Konge River: the cauldron grave and the boat grave were probably the richest graves known from this period in West Jutland as a whole. However no aerial reconnaissance, detector-searching, hedgerow surveys or other topographical studies have yet succeeded in finding any secure evidence of a later life.

In the extensive village lands of Store Darum, as early as the pre-Roman Iron Age a torque was sacrificed in the same bog that in the 6th century received a set of jewellery that was found by small-holder Eskild Pedersen when cutting peat in 1884, *the Darum bracteates* (Fig. 82). The find comprised not only twelve bracteates but also a pendant, a red glass bead and a gold scabbard-mouthpiece from what must have been a sword with its own name. This can only have been a chieftain's gold treasure which had been sacrificed. On the crest of the bank just above where the bracteates were found two building plots from the pre-Roman Iron Age have been excavated, and immediately above the find-place a small-scale excavation has revealed a saddle-roofed fence more than 80 m long which can be linked to a large number of building foundations and other evidence of settlement observed from the air to the east (Fig. 83).

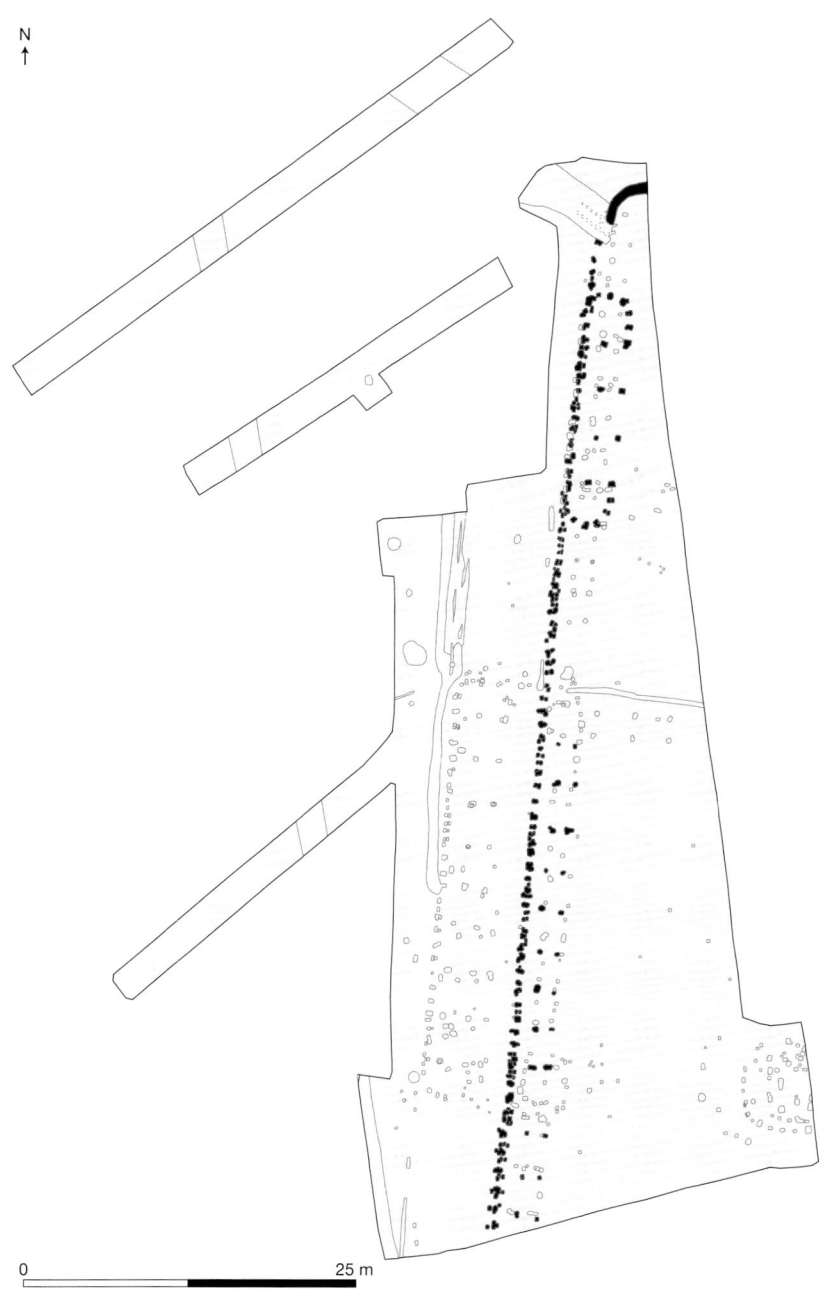

N
↑

Fig. 83. The saddle-roof fence over 80 m long, from excavation ASR 1775 of 2003, must enclose a very large farmstead, radiocarbon-dated to the Early Germanic Iron Age. The site of this excavation is shown on Figure 82.

0   25 m

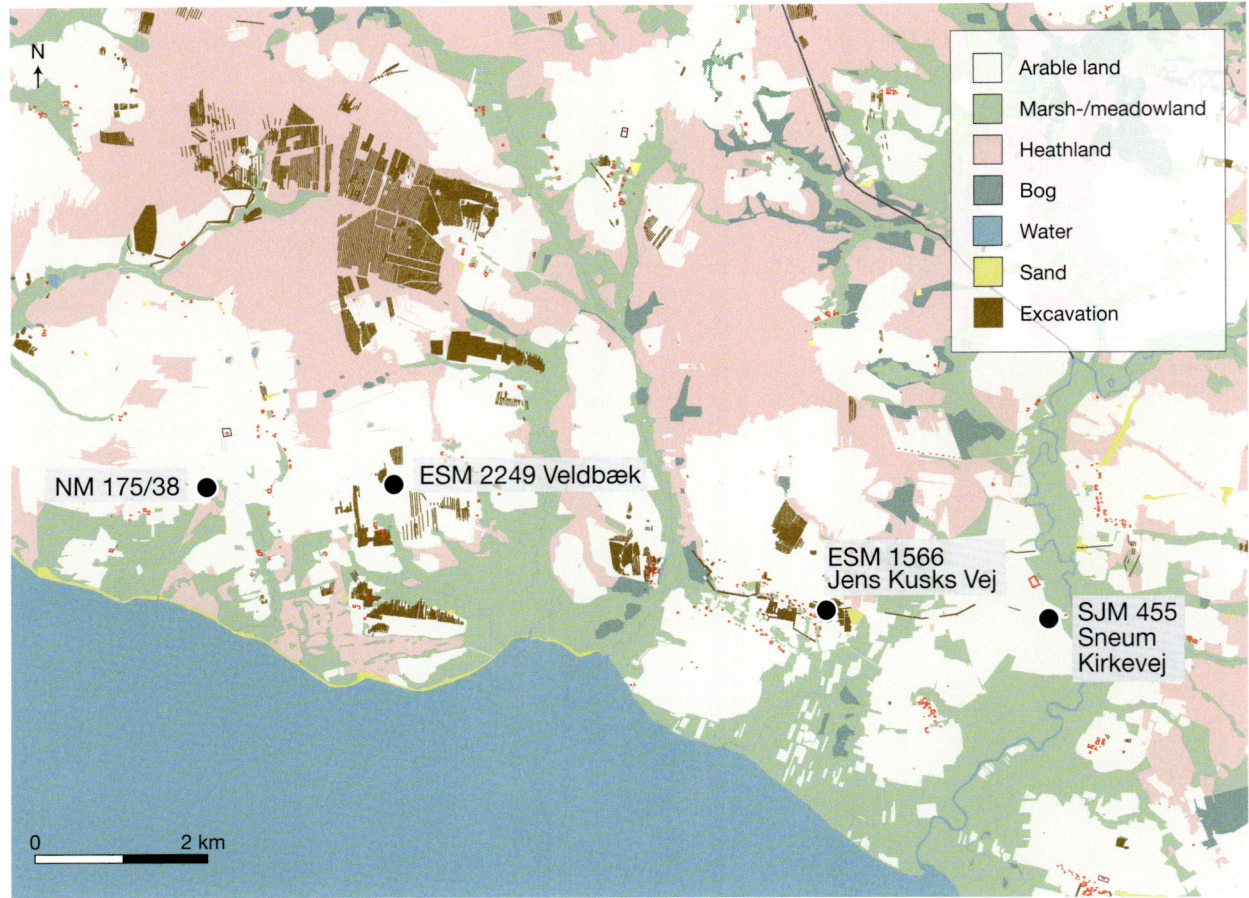

Fig. 84. In Skast District a number of rich graves of the Roman Iron Age are known, all of which lie in the coastal zone. They are conventionally understood to be the burials of chieftains who are supposed to have held power over a larger although rarely specifically described area of territory. In that case power will have changed hands in the area quite freely. Rather than chieftains, the rich graves represent a distinct aristocratic stratum of society in this period.

This must have been an exceptionally large farmstead, which may possibly have been the home of the owner of the bracteates. On the basis of what is not strong evidence, one can nonetheless make out cultic and settlement continuity from the pre-Roman Iron Age through to the 6th century AD.

Besides this, in Darum, we know of a large number of other sites which have been found from the air (S. Jensen 1985). Together with small-scale excavations these show that the large number of farms that were known around 1800 can apparently be traced far back into the Iron Age (Søvsø 2010b). A major cemetery is also known, Bavnehøj, just a little to the north of the church, excavated by the National Museum in 1924-9, where amongst other things the discovery of a wagon body points to an aristocratic presence in the Late Viking Period. Here too can be seen burials ranging in date from the pre-Roman Iron Age to the Viking Period. Both in votive and funerary practice, then, there was continuity throughout the 1st millennium AD.

4.3.5.5 Skast District

By Sneum church, on a prominent tongue of land projecting into the Sneum River and the marsh, in 2015 metal-detecting found a cauldron burial of the 2nd century AD which together with the earlier find of a serpent-head ring slightly further north – the most eminent of several earlier finds around here – indicates the presence of an aristocratic milieu in the Roman Iron Age (Fig. 84) (Feveile, Frandsen & Stoumann 2006).

In Tjæreborg, a rich cemetery with graves of the Roman Iron Age has been excavated on Jens Kusks Vej (Siemen & Stoumann 1996), while in 1997, purely by chance, a chieftain's grave of the 4th century which had been dug into an earlier barrow of the Single Grave Culture was found in Veldbæk (excavated 1999). The latter grave remains unpublished but it contained a sword with silver and gold-foil fittings, a spear, a gold ring, a set of gaming pieces, a silver brooch, and more (Fig. 85).

Around the Varde River too, the Roman Iron-age cemetery at Næsbjerg (Sb nr. 190509-105), the

Fig. 85. Items from the grave goods of the rich grave excavated at Veldbæk in 1999. Gem: ESM 2249x77 (2:1), Gold ring in two pieces: x87, x88 (2:1), Fibula: x89:4 (1:1) and sword belt garnish: x89:1 (1:1). Photograph: SJM.

Skonager bracteates (Sb nr. 190509-50), and the cemetery at Billum, all testify to rich milieux in the Roman and Germanic Iron Ages (Frandsen 2001).

In Skast District, therefore, up to the meadowlands around the Varde River, one can document a particularly aristocratic presence down to the Germanic Iron Age while comparable evidence from the subsequent period is sparse. To an extent that may be due to a near-total lack of metal-detecting before 2013, but that can hardly be the only explanation. The few and small medieval estates in this area could also show that, for unknown reasons, the local aristocracy did not come to play as prominent a role as before.

4.3.5.6 Horns District

In King Valdemar's Danish Census Book of c. 1231 the area between Varde and Skjern River was referred to as *Hornsheret* but by 1300 it had been divided into Western, Eastern and Northern Horns Districts; the latter two were recombined in 1687. The District seals that are known from the late 16th century depict two or three horns, possibly drinking horns, while the interpretation of the district name assumes that it refers to Horns Rev/Reef which was in all probability still

in existence as a promontory jutting into the North Sea when the district gained its name in the earlier Middle Ages (Fig. 86).

In the district town of Horne, which the Droveway passes through, an incomplete runestone which was built into the church wall is referred to first in the 17th century, with the inscription: 'Ravnunge-Tue made this [Thyra's mound]'. A man of the same name, and probably the same person, is referred to on both of the Bække runestones, from the ship setting and from the church wall, and on the Læborg runestone. The interpretation of the man Ravnunge-Tue and his relationship with the Thyra referred to is debated. Ravnunge-Tue was probably a retainer of King Gorm, and the runestone can be dated to around the middle of the 10th century (Imer 2014). The stone must, of course, originally have stood at another location, probably beside the public highway, and possibly in the vicinity of the later church (Lerche Nielsen 2001).

Just east of the church, in Hornelund, in 1892 two beautiful large disc brooches in gold filigree work were found together with a gold armring while harrowing a field, dated to around the year 1000. In 2014 this old find could be supplemented with a number of coins and other fragments of jewellery found by metal-detector around 175 m south of the older find-spot. From the coins, the new finds could be dated to shortly after AD 1056. It is a matter of debate whether these represent a single hoard or two. Arguments for the latter case are the substantial distance between the finds and the fact that the hoard found in 1892 consists of whole objects while that found in 2014 comprises fragments plus coins. Whether this is one deposit or two, it or both can be inferred to have been made in the Christian period, and the finds are reminiscent in many respects of the only slightly earlier Vester Vedsted hoard. The quality

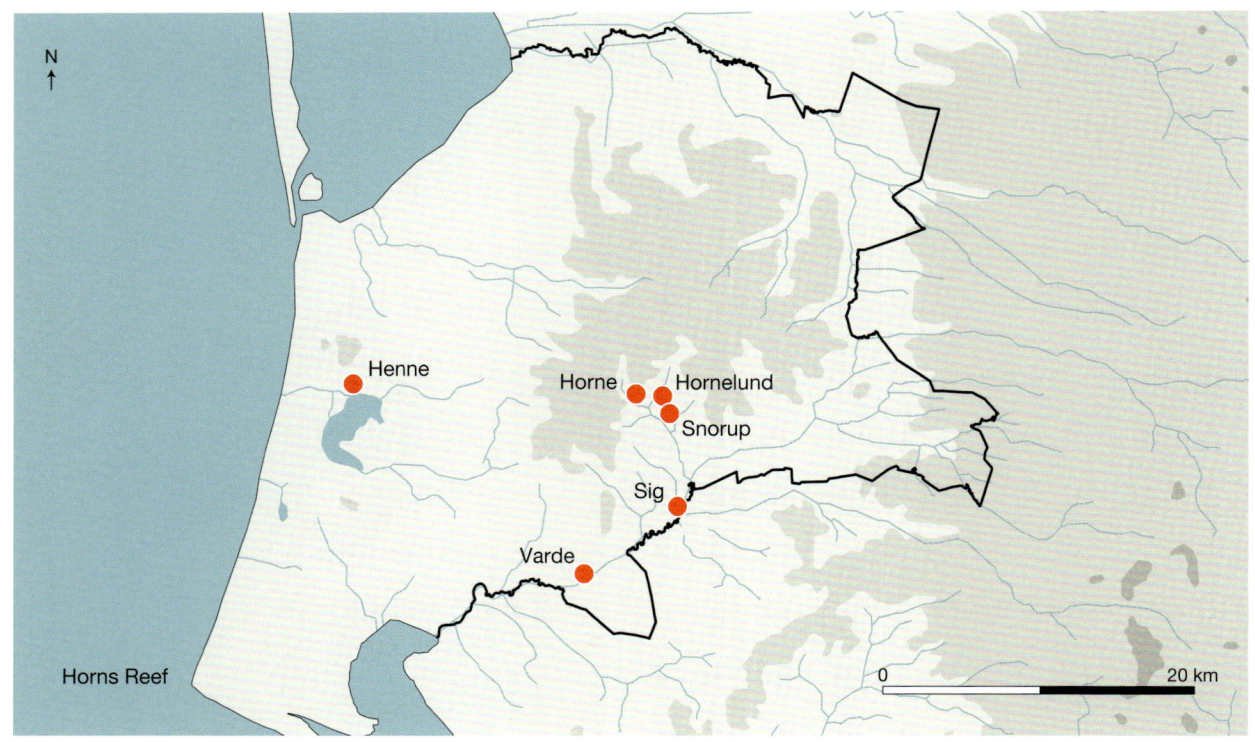

Fig. 86. Map of Horne District at its earliest known extent with the sites referred to in the text. Below can be seen the two magnificent Hornelund brooches. 1:1. Map by the author; photograph: NM.

120

of the jewellery indicates a high social level, as does the runestone, and it is noted that the second element of the place-name is the potentially religious term *-lund*.

The finds from Horne point to a prominent sacral-aristocratic memorial culture of the Late Viking Period and earlier Middle Ages. If these acts of display had earlier roots or can be attributed to the desire of new holders of power to establish themselves in the area we cannot tell (Randsborg 1980, 25ff). A nearby detector-site, Sig Syd, does not appear to stand out in any particular way from many others, with the possible exception of a single gold-foil figure (Lauridsen 2014). At Snorup in the next parish of Tistrup a settlement of the Late Roman and Early Germanic Iron Ages has been excavated where iron-production was an important activity, and that may have still been the case later on.

At Henne, north of Lake Fil, excavations, geophysical surveys and metal-detecting have revealed a remarkable site of the Viking Period (Ploug, Jepsen & Franden 2012, 28ff). Either side of a N.-S. roadway are small, broadly equal-sized, fenced tofts; probably around 50x50 m, and consisting of buildings built on to the fence-line and sunken feature buildings alongside the roadway (Fig. 87). Unfortunately none of these fascinating tofts has been excavated yet, but their size is considerably less than at the many well-known farming settlements of the Viking Period which could indicate that the activities at Henne were not primarily agrarian. To date, the investigations indicate that the site was at its peak in the 9th century.

West of here is the estate centre of Hennegård where the buildings of 1831 incorporate earlier elements. The buildings stand on an undated castle site. Bishop Elias of Ribe signed the letter establishing the cathedral chapter at Ribe on 13 June 1145 at Hennegård, and many suppose that the site was then in the bishop's possession and thus linked to the leading aristocracy. A possible interpretation based upon current knowledge is that Henne had had an elite farmstead in the Viking Period too, close to which a landing place based upon trade and craftwork developed.

4.3.5.7 Dejbjerg and Sønder Haurvig

The site of Dejbjerg lies within a parish of the same name on the eastern side of Ringkøbing Fjord, barely 10 km north of the Skjern River. The Droveway cuts across the parish, and many traces of the road are preserved east of the church. The place-name means 'the hill of those who are killed' and has previously been proposed as having a religious character and linked to finding of the two famous wagons of the Late pre-Roman Iron Age that were discovered during peat-digging in 1881 and 1883 in the wetland of Dejbjerg Præstegårdsmose (Fig. 88) (H. Petersen 1888). The two wagons are not identical and we do

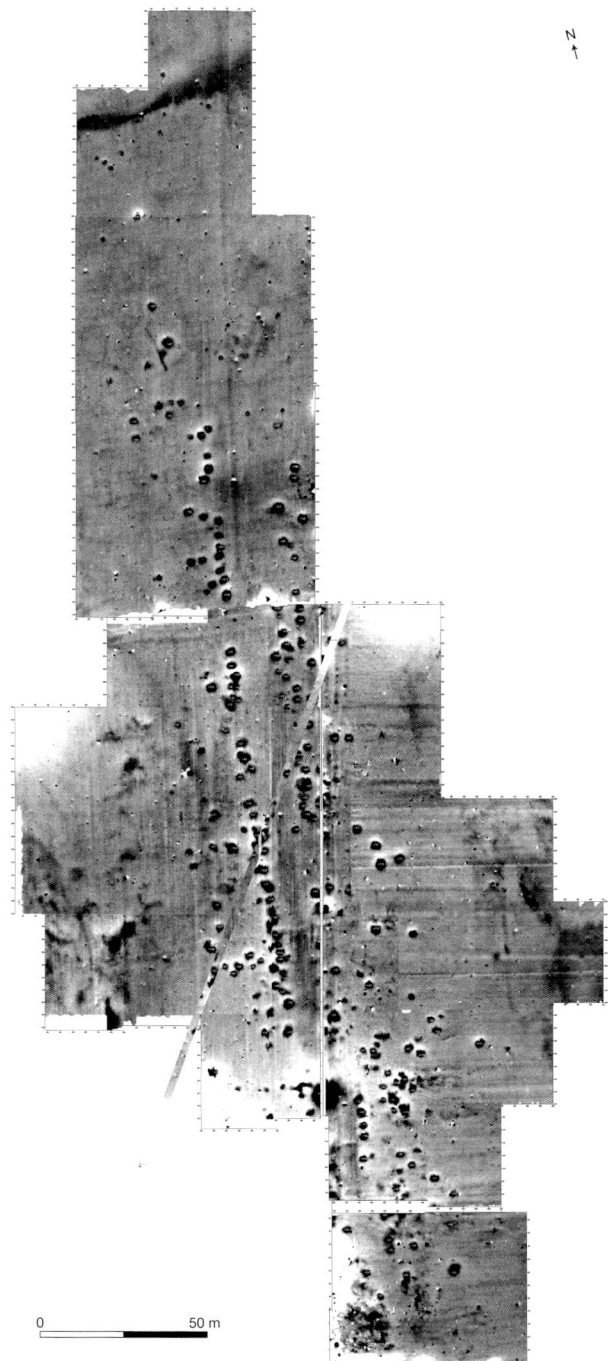

Fig. 87. Magnetometric plan of sunken feature buildings at the Henne site. Excavations have confirmed that the dark signatures represent sunken feature buildings which lay alongside a roadway passing through the site over a distance of several hundred metres. After Ploug et al. 2012.

not know whether or not they represent one or two sacrifices: either is possible. Also known from the bog are wagon axles of a Late Roman Iron-age type and pottery and weaving tablets dated to the Early Roman Iron Age: these document both a wagon cult and

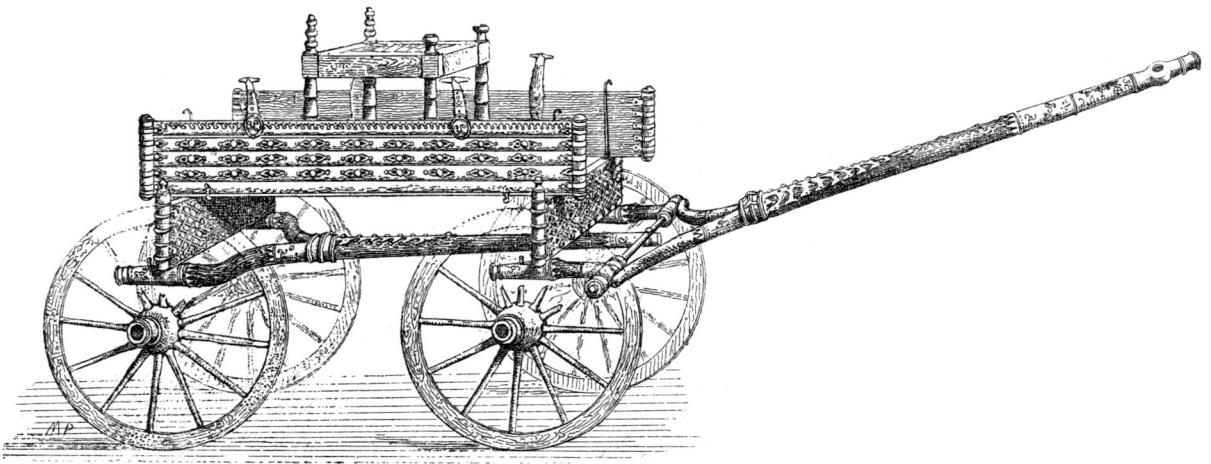

Fig. 88. Reconstruction of one of the two cult wagons from Dejbjerg Præstegårdsmose. After H. Petersen 1888.

sacrificial practice over a period of several centuries (Schovsbo 1987, 240; Egeberg 1996).

In 1969, during the development of the area northwest of the Romanesque parish church, a Viking-period tool chest was found which contained two pairs of tongs, a hammerhead, a whetstone, a rivet plate, an axe, an adze, a gimlet, a fragment of iron and four iron chest-mounts (Egeberg 1990). These buried chests, of which nine are known from Scandinavia, were formerly thought of as hidden valuables or accidental losses, but their meaningful location in the landscape and their clear association with sites with religious functions shows beyond any real doubt that they were in fact sacrificed, which seems to have been a practice within a brief period in the Late Viking Period (Lund 2006).

In 1992-3 a small-scale excavation was carried out over only about 500 sq m in the area west of the church, which is situated about 700 m from Præstegårdsmosen where the wagons were sacrificed and just 100 m from where the tool chest was found (Fig. 89). In addition to settlement of the Early Iron Age a hall of several phases, 16.5 m long and with bowed sides, was found. It was around 6 m wide in the middle. The dimensions of this building do not stand out from many other excavated examples of the 5th-6th centuries but its roof-bearing posts were exceptionally strong. The hall had burnt down, but remarkably had practically no pottery inside, which may be evidence that the burning was deliberate rather than a destructive accident. Besides the sparsity of pottery, other facets of the finds were highly unusual. These came from the cleaning out of the roof-bearing post-holes and subsequent sieving of this material, and some of the machine-dug topsoil. The area was also metal-detected. The finds assemblage consists, amongst other things, of:

- About 160 sherds of blown glass of various types
- A copper-alloy neckring
- An unusual piece of copper-alloy jewellery in openwork
- A 6th-century sword pommel
- Two spearheads
- A shield-on-tongue buckle

Although the construction of the building does not differ significantly from a large number of other excavated examples of the 5th-6th century, the assemblage of finds is so unusual that the building has to be regarded as a hall designed for presumably religious cemeteries and *conspicuous consumption* of the same pattern as is known from the much more comprehensive excavations at Dankirke.

The areas close to the church to the north and west were developed in the 1960s and 70s, leading to the finding of the tool chest noted above but unfortunately without wider excavations in that case. Through a later minor excavation immediately north of the church sunken feature buildings with large quantities of iron slag were found, while the church wall also now includes a large number of whole iron-smelting slags. A barrow a short way north of the church was called *Smedebierg* ('Smith's Hill') on the earliest cadastral map. The fields to the west have a large number of crop-marks which are interpreted as SFBs. The only neighbour to the church was the former manor house of Dejbjerglund, which forms the village lands (ejerlav) and is known by that name from around the year 1500. The second element *-lund*, which may be of sacral character, is again to be noted; if this is put together with the finding of

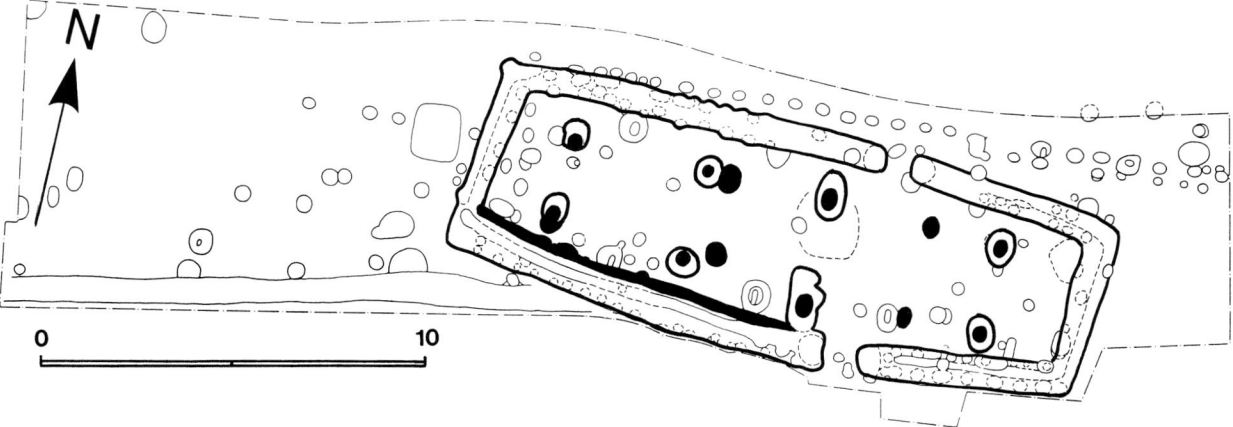

Fig. 89. Plan of the hall building at Dejbjerg of the 5th-6th centuries AD. After Egeberg 1996.

the Late Viking-period tool chest, the hall of the 5th and 6th centuries, and the sacrificed wagons of the 1st and 2nd centuries, at least the outline of an important *central place* emerges: a chieftainly milieu, centrally located in the landscape of communications, and with clear evidence of votive acts. The chieftain may be supposed eventually to have raised the church in the earlier Middle Ages, and the manor house of Dejbjerglund may be the last surviving remnant of an elite farmstead whose history could run in a straight line right back to the Early Iron Age.

At Holmsland Klit at the site of Sønder Haurvig, a large number of coins have been found since the 1800s, and still appear as a result of coastal erosion (J.Aa. Jensen 1988). The coins include a number of denarii, a sceatt, and many coins of the 11th century onwards. The find-bearing culture-layers are covered by dunes and the form of activity that the coin finds represent is unknown; however the best suggestion has to be that there was a landing place here, apparently in use from the Roman Iron Age down to the Renaissance Period, when the landscape changes caused by the Little Ice Age put a stop to the activity. Following the same model as that proposed for the Tønder Marsh (Segschneider 2014), this landing place may have been controlled by the chieftain at Dejbjerg.

4.3.5.8 Omgaard

At Omgaard in Nørre Omme parish two large farmsteads of the Late Iron Age and Viking Period have been excavated, characterized amongst other things by impressively large buildings (Fig. 90) (L.C. Nielsen 1979). The farmsteads lie alongside an important routeway, a predecessor of trunk road 11, the earlier roots of which are revealed by lines of burial mounds and wheel-tracks. But from the published evidence

the farmsteads appear to have been primarily agrarian and not to have housed any religious functions such as characterize both Dankirke and Dejbjerg. Omgaard is thus highly reminiscent of Kalvsund, the site close to Ribe discussed above where a farmstead of dimensions comparable with those at Omgaard has been excavated alongside the land-route between Ribe and Kolding, immediately south of the church (see Fig. 54) (Søvsø 2011a; 2013).

Although not rooted in thorough studies, it should be noted that *Omgaard* apparently means 'the farm by the watercourse', quite a precise description, and it is highly likely that it was this farmstead which came to give a name both to the later church and its parish.[13]

4.4 Summary, Topography

The rich grave finds of West Jutland from the period down to the Germanic Iron Age reveal a distinctly aristocratic layer of society which, in combination with the weapon hoards principally from East Jutland and Fyn, have constituted the traditional foundation stones for various reconstructions of social structure and social relationships in the Roman Iron Age (Ethelberg 2014). On the basis of this processual model, the high-status graves are interpreted as expressions of a hierarchical power structure within society that was recognized at the time, and in which, with minor variance, the richer the grave, the greater the power. The inspiration for this social model comes, like so very much else in this period, from the Roman Empire. On the basis of this model one has, in the end, to conclude that the many elite milieux in the West Jutlandic coastal zone either could not have had very great endowments or that the area must have been the stage for intense power-struggles between rival aristocratic alliances.

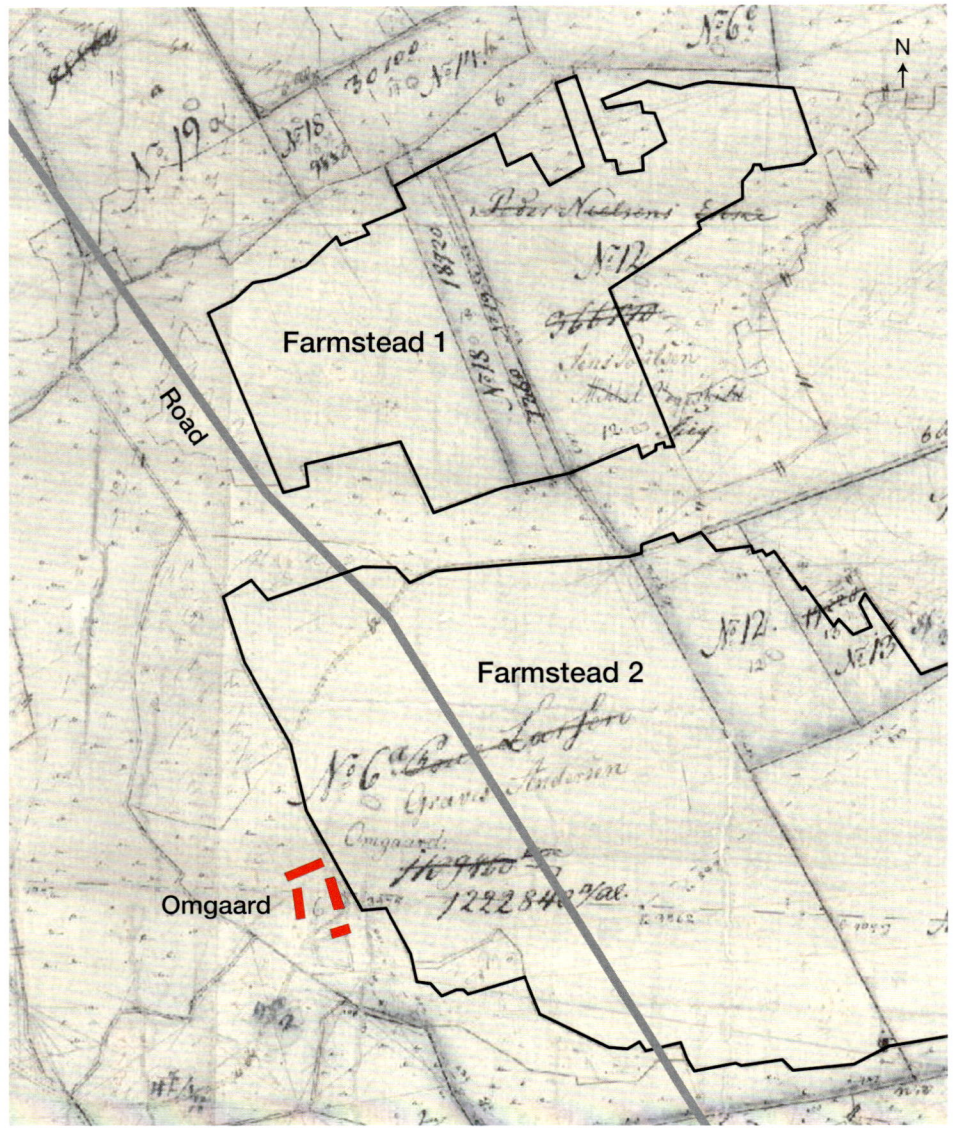

◄► *Fig. 90. Left, Omgaard in Nørre Omme parish on the Original 1 cadastral map surveyed in 1799 with additions to show the location of the two excavated farmsteads and the routeway. Right, the excavation plan. Farmstead 1 is uppermost and Farmstead 2 below. The fields on the map of 1799 show exactly what the potential for settlement was in the Viking Period too. After the Original 1 cadastral map at the Geodata Agency and L.C. Nielsen 1979.*

A different and in my view more plausible alternative is that there was no one-to-one relationship between burial practice and the social structure in the society of that time, and that the aristocratic level in the society may have been moulded more by local variations such as familial custom; more differentiated; and not internally sub-divided into clearly defined aristocratic strata. This does not change the fact that common religious and social conceptions and ideals were held, and that the burial practice on the whole was directed towards expressing both the former social role of the deceased and focused upon an afterlife; burial practice could, however, within the cognitive framework of the period, otherwise have been just as varied as the landscape in which the dead were laid to rest.

From the following period the archaeological source evidence is radically different. Many fewer graves are known, and the great weapon deposits had ceased. In contrast there is a comprehensive body of evidence from settlement archaeology and detector-finds, and both sources point to extensive continuity from the Roman Iron Age on through the Early Germanic Iron Age until the AD 536 environmental catastrophe and the cold period which followed it. Both the sacrificial practices and the dendro-datings indicate that this event was an all-encompassing disaster without parallels, followed by a sharp decline in population. The consequences were probably varied, governed entirely by how the local resource landscape reacted, and the ongoing impacts may conceivably have been different in the sandy west of Jutland than in the moraine landscapes of East Jutland.

The fall in population must also be assumed to explain why this period is still unclear in terms of settlement archaeology, although detector archaeology shows that already in the course of the 7th century the population must have reached a level which means

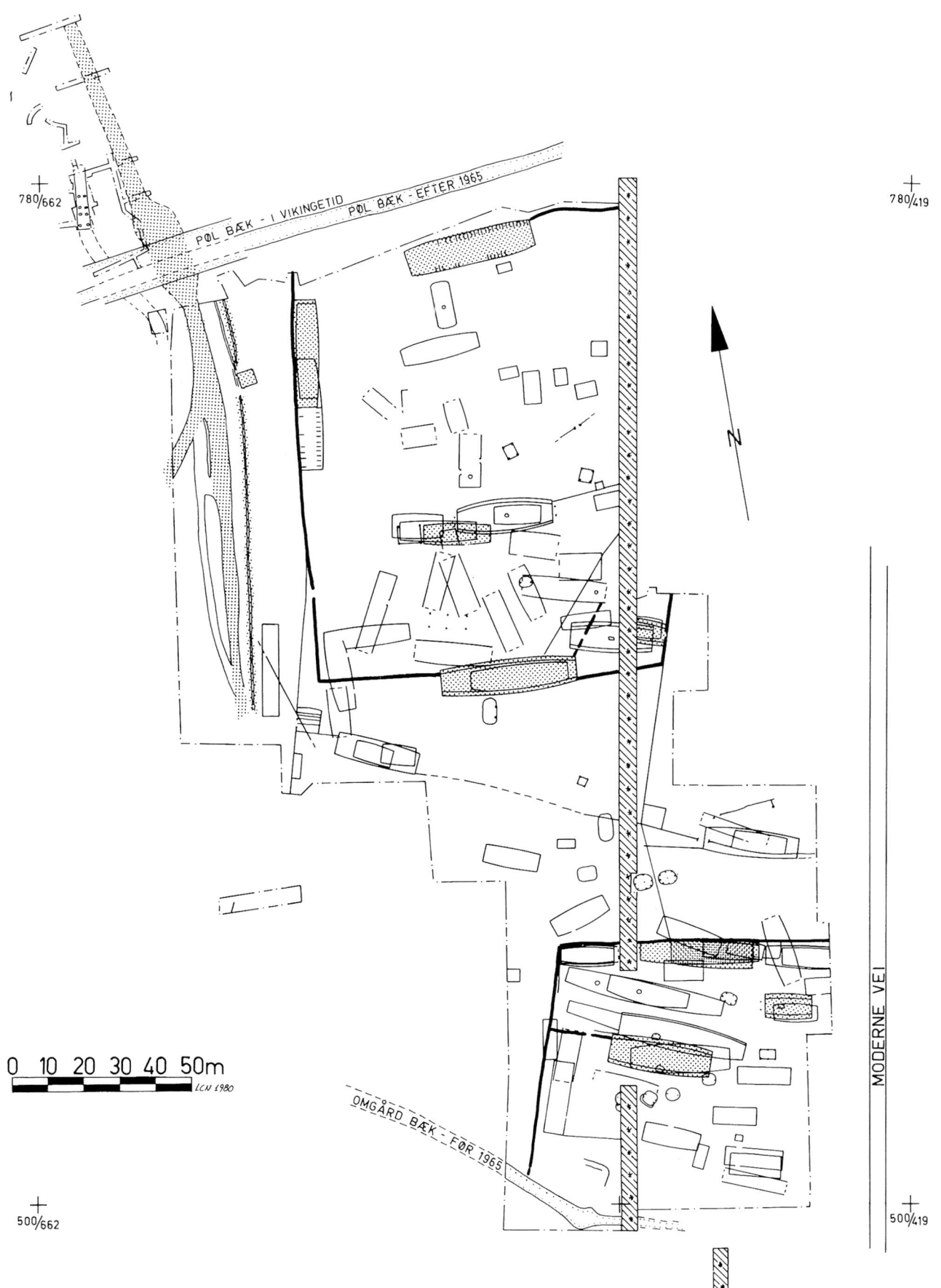

PØL BÆK - I VIKINGETID

PØL BÆK - EFTER 1965

780/662

780/419

N

0 10 20 30 40 50m

LCN 1980

MODERNE VEI

OMGÅRD BÆK - FØR 1965

500/662

500/419

that brooches of the 7th century (and of other periods of the Iron Age, the Viking Period and the Middle Ages) are now found in what would appear to be practically every single parish of Denmark.

From East Denmark, research into a number of aristocratic sites, the so-called 'central places', has set the tone of the debate concerning the religion and social context of the Late Iron Age. Excavations have uncovered a series of elite residences consisting of impressive halls with outstanding traces of a rich cult life (L. Jørgensen 2014; T. Christensen 2015). The striking absence of places of that kind in the archaeological evidence from Jutland has been noted by many scholars, and taken as evidence for the existence of a fundamental cultural difference between East and West Denmark in this period (Holst 2014).

The discovery of the site of Erritsø near Fredericia, with a 39-m long hall with bowed sides and external sloping supporting posts, and with a familiar form of fenced off special area adjoining it, all enclosed within a strong palisade fence, appears, however, to match all of the criteria for an 'East Danish' hall, even though the dimensions are a little less. This structure is dated to the 9th century (P.M. Christensen 2009).

Similarly, the site of Toftum Næs near Stoholm west of Viborg, has to be regarded as an aristocratic site. The excavations so far have revealed a series of unusual buildings, including several halls, which are radiocarbon-dated to the Late Germanic Iron Age and Viking Period (Fiedler Therkildsen 2014; 2015). Together with a number of exceptional detector-finds from the area in the form of rare Anglo-Saxon coins and more, both the architecture and the range of artefacts appear to distinguish the settlement at Toftum sharply from a normal village of this period, even though both the sizes of the buildings and the quantity of finds lie markedly below those of the largest sites of the east of Denmark. The major farmstead at Toftum Næs is neighbour to the later manor house of Lundgård, which in 1454 was called *Lundgardh*.[14] This possibly religious place-name may have been the farmstead's original name.

In the foregoing chapter it has been argued that Dankirke, Hornelund and Dejbjerg should also be regarded as chieftainly residences and cult sites, and thus as expressions of the same basic set of concepts that made themselves dominant across southern Scandinavia as a whole and which find expression in the relatively uniform aesthetic of the period. This does not affect the fact that as of yet there is a major difference in scale between west and east in Denmark. It corresponds with the better known, later cultural differences of the Middle Ages, when eastern Denmark was dominated by a high aristocracy to a greater degree while a more differentiated and on the whole also a less wealthy aristocracy was typical of Jutland. One could claim with some validity that this is also the case nowadays. The archaeological evidence could indicate that these conditions were

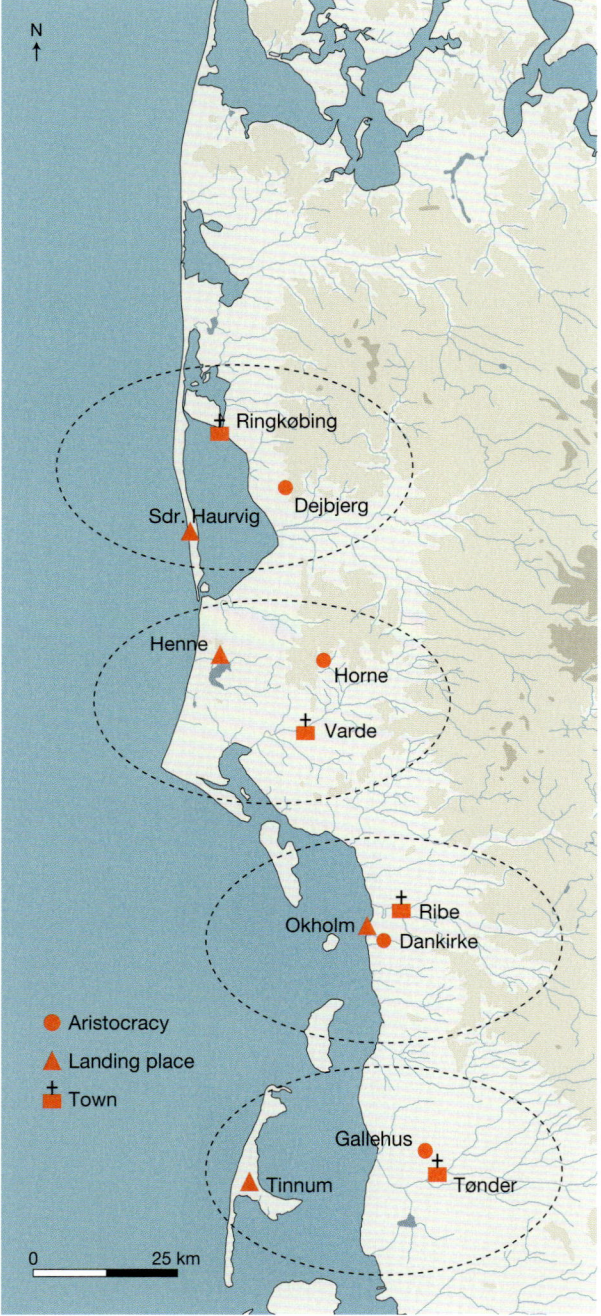

Fig. 91. Aristocratic sites, landing places and medieval towns in West Jutland. In the near hinterland of all four towns we know of aristocratic sites of the 1st millennium and in many cases also of associated landing places. The towns did not arise in a vacuum but built upon centuries-old and well-established structures of communication and exchange.

also in force in the Late Germanic Iron Age and the Viking Period, but one must not forget either that the extent of excavations on the Jutlandic sites referred to above has been very limited so far.

The trading networks around the North Sea that were expanding in the course of the 7th century must have had contact with greater or lesser sections of the aristocracy of southern Scandinavia, whether their role was that of suppliers of goods or they were trading visitors to the earliest emporia. The shorter the distance, the easier the contact was, and at latest with the emergence of Ribe around the year 700 firm connexions between the agents of the trading network and a local interest group was established. Up along the west coast and into the Limfjord there was village after village dominated by local leaders and a large group of presumably free farmers occupying farmsteads that were run as family enterprises. There are at present no grounds for adopting a strong position on whether these farmers played a part in state-formation or were possibly just minor political entities.

It is proposed in this book that the climatic catastrophe of AD 536 was a *game changer*, in the wake of which there was a great fall in population level, which may have had a range of chaotic consequences in the form of conflict or raiding, but which in the larger view reduced rather than increased the potential for conflict amongst the survivors. The archaeological vacuum in the 6th and 7th centuries has previously led to speculation about the emergence of a Danish centralized power possibly as early as the 6th century (Näsman 2006), but from the demographic picture that is put forward here it appears more reasonable to point to the construction of the Kanhave canal in 726 and the massive extension of the Danevirke in 737 as the first unambiguous signs of royal power in Denmark. As is argued later, in Chapter 6 of this book, we can add the emporia to this evidence, and the monopoly over coinage linked with them, as introduced in Ribe around the year 725.

Finally, Ribe Diocese seems to have had a significant, virtually a one-to-one connexion, between the most important central places of the Iron Age and later towns (Fig. 91). Unlike the central places, however, the towns needed access to the sea. In the case of Ribe the predecessors were at Dankirke and Okholm, the aristocratic central functions of which in combination with the favourable location of Ribe in respect of land traffic must be regarded as the precondition for the birth of the town around the year 700.

In the case of the Tønder Marsh, it is proposed that there ought to be evidence of the aristocratic milieu around Møgeltønder which – possibly as a consequence of the climatic catastrophe of AD 536 – sacrificed the gold horns, and that the manorial seats which are known in the area from the 13th century are a latter reflex of the same phenomenon, which in turn was the precondition for the town of Møgeltønder/Tønder appearing in the 12th-13th centuries. Storm floods have made major inroads into the landscape of the Tønder Marsh and may be one reason why the picture here remains fragmentary.

In Horns District the Hornelund hoard(s) and the runestone at the church show that at the latest in the Late Viking Period a high-aristocratic central function can be proved, which must be the background to both the district name and the emergence of the town of Varde in the course of the 11th-12th centuries.

Dejbjerg did not come to provide a district name, and no town emerged by the Skjern River. Why that was so is hard to say, but the opportunities for traffic around the watery river could perhaps have been a factor. At the same time there was the site of Sønder Haurvig, which was too out of the way for land traffic to become a town in its own right. Rather, Ringkøbing emerged in the course of the 13th century, and remained a relatively small town. The town was taken out of the already extant land parish of Rindum and the suggestion of a link between Dejbjerg and Ringkøbing may have been influenced by other interests too – but this does not alter the fact that the distance between Dejbjerg and Ringkøbing is only 15 km.

Further north in the diocese only the market towns of Holstebro and Lemvig were found, both of them quite small towns in the Middle Ages. From the northern part of the diocese there is similarly limited information on aristocratic sites of the Iron Age.

In bullet-point form, this chapter has attempted to document the following general points:

- West Jutland is relatively under-explored archaeologically in comparison with other regions of Denmark.

- The conditions for settlement in the Iron Age, Viking Period and earlier Middle Ages were generally favourable. The Late Antique Little Ice Age (LALIA) appears to have hit the population extremely hard and the Little Ice Age (LIA) also caused a severe reduction in scope for life.

- West Jutland was part of a common southern Scandinavian social system. At suitable places in the landscape there were elite farmsteads with halls and evidence of a rich sacrificial cult.

- The known elite farmsteads of the west of Denmark are smaller than their counterparts in the east, while the average farmstead was apparently larger. This is assumed to reflect a society in the west that was less aristocratically moulded than was the case in the east.

- A conspicuous continuity in the power structures within society. The towns of Ribe, Tønder, Varde and Ringkøbing are all suggested to have had elite farmsteads/central places as predecessors.

- The combination of archaeological data from excavations and metal-detecting with studies of historical maps, LIDAR scans of the surface of the landscape, and place-names plus the development of the areas in historical times is a powerful tool for the reconstruction of the conditions back in the Iron Age.

- Around the year 700, Jutland was a densely settled community with a well-established system of power and infrastructure which, in light of the archaeologically visible range of goods available in Ribe, must be understood to have been the primary target market for the traders at Ribe.

5. Ribe AD 700-1050

5.1 The meaning of the place-name Ribe

The name of Ribe, *Ripa* in Latin, is known from as early as the Life of Ansgar, dated around AD 870. We do not know whether or not the town had this name from the outset, but it is overwhelmingly probable that it was so. The meaning of the name has been debated, and there are two possible explanations. *Ripa* may come from a common European word meaning 'a river bank' or 'riverside', or from a common Norse word with the sense of 'stripe' or 'strip'. After the discovery of the narrow tenement plots it was suggested that those could have produced the name of the town. That, however, would be a highly unusual element to choose in name-formation, and it is thus more probable that *Ripa* does mean 'river bank' instead. This would then be the only example of a town in Denmark which does not have a name of Danish origin.[15] The same name may have been used for emporium of Åhus in Skåne: see Chapter 6.

5.2 The taphonomy of Ribe

At this point in the book, before the account of the emergence and development of Ribe as they can be portrayed from the archaeological evidence, it should be helpful to analyse the ancient monument that is Ribe at a general level, with particular attention to an explanation of the taphonomic conditions. Ribe differs markedly from most of the other Viking-period towns of the North – Reric, Hedeby, Birka and Kaupang – in that it survives in the present as an existing and functional town with a history of over one thousand years in the same location. In essence this means that some of the stratigraphy of Ribe is extremely well preserved because the layers were sealed beneath thick medieval culture layers from an early date (Fig. 92), while other areas did not benefit

from that protection and have correspondingly been more extensively destroyed by the proximity of the town and the large amount of digging that has been carried out over time. This also means that it has rarely been possible to place excavations in the town in accordance with research-directed questions but rather that they have had to be fitted into the framework which the built environment imposes (Plate 1). Both circumstances have had decisive significance in relation to the production and the interpretation of the archaeological data alike. Amongst the Viking-period towns of Denmark from before the year 1000, it is only Aarhus where the taphonomic situation is on the whole comparable with that of Ribe.

Fig. 92. Stratified sequence of layers covering the period c. AD 700-850. From a photograph in case ASR 9 Posthuset.

5.2.1 The north side of the river, the oldest Ribe

Ribe is rightly famed for the well-preserved sequences of layers from the 8th and 9th centuries in the area around Sct. Nicolaj Gade (Fig. 92). In this highly constrained area excavations have been able to reveal the structure of the oldest Ribe. The vital artery of the town was a street along the river, around which small tenement plots lying side-by-side were occupied by craftspeople and traders. The stratigraphic sequence in this area is still partially saturated and has preserved a large number of organic artefacts, including a quantity of wood for dendrochronological datings; however the layers both above it and below it have now deteriorated and do not contain preserved wood any longer. Thus there is a wet core in the stratigraphy that is in the process of breaking down.

The extent of the well-preserved series of layers has, up to now, been regarded as reflecting the extent of the street with the plots along the river (S. Jensen 1991b; Feveile 2006a). However a series of circumstances, which are reviewed below (section 5.3.3.1), indicate that to the south-west the stratigraphy of the 8th and 9th centuries was dug away in connexion with the establishment of the Outer Mill Stream, and that Nederdammen was originally part of the northern side of the river (Fig. 93).

The most recent excavations in Sct. Nicolaj Gade, in 2013, showed that the plots can be assumed to extend as far as Saltgade, and it is quite likely that they extend even further. During the replacement of drains in Sct. Peders Gade in 1960s there was found, according to the report of the workers, a quantity of goat horns in the layers: a type of find that occurs very frequently in the layers of the 8th and 9th centuries.[16] No archaeological recording was undertaken on that occasion.

To the south-west, the stratified sequence is bounded first by the Droveway, which, until the dam was constructed, crossed the river at this point, extending the line of Badstuegade. The heavily used crossing road lines have cut down into and removed the stratigraphy of the plots in the form of a hollow-way. The Droveway was flanked to the south-east by the flattened castle of the earlier Middle Ages which was first revealed in 1993 (Feveile 2006i). This significant structure covering 60 x 100 m must have occasioned extensive earth-shifting when it was established, and further damage will have taken place with the building of the town's first gasworks here in the 1860s.

Fig. 93. Excavations carried out down to 2016 are marked in yellow on the plan. The red zone shows the suggested extent of the stratified layers while the black lines show the course of the Droveway before the dam was built. In blue is marked the rampart beneath Ribes Vikinger *and the Outer Mill Stream. Aerial photograph of 2011 with additions by the author.*

The excavation of 1993 was able to demonstrate that the whole ground surface has now been dug away in this area; in some preserved cut features, however, finds of the 8th and 9th century were made, of precisely the kind that characterize the tenement plots and are only found in those contexts. We must, consequently, reckon that the street with the plots extended into this area too, although regrettably it is largely destroyed now. Further to the south-east there are no further sites of archaeological investigations until the Ribelund area is reached.

It was, therefore, proximity to the medieval town which meant that sections of the core element of the oldest Ribe, the street with its tenement plots, were sealed by the earlier Middle Ages so that excellent preservation was secured, while other parts were dug away even at that early date.

In the area behind the main street of the Viking Period, towards the north-west, there were three medieval parish churches, a nunnery and a leper hospital, together with a certain amount of housing. The area has also been cultivated – involving deep trenching – most recently for a while during the modern period. This has meant, on the whole, that only cut features are preserved in these areas, and only exceptionally remains of actual culture layers. As a rule-of-thumb, the groundworking seems, however, only to have affected the culture layers, as it was of no benefit to productivity to mix in the sandy subsoil. The situation in this part of Viking-period Ribe is therefore rather reminiscent of the situation out in an arable field: there is an overlying ploughsoil covering the natural subsoil with cut features.

5.2.2 The south side of the river, the medieval town

On the cathedral island there are medieval culture layers up to 5 m thick that have accumulated from around AD 1050 onwards (Plate 1). In the core of the town the thickness of these layers varies from 3 to 5 m and the layers become thinner out to the western and southern edges of the town. Our knowledge of this massive stratigraphical sequence is very limited on the whole, as the old heart of the town is still preserved and consists of historic protected buildings or buildings which merit such protection.

For the same reason, knowledge of what is still hidden in the depths beneath the town is also limited. If Ribe were now a large town, as in the case of all the other important medieval towns of Denmark, the majority of the large buildings would have gone, and new buildings with deep cellars as well as infrastructural projects would have destroyed and unearthed the secrets of the culture layers, whether that was done by earth-shifting machinery or archaeologists.

The high level of activity in the Middle Ages, especially the 12th and 13th centuries, produced most of the stratigraphied sequence (Fig. 94). Out in the streets, where many archaeological excavations have been undertaken, the sequence is usually simple, characterized by typically horizontal layers containing the remains of the earlier road decks (Søvsø 2006). On the occupied plots, where the number of archaeological excavations has been quite low, the situation is different. The stratigraphy here is characterized by a large number of pits, usually waste pits located

Fig. 94. Well-preserved culture layers. During the excavation in Grønnegade of 1955-6 large quantities of wood preserved in these layers were found from a depth of about a metre downwards. From a photograph in case ASR 52/64 Grønnegade.

Fig. 95. Decomposed culture layers. The excavation ASR 11 in Danielsen's Timber Yard in 1999-2000 in the western quarter of Ribe was concerned primarily with relatively degraded layers where, for instance, there was no longer any wood. At one stage in the process of decomposition of the layers they were reminiscent of the situation in Grønnegade (Fig. 94). ASR 11 Danielsen's Timber Yard.

up alongside a boundary, which have for the most part destroyed the earlier layers there. In many cases more than half of any occupied plot will have been destroyed by later, usually medieval, digging. For the same reasons, the old ground surface underneath the culture layers has also been extensively removed by later digging, and this inevitably makes it difficult to achieve any secure knowledge of the earliest use of the cathedral island. Only beneath Fiskergade and Skibbroen are there real sequences of deposits related to land reclamation undertaken in the 14th century (Kinch 1869, 554; I. Nielsen 1985, 114; T.B. Jensen 2011).

The sequence of layers survives in a highly variable state, and its condition is generally worse the further from the river, but there can also be more local circumstances which affect things (Fig. 95). In the streets, where the earliest sequence of layers is one of horizontal, organic layers, wood survives better than on the adjacent plots, affected as they are by cut features. On the whole, this archaeological *swamp* can be regarded as decomposing, and progressing towards a condition corresponding to that in the western town.

While the culture layers of the later Middle Ages are usually thin, and have frequently been removed either by later building work or cultivation, the situation is completely different for the sequence from the earlier Middle Ages. To a considerable extent this colossal series of layers has only marginally been impacted by later activities and is protected by a covering of culture layers 1 to 2 m thick. Within the medieval area of Denmark it is only in Lund and in Schleswig where similarly massive deposits are known, and their

potential in those towns has been demonstrated by a number of research or rescue excavations (Vogel 1989; S. Larsson 2000).

The three worst archaeological losses on the cathedral island came about, thought-provokingly, in connexion with restoration projects. Along with the comprehensive principal restoration of the cathedral in 1882-1904 there was extensive digging within and outside the church in the form of replacement of the foundations, the insertion of a heating system, and the widespread digging away of the entire cathedral square. These enormous undertakings were carried out with no archaeological presence from the authority in this field at the time, the National Museum. Only with the excavations alongside Ribe Cathedral in 2008-12 was it possible to determine the extent of the loss that caused (see section 5.9.8.3).

The restoration of Sct. Catharinæ Church, the former Dominican friary church, in 1918-32 also occasioned a massive amount of digging into the thick culture layers beneath the church building. This revealed, amongst other things, deep, filled up moats which are possibly remains of the royal court in Ribe (see section 5.11.3) but produced no documentation apart from a couple of lines in a notebook (*DK*, Ribe amt, 699).

Riberhus castle mound was restored in the years 1940-1. That involved the emptying out of the completely overgrown moat, which must have contained vast quantities of finds as well as vital information about the appearance of the medieval castle. This work, however, has left us relatively few finds and practically no documentation.

5.2.3 Summary, taphonomy

The remains of the oldest Ribe north of the river are very unevenly preserved, and vary within short distances from exceptionally fine preservation to complete loss. The explanation of these challenging circumstances has, of course, been a major challenge to research, and an understanding of the taphonomy must be the prism through which the archaeological data are interpreted.

In the case of the cathedral island the situation is completely different. To a great extent the earliest strata are still preserved beneath a thick, protective layer of later deposits. The high level of survival of the earliest culture layers of the cathedral island is exceptional within both Danish and international contexts, and is due to the fact that since the 17th century Ribe has not experienced any significant economic growth. This has helped to preserve the town and the stratigraphy below it. The negative consequence, however, is that our knowledge of the earliest state of affairs is limited, and we have to suppose that the culture layers of the cathedral island must still contain many archaeological surprises for the future.

5.3 The topography and hydrography of the area around the town

The first attempt to map out what the landscape of the area around the town would have looked like when Ribe emerged was undertaken through a programme of geological core sampling, which provided the foundation for a general reconstruction of the original landscape beneath the culture layers (Mertz 1977; I. Nielsen 1985, 26f). The Ribe River and the entire, artificial water system that surrounds the town have not attracted the same level of interest and attention but have been discussed in a number of minor studies (Edelberg & Bencard 1962; Kann 2001). Successive archaeological investigations have since been able to add many new details to our image of the topography and hydrography of the area of the town, leading to the reconstruction which is presented here.

Ribe owes its existence to the river and the sea, but both of these linked water zones have changed greatly since the earliest merchants made their way up the river around the year 700. As is the case with the development of vegetation in the region, there is a lack of palaeoenvironmental analyses of the wetlands which could provide information on how they developed; by integrating a range of archaeological and cultural historical sources, however, it is possible to produce a number of propositions about the appearance of the landscape around the town which in a number of instances will differ from the reconstructions produced by previous research (I. Nielsen 1985, 22ff; Feveile 2006a, 15ff).

5.3.1 The Droveway

Lines of barrows and traces of hollow-ways north and south of Ribe show that the Droveway must have been in existence since the Stone Age in some form or another (Fig. 50); whether or not the crossing of the river at Ribe goes that far back too, however, is not known. There are only a few preserved barrows around the Ribe Marsh, and the only indirect trace of the course of the road is a pit-strip – a defence work or boundary marker of the pre-Roman Iron Age – which was discovered in 2011 at Øster Vedsted, 1.5 km south of Ribe, excavation ASR 2423 (T.B. Jensen 2018). With caution, then, it can be inferred that, since the pre-Roman Iron Age at least, the Droveway has crossed the Ribe River at a location where the town was eventually to stand. In the 13th century a dam was constructed across the river (I. Nielsen 1985, 86ff). In the earlier Middle Ages, and possibly before then too, there may have been a bridge to connect the two parts of the town, but no traces of this have been found.

5.3.2 The Ribe River

The strong-flowing Ribe River runs through Ribe (Fig. 96). East of the town the watercourse splits into a number of tributaries which spread out like a fan over the central areas of southern Jutland. The watercourses drain an area of 940 sq km stretching all the way to the principal watershed of East Jutland, and the basin also provides the meadowlands over which the Farris Forest once extended (see section 4.2.7; Pilgaard 2009).

The Ribe River is recorded under that name, *Amnis Ripensis*, as early as 1294, while an alternative, relatively old name is Nibs River, after the miller Svend Nib who built the Middle Mill of the town in the first half of the 16th century (Kinch 1869, 1). The villages of Sønder and Nordre Farup on either side of the river west of Ribe may bear witness to an even earlier name, *Far Å*, meaning the river along which one can travel ('fare') or the navigable river. It may very well also have been the Far River which gave the Farris Forest its name. Until the Kammer (Chamber) Sluice was built in 1912 the river was tidal, and the water-level was governed by the astronomical and meteorological conditions. Exploitation of the tidal flow facilitated navigation up to the town and it was probably possible to reach the town on a single in-

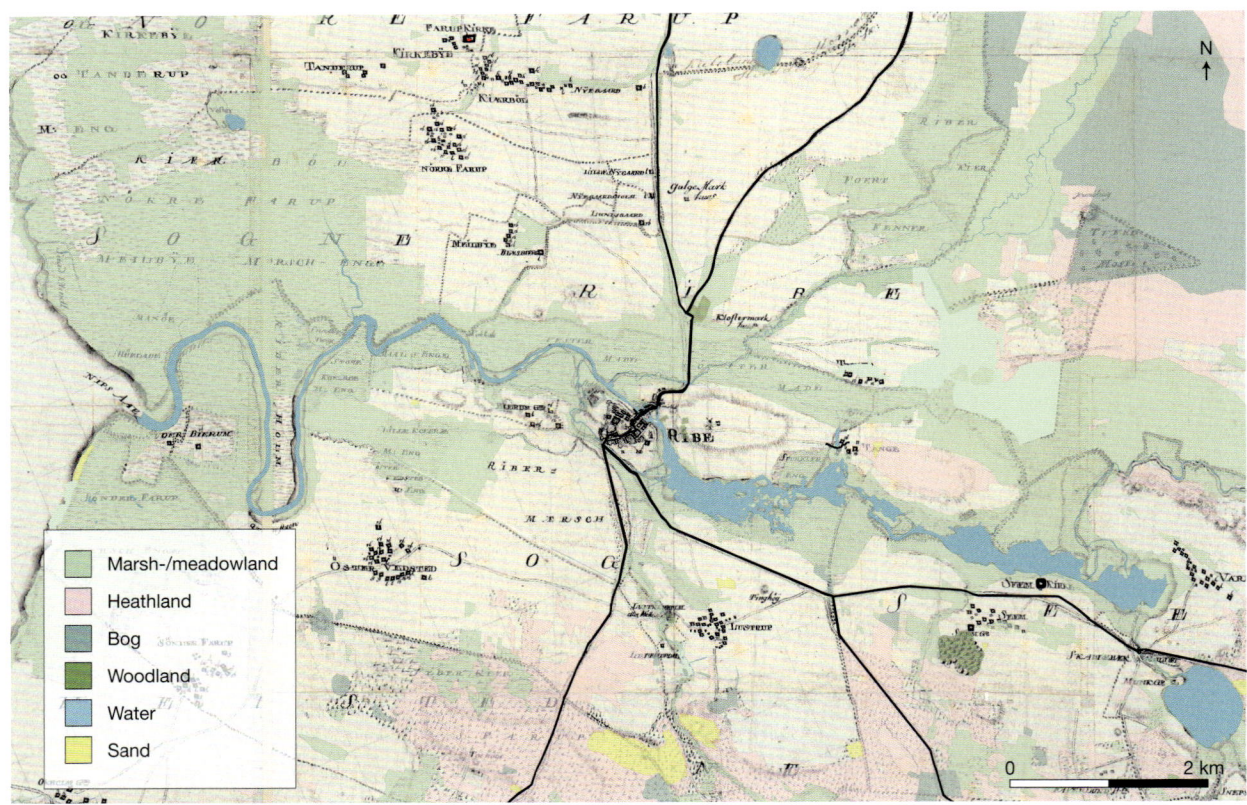

Fig. 96. Ribe is sited where the main land route of West Jutland, the Droveway, crosses the Ribe River. West of the town stretch the marsh flats while to the east there are extensive wetlands around the Ribe River. The base map is Videnskabernes Selskab's primary survey map of 1794 with the landscape classification added from the Original 1 cadastral map. From the original with the Geodata Agency with additions by the author.

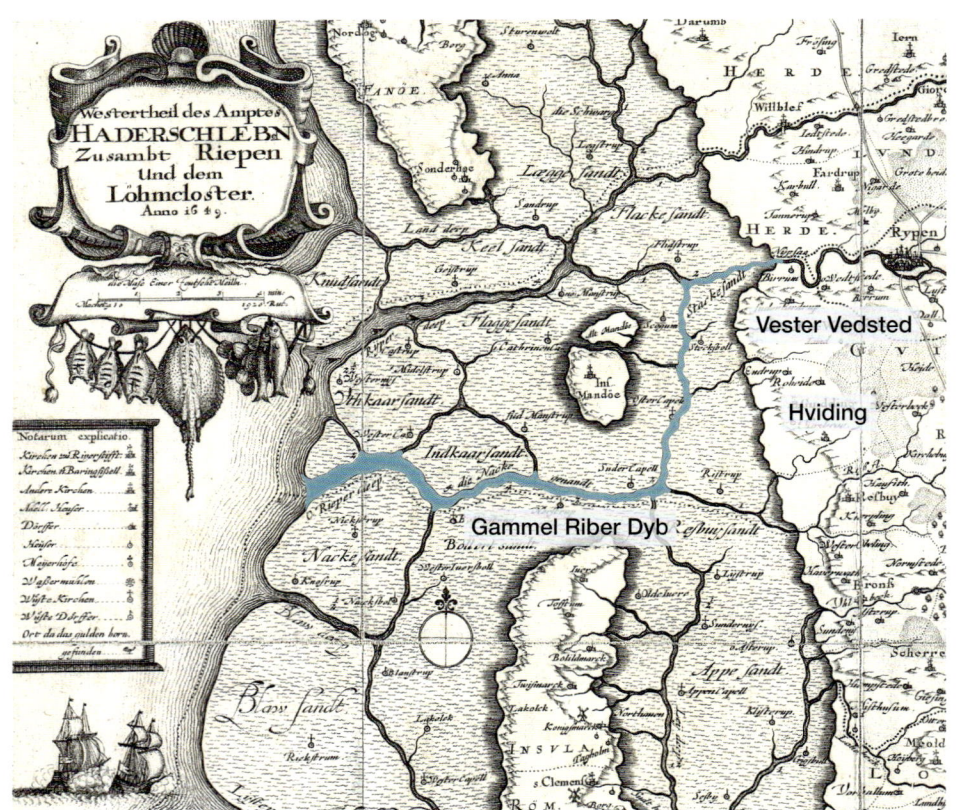

Fig. 97. On Johannes Mejer's map of 1649 Gammel Riber Dyb (Old Ribe Depth) is marked. The finds from Hviding and Okholm in Vester Vedsted indicate that the sailing route of the Viking Period also passed to the south of Mandø. Extract from the original in the Royal Library with additions by the author.

134

coming tide. This could also be the reason for Adam of Bremen's description of Ribe as lying upon a river *qui ab oceano influit*, 'which water flows into from the sea' (Skovgaard-Petersen 1981, 51).

5.3.2.1 The sailing route into Ribe, Ribe Western River and the marsh

The first traders who sailed in towards Ribe came in sailing ships of Frisian or Scandinavian types, the appearance of which is known from both wrecks and from pictorial evidence, especially on coins (Malmer 1966, 60ff, pl. 1). Each ship was a trading unit comprising both the ship and its crew, a storage space, and one or more merchants and/or craftsmen. Protection of the cargo in transit must have been the responsibility of the crew. For the same reason we have to suppose that the trading ships sailed up along the river and anchored or beached at the town itself where strict rules were in force. Only in the course of the Middle Ages did cargo ships become so large that they anchored, instead, out by the town harbourage and subsequent transportation into the town used trolleys or carts. In the period under discussion here, we can therefore assume that Ribe had a significant harbour where the sea-going ships landed, and that this structure must have been right alongside the town.

The Ribe River now flows north of Mandø, but until the 17th century the sailing route ran south of the island (Fig. 97). This is indicated, for one, by the place-name of Gammel Riber Dyb for this area but is also revealed by preserved chart information, and can be inferred indirectly from a privilege of 1292 which refers to the harbourage of Ribe town, which then extended as far north as the northern point of the Wadden Sea island of Sylt (Kinch 1869, 110; I. Nielsen 1985, 40). That the sailing route south of Mandø goes back even further in time is implied by Hviding Church, which lies alongside the entrance to Gammel Riber Dyb. In the 13th century this church was adorned with a striking double-tower façade, and one of the motives for its building may have been to create a seamark. Vester Vedsted Church was also provided with a tower as early as the Romanesque period, and together with the cathedral in Ribe they were able to protect and direct seafarers to a safe harbour.

The level of water in the river was formerly determined by the sea, the wind and the level of rainfall, and water was constantly overlying the surrounding marshlands which rose slowly because of the deposition of alluvial clay particles and silt (Thamdrup 1998). The rise was not chronologically consistent but must have been a function of sea-level: in periods with a rising water-level clay was deposited while in periods of stable or falling water-level the surface of the marsh may have been drier.

Another factor that influences the effective power of the sea is the sinking of the land, and such a phenomenon is well documented in geological studies while also clearly implicit in a series of archaeological observations made along the Wadden Sea coast. At the northern end of the Wadden Sea the lowest recorded level of prehistoric settlement both in the Varde River valley and around Esbjerg is slightly above 4 m over sea-level.[17] In the Ribe Marsh the lowest-lying settlements are found around 2.5 m over sea-level while in the Tønder Marsh one can find settlement sites at levels which were habitable in the Viking Period and earlier Middle Ages as low as just above 1 m over sea-level (Krants Larsen 2010, 30ff). The reducing settlement levels along the Wadden Sea coast continue further south, and must be the result of a consistent sinking of the land: isostasy.

Storm floods do not appear to have been a problem for Ribe before the second half of the Middle Ages. In the town itself, areas lying 2 m over sea-level could be occupied in the earlier Middle Ages, and down to around the year 1100 the main street of the town, Sønderportsgade, lay around 2.3 m over sea-level. This level coincides closely with observations from the geest edge around Ribe, where settlement is found down to around 2 m over sea-level, as in excavation ASR 440 Gl. Hviding. There is therefore little to suggest that storm floods were a problem in the period before AD 1362 but from then they appear to have become a growing threat as a result of both land-sinkage and worsening climatic conditions.

The sinking of the land also brought with it the deposition of clay, and it is possible to indicate the extent of this growth in the period from the middle of the 11th century to the present day. Beneath the culture layers in the town of Ribe there are sealed marsh surfaces in areas close to the river around 2 m over sea-level (Søvsø 2007a). From a series of investigations it is known that this surface was sealed by culture layers around the year 1100. The present marshland around Ribe, as it can be seen at Hovedengen, now has a surface around 2.5 m over sea-level (Thamdrup 1998) and there appears, therefore, to have been an accumulation of clay of around half-a-metre in the period from the 11th century to the establishment of the Kammer Sluice and the sea-wall in 1911-15 which stopped the sea from flooding the Ribe Marsh.

5.3.2.2 Ribe East River and Lake Varming

Upstream from Ribe, the Ribe East River is now entirely as shaped by the dam that was built across the river in the middle of the 13th century and which has been attributed with the decisive role in the formation of the extensive, lake-like area of wetland that now stretches all the way to Varming, 6 km east of Ribe (Fig.

98). There are, however, a number of factors which indicate that there was in fact already an elongated lake in this area before the dam was constructed, and that this is of significance for our understanding of the topography of Ribe in the period under discussion in this book.

The whole of the wetland around the East River consists of freshwater alluvium, and it must at some stage in prehistory have been a lake that the river flowed through. In more recent times, sedimentation in the area has been very extensive, as is clearly shown not only by written sources but also in older maps (Kann 2001; Mulvad & Søvsø 2011). The earlier presence of the lake is implied in the parish-name Seem, *the settlement by the lake* (Aa. Andersen 1998). This place-name belongs to the earliest stratum of names, which is believed to go back to the Iron Age, and Seem Church, which stands close to the East River, indicates that this lake was what is now the overgrown Ribe East River. In the field west of Seem Church a number of metal finds from the Late Iron Age, Viking Period and Middle Ages have been made, and excavations have also revealed settlement from the Late Roman or Early Germanic Iron Age close to the church: investigations ASR 1021, ASR 1327 and ASR 1328. The finds appear to show, therefore,

that the settlement of Seem can be traced back in approximately the same location to at least the middle of the 1st millennium AD.

The lake around Ribe East River may have been called Warmi. The place-name Varming is understood to mean *the barrow by Lake Warmi*, and it is tempting to identify the barrow referred to with the group of conspicuous prehistoric barrows which are still in situ alongside the road between Skallebæk and Varming (Fig. 98) (Aa. Andersen 1998). Nowadays, these constitute the most prominent heights in the area.

The obstruction of the flow within Ribe around the middle of the 13th century is usually supposed to be the real cause of the creation of the wetland of Ribe East River (Kann 2001, 64; I. Nielsen 1985, 28f). That the construction of the dam did have an impact is implicit in the settlement of 14 March 1255 when King Christoffer I promised compensation to Esger Bishop of Ribe for the meadows in Lustrup which the construction of the royal mill had flooded (Kinch 1869, 67).

Since the end of the Ice Age, the Ribe River has carried huge amounts of sediment in its flow. Studies from Storåen, a watercourse in West Jutland of around the same size and rate of flow as the Ribe River, have shown that during the 20th century around 25,000 cu

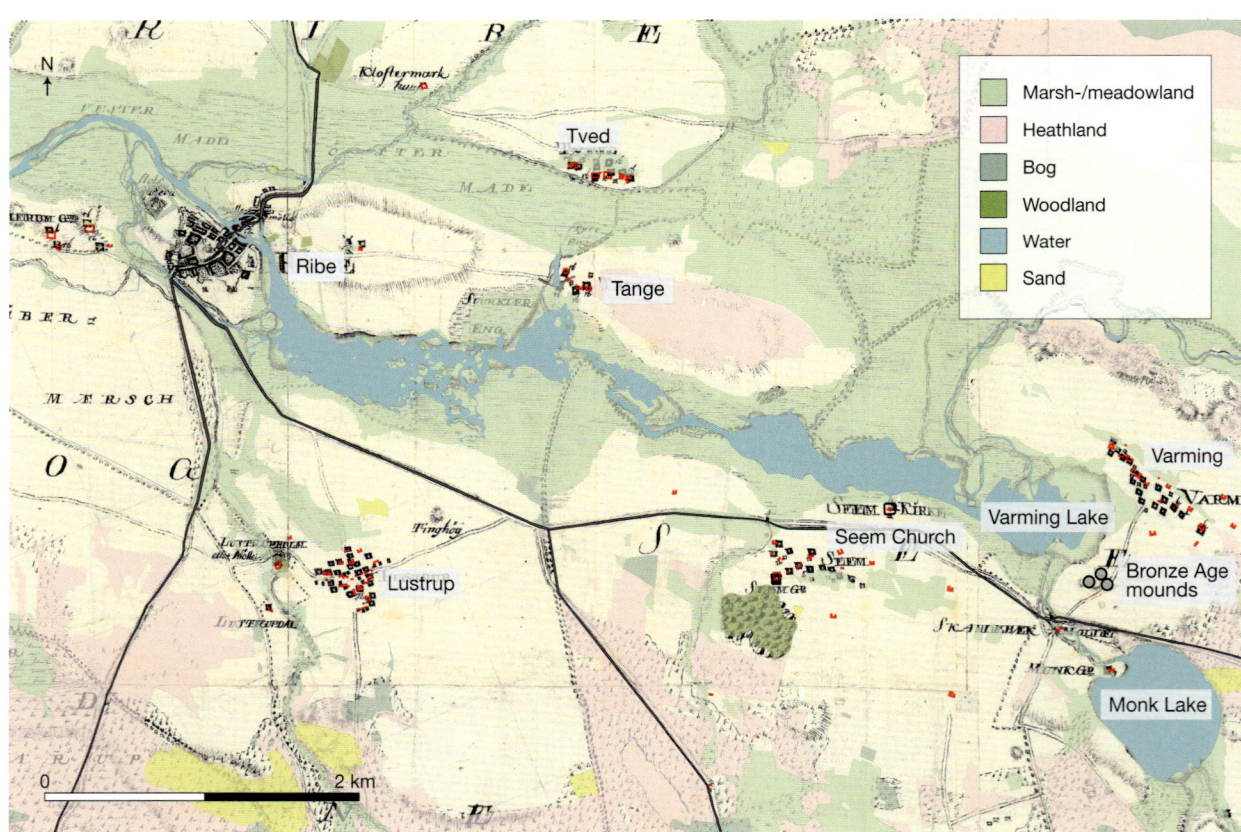

Fig. 98. The earlier lacustrine character of Ribe Østerå was still preserved around 1800 and has been overlaid upon Videnskabernes Selskab's primary survey map. Note the position of Seem Church.

m of sediment were deposited annually at the mouth of the river in Nissum Fjord, corresponding to an annual removal of 25 cu m per square kilometre in the area of drainage (Odgaard & Dalsgaard 2014). Comparable processes are in action in the Ribe River, and even if the assumed level of sedimentation is put at just half the rate that has been recorded in the case of Storåen in the 20th century it would still mean that through a period of a thousand years the Ribe River has deposited more than four metres of sediment in the whole of the former Lake Varming area.[18]

When Ribe first appeared, around the year 700, there was quite a substantial, extended lake immediately east of what would be the location of the town, upstream of the ford which crossed the river. The presence of this lake is of course significant in relation to the question of the earliest harbour facilities at Ribe. The lake would not only have provided ideal opportunities for turning ships but also a good place for anchorage. Where the lake adjoined the town is where we should look for the earliest harbour of Ribe.

5.3.3 The terrain beneath the culture layers of the town

If you walk around Ribe nowadays you are moving over the top of culture layers up to five metres thick, the majority of which were formed during the first two major periods of the town's history. On the north side of the Ribe River, beneath Sct. Nicolaj Gade, there are layers of the 8th and 9th centuries up to 2.5 m thick, while in other places on that side of the river there are layers several metres thick which accumulated in the course of the Middle Ages. On the cathedral side, south of the river, there are layers up to 5 m thick, mostly formed in the 11th-13th centuries. The reason for the accumulation of these enormous quantities of material is primarily the absence of renovation, while the thickness of layers at specific locations and the period in which they were formed are also determinative functions of both the key geographical and the key chronological phases in the history of the town. These culture layers completely disguise the original faces of the terrain, and the reconstruction of the original surface relief of the landscape has long been a crucial factor in research into Ribe's history. What did it look like when the first traders arrived here around the year 700? The first reconstruction carried out appeared in *Middelalderbyen Ribe* (Fig. 99) (I. Nielsen 1985, 28). The majority of the data used was from corings, many of them undertaken in the course of an engineering/geological investigation of the layers beneath Ribe (Mertz 1977). The mapped results showed a dramatically uneven landscape beneath the culture layers which in many places was

thought to contain low-lying areas with freshwater alluvia which were interpreted as blocked meander loops created by the watercourses in the period before the town appeared.

More recent archaeological studies in the town area have repeatedly shown that the results from these corings cannot be confirmed. In many cases anthropogenic culture layers, rubbish pits or wells have been identified as natural freshwater silts with radical misinterpretations as a result.

The archaeological investigations within the town area have laboriously, bit-by-bit, established a more secure set of basic data, on the basis of which it is possible to reconstruct the original topographical conditions beneath Ribe (Fig. 100) (Feveile 2006a). In very recent years the number of new observations has grown remarkably, and especially in the case of the areas by the river interpretations can be offered which differ substantially from earlier maps (Fig. 101).

5.3.3.1 The wetlands and watercourses

Around the drier islands which the suburbs of Ribe have expanded over there are wetlands in the form of sea-marshes that gradually give way to freshwater alluvia further inland towards the east. The relationship between these two forms of deposit is dynamic and complex, governed as it is by sea-activity, the sinking of the land, rainfall and more. Investigations beneath Ribe have shown that below the culture layers in the areas close to the river there are marsh flats with a surface around 2 m over sea-level that were deposited on top of heath-sand flats. As noted, at that level of 2 m over sea-level a number of investigations have revealed that this level was still habitable in the period under discussion here (Søvsø 2007a). 2 m over sea-level is therefore regarded as a more reliable indication of the boundary line between the drier land and the wetlands in respect of the period before the year 1200. One may therefore describe the later urban areas of Ribe as drier islands formed of sand which, up to 2 m over sea-level, were overlain with marsh and meadow formations. Later sinking of the land has moved the interface between the drier land and the wetlands up to around 2.5 m over sea-level.

The wetlands around the town contained four different watercourses which, listed in order of flow, are the Ribe River, the Tved River, Haulund Bæk and Kovad Grøft, all of which to a greater or lesser degree were managed for the benefit of the defence of the town and the operation of mills (Fig. 102). It has been suggested that the islands Mellemdammen and Nederdammen which form part of the dam in the Ribe River were originally parts of an inland delta within the river, but an excavation of 1994 showed that beneath Nederdammen there is a layer of clay more

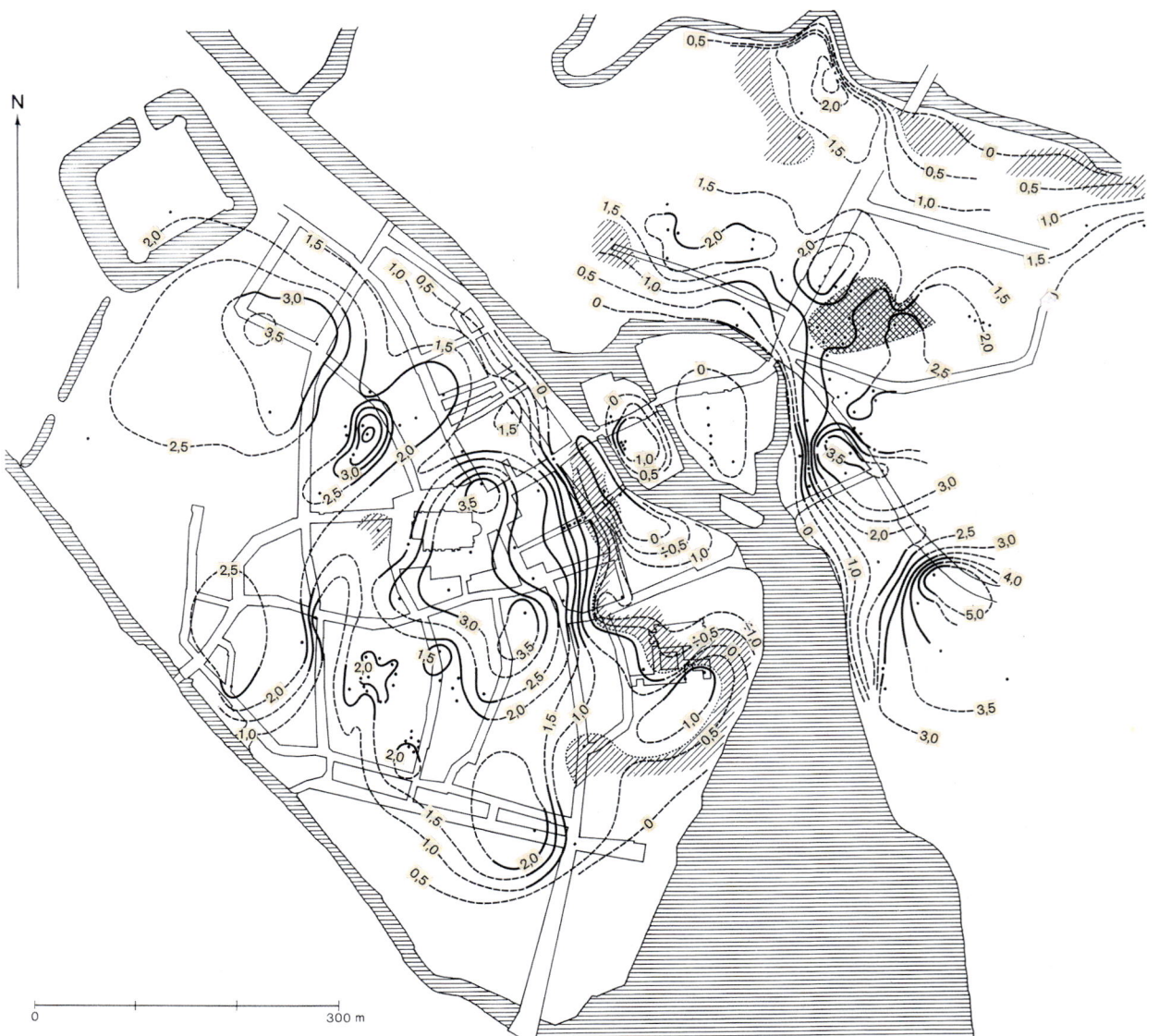

Fig. 99. On the basis of cored samples, the landscape beneath the culture layers was reconstructed in this manner in Middelalderbyen Ribe. After Nielsen 1985.

than 3 m thick which cannot have been deposited to form an island in an inland delta (I. Nielsen 1985, 79; H. Skov 1995).

One may rather draw attention to the remarkable fact that, in the Middle Ages, Mellemdammen and Nederdammen each belonged to separate parishes either side of the river: the cathedral parish of Our Lady and St Peter's (I. Nielsen 1985, 60). The most logical way to explain this situation must be that Nederdammen was originally part of the northern side of the river and was separated off by canalization in the course of the refortification of the town that took place in the second half of the 13th century (Søvsø 2010b). The sequence of layers in excavation ASR 7 in Sct. Nicolaj Gade 8 shows, indeed, that stratified layers of the 8th century are overlain by a dug-away level of the 13th century, and thus supports this proposition.

For this reason, evidence rather suggests that the Ribe River originally flowed between Mellemdammen and Nederdammen. When the Royal Mill was established shortly before 1255 the structure was located alongside a newly dug canal that created Mellemdammen. This developmental model is corroborated by the fact that the exit lock (frislusen) of the Middle Ages ran between Mellemdammen and Nederdammen (Kinch 1869, 471).

5.3.3.2 Paypyt and the digging away hypothesis

In the Landbook of Ribe Town of the mid-15th century, a wet area is referred to, *Paypyt*, the location of which can be narrowed down to the area east of Saltgade on the northern side of the Ribe River (Figs. 99-100) (I. Nielsen 1985, 81ff; Feveile 2006a, 19f).

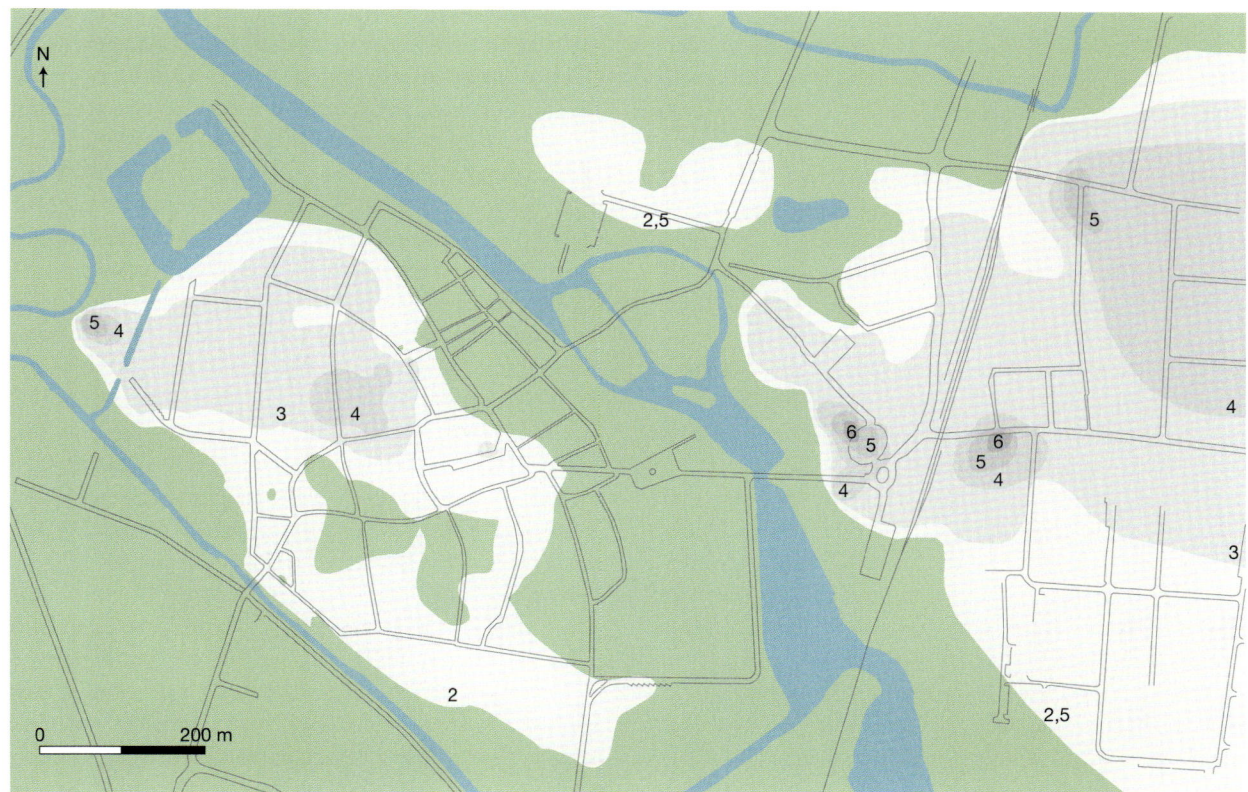

Fig. 100. Reconstruction of the form of the terrain based on information available in 2006. Levels below 2.5 m over sea-level are shown in green, and considered unsuitable for occupation. The contour levels of the drier land are given in figures. After Feveile 2006a.

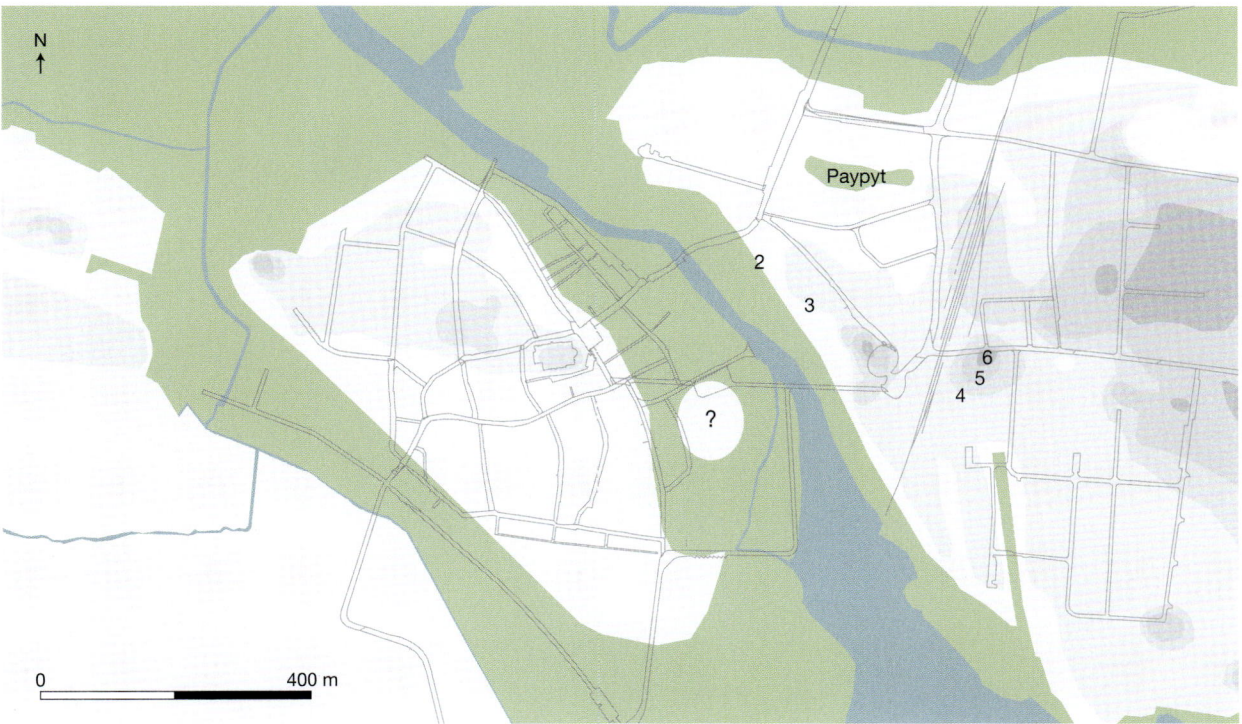

Fig. 101. Reconstruction of the form of the terrain and the course of the Ribe River based on information available in 2020. The green areas are those below 2 m over sea-level while the drier areas have contours in metres. The majority of the later town area both north and south of the river was relatively flat, with a surface varying from 2 to 4 m over sea-level.

The first element of the name means 'toad' and can hardly mean anything other than that there were frogs in the pit. Paypyt was the basis for a large-scale digging away hypothesis which was of consequence for archaeological research into this area and was proposed as the explanation of *the gap in the history of the town* – the apparent absence of archaeological remains from the Late Viking Period. The digging away hypothesis proposed that the deposits removed would have been used in the dam over the Ribe River, but this has found no confirmation in the stratigraphical sequences seen during later excavation in Overdammen, Mellemdammen and Nederdammen, and so must now be rejected (S. Jensen et al. 1982; 1983; H. Skov 1995; L. Andersen 1997).

The identification of Paypyt followed geological sample-coring (Nørnberg 1979). This revealed, at the bottom, a layer of peat up to 1.5 m over sea-level, the identification of which as a naturally formed deposit was not contradicted by its level. It thus appears probable that there had been a natural hollow in this area which became overgrown with peat during prehistoric times. The peat layer was overlain by a 'mud layer' which was understood to have been 'deposited in a waterhole with the character of a village pond' – and in this way Paypyt was discovered (I. Nielsen 1985, 81). Later cores and excavations identified the same 'mud layer' across an astonishingly large area, leading to the conception of the digging away hypothesis (S. Jensen et al. 1982; 1983). Through a series of trial excavations in

the Paypyt area subsoil in the form of yellow sand was found directly underneath the uniformly dark culture layer with no sign of the overlying podsol profile containing bleached sand and humus, and the area must then have been dug away.

The presence of the homogeneous mud-like layer in *Paypyt* can, however, also be explained in another way. In the course of excavations on the cathedral side, in the western part of Ribe, a number of major investigations have shown that the upper 1.0-1.5 m of the culture layers consisted of uniform, dark soil with no layering but with a large amount of brick included which showed clear signs of mechanical wear: excavations ASR 1015 Dagmargården, ASR 1200 Bakelitten, and ASR 11 Danielsen's Timber Yard. At the interface with the underlying culture layers, on several occasions, evidence of systematic deep trenching was found – a product of large-scale gardening activity in more recent times. Similar evidence of trenching was found in the excavation at Viborg Søndersø in 2001 (Thomsen 2005, 76ff).

The Paypyt area had been used in a similar way, and the so-called 'mud layer' in the area is suggested here to have been a similar deposit formed through intensive gardening in more recent times. In the excavation in Sct. Nicolaj Gade in 2010 the boundaries between these beds and the road area could be identified in several cases (Alrø Jensen 2013).

This perception of the formation of layers in the Paypyt area means that the stratigraphy of the youngest culture layers must be presumed to have been

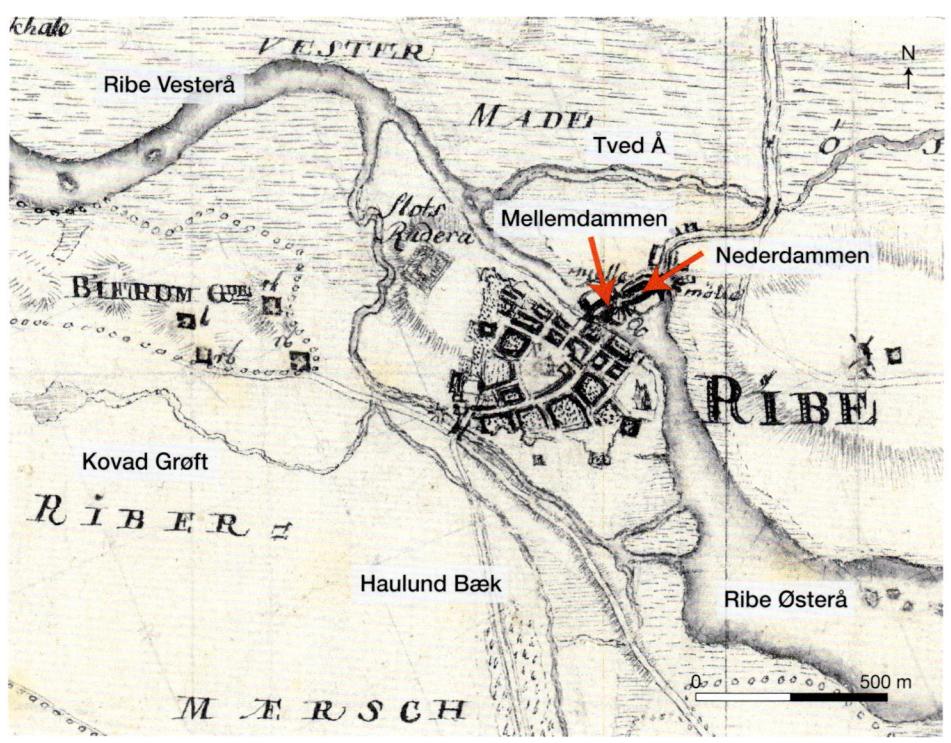

Fig. 102. The watercourses around Ribe as shown on Videnskabernes Selskab's primary survey map of 1794.

largely destroyed by the historically known gardening activity here. The trenching could have started as early as the Middle Ages, and continued through to the building over of the area in the course of the 19th century. The finds which were once within these layers must still be there, depending on the conditions for preservation. The course of events allows little of Paypyt itself to survive, but there appear to be no substantial culture layers deposited in the area east of Saltgade and north of Sct. Nicolaj Gade, and it is likely that this area, which coincides quite closely, in fact, with the original hollow, remained as a wet spot, *Paypyt*.

5.3.3.3 Driftsand

Wind-blown sand, known as 'driftsand', is a familiar feature of the West Jutlandic landscape. It has played a disproportionately large role in research into the earliest history of Ribe, because a massive driftsand deposit around Sct. Nicolaj Gade was for a time thought to have been put there by human intervention as part of a large-scale foundation of the market place (Jensen 1991b). Several scientific datings of the sealed vegetational surface below the layer of sand have shown, however, that this dune was formed around the beginning of the Christian Era (Dalsgaard 2006; Feveile 2006a, 21f). Since then, on both sides of the river, driftsand has been found beneath the culture layers of the town on several occasions (Figs. 103-4). In Albert Skeels Gade on the cathedral side even more layers of driftsand separated by culture layers of the earlier Middle Ages have been found (Fig. 104) (Post 2011, 49f). Outside of the town area there are also extensive areas of driftsand. The deposition of driftsand is therefore a dynamic process which has taken place on several occasions in the period from the Early Iron Age through to more modern times.

5.3.4 Summary: the original topography of the urban area beneath the culture layers

The arguments presented above form the basis for a reconstruction of the terrain underlying the town as presented in Figure 101. In comparison with earlier studies, 2 m over the present national sea-level is believed to be the most realistic line of division between wetlands and the habitable drier land in the period under discussion here. This means, as a result, that the habitable area has to be seen as considerably larger, and that the wet zone of Paypyt shrinks considerably, while Nederdammen is suggested to be an artificially constructed island on the northern side of the river. A major question concerns the natural ground conditions beneath the Dominican friary. Excavation

Fig. 103. Driftsand by Ribe Cathedral. The light grey layer beneath the skulls is driftsand deposited on top of a layer of humus. From a photograph in case ASR 2391 Ribe Domkirkeplads.

Fig. 104. Driftsand in the western quarter of Ribe. The light stripe in the middle of the picture is driftsand incorporated within a medieval stratigraphical sequence and therefore deposited sometime in the course of the earlier Middle Ages where Albert Skeels Gade is now located. From a photograph in case ASR 1988, kloakering, Ribes Vestby.

◄▼ *Fig. 105. The microliths and transverse arrowheads that were found in 2005 through the sieving of the layer of soil beneath the 4.5-m thick culture layer in front of the Old Town Hall in Ribe. 2:1. Excavation ASR 2090 von Støckens Plads. After Søvsø 2007a.*

around the friary buildings has revealed natural sand above 3 m over sea-level, and other investigations have shown this area to be completely surrounded by wet areas (Madsen et al. 1984, 63). If all of these conclusions are right, there must be a separate small island of heath sand underneath the friary.

5.4 Earlier activity below the area of the town

The earliest occupants of the town discovered were Stone-age hunters, traces of whose presence in the form of flint have been found during excavations in the cathedral area. The datable artefacts range in time from the Maglemose Culture to the Funnel Beaker Culture, and there seem to have been hunting stations here (Fig. 105). Scattered signs of settlement from the Neolithic or Early Bronze Age were recorded during excavation ASR 1357 but the earliest ancient features otherwise known from the town area so far are narrow ardmarks. These marks are known from a number of excavations on both sides of the river and in appearance closely match ardmarks found in association with 'Celtic fields' (Fig. 106). A dating to the period BC has been obtained from the excavation at the Post Office site, ASR 9 (Feveile 2006a, 24). It appears that extensive parts of the town area on either side of the river were cultivated fields in the Early Iron Age.

Through several excavations on both sides of the river it has been recorded that the ardmarks were overlain by another type of ploughmark consisting of wider furrows with a common orientation and regularly spaced (Fig. 106). These marks are interpreted here as those produced by a mouldboard plough and are surely evidence of the unsurprising state of affairs of the later urban area having been under the plough in the period from when the mouldboard plough was introduced in the Late Iron Age until it was sealed by culture layers (Agersnap Larsen 2015).

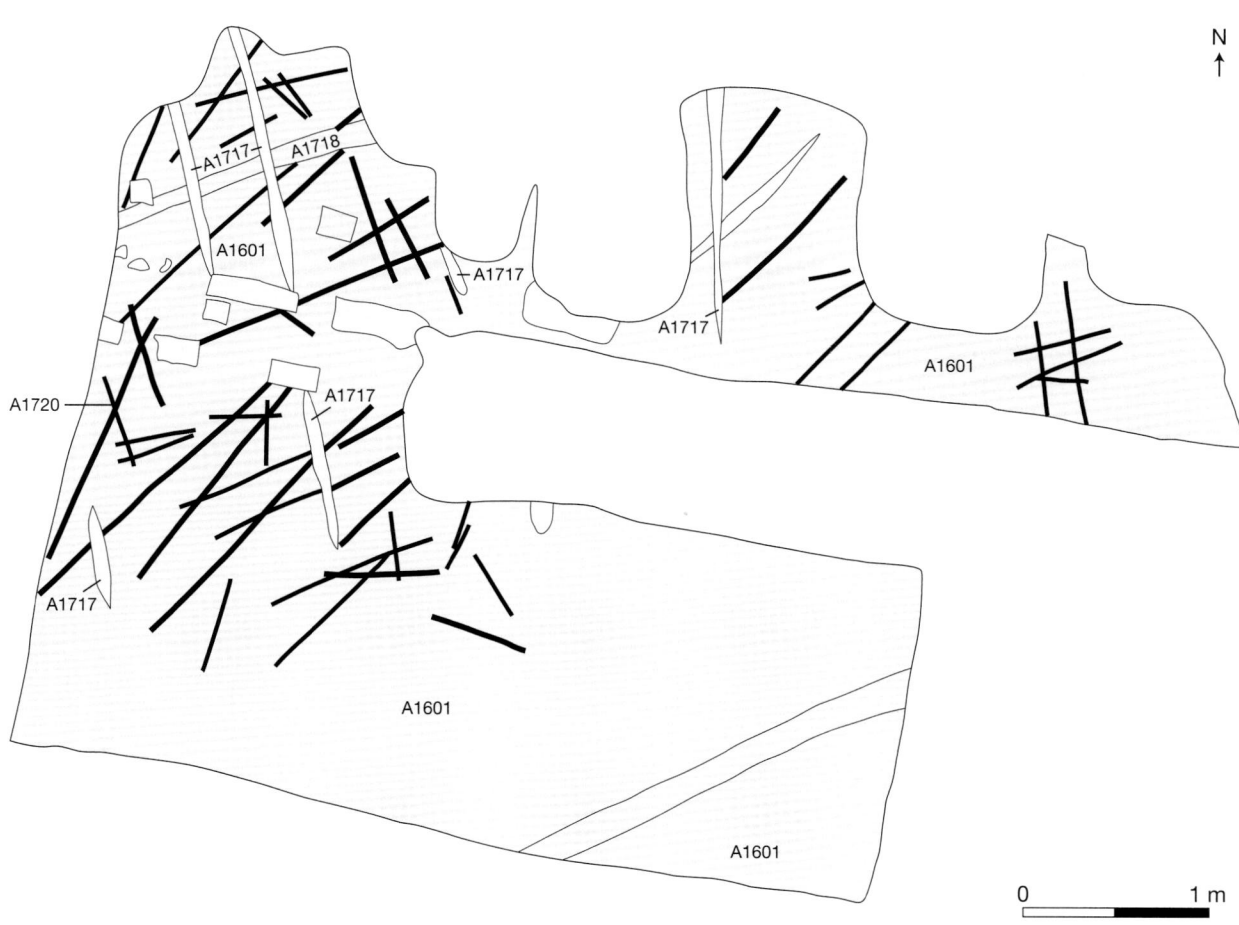

Fig. 106. Ploughmarks are often found at the interface between the soil layer and the underlying bleached sand below the culture layers of Ribe. The oldest are always ardmarks, thin lines of varying alignment (shown in black, A1720) which are overlain by wider marks that are regularly spaced and aligned — the marks of a mouldboard plough (A1717). Illustrated here from a preserved natural undersurface from the excavation under Danielsen's Timber Yard, ASR 11 T811.

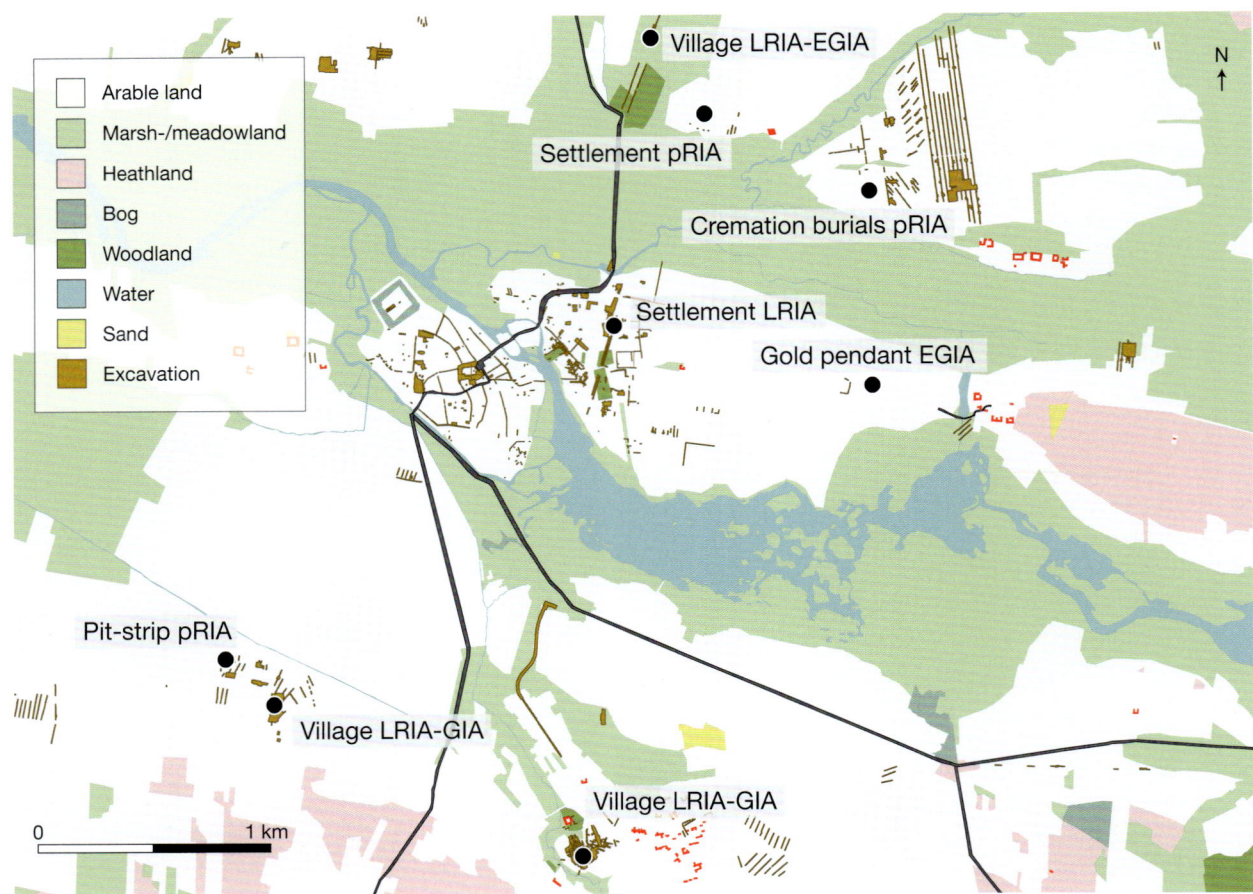

Fig. 107. Iron-age finds around Ribe from before AD 700. The distribution map has to be viewed in light of the excavations undertaken, which are marked in brown. pRIA = pre-Roman Iron Age; LRIA = Late Roman Iron Age; GIA = Germanic Iron Age; EGIA = Early Germanic Iron Age.

The mouldboard ploughmarks from a series of excavations all have *ante quem* datings determined by when they were succeeded by urban activities. During the excavations of the 1970s these wide ploughmarks were also supposed to have been produced by the ard, but on the basis of the most recent evidence this conclusion is now to be rejected (Bencard & Jørgensen 1990; Agersnap Larsen 2015). Down to the 1990s they were thought to have been produced by the first inhabitants from the town in its supposed village phase, but as the understanding of the earliest phases of the town has changed, this inference also has to be abandoned.

Viewed in the round, it has to be considered most likely that the wide ploughmarks derive in most case from the period preceding the establishment of the town, presumably the Germanic Iron Age, and it is typical that apparently there is evidence of only one or two ploughings at many sites where ploughmarks have been found.[19] This may either be due to the fact that there was a system of rotation with long periods of fallow or that the objective was to loosen the turf in order to make use of

it somewhere else. In any event they indicate that the later urban area was marginal in relation to the systems of cultivation and settlement structure of the relevant period.

The location of the farms from which this area was cultivated in the Early and Late Iron Ages is not known for certain (Fig. 107). The closest known settlement of the Early Iron Age has been discovered in Obbekjær-parken, exactly a kilometre north of the Sct. Nicolaj Gade, while a larger village of the Early Germanic Iron Age was situated by Øster Vedsted just two kilometres from Sct. Nicolaj Gade. Archaeological investigations were undertaken in advance of the laying out of the residential suburbs and industrial quarters of Ribe in the 20th century only on a very limited scale, and there may have been farms of the Iron Age here, and more, that we know nothing of now. In 2019, a village from the Late Roman and Early Germanic Iron Age was found just 1 km north of Ribe, case no. SJM 404. And the same year a post-built house of Late Roman-Early Germanic type excavated in 2016 on Rosen Allé within Ribe was C14-dated to Late Roman Iron Age, case SJM 348. However, these settlements were long gone before the emergence of Ribe. The roadway leading to the crossing point of the Ribe River must be assumed to have been been in continuous use.

Where the Droveway crosses the Konge River 7.5 km north of Ribe is the location of the two Brokær graves and the place-name Gredsted, *the place of sanctuary*, both of which imply a politico-religious central function for this place. This does not appear to have been the case in respect of Ribe, however, either from the testimony of the known place-name evidence or from the archaeological finds. This seems rather to have been a marginal agrarian zone in which there is not even any sign of the area having been attributed any particular significance in the form of votive deposition or burials. The later urban area was presumably heath or pasture when the first traders came there.

There is just one stray find which is earlier in date than the town from the later urban area, in the form of a small gold pendant of the Early Germanic Iron Age found at Tange (Figs. 107-8). The circumstances of the find do not permit any further conclusions to be drawn, but there could possibly be some religious connexion between this find and the gold armrings that were deposited some four to five centuries later in the wetlands slightly further north (see section 5.10.5).

5.5 Methods of excavation and recording

Before the archaeological evidence is presented, it will be helpful briefly to outline the various methods of excavation and recording that have been used for the Ribe excavations to date, and to give a short account of the funding of the excavations. Both aspects are essential keys to understanding why the archaeology of Ribe is not directly comparable with that of, for instance, the archaeology of the other Scandinavian Viking towns.

After the discovery of the earliest Ribe in 1972, comprehensive research excavations were carried out under the direction of Mogens Bencard in 1973-5. The two open area excavations ASR 5M74 Dommerhaven and ASR 4M75 Kunstmuseets have proceeded by means of the excavation of 10-cm spits within a fixed grid system (Fig. 109), like the methods employed in Kurt Schietzel's excavations at Hedeby. This artificial stratigraphy would have been suitable if the layers are horizontal, but in both of the excavations in Ribe the layers slope slightly, and in combination with a range of variations within the layers as a result of cut features and decomposition this meant that the digging did

Fig. 108. A gold pendant of the Early Germanic Iron Age found in 1878 in 'the gravel on the Tange road': see Figure 107. NM C3215. SB no. 190409-104. 2:1. Photo: Laila Malene Pedersen & Kirsten Lindhard, Nationalmuseet.

not end up following the stratigraphy, with all of the problems that then ensue.

In terms of recording, a series of capital letters were used as codes (A, B, C… AA, AB, AC etc) to label all of the excavation data: plans, profiles and sections, the individual units of the grid, and the stratigraphical entitities excavated in the form of layers or features. The finds from the individual grid blocks were labelled using the letter code of the segment and the level, which it was sought later to correlate with the layers in the sections.

The finds were registered in the museum's overall, continuous, accession register, which at that time was sub-divided chronologically into A: Stone Age; B: Bronze Age; C: Iron Age; D: Middle Ages; E: Modern Period. Presumably with the objective of at least keeping the finds in a single register, D-numbers were selected for all of the finds that were progressively recorded. The finds from the separate excavations thus do not form continuous numbered series but are mixed up in relation to the sequence in which they were recorded, which in turn was dependent upon conservation, staffing, and other circumstances. The decisions made in respect of cataloguing meant that forming an overview of the finds, and of their relationship with the stratigraphy, was particularly difficult. This problem was only resolved with the digitization of the information in the catalogues in the museum finds database, which did not come about until the publications of *Ribe Excavations 1970-76* were completed.

In the publication of the excavations of the 1970s it was attempted, to some extent, to hide the unstratigraphical, mechanical method of excavation, which appears in only an introductory and otherwise marginal place in the presentation of the excavations themselves (Bencard & Jørgensen 1990). This

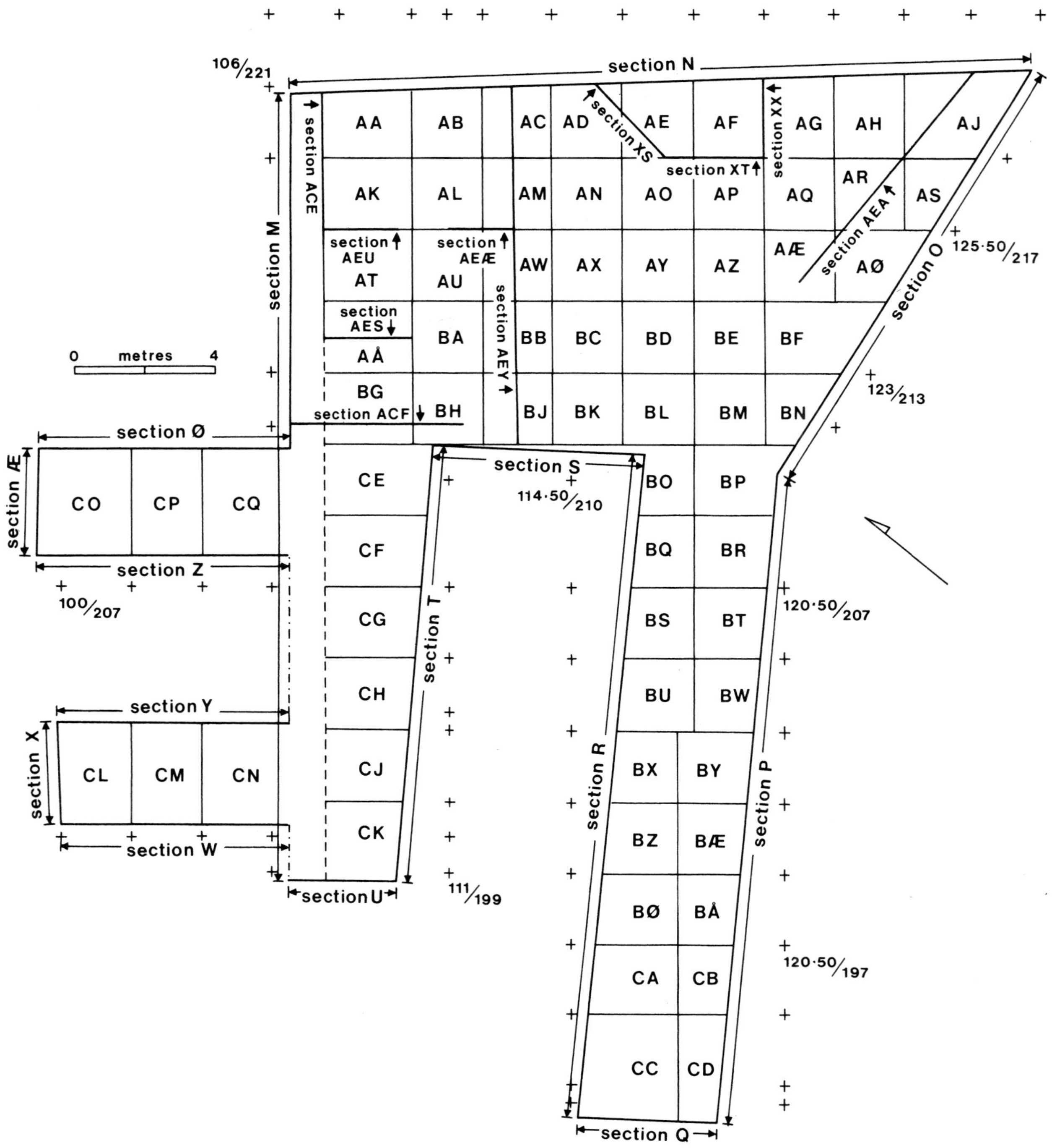

Fig. 109. The grid system used for the excavation in Kunstmuseets Have, ASR 4M75. After Bencard & Jørgensen 1990, p. 88.

is a shame in a way, because the grid system offers admirable opportunities to work on the distribution of finds for instance – but amongst the many contributions across the six volumes only two authors make use of this (Brinch Madsen 1984; 2004; Feveile 2010).

With the appointment of Stig Jensen in 1980 the museum moved over to the present model of cataloguing, in which all finds are given an x-number which is linked to an archaeological context, which

in turn is linked to a journal number: typically an excavation. The recording system thus began for the first time to correspond with the stratigraphically based model of excavation, and this structure has been maintained since then. The change coincided with the introduction of the stratigraphical method of excavation in the museum by Ole Schiørring and Per Kristian Madsen, and meant that both post-excavation work and the publication of the excavations became considerably easier.

While Bencard's research excavations were relatively well funded, that was the case only for some of the later rescue excavations, which were normally financed by Ribe Kommune (municipality) or the State Antiquary, depending entirely upon whether the developer was public or private. In a few cases research excavations were carried out that were paid for by the museum. In most cases the money available was not much in comparison with the extent and complexity of the archaeology. This rarely had a clear impact on the fieldwork itself but did lead to decisions to exclude certain additional procedures such as laboratory analyses: dendrochronological datings, radiocarbon datings, physical anthropological examinations, material analyses, etc. In these respects the archaeology of Ribe is still under-studied.

Since the Grønnegade excavation of 1955-6 it has been clear that the extraordinary volume of finds from the culture layers of the town posed a particular challenge. In the 'analogue age' it was attempted to cope with this challenge through card-record systems, but with the appearance of databases there were new opportunities to develop digital systems for the classification and analysis of the huge quantities of evidence (Tab. 3).

The museum's first database was developed in connexion with excavation ASR 7 in 1986 by an IT specialist who was married to someone who was involved in the excavations. The DOS system with the name *Dbase2* was adapted in a bespoke manner to the finds from this particular excavation, which came to inspire the next database, *Ribefund*, developed in 1991 for the management and recording of the large amounts of finds from excavation ASR 9 Posthuset. The database, programmed in the Danish-developed *DSI* of Dansk System Industri, was developed by Claus Feveile in collaboration with an IT-qualified acquaintance. Several other excavations were also subsequently recorded in this database.

On the basis of good experiences with this digital cataloguing, the next major step was the development of an all-in case-management and artefact database covering the whole museum: both archaeology and more recent history. Work on this was undertaken in 1998-9, again with Claus Feveile and his colleague in IT as the driving forces. The result, *ASR SYS*, came into operation in 2000. After that, a large-scale digitization of the museum's analogue data was launched. Case archives, find registers, blue cards and finds lists were typed into the database: a comprehensive process that continued to the year 2006 and was linked to the transfer of the museum collection to the newly built store which also opened in 2006. Since then the information in the database has been linked to the actual objects in the store and in the exhibitions, a job that is every bit as extensive and is still underway, and which will lead to the situation in which at individual find level there is a 1:1 relationship between the information in the database and the collection's physical contents.

Within the database, the archaeological objects are classified according to material in a hierarchical classificational tree, the purpose of which is to serve as a precise and operational mirror of archaeological reality and the research tradition. The types defined in the database are intended to coincide with the research tradition of the field in question, a straightforward matter in some cases but difficult in others. A guiding principle has also been that transparency and user-friendliness should not be sacrificed in favour of a largely incommunicable atomization into innumerable sub-types.

When ASR SYS was implemented in 2000 the programming language DSI was already out-of-date, a problem which became more and more serious as time went on. The difficult circumstances of the museum's fusion in 2008 imposed a temporary stop on plans to convert the data to another platform, but in 2013 the opportunity arose to upgrade to an up-to-date *.net* platform, which came into operation on 25 January 2014 as *SJM SYS*, linked via web-services to the national register *Regin*. The museum side of the work of development and conversion was on this occasion undertaken by the present author, while the technical side of the task was dealt with by the IT-trained amateur archaeologist Henrik Brinch Christiansen.

The present database therefore is the product of developmental work which, with breaks, has been ongoing since the 1980s and has been achieved at very limited cost by the staff of the museum in cooperation with IT-skilled acquaintances. Despite that, an all-embracing retrospective digitization of the museum collection has been successfully put in to a database structure which is defined by research questions. This probably makes this museum's collection without parallel the best recorded and most readily accessible archaeological collection in Denmark – a level of accessibility which is reflected in the comprehensive publication of evidence in *Ribe Studier I.1* and *I.2* as well as in a wide range of other research studies and collaborative work both within Denmark and overseas. In 2019 the entire archaeological collection including more than 100,000 photos was made accessible on line at http://sol.sydvestjyskemuseer.dk

This thorough cataloguing of the museum collection is also a key precondition for the work on the present book, which has been able to work up and down through the huge archaeological archives of the museum without difficulty.

5.6 Chronological schemes

Following Mogens Bencard's excavations down to 1976, an initial scheme of phasing of the stratigraphy on the tenement plots was constructed, although the structure of the latter was not yet known then. The stratigraphical sequence was divided into four phases:

- "Phase 1 is the natural ground surface. Plough-marks have been seen with this."

- "Phase 2 is essentially a midden layer, the principal content of which is more or less decomposed animal dung mixed with waste from settlement activities."

- "Phase 3 consists of series of workshop layers, from activity which was carried out in the open air (or in tents?)."

- "Phase 4 is a midden layer which has completely mineralized. Above this come layers from the Middle Ages and Modern Period."

"The dating of this entire phased stratigraphical sequence is assigned to the period 725-800." (Bencard 1981, 17)

On the basis of Stig Jensen's excavation in Sct. Nicolaj Gade 8, ASR 7, in 1985-6, a new phasing was developed which incorporated the newly recognized plot divisions, in which the layers in the tenement plots were assigned to six 'workshop horizons' (VH 1-6) while the layers in the boundary ditches were divided into two phases (G1-G2) (Fig. 110) (Frandsen & Jensen 1988).

Following a debate with Stig Jensen, Mogens Bencard added, without arguing the case specifically, a phase 1A and also pushed the start date back to AD 704-10 after the dendrochronological dating of well NS had been undertaken (Bencard 1990; Bencard & Jørgensen 1990, 22).

The Post Office excavation of 1990-1 led to the construction of yet a further phase scheme based upon the most thorough stratigraphical sequence to date, which could be underpinned with a series of absolute dendrochronological dates (Tab. 7) (Feveile & Jensen 2000).

With the benefit of this, Bencard adjusted his chronology once more (Bencard 2004). Most recently, Claus Feveile has attempted to correlate the chronological schemes without linking them up directly to absolute dates (Tab. 8) (Feveile 2006a).

The sequence of layers on the plots includes a number of recurrent features relating to the physical structure of the layers and their visual appearance. A lower core of the sequence can be particularly well preserved and has become Bencard's phase 2/ Posthuset phase C. The layers below this are markedly less well preserved, as is also the case with the layers above it. Towards the top of the sequence of layers the stratigraphy becomes more and more affected by bioturbation and more recent disturbance.

All of the circumstances referred to above are taphonomical in character, and involve post-depositional processes. The best preserved core of the stratigraphy can itself vary in exent within a single excavation, and it is consequently hazardous to argue for a close inter-relationship between the stratigraphically based chronology of the Post Office site excavations

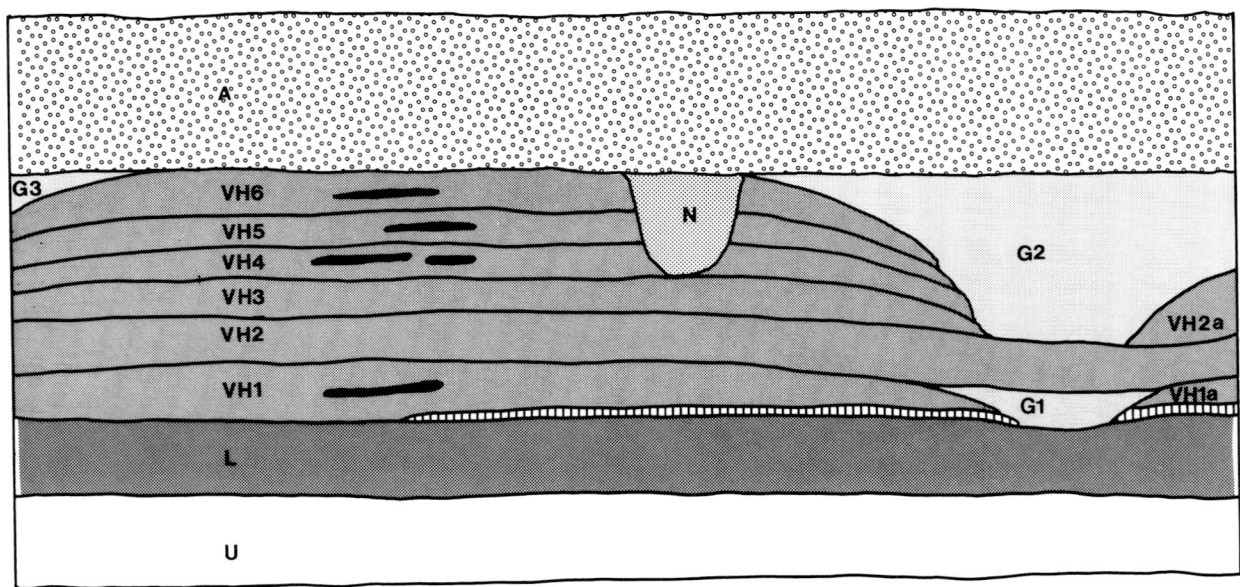

Fig. 110. The phasing scheme from excavation ASR 7, Sct. Nicolaj Gade 8. After Frandsen & Jensen 1987.

Period	Phases	Dating	Sceattas <> W/M	Sceattas = W/M (fig. 7a)	Dirhems, Arabic (note 10)	"Hedeby"-coins (fig. 7b)	Byzantine lead seal c. 840 (fig. 7c)	Muschelgrus (fig. 8a)	Badorf (fig. 8b)	Relief Band (fig. 8c)	Type N (fig. 10a)	Ribe 9 (fig. 10b)	Berdal brooch (fig. 10c)	Equal-armed brooch (fig. 10d)	Round brooch (fig. 10e)	Sword-guard-shaped brooch (fig. 10f)	Rectangular brooch (fig. 10g)	Phases
	J	12.-13. Årh.						1					3					J
Viking Age	H and I	820-850				>5	1	21	17	5			161	11	2	1	19	H and I
Viking Age	G	800-820		2				37	2	2		1	120	40	9	4	3	G
Viking Age	F	790-800		4				45	2			12	81	2	2			F
Late Germanic Iron Age	E	780-790	1	7	>4			33				11	2					E
Late Germanic Iron Age	D	760-780	2	5				5			3							D
Late Germanic Iron Age	C	725-760		16							12							C
Late Germanic Iron Age	B	705-725	7	2														B
	A AA																	A AA

Table 7. The phasing of the stratigraphical sequence from the 8th–9th centuries in phases from AA–J constructed on the basis of excavation ASR 9 Posthuset. After Feveile & Jensen 2000.

and that of the 1970s excavations. Not least in light of the artificial stratigraphy of the 1970s excavations a connexion can never be more than approximate. Only the stratigraphically directed excavations ASR 7, Sct. Nicolaj Gade, and ASR 9, Posthuset, can be used for fine-grained schemes of phasing, and since only the Post Office site has produced absolute dendro-chronological datings that is basically the only one which can be used for a calendrically dated phasing. As pointed out above, however, a range of taphonomic factors prevent this chronology being extended over the remainder of the stratigraphy of the plots.

These circumstances are the reason why the following presentation is not based upon the phasing of the Post Office site but rather follows more broadly defined periods in the form of round centuries.

MB 1973-76	LBF/SJ 1985-86	CF/SJ 1990-91
4	G2	H/I
		G
3		F
	VH3-6 + VH2a	E
		D
2	VH2	C
1a	G1 + VH1	B
	L	
		A
1		AA

Table 8. Diagrammatic comparison of the three chronological schemes found in publications on 8th- and 9th-century Ribe. After Feveile 2006a.

5.7 The principles for the presentation of archaeological evidence: inclusion and exclusion

The archaeological evidence from Ribe is overwhelmingly large, and could provide material for many books. In the following, I have decided to focus upon the archaeological features and only to a lesser extent upon the massive finds assemblage, except for coins. The principal focus will lie upon the archaeological structures and what their excavation can reveal about the town of Ribe and its development. The presentation is chronologically progressive, except for the section on the excavations at Ribe Cathedral, which are described as a unit.

5.8 Ribe in the 8th century

5.8.1 The foundation of Ribe?

In what would later be the area of the town on the northern side of the Ribe River, it is only in the limited areas where the stratigraphy is intact that the original ground surface is also preserved. In other areas it has been lost through cultivation, or dug away. There are, therefore, only minor patches which have been able to provide information on the earliest activities. However, since excavations in the intact stratigraphy also include the area immediately around the course of the Droveway which, all other things being equal, has to be considered the core of the settlement as it is where land and water traffic met, it seems probable that those really *are* the earliest traces if Ribe that have been found in the excavations around Sct. Nicolaj Gade (Fig. 111).

These traces comprise a series of so-called 'irregular ditches', the alignment of which differs from the later 'regular plots' (Feveile 2006a). The function of the irregular ditches is unexplained, but they could reflect some form of ad hoc, pragmatic division of the area. Within the ditches and scattered across the patchily preserved ground surface a small number of finds have been made which include the remains of a glass-bead workshop, sherds of blown

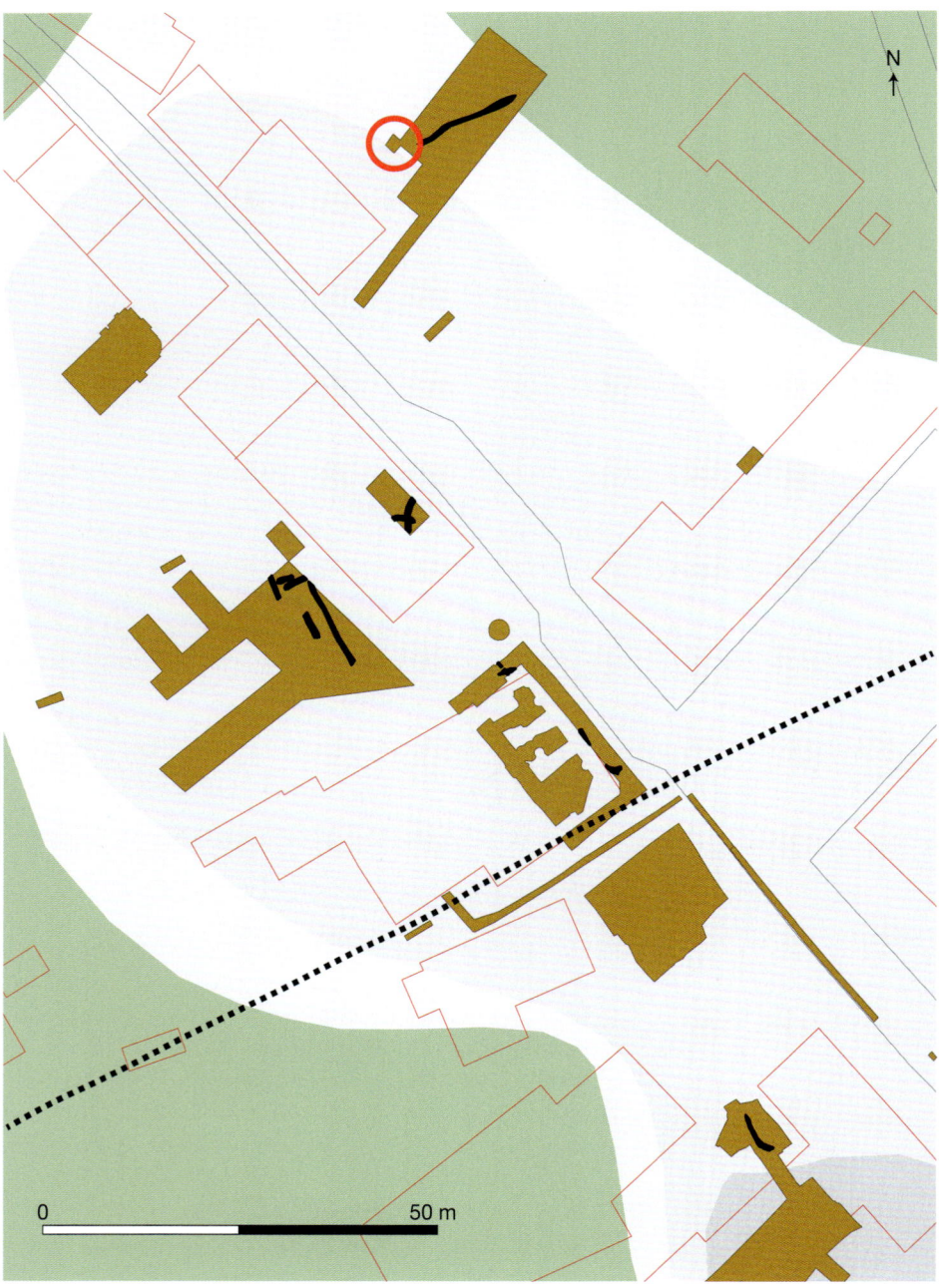

Fig. 111. The so-called 'irregular ditches' (in black) constitute the first identified traces of land division in the trading area on the bank of the Ribe River. The red ring marks the position of well NS of c. AD 704 while the dotted line marks the postulated course of the Droveway. After Feveile 2006a with additions by the author.

glass, a basalt quernstone, and some evidence of combmaking in the form of red deer antler with saw-marks (Feveile 2006a, 24). Both trade and skilled craft were therefore present as primary activities from the very start in Ribe, although not at a volume that produced a distinct culture layer. No remains of structures from the earliest phases have been identified, and it can be postulated that this was a seasonal activity, with the visitors living in tents they brought with them or, in the case of the traders, perhaps in their own ships.

If the hypothesis that the harbour of Ribe is to be sought on the shores of the lake to the east is correct, one must suppose that this was also the ideal place for the first ships to moor at. What follows from this is that there should have been some activity across in the whole area towards the harbour in the earliest period but that the scattered traces in these areas have been destroyed by later interventions (see section 5.2, Taphonomy).

When this all began we do not know. The earliest dating we have so far is from a well, NS, excavated in Dommerhaven in 1974. From stratigraphical evidence this must have been constructed from the ground surface and so belong to the original phase. In structural terms the well consisted of an originally c. 1.5-m deep pit in the base of which was set a four-sided, laft-jointed framework of radially split timbers which must have reached up to the original surface, possibly secured at an upper level too by a frame similar to that at the base, producing a four-sided, wooden-lined well-shaft.

Only on two sides of the well were there vertical timbers still more or less in situ, and the remainder must have been removed when the well was decommissioned; not an unusual phenomenon, and one confirmed by the fact that loose timbers from the well-shaft were also found a little higher in the fill.

Excavation photographs show that the timber had bark on and thus was presumably newly felled. Unfortunately the subsequent fate of this bark in the process leading to the timber's dendrochronological dating is unknown. Three pieces of vertical timber that had not been re-used were dated (K. Christensen 1990). All three of these had sapwood but no longer any identifiable bark. Two of the pieces were apparently from the same tree and had a terminal ring of AD 695 while the other had a terminal ring of AD 704. The well must therefore have been constructed in 704 or in the years immediately after that. Amongst the vertical timbers of the well were four former barrel staves, all lacking sapwood, which were also dated. The terminal rings of the heartwood lay between AD 660 and AD 679, and with the removed sapwood added in the felling year could be set at *hardly before 707*. We do not know if the barrel staves were parts of

the original construction of the well or a later repair, but the latter seems likely. Since there was more than 1.5 m from the water-level in the well to the ground surface one must presume that the barrel staves were also originally of this length or more, like the large barrels of around 800 litres that are known from Dorestad (Eckstein 1978). After first having been provenanced to Niedersachsen, more recent studies have been able to fix the source of the barrel staves in the Upper Rhineland: the region around Mainz (Bencard & Jørgensen 1990, 59; Daly 2007, 159f). The well was abandoned, some of the timbering pulled up, and the cavity filled before or at the transition to Mogens Bencard's phase 2, corresponding to Posthuset phase C, around the year 725.

Well NS thus reveals a number of striking points about early Ribe. For one, the construction of the well itself shows that even at this date there was investment in a permanent water supply despite the fact that the river was adjacent. All other things being equal, this indicates that activities went on for weeks or months rather than merely for days – if they were not, in fact, permanent. At the same time we can see that a large barrel from the Upper Rhineland reached Ribe early in the 8th century and ended up as re-used timber in a well.

There is no guarantee that well NS also dates the first visit made by traders to Ribe, and there is nothing therefore to prove that the earliest such visits could not have taken place before the year 700. *Around the year 700* must therefore remain the best suggestion for the date of the emergence of the trading site. At that date the emporia were already *old news* in north-western Europe. Dorestad and a number of other major sites both on the Continent and in Britain had been functioning for decades within the frameworks of various political systems. The networks of agreements and customs which linked the traders together and which contributed to the formation of a particular urban material culture were well developed. The elite of southern Scandinavia in the period up to the year 700 can hardly have been ignorant of a site such as Dorestad and probably had had contact with the growing trade network either directly or through agents.

The topographical study above has suggested that Ribe is located at a natural node for communication, where land- and water-borne traffic were able to meet, but that there is little to suggest that there was any prior use of the town area itself for anything other than traffic. Current knowledge rather indicates that a local elite had been resident in the area south of Ribe since the Early Iron Age. The first visits of the traders can hardly have taken place without the consent of the local elite, and the outcome for the traders must also have been strongly dependent upon the goodwill

of this local elite. One may presume, therefore, that the origin of Ribe was based in an agreement between one or more agents in the trading network of the emporia and the 'Dankirke dynasty', but whether the first visit took place on the initiative of one party or the other will probably never be known. It appears to be firmly supported by the archaeological data that the origins of Ribe were modest, and not the product of any large-scale initiative.

An alternative possibility is that a major regional power, possibly even a king, was responsible. There is no reason from the archaeological evidence to reject this possibility either, although there appear to be no unambiguous archaeological or historical sources which imply the existence of a royal power in this area before somewhat later in the 8th century (Näsman 2006). Should further research produce new archaeological data that might point towards the

◀▼ *Fig. 112. Well NS during excavation in 1974. Plan below. After Bencard & Jørgensen 1990.*

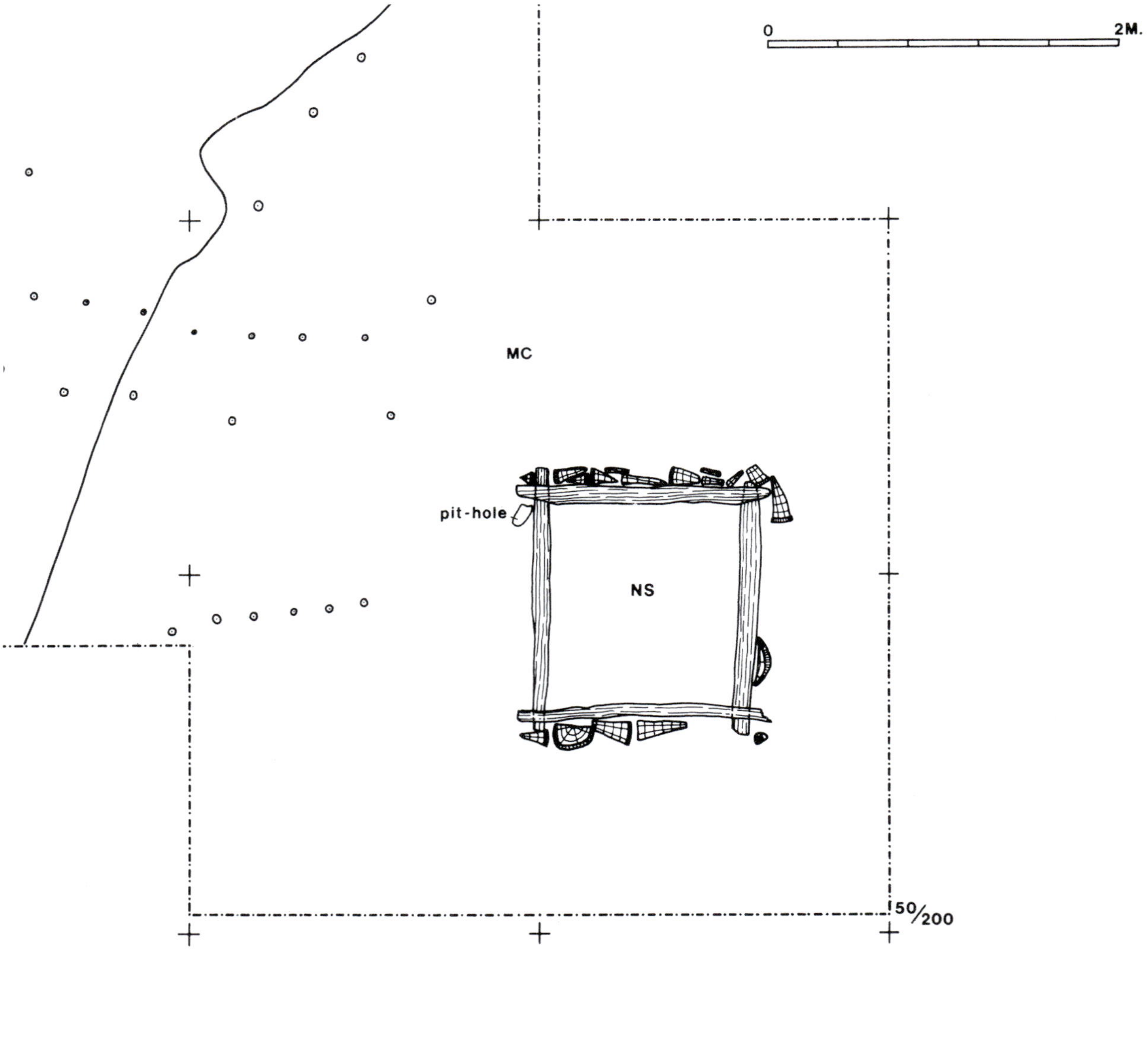

MC

pit-hole

NS

0   2M.

50/200

presence of a royal authority as early as around the year 700 this topic would become a live one again.

The question of the origins of Ribe can hardly, in any event, be ascribed to a single actor's decree and must be the result of an agreement between several parties. From a Marxist/substantivist viewpoint, Ribe could have been established by agreement between a Danish and a Frisian king, who agreed to found the town, after which a number of bound actors were directed to Ribe in order to trade. More liberal models would assign non-royal actors more space to make their own decisions. In relation to these two models, the apparently scattered and disorganized traces of the beginning of Ribe appear to point rather towards the latter.

5.8.2 The regular plot layout

In the face of massive challenges and problems to research into the earliest Ribe posed by the built environment of Sct. Nicolaj Gade, a large number of often small-scale excavations have made it possible to reveal the plot layout which either emerged or was laid out in this area early in the 8th century, and which for centuries to follow would form the backbone of the town of Ribe. Recognition of the tenement plots came about first in 1985-6 with Stig Jensen's excavation trench ASR 7, Sct. Nicolaj Gade 8, fortuitously located as determined by new development, but was not revealed on a larger scale until the Post Office site excavation ASR 9 of 1990-1 (Fig. 113).

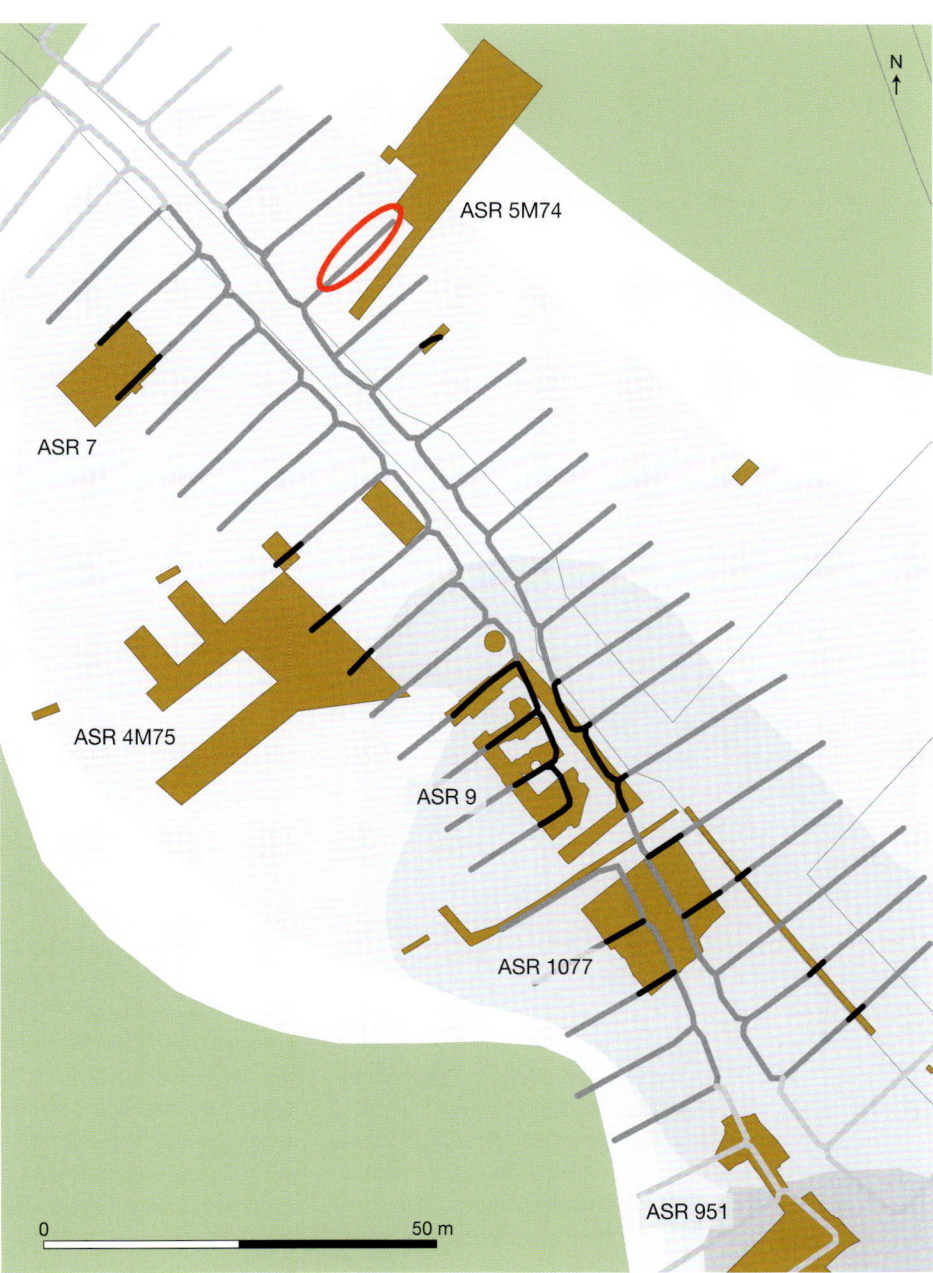

Fig. 113. Reconstruction of the plot layout beneath Sct. Nicolaj Gade. Mogens Bencard's excavations, ASR 5M74 and 4M75, had little chance of revealing the pattern of tenement plots. The find spot of the anchor discussed below (Fig. 116) is marked with a red oval. After Feveile 2006a with additions by the author.

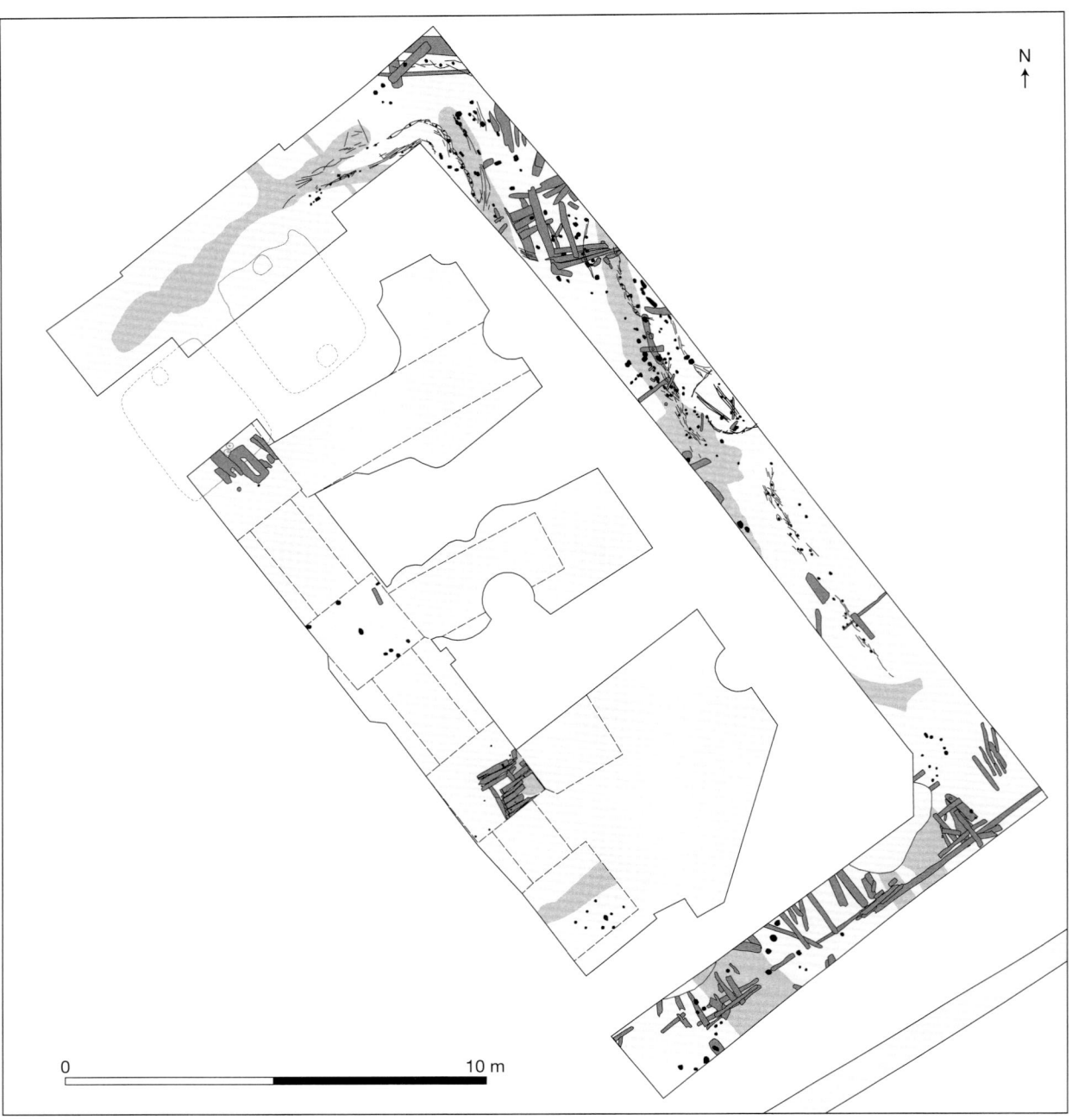

Fig. 114. ASR 9 Posthuset. The boundary ditches of the earliest phase, B, are shown in light grey together with remains of the plot system in the form of wattled fencing, and remains of wooden street paving. On the uppermost plot the outline of two sunken feature buildings is also marked. After Feveile & Jensen 2006b.

In relation to the now recognized pattern, it is manifest how unlucky Mogens Bencard was with the positioning of the first major excavations in Sct. Nicolaj Gade in 1973-5. Things would have been very different if the earliest excavations had been sited closer to the lane running through the site.

With regard to the emergence of the plot layout and its development, it is the Post Office site excavation that has produced by far the best information, not least in the form of a range of dendrochronological datings of timbers from the excavation. The fine

conditions for the preservation of organic material in parts of phases B and C have also meant that this excavation has also yielded the best evidence for street paving, plot boundaries and other features within the individual plots. Unfortunately, however, these are not from large, coherent areas, which could have shed more precise light on many aspects than was the case with the trenches of the Post Office site.

The actual marking out of the plots in this area appears to have been done by digging not particularly regular boundary ditches, typically of around half a

154

metre in width, which delimited a row of plots 6-8 m wide on both sides of a street or lane just 2 m wide. The haphazard appearance of the boundary ditches and their slightly curving line does not suggest that they were all dug together but rather as successive additions, one after the other. The narrow roadway can hardly have been meant for anything more than foot traffic. Wood was only patchily preserved in phase B, and it is not known whether or not the street was paved with planks from the outset, although that is considered likely. The accumulation of culture layers as a result of activities began in this phase, and after the refilling of the boundary ditches new boundary lines were marked out in the form of many successive phases of wattled fencing, within which in some cases were preserved entrances to the plots in the form of an opening with a step (Fig. 115). One of these is dendro-dated to AD 721/2 and thus provides a firm *ante quem* dating of the regular plot layout. In other cases the plot boundaries were refurbished through cleaning out and the recutting of ditches, creating a particularly complicated stratigraphical sequence in these areas.

To judge from the available information, there is a good deal to suggest that the laying out of the plots was a progressive phenomenon rather than a single act. The uniform result may be due to the widths of the plots having been determined in advance, or because those responsible for them had a common plan in mind, such as a desire to copy the arrangements in Dorestad.

If we follow that line of thought, one may infer that the plots were created at different rates, presumably starting in the core of the settlement, which must be assumed to have been the crossroads between the Droveway and the walking/river passage, and spreading out in both directions along the bank of the river. This process probably took place within the area in which plots have so far been identified in the period of c. AD 710-20. If the construction of the regular plots was a process rather than a single act there is not necessarily any sharp transition from the irregular trenches of the preceding phase.

At the southern end of the Post Office site the lane alongside the river with its plots was cut by another street line, probably the Droveway, which could be followed from phase C (Fig. 114). Both the lane with the plots and the crossing street were paved with planks but only patches of the planking were still in situ. This is probably due to the missing section have been lifted for re-use in connexion with the remaking of the roadway at a higher level. The same state of affairs affects the medieval streetways of Ribe on the cathedral side (Søvsø 2006). The northern course of the crossing street was apparently later erased, but conceivably this is just a matter of the street having been shifted towards the south-east, outside of the area of excavation. This cross-roads can be considered the first centre of the town.

Fig. 115. ASR 9 Posthuset. The front of a plot bounded by wattle. From a photograph in the case.

5.8.3 The arrangement of the plots and the pattern of activity

What we know about the internal organization of the individual plots is severely limited, because excavations to date have only uncovered small parts of any one plot, and only in a few cases the more central zone. The overall picture is still diffuse, consisting of a collage of individual observations from many different excavations, each minor in themselves.

A number of general features of the stratigraphical sequence on the plots seem to be typical, nonetheless. The activities in the area created a massive accumulation of culture layers which concentrates very distinctively precisely within the area of the plots. Although the problematic taphonomic circumstances affecting the earliest Ribe do not allow us to determine the situation with certainty, there is no definite evidence that in the 8th and 9th centuries there was any significant growth of culture layers anywhere other than over the plots, while the accumulation of layers was strongest around the lane that ran through the area and diminishes towards the back of the plots. The culture layers in the area, typically consisting of thin, alternating layers of dark, originally organic deposits and lighter clay, sand or ash etc, represent pretty much the entire known sequence which undoubtedly continues through to the middle of the 9th century and probably also had similar even later layers that have for the most part been removed by later activities (see section 5.2). This basic homogeneity, which clearly distinguishes the sequence from the well-known medieval strata at Ribe and other towns, must reflect a range of common features within the pattern of activity that led to the formation of the layers – a range of elements that did not alter fundamentally throughout the long period in which the sequence accumulated. One constant feature appears to have been the overall physical framework in the form of the plot layout and the lane running through the plots. Another

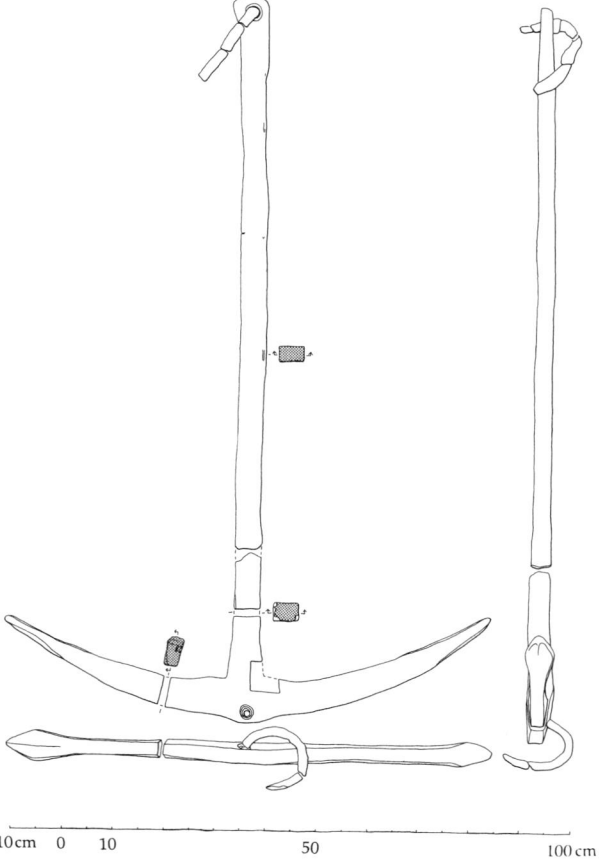

10 cm 0   10   50   100 cm

Fig. 116. The ship's anchor of the 8th century found under the gable end of the Judges' Office. ASR D7887. After Rieck 2004.

is the absence of reconstruction. Both human and animal waste remained in the area and must have been continuously levelled out in connexion with the renewal of the plot boundaries, new constructions, and repairs to the paving. More than anything else, it must have been the role of the lane as a place of trade and and for various forms of craftwork that led to the accumulation of the rich culture layers.

The steps found at the entrance to plots lay approximately centrally and show that access for foot traffic was anticipated. What those who stepped into the plots would have seen there is less clear. We know for a fact that some had sunken feature buildings towards the back of the area; there is little evidence that these were used for anything other than weaving.

The majority of the well-documented craft activities took place in the open air. Whether there was any actual housing on the plots – or to what extent – remains an unanswered question.[20] From a recent review of excavation ASR 7 it has strongly been argued that a house was built on this plot at the beginning of the 8th century (Croix 2015). On this issue, see further the summary below (section 5.8.8.2).

At the very back of the plots, in addition to well NS already referred to, well AGF was explored in the course of excavation ASR 4M75 Kunstmuseets have. This well from Bencard's phase 1A must also belong to the very first phase of the town and consisted of what, when excavated, was a rotten barrel. If there was only the one barrel in the cut, its height can be put roughly at around 2 m while the diameter at the base seems to have been around 0.6 m.

The largest single find from the plots is the ship's anchor that was found in 1975 in the course of foundation support work on the south-eastern gable of the Judges' Office (Fig. 116). Since it was found during building work the contextual information is regrettably poor (Bencard 1979b), but it was found lying on the surface with the stock parallel to the river lane on the upper edge of the well-preserved phase 2 layers and thus would appear stratigraphically datable to the period 750-800, which is consistent with the typological dating of the anchor.

The anchor is a mysterious find which cannot have been a casual loss but must have been either cached or a votive deposit. It weighed 27.5 kg when found and the metal alone must have been worth a fortune. No interpretation of the find can be anything much more than speculative but the anchor must, for whatever reason, have been separated from the ship it belonged to and may have been buried in a period of conflict in order to hide it while the owner was away from the town. Whatever the case, the individual involved did not return. It is not possible, either, entirely to rule out that this was a deliberate, votive offering.

156

5.8.4 The river lane

The re-assessment of the original topography of the town area which is offered in this study (Fig. 101) proposes that the harbour of Ribe was located at the shore of the lake which then lay immediately east of the town area. No archaeological work which might shed light on the question has been undertaken in that area yet. Nor do we have any information on other interventions in more recent times which might have uncovered the potentially rich deposits that could be hidden in the saturated contexts around the edge of the lake. The closest excavations have been undertaken at Ribelund, excavation ASR 926 Ribelund I (Feveile 2006d). Here, in the course of a traditional open-area excavation, a roadway was revealed and several phases of settlement (Figs. 117-18). The datings from this excavation are based upon the artefactual finds.[21] West of the roadway the area had been destroyed by later disturbance which was understood to have been a produced of erosion from the Ribe River although later discoveries of natural sand at high levels even further to the west now preclude that explanation.

East of the roadway several phases of well-preserved settlement consisting of post-built buildings and SFBs, which from their associated artefacts are dated as having been constructed around the middle of the 8th century and to have remained in use into the 9th and possibly on into the 10th century (Feveile 2006d, 225f).

The architecture of the post-built buildings did not appear to be very different from farmsteads out in the countryside, but the positioning of contemporary buildings side-by-side and the absence of any toft with them together with the absence of any stalling, does not point to their having been agrarian buildings. The buildings were clearly aligned upon the roadway and so are dated by association to the same period. The later town ditch (see section 5.9.5) also starts from this road line.

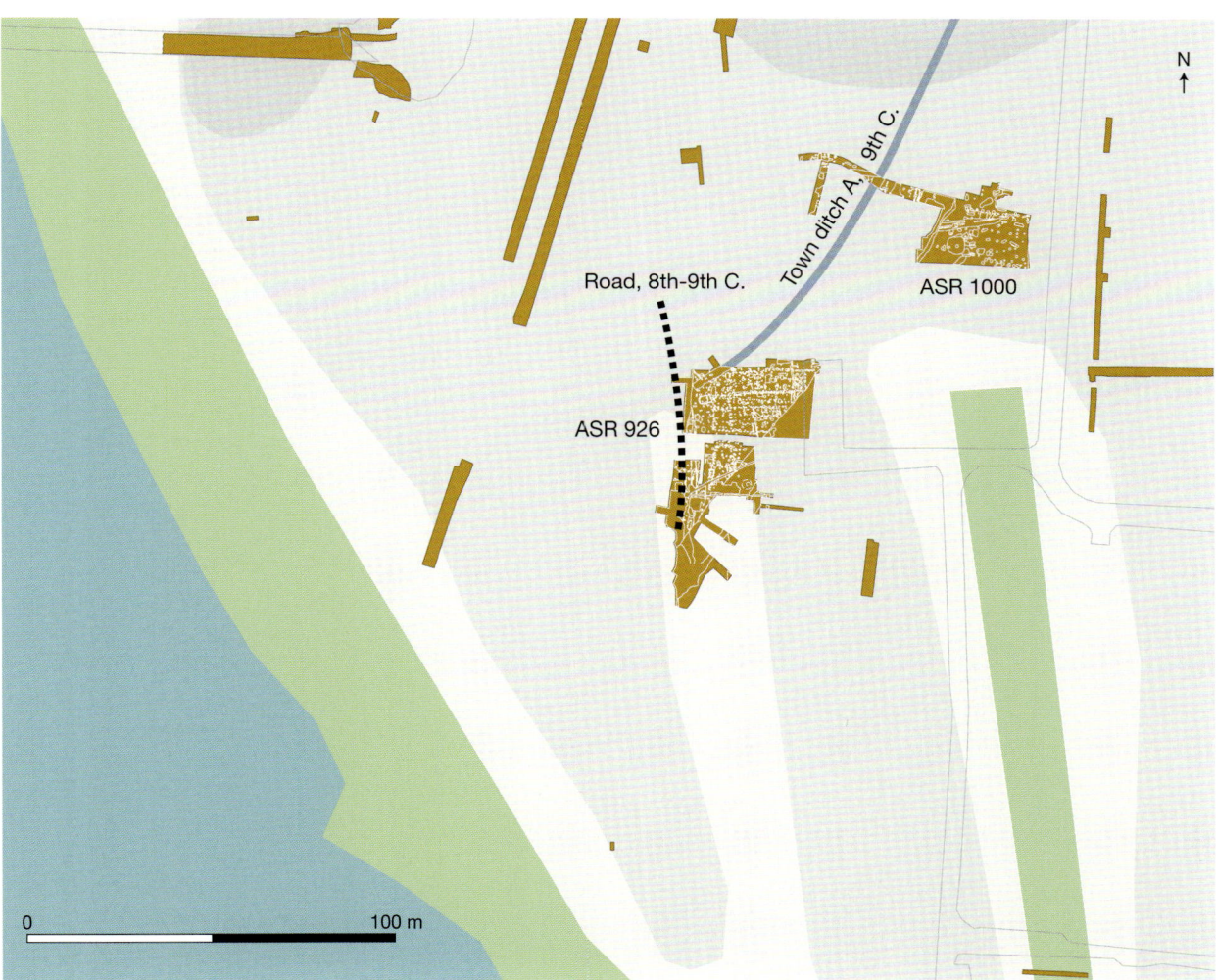

Fig. 117. The excavations ASR 926 Ribelund I and ASR 1000 Ribelund II overlying what is currently considered the most reliable reconstruction of the terrain. The elongated meadow strip in green is also an anthropogenic feature, probably a moat, which is as yet undated.

N

Modern interventions
Road
Town ditch A
Moat C

0   20 m

Fig. 118. Excavation ASR 926 Ribelund I with the buildings and other features shown.

This, then, was an important road or lane which, on the strength of the datings of artefacts found in the individual features, appears to have been in use at the latest from the middle of the 8th century and on into the 9th and possibly into the 10th century. This roadway led down towards the postulated harbour area and it would be entirely logical if it were the other end of the lane through the plots. That suggestion is not contradicted by any archaeological evidence. The relatively sparse finds assemblage from the Ribelund I excavation does not point towards any major, specialized, craft production in this area. One might rather suggest that the post-built structures of the 8th century served as packing or warehouses, or may have had some other function governed by the proximity of a harbour.

This interpretation of the topography and the results of excavation indicates that the key formative component of the earliest Ribe was a lane running alongside the river which connected the harbour area on the lake with the laid-out market area, which was centred where the Droveway crossed the Ribe River. The original Ribe can thus be described more or less as an *Uferparallelle Einstraßenanlage* ('a single-street layout parallel to a river bank') like many other trading towns of this period (Ellmers 1984, 178ff).

5.8.5 The area behind the river lane

In the area towards the north-east behind the river lane, several separate excavations have discovered scattered traces of settlement from the 8th century and later. Our picture of the structure of settlement here remains utterly diffuse, however. Apart from the excavations in Rosen Allé, which are discussed below under 'The Cemetery', the largest excavation has been ASR 1357 Giørtzvej, where 950 sq m were excavated in 2000 (Feveile 2006j). Despite its proximity to the plots, the majority of the cut features of the 8th-9th centuries were considerably smaller than those beneath the plots, and the sequence of culture layers and the finds within it were of a quite different and modest quantity in comparison with what is typical on the plots. To a minor extent this state of affairs might be explained taphonomically, as the area had not been sealed under any protective culture layers but rather left open both to cultivation and animal activity. Even with these circumstances in view, however, there is no doubt that the level of activity in the 8th-9th centuries was low.

The excavation in Giørtzvej (Fig. 119) demonstrated that the extraordinary quantity of finds and structures that characterizes the lane with the plots is indeed limited to the area immediately alongside the lane, and

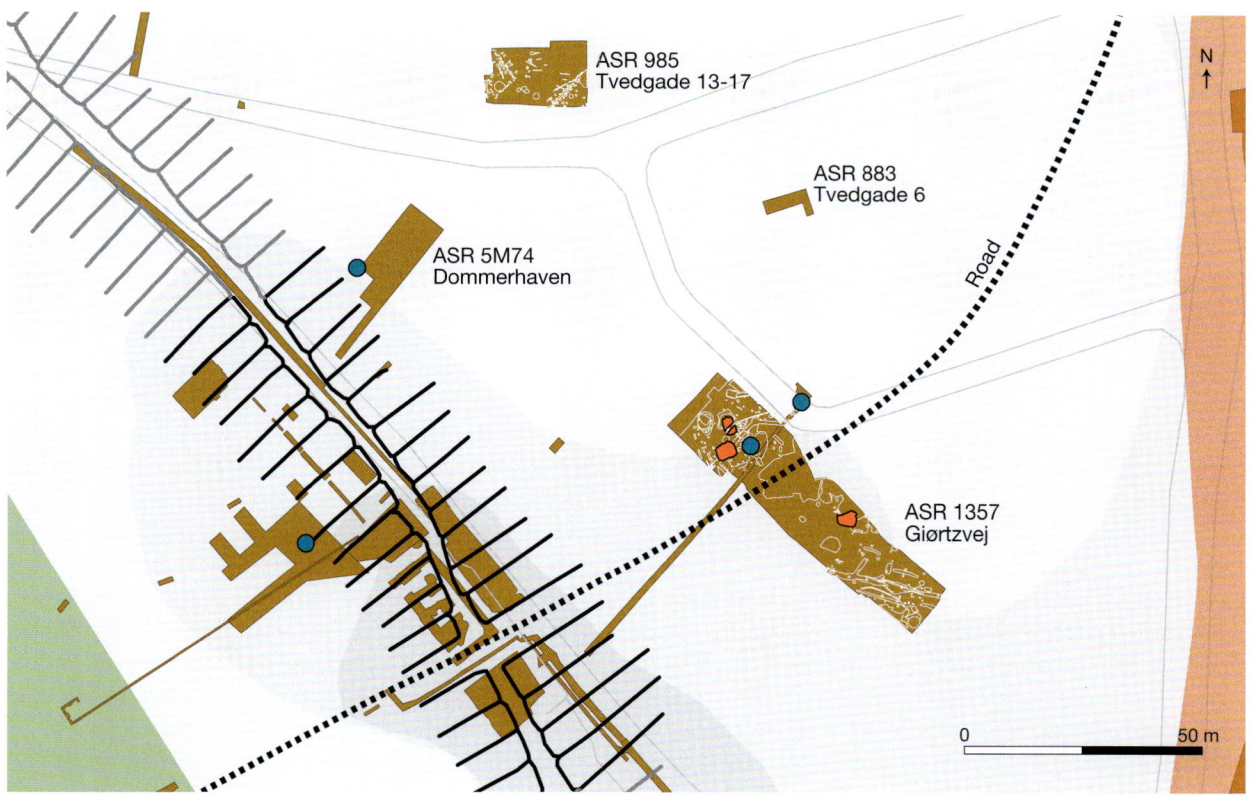

Fig. 119. North-east of the area with the plots the thickness of the culture layers rapidly diminishes and the area contains only a few structures of the 8th and 9th centuries. Most of the time it must have remained very thinly built upon. Despite its proximity to the Droveway, ASR 1357 contained only three short-lived sunken feature buildings (red). Blue dots represent wells.

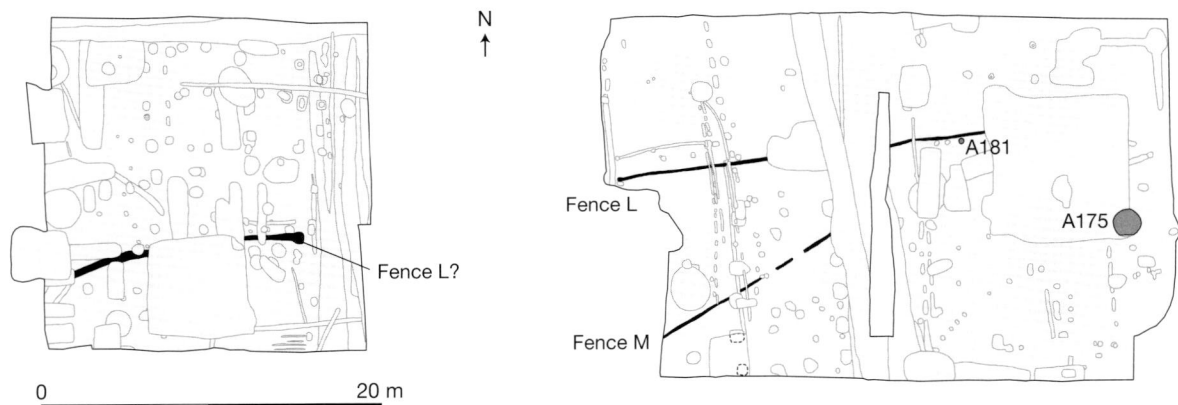

Fig. 120. The excavation at Seminarievej 4-8 produced only one definite structure of the 8th-9th centuries: well A175, constructed sometime after the year 751 and maintained through a number of phases. After Feveile 2006c.

the quantity of both of those components is fundamentally less in the area to the north-east. Another aspect of this view is that there is no indication that there was anything other than a slight accumulation of culture layers in the area north-east of the plots, which is why the natural ground surface contains all the evidence of significant digging activity in the 8th and 9th centuries.

At Giørtzvej a multi-phase ditch and fence line was found, the alignment of which diverges from that of the plots and which must thus show that there was a different layout in this area to that around the lane with the plots. Three SFBs were also found: SFB I from early in the 8th century; SFB II from around the year 800; and SFB III from later in the 9th century. There were also two wells: A7, a large barrel with a suggested diameter of around 0.85 m and a height that can be determined to have been around 2 m and which can be dendro-dated to post-AD 715 and provenanced to the area of the Rhineland around Mainz (Daly 2007, 159ff). In the fill of the well was found a separate piece of wood that could be dated post-AD 855. The well was therefore in use from sometime post-715 down to after the middle of the 9th century. The other well, A111, contained a coopered vessel at the bottom, probably a sawn-off barrel, the base of which had been removed and which had been deposited upside-down. Down over the inverted barrel another large barrel had been placed, with a diameter at the base of 0.66 m and a height probably of around 2 m. Dendrochronological investigation showed that the wood for the inverted barrel was felled around the year 712 and its provenance was also in the Upper Rhineland (Daly 2007, 162). From its stratigraphical relationship with SFB I the construction of this well can be dated to the middle of the 8th century.

In topographical terms, the area was relatively plain, highly suitable for settlement and lying adjacent to the course of the Droveway through the town.

Nevertheless it was apparent that the exploitation of these 1,000 sq m in the 8th and 9th centuries was limited to one boundary and one or two wells even though, to all appearances, the Droveway ran through this area.[22] For some of the time there was also a single SFB in the area – very thin occupation.

At Seminarievej 4-8 in 1990, an area of 1,010 sq m was excavated with very little funding, ASR 863 (Feveile 2006c). Even though the inadequate budget may have affected the results negatively, it is striking that only one definite structure of the 8th-9th centuries was found here, well A175 (Fig. 120). This consisted of the remains of three barrels placed inside one another. On the inside were two barrels of coniferous wood and on the outside an oakwood barrel of about 1 m in diameter that could be dated as having been felled post-AD 751 and provenanced to the Rhine region. The coniferous timber barrels were poorly preserved and could not be analysed dendrochronologically. They must represent later repairs, and could therefore indicate that this well had an extended functioning life, probably continuing into the 9th century.

In Tvedgade an area of 275 sq m was excavated in 1992, ASR 985 (Fig. 121) (Feveile 2006g). From the expectation that the area only contained the so-called Paypyt layer, the sequence of culture layers was removed by machine down to the level of the natural, where a number of features appeared, including the remains of three buildings, buildings I-III, which were located more or less partially within the excavation trench. In topographical terms, the area was low-lying, with a ground surface between 2.3 and 2.5 m over sea-level.

Building I was 6 m wide, had straight side walls and ends and sloping outer supporting posts which in combination with the sets of roof-bearing posts inside the building supported the roof: architectural

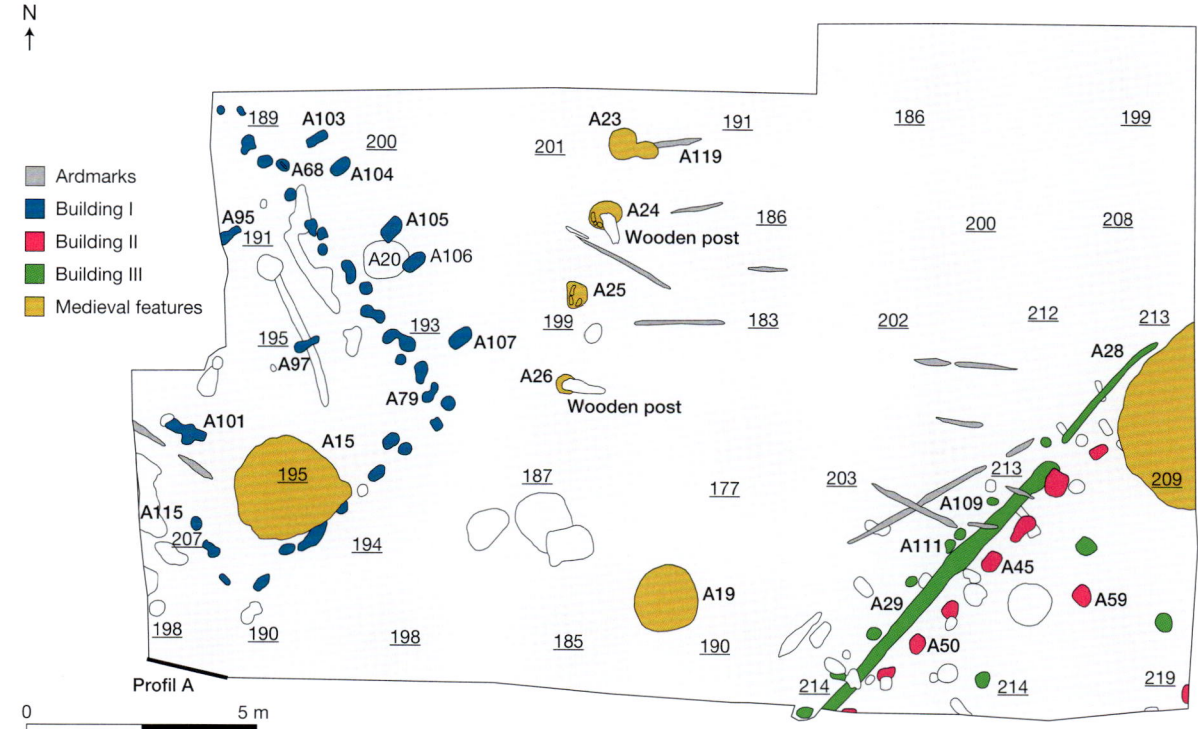

Fig. 121. Plan of the building foundations I-III from ASR 985 Tvedgade 13-17. After Feveile 2006g.

features which are highly reminiscent of what is known as the 'Hedeby house' (Schietzel 2014). Buildings II and III were successive, but only sections of a wall line and a few sets of roof-bearing posts were uncovered; these demonstrated that both buildings were straight-walled, with internal roof-bearing posts and a width of around 6.5 m. There was no dating evidence from the buildings, which typologically can be dated to the Viking Period. All three building foundations appear to be aligned in accordance with the plot layout.

The Tvedgade excavation was thus the only field-work that could show the presence of genuine build-ing foundations in the area behind the lane along the river. Considering the life-span of the slender building foundations they cannot have been of anything other than an episodic character, and their date-range can-not be made more precise than the 8th-10th centuries.

5.8.6 The cemetery[23]

In 1970, the acting Antiquary, Aino Kann Rasmussen, undertook a research excavation right alongside the water tower of the welfare centre of Ribelund east of the railway: ASR 43M70, S. Nikolaj kirkegård (Figs 23 and 122). The aim was to find the nunnery of the town which had been associated with the parish church of St Nikolaj, and the expectations were fulfilled in the form of a number of medieval burials. Beneath one grave, however, purely by chance, was found a N.-S.

inhumation grave in which the deceased had been interred along with a copper-alloy armring and there was a rusted mass of iron by the waist: possibly a toilet set (Kann Rasmussen 1971, 15). The armring was dat-able to the Late Germanic Iron Age and it was clear to the excavators that they were now on the track of Viking-period Ribe. The finds below Ribe Art Museum in 1972 meant that efforts in the following years were focussed around Sct. Nicolaj Gade and it was only with the excavation in Rosen Allé in 1989 that a wider area of the cemetery was uncovered: excavation ASR 8, Rosen Allé (Figs. 30 and 122) (Feveile & Jensen 2006a).

At Rosen Allé the remains of a very diverse burial ground were found comprising both cremations and inhumations of very different types, which in some cases could be dated to the 8th-9th centuries. Many of the cremations lay very close to the present ground surface and some have probably been destroyed by the use of the area in later times either for building or for cultivation. In 2014-16, in partnership with Aarhus University, the museum organized training excavations of the area adjacent to the southern end of the Rosen Allé excavation. In the course of these three seasons 17 cremations and 14 inhumations have been excavated: excavation SJM 348, Rosen Allé II. At Ribelund 2 cremations and 14 inhumations were found, the latter group entirely without grave goods: excavation ASR 1000, Ribelund II. The inhumed bodies were laid in a disorderly fashion in irregular

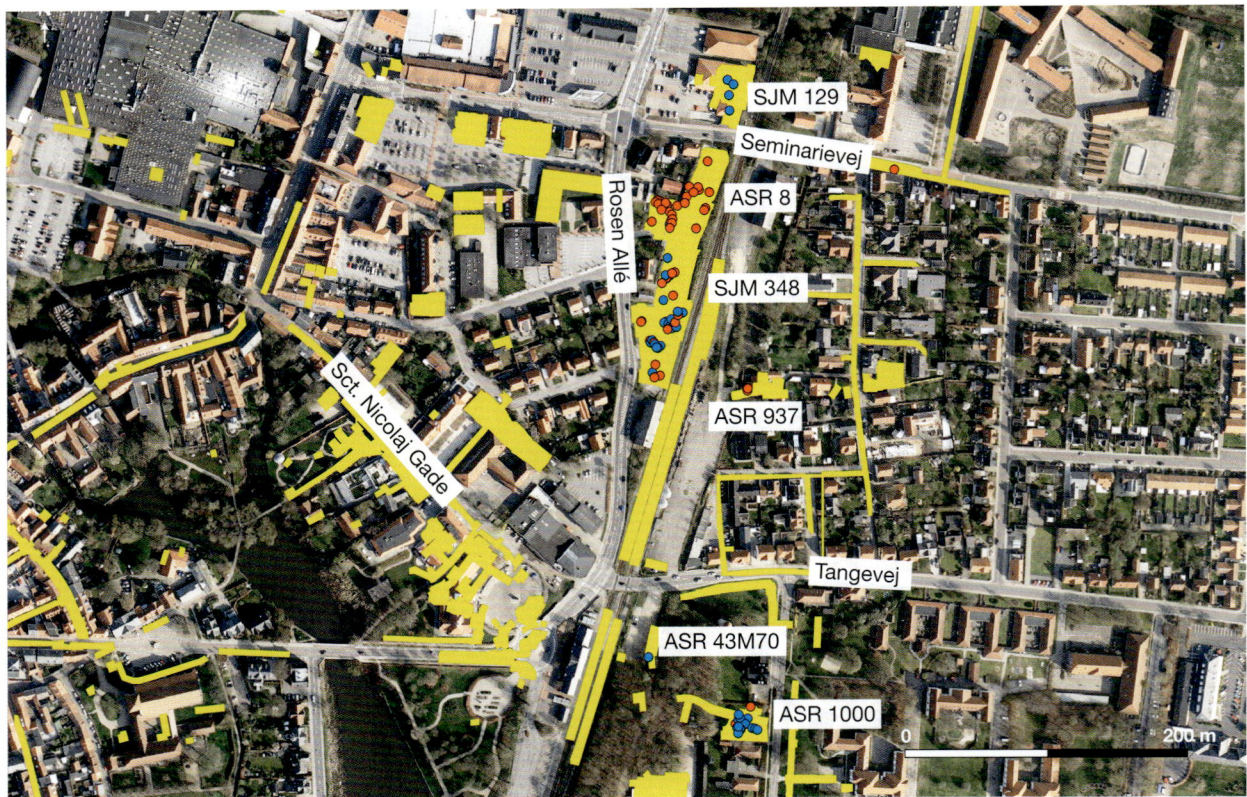

Fig. 122. Overview of the cemetery with the trenches in yellow and the cremations (red) and inhumations (blue) found up to 2016.

grave pits – in some cases virtually thrown into the grave – and two subsequent radiocarbon dates put them into the 10th century (Feveile 2006h). There is nothing in the burial rite that contradicts these graves having been Christian.

The building of a new Netto shop on Seminarievej resulted in the excavation of five inhumation burials. The high level of disturbance in the area had removed any possible remains of cremations: excavations SJM 129 Seminarievej (Qvistgaard & Søvsø 2018). Thus a total of c. 89 burials has been excavated: 49 cremations and 40 inhumations (Søvsø 2016).

In topographical terms, the position of the cemetery is classic: a slight elevation immediately east of the line of the Droveway northwards from Ribe. The burial ground is very large, covering more than 9 ha. Graves dated to the both the 8th century and the 9th are found at both ends of this area, so there does not appear to have been any geographical shift in the cemetery over time, although the whole area cannot have been used to a uniform density. The stretch alongside the land route appears, unsurprisingly, to contain most of the graves. The only sign of above-ground grave-marking comes in the form of ring ditches of varying size found, the outer diameter ranging from 6 m to 13.5 m, while the ditches themselves can have a more or less haphazard appearance. These must

be the remains of low mounds, and in a couple of cases a cremation patch was found in the interior of the ring ditch which is assumed to be associated with that ditch. The absence of preserved burial remains enclosed by the other ring ditches shows that the associated graves must have laid quite high and were probably also cremation patches.

Amongst the preserved cremation burials the following types have been distinguished, although the poor preservation may mean that the range of variance was greater still (Feveile & Jensen 2006a, 65f).

- *Cremation urn pits*: Remains of the pyre are deposited in an urn which is placed into a pit. The fill of the pit can contain larger or smaller amounts of pyre debris, after which the pit is refilled.

- *Cremation pits*: Small pits in which remains of the pyre have been buried after which the pit is refilled.

- *Cremation patch*: A concentration of charcoal either on top of the ground or in a rather shallow pit. Great variation in size is found.

- *Grave pit*: Usually quite a large, shallow pit, with a variable content of charcoal or burnt bone which apparently was not deliberately refilled but filled up by naturally produced layers, blown or alluvial sand.

162

In the case of the inhumation burials, the state of preservation is better, although generally all of the organic material is largely decomposed; often even the large limb bones are only present as outlines of different colour in the sandy fill. S.-N. graves have been found in which the deceased are lying either on the side, with the legs tucked up, or on the back (supine) with the arms down along the sides; in all cases the dead have their heads to the south. There are also oriented W.-E. graves in which the deceased are always supine and the head to the west. In some cases there are preserved traces of a coffin. Amongst the latter is a log boat 3.5 m long. In addition to humans a horse was found buried with a saddle and bridle. This is apparently datable to the 8th century (Sindbæk & Croix 2016).

The grave goods vary too. The inventory can generally be described as modest, and to date the most spectacular object is a gilt silver Frankish scabbard mount re-used as a pendant. This was found in a cremation patch at Seminarievej (S. Jensen 2006, Pl. 10).

By inference from the grave goods and the grave forms but not from osteological examination of the human skeletal remains which do not survive, the proportional distribution of males, females and children appears as in Table 9. Women and children are a clear majority, and this disproportion goes back to the earliest burials. The clear prominence of women in the grave goods can hardly mean that they were a majority in Ribe at that time but it does nonetheless argue strongly for a substantial presence of women and children in 8th-century Ribe.

In addition to the various forms of burials found, a few features have been identified which may have been connected to death or sacrificial rituals in the form of buried animal parts. These include equine limb bones, which formed the basis for Flemming Bau's frequently reproduced reconstruction drawing of the cemetery. It should be noted, however, that the relevant feature is undated, and contained no skull remains from a horse, and none of the teeth (Feveile & Jensen 2006a, 78f). In several of the graves bird bones have been found as well, which must have come from the pyre.

The pre-Christian cemetery of Ribe is an extensive and complex ancient monument with few parallels. In all of its composite character it reflects not only the extent of the emporium but also its cultural diversity in the 8th and 9th centuries. The closest parallels in southern Scandinavia are the largely later graves from Hedeby (Arents & Eisenschmidt 2010) and the graves from Groß Strömkendorf, the emporium of *Reric*, whence in 808 King Godfred removed the merchants to Hedeby (Gerds 2015).

Amongst the elements which are lacking in the cemetery of Ribe are high-status graves. There can

Excavation	Site	Male	Female	Child
ASR 43M70	S. Nikolaj kirkegård	1		
ASR 8	Rosen Allé	1	8	1
ASR 1000	Ribelund II		2	
SJM 129	Seminarievej	1		
SJM 348	Rosen Allé II	1	2	2
Total		4	12	3

Table 9. The distribution of males, females and children in the pre-Christian cemetery of Ribe as indicated by grave goods and grave form. Spindle-whorls, pins, chest keys and glass beads are regarded as female grave goods. Folding knives, armrings and horse harness are regarded as male. Males: ASR 43M70 grave O, ASR 8 G12, SJM 129 G3, SJM 348 K274. Females: ASR 8 G2, G8, G9, G11, G13, G14, G16, G24. ASR 1000 G1, G2. SJM 348 K45, K141. Children: ASR 8 G10. SJM 348 K198, K562. Data from Bencard & Jørgensen 1990, Feveile 2006, and unpublished excavation reports in the SJM archive.

be little doubt that special regulations to maintain the peace in the market site were in force, imposed either by the king himself or a high-ranking governor and probably enforced by a group of armed men. The graves of that social group have not as yet been found. Were one to point out a plausible site for such graves from topographical considerations, it would be the higher ground which later came to house St Nikolaj Church. No archaeological investigations have been undertaken on this rise itself but much of the area appears to contain medieval burials from the period of the parish church.

The excavations down to 2016 show that the pre-Christian cemetery of Ribe is one of the largest in Denmark (Fig. 123). How many graves it originally held one can only guess at, but it is clear that the great majority are of the 8th and 9th centuries.

5.8.7 Coin finds and economy in the emporium of Ribe

One of several sensations from Mogens Bencard's excavations in the 1970s was the finding of a number of small silver coins of the Frisian/Anglo-Saxon type called *sceattas*. The sceatt is a silver coin of only about a centimetre in diameter struck from a thick blank. Their weight is typically just over a gram in the case of well-preserved specimens. Coins of this type were used and circulated around the North Sea in the otherwise silver-poor 7th and 8th centuries (Metcalf 1993; Gannon 2003; Feveile 2008). From around the middle of the 8th century the sceatt as a form was gradually superseded in the North Sea area by a larger

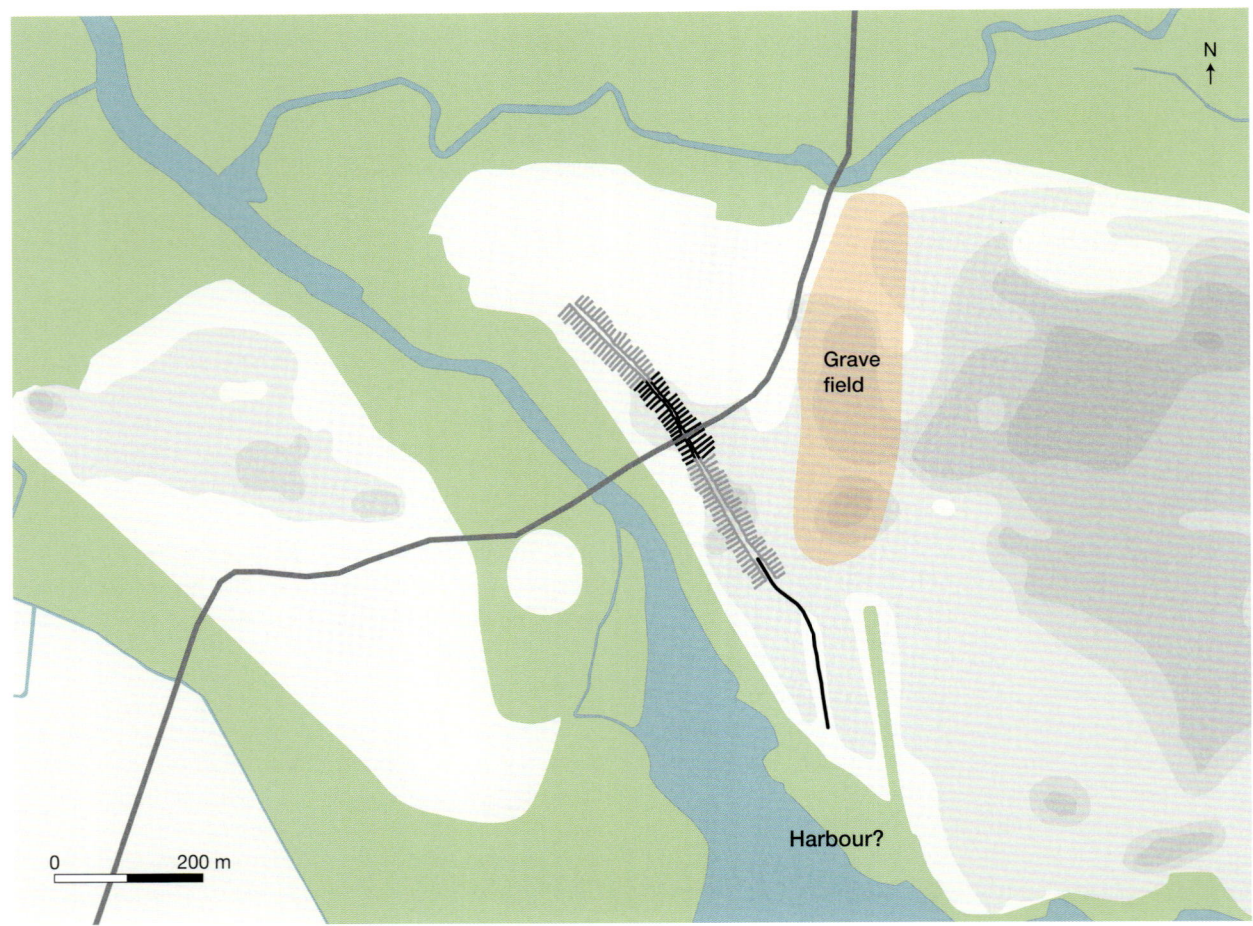

Fig. 123. Reconstruction of the topography of Ribe in the 8th century. The cemetery covers more than 9 hectares. In the centre of the southern third of the burial ground can be seen the higher ground which will have been the most conspicuous element of the area and where the parish church of St Nikolaj was later built.

coin struck on a thinner flan, known as the denier or the penny – this was to be the standard coin format for centuries subsequently. Down to 2016, 218 sceattas have been found in Ribe (Bendixen 1985; Feveile 2008). With three exceptions, all of these are single finds discovered narrowly within the area along the lane parallel to the river (Tab. 10; Fig. 124).[24]

The fact that the coins occur as single finds scattered through the layers shows beyond question that they represent casual losses as a result of their use in deals and transactions (Coupland 2010, 100). The insistent and well-documented concentration of the finds in the area immediately around the lane along the river is firm evidence that this business was taking place just there. The coins are regrettably in a poor state of preservation overall, and the scope for die-studies is limited.

Despite its condition, this large collection of material does allow us to deduce several typical features of the use of the coins. The coins are, practically without exception, whole (or had been whole before disintegrating while lying in the ground) and show

Journal no.	Site	Quantity
ASR 6M73	Site 5, Kunstmuseets Kælder	5
ASR 6M73	Site 7, Plejehjemmet Riberhus	2
ASR 6M73	Site 11, Sct. Nicolaj Gade	1
ASR 5M74	Dommerhaven	8
ASR 4M75	Kunstmuseets Have	16
ASR 7	Sct. Nicolaj Gade 8	34
ASR 9	Posthuset	54
ASR 926	Ribelund I	1
ASR 951	Plejehjemmet Riberhus	25
ASR 1077	Sct. Nicolaj Gade 14	7
ASR 1085	Gasværksgrunden	9
ASR 1357	Giørtzvej	41
ASR 2087	Dagmarsgade	1
ASR 15	Kunstmuseets kælder II	8
ASR 2360	Sct. Nicolaj Gade	3
SJM 348	Rosen Allé II	3
Total		218

Table 10. Finds of sceattas in Ribe, all types, as distributed per individual excavation; cf. Figure 124.

164

Fig. 124. The distribution of the total of 218 single finds of sceattas made in the Ribe to the year 2016 represented by circles, the size of which represents the relative quantity of coins from the sites in question. The areas excavated are shown in brown. It is clear that the 8th-century coins are concentrated in the area laid-out in plots, where those coins must have been changing hands.

no sign of having been bent or having had their fineness tested in any other way through peck-marks from a knife. There are also no examples of perforated coins.[25] There is therefore no reason to doubt that the coins were used within a system wherein the individual coins were respected and attributed with a fixed, symbolic value: in other words, a system comparable to our contemporary understanding of 'money' (Kilger 2008; Metcalf 2014).

It must be considered doubtful that all trading transactions in 8th-century Ribe involved sceattas. Barter and a goods economy can be assumed to have played a major role, and one may guess that the majority of exchanges were effected by those means.

5.8.7.1 A weight economy?

In the second half of the 9th century, a weight economy based upon the weighing of hacksilver spread across Scandinavia, driven first and foremost by the large quantities of silver from the Caliphate which came to

Scandinavia via the easterly trading network (Steuer 2002). The hacksilver economy was, predictably, accompanied by weights and balances, which start to appear both as grave goods and in the assemblages of finds from trading sites and other sites of this date. The small, light weights were typically shaped as what is called a 'cubo-octahedron' while the larger and heavier weights were the flattened globular 'oblate spheroid' type. Along with the gradual displacement of the weight economy by a regulated monetized economy, both the quantity of hacksilver and the use of weights grew less, but the process advanced at different times in different places.

The well-dated stratigraphical sequences from Ribe allow us to assess whether the archaeological evidence shows any sign of some form of weight-based economy in 8th-century Ribe. From Table 11 it is quite clear that hacksilver does not occur amongst the material from the earliest Ribe in any significant quantity. It appears more probable that the small pieces of silver found may have been lost by silversmiths. A certain number of flattened cylindrical, almost pill-shaped

Journal no.	Site	x-no.	Dimensions (mm)	Weight (g)	Description
ASR 6M73	Kunstmuseets kælder	D06906		< 1	Silver globule of the size of a small pea
ASR 8	Rosen Allé	x011	16x8	< 1	Silver foil
ASR 9	Posthuset	x102		< 1	Melted drop
ASR 9	Posthuset	x329		< 1	Silver shaving
ASR 9	Posthuset	x440	10x7	< 1	Gold foil
ASR 951	Plejehjemmet Riberhus	x052		< 1	Melted drop of gold
ASR 1085	Gasværksgrunden	x013		< 1	Silver drop
ASR 1357	Giørtzvej	x045		< 1	Melted drop
ASR 1357	Giørtzvej	x053	Length 19, diameter 3.5	< 1	Twisted piece of silver
ASR 1357	Giørtzvej	x070	42x7x4	11.2	Ingot
ASR 1357	Giørtzvej	x082	33x5x4	c. 5	Ingot
ASR 1357	Giørtzvej	x139		< 1	Melted drop
ASR 1357	Giørtzvej	x147	Length 15, diameter 3	1.0	Fragment of an armring with rhomboidal decoration
ASR 1357	Giørtzvej	x166	24x11x3.5	3.3	Fragmentary ingot
ASR 1357	Giørtzvej	x278		< 1	Two very small pieces of silver
ASR 2165	Dagmarsgade	x11	Length 23, diameter 2.5	< 1	Small twisted rod
ASR 15	Kunstmuseets kælder	x034	11x2.5	0.11	Fragment of gold jewellery
SJM 348	Rosen Allé II	x478		< 1	2 dirham offcuts

Table 11. Table of all finds of hacksilver or hackgold of the 8th and 9th centuries from Ribe. Although large quantitites of earth have been sieved, the total weight is less than 25 g. Precious metals are, on the whole, lacking in the archaeological evidence of the Viking Period from the town.

lead weights are known from 8th-century layers, but the absence of hacksilver suggests it is more likely that those were used by metalcasters or for weighing something other than silver (Feveile & Jensen 2006b, 144). We may conclude that there is no trace of any form of hacksilver economy in 8th-century Ribe.

5.8.7.2 The find contexts of the sceattas and change in the composition of the coinage over time

In respect of the contexts in which the sceattas have been found, it is once again the stratigraphical excavations which have produced far and away the best evidence (Tab. 12). From the inclusion of the coins in the layers it has been possible to track a significant course of development in the types of coin that were used on the plots in the 8th century (Metcalf 1986; Feveile & Jensen 2006b; Feveile 2008).

In the earliest phases we see a mixture of various coins. The Continental Runic, Porcupine and Wodan/monster types were in circulation along with several other, rarer forms of sceatt. This seems to reflect a pattern of trade in which the participants used the coins they had brought with them in business transactions. The picture changes markedly around the year 725. The best dated evidence of this is again from the Post Office site, where this change takes place at the transition to Phase C, in other words around the year 725. The coinage in circulation is subsequently dominated by the Wodan/monster sceattas, a state of affairs that continues down to around the year 800 when the type is superseded by a coin with a similar design but struck on a broader and thinner flan known as the Rayface/deer A penny (Fig. 125) (Malmer's KG 4 and later 5-6) (Malmer 1966; Varenius 1994).

The significant distribution of the coin-types stratigraphically, which has been reproduced in several excavations, leaves no room for doubt that it was palpably the case that a single type of coin became the sole coin in use and continued as such into the 9th century (Metcalf 1993, 275ff).

- c. AD 700-725: Sceattas of many different types

- c. AD 725-800: Monopoly coinage: the Wodan/monster sceatt

- c. AD 800-850: Monopoly coinage: the Rayface/deer penny

Monopology coinage has to be explained in terms of an issuing authority having the power to enforce the use of only one type of coin in Ribe, and this system, which will have required a functional mint, functioned for more the a century. The best suggestion as to whom this issuing authority will have been must be the Danish king.

For these reasons, it has been proposed that the Wodan/monster sceatt was a Danish issue struck

Phase	Dating	Wodan/monster	Porcupine	Continental Runic	BM C 37 Series J	Unique	Unclassified sceatt	Pennies	Dirhams	Roman
Un-phased										
J	12th-13th c.									
H and I	820-850							7		
G	800-820	1 1								
F	790-800	4 1								
E	780-790	7							4-7	
D	760-780	4	1		1		1			
C	725-760	17 3								1
B	705-725	4	3	3	1	1				
A										

Table 12. The distribution of coins in the Post Office excavation. Before c. 725 several different types of sceattas were used, after 725 the Wodan/monster sceatt became dominant. The same picture emerged from the stratigraphic excavations ASR 7 and ASR 1077. After Feveile 2006b, 281.

in Ribe (Metcalf 1986; Feveile 2006b; 2008; 2019). This matter has been and continues to be debated (Jonsson & Malmer 1986; Williams 2007). The coin finds from Ribe support the case strongly, but the clear geographical distribution of Wodan/monster sceattas also in Anglo-Saxon Engand and the Frisian region shows that this coin-type was struck at more than one location.

Detector-searching at the emporium of Reric alongside the modern village of Groß Strömkendorf in Wismar Bay has recently added new material for this discussion. Down to 2014 34 sceattas have been found, 24 of them of the Wodan/monster type.[26]

An overview of this patchy find picture could propose that the Wodan/monster iconography was not invented by a Danish king but rather was a Frisian or Anglo-Saxon coin-type which a Danish king chose to copy around the year 725. Copying of familiar foreign coins was certainly seen at Hebedy early in the 9th century, where coins from Dorestad formed the immediate

Fig. 125. To the left are shown the obverse and reverse of the so-called Wodan/monster or Series X sceatt, which was the sole coinage in Ribe in the period c. AD 725-800. It was then superseded by a coin with the same basic design but struck on a larger flan, known as Combination Group (KG) 4 (Rayface/deer A), and 5-6 (Rayface/deer B). The diameter of the sceattas is c. 11 mm and that of KG 4/5/6 is c. 18 mm. 2:1. Photo: ASR. ASR9x526, SJM810x014, coin in NM.

prototype for the first Hedeby coins (KG3 and later KG 7-9: Malmer 1966; Williams 2010). The coins of Svein Forkbeard and Cnut the Great were also direct copies of English prototypes. It appears to have been the rule rather than the exception for Danish kings to imitate foreign coins – so why should that not have been the case at Ribe around the year 725?

In this view, the Wodan/monster sceatt could therefore be either 'foreign' or struck by a Danish king. The dominance of the type at both Ribe and Reric and its almost complete absence amongst archaeological finds from Denmark otherwise could indicated that it was intended exclusively for use at the king's trading sites (Feveile 2019). Possibly future die-studies will be able to shed light upon this complicated set of issues. If the assumption that the Wodan/monster sceatt is a copy of a foreign prototype is valid, the actual designs and their ideological background become less interesting (Gannon 2003).

It follows from the above that the traders who came to Ribe in the period following c. 725 were obliged to exchange the coins they had brought with them, presumably at the cost of a specified commission as payment to whichever king assured the security of the traders. The Frankish Royal Annals report that before 808 Reric had produced a large income for the Danish

king, and the coin must have played a part in this. The coin finds from Ribe and their distribution in the stratigraphy indicates very strongly that the town either already was or came under royal control no later than the year 725 (Näsman 2000). When Ribe was first referred to in connexion with the permission given Ansgar to raise a church at the site around the year 855, the town was under royal control (Skovgaard-Petersen 1981).

5.8.8 Summary and interpretation: Ribe in the 8th century

In Chapter 4 of this book (Topography), it was argued that Vester Vedsted and Hviding parishes had been the home of an aristocratic group, probably a family or dynasty, throughout the 1st millennium AD. In the first half of the millennium, the site of Dankirke was a religious centre and the residence of this family, and it is proposed that this centre was then relocated to Okholm, on the strength of a sketched out case based upon hoards, excavations and detector surveys. From this area the sailing route up the Ribe River could be managed, and it is suggested that these aristrocrats had contacts with the growing trading networks of the late 7th century and might themselves have visited Dorestad.

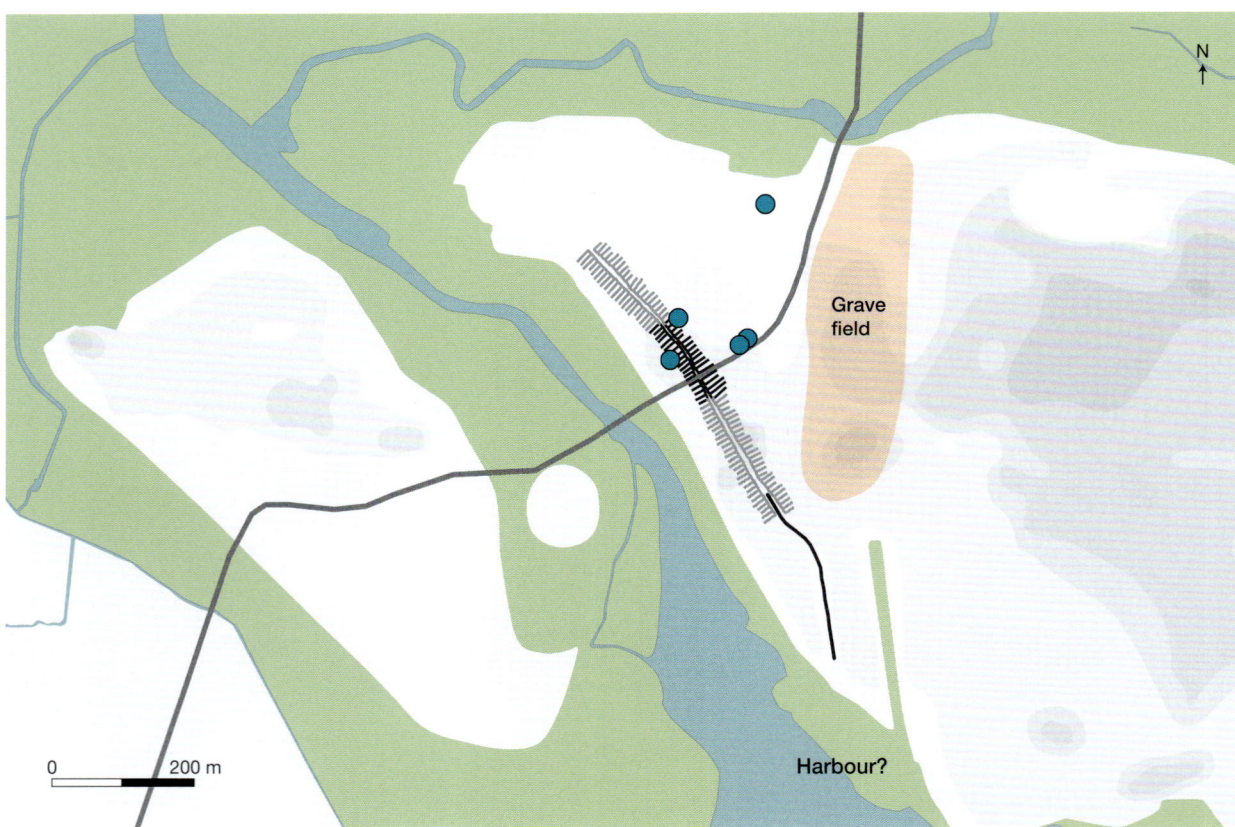

Fig. 126. The topography and fundamental structure of Ribe in the 8th century. The securely mapped plots are shown in black while their postulated counterparts are in grey. Blue dots mark 8th-century wells.

5.8.8.1 The birth of Ribe and its fundamental structure

The origins of Ribe are perceived as an agreement between the local aristocracy and Frisian traders, which on the basis of the archaeological data has to be dated to around the year 700. It is possible that a Danish king was involved as well. It is argued that the later town area was an unsettled, marginal area around the principal N.-S. landroute, the *Droveway*. From an essentially land-based traffic's perspective there was also easy access from Ribe to the main land route of Jutland, *Hærvejen*, and a desire to be able to access an extensive upland could have lain behind the choice of location.

Following an analysis of the problematic topography, hydrography and taphonomy of Ribe as an archaeological site, an account is given of the earliest traces of the town. The existence of a major, elongated lake immediately upstream of the town area is suggested to provide the location of the harbour of Ribe. The specialized craftsfolk that are typical of the emporia were present from the outset. After a short and apparently unstructured preliminary phase the street running alongside the river emerged, and it is suggested that this connected the harbour area with the excavated tenement plots (Fig. 126). A range of circumstances indicate that the plots extended further in both directions than currently observed. In contrast to inferences previously published, the regular plot structure is not regarded as a single, unified layout but rather the product of continual additions as the town grew. For the same reason, a sharp distinction between the first phase's 'irregular ditches' and the slightly later 'regular plots' is not employed. The reason for the uniform appearance of the regular plots could be that their width of 6-8 m had been prescribed in advance and that the parties involved shared an understanding of what was wanted – such as knowledge of what other emporia looked like. The area towards the north-east behind the plots is suggested to have had thinly dispersed building.

The spread-out cemetery of Ribe lay east of the course of the Droveway through the town, covering a massive area of c. 9 ha. The excavations in this area have revealed a rich variety of cremation and inhumation practices, reflecting the diverse ethnic and cultural composition of the town. The majority of the 89 graves excavated to date must have been heathen, but a few are compatible with Christian practice, and it is not impossible that they were the resting places of Christians who had come from the south. The closest parallel to the Ribe cemetery has been excavated at Groß Strömkendorf, the emporium of Reric.

From this interpretation of the many archaeological data, Ribe in the 8th century was essentially an *Einstraßenanlage* like Dorestad. The street/lane along-side the river was just 2 m wide, probably paved with planks and to judge by its width intended for foot traffic. The activities of the town took place principally on the tenement plots, and the wide range of trading and craft activities created thick culture layers. We do not have good data on the density of building on the plots. However, this important question was answered in the research excavation Northern Emporium, case no. SJM 3, conducted in 2017-18. It proved the existence of permanent houses on the plots and the main results of this ground-breaking investigation will be published shortly (Sindbæk ed. in prep). Just behind the plots sunken feature buildings have been found, but to what extent there may have been actual houses at the front parts of the plots is as yet unknown. If this was the case, they were of slight build. The density of building is linked to the debate over whether Ribe was a seasonal trading place or a permanently occupied town (Hodges 1982; 2000; Skre 2007c; Croix 2015).

5.8.8.2 Seasonal trading place or permanently occupied town?

The evidence from Ribe includes both loomweights and spindle-whorls, alongside SFBs which, from finds of loomweights, were used for textile production. These activities were present from early in the 8th century. If we turn our view to the burial ground of the town it is also evident from the grave goods and grave forms that women and children were in a clear majority. Thus various sources of evidence indicate that, from early in the 8th century, Ribe housed both women and children in considerable quantity. As hardly all of these could have been prostitutes or slaves, one must recognize that the population does not correspond in composition to what one would anticipate were Ribe only a seasonal trading site populated by merchants who had arrived by ship with the limited crews those would involve alongside those who had travelled to trade via the land routes.

Despite the apparent absence of substantial structures on the plots, quite a number of strongly constructed wells associated with the plots and maintained over longer or shorter periods have been excavated. Larger buildings have also been excavated in the vicinity of the proposed harbour area (ASR 926 Ribelund I). Altogether, this suggests that Ribe was already permanently occupied from early in the 8th century. It does not mean that the level of activity did not almost certainly fluctuate considerably from season to season, with possible high seasons in the form of markets at fixed dates.

In an integrated assessment of the stratigraphy, the finds and the archaeological features, the growth of Ribe at the beginning of the 8th century looks to have been rapid and dramatic. The location of the excavations and the taphonomy pose a challenge in this respect too, but finds from the 8th century appear to be present all along the lane parallel to the river, and in the cemetery the graves that can be dated to this century are also in the majority.

5.8.8.3 Wine barrels as wells

The large number of wells of the 8th century are particularly interesting because they are very little affected by taphonomy, and reveal that there was manifestly a demand for quite a substantial water supply on the plots despite the proximity of the river.

Table 13 shows that all five wells of the 8th century were either constructed using large oakwood barrels or contained staves from a barrel. There are precise measurements only of the diameter of the barrels while their heights are calculated from the distance between the base of the barrel and the then land surface. Although it is unknown what the decomposed upper parts of the barrels looked like there is no doubt that they were all large, with capacities that may have approached a thousand litres. The three oldest are provenanced to the Rhine lands around Mainz while the slightly later barrel from Seminarievej could not be determined more precisely than to 'probably the Rhine lands' (Daly 2007, 159).

The barrels from Ribe correspond exactly in date, size and origin to barrels found re-used in wells at Dorestad (Eckstein 1978). There is no reason to doubt

that they were originally wine barrels; and as they ended up in wells it would appear equally certain that they either were intended to invigorate the water with some of the qualities of the wine or were not attributed with any special value after they had been emptied of their contents.

The crucial question is, naturally, whether or not they also contained wine when they arrived in Ribe. This cannot be answered, but since the subsequent use of the barrels at both Dorestad and Ribe is the same why should their previous use not be so too? With considerable plausibility one may therefore add Rhenish wine to the list of goods on sale in 8th-century Ribe – a suitable drink from the many fine blown glass vessels that were also for sale (L. Feveile 2006).

5.8.8.4 Specialized craftsmen on the plots

The town served as a centre for specialist craft. Combmakers, amberworkers, beadmakers and metalcasters were all subject to the need for the raw materials for what they would make to be brought to the site. That might be over long distances, in the cases of glass and brass, or shorter distances in the cases of antler and amber. The presence of these craftworkers must itself have created a market for dealing in raw materials such as antler and amber. Likewise iron, wood, leather and wool would have been worked in the town in considerable quantities, but the traces of these crafts have survived very poorly on the whole in the culture layers.

Journal no.	Site	Well	Description	Barrel diameter	Barrel suggested height	Dendro-dating	Prove-nance	Period of use
ASR 5M74	Dommer-haven	NS	Barrel staves used in the repair of a well		c. 2 m	post-704	Mainz	c. 704-725
ASR 4M75	Kunstmuseets have	AGF	Complete decomposed barrel	c. 0.6 m	c. 2 m			c. 700-725
ASR 863	Seminarievej	A175	Oakwood barrel with two later pinewood barrels inserted as repairs	c. 1 m	c. 2 m	post-751	The Rhine lands?	c. 750-850
ASR 1357	Giørtzvej	A7	Oakwood barrel. The fill Contained loose timber dendrodated post-855		c. 2 m	post-715	Mainz	c. 715-855
ASR 1357	Giørtzvej	A111	Coppered vessel and oakwood barrel in the well	c. 1 m	c. 2 m	post-712	Mainz	c. 712-800

Table 13. The five wells of the 8th century excavated to date. Data from Feveile 2006c and 2006j and Daly 2007.

The stratigraphy of the plots is characterized by a large number of thin layers, some of which are extremely rich in finds and include concentrations of a range of waste products from craftworking, while others have more diverse contents composed of waste from a range of different crafts plus domestic waste in the form of animal bone, potsherds and more. It seems clear that there was a continuous levelling out of waste heaps and removal of material as part of a system of maintenance, and yet the waste does not appear to have been taken out of the area that was divided into plots. The layers thus essentially represent secondary or even tertiary deposits, and for the same reason only few intact interfaces have been identified as of yet – in other words the actual surfaces on which the crafts were practised. This is the reason for the apparent disproportion between the huge quantities of waste from craft activity compared with the few concrete, demonstrated, remains of workshops. The distributions of the finds appears to show that the lane with the plots was not divided into quarters for, say, beadmakers or bronzecasters, but rather housed a variety of crafts through time.

5.8.8.5 The trade of Ribe in the 8th century

It would be difficult to represent the emergence and development of Ribe in the 8th century as anything but a great success: a mini-Dorestad in Scandinavia which helped to lay the foundation for the growth of Åhus and Reric on the Baltic a little later in the century. But why did the traders and craftspeople come there, and why did they stay? The really crucial reason must be that the economic conditions for sustaining an urban community whose subsistence basis was not (solely) agricultural were met.

In addition to wine and blown glass, plus raw materials such as glass, brass and lead, the visitors also imported quernstones of Mayen basalt and a small amount of pottery which can be identified as imported through its fabric. The quernstones were sold on in large quantities, and the concentration of finds in south-west Jutland that can be documented must mean that these customers lived locally or in the region (Fig. 127).

At the moment, research is underway on whether the whetstones of the 8th century were what is known as Caledonian slate from Norway (Resi 2011), while amongst the assemblage of antler a small quantity of reindeer antler has been identified which must also have been imported from the north (Ashby et al. 2015). In this way it appears that contacts facing northwards can be traced as early as the 8th century, although in quantitative terms the connexions do not look massive.

The quantities of finds from Ribe show that there was a copious production of glass and amber beads, and of brass jewellery and antler combs, in the town, with a view to sale. This production cannot be regarded as having been directed at the uppermost level of society but rather to correspond in level with what one would find with the jewellery-wearing ranks of society whose former possessions are now found by metal-detecting all over Denmark (see Ch. 4, Topography). In other words, a sort of costume jewellery store with a large circle of customers.

While it is relatively easy to identify some of the categories of goods that visitors brought with them, there is much less evidence of what they received in return. A simple inference would be that such payment must have been in goods which do not survive archaeologically.

The emporia functioned, at that time, as international trading sites, and the exchange of luxury items such as furs, precious metals, gems, dyes, spices etc will not necessarily leave much archaeological trace although it could have been of considerable economic importance. In the 7th and 8th centuries, a time of relative poverty in precious metals, there is, however, little sign that these elite exchange networks had much to do with Ribe.

The craftspeople in the town who made use of local raw materials – the combmaker and the amberworker, and those who worked with textile, leather and wood – could basically depend on barter for their crafts: gathered antler and amber together with foodstuffs in exchange for finished products. Both beadmakers and metalcasters, however, were dependent upon a supply of raw materials from outside, and it is equally inconceivable that the wine merchant did not receive payment for the drinking glasses and their contents. What, then, did the traders from overseas take home or further on on their travels?

One possibility that is frequently suggested is slaves: heathens meant for a future on Frankish estates (McCormick 2007, 606ff). Once again this is a category of goods that leaves little archaeological trace; and in the absence of such evidence one has to ask whether other sources could shed light on this key question. Climatic studies, dendrochronology and settlement archaeology (see Ch. 4, Topography) all appear to show that the level of population remained low in the 8th-century Jutland, meaning a reduced probability of conflict over territory. Apart from the Danevirke no land dykes or votive hoards of weaponry are known from the 8th century. It is proposed, rather, in the present work, that the kingdom was or became unified under a single king in the 8th century (Näsman 2006) with his seat at Lejre (see Ch. 6). This hypothetical unification of the kingdom could naturally have involved the taking of a number of

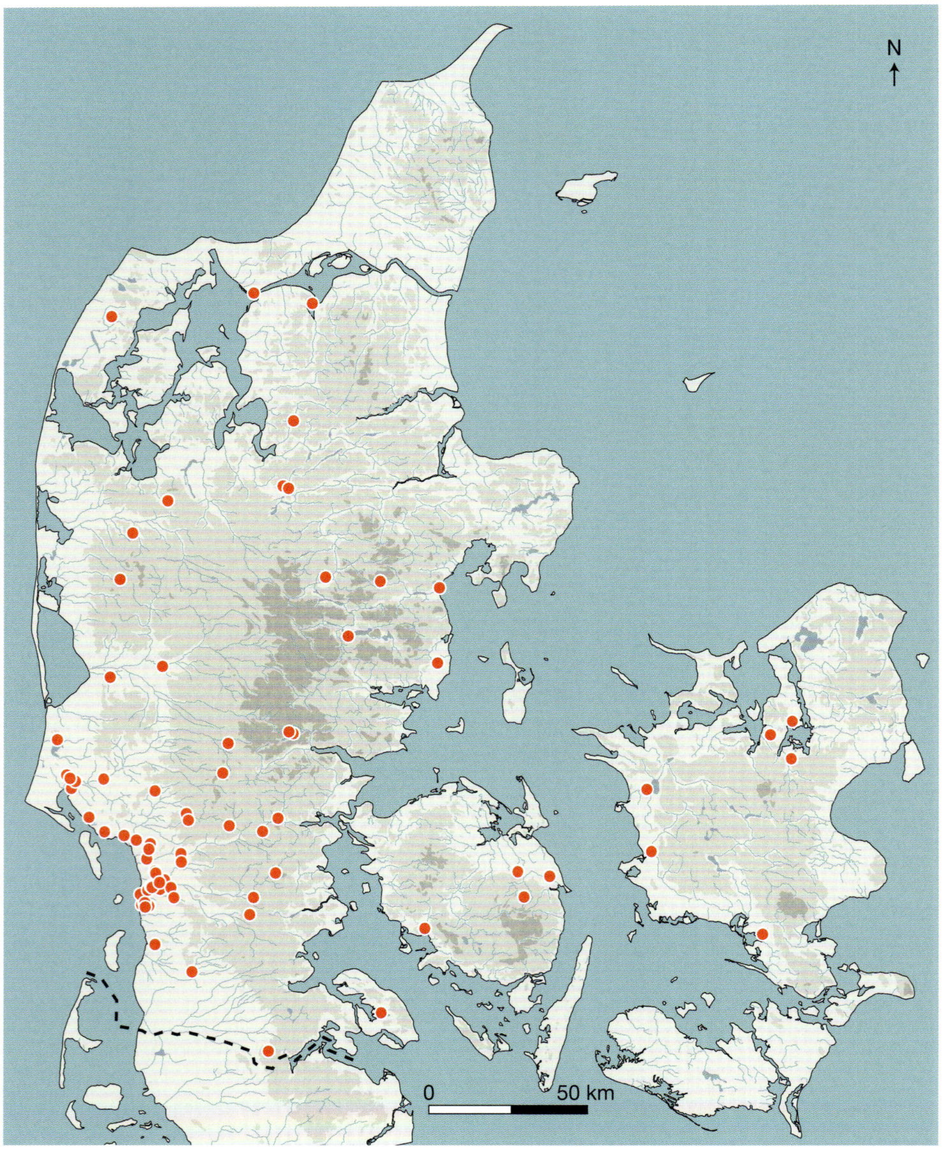

Fig. 127. Finds of basalt quernstones in Denmark. After Feveile 2010.

captives, although no evidence of slaveholding at that date is currently known. For this reason there does not appear to be much to imply that slave trading constituted a significant component of the economy of Ribe in the 8th century.

What remains is the surplus production which the farming population might deliver: iron, textiles, wool, skins and other animal products, as well perhaps as live beasts. It is difficult to estimate the extent of iron production, but there are remarkably few and only small finds of iron ingots in the archaeology of Ribe, and no substantial quantities of forging slag that would serve to show that iron played any major role as a commodity. Consequently one has to suggest that textile, wool, hides and animal products, as well perhaps as live beasts, would appear to have been the goods that the merchants would have taken home with them. Such was the situation later in the Middle Ages too.

5.8.8.6 Sceattas, kings and moneyers

The first attempts to make a case for the foundation of Ribe by a Danish king were based upon the famous layer of driftsand and subsequently through the regular plot layout, which was regarded as a single, designed feature. Neither of these explanations seems to work any more, and rather than having been a unitary, ready-made foundation Ribe appears to have evolved through an agreement between Frisian traders and the Dankirke family – and yet one cannot entirely rule out the possibility that a Danish king was also involved in the process.

In the well-preserved stratigraphy of Ribe it has been possible to analyse the use of sceattas, and to observe that in the earliest decades of the history of the town many different types were in use, a situation which changed from the year 725, after which only Wodan/monster sceattas were in use. This coin profile is viewed

172

as a reflex of the fact that a single monopoly coinage was introduced, and that implies that there was also an authority with the power to impose and maintain this reform. A further implication is that there must have been an operative mint, presumably under the leadership of a master moneyer. This interpretation of the numismatic evidence further means that a Danish king must be inferred to have taken control over Ribe around the year 725, and that this royal hold was maintained through to the second half of the 9th century. The motive behind the system of coinage was to secure income based upon compulsory exchange. That presupposes that there was also some system of tolls on imported goods and another fee for keeping the peace in the market site (Middleton 2005).

It is not really possible as things currently stand firmly to establish whether or not monopoly coinages were in use in the same way in the other 8th-century emporia, because insights of this nature depend upon both well-preserved stratigraphy and a careful method of excavation. In respect of the former in particular, Ribe is in a class of its own. The formation processes in the largest of the emporia, Dorestad, were fundamentally different from Ribe, as the town followed the shifting course of the Rhine, producing a horizontal rather than a vertical stratigraphy, which has also been highly vulnerable to taphonomy (van Es & Verwers 1980). The many finds of Wodan/monster sceattas at Reric/Groß Strömkendorf could indicate that a system reminiscent to that in Ribe functioned there, but there is no intact stratigraphy there which could confirm that. The moneyers Rimoaldus and Madelinus are known from Dorestad, and since Ribe was similar to Dorestad in many other ways its coinage system was probably modelled on the latter site's too (Pol 2010).

The coin system appears to require there having been a royal representative in 8th-century Ribe, probably a *comes vici* as known at Dorestad, Hedeby and Birka. In the archaeology of the town there is as yet no sign of either finds or structures which could apparently be linked to an office of that kind of military/aristocratic character; but if we were to suggest a location from the reconstructed topography of the town area it might be the hill below the later parish church of St Nikolaj, or the raised ground beneath the museum Ribes Vikinger (Fig. 128) (S. Jensen 1990; 1991b).

The special legal status of the town was later expressed through physical separation from the surrounding territory in the form of ditches – what is called the 'town ditch' (see below), which appears to date back to the 9th century. In the preceding period too, when the level of activity was considerably greater, there must have been a jurisdictional boundary between the town and the surrounding countryside. In the absence of evidence of that, it may be suggested to have followed the wet areas in such a way that the whole of the dry island between the Ribe and Tved Rivers was incorporated within what was later known as *the peace of the town*.

5.9 Ribe in the 9th century

At the transition to the archaeological Viking Period, traditionally put at around the year 800, Ribe was a town a century old in which the level of activity was still high. The lane along the river with the plots was still the main element of the town, and several of the wells from the 8th century were maintained and used into the 9th. Building in the area behind the

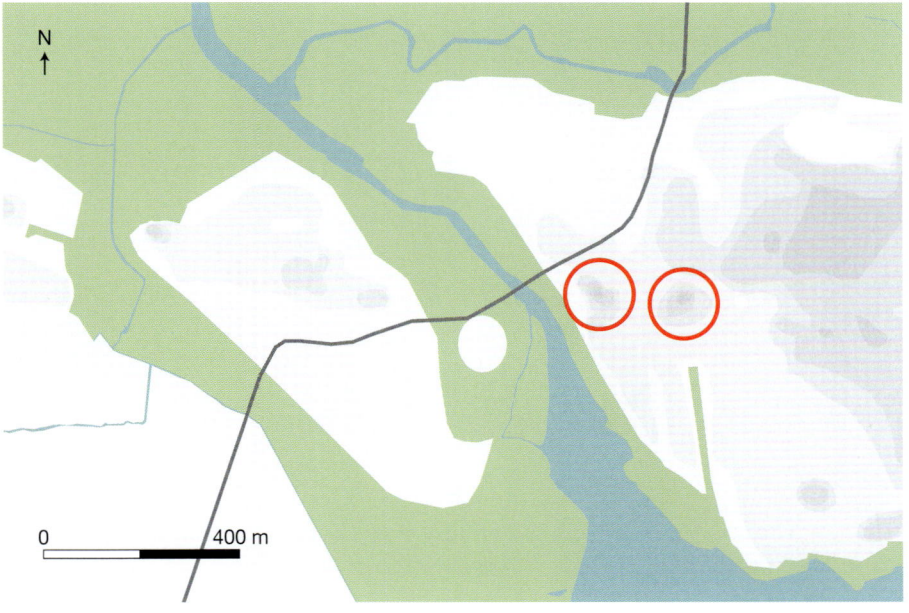

Fig. 128. The circles surround the two natural slightly raised areas which were the most prominent hills of the earliest Ribe. The hill to the west has been almost entirely removed by a castle of the Middle Ages and the construction of the gasworks and electricity power station there in the 19th and 20th centuries. The hill to the east has been the location of the parish church of St Nikolaj and its associated nunnery since the Middle Ages, and burials and buildings have largely removed any possible earlier remains.

river land was still very thin. In the course of the 9th century, however, there were major changes. The town was provided with its first known physical boundaries against the surrounding countryside, a church was founded on the opposite side of the river, and a little later in the century the level of activity fell sharply.

5.9.1 Stratigraphy from the 9th century

In many respects, the archaeological state of affairs from the 9th century is more problematic than from the previous phase. No wood is preserved in the layers from this period, and despite the fact that the finds from the plots are otherwise comprehensive we have only one dendrochronological dating from the 9th century in contrast to 55 from the 8th. As well as the preservation of organic remains being worse, the 9th-century layers are also far more damaged by taphonomic factors. These circumstances mean that the dating of various features in the excavations is almost entirely based upon artefactual finds from the excavated structures (Fig. 129).

5.9.2 Settlement and activities on the plots and in the lane alongside the river

Through the Post Office site excavation, and the most recent resurfacing of Sct. Nicolaj Gade in 2010-11 (ASR 2360), considerable areas of plots of the 9th century were uncovered which show very clearly that the pattern of the 8th century involving narrow tenement plots either side of the lane alongside the river was maintained (Fig. 130). Only around this central part of the lane are stratigraphic deposits of the 9th century preserved (see section 5.2, Taphonomy), but as the line of the street from ASR 926 Ribelund I was also in existence in the 9th century there is at least slender evidence for a case to be made that the lane survived over its full extent.

On two of the only partially uncovered plots in the Post Office site traces were found of what are suggested there to have been permanent buildings with clay floors and post-holes or wall trenches in the wall lines; only smaller sections of these probable houses were revealed, however (Feveile & Jensen 2006b, 184ff). On this slender basis one may conclude that

Fig. 129. The silver pin from ASR 9 Posthuset. Apart from coins, finds in precious metal from 8th- and 9th-century Ribe are few and small. The only really high-status artefact that is know from the layers is this silver pin of phase G (AD 800-820). The head was originally decorated with gripping beasts, and gilt. ASR 9x377.

Fig. 130. Composite plan of the plot structure of phase D ASR 9 Posthuset and ASR 2360 Sct. Nicolaj Gade. Light grey areas are modern pipe trenches. The plot structure on the Post Office site is of phase D, the period AD 760-80, at c. 4.0-4.4 m over sea-level, while the plots uncovered out in the street area were more than a metre higher and must date to the 9th and 10th centuries. There is therefore a chronological span of about a century between the layout mapped from the Post Office site and the situation out in the street. It can be seen that there was a minor realignment of the lane towards the north but that the pattern involving narrow plots was maintained.

N
↑

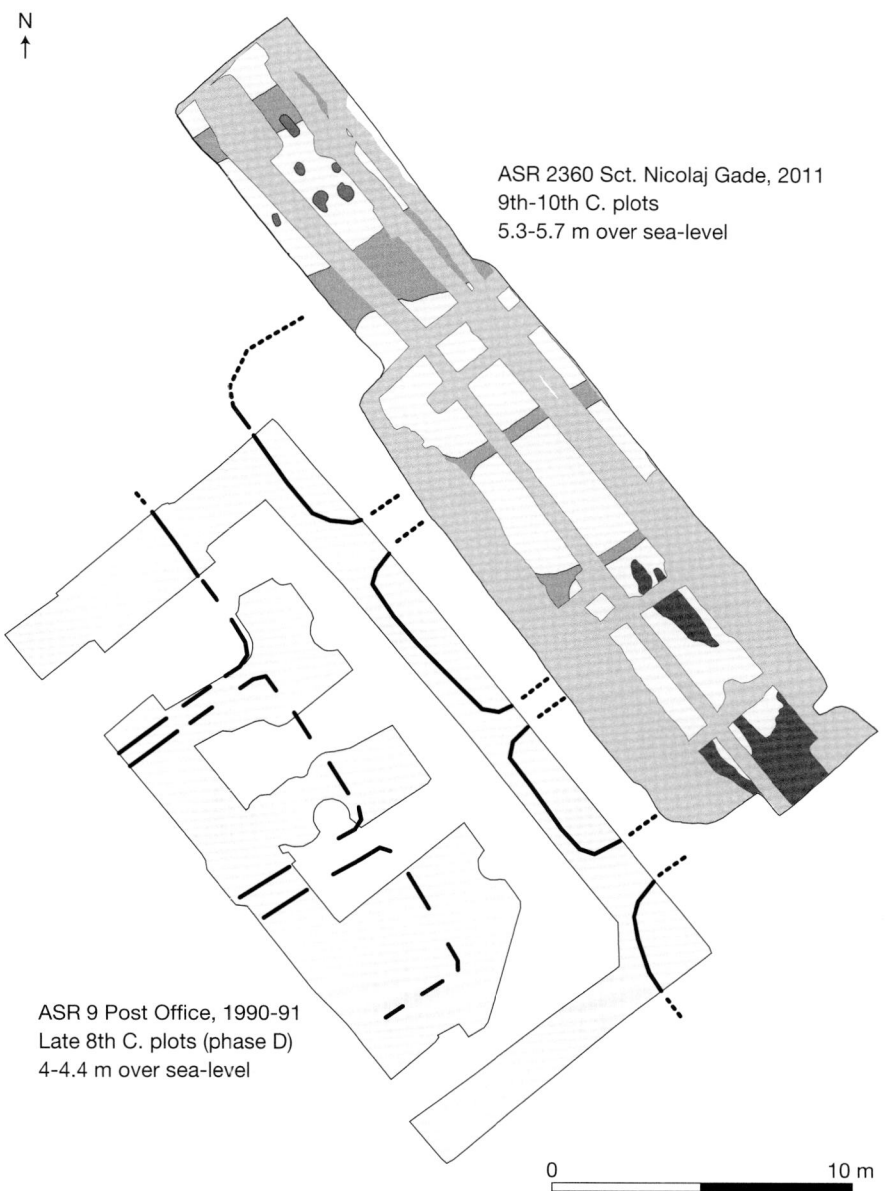

ASR 2360 Sct. Nicolaj Gade, 2011
9th-10th C. plots
5.3-5.7 m over sea-level

ASR 9 Post Office, 1990-91
Late 8th C. plots (phase D)
4-4.4 m over sea-level

0   10 m

the great majority of the stratigraphy of the plots from the 9th century has long been lost. To judge by the surviving remains, there were regular buildings alongside the lane, although it seems equally certain that other plots did not have any major structures but were rather work spaces or may have housed tents, windbreaks or other light structures.

The rich finds assemblage from the 9th-century layers on plots shows that trade and specialized craft production were continuing there. The artefact inventory and the waste products changed as a consequence of changes in the pattern of trade (see section 5.9.3, below), but essentially both the sequence of finds and the stratigraphy appear to reflect continuity in the pattern of activities that had been characteristic of the plots in the previous century too.

At Ribelund, a number of the excavated longhouses have been dated on the basis of finds from the post-holes primarily to the 8th century, but the evidence is slight, and a programme of radiocarbon dating here could have paid off handsomely. Some of the SFBs are from the 9th century, and overall it can be said that this area was also occupied in the 9th century (Feveile 2006d).

5.9.3 9th-century trade

When King Godfred moved the merchants from Reric to Hedeby in 808 a thrust was given to the growth of the largest and most important town of Viking-period Scandinavia, and the archaeological results from Hedeby clearly show that it was only from this date that a streetway surrounded by plots which formed the backbone of the 9th-century trading town was established along the bank of Haddebyer Nor (von Carnap-Bornheim et al. 2007; Arents & Eisenschmidt 2010; Schietzel 2014). Like Ribe a century earlier, the growth of Hedeby seems to have been rapid, but Hedeby was to become considerably larger than Ribe and must have had a major impact on the patterns of trade in Ribe as well. Aarhus similarly seems to have emerged around this date, but in the 9th century was apparently a very small trading site (H. Skov 2008).

In the well-dated stratigraphy in Ribe, it is possible to follow a series of changes in the pattern of trade from the end of the 8th century to a short way into the 9th. The north-facing contacts begin to become far more conspicuous in the archaeological evidence, in the form of both soapstone and whetstones of dark grey/violet Caledonian slate (Feveile & Jensen 2006b, 140f). All in all, we must reckon with traders from Norway being present amongst the visitors to the town to a growing extent.

The well-known contacts with the Rhineland and the Frisian zone are underscored by the presence of the imported pottery *par excellence* of the Viking Period, Badorf Ware (Sindbæk 2007), as well as the even larger Reliefband amphorae. The attractive foil-decorated jugs that are known as Tating Ware also start to show up. The occurrence of these wares in the layers at Ribe is not a reflex of new trading contacts but rather evidence for the growth of the near-industrial production of those high-quality vessels, jugs and amphorae that came to accompany the traders around the North European trading network. The Frisian grey ware tempered with crushed mussel shell, Muschelgrus Ware, appears in the layers from the end of the 8th century and forms another characteristic feature of the layers dated to the 9th century.

In the sphere of beadmaking, there were fundamental changes. Production in Ribe appears to cease, clearly reflected in the absence not only of production waste but also of raw materials in the form of tesserae, raw glass and blown glass sherds (Feveile & Jensen 2006b, 146ff). Alternatively, finished beads were now imported in the form of metal foil covered beads, green lead glass beads, drawn cylindrical glass beads, mosaic eye beads, and more (Sode & Feveile 2002).

It is not possible to exclude the possibility that this is due to chance because of just where the excavations have been placed – nonetheless the layers of the 9th century contain a large quantity of fragments of moulds from the production of a mass of the dress-accessories of the period: oval brooches, equal-armed brooches, lozenge brooches, large disc brooches, horse brooches, and more. This form of production appears to have been on a large scale in 9th-century Ribe.

5.9.4 The coin economy

The finds from Ribe show that the Wodan/monster sceatt was used on the plots down to around the year 800. After that a new and larger coin appears in the stratigraphy, with a diameter of around 18 mm but struck on a markedly thinner blank: the form of the denier/penny which was to become the standard coin-form far into the Middle Ages (Tab. 14; Fig. 131) (Feveile 2006b, 284). These are coins of Combination Group (KG) 4-6 (Malmer 1966; Williams 2007), which is also known as the Rayface/deer penny. The design of this coin matches that of the Wodan/monster sceattas. On the objverse is a staring face with spiky hair and beard, and on the reverse a forward (KG 4) or backward-facing (KG 5-6) animal (Figs. 125, 131). In the disturbed layers of the 9th century these thin coins are particularly poorly preserved, but none of them has any visible sign of having been tested, bent or re-worked as jewellery. From the material available to us, the Rayface/deer penny appears to continue in the role of the Wodan/monster sceatt as the monopoly coinage of Ribe: the royal Ribe coinage. The evidence from the town is supplemented by finds of exactly the same type of coin from excavations and detecting at Okholm (Feveile 2001). The finds from there also show no sign of having been treated as anything other than coins.

This coin-type is also known from several other sites in Scandinavia, including a number of graves at Birka (Malmer 1966), but in those cases has typically been re-worked into jewellery and thus is no longer 'money' (Kilger 2008). The distribution has in the past led to an unfinished debate over where the coin-type was struck (Malmer 2002; Williams

Journal no.	Site	KG 5-6	KG 5-6?	CEIII KG 7-9	?
ASR 8	Rosenallé	1			
ASR 9	Posthuset	3	3		1
ASR 926	Ribelund I	1		1	
ASR 1077	Sct. Nicolaj Gade 14		1		

Table 14. Finds of coins of the denier/penny type of the 9th and 10th centuries in the town of Ribe. After Feveile 2006b, 285.

2007; 2011). The sensational find of the Damhus hoard just outside Ribe in 2018 consisting of 258 Rayface/Deer A coins (KG 4) and four Ship/Deer coins confirmed the association of also this coin type with Ribe (fig. 131, 168) (Moesgaard 2018, Feveile & Moesgaard 2018).

The Wodan/monster sceattas from Reric noted above suggest that these coins were also used as the sole coinage there. When the merchants of Reric were moved to Hedeby in 808 a change seems to have taken place. From Hedeby just one single Wodan/monster sceatt has been found, and minting at the site began with what are known as Dorestad imitations. The earliest of these, KG 3, is dated to the beginning of the 9th century, and the type is understood to have been the prototype for coins minted in Hedeby down to the middle of the 9th century (KG 7-9: Malmer 1966; Williams 2007). The Dorestad imitations appear therefore to have been the royal *Hedeby coin*, and the selection of Dorestad as the model may possible express a desire for Hedeby to be 'the Dorestad of the North'.

The finds from Ribe, conversely, show that the Rayface/deer pennies were used in this town, in light of which it is entirely reasonable to describe it as a Ribe mint product. From early in the 9th century, then, it can be seen that, rather than controlling one single coin-type, namely the Wodan/monster sceatt, the royal authority introduced several types for use in the different towns. Further types of coin are known besides KG 3 and KG 4-6, the mint sites of which are a matter of discussion.

Despite the poor conditions for preservation, the coin finds from Ribe and the surrounding area together with the absence of evidence of any hacksilver economy point quite unambiguously to the maintenance of a functional monetized economy in the town based upon the Rayface/deer penny.

5.9.5 Town Ditch A

During excavation ASR 8 Rosen Allé in 1989 a mass of dug features were found: not only a cemetery and settlement but also street-lines and defensive structures, covering a period from the 8th century to post-medieval times. A ditch with a curved course was found, and two non-aligned stretches of a true moat with an opening between them (Fig. 132).

For the first time, traces of both a boundary and the defence of the town had been found, and in later excavations it was possible to find more of both the minor ditch and the moat and it could be seen that the smaller ditch underlay the larger moat and so must be older. The smaller ditch has been labelled Town Ditch A while the true defensive structure is Moat B. The town ditch could be

Fig. 131. At the top, a fragment of a Rayface/deer B penny found by metal-detecting at Okholm. SJM 154x18. Below, complete specimens of Rayface/deer B (middle) and Rayface/deer A (bottom). Photo: ASR and NM.

dated as having been dug in the first half of the 9th century on the basis of the finds from the fill in the Rosen Allé excavation combined with the stratigraphical relationships that can be identified. Measured from what was then the ground surface the width of the ditch was around 2 m but it was only around a metre deep.

In 2014, together with the Department of Medieval and Renaissance Archaeology of Aarhus University, the museum undertook a training excavation that extended the area of the ASR 8 site to the south, excavation SJM 348. Beneath Moat B was found a smaller ditch, K200, which matches Town Ditch A in size and was running parallel to the later Moat B. Radiocarbon dating from the fill of the smaller ditch puts its refilling in the 10th century: see section 5.10.3.

From the available evidence, it would thus appear that there are at least two courses of town ditch that are not contemporary. It would appear most likely that

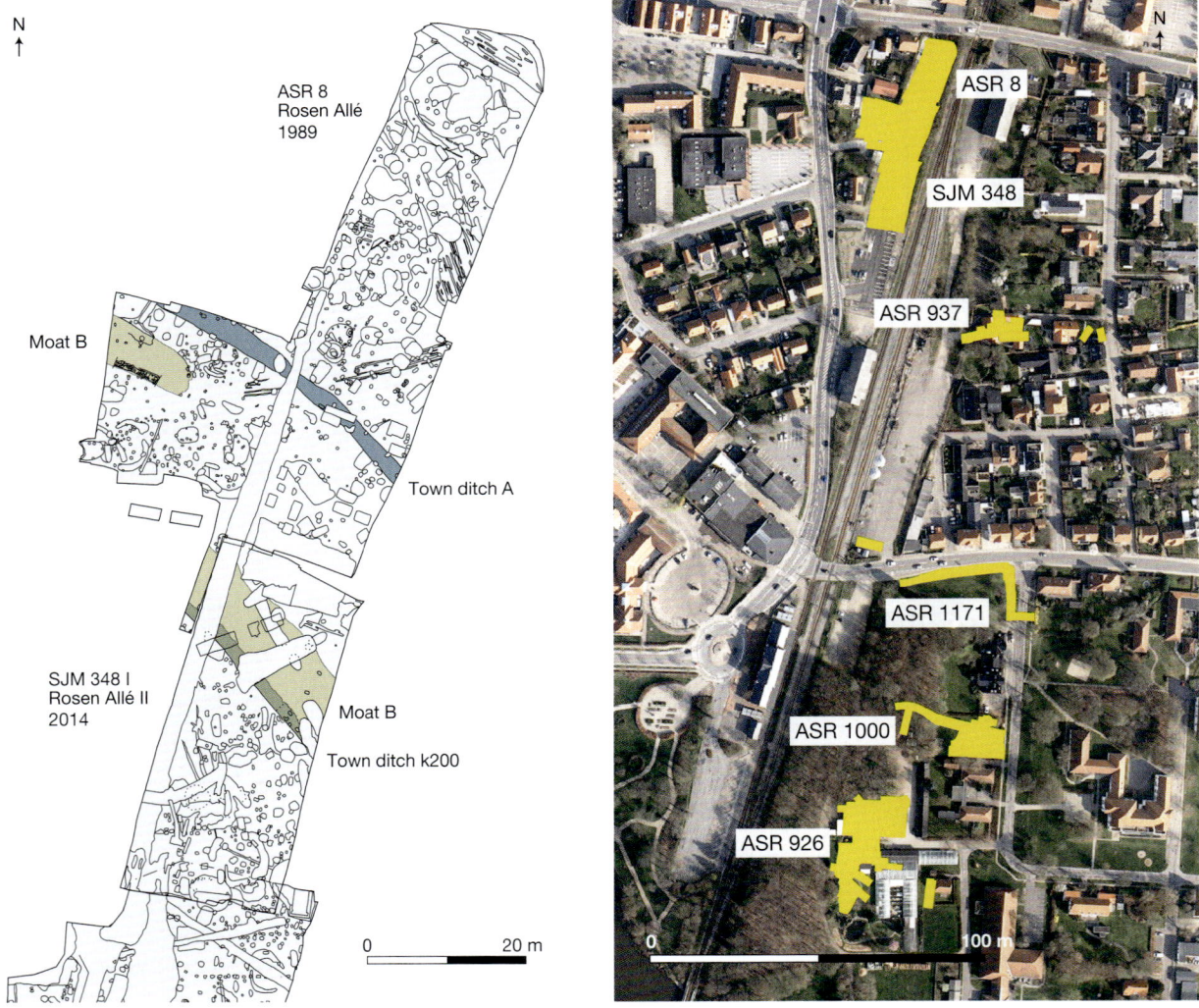

Fig. 132. Town Ditch A and Moat B as they were seen in the excavations ASR 8 Rosen Allé (1989) and SJM 348 Rosen Allé II (2014). To the right, an overview of the excavations that have revealed sections of the defences of Ribe in the 9th and 10th centuries.

the town ditch that was found underneath Moat B in the excavations ASR 937 Øst, ASR 1000 and SJM 348 is part of the the same course which must then have been functional in the 10th century; there is nothing, however, to show that Town Ditch A of ASR 8 was not constructed in the first half of the 9th century. If the isolated town ditch in ASR 926, Ribelund I, belongs to one of these two ditches or the other is indeterminable (Feveile 2006e; Feveile & Jensen 2006a; Munch Kristiansen et al. 2019) (Fig. 132).

The present interpretation is, then, that the first boundary marker of Ribe was Town Ditch A, constructed in the first half of the 9th century and re-filled deliberately or with blown sand relatively soon. That the feature may have successors in almost the same position may be because this ditch had a bank on the inner side that was still visible after the ditch had re-filled. On current evidence, the successor should have been ditch K200.

5.9.6 The 'heathen' cemetery

Town Ditch A and the later town boundaries cut through the cemetery area of the 8th century. We do not know for certain that the marking of this boundary represents the regulation of the burial area but that does appear likely. Unfortunately no radiocarbon dating has yet been carried out on any of the many cremation burials, whose dating therefore depends entirely on the evidence of the grave goods. It is nonetheless striking that the few more or less securely dated burials of the 9th century lie outside the town ditch (Feveile 2006h). On slight evidence it may therefore appear that the town ditch of the 9th century also came to define a new boundary line between the town and its heathen burial ground. The fact that only one to three graves have been found dated to the 9th century in comparison with the large number of the 8th century would appear also to show that there was a major difference in the frequency of burial; whether, however, that was really the case has to wait upon the results of a research project that is currently underway.[27]

5.9.7 Settlement in the area behind the lane parallel to the river

The archaeological situation in respect of the settlement in the area behind the lane along the river and its relationship with the cemetery area and the town ditch discussed below is extremely complicated. In summary, one can say that the settlement must have been thinly dispersed and still, as in the 8th century, concentrated around the river lane. The datings of various features as based on the whole on artefactual finds alone but many of those can be older, residual finds or types with broad date-ranges.

Just one well discovered in this area could have been functioning in the 9th century. Well ASR 863 A175 from Seminarievej was constructed in the second half of the 8th century and refurbished twice with the sinking of undated pinewood timbers, implying a functioning life continuing into the 9th century.

The largest continuous excavated area consists of sites ASR 8 Rosen Allé and the three seasons of SJM 348 (Fig. 133). The results of the latter excavation have not yet fully been worked through and a number scientific datings are still awaited; nonetheless, a series of points are striking. Practically all of the area excavated has to be regarded as part of the town in the 9th century as it lies inside the boundary marked by Town Ditch A. Despite the many features in the area that are both earlier and later, in the form of 8th-century graves and various types of settlement evidence from the Middle Ages and later, there is nothing which could argue that hypothetical traces of evidence for settlement from the Viking Period would not have been preserved, and yet such are very few – considering the functioning life of SFBs, this area must have been left more or less empty during the 9th century. In this whole large area there are traces of just three post-built houses that are not of the Middle Ages, of which only two appear to be of the Viking Period, and ten SFBs.

Settlement was densest around street-line A42. The traces of the roadway must be assumed to be Ribe's northern exit route, and since it runs right across the backfilled Town Ditch A and cannot be contemporary with Moat B and its bank it is most likely that the remains of this road are contemporary with Town Ditch K200: the second half of the 9th century and into the 10th century. This date-bracket is supported by the finds from SFBs I and V (Feveile & Jensen 2006a, 79ff) but does not explain why, then, the settlement lies outside Town Ditch K200.

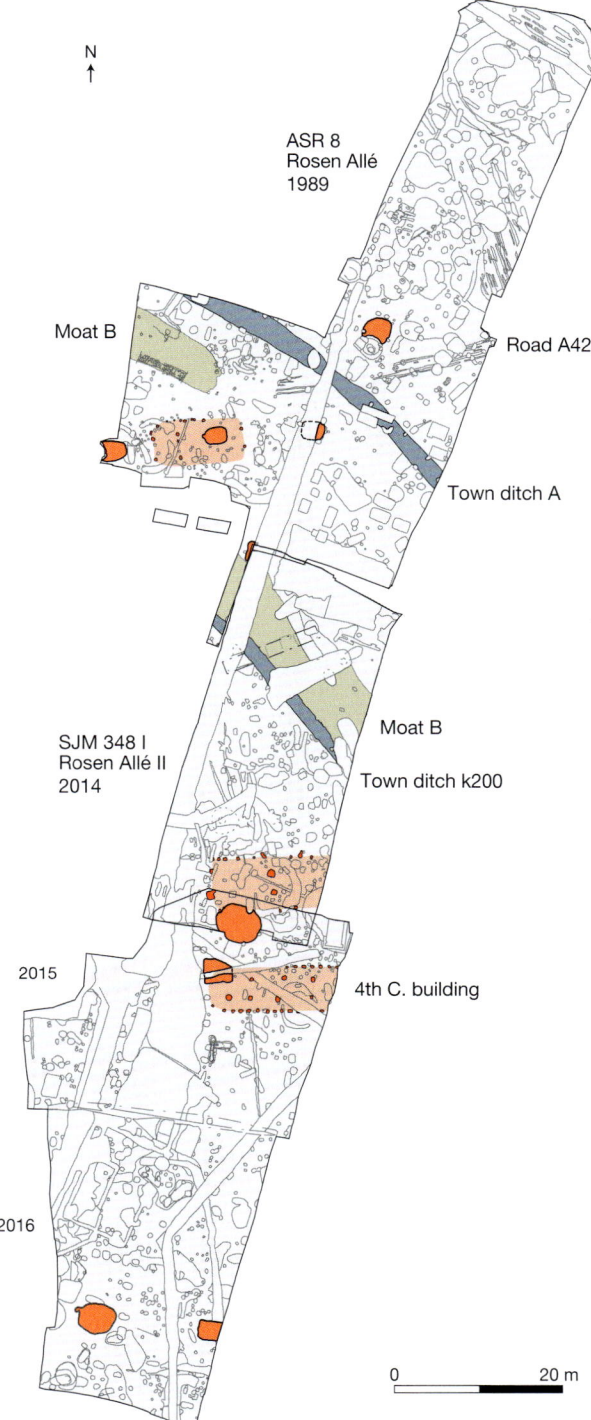

Fig. 133. At Rosen Allé, a continuous area of 4,133 sq m in total has been uncovered, which made it possible to assess the density of settlement in the area after the discontinuation of the cemetery on a large scale. The large area contained a total of ten sunken feature buildings (red) and three longhouses (also red) of which only two are of the Viking Period. All of this settlement appears to belong to the 9th century, when the area had very dispersed occupation, while it was void of settlement in the 10th century. No wells of the Viking Period were found in this area.

5.9.8 The Church of Our Lady in Ribe in the period c. AD 855-1050

The possibility that below the culture layers on the cathedral side there might be layers and features from the Viking Period was a decisive factor in the earliest excavations in Ribe up until the discovery in the cellar of the Art Museum (*Kunstmuseets kælder*) in 1972. As the result of that work was clear, the question concerning the Viking Period of Ribe was reduced to that of a lacuna in the history of the town; where, then, was the Viking Period proper? Excavations at the western end of the cathedral island produced no evidence for activity before the Middle Ages, and in the absence of better knowledge the digging away hypothesis was formulated: the layers of the Viking Period had lain north of the river but had been dug away and used in damming the river, while Paypyt was left in the hollow which this earth-shifting left. However excavations in the dam itself were unable to produce Viking-period finds.

Successive excavations in the streets of the town and large area excavations in the western quarter of Ribe during the 1980s and 1990s had also failed to produce finds from the Viking Period, and the view of the museum gradually came to be that the information in the Life of Ansgar about King Haarik II

Fig. 134. Side C of the large Jelling stone with the portrayal of Christ above the inscription ok Dani gærþi kristna, *'and made the Danes Christian'. Drawn by J. Magnus Petersen. After Wimmer.*

granting a plot for the building of a church in Ribe and the presence of three Danish bishops at the Synod of Ingelheim in 948 did not necessarily mean that a church had been built (Kieffer-Olsen 2008).

In the year 2000, a larger block of flats immediately south of Ribe Cathedral was destroyed by fire. The plot was excavated in two campaigns, in 2008-9 and 2011-12. In addition, the whole Cathedral Square was remodelled in 2012 which also led to extensive excavations which have altogether multiplied the archaeological understanding of Ribe Cathedral many times over. The excavations have shown that beneath the thick culture layers at the site lies a large Christian cemetery from the Viking Period, in which an estimated two to three thousand people were buried in the period c. AD 855-1050.

In the following section the results of the excavations in the Viking-period churchyard connected to Ribe Cathedral are presented. In this context the chronological scheme which the presentation of the material otherwise follows is temporarily suspended. After that we return to the chronological framework, and the significance of the church for Ribe will be discussed in those sections.

5.9.8.1 The missionary period in Denmark

When King Harald Bluetooth raised the great Jelling stone, he had the long inscription conclude with a line of text which is transcribed as *ok Dani gærþi kristna*: 'and made the Danes Christian' (Fig. 134). Harald's own conversion must have preceded that, and according to the Saxon chronicler Widukind of the monastery of Corvey that had been after Harald had witnessed the missionary Poppo undergo his famous ordeal by hot iron. The event is thought to date to the year 963, and it has been corroborated that the successful missionary was one and the same as Volkmar the Canon of Cologne who became Archbishop of Cologne in 965 (Gelting 2007).

Harald's conversion is rightly regarded as a watershed in the history of Denmark, and it is the natural starting point for the majority of discussions about the progress of the conversion of Denmark to Christianity. Before Poppo's ordeal, however, there had been a period of around 250 years in which missionaries had intermittently been operating in Denmark, and many Danish merchants, aristocrats, seafarers and pirates were personally familiar with the flourishing Christian areas to the south and west.

The written sources which shed light on the conversion are both few and controversial. Our knowledge of the first missionary efforts is based primarily on the hagiographies of Willibrord and Ansgar – problematic sources if one wishes to discover what the impact of their visits really was (Knibbs 2011).

The first missionaries whose efforts in Denmark we have some information about included the Anglo-Saxon Willibrord, who probably met a Danish king, Ongendus or Angantyr, as early as the 690s, with little success (K.H. Andersen 2017, 402). King Angantyr is described as crueller than a wild beast and harder than a stone, and Willibrord had to travel back to his cloister of Echternach in what is now Luxembourg having failed in his mission. According to his hagiographer, Alcuin, Willibrord brought thirty young boys with him from the meeting who may perhaps have been converts intended to play a role as missionaries (Skovgaard-Petersen 1981, 27f).

As a consequence of Charlemagne's successful Saxon wars through the latter part of the 8th century the northern boundary of Christendom was pushed forward to the Elbe. The next Frankish emperor, Louis the Pious, tried to establish influence in Denmark from around 815 through an alliance with Harald Klak, who had formerly had a share in the Danish royal power but had been driven out by the sons of King Godfred. This alliance briefly opened the way for missionizing in Denmark in the years 823-7, when various missionaries with Archbishop Ebo of Reims at their head were at work in the country (Fig. 135). It is possible that Ansgar also took part in this campaign, which may have had more impact than we can now know (Knibbs 2011, 66ff). The power-relationship between Denmark and the Frankish Empire, including the expulsion of Harald Klak from Denmark in 827, was not, however, favourable for the evangelization of Denmark in the following decades.

In 829 Louis the Pious sent a delegation of missionaries to the flourishing trading site of Birka, where the Swedish king Bjørn received them warmly and permitted them to build a church – apparently the first church in Scandinavia.

A new critical reassessment of *Vita Anskarii* in relation to contemporary Frankish sources points out that in 834 Louis the Pious had Ansgar consecrated bishop of a newly established missionary see in Hamburg which was subject to the archiepiscopate of Mainz and so was not initially a metropolitan see itself (Knibbs 2011). The new missionary establishment faced hard times, characterized by growing pressure on the northern boundaries of the Frankish realm. A Viking force burned Hamburg in 845 and the missionary see was transferred to Bremen which then was subject to the archiepiscopate of Cologne.

From here, the missionary bishop Ansgar carried on with his work, and was in Hedeby around 850, at that time the most important trading site in Denmark, where King Haarik I gave permission for a church to be built, the first in Denmark. It has not so far been possible to find this church archaeologically, but a considerable proportion of the many excavated graves

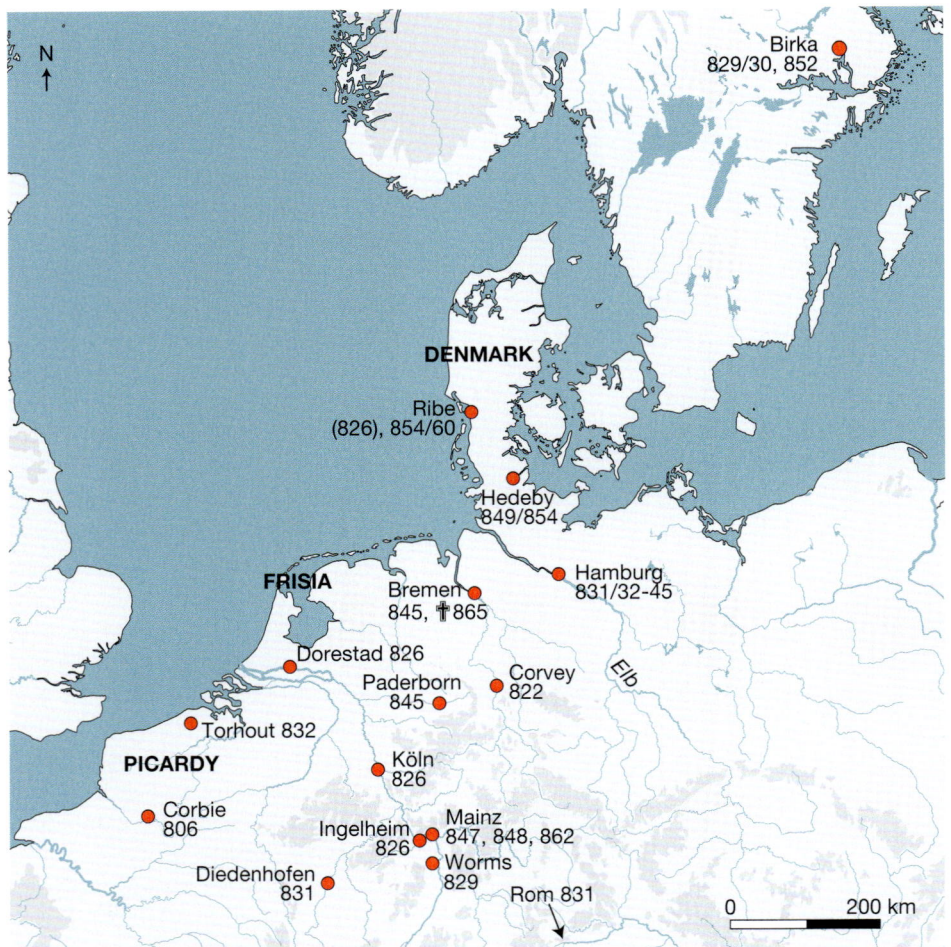

Fig. 135. Places visited and resided in by Ansgar. The River Elbe was the boundary between the Christian and heathen zones down to the 960s. After Müller-Wille 2014.

from Hedeby show clear Christian influence, especially in what is known as the *Flachgräberfeld*: 'the flat-grave cemetery' (Arents & Eisenschmidt 2010, vol. I, 292ff). The finding of a church bell, typologically datable pre-1050, in the harbour at Hedeby may also indicate that the church was nearby and may be taken as evidence that the church in question was demolished at some stage and not rebuilt (Kalmring 2010, 441).

A few years after the building of the church in Hedeby, around 855, Ansgar received a plot of land in Ribe from King Haarik's successor the young Haarik II. A church is supposed to have been built here and a priest could take up permanent residence (Skovgaard-Petersen 1981, 34ff). The excavations at the cathedral church of Our Lady (*Vor Frue*) in Ribe show that that was the site at which Ansgar's church was raised, and it has survived without interruption to the present day.

The presence of one or two churches in Denmark was, however, only a small step towards the conclusive triumph of Christianity over heathenism. Our knowledge of the history of Denmark in the 10th century is regrettably highly fragmentary, especially before the breakthrough of the Jelling dynasty around the middle of the century, and even after that there are major

areas that remain obscure. However the archaeology shows that throughout the 10th century we are faced with growing Christian influence on burial practice in terms of the positioning of the dead in the grave, with the Christian custom of an W.-E. orientation, lying supine, becoming predominant (Eisenschmidt 2004b). Various cross motifs also occur occasionally amongst the grave goods. This trend is reinforced by a continually increasing number of detector finds of metalwork that includes the cross amongst the decorative elements, both imported pieces and locally made (Baastrup 2009; Feveile 2011; for the Saxon region, see Müller-Wille 2003).

Heathen cult sites like Uppåkra in Skåne and Lejre and Tissø on Sjælland were also flourishing at this date (Gelting 2007; L. Jørgensen 2014).

In 948 there were three Danish bishops, from Schleswig, Aarhus and Ribe, at a synod in Ingelheim. The character of these early bishoprics is a matter of discussion (Gelting 2004; Lund 2004; Refskou 2004) but it cannot be coincidental that all three sites were trading centres in the southern half of Jutland – those areas of the country which had the greatest degree of contact and exposure to Christian territories.

Around the year 963 King Harald Bluetooth adopted Christianity (Gelting 2007) but, as the excavations at Ribe Cathedral described below show, there was already at that date apparently a greater or smaller Christian minority in Denmark. Harald's conversion was a major victory for the metropolitan see of Cologne but created a particular field of problems in terms of power politics for the Danish kingship which now hosted an ecclesiastical institution that was subject to the German Emperor. It has been proposed that an independent Danish Church may been dangled in front of Harald's eyes by Otto I but the German Emperor's need for support from Hamburg-Bremen in 964 brought the process to a halt and created a seed bed for growing Dano-German tensions in the following decades (K.H. Andersen 2017, 407). This may be the real reason why around 987 the next king, Svein Forkbeard, proposed the expulsion of the bishops of the now four Danish sees, Schleswig, Ribe, Aarhus and Odense (Gelting 2004, 172ff). Only the missionary bishop Odinkar the Elder, who was trained in Bremen, is thought to have been tolerated by Svein, possibly because they were related. Odinkar the Elder was active in Sweden and eastern Denmark and was buried in the cathedral of St Peter in Bremen (Gelting 2004).

Svein Forkbeard re-oriented the Danish Church towards England, and around 1020 his successor, Cnut the Great, divided the country into four bishoprics – Jutland, Fyn, Sjælland and Skåne – subordinate to the archiepiscopate of Canterbury. This structure and the close ties with the Anglo-Saxon Church continued until the redistribution of dioceses under King Svein Estridsen c. 1059, which resulted in seven Danish dioceses subordinate to Hamburg-Bremen (Gelting 2004).

The names of Cnut's first bishops in the Diocese of Ribe are not known, but probably around the year 1030 Odinkar the Younger was installed, nephew to both the king and to Odinkar the Elder. The Episcopal Chronicle of Ribe understood that it was during his episcopacy that half of all the king's rights in Ribe were granted to the see. On his death in 1043 Odinkar bequeathed a great deal of property to the Church.

5.9.8.2 Earlier excavations at the cathedral

Prior to 2008 no major archaeological excavations had taken place at Ribe Cathedral. The lack of investigations down to the middle of the 20th century can to some extent be explained by the distance from the National Museum in Copenhagen, but whatever the reason it is lamentable, as the principal restoration of the cathedral of 1882-1904 was a ham-fisted undertaking which may indeed have saved the church from demolition but in the process destroyed numerous ancient monuments lying underground. Large parts of the church were underpinned, an extensive heating system was sunk into the ground beneath the floor of the church, and finally the whole area around the church was reduced by 1.0-1.5 m. The digging work destroyed thousands of medieval graves, including burials in sandstone tomb chests and many graves lined with tufa or brick as well as innumerable burials in wooden coffins – on the whole with no surviving documentation (*DK*, Ribe amt, 522ff). In 1930-1 the foundations beneath the apse and the eastern transept wall were renovated, likewise without antiquarian supervision (Fig. 136).

Fig. 136. Photograph of the digging work east of the northern transept in 1931 where the former chapter house had stood. A sandstone tomb chest of the 12th or 13th century can be seen, and the light layers beside the red dot are the naturally deposited driftsand which the first church on the site had been built upon. When this hole was dug a very large number of graves from the Viking Period and the Middle Ages must have been destroyed. After a photograph in SJM.

Fig. 137. Prior to 2008 only three proper archaeological excavations had taken place around the cathedral, and all of them were quite small. The areas of excavation are in yellow. South of the cathedral can be seen excavation area ASR 13, divided into stage I (2008-9) and stage II (2011-12). The base plan is an aerial photograph of 2016.

The first proper archaeological excavation was in 1986, when a limited investigation of the ground beneath the grave of King Christoffer I (1252-9) in the crossing was undertaken (Fig. 137). Beneath a tomb walled with tufa were found graves on an alignment which differed from that of the extant church. There was no sign of stonework in the graves, nor any other datable evidence (Frandsen, Madsen & Mikkelsen 1990, 14ff).

In 1987 a trial trench of just 5 sq m south-west of the preserved section of the cathedral's processional circuit was dug. The earliest discovery at this spot was a burial which it was not possible to radiocarbon-date. The grave was covered by settlement layers and had no trace of stonework (Frandsen, Madsen & Mikkelsen 1990, 16f). In 1995, 6 sq m were excavated at the address of Torvet 9, south-east of the cathedral. Below metre-thick settlement layers an original ground surface was found in which two cuts were recorded of

the form and size of children's graves, containing a number of nails but no skeletal remains. Towards the south-east the ground surface had been removed by a large ditch (Klemensen 1996).

5.9.8.3 The excavations of 2008-12

After the fire of the year 2000, the plot south of the cathedral remained empty. In the meantime the developer-pays principle was incorporated into the Danish Museum Act that came into force in 2002, as a result of which the bill for the archaeological excavations on the plot would land on the local authority's desk. After a considerable period it proved possible to achieve the funding needed for a partial excavation of the plot paid for by the property company Realea A/S.

The excavation *ASR 13 Lindegården I* took place in 2008-9, and was archaeologically planned out on the basis of a desire to achieve the greatest possible information about the earliest state of affairs in this area. As the answer to that question lay up to 5 m below the present ground surface it was impossible to carry out the excavation with vertical sections. The precise positioning of the excavation trench also had largely to take into account a safe distance from standing walls and the scope for creating supporting steps for the sections. For the same reasons the extent of the excavation was reduced as it progressed deeper. The area of excavation at the upper levels was c. 230 sq m but at the bottom of the trench it was 127 sq m. The results were thought-provoking, and made it possible to raise funds from various quarters for a complete excavation of the plot in question (Søvsø 2009, 2011b). This excavation, *ASR 13 Lindegården II*, was carried out in 2011-12 and paid for by the council of Ribe Cathedral with support from the Velux Fund and the Culture Agency. The area of excavation was 585 sq m at the upper levels and 408 sq m at the base.

Concurrent with these excavations, plans were introduced to reshape the entire cathedral square in Ribe. The successful plan proposed that the large number of differences in level created by the digging away of the site in the 1890s should be levelled off to create steadily sloping surfaces leading into the church itself. The architect Torben Schönherr won the competition and the project was funded by Realdania and Esbjerg District Council. It was carried out in 2011-12 and led to comprehensive excavations and recording in the upper earth layers together with, in places, trenches and minor excavations which also provided information on the earliest state of affairs at the site: excavation *ASR 2391, Ribe domkirkeplads*.

5.9.8.3.1 The terrain underneath Ribe Cathedral

In the course of the Middle Ages, organic culture layers from 3 to 4 m thick were deposited in the cathedral area. These layers containing settlement detritus and burials completely seal the original form of the landscape, the character and appearance of which was largely unknown before the excavations of 2008-12: see section 5.3. From the middle of the 12th century the present cathedral building has stood here, and the accumulation of culture layers had already begun when it was first raised. Towards the south the area is bounded by Sønderportsgade, the Droveway, the earliest line of which shown by wheel ruts followed the terrain at around 2.35 m over sea-level (Søvsø 2006, 8ff).

The excavation at Lindegården showed that the original ground surface here rose slightly towards the north to reach a level of about 2.75 m at the northern limit of excavation. Around the cathedral itself, the density of burial had removed the majority of the

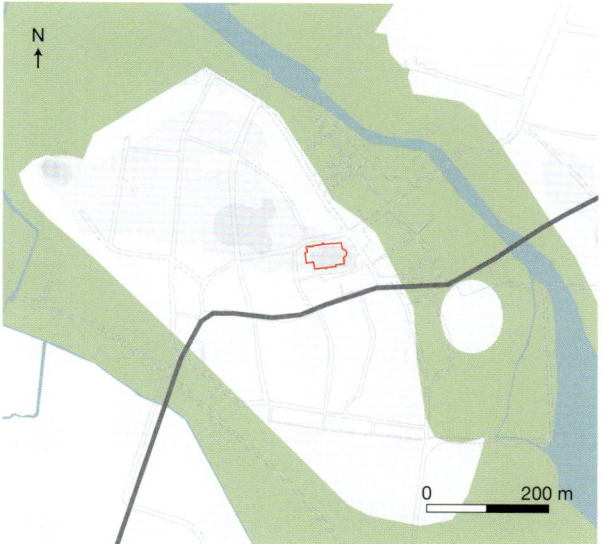

Fig. 138. Reconstruction of the terrain of the cathedral island beneath the culture layers. Green areas are low-lying land, below 2 m over sea-level while the contours of the drier areas are at 1-m intervals. The sand dune underneath the cathedral can be seen to reach a height of just over 4 m over sea-level.

ground surface, but east and north of the church building a prominent blown sand dune was found, the surface of which had reached around 4 m over sea-level. This dune is just one of many that have been discovered in and around Ribe, and the story of how it formed can hardly have meant anything to the earliest users of the site, although what really matters is that this formed a marked and naturally bounded terrace standing more than 1.5 m above the roadway to the south which would have been striking to passers-by and to those using the market site on the other side of the river. The top of the dune appears to have been beneath the eastern end of the cathedral with falling slopes recorded to the east, west and south.

5.9.8.3.2 The Viking-period churchyard at Lindegården

The excavation of the area started from a level of 6 m over sea-level, and both of the campaigns noted above were carried out stratigraphically with layers and features removed in their reversed chronological order. This revealed a dynamic history of settlement through which the changing use of the site through time could be traced in the culture layers deposited. At a depth of around 3.5 m the original ground surface was found in the form of a greyish, leached soil layer with underlying podsolization in patches in the form of pale sand formations and further down some hard pan in the natural sand.

Fig. 139. ASR 13 Lindegården. General plan with Viking-period graves recorded at the level of the original ground surface. Later disturbances which extended into the ground are shown in light grey. The two cemetery ditches are shown in a darker grey.

A total of 83 graves were found dug from the surface of the soil layer along with two ditch lines and various further features all of which were sealed by the earliest true culture layer (Fig. 139). The sealing culture layer was formed by settlement on the site which was also evidence in boundary markers, waste pits and buildings. It was quite clear that a former burial ground had been given up for urban settlement, the archaeological footprint of which corresponded closely to what is known from other excavations in Ribe. At the same time it was noticeable that the same sequence of development could be recorded in the minor excavations of 1987 and 1995 west and east of Lindegården respectively (Fig. 137). This must reflect the growth of a genuinely urban settlement around the principal routeway of Sønderportsgade that took over an area of the extensive churchyard around the cathedral.

The dating of the sealing settlement layer is important for an understanding of the underlying cemetery. In the southern part of the area remains of a timber building constructed in 1077 (Fig. 174) were found in the culture layers deposited over the original soil layer. Beneath the building was a culture layer of some 0.4 m containing, amongst other things, several pits. Dendrochronological datings and coin finds place the appropriation of the former churchyard area by settlement closely around the year 1050: see section 5.11.2.2. The imposition of the settlement is understood to have been the result of parcelling up of land which brought this phase of the use of the cathedral area as a cemetery to an end. The graves discussed here are therefore all certainly earlier than 1050.

5.9.8.3.3 The churchyard ditches

Two substantial E.-W. ditches were recorded in the excavation which from stratigraphy and their finds belong together with the graves (Fig. 139). The ditches are understood to have been cemetery ditches which created a boundary between the consecrated earth of the cemetery and the outside world. The northern ditch was cut by wagon-body grave G1140 and several earlier graves were found below the ditch. The ditch itself had been scarcely 2.5 m wide, with a rounded profile, but its depth was only just over 0.5 m. On the base were found thin, water-deposited sand layers, but the main fill above those consisted of dark grey, muddy clay, probably material transported for the backfilling of the ditch. Only one reduced body sherd of pottery and animal bones were found in the ditch. The presence of graves that are both earlier and later than the ditch show that this represents one phase of the history of the churchyard.

At the extreme southern limit was recorded a markedly larger ditch which could not be excavated to its full width although that can be estimated as c. 2.5 m while it was c. 1.5 m deep. Cross-sectioning showed that this ditch had been cleaned out several times but its position at the limit of excavation left limited scope for separating out the individual layers within the ditch.

The excavation to the east of 1995 (Fig. 137) revealed the edge of a major ditch with the same stratigraphical contents. In the cathedral square itself similar ditches have been discovered in several locations. Altogether, these observations indicate that the entire Viking-period churchyard was enclosed by ditches. A churchyard is consecrated ground, and the boundary to the surrounding world is rooted in Christian liturgy (Ottosen 2004). There are also numerous examples from other churchyards, and boundary ditches are unknown from heathen Viking-period cemeteries (Engberg & Kieffer-Olsen 1992; Eisenschmidt 2004a).

5.9.8.3.4 The graves

During the excavation, the removal of later cut features which reached into the undersoil had revealed that there were earlier graves in the area of excavation. Through shovel-scraping of the soil-layer surface and its growth horizon which was still preserved in some places several became visible: evidence that these graves must have been fully overgrown by the time that the culture layers sealed the cemetery. Traces of above-ground grave markers were assiduously sought but without success. The sealing growth horizons showed that the graves had been level with the surface, but it is likely that since-removed stones, slender hammered in wooden crosses or other structures, marked the positions of individual graves – despite careful searching, however, no surviving traces of any such embellishments were found. Some graves appeared to respect others in a way that presupposes either contemporaneity or grave markers, while other examples of intercutting graves show that any possible grave monuments were not particularly long-lasting. Of the total of 83 graves identified 77 could be excavated. In all cases the graves held just one individual. Amongst the graves examined some had been almost totally removed by later interventions, two were interpreted as intentionally emptied already in the Viking Period, while the bones in other graves no longer survived. In light of the sandy natural undersoil of the site the general state of preservation of the bones can nonetheless be described as relatively good. It is without question being sealed underneath thick culture layers from as early as the 11th century that has slowed the decomposition of the bones. The overlying layers have also reduced bioturbation of the level of the burials with the result that the edges of the grave cuts, as well as traces of coffins and other decomposed features within the graves, were still sharp.

In comparison with other excavated Viking-period graves from Ribe which had not been covered by a similar thick, protective culture layer, the difference in condition is manifest (Fig. 140) (Feveile 2006h, 280f). The good conditions for observations in Lindegården also meant that the potential for missing the graves of infants was reduced, although simply in terms of size there is inevitably a greater risk that such have been completely removed by later cut features.

The dimensions and depths of the graves could be measured precisely thanks to the partially pre-

Fig. 140. G1559 lay against the western baulk of the trench and may serve as the typical example of the mottled appearance of the grave fill and the pin-sharp differentiation of layers that are due to having been sealed beneath thick culture layers. Photograph: SJM.

Coffin-type	n	%
Plank coffin without nails	42	61
Plank coffin with nails	5	7
Plank coffin of re-used materials	2	3
Hollowed out coffin	14	20
Hollowed out coffin in chamber	1	1
Logboat	1	1
Logboat in chamber	1	1
Wagon body	1	1
Uncoffined	2	3
Total	**69**	**~ 100%**

Table 15. The various types of coffin found in the Viking-period graves at Lindegården.

served ground surface. The grave pit itself appeared to have been carefully dug and to have had a clearly rectangular shape, vertical sides, and a flat base. Some graves were more than 1 m deep but adults were usually buried 0.6-0.8 m below the ground level while children's graves were shallower. One infant's grave, G1565, was only 0.26 m deep.

In two graves, G1556 and G1559, the sides of the grave pit had been protected by staves producing a form of chamber grave. The planks had not been sunk into a slit trench in the base of either grave pit, as otherwise was typical with chamber graves. The width of these graves was only 0.60 and 0.65 m while their lengths are not precisely known because the heads lay beyond the limit of excavation. Considering the position of the bodies in the graves, the lengths of the graves would appear to be consistent with other burials, and in both cases the deceased was also laid to rest within a coffin, which in one of these cases was a logboat and in the other was a log coffin. Perhaps we can imagine that the staves stuck out above the ground surface after the grave was filled to serve as a grave marker?

After the burial rite, all of the graves seem to have been backfilled with the soil that had been dug out of the pit, consisting typically of a mixture of lumps of soil, pale sand, and natural sand mixed with hard pan (Fig. 140).

5.9.8.3.5 Types of coffin

The overwhelming majority of the graves had surviving evidence of some type of coffin in the form of decomposed traces of wood, in some cases supplemented with rusted iron lumps from material that must have been part of the construction of the coffins. In a single case, G1603, wood was preserved undecomposed; this has since been identified as ash. In 69 of the 83 graves the disposition of the evidence of the wood provided secure evidence of what the coffin was like (Tab. 15). The remaining 14 burials in which the coffin-type was indeterminable were all graves that had either been completely removed by later interventions or were only partially within the limits of excavation. If these are discounted, coffins have been identified in 67 out of 69 graves, or 97%. The other two graves appear, from the position of the body and the absence of evidence of coffining, to have been uncoffined (Fig. 141).

On the whole, the coffins fall into two principal groups. The largest group consists of planked coffins, found in 71% of the graves. The majority of these were rectangular in shape, although trapezoidal coffins are also recognizable. The degree of decomposition renders it difficult to determine with certainty, but the traces of a number of coffins are

Fig. 141. In G1578, the grave of a man of around 1.60 m aged 18-25 at death, no signs of a coffin were found. The position of the arms also indicated that this was an uncoffined burial. Photograph: SJM.

Fig. 142. In G1548, the grave of a man of around 1.65 m aged 45-55 at death, the shadow of the wood of the hollowed out coffin was well preserved. Photograph: SJM.

widest at the head end, and the inverse has not been recorded. The majority were jointed without iron nails and as far as one can judge from the surviving evidence the great majority of the coffins also had both bases and lids. No traces of slatted coffins were found. In a number of cases it was observed that the mark of the end of the coffin stood pushed in from the sides of the coffin, but it was not possible to determine with confidence whether or not this state of affairs came about only after burial, as the coffin broke down in the ground.

With a few exceptions, the lengths of the coffins appear to have been right for the deceased, and they have to be supposed to have been purpose-made. The widths varied somewhat, fluctuating from 25 to 50 cm for adults. A neonate was buried in a trapezoidal coffin only 10-15 cm wide. Two planked coffins appear to have been made of re-used materials. In one of these

cases, G1573, 11 rivets were found in the northern side of the coffin which could indicated that this part of the coffin was produced using one or two re-used boat-planks. In the other case, G1549, rows of small nails were found in the base of the coffin and rivets in each corner. What the earlier use of the material of this coffin may have been has not yet been determined with confidence. The overall impression given by the planked coffins is that the great majority were made for purpose with only a few signs of re-used materials having been made use of.

The other primary coffin-type is labelled here hollowed out coffins (Fig. 142), but probably comprises various phenomena. In a number of graves the mark of the wood of the coffin revealed the impression of a round-bottomed container, the shape of which in plan might be practically rectangular but with rounded corners, oval, or more or less pointed.

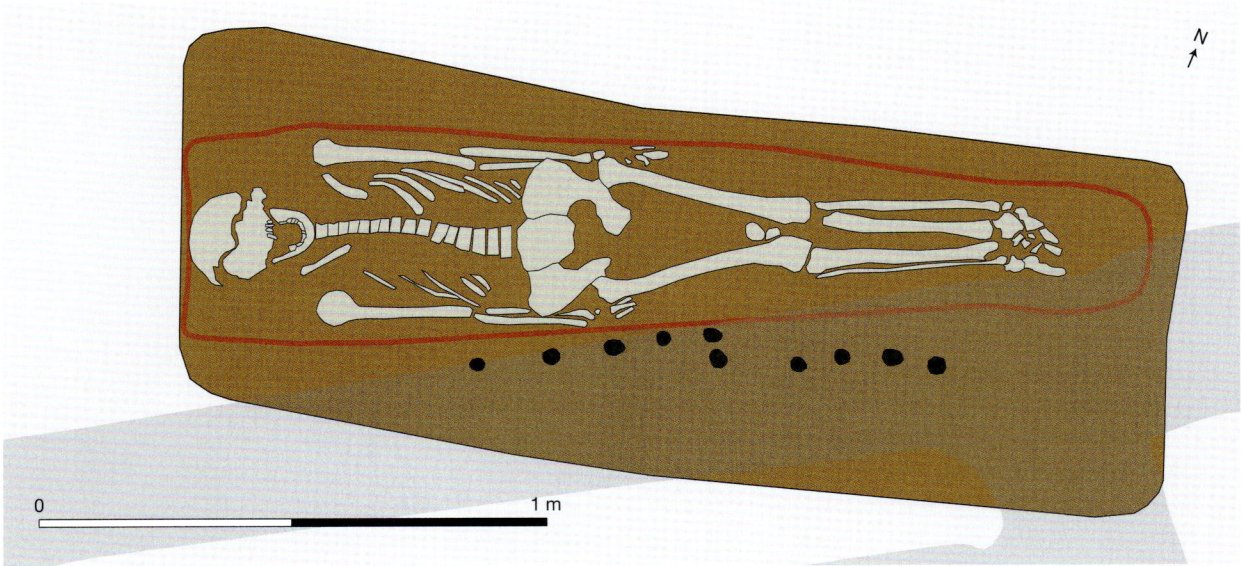

Fig. 143. Grave K1132 was the burial of a woman of around 1.55 m aged 40-50 at death. The shape of the coffin stain in plan and section indicates that she was laid to rest in the prow of a logboat. Above the grave lay a decomposed lid in which 10 small nails stood vertically (black circles).

From excavations where the preservation has been better it is known that split and hollowed out tree trunks, sometimes with lids made of half of the log, logboats or troughs, could be used as coffins early in the Christian period (M. Cinthio 2002; J.N. Nielsen 2004). In this excavation, the impression left by the coffin was in some cases sufficiently unambiguous for us to be able classify the coffin as a logboat or a tree-trunk coffin, but in most cases it has not been possible to determine with certainty whether it is a case of a re-used trough, a logboat or a specially made tree-trunk coffin. It is striking, nonetheless, that there appears to be a very close fit between the stature of the deceased and the length of the hollowed out coffins, and altogether one may assert that there is no definite sign that re-used troughs were made use of as coffins at Ribe Cathedral such as is the case at the edge of the churchyard of Skt. Drotten in Lund (M. Cinthio 2002, 63ff). Andrén has suggested that the distribution of re-used coffins in that churchyard reflected socio-economic factors (Andrén 2000).

There were two cases, both the graves of women, in which the traces of wood had a distinctly pointed shape that indicates that both coffins had been re-used logboats, G1559 and G1132 (Figs. 140, 143). Only one of these graves was excavated in full, and this seems to have contained a truncated boat. Similar boat graves are well known from both heathen and Christian cemeteries of the Viking Period and earlier Middle Ages, and apparently have their source in a pre-Christian conception of death as a journey to the realm of the dead (Müller-Wille 1995; Price 2008;

Stoumann 2009, 221). There are parallels to the impressions left in logboats of the Viking Period and Middle Ages found in wetlands (Bork-Pedersen 2011).

In one case, G1556, the outline of the wood was of such massive size that the coffin is understood to have consisted of the two halves of a split and hollowed out trunk, a rather less familiar type of coffin but nonetheless one that has been found even in Christian churchyards here and there when the conditions for preservation are suitable (M. Cinthio 2002, 72ff with refs.). This type of coffin is known from as early as the Late Neolithic and occurs widely in northern European funerary evidence in exceptional preservative conditions. This is a distinctly aristocratic coffin-type, and significantly, indeed, King Arthur was buried in a log coffin according to the historian Gerald of Wales in the context of the excavation of Arthur's alleged grave at Glastonbury Abbey in 1191.[28] In this light one may surmise that the woman buried in a log coffin alongside Ribe Cathedral also belonged to the uppermost social class. The aristocratic character of the grave was further emphasized by the fact that the sides of the grave were planked: in other words, it was a chamber grave. It was also possible in many cases to recognize remains of a cover in the form of thin shadows of wood in the graves containing hollowed out coffins. With the great majority of the hollowed out coffins the cover appears to have been planking.

In one case, a clinker-built wagon body was found used as a coffin, but this grave no longer contained any remains of the deceased as it had been emptied

Fig. 144. G1140 was emptied at some point after the burial and no longer contained any remains of the deceased. Only this clinker-built wagon body measuring 2 x 1 m was left in the grave. Photograph: SJM.

out shortly after the burial (Fig. 144). This behaviour was clearly recognizable in the form of a very distinct robber trench that surrounded the whole grave. The grave fill was therefore sieved but it contained no finds or bones. The impression of the wagon body was well preserved, showing a clinker-built structure of 2 x 1 m containing seven base and side planks and two end planks. In the middle of the box on either side were found the two typical iron rings while brackets and nails provide precise information on how the ends and sides were joined. In the middle of the western end there were two strips of iron, one over the other, which may have held a vertical staff; apart from these, however, all of the other iron components served to fasten the structure together.

We shall unfortunately never know who was interred in this intriguing grave, nor who it was who then exhumed that person. The grave-type, however, is a regular feature of cemeteries of the Viking Period, particularly in Jutland where in the great majority of cases they are the graves of wealthy women and of the 10th century (Eisenschmidt 2004a, 61ff). They are perceived to have been a counterpart to the elite male graves of that period, the equestrian graves. It is likely, therefore, that this was the grave of a high-status woman who died sometime in the course of the 10th century. We must also assume that this grave was marked at the surface since its reopening surrounded the grave itself very accurately. One motif for exhumation could have been a desire to translate the body to another churchyard –perhaps the private church of the family? Another grave appeared to have been deliberately emptied, G1595, and here too the exhumation was very accurately placed around the original grave.

5.9.8.3.6 Those buried

A total of 74 graves were able to provide data for determination of sex and age at death (Figs. 145-6 and Tab. 16).[29] Ten of the skeletons from these graves were adults but did not display clear male or female morphology and so are not included in the figures in Table 16. The majority of these unsexed adults were skeletons of a poor state of preservation but corresponding with the women in stature, so that the majority of them are suspected to have been female. The preponderance of men can thus partly be explained through male skeletons being more robust and having survived better in the ground than women's.

The occurrence of considerable numbers of both children's and women's graves clearly shows that the population which was buried at Ribe Cathedral included men, women and children, and no tendency towards sexual differentiation is evident. Amongst the 17 children buried 7 were infants under 1 year of age and one, G1550, was born premature, with a length in the grave of c. 0.30 m. This clearly shows that even neonates were buried.

All of the dead were lying on their backs with the head to the west. The arms lay predominantly straight alongside the body, known as arm-position A, with only a few variants. There was one grave with arm-position D, G1552. In the apparently uncoffined grave G1578 the deceased appeared to have been laid carelessly on the base of the pit with one arm crossing the stomach (Fig. 141). In the round-bottomed hollowed out coffins the arms in some cases lay in across the pelvis because of the shape of the coffin.

The provisional osteological examinations of the skeletal remains have revealed a range of traumas and

Fig. 145. Sexed graves. Red: female; blue: male. Sexing is based upon the physical anthropological report and skeletons with 'clear' or 'convincingly' female or male morphology have been classified as women and men respectively. Children and adults, women and men, appear fully interspersed.

pathologies which will not be dealt with in more detail here as a more extensive analysis is in progress. One case was so serious, however, that it must be noted. G1563, a man of about 50, was found to have been decapitated, and his separated head was placed by the right arm of the body (Fig. 147). What is more, a collection of animal bones had been placed on top of the coffin when the grave was being refilled – from a provisional assessment these included the jaw bones of a cow and a pig and several larger limb bones.

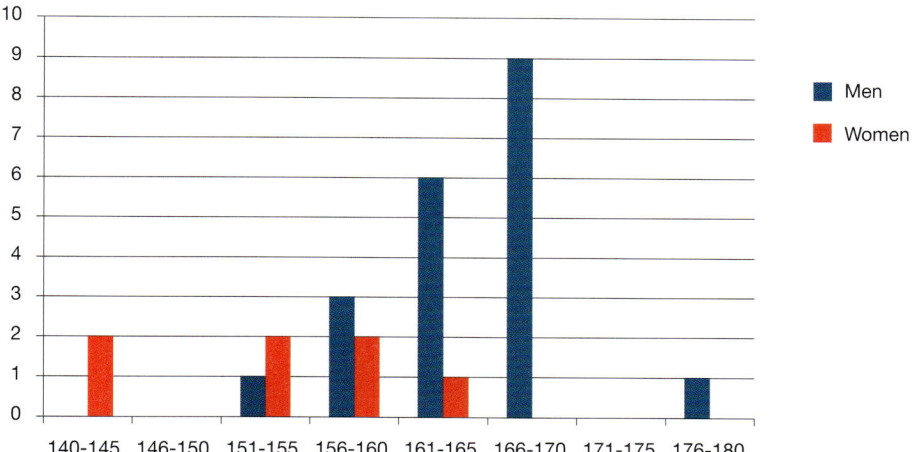

Fig. 146. The stature of the adult individuals from dimensions in the graves. The women had a mean height of 152 cm, the men 165 cm.

Sexual classification	*n*	%
Men	30	47
Women	17	27
Children	17	27
Total	**64**	**~100%**

Table 16. The sexed burials.

The collection of bones looks more like butchery waste than a food offering. There was room in the coffin to have put the separated head in the correct anatomical position so it must have been deliberate in this case for the cause of death to be represented within the grave.

5.9.8.3.7 Grave goods

Only two graves had surviving grave goods. G1133, a child of around 6 in a planked coffin joined with nails, was buried with a string of beads around the neck which consisted of a total of 9 beads: 7 of glass, 1 of amber, and greatly decomposed spherical corroded flakes which were eventually identified as silver, most probably the remains of a silver bead (Fig. 148). The beads are worn and cannot be dated closely although similar necklaces are known from graves dated to the 10th century (Roesdahl 1977; 1978; Christiansen & Sarauw 2010). G1607, a man of 25-45 in a planked coffin, had an iron knife some 16 cm long at the hip, a divergence from the Christian burial practice that is unique amongst the graves excavated.

If the graves had contained organic grave goods such as the hazel rods that are known from a number of early medieval contexts, those no longer survived (Krogh 1965; M. Cinthio 2002, 83ff).

Fig. 147. G1563 after the coffin was fully exposed. The deceased had been decapitated. Photograph: SJM.

Fig. 148. G1133 was the grave of a child aged around 6 at death who was buried with a string of beads of which seven were glass and one amber plus a sheet-silver bead which survived only as corroded flakes. Photograph: SJM.

5.9.8.3.8 The dating of the graves at Lindegården

A series of samples were dated, and the calibrated and marine reservoir effect-corrected results coincide overwhelmingly with the period before the official conversion of Denmark under Harald Bluetooth (Fig. 149). In the cases of G1135 and G1145 by far the majority of the range of probability remains in the 9th century. The radiocarbon dating of human bone is a debated issue in Denmark that has, in the past, led to keen discussion particularly of correction for the reservoir effect (Christensen & Lynnerup 2004; J.N. Nielsen 2004).

To help us evaluate the datings of those buried alongside Ribe Cathedral we have a range of supplementary archaeological details at our disposal. First and foremost, the terminal date of the cemetery at around 1050 is firmly grounded. Actual finds from the cemetery are very few, but the collection of beads in G1133 is to be dated typologically to after the mid-9th century while the wagon body grave G1140 is a type with parallels in the 10th century (Roesdahl 2006). The later churchyard ditch is dated to the first half of the 11th century on the strength of a more substantial assemblage of finds, while its predecessor must be older without necessarily going any further back than the 10th century.

The form of the graves themselves and their location may also imply an extended period of use. The varying alignments could possibly reflect a long period of burial in which the graves were, perhaps, oriented on the basis of various successive church buildings; it could also be due to the cemetery have been aligned upon various structures that indicated orientation. The most important evidence of the period of use must, however, be the number of cases of intercutting, which has to mean that above-ground grave markers had been lost before a new grave was dug.

The inconsistent degree of preservation of the skeletons is another indication that the period of use was extended. These differences were most significantly expressed in the stratigraphically related graves K1138 and K1139 in which a later child's skeleton was markedly better preserved than the earlier skeleton of an adult woman – both of them buried at the same level in uniform soil conditions.

A sorting of the human skeletal remains according to stratigraphical relations, the observed state of preservation, the measured collagen content of the bones, and radiocarbon datings all essentially give the same results. This indicates that the radiocarbon datings are essentially correct.

5.9.8.3.9 Viking-period graves in the cathedral square

The excavations of 2012 in the cathedral square made it possible to investigate the earliest phenomena at the site in small areas and minor trenches. In the old churchyard area, every excavated location has produced graves that were cut from the original ground surface which match those from Lindegården in appearance and type. They do not, however, all have the same useful *terminus ante quem* dating as the burials at Lindegården as these parts of the churchyard continued in use throughout the Middle Ages.

Fig. 149. The calibrated results of the 35 radiocarbon dates from in situ human skeletal remains taken to date, corrected for the marine reservoir effect. The datings were undertaken by Aarhus University radiocarbon laboratory and have been modelled by the author with the help of colleague, Museum Inspector Tobias Danborg Torfing using the OxCal programme, with AD 1060 as the latest possible date. From x1138 the marine fraction *was so low that there has been no reservoir effect correction. The green dotted line is placed at the date of the conversion of Harald Bluetooth c. AD 963.*

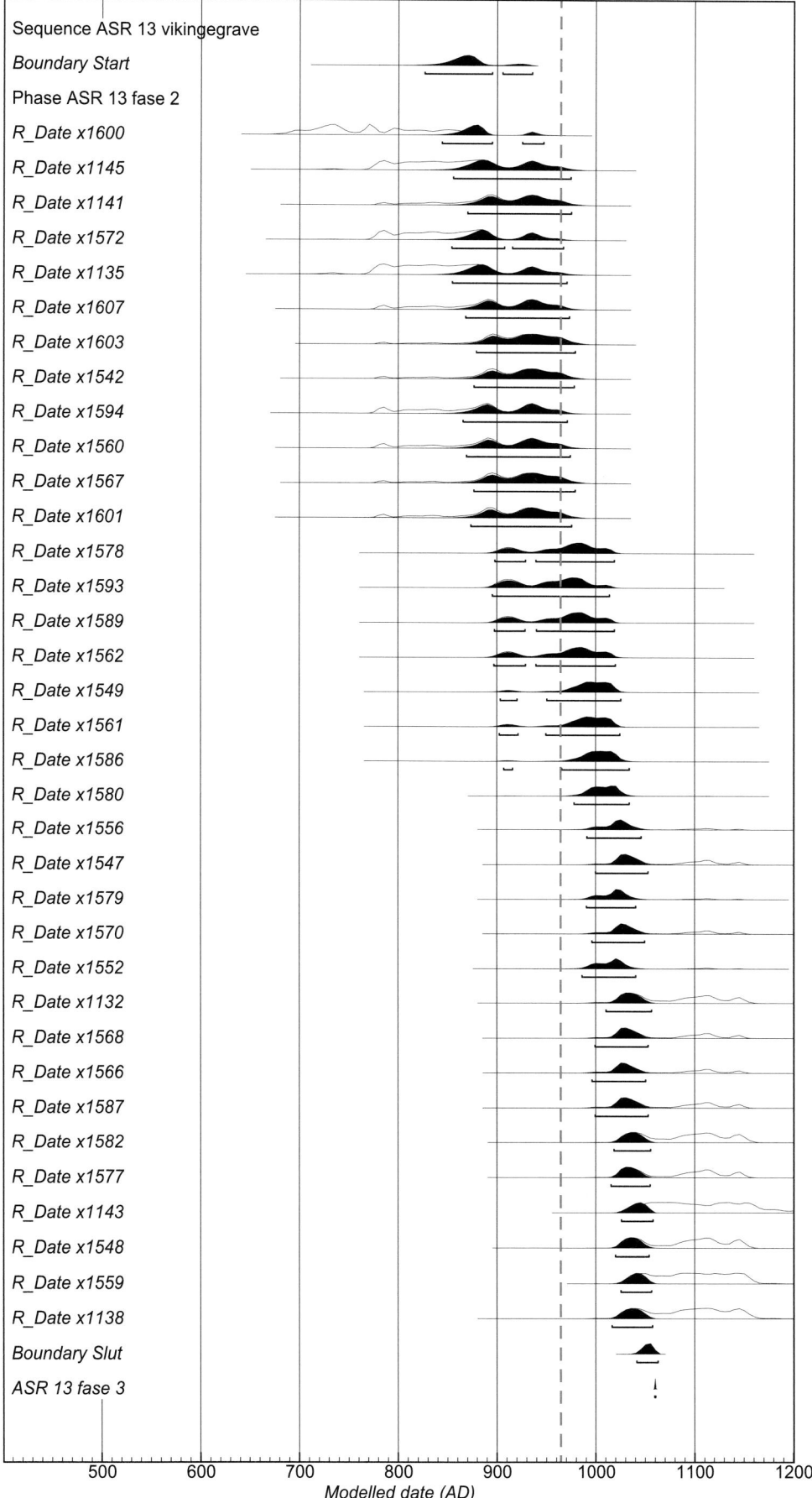

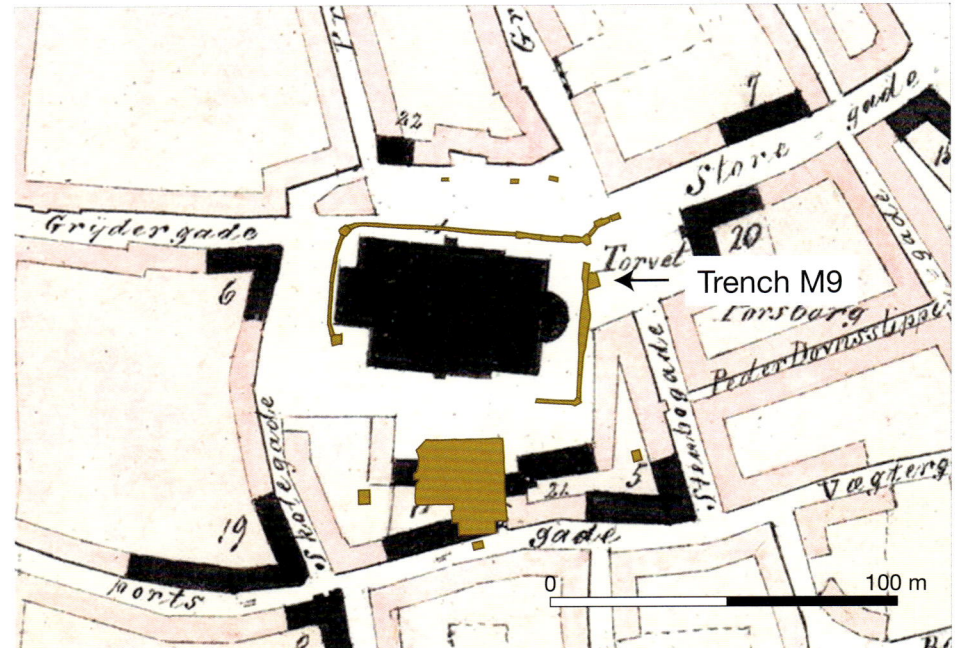

The number of graves cut from the ground surface is considerable in all of the areas excavated. Post-holes from possible timber churches or areas without graves which could represent the location of a church were assiduously sought but not finds of remains of timber churches have been made.

One trench, M9, produced especially good information and will be discussed in greater detail (Fig. 150). North-east of the apse of the cathedral an area of 16 sq m was excavated on the blown sand dune, the well-drained sand of which regrettably meant particularly poor conditions for the survival of bone. Below seven graves of the Viking Period or earlier Middle Ages, one of which appeared to have been in a large log coffin, the two earliest burials at the site were found (Fig. 151). The earliest was a chamber grave, the staves of which had been placed in a shallow trench at the base of the grave pit. They formed what appeared to be an oval chamber. The grave had been disturbed on both the western and southern sides and unfortunately no longer contained any remains of the deceased.

Towards the south, this grave was cut by another chamber grave of unusual type. The chamber itself had consisted of planks lying on edge, and measured 1.5 x 2.5 m. A clinker-built wagon body of 1.0 x 1.9 m had been placed in the chamber, which left a well-preserved impression (Fig. 152). This chamber had no base but had had a planked cover.

The wagon body, unfortunately, no longer contained skeletal remains, but did have grave goods deposited at the western end of the wagon box in the form of a necklace made up of four glass and one amber beads together with a disc brooch of silver filigree-work in the form of a shield amulet (Fig. 152).

The amulet has a close parallel in one of the best known graves from Birka, grave 660, and they could perhaps have been produced in the same workshop (Arbman 1940, Taf. 97; 1943, 231f). Shield amulets occur in graves, as stray finds and in hoards of the period, and like the wagon body graves are dated to the 10th century (Skovmand 1942; Trotzig 2004; Roesdahl 2006). The graves in trench M9 could indicate that closer to the church there was a greater concentration of aristocratic burials.

5.9.8.3.10 The extent of the Viking-period churchyard

The cathedral area is the natural centre of the town quarter on the southern side of the Ribe River, and even early town historians noted that the old streets of the town radiate out from the cathedral on all sides, which would thus seem to imply that the church was present when the streets were laid out (Galthen 1792). The majority of these streets have since been investigated by archaeologists and it has transpired that most of them were laid out in the second half of the 11th century (Søvsø 2006; 2007a).

The earliest survey plan of the churchyard area is from 1797 (Fig. 153) and a striking feature is that the northern and western churchyard walls followed a curved line. The excavations in the cathedral square have shown that these churchyard walls go back to the 13th century. Dispersed observations at deeper levels have revealed that there are earlier ditches outside

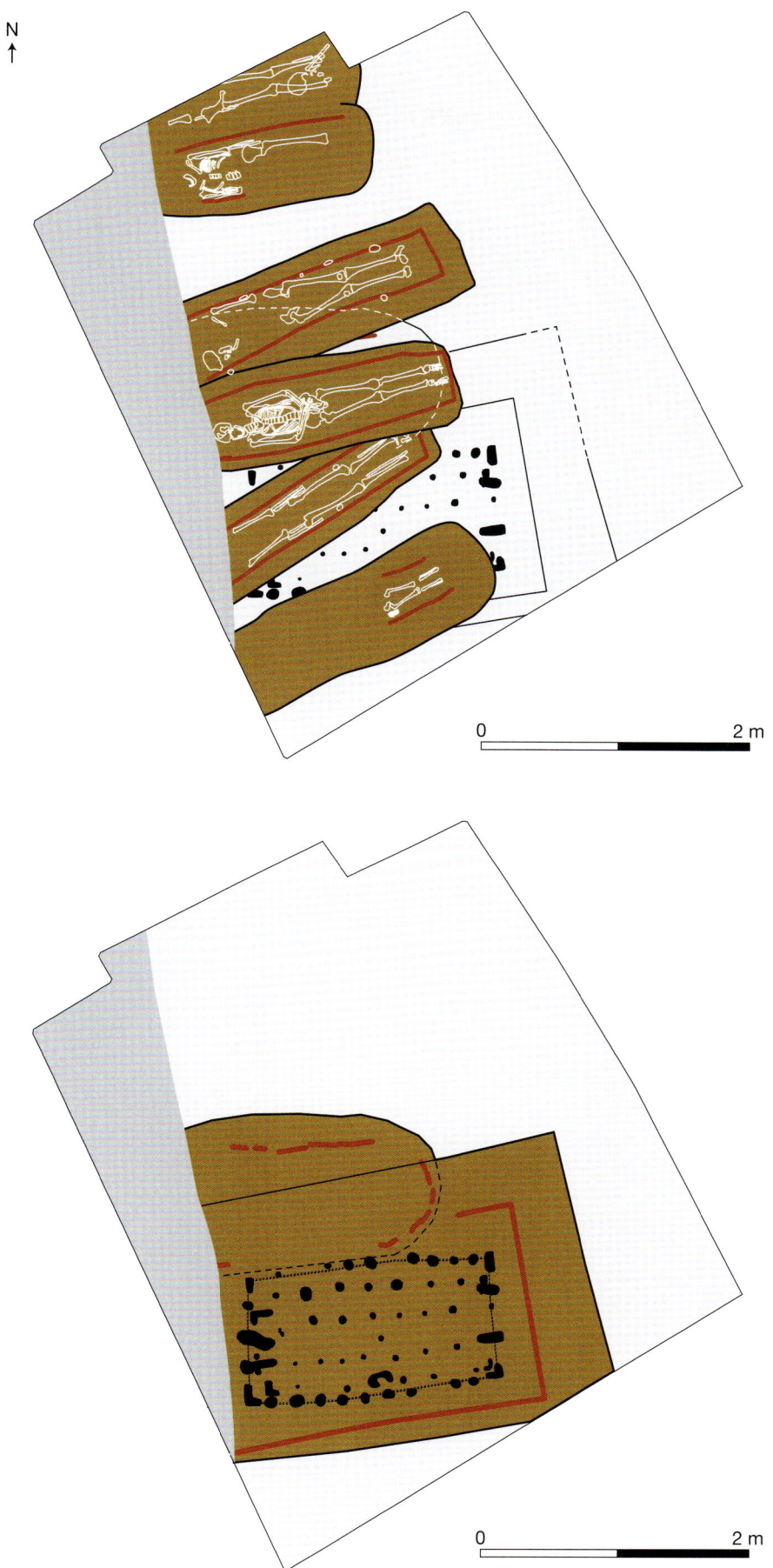

Fig. 151. Top: Plan of all the graves surviving in trench M9. Bottom: Diagrammatic plan of the two earliest chamber burials.

N

0   2 m

0   2 m

Fig. 152. In the wagon body grave by the cathedral there were no longer any human skeletal remains but in the western end, where the arrow has been put, grave goods in the form of a scutiform disc brooch in silver filigree-work and a necklace consisting of four glass beads and one amber bead were found. Scale 2:1.

the churchyard walls. If the cartographic evidence is combined with the extensive archaeological excavations, the Viking-period churchyard area can be reconstructed as an approximately circular area of c. 9,000 sq m with the present cathedral in the centre. The present curved line of Skolegade appears directly to reflect the boundary of the first churchyard.

Were one to attempt to calculate the total number of burials at Ribe Cathedral in the Viking Period – the period down to c. AD 1050 – one could start from the recorded density of burial at Lindegården. This area comprised the edge of the cemetery as well as more central zones, and the density of burial at the former appears to be lower than in the more central parts. The density of graves at Lindegården is 0.2 graves per sq m.[30] As the area of the churchyard can be estimated as around 9,000 sq m, 1,800 burials has to be regarded as a minimum figure, and with regard

to the apparent and anticipated greater density closer to the church building, a figure of 2,000-3,000 burials in the period of AD 855-1050 appears to be a realistic suggestion – a considerable sum, but in relation to a functioning period of two centuries corresponding to only 10-15 burials per year.

5.9.8.3.11 Ansgar's church, summary and discussion

The excavations at Ribe Cathedral of 2008-12 have shown that beneath the thick culture layers with burials and building remains there lay an approximately round churchyard of the Viking Period. The churchyard was separated off from the surrounding land by a substantial ditch, and in its area of around 9,000 sq m it can be estimated that two to three thousand people were buried in the period down to AD 1050.

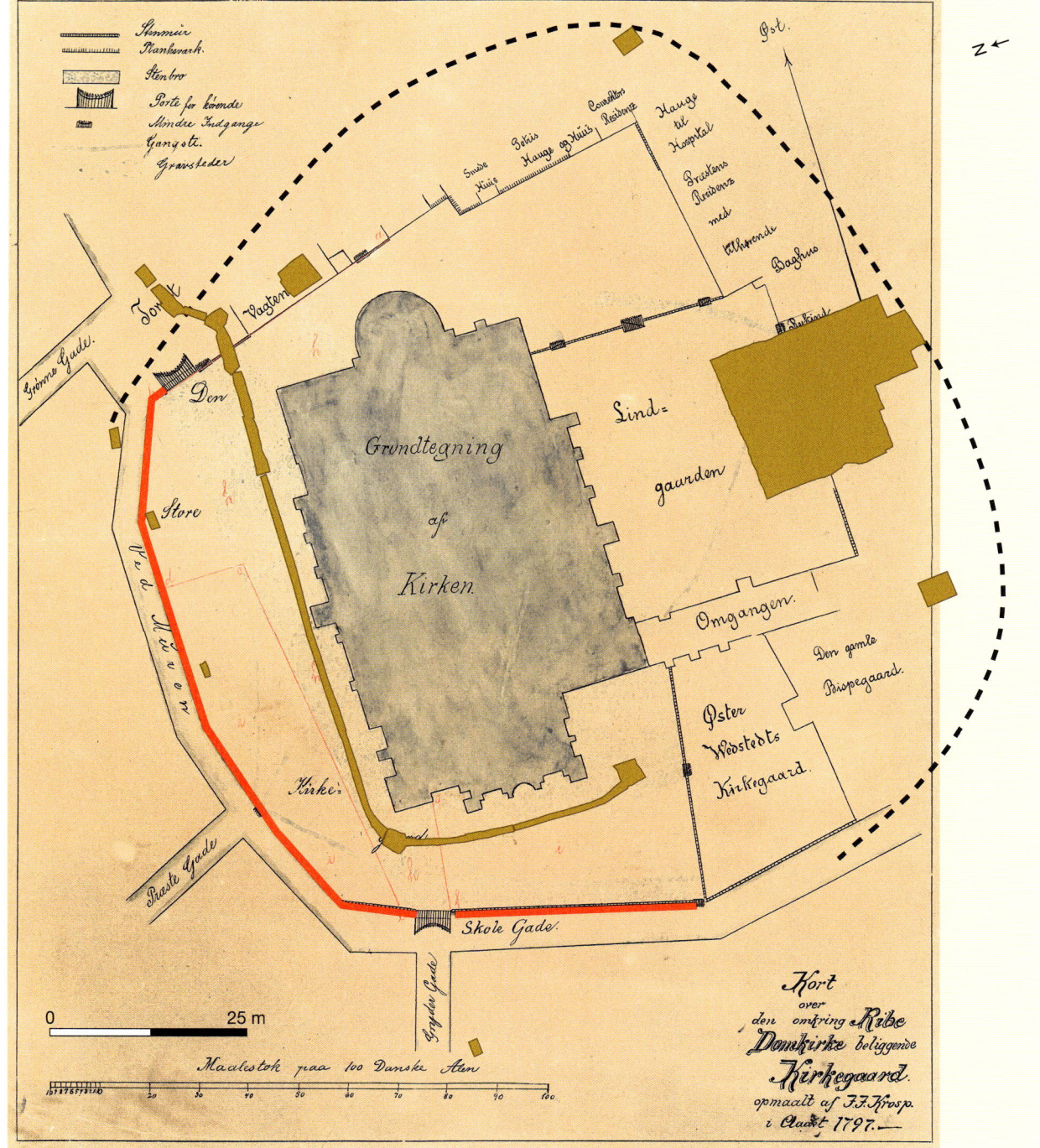

Fig. 153. Survey plan of the cathedral churchyard from 1797 by I.I. Krosp. The areas of excavation are in brown. Highlighted in red are the then still standing churchyard walls which were constructed in the 13th century. The black dotted line shows the course of the Viking-period ditch line found through excavation that bounded the first churchyard at this location. After a copy of the map, ASR M8179, with additions by the author.

From the radiocarbon datings of those buried here obtained so far, some fall in the 9th century, some in the 10th and many in the 11th century (Fig. 149). Looked at in the round, this is not contradicted by any other archaeological discoveries, and there is good reason to believe that the earliest Christian burials at Ribe Cathedral took place long before the official conversion of Denmark to Christianity – probably as a direct consequence of the German mission to Denmark, whether the missionary was called Ebo of Rheims, Ansgar, or was someone quite different.

The boundary ditches of the churchyard, the Christian burial practice, and the documentary references to the permission obtained by Ansgar to build a church in Ribe leave no room for doubt that these are Christian graves. From the historical sources and the extent of the churchyard found there is also no reason to doubt that a church continued to stand at this spot with no significant break. In the 250 years to when Bishop Thure launched the building of a stone church early in the 12th century these would have been timber churches. It is not unreasonable to postuate several generations of timber churches, and remains of these could well still be preserved beneath the current church building.

The episcopal chronicle of Ribe relates that in Liufdag's time, as today, the church was dedicated to Our Lady, a well-chosen patron saint for a baptismal church. This too can be believed to go back to Ansgar (Skovgaard-Petersen 1981, 59). The church in Schleswig, which is just a few years older, was also dedicated to Our Lady according to Ansgar's Life (Skovgaard-Petersen 1981, 37).

The physical anthropological studies of the deceased are not yet complete, but the interim results show very clearly that the group of people whose successors buried them alongside the church in Ribe comprised men, women and children alike. The sex- and age-ranges do not differ significantly from other excavated churchyards of later periods, and it therefore appears reasonable to suggest that those buried at Ribe Cathedral represent a population of men, women and children – families, in other words.

The deceased all lay in coffins that were placed in neatly rectangular graves. Combined with the position of the bodies inside the coffins, the actual burial rite appears to have been thoroughly characterized by order and care.[31] There are few coffins produced from re-used material, and the presence of occasional chamber graves, log coffins and wagon body graves indicates that those buried there belong to the upper strata of society.

Who were the first Christians? Ongoing detailed osteological analyses of the skeletons excavated, including strontium isotope analyses, indicate that they were 'local', but the results are not yet published.[32]

All in all, excavations of heathen burial sites close to Ribe itself show that non-Christians were still living in the area far into the 10th century (Stoumann 2009). An example is the cemetery at Hunderup, only 10 km north of Ribe, where 15 graves were excavated in 2007 (Feveile & M.H. Søvsø 2009). These were typically heathen graves, with grave goods in the form of knives, an axe, spurs, beads and even a Thor's hammer. Nothing suggests that the inhabitants of this village were then Christian.

It has long been pointed out that conversion in Denmark was a process that extended over a long period of time (Brink 2008). Up to now, it has been difficult to point to concrete evidence of this process and its course, but the excavations at Ribe Cathedral demonstrate the existence not only of churches but also of Christian minorities in Denmark from the middle of the 9th century.

5.9.9 A decline of Ribe in the second half of the 9th century?

Mogens Bencard's excavations of the 1970s solved the problem of where the earliest Ribe had been. The next problem was the lacuna between the series of layers around Sct. Nicolaj Gade, which covered the period of c. AD 700-800, while the layers of the Middle Ages could not, it appeared, be dated earlier than around the year 1100. Only with the excavations in Rosen Allé was it possible to identify definite structures from the 9th century, while a couple of years later the Post Office site excavation revealed that the stratigraphy there continued to around the middle of the 9th century.

As this section, 5.9 Ribe in the 9th century, has shown, taphonomic factors have destroyed by far the greatest part of the stratigraphy from the 9th century on the plots. Only in a small area around Sct. Nicolaj Gade, including the Post Office site, are layers from this period preserved. However they do reveal that not only was the monetized economy still functioning in the first half of the 9th century but also that trade and craft continued at high levels. Nonetheless the series of layers did appear to thin out after that, and to be overlain in several places by culture layers of the Middle Ages. The hunt for finds or features that would fill this gap in the history of the town has been continuous since the 1970s. Practically all of the datings have been based upon artefact typology, which involves a series of problems, as relatively few artefacts can be dated narrowly.

The absence of finds of the second half of the 9th century on the plots can therefore, to a great extent, be explained taphonomically. In respect of the area behind the lane along the river, it has been argued above that both in the 8th century and the 9th it was very thinly built upon so that the absence of structures in this zone cannot be used as an argument for a radical reduction in the 9th century. The almost complete absence amongst the finds from the town of dirhams, hacksilver and the linked cubo-octahedral and oblate spheroid weights and balance pans which came to Scandinavia from around the year 860 (Steuer 2002) could also be used as an argument for a decline, but the opposite could be argued too,

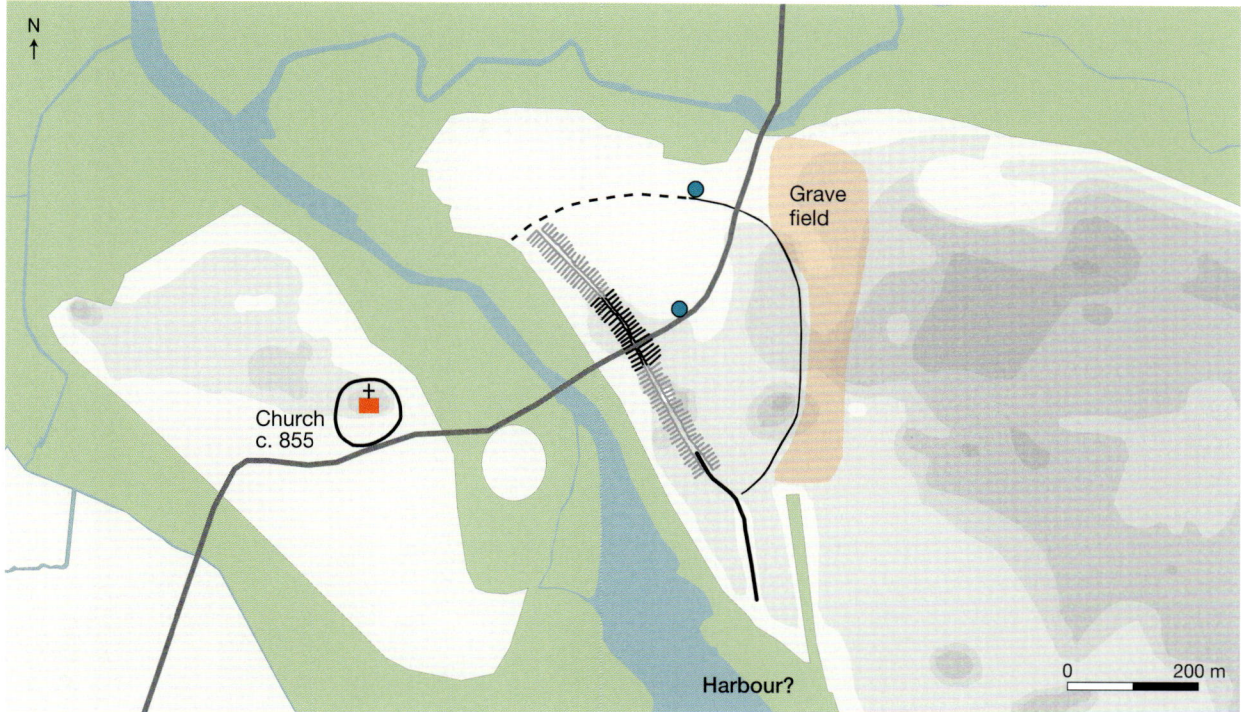

Fig. 154. Ribe in the 9th century. The town is enclosed by the town ditch and the two blue dots mark wells which were in use in this century. South of the river the Church of Our Lady was founded around the year 855.

by claiming that it was the monetized economy of the town that kept hacksilver out of the finds assemblage. The relatively few graves of the 9th century from the heathen cemetery of the town can also be used to support the argument for a reduction, but the arrival of a church on the other side of the river might explain this away as well.

Other factors point rather towards continuity. The presence of a church has just been noted, but Town Ditch K200 and Moat B, which both maintain the course laid out by Town Ditch A in the first half of the 9th century, are difficult to understand as anything other than later defences, which presupposes, of course, that there is something to defend.

None of this should obscure the fact that the archaeological evidence from Ribe of the later Viking Period is especially slight compared with the preceding period, and while Stig Jensen explained this principally on taphonomic grounds (S. Jensen, Madsen & Mikkelsen 1983), Claus Feveile has very recently argued that there was a dramatic reduction and possibly even a cessation in the second half of the 9th century, and has further discussed possible reasons why that should have been the case (Feveile 2006a). The stimulus for that position came from international emporium scholarship and in particular the demise of Dorestad in this period, and it has been incorporated into various models representing the emporia/towns of this date (Hodges 1989; 2012; Skre 2007c).

From what is known now, there is no doubt that Ribe in the second half of the 9th century was still to be found where it had been since around the year 700 (Fig. 154). The lane alongside the river was still its principal structuring component and the town ditch of the first half of the 9th century was subsequently superseded by Town Ditch K200. The problematic taphonomic circumstances and the relatively few scientific datings make an assessment of the archaeological evidence harder, but both the absence of wells and an almost total absence of artefacts that can be dated to the later Viking Period are strong arguments for the proposition that there was a concrete and marked fall in the level of activity. It would appear just as certain, however, that the town did not disappear. The date of this reduction should, in my view, be placed in the period 850-900. What may have caused it is discussed below.

5.9.10 Summary and interpretation: Ribe in the 9th century

King Godfred's new foundation of Hedeby in 808 and the *boom town* growth of that town in the 9th century must have led to aggressive competition with Ribe. Thanks to its location, Hedeby opened up contacts into the Baltic, and in the course of the 9th century the town became the largest and most important emporium in Scandinavia, the central node in *the northern arc*: the most important trade route between Asia and western Europe of the Early Middle Ages (A.E. Christensen 1969, 185ff; McCormick 2007, 562ff). But the king did not forget Ribe. The Rayface/deer penny was introduced in the town while Hedeby got its own pennies modelled on coins from Dorestad.

Around the year 800, Ribe was still fundamentally an *Einstraßenanlage* consisting of the lane alongside the river and greatly dispersed settlement in the area behind the lane. The large heathen cemetery was still in use. Some time during the first half of the 9th century this pattern was disrupted with the construction of Town Ditch A, which has to be supposed to have formed a semicircular line which marked off a town area of around 14 ha. On the inner side of the ditch there was a small bank that survived as the visible boundary marker following the rapid refilling of the ditch and came in turn to lay out the course for the succeeding Town Ditch K200. The complicated circumstances surrounding Town Ditch A have been reviewed above, but it seems certain that its construction belongs to this period. The ditch is not military in character but must instead have formed a juridical or fiscal boundary and thus indirectly express the fact that there was a town in existence, as is also known in the case of Hamwic (Hodges 2000, 76ff).

In the archaeology of the town, the northerly-oriented connexions now appear more prominently in the

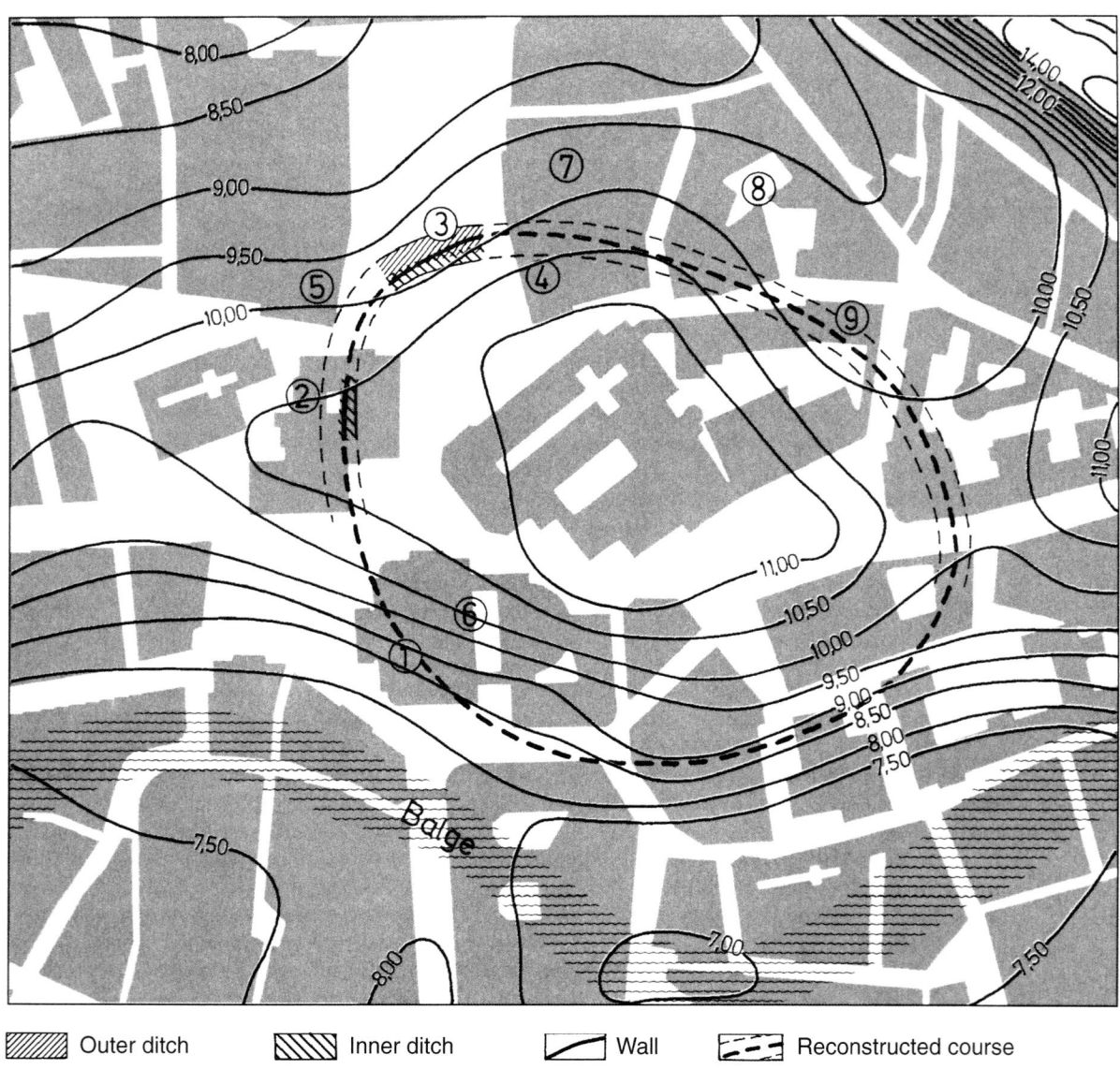

| Outer ditch | Inner ditch | Wall | Reconstructed course |

Fig. 155. In Bremen, the cathedral was sited on the crest of natural raised ground and was soon surrounded by a roughly circular ditch of several phases, the reconstructed course of which is shown here. The ditches are thought to date back to the 9th century and they enclosed an area of around 5 hectares. After Wilschewski 1998.

202

form of Norwegian soapstone and whetstones. Beads were not being manufactured any more but rather being imported ready-made. This means, of course, that the raw materials for making glass beads were also no longer coming to the town, and has to mean that the blown glass sherds in the layers of this date are evidence of trade in such glass and not cullet for beadmaking.

The excavations at Ribe Cathedral of 2008-12 have revealed a large Christian churchyard from the Viking Period, approximately round in shape and with an area of c. 9,000 sq m. A number of graves have been radiocarbon dated to the 9th century and the dating of the earliest graves is supported by various stratigraphical details. All in all there is reason to believe that Ansgar not only obtained land on which to raise

a church, but that it was dedicated to Our Lady like the church in Hedeby and has remained in use continuously through to the present day. The size of the churchyard contrasts starkly with the practically absent traces of Ribe from the period after AD 850, and rather than regarding the church as directed solely at the urban population it makes more sense to regard it as a *minster church*, a missionary and baptismal church aimed at a larger hinterland – in principle, the whole northern part of Jutland (Carelli 2001a). The large round churchyard is also found at a series of Carolingian foundations that are just a little older: Bremen, Osnabrück, Halberstadt etc (Figs. 155-6). It is not known what the church in Hamburg, Ansgar's missionary see, was like (Bischop 2014; Lobbedey 2014).

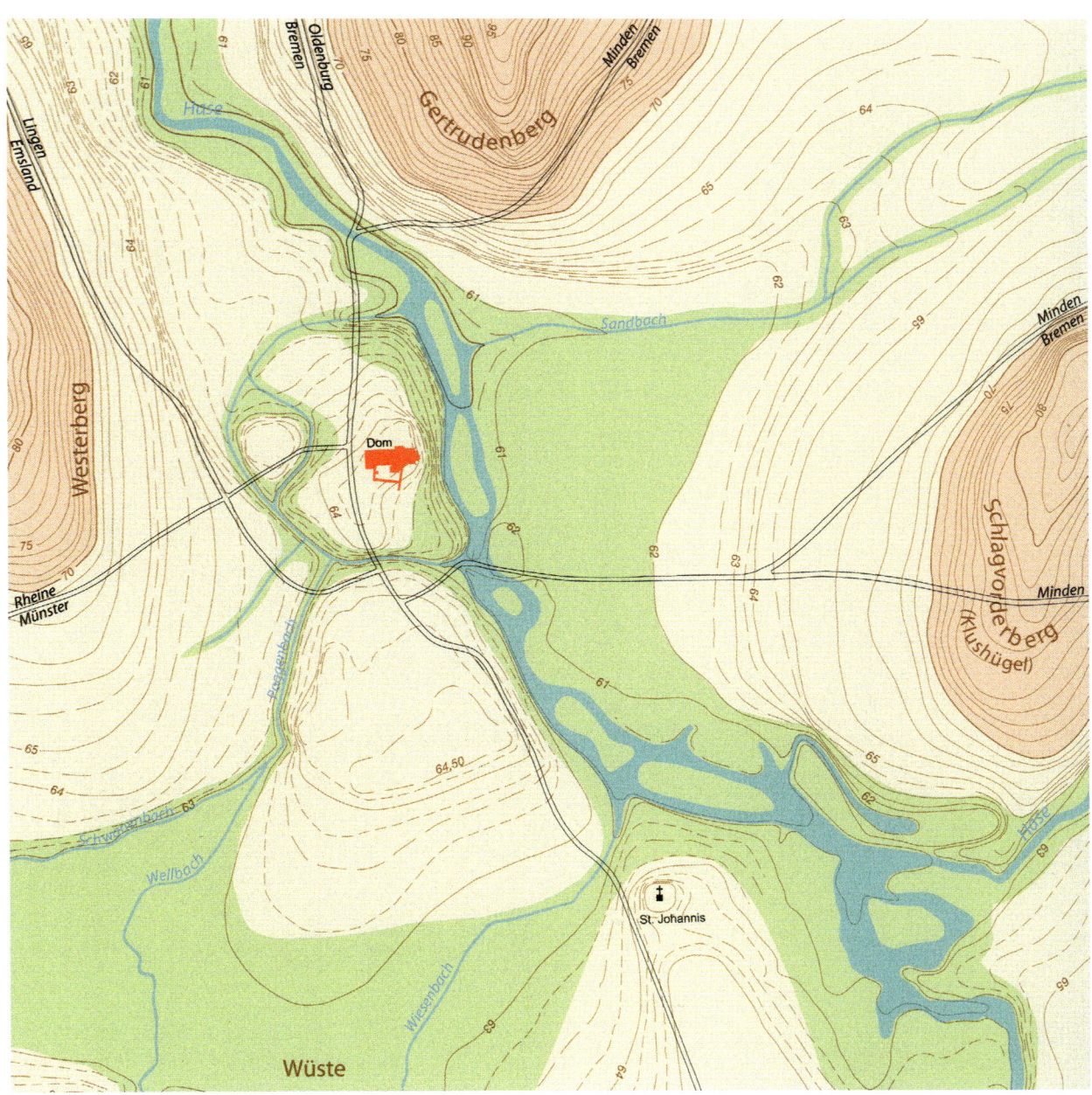

Fig. 156. Reconstruction of the church and the terrain at Osnabrück in the 9th century. After Lobbedey 2014.

The siting of the church on the far side of the river could have had a number of objectives. One possibility is that both the heathen king and the presumably largely non-Christian residents of the town preferred to have the church at a bit of a distance, but it is possible that the otherwise unoccupied cathedral island, completely surrounded by wetlands and watercourses (cf. Fig. 156) was also an attractive site offering the chance to create a Christian island in a heathen landscape.

While the powerful growth of Hedeby in the 9th century challenged Ribe's role as a centre of long-distance trade, the comparable, rapid decline of Dorestad in the 840s must have weakened the trade network around the North Sea which Ribe was part of (Coupland 2010). The reason for the collapse of Dorestad was partly the weakness of the Frankish realm after the death of Louis the Pious in 840. Following a civil war, the Empire was divided into three through the Treaty of Verdun of 843, with Dorestad coming under Lothar I, who died in 855 after which his kingdom was divided further. This division meant that defence against Viking attacks was weakened, and following a series of Viking raids from 834-7 a Danish Viking force took Dorestad in 841 and controlled the harbour over the following decades after concluding a peace treaty with the local powers. The result was that the largest emporium of northern Europe collapsed irretrievably, and its failure is clearly visible in the town's formerly enormous mint output, which fell dramatically from the 840s and ceased completely around 855 (Coupland 2010). The fall of Dorestad ran in parallel to the growth of Hedeby, and behind the events can be discerned the contours of a successful Danish trade war which led to Hebeby taking over Dorestad's former role as the primary trading node of northern Europe from the middle of the 9th century – but also at the expense of the other Danish emporia.

Later in the century, political chaos came about in Denmark too. Although the sources do not allow for firm conclusions, there seems to be a strong case for suggesting that the royal dynasty which had held power in Denmark since the beginning of the 8th century and which counted kings such as Angantyr, Sigfred, Godfred, Hemming and Haarik in its king-list, fell around the year 870 (Sawyer 1991).

5.10 Ribe in the 10th century

Until 2008, palpable traces of the town of Ribe in the 10th century were limited to a single coin found in excavation ASR 926 Ribelund I, a so-called Dorestad imitation struck in Hedeby of type KG 7-9, together with a group of highly problematic inhumation graves

uncovered in course of the excavation ASR 1000 Ribelund II. However the discovery of the first Viking-period churchyard alongside Ribe Cathedral in 2009, and then the street excavation in Sct. Nicolaj Gade of 2010-11, changed the situation markedly (Alrø Jensen 2013; Søvsø 2014).

5.10.1 Stratigraphy of the 10th century

Sct. Nicolaj Gade was renovated in 2010-11 (Fig. 157). After the old road surface immediately east of the Art Museum was removed, intact stratigraphy appeared at an unexpectedly high level. Beneth the pavement on the southern side the layers survived at an even higher level, and it was possible to clean a length of section with clearly striated culture layers consisting of charcoal-rich dark layers alternating with lighter sand or clay layers (Fig. 158). The gently undulating course of the layers revealed the plot structure.

The thin deposited layers are entirely characteristic of the series of layers on the plots themselves and are unknown from other contexts in the archaeology of

Fig. 157. Working photograph of the excavation in Sct. Nicolaj Gade. In the area between the red-coated Art Museum and the former Post Office can be made out a small piece of section, a drawing of which is Figure 158. Photograph: SJM.

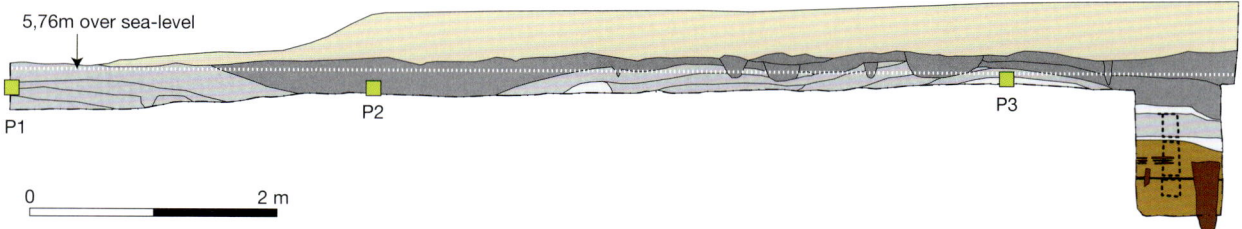

Fig. 158. Section from Sct. Nicolaj Gade from the area between the Art Museum and the former Post Office. Undisturbed stratigraphy was preserved in some parts up to above 5.80 m over sea-level. By the three green squares flotation samples were taken, from which three carbonized grains, three from each sample, were dated: see Figure 159.

Ribe. The layers must then be considered to have been produced from the pattern of activity that since the 8th century had led to the formation of the thoroughly distinctive and particular stratigraphy of the plots. The insertion of a new drain-pipe chamber meant that a hole of 0.6x0.6 m had to be taken a little deeper into the layers on the boundary between two plots. Below this the layers were distinctly better preserved, and various forms of evidence of fencing were found. One piece which included a re-used piece of wood had been burnt down and corresponded with a burnt layer. The piece of wood was subsequently dendrodated as having been felled in AD 775. Considering the re-use, the burnt layer at 4.95 m over sea-level can hardly date earlier than c. 800. This site therefore has a recorded sequence of layers of about a metre's depth which had formed after the year 800.

The dating of the latest layers in the sequence was naturally of especial interest, and in order to date the stratigraphy small flotation samples were taken from three points in the section. Three carbonized grains were then dated from each flotation residue (Fig. 159). The datings show that the relevant layers must have been formed in the period up towards the year 1000. The character of the layers corresponds with the stra-

tigraphy on the plots otherwise, and the results indicate that the particular pattern of activity of the plots, and thus also the plot system, were still extant at that date.

The line of Sct. Nicolaj Gade must have existed in some form or other since the construction of the Dam in the second half of the 13th century. After this, the traffic out of the North Gate in the direction of St Nikolaj's Church and further on to Tange followed this route. It is probably the existence of the street that protected these layers from cultivation and other digging activity while practically everywhere else they have been destroyed by later interventions.

5.10.2 The graves at Ribelund

The actual objective of research excavation ASR 1000 Ribelund II of 1991-2 was to examine the so-called water tower hill on which the parish church of St Nikolaj and the associated nunnery were located in the Middle Ages. It was hoped that the mound might contain evidence from the Viking Period, possibly a royal residence (S. Jensen 1990; 1991b). In order to reveal the process of formation a trial trench down to natural was dug in 1991: a difficult undertaking because of the vegetation in the area.

Fig. 159. Five of the nine dated carbonized grains from the layers in the section in Sct. Nicolaj Gade produced dates around the year 1000. The datings were carried out by Aarhus University radiocarbon laboratory.

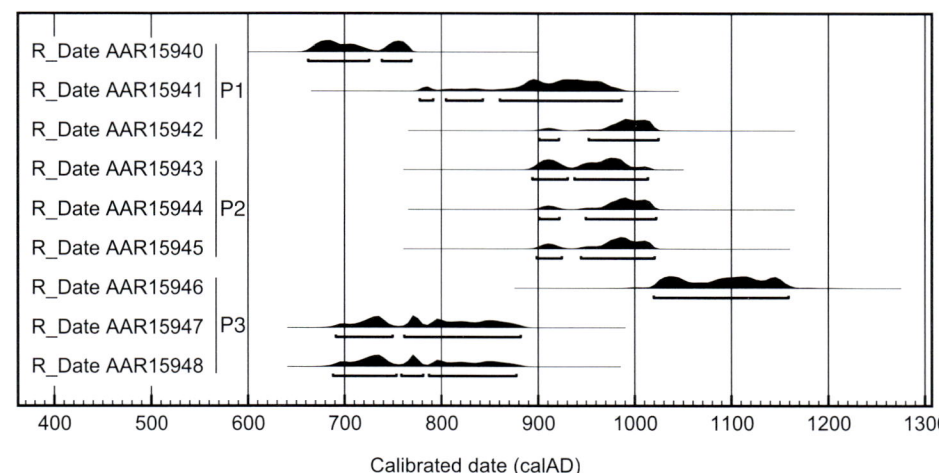

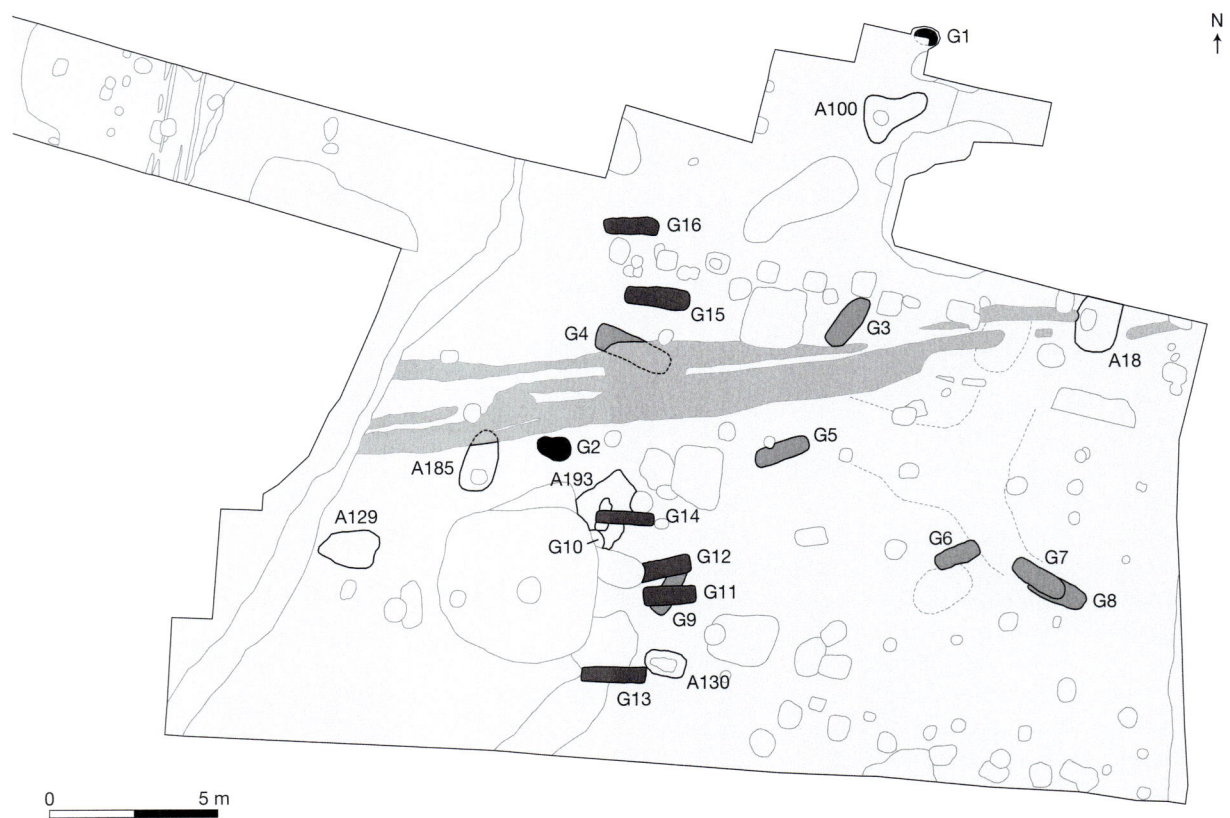

Fig. 160. The graves at Ribelund. After Feveile 2006h.

Fig. 161. ASR 1000 Ribelund II. G11 and G12. The bodies lay with their arms and legs crossed.

At one end of the trench, away from the mound upon which the excavation was targeted, inhumation graves were found, and in 1992 the excavation was conintued; now focussed, however, upon the graves discovered: 16 in total – 2 cremations and 14 inhumations (Fig. 160).

The two cremations, G1 and G2, and inhumation grave G15, in which the deceased lay on one side with the legs drawn up, have a character that agrees closely with the other graves of the 8th and 9th centuries from the town cemetery. The other 13 inhumation graves, however, were very different both from the other inhumations in the heathen burial ground and the graves subsequently found by the cathedral.

Two radiocarbon dates place the Ribelund inhumation graves in the 10th century (datings from AU radiocarbon laboratory: AAR 4851 and AAR 4853, corrected for the reservoir effect) (Feveile 2006h, 276), but many cases of intercutting between the graves show that the burials must have been carried out over a longer period. The distribution of the graves within the area excavated might indicate that the cemetery has been fully uncovered, but this impression could also be due to sheer chance in respect of the location of the area of excavation.

The group of inhumation graves is characterized by consistently haphazard burial practice, not only in

Table 17. Stature of the bodies in the inhumation graves in the ASR 1000 Ribelund II excavation.

Grave no.	G16	G3	G15	G6	G5	G4	G7	G11	G12	G13
Height in cm	135	144	144	145	147	154	156	162	163	167

terms of the alignment of the graves and their widths and lengths but even more in respect of the position of the bodies in the graves (Fig. 161). The deceased lay with randomly crooked or crossed legs and arms, and G7 lay prone. The bodies give the impression of having been virtually thrown into the graves, in stark contrast to the care in the placement of the bodies that is typical of the other inhumation burials both in the heathen cemetery and at Ribe Cathedral.

The poorly preserved bones and dental evidence have not been studied osteologically, but the stature of the dead, in those cases where it can be estimated on the evidence of their skeletal remains, is shown in Table 17.

The meagre heights must mean that the majority of those buried here were children or women, and yet that probably some men were buried here too. The Ribelund graves appear to show, then, that over a considerable period of the 10th century, within what was apparently a delimited zone, a series of disordered burials of men, women and children were carried out which one cannot classify in terms of having been either Christian or pagan although either remains possible. Behind this state of affairs must lie some early group identity, whether that were shared by the deceased or was imposed upon them by those who buried them. The graves lie outside the line of Moat B and the town ditch underlying it, probably Town Ditch K200.

One possibility is that this was a burial place for slaves, the poor or others who had no social network to ensure a decent burial for them. The population profile and the period of use appear to rule out episodic events such as warfare or epidemics.

5.10.3 Town Ditch K200

The identification of two lines of town ditch in 2015 (see section 5.9.5) shows that the history of the boundaries of the town was more complex than had been recognized hitherto (Fig. 162). On the strength of the data now available it appears that Town Ditch A of the 9th century was succeeded by Town Ditch K200 in the 10th century. The excavation in Rosen Allé in 2014 uncovered a ditch that ran under the southern edge of and parallel to the later Moat B. The trench had been around 2 m wide at the top and around 1

Fig. 162. Features of the Viking Period from the excavations along Rosen Allé.

Groups of finds	n	Weight
Greyware, body sherd	33	
Greyware, rim sherd	3	
Glas beads	1	
Basalt	2	9 g
Iron	4	
Porous slag	4	38 g
Iron slag	3	206 g
Total	**50**	

Table 18. The finds from Town Ditch K200 under Moat B.

m deep. The lowest layers of fill were water-deposited sand, above which there was a vegetation level overlain by a greyish layer of fill. On the southern side of that layer a series of separate grass turfs were found, the position of which along the southern edge must be due to them having been part of a collapsed associated bank built of turf.

The layer of fill from the trench was sieved, and thanks to its considerable depth there were no intrusive finds (Tab. 18). The meagre amount of finds does not permit any firm conclusions, but the three rimsherds were all from hemispherical pots. Two samples for radiocarbon dating were taken from the fill: a piece of unidentified charcoal and a piece of the short-lived species willow. Both datings fall with a very high level of probability in the 10th century, which must have been the period in which Town Ditch K200 was in use (Tab. 19).

It may be that Town Ditch K200 was in use at the same time as a number of SFBs that were found in ASR 8 but did not appear to be contemporary with either Town Ditch A or Moat B, while the finds from these SFBs fit better in the 10th century than the 9th, as has been noted before (Feveile & Jensen 2006a). With the discovery of Town Ditch K200 beneath Moat B it seems more likely that it was also the course of this ditch rather than Town Ditch A which was found underlying Moat B during a number of other excavations.

5.10.4 Moat B

With the construction of Moat B, the character of the town's boundary changed into a truly defensive one (Figs. 162-3). It has not so far been possible to date the construction of Moat B closely, but it must naturally have been after the refilling of Town Ditch K200 in the 10th century and before Moat B itself was refilled in the first half of the 11th century (see below). Before it collapsed there was a period of use involving cleaning out at least once, and it therefore appears most plausible to assign the raising of this defence work to the 10th century (Munch Kristiansen et al. 2019).

Moat B has been discovered during a series of excavations, and appears very consistently as a ditch 1.0-1.5 m deep and from 7 to 8 m wide. On the inner side in one case remains of a 6-m wide turf-built rampart have been found which can be reconstructed as a bank around 2 m high with a platform on the top 2 m wide upon which there may have been a palisade.

By chance, the excavation in Rosen Allé in 1989 came across an opening in the defensive structure, where the ends of the moat are not aligned directly on one another so that the roadway between them had to take a turn (Fig. 162). The most thorough excavation of the moat has been that in Rosen Allé in 2014, where a 20-m long section was examined. After the soil had been removed the moat was visible as a dark grey-filled feature across the area of excavation in which the two ditches from ASR 8 and a number of other interventions of various periods stood out more or less clearly. Work proceeded very thoroughly to distinguish a series of later cuts that were excavated, emptied and sieved one by one until only the uniform grey fill of the moat remained. The earliest of the cuts which overlay the fill could be dated to the 11th or 12th centuries, which shows, then, that the moat had filled up completely by this date at the latest.

After this, a series of sondages were dug through the fill, which was sieved. In the course of removing the fill it transpired that there were clear, longitudi-

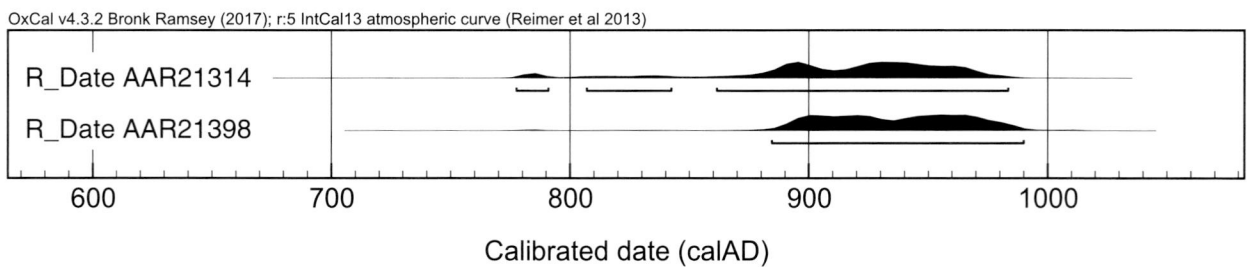

Table 19. The two radiocarbon dates from the fill layer in Town Ditch K200. From AAR Report 1357.

Fig. 163. Longitudinal ploughmarks in the base of Moat B. In the foreground can be made out Town Ditch K200 as a brown fill. Excavation SJM 348 (2014). Photograph: SJM.

nal ploughmarks in the base of the moat, like those which the first excavation in 1989 had discovered (Fig. 163). A considerable part of the base was revealed by excavation and planned. The fill was completely uniform and lacked no visible stratification other than a series of wavy, horizontal precipitation levels, a phenomenon that occurs as a secondary result of water penetration. How the whole decomposed and bioturbated fill layer had been formed was not fully determinable. Its homogeneity could indicate that the contents had come from parts of the associated turf-built bank, but the actual structure of no preserved grass turfs was observed within the fill.

In the absence of stratigraphy within the fill of the moat, 5-cm spits were removed within a grid framework in order to reveal any later disturbances that were not discernible by eye. The sieving of the fill produced a considerable collection of finds. The bioturbation observed shows that a certain amount of material from later contexts is to be anticipated, and it is evident that the uppermost assemblages include a small amount of intrusive material in the form of very small pieces of later pottery, glass sherds and clay-pipe stumps – but this does not occur lower down. The artefactual evidence shows quite clearly that the large quantity of other finds represents a contemporary assemblage which supports the inference that the fill is the product of rapid refilling. The many small sherds amongst the finds and the homogeneity of the soil matrix show that the layer had been cultivated, and it is perhaps possible to im-agine that the refilled ditch around the town offered an especially fertile field in the earlier Middle Ages. The analysis of how the fill had been formed vindicates the treatment of the considerable assemblage of finds as one collection, and the most important categories of find from the moat are made up as shown in Table 20.[33]

Groups of finds	*n*	Weight
Greyware, body sherd	893	
Greyware, rim and bottom sherd	44	
Pingsdorf ware	18	
Coins	3	
Glass beads	2	
Glass vessel sherd	4	
Amber	4	0.1 g
Basalt	21	587 g
Whetstones	5	
Loom weights	7	36 g
Spindle whorls	3	
Iron	75	
Glass bead production waste	1	
Crucibles	5	
Forge stone	10	46 g
Porous slag	69	276 g
Iron slag	25	506 g
Total	**1189**	

Table 20. The finds assemblage from the fill of Moat B.

Fig. 164. A coin struck in Aarhus under Magnus the Good (AD 1042-7), Hauberg 33, found in the fill of the moat. SJM 348x259. To the right a drawing of this coin-type after Hauberg 1900. Scale 2:1.

The finds are completely dominated by household waste and basic craft in the form of ceramic fragments, quernstones, whetstones, iron nails, spindlewhorls and loomweights. The smithing of iron and casting of copper alloy is sporadically represented by iron slag, porous slags, tuyères and crucible sherds, but the quantity of such finds is low. The one piece of waste from glass-bead manufacture cannot in itself be treated as evidence for the practice of this craft as it could just as easily be a matter of older, residual material.

The coins are of course of particular interest in chronological terms. One of them is a fragment of a short cross penny of Cnut the Great struck in London AD 1029-35; a second is a German coin from between the end of the 10th century and the first part of the 11th. The final coin is complete, and was struck under Magnus the Good in Aarhus (Hbg. 33) in the period 1042-7 (Fig. 164). The latter two coins were found in the same sample from the moat and could have been lost as one, but this does not alter the fact that they point to the refilling of the ditch in the first half of the 11th century.

From the sieving of the fill from a pit cut into the fill of the moat came an oblate spheroid copper-coated weight with decorated faces which may also have come from the fill of the moat (Fig. 165).

Grey-fired pottery accounts for what is clearly the largest group of finds, and amongst the 893 body sherds there are both thick-walled sherds which probably come from hemispherical pots and thin-walled sherds which could be from either hemispherical pots and globular pots. They do not bring us very much closer to a description of the vessel-forms. Amongst the rimsherds, 16 can be identified as from hemispherical pots while 25 can be assigned to globular pots with out-turned rims. Only one of the sherds is decorated: from a hemispherical pot with two rows of ring punchmarks around the rim. There is also a single base sherd from a flat-bottomed vessel, possibly of Slavic type. The grey-fired pottery thus consisted of both hemispherical pots and globular pots with out-turned rims. The rims of the globular pots are consistently coarse and simple and differ both in fabric and profiles for those of later globular pots.

Only one type of imported pottery is represented, in the form of 18 sherds of Pingsdorf-type ware. These were found dispersed and so form a small but unmistakable group of finds. Some of the sherds have the characteristic painting but otherwise these sherds differ from the 12th-century Pingsdorf Ware of which more than 7,000 sherds have been found in Ribe by consistently being of lighter fabric and having a chalkier body, perhaps the products of a lower firing temperature.

Fig. 165. Oblate spheroid weight of the late Viking Period. SJM 348x179. Scale 2:1.

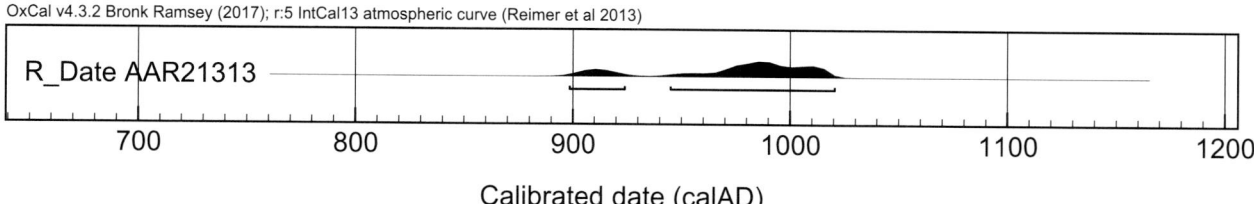

OxCal v4.3.2 Bronk Ramsey (2017); r:5 IntCal13 atmospheric curve (Reimer et al 2013)

R_Date AAR21313

| 700 | 800 | 900 | 1000 | 1100 | 1200 |

Calibrated date (calAD)

Table 21. The C14-date obtained from a carbonized rye grain retrieved from the bottom of the fill layer in Moat B.

Altogether, we can say of the finds assemblage from the moat that there are good reasons to treat it as the product of a single act of refilling, possibly the consequence of a deliberate removal of the defences, and that this event can be dated to around the middle of the 11th century. The finds must reflect the Ribe of that time to some degree or another, and if that is true, the specialized craftwork that left such great quantities of waste in the 8th and 9th centuries appears not to be playing the same role. The presence of imported pottery, coins and weights, however, points to international contacts and trade, albeit to a lesser degree than both previously and subsequently. The imported pottery constitutes just 2% of the whole ceramic assemblage. A century later 20% of the pottery in the town was imported (Søvsø 2006; 2007a).

From the base of the moat one flotation sample was taken. Out of this, one carbonized rye grain was retrieved for dating (Tab. 21).

The ploughmarks at the base of the moat must, beyond any reasonable doubt, have been produced by a mouldboard plough. Whether their purpose was agrarian or military we do not know, but it is considered most likely that it was the latter: to reinforce the defences by raising the rampart with grass turf from the moat. Finds sealed within the moat would thus have been removed, but if they were redeposited in the rampart they could, of course, have been returned through the final demolition of that bank.

Nothing of the rampart remained, but later features on the site have shown that no later than the 12th century it must have been more or less completely levelled and removed from the topography of the town, at least in this location. Traces of possible earth-fast timber structures within the rampart such as are known from other 10th-century military structures might have been preserved in the form of post-holes, but this can in fact be ruled out. The rampart appears to have been a pure turf construction, at least in its lower part, and it is possible that there was a palisade on the crest. With a demonstrable width of 6 m it must have been around 2 m high. This would provide room for a palisade with a 2-m wide walkway behind it (Fig. 166).

For a bank of this size about 8 cu m of material per metre length would be required. If the defences formed a semicircle, the length would have been at least 800 m and thus have required at least 6,400 cu m of grass turf and sand. This cannot really be described as anything other than minor in comparison with, for instance, Hedeby's defences – even if those are multi-phase – but was nevertheless a much greater undertaking than the first defences of Aarhus (H. Skov 2008).

5.10.5 10th-century hoards around the town

On three occasions, in 1874, 1883 and 1919 respectively, in the meadowlands of Ribe Østermade between Tange and Tved, gold armrings of the Viking Period were found which, from the circumstances of the

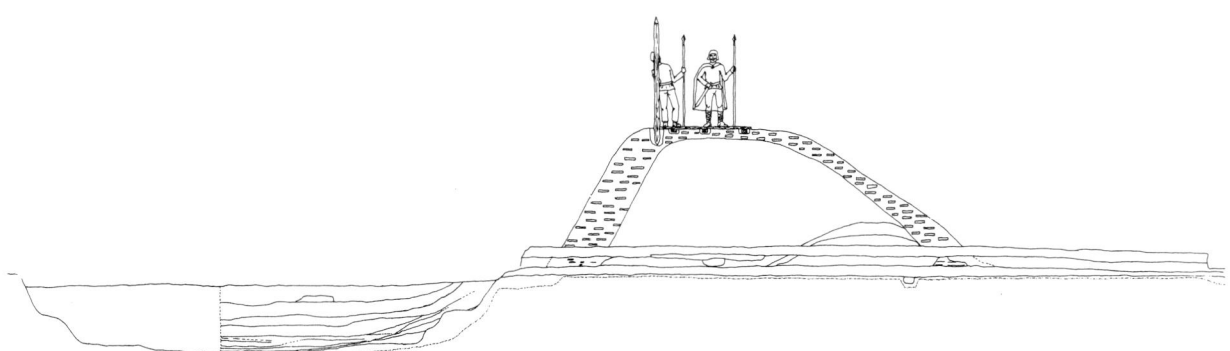

Fig. 166. Reconstruction: diagrammatic section of the defences. After S. Jensen 1990.

finds, have to be understood as wetland hoards (Figs. 167-8) (Skovmand 1942, 76). The armrings weigh 48.7 g, and 101.8 g and 83.8 g in the case of the two first finds, corresponding approximately to 2 and 4 *aurar* (øre) in the weight-units that can be traced in a range of Viking-period treasure hoards, including that from Vester Vedsted (Skovmand 1942). Typologically, the armrings from Ribe are dated to the 10th century, and it is not possible to determine if they represent one, two or three subsequently dispersed deposits.

Beside the roadway heading north out of Ribe towards Kolding, in 1908 the so-called Ribe beaker was found (Fig. 169). This is a Carolingian pyxis of gilt silver and niello from the late 8th century and decorated with Christian iconography in the form of a Tree of Life design (Wamers 1992). Vessels of this type were manufactures in Frankish monastic workshops and were sacred vessels meant to be used in Church ritual as the storage place of the communion bread, *the host*. It would originally have had a lid. Inside the beaker were found six small drinking cups of hammered/driven silver, of which only five remain today. They were each different, and of Scandinavian work. The cups show that the function of this set before it

Fig. 167. The gold armrings found east of Ribe. From the left, C1736 found in 1874; C5031 found in 1883; and DNF 3/19 found in 1919 on the tine of a harrow and therefore presumably moved from its original location. Whether these represent one single hoard or several successive deposits is unknown. Photograph: NM.

Fig. 168. Viking Age hoards around Ribe. In 2018 262 local coins from the early 9th century was found by a detectorist in Damhus. Gold armrings presumably from the 10th century were found in the wetlands between Tange and Tved in 1874 and 1883. In 1919 another gold armring was found stuck on the spike of a harrow, its original place of deposition being uncertain. Archaeological trial excavations around the find spot of the Ribe beaker revealed only wheel ruts from the roadways out of the town. The base map is Videnskabernes Selskabs topographical map of 1794. After the original with the Geodata Agency with additions by the author.

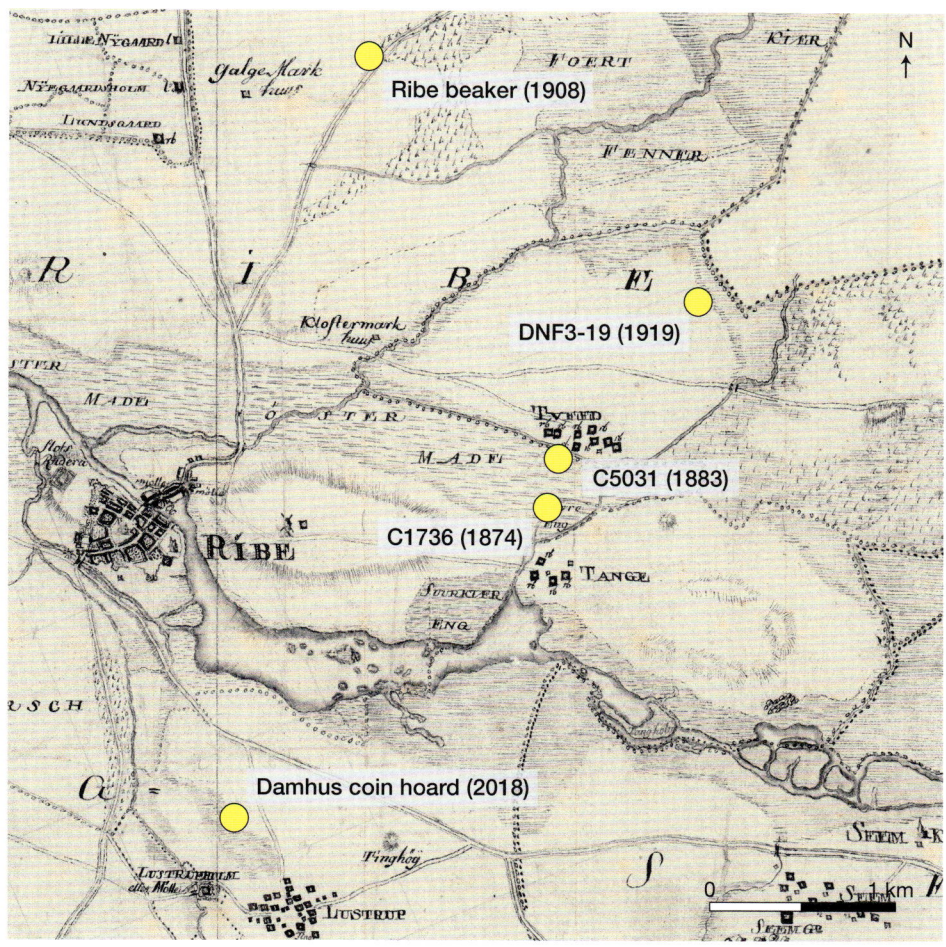

Fig. 169. The Ribe beaker. Height 8 cm. Photograph: NM.

was buried must have been some form of drinking ritual, perhaps with drink poured into the small cups from the pyxis. From the form of the smaller cups the hoard is dated to the 10th century.

The find from Ribe is a perfect parallel to the Fejø beaker, likewise a Carolingian pyxis, which was found in 1872 together with five small drinking cups. Detector searching on Fejø in 2015 produced eight small cups, making up a total of 13 small drinking cups to date. Archaeological preliminary excavations were carried out where the Ribe beaker was found in 2005: preliminary investigation ASR 2091. No sign of any settlement evidence was found, but rather the actual place of deposition appeared to have been a small wet area. The only archaeological feature present was a large number of undated wheel tracks from the aforementioned road out of Ribe. The Ribe beaker appears to be a wetland deposit beside a major routeway remote from settlement.

5.10.6 Summary and interpretation: Ribe in the 10th century

In the archaeological evidence from Ribe, there is a near total absence of securely datable finds of the 10th century such as coins and jewellery, but despite that the excavations of the most recent years have been able to demonstrate that there was a functioning church in this period on one side of the river while within the town itself on the other side of the river culture layers were being formed on the plots. The marking of the boundary of the town was first renewed in the form of Town Ditch K200 and replaced later in the century by a true defensive work, Moat B (Fig. 170). Burials were also placed in a small part of the originally heathen cemetery. Especially in comparison with the massive quantities of finds from the 8th-9th centuries this is a paradox which must somehow or other reflect equally radical changes in the economy of the town.

The presence of three Danish bishops from Hedeby, Ribe and Aarhus at the Synod of Ingelheim in AD 948, and what we can conclude from that about the character of the early Danish Church, has been discussed vigorously (Gelting 2004; Lund 2004 with refs.). There is no reason to doubt that there was a church in Ribe at this date; and that there could have been churches in all of three of the towns named, each with a bishop associated with it, is as yet unproven but quite conceivable.

In the 10th century the town of Ribe lay where it had been all the time. The renovation of the town ditch and the later construction of true defences clearly underline the continued importance of the site, and both works must have been initiated on the orders of the governor of the town, quite plau-

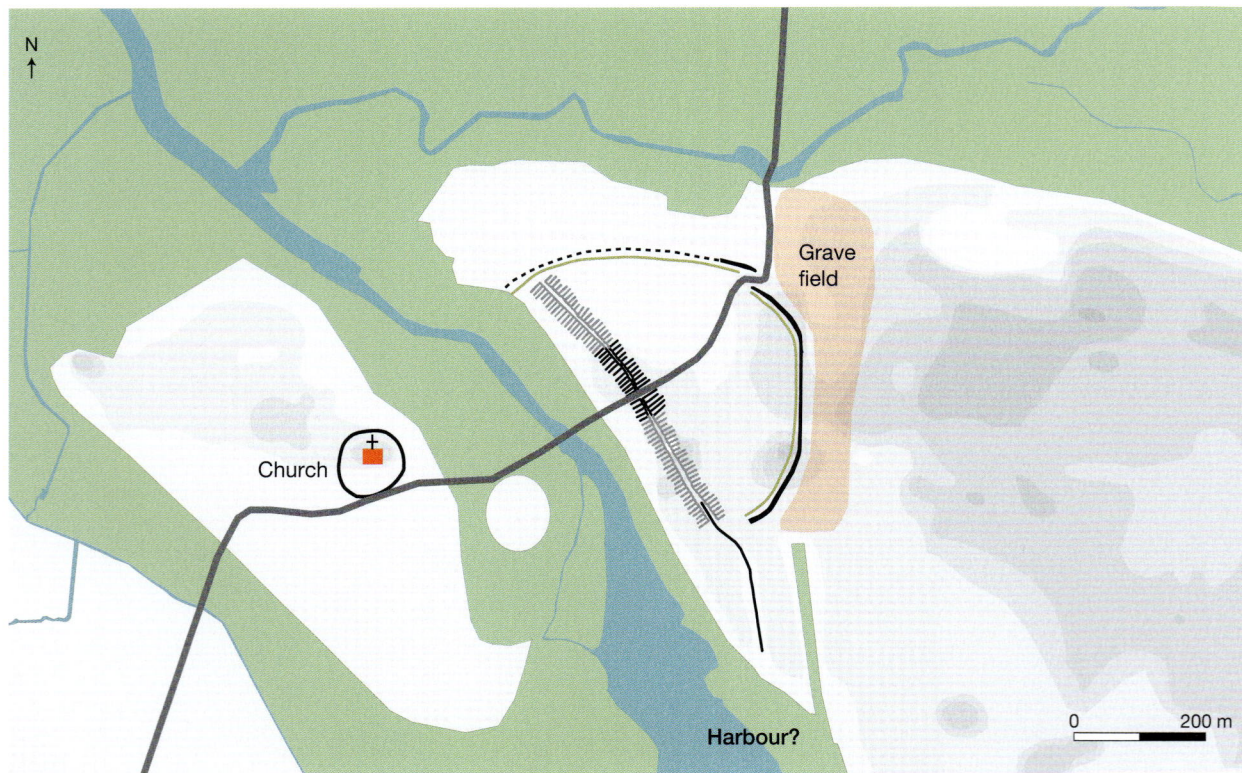

Fig. 170. Ribe in the 10th century.

sibly of the king himself. Where are the finds then? Taphonomy has removed a considerable part, and as for the remainder the answer should probably be that the finds have already been made but have previously been dated as '8th-/9th-century' on the assumption that there was no town here in the 10th century. This is quite possible for series of not narrowly datable categories of finds such as pottery, blown glass and the imported glass beads from c. 800 onwards, and more; and it is not least the use of radiocarbon datings in recent years that has helped to shed light on this state of affairs.

Nevertheless, this does not alter the fact that the finds assemblage from 10th-century Ribe remains unusually slight, and in particular the paucity of coins, hacksilver, and cubo-octahedral and oblate spheroid weights (see sections 5.9.3-4) can hardly mean anything other than that exchange depending upon precious metals was at a low level, or perhaps was carried out within the harbour area which has not yet been definitely located (Kalmring 2010). The complete lack of copper-alloy jewellery of the 10th century also suggests no great activity, but once again it is necessary to remember that the quantity of items of jewellery found from the preceding centuries is barely more than ten or so pieces.

Despite the picture painted by the finds, the renewal of the town ditch and subsequently the construction of the true defences indicate that whoever was in charge of the town insisted to begin with upon the maintenance of the boundaries of the town and later upon defending it against hostile attack. In its construction and size, the rampart around Ribe is highly reminiscent of the earliest rampart at Aarhus (H. Skov 2008) but the circumstances surrounding the construction and development of the defences of Hedeby are less clear.

The defences of Hedeby, Ribe and Aarhus are mutually similar in that they were not laid out with the geometrical precision that characterized the royal building complex at Jelling, probably in the course of the 960s, or the ring forts of the 970s onwards (Holst et al. 2012; Roesdahl & Sindbæk 2014; Sindbæk 2014b). The opening in Moat B at Ribe also differs strikingly from the architecture of the ring forts. Altogether, this constitutes an argument for placing the defensive works at the three royal towns of Hedeby, Ribe and Aarhus in the period before Harald Bluetooth's interest in monumental architecture and geometry took root; and that is not contradicted by archaeological evidence. The enclosed area of Hedeby was around 27 ha, that of Ribe can be estimated as around 14 ha, and Aarhus was around 6 ha.

Town Ditch K200 and Moat B of Ribe of the 10th century clearly show that the town itself was still the area north of the river despite the presence of the church on the opposite side, and the significant extent of the defences has to express the existence of a not insignificant town.

At the cathedral, however, the radiocarbon dates indicate that many burials took place in the 10th century. A single find from the excavations at Ribe Cathedral deserves special mention. In the foundation of a building of 1850 was found a substantial fragment, about a fifth of a highly decorated runestone from around the year 1000 (Figs. 171-2) (Imer, Knudsen & Søvsø 2012; 2013; Imer 2014). The stone carried the marks of having been split on at least three different occasions, and from the inscription in the looped runic ribbon only the word *fultrua*, 'trustworthy', could be read. Although it is unprovable, it is probable that the stone was originally raised at Ribe Cathedral out by the Droveway and the crossing place of the river. This is the first known runestone from Ribe although there may have been more. Large stones would have attracted the attention of stonemasons in this otherwise completely stone-free area from an early date.

The history of the town of Ribe in the 10th century has become much better understood in the course of excavations in recent years, and yet it appears still to have been a low point in terms of trading and other activities which contrasts quite paradoxically with the extent of the defences of the town and the density of burial at the cathedral.

5.11 Ribe in the 11th century

In the course of the 11th century, probably around the middle of that century, the defensive work around the Viking-period town north of the river was removed (section 5.10.4); at the same time, a settlement of urban character appeared around the cathedral on the other side of the river. In this way, the town changed character fundamentally, and was transformed from a typical emporium pattern to an equally typical civitas pattern in which a church was the physical and ideological heart of the town. Whether or not one or more of the other five parish churches of the town were founded during this century we do not know, but that must be considered likely.

5.11.1 Ribe north of the river in the 11th century

The excavations around Rosen Allé in 1989 and 2014-16 form the largest continuous area excavation in the urban area north of the river, and the finds from the fill of Moat B made during the course of that work constitute by far the largest collection of finds which shed light on the life of the town in this period.

Fig. 171. Runestone fragment 'the Ribe stone' being lifted out from the excavation on 26 April 2011. In the foreground, Museum Inspector Troels Bo Jensen while behind him the author is lending a hand. In the background is Ribe journalist Ole Sønderstrup who for decades was a loyal guest on the edges of excavations in the town. Photograph: Henrik Dons Christensen.

Fig. 172. The stone has been decorated with an animal with the inscription within its body. Only one word of the text can be read: fultrua, *meaning 'trustworthy'.*

216

As discussed in section 5.10.4, Moat B, the finds from the moat with its functioning period from around the middle of the 10th century to the middle of the 11th do not imply that Ribe was a flourishing trading town during that time, although since the heart of the town was still the lane alongside the river a long way from the moat, the paucity of finds can to some extent be explained by that distance. Despite everything, the fill of the moat contains a small but distinct amount of early Pingsdorf pottery which shows that there were connexions with the Rhine regions in this period (Tab. 20).

North of the Ribe River, five coins of the 10th-11th centuries have been found to date (Fig. 173). These coins have no signs of having been tested or bent, and apart from one broken-off fragment they are either whole or quartered, and thus some slender evidence of a monetized economy at the site. None of the coins is one of Cnut the Great's so-called Ribe issues, which have in the past been viewed with growing scepticism while the most recent coin finds from Ribe give less and less reason to think that coins were

struck in the town before the end of the 11th century at the earliest. The two coins of Cnut and the coins of Harthacnut and Magnus the Good clearly show that use of coinage and probably trade was still going on inside the old town area.

5.11.2 Ribe south of the river in the 11th century

5.11.2.1 The cathedral

Notwithstanding the varied history of the Danish Church in the late 10th and early 11th century (Gelting 2004), the church in Ribe appears to have continued to function and, perhaps because of the official conversion of the nation, the number of burials seems to increase in this period (Fig. 149). Several phases of churchyard boundaries in the form of ditches, probably with banks on the inner side, belong to this period and thus also demonstrate the continued maintenance of the boundaries of the institution. The earliest dendro-

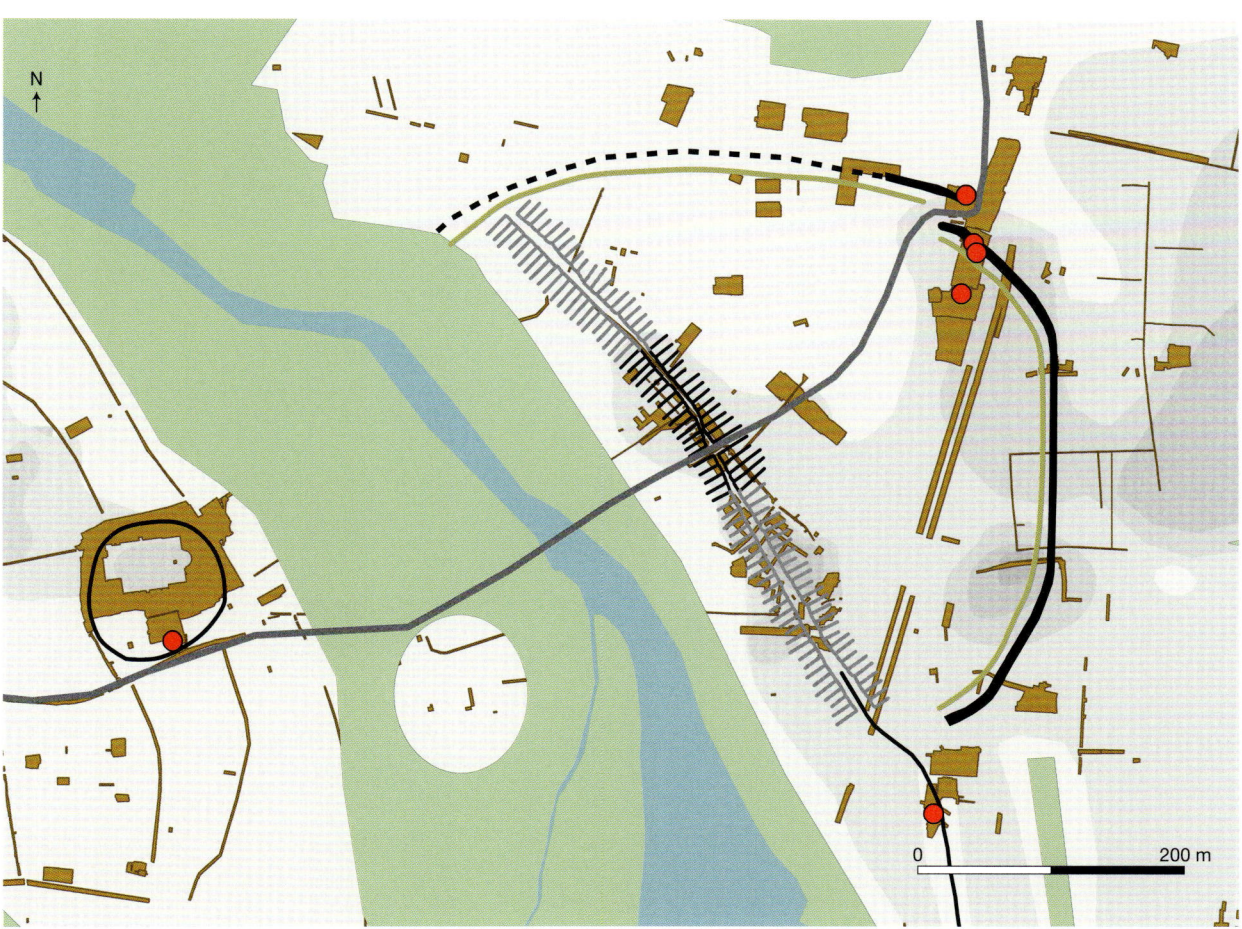

Fig. 173. The six Danish coins (yellow dots) of the period AD 900-1050 found to date have, with one exception, been found north of the Ribe River. Also known, from north of the river, are a few clipped dirhams and a couple of fragments of German coins; since those cannot be dated precisely, however, they have not been shown on the plan. Areas excavated are shown in brown.

datings from planked structures around the churchyard are '1037', 'after 1028' and 'after 1029' (see Appendix 1: Dendrochronology in Ribe), the period in which Odinkar the Younger served as bishop.

5.11.2.2 The town moves to the church

Around 1050 the southernmost part of the churchyard, the area north of the main artery route, was laid out and subsequently was occupied by settlement of an urban character over what had been part of the churchyard. The process could be followed in detail through excavation ASR 13 Lindegården, and a matching stratigraphical sequence has been recorded both to the west and the east in trenches ASR 564 and ASR 1150. This change of use must therefore cover the whole of the southern part of the churchyard.

The churchyard ditch was filled and in the one section that has been excavated datable objects in the form of a halved coin of Cnut the Great (from London, AD 1029-35), a coin of Svein Estridsen struck in Viborg (Hbg. 65), and a clipped fragment of what was prob-

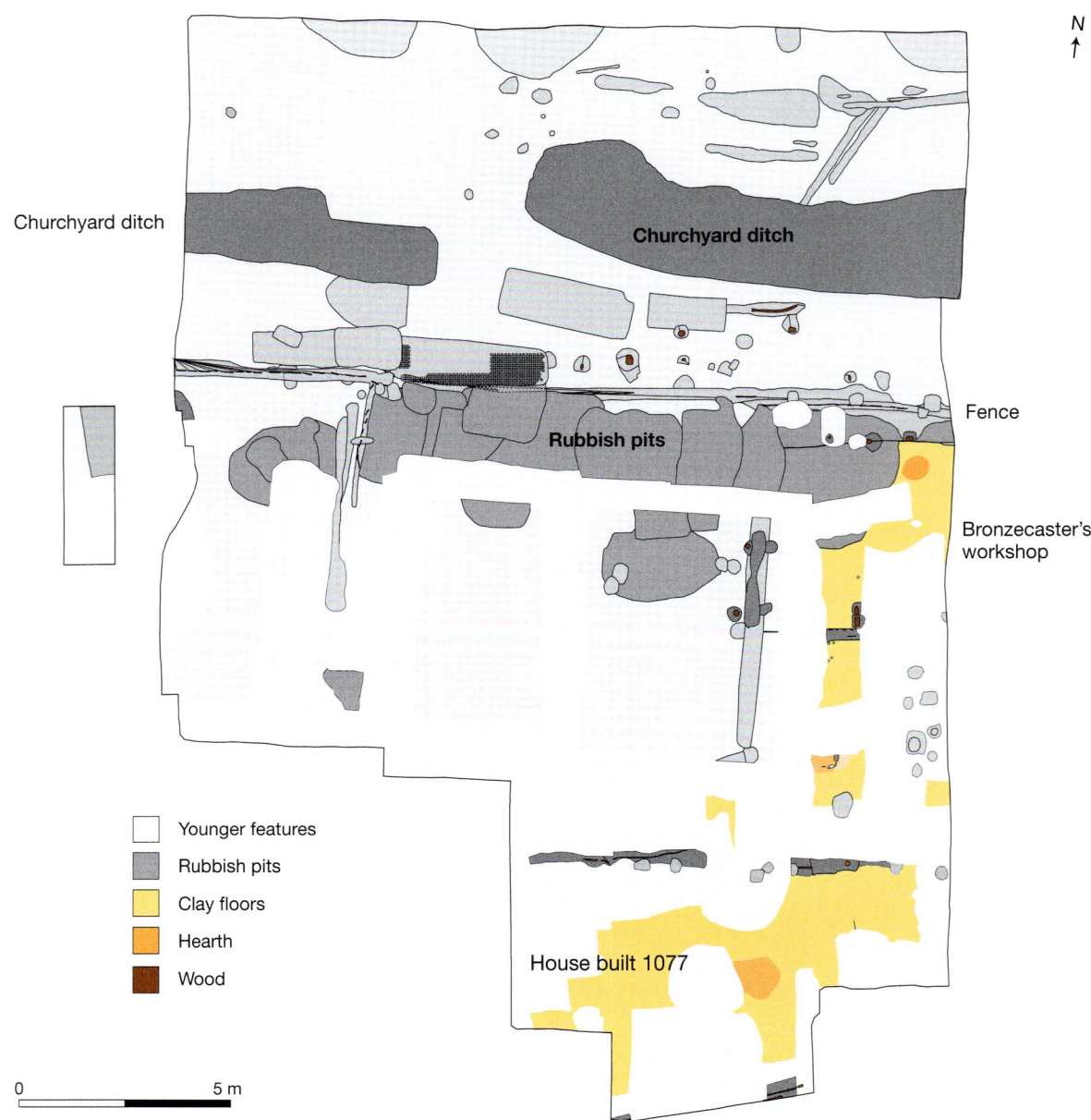

N ↑

Churchyard ditch

Churchyard ditch

Fence

Rubbish pits

Bronzecaster's workshop

☐ Younger features

▨ Rubbish pits

▨ Clay floors

▨ Hearth

▨ Wood

House built 1077

0   5 m

Fig. 174. The earliest phase of building overlying the earliest churchyard at ASR 13 Lindegården: cf. Figure 139. To the south lay a building with bowed walls and a central hearth, raised in 1077. North of here were slight wooden buildings of which the northernmost was a bronzecasting workshop which produced Urnes brooches, bird brooches and 'animal in ring' brooches. The plot was enclosed by a planked structure along which a series of successive rubbish pits were sited.

ably a foreign coin were found. Amongst other finds of interest can be noted several human bones and a horse's skull. The coins and the other finds point to a dating from around the year 1000 up to when final refilling took place after 1050, but cleaning out could have removed evidence of earlier phases.

In the southern part of the area of excavations the culture layers deposited over the original soil layer contained the remains of a timber building with a clay floor and a hearth (Fig. 174). Some of the southern wall had been preserved, built of 40- to 45-cm wide planoconvex vertical planks with the convex side facing outwards. Three of these oakwood planks have been dendrochronologically dated to 'after 1037', '1077' and '1077-89' respectively.[34] 1077 is considered to have been the year in which the building was constructed. Beneath the building was a culture layer some 40 cm thick which contained, amongst other things, a number of pits. From two of those there are dendrochronological datings of pieces of wood with felling years of, respectively, 'after 1039' and 'after 1048'. These datings are supported by a coin struck in Emden sometime in the period 1059-86 (Dannenberg 773). which was found in a context beneath the timber building.[35]

The oldest traces of building at ASR 13 Lindegården comprise a planked structure which stood as a boundary between the churchyard and the built zone (Fig. 174). On the inside of the planking the earliest features were a series of pits whose contents were typical of urban settlement – pottery, animal bones etc – in stark contrast to the churchyard's features, which are virtually void of finds. The town had thus now moved to the church, and this event or process can be dated to AD 1050 ± 10 years when the radiocarbon datings are considered along with the buried finds from the sealed settlement horizon. No remains of buildings from the very earliest settlement have been found, but they are probably to be found outside the area excavated.

To the north of the area a bronze-/brasscasting workshop was set up in which large quantities of Urnes brooches, bird brooches and animal-in-ring brooches were produced (fig. 175). The workshop left behind it a large quantity of moulds and crucible sherds (M.H. Søvsø & C.V. Jensen 2020). A number of the animal-in-ring brooches include a conspicuous cross motif, and both the small bird brooches and the larger Urnes brooches, the design of which is a beast struggling with a snake, have convincingly been argued to be Christian designs (Wood 2014). This output can therefore be described as one of Christian amulets: in other words objects which were attributed with some innate power, probably in continuation of the tradition leading from the enamelled cross brooches and other cross-decorated jewellery of earlier times.

Fig. 175. Moulds for an Urnes brooch, a bird brooch, and an animal in ring brooch, together with crucibles from the jeweller's workshop. Not to scale. Photograph: SJM.

Around the middle of the 11th century, then, a minor part of the large churchyard was given up for an urban settlement along the main arterial route of Sønderportsgade. This is as yet the earliest securely dated evidence of urban settlement on the cathedral island, and with its utterly central location in mind this is presumably the actual occasion on which the town was moved across to the cathedral.

Why some of the churchyard was appropriated we do not know, but by then, probably, one or more of the five parish churches of the town had been raised, which could have lessened the pressure on the cathedral churchyard. It is to be supposed that the king or the bishop was responsible. The metal workshop was positioned close by the churchyard and was producing Christian amulets.

5.11.2.3 The street plan

The streets of Ribe have been subjected to a long series of archaeological examinations since the 1980s in connexion with the renewal of their surfaces and pipe-trenching below them. In combination with the information from excavations of abandoned street lines in the western quarter of Ribe it has transpired that the stratigraphy of the street plan is uniform, involving the same sequence of successive forms of paving which in some cases have been datable with the help of dendrochronology.

Beneath the principal artery, Sønderportsgade, wheel ruts have been found which probably go back to the Viking Period or possibly even earlier. In some other streets too, wheel ruts are the earliest features. Around the year 1100 the first proper paving was laid in the form of a layer of animal bone and stone, which has been discovered in a large number of streets (Fig. 176) (Søvsø 2006; 2007a).

The reason for this rather macabre form of protection is probably the lack of stone around Ribe. A little later, the bone and stone paving was superseded by woven matting laid upon sand (Fig. 176) and from the 1120s proper planked streets were constructed consisting of oakwood planks lying across the street. The same sequence is found in all of the streets examined, and the infrastructure must therefore have been under a centralized administration.

The extensive street plan must reflect an overall plan which was put into effect in the second half of the 11th century. Starting from the two principal features of the cathedral island, the main street of Sønderportsgade and the cathedral itself, streets were laid out which radiated out in all directions from the heart of the town, the cathedral. The bishop or the king must have been behind this regulation of the street plan, which in its own way constitutes a refoundation of the town (Fig. 177).

Fig. 176. At the top, bone paving from around the year 1100, and below, woven matting from around the year 1120. Top: from excavation ASR 1200 Bakelitten; Bottom: from excavation ASR 1843 Sønderportsgade.

5.11.2.4 The plots of the town

The spaces in between the streets were laid out in plots. Our knowledge of these areas and how they developed is very limited, but it does appear to be clear that there were great discrepancies in size, and that despite the slender data from the 11th century there is evidence of a large number of adjustments

Fig. 177. Ribe in the 11th century. The orthogonal street plan on the cathedral side is based upon a large number of observations and is quite certain. The other five parish churches of the town are also marked. That all of them were in existence in the 11th century is uncertain. The blue dot marks a well constructed in AD 1077, so far the only known well of the 11th century.

and sub-divisions of the individual tenement plots. The dynamic thus appears to have been fundamentally different from that on the plots north of the river. As boundaries between the parcels of land we know of planked structures, wattled fences and ditches.

The tenement plots adjacent to Sønderportsgade were not very long. These attractive plots probably housed traders and artisans as at the metal workshop beside the cathedral which could profit from the traffic.

Extensive areas were excavated in the western part of Ribe in 1990s which have only been summarily studied. The earliest dating from this area is a well from excavation ASR 1200 Bakelitten which was constructed in AD 1077 (Fig. 34; 177) (L. Andersen 1999). Since the whole area is also united by a network of streets paved with bones there is no reason to doubt that this was laid out as a quarter of the town, and at the very least parts of the area must have been built upon already in the 11th century. The most informative evidence about the plot structure is from excavation ASR 11 Danielsens Tømmerhandel. North of a paved street, the earliest phase of which is represented by wheel ruts followed by bone paving, one large plot of 35x20 m could be identified. To the south, west and east this was bounded by ditches

but to the north by a wattled fence which might therefore represent the subsequent sub-division of what was originally an even larger area. In the south-eastern corner of the plot a large house of c. 8x10 m with substantial earth-fast posts was excavated, which had stood through several phases down to the beginning of the 13th century. In and around this house a number of fascinating artefactual finds were made: a decorated Hanse bowl (Hanseschale) of the 12th century, several coins and weights, a coin brooch, an 'animal-in-ring' brooch, 12th-century coins, and more. The finds assemblage shows that the residents of this house were involved in trade and that probably several generations of merchants lived here who were responsible for foreign trade which, amongst other things, brought quantities of imported pottery to Ribe. On the western side of the plot there was a lighter building, possibly a stall, while the water supply came from a series of wells. The earliest of those was a pinewood well that was undatable but was followed by four framed wells dated to AD 1134, 1141, 1175/6 and 1207. The household waste, as could be seen in the excavation of Lindegården, was deposited in rubbish pits that were grouped along the northern boundary line.

5.11.3 Summary and interpretation: Ribe in the 11th century

While traces of 11th-century Ribe were virtually non-existent only a few years ago, the situation is now completely different (Feveile 2006a; Kieffer-Olsen 2008). From the northern side of the river radiocarbon dates from the latest layers in Sct. Nicolaj Gade, the finds from the refilled moat, and coins – three separate datasets, in other words – show that urban activity continued to the middle of the 11th century. On the opposite side of the river the excavation at the cathedral showed that urban settlement was introduced to the site around the year 1050. There are no strong grounds from the evidence at present available for adopting a categorical position over whether this was one coordinated move or a more gradual process. One possibility is that the northern side of the river was not completely abandoned, and the presence of three parish churches in that area could argue in favour of that; it appears unquestionable, though, that the level of activity on the cathedral side was a great deal higher and that the new centre of the town was the cathedral.

Unfortunately, archaeological information about the other parish churches is poor, nor is the documentary evidence of much help. St Klemen's and St Peter's churches are the first churches in addition to the cathedral referred to, in the foundation document of the cathedral chapter in 1145, showing that by that date at least there were churches on both sides of the river (*DK*, Ribe amt, 64).

The laying out of the street plan and its early decking with animal bone are clear evidence that the organization of the new town was taking place according to an administered scheme. Whether before that plan there was less controlled, topographical preliminary phase is difficult to determine, but in any case some central authority laid out the framework of the structure of the town. The reconstruction of the earliest street plan indicated that this started from the cathedral and the extant main artery Sønderportsgade, and attempted, from these fixed points, to lay out a network of streets with the church in the centre which defined more or less square zones. The newly planned layout was at least 20 ha in area, and therefore much larger than Viking-period Ribe, and the archaeological data to hand imply that the framework was quickly filled up.

The governor of the town has to be assumed, *a priori*, to have been the king, although down to 1234 the bishop held 'half of all the royal rights in Ribe' (Kinch 1869, 51), and it is possible that this sharing of power goes back to before the year 1100. On a Danish coin of c. 1100 found at von Støckens Plads the obverse depicts a bishop, which may indicate that the bishop then already controlled the newly established mint in the town (Fig. 178).

It is not known for certain whether or not the bishop's residence was already within the town of Ribe in the 11th century, but the finding of a coin die in Grydergade in 2006 used by Bishop Tue in the period 1214-30 (Søvsø 2007b) strongly suggests that the mint, which would usually have been at the lord of the mint's residence, was here. This find would therefore indicate that, before it was moved to Bispegade in the late 13th century (Kinch 1869, 147ff), the bishop's residence lay immediately to the west of the cathedral – a position which might go back to the Viking Period.

Whether or not the king had a residence in the town before the construction of Riberhus in 1268 is also unknown for certain but can be considered overwhelmingly probable. The merchants of the 11th century still needed protection, and the income from the trade of the town must already have been considerable. The evidence known includes no direct sign of a royal residence or a market square but a range of disparate observations suggests possible locations.

North of the river in 1993 a moat which surrounded a large area of 60 x 100 m was found in an area which had been completely levelled (Feveile 2006i). One possibility is that this was the royal court, but if so its date should precede the removal of the town to the cathedral island around 1050 – a period in which there is otherwise no evidence for fortified structures.

On the other side of the river, the Dominican friary appears to have been built on a natural hill of heath sand which was surrounded by wetland on all sides. When the church was being renovated in 1918-32 deep, refilled ditches were found which must have been older than the foundation of the friary in 1228 (*DK*, Ribe amt, 697 with refs.). In a smaller trench located immediately east of the east wing in 1988 below a layer of 18th-century burials the substantial foundation of a brick building was found, the level and alignment of which did not agree with any known building plan for Danish mendicant houses (Frandsen et al. 1990, 13). In the demolition material above the wall was found a moulded brick that was fluted and glazed, fine features

Fig. 178. A presumably danish coin of c. 1100 found in von Støckens Plads. The obverse shows a bishop with a crook. ASR 2090x3. Scale 2:1.

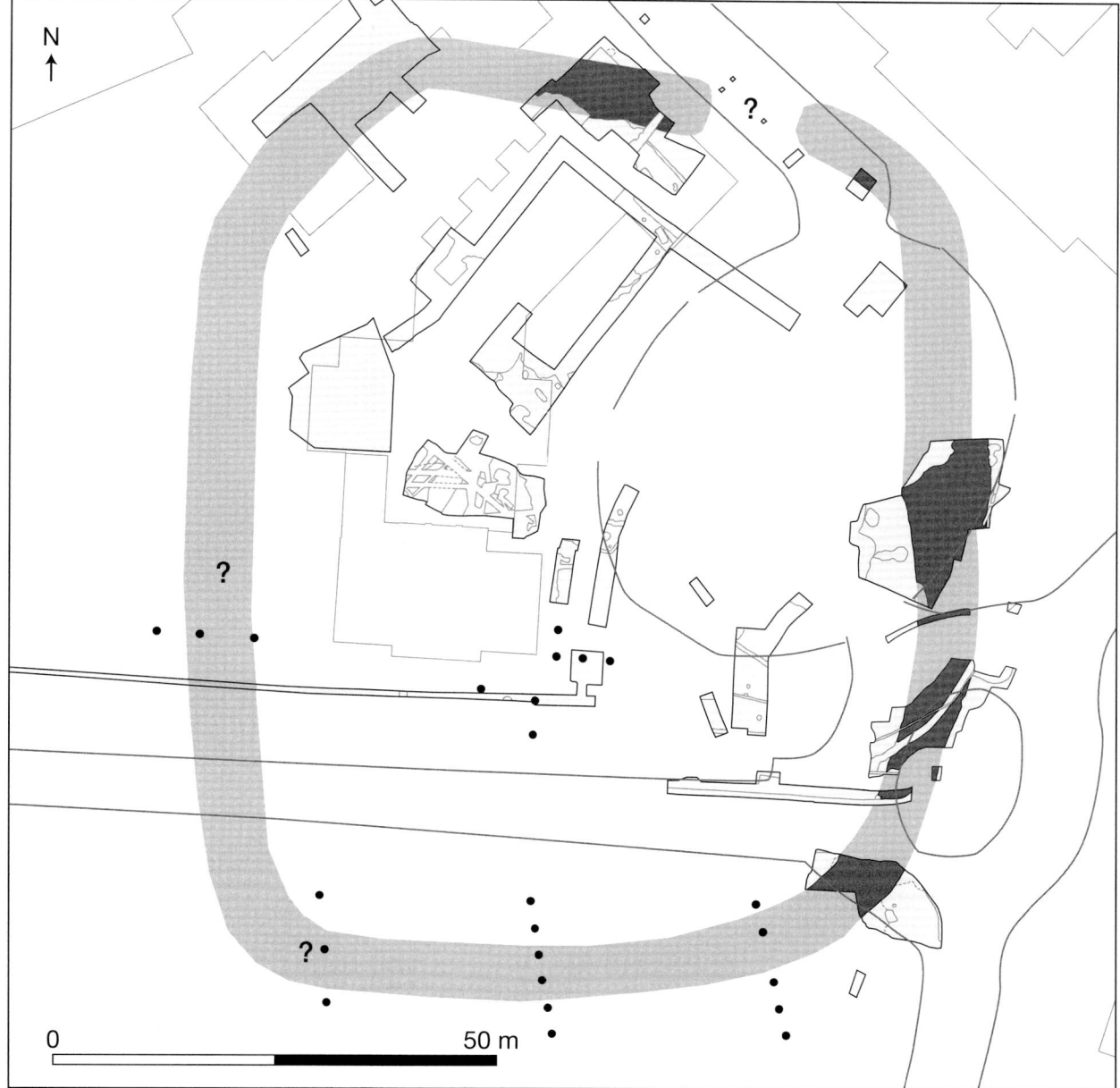

N

0   50 m

Fig. 179. The castle north of the river; cf. Figure 93. More recent excavations have revealed the moat alongside the postu-lated opening to the north too. After Feveile 2006i.

which belong to Romanesque brick architecture. This find appears therefore to document the presence of a fine brick building pre-dating the foundation of the friary in 1228. A number of mendicant houses took over earlier royal structures, for instance the Franciscan friary in Schleswig, and that could have been the case in Ribe too. This also concurs with the strategic posi-tion out by where the main roadway crosses the river. In the river area north of the friary, where the street Sortebrødregade now runs, several minor archaeologi-cal excavations have been carried out. In all cases no buildings have been found in the lower culture layers but entirely organic layers on the whole, within which

surfaces decked with wood have been seen (Klemensen 2000). This stratigraphical sequence could agree with the area down by the river having been laid out as a market square, possibly as early as the 11th century, and would also fit with the proximity of the postulated royal residence. For the time being, however, this can only remain a hypothesis.

The year 1050 was selected as the upper chronologi-cal limit of this book, but in this section threads have been followed up to the period around 1100. The academic reason is that Ribe then had achieved the basic form which remains intact in respect of parts of the town. This does not mean that the town has not

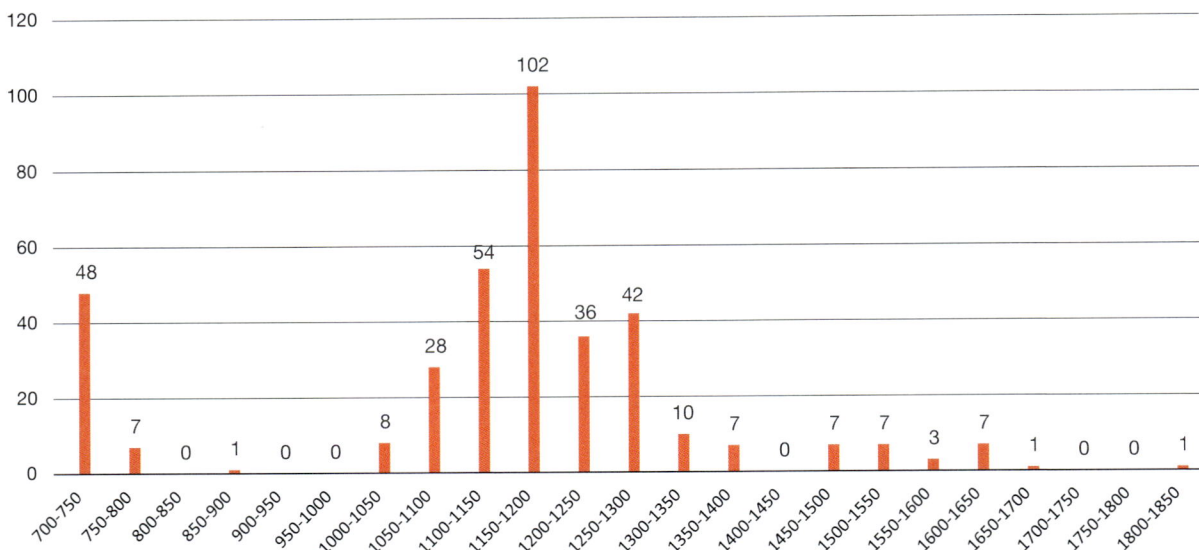

Fig. 180. Overview of the total of 369 dendrochronological samples from Ribe from down to 2016, grouped into 50-year intervals. For datings without sapwood a judicious chronological position has been assigned based on the archaeological context of the sample. See Appendix 1.

subsequently changed. Later in the Middle Ages Ribe experienced both dramatic growth and radical decline, and was profoundly transformed as a result of the royal appropriation of the town. But the extent of all of those changes really does lie beyond the scope of this study.

Access to timber, the conditions for preservation, and the pattern of waste disposal, all of course play roles affecting the data in Figure 180, but the indication that the 8th and the 12th centuries were Ribe's two major peaks is consistent with the other archaeological evidence from the town, and shows that the towns of the Viking Period and the Middle Ages were not slowly and steadily growing constants but mechanisms which were extremely dependent upon conditions and opportunities and whose growth and deterioration followed the streams of goods which were the *raison d'être* of the emporia as towns.

5.12 Summary: Ribe AD 700-1050

In bullet-point format, this chapter has attempt to document the following key points:

- In what was formerly a marginal zone where the main land route of West Jutland, the Droveway, crossed the Ribe River, around the year 700 a trading site either emerged or was founded with specialist craftspeople present from the outset. The inspiration must have come from the expanding emporia network of the North Sea region with Dorestad at its heart.

- The earliest traces of Ribe appear to be scattered and unsystematic, and so there can hardly have been an overall plan. It is possible that Ribe had a royal founder, but it has been proposed above that the local aristocracy of Dankirke/Okholm could also have been the founders, possibly in collaboration with merchants.

- Various types of sceatt were used from the beginning, but these coins were superseded around 725 by a single type, the Wodan/monster sceatt, which must have been a monopoly coinage of a Danish king.

- The plot structure focused upon a lane along the river was established through a progressive process in the early decades of the 8th century in pace with the powerful growth of the town.

- The artefactual finds from the town and its cemetery point to a mixed population and permanent occupation from early in the 8th century.

- There was a decline from the second half of the 9th century and few archaeological remains down to the 11th century, but the plot structure was maintained, a church was founded, and the town was defensively enclosed.

- Around 1050 the town moved from the north side of the river to beside the church on the southern side, and changed in structure from an emporium to a civitas.

6. The urbanization of southern Scandinavia, AD 700-1050

Having now presented and analysed the archaeological evidence relating to Ribe in the period of AD 700-1050, the final chapter of this book will expand the view to southern Scandinavia as a whole. The aim is to investigate whether the lines of development that have been proposed in the case of Ribe in the foregoing chapters can be matched at other sites and thus will form the basis for a more general model of urbanization in what was then the territory of Denmark.

6.1 The first emporia

There are only two known sites of the 8th century in southern Scandinavia besides Ribe whose structure, range of finds and pattern of activity are so clearly different from other known sites that they can be classified as *emporia*: higher level nodes of 8th-century international, regional and local trading networks. These are Reric in Wismar Bay and Åhus in the north-east of Skåne (Callmer 2007; Sindbæk 2007; Kleingärtner 2014).

From several coastal landing or trading sites, and from central places, there may also be information on various forms of evidence for specialized craft and trade, but these traces are either poorly dated or spread out over a long period of time. The quantities of finds from these sites correspond only to fractions of the masses of material from the emporia, although they do indeed show that trade and specialized craft were not monopolized by the emporia but rather could take place at a wide range of sites of varying character (Ulriksen 1998). In terms of volume in those respects, however, none of these sites comes anywhere near the emporia.

6.1.1 Reric

In Wismar Bay, 7 km north of the later Hanseatic town of Wismar, the remains of a coastal trading site of the 8th and very early 9th centuries have been excavated, along with an extensive cemetery. The Frankish Annals record under the year 808 that the site was known as Reric in Danish, a name which toponymical research attributes with reeds or 'bay with reeds' (Kleingärtner 2014, 305 with refs.). This is consistent with the reconstruction of the former, now eroded, coastline (Fig. 181). Nowadays, the site lies right on the shore and is cultivated land. Both erosion as a result of rise in sea-level and agriculture have damaged or completely removed the archaeological deposits over a large area. Only cut features survived when extensive excavations of both the settlement and the cemetery were undertaken in the 1990s (Pöche 2005; Tummuscheit 2010; Kleingärtner 2014, 303ff; Gerds 2015).

Around 100 SFBs have been excavated. They are concentrated in a N.-S. strip and in several cases are so regularly spaced that they must represent an organized division of the area around one or more N.-S. street lines running parallel to the shore; however all traces of streets and plot boundaries are now lost. The majority of the 30 excavated wells, which have produced most of the c. 90 dendrochronological datings from the site, are in the same area. These date the period of functioning of the site to AD 735-811.

The SFBs are overwhelmingly of the Saxon, square type with corner hearths, and so could be used not only as weaving huts or workshops but also as proper housing. The zone of the settlement by the shore has been lost to erosion. To the extent that the situation in the 8th century can be reconstructed, however, the settlement appears to have covered an area estimated as 10-20 ha, probably organized around a street which ran through it and led down to the postulated harbour. The basically elongated layout is similar to that of Ribe in the 8th century.

Similarity to the state of affairs in Ribe is also evident in the cemetery placed to the north, which is spread out over around 2.5 ha of a clearly defined low hill. About 300 graves have been excavated, the majority of them inhumations of a wide range of forms while

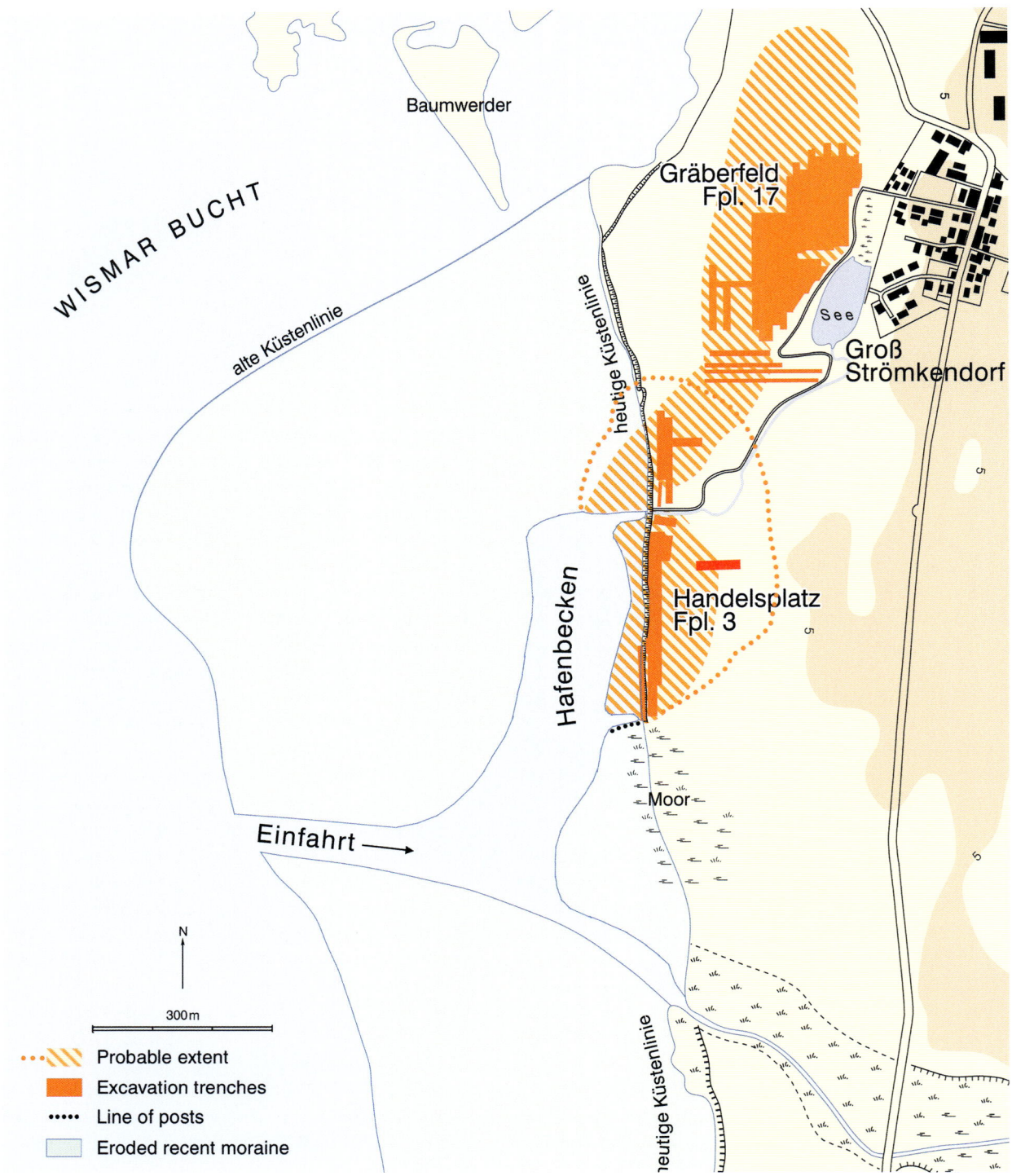

*Fig. 181. Reconstruction of the basic structure of the emporium of Reric. The sunken feature buildings were found primarily in the long narrow area labelled Fpl. (*Fundplatz*) 3. After Messal et al. 2020.*

the remainder comprise urned cremations and other types (Gerds 2015). As in Ribe, it is to be supposed that a large number of relatively shallow cremation graves have been lost through cultivation, while at Reric the cemetery is also characterized by a number of irregular traces of more or less clear ring ditches, presumably the remains of low barrows.

The comprehensive finds assemblage, like that from Ribe, is marked by specialized craftwork making use of amber, antler, glass and metal as raw materials, while the palette of finds reveals trading links with both the Frankish realm and Scandinavia. More recent metal-detecting has, down to 2014, also added 34 sceattas to the list of finds, 24 of them of the Wodan/

monster type.[36] Ribe and Reric therefore stand out as the two major find spots of sceattas in Scandinavia, and the finds indicate that the monetary system of Reric could have been parallel to that in Ribe.

As this shows, Reric and Ribe are structurally practically identical on a wide range of parameters. One might form the judgment that the architecture of the buildings and the finds representing domestic life, especially the pottery, express a difference, but here too there is in fact a similarity in so far as the finds at both sites are the products of the local building practice and local domestic traditions. At Reric these are consistently extremely modest buildings, and to the extent that there were any buildings on the plots in Ribe they too may have been slight (Croix 2015). The large number of wells is a feature of both sites, although not in the form of wine barrels at Reric. Possibly the Slavs did not drink wine.

Reric is referred to in the Frankish Royal Annals under the years 808 and 809. Under the first of those years it is reported, in relation to the Danish king, in this case Godfred, that the town had formerly 'brought his kingdom large benefits from the collection of taxes' (*Vikingerne i Franken*, 16): a strong reason to claim that, for some of the 8th century at least, Reric had been subject to Danish royal rule. The many recent finds of the Danish king's Wodan/monster sceatt (see section 5.8.7.2) corroborates this political and economic connexion.

6.1.2 Åhus

Since 1979, sections of a trading site of the 8th and 9th centuries have been excavated alongside the most substantial river of Skåne, the Helge River, two kilometres from where it debouches into the Baltic. The structure of and activities at this site are highly congruent with those at Ribe in several respects. The name of the river means 'the holy river', while Åhus means 'river mouth'. The closest village on the northern side of the river has been called *Ripa* since the Middle Ages, which is also a completely unusual place-name in Skåne.[37] The coincidence of the common European place-name *Ripa* and the archaeological site on the Helge River cannot be a matter of chance, and could indicate that at least one of the names of the site at Åhus in the 8th-9th centuries was *Ripa*. Perhaps, like Hedeby/Schleswig, the site had several names even at an early stage?

The Helge River flows through an important agrarian landscape with a profusion of archaeological sites (Callmer 1991). The most important of the many sites was probably Vä, a pre-Christian religious place-name meaning 'shrine'; here there is evidence of a major settlement site of the Iron Age, probably a central place. In the earlier Middle Ages a royal presence in the area

can be traced not only in documentary sources but also through the foundation of Premonstratensian monastery and a town. The landscape around Åhus does not, therefore, lack evidence of an elite presence, reflected in place-names, a concentration of estates, and urbanization, and this picture would probably be much enhanced if metal-detectors were used in Sweden more.

The topographical and hydrographical circumstances around the archaeological site of Åhus have been changed fundamentally, and it is difficult to reconstruct the state of affairs in the 8th century. It could, however, be that the trading site was located where the course of the river changed from wide and slow-flowing to being narrowed to a width of just 20-50 m with a more rapid flow and less depth (Callmer 1991, 33f). This discussion could unquestionably be modified by more thorough studies of the historical cartographic evidence, but on the basis of this reconstruction a logical place to locate a crossing of the river would have been where its course narrowed, and the same place must mark the limit of navigation up the river. If that is correct, the location can be described as a natural meeting point of traffic by land and sea.

The site has been under excavation led by Johan Callmer from 1979 onwards, and some of the evidence has been published in a series of articles although a presentation of the basic excavation data in the form of the archaeological structures and finds is badly needed. Callmer distinguishes two sites: Åhus I, on the southern side of the river, was functioning in the first half of the 8th century, and succeeded by Åhus II on the northern side of the river a little further downstream (Fig. 182). Åhus II was operative from later in the 8th century through until after the middle of the 9th century. Åhus I is interpreted as an intermittent market site while Åhus II was a more permanent trading site. Both sites were subsequently abandoned and were subject to ploughing after the end of settlement (Callmer 2002). There is no intact stratigraphy left, but some of the plough-layer overlying Åhus II was sealed under soil from a canal that was dug as early as the later Middle Ages. Altogether three sceattas are known from Åhus I, all of the Wodan/monster type, while the remaining Viking-period coin finds recorded in Lunds Historiska Museum consist of just four dirhams, two complete and two fragments, together with a halved German denier, a Cologne-imitation of c. AD 1030 (Callmer 1991, 41).[38]

Callmer's plotting of the settlement is based upon a combination of excavation and phosphate mapping. The latter approach in particular may be problematic when one considers that the area is part of the intensively manured town-field of the later medieval town. Åhus I is estimated to have covered an area of 2-3 ha while Åhus II covered a considerably larger area, of more than 12 ha (Callmer 2002, 127).

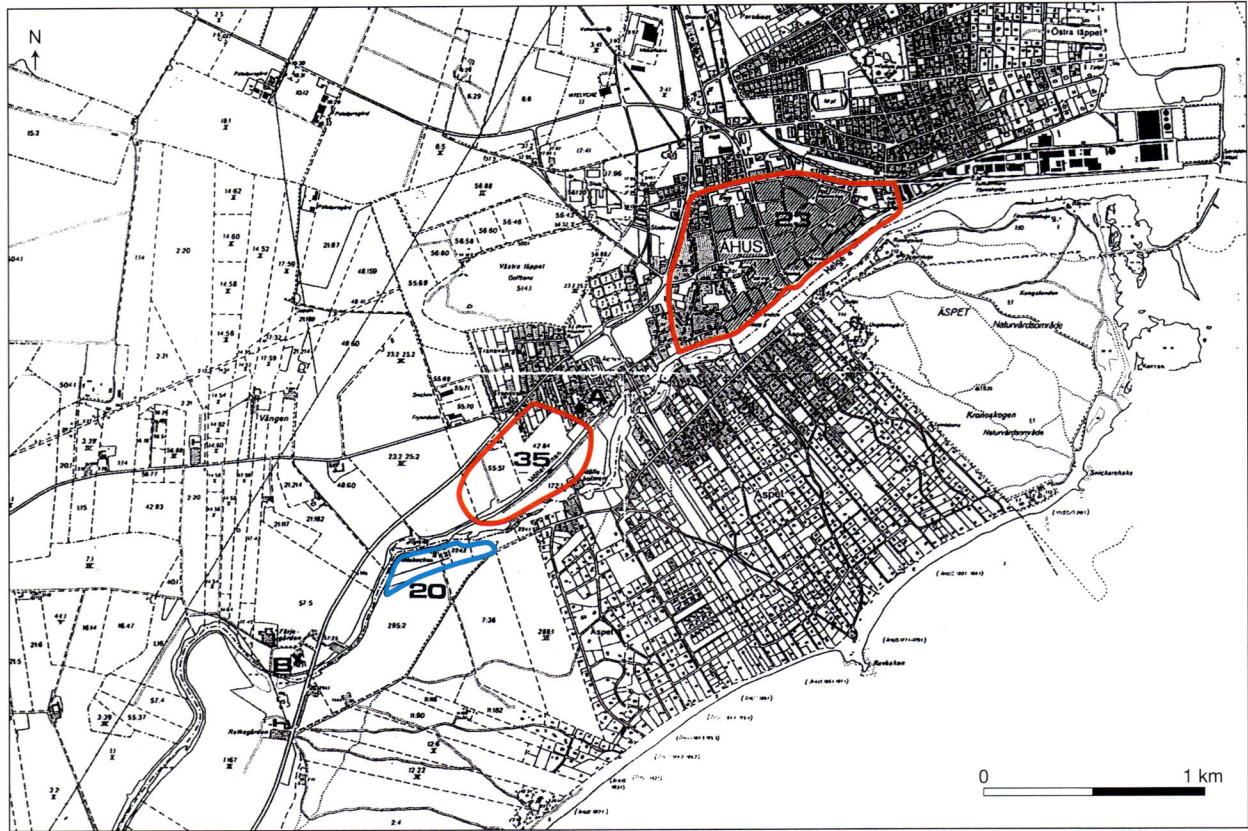

Fig. 182. Åhus in Skåne. The blue area numbered 20 marks the site of Åhus I, functioning in the first half of the 8th century. The red loop around the number 35 marks Åhus II of c. AD 750-850, which is cut by a later millstream while the medieval town of Åhus is the larger red loop to the right. The village of Ripa in Åhus parish lies slightly to the left of the edge of the map. After Callmer 2002 with additions by the author.

The lack of access to the empirical evidence renders it difficult to compare Åhus with other sites, since the starting point in the case of Åhus has to be Callmer's interpretations of the archaeological data rather than the actual data themselves. On that unsatisfactory basis, the development of the site across the 8th century appears to be as follows:

Åhus I was founded or emerged in the first half of the 8th century on the southern side of the Helge River. After the demise of that settlement the area is thought to have been left as pasture until the 19th century, and the level of destruction is limited to the consequences of ploughing for what was in fact a limited period. The natural subsoil does not appear to contain significant cut features; conversely the plough-layer, culture layers and archaeological structures contained significant quantities of finds, principally waste from specialist craftwork: the beadmaker, combmaker and metalworking in the form of the casting of copper alloy and blacksmithing. Although there are numerous crucible sherds and other evidence of metalcasting the material includes no clay moulds. The 'flimsy' structures of the site

and the paucity of ceramics are proposed as the most important arguments for interpreting Åhus I as an impermanent market site. Nonetheless the question can be asked, as to whether the absence of both clay moulds and pottery could not largely be explained through degradation as a result of frost and cultivation?

Both the finds and the structures were concentrated in a strip along the river that has been identified over a distance of about 200 m; within this zone the distribution of finds is highly uneven. If we take taphonomy into account, these circumstances appear to have many similarities with the state of affairs in the oldest Ribe, where waste heaps from a range of crafts on the individual plots produce similar concentrations of finds (see section 5.8.3). When the first artisans and traders came to Åhus I cannot be dated any more precisely than to the period AD 700-750. Why the settlement moved downstream and across to the other side of the river is also unknown.

The quality of preservation of the Åhus II site, which was functional in the period c. AD 750-850, is very inconsistent, but both the impressive quantities of finds and the archaeological structures, including 149 SFBs, show beyond doubt that this was a true emporium, of which more than 3 ha have been excavated: twice the excavated area of the oldest Ribe. It is no surprise that this has produced large amounts of finds characterized by the specialist craftwork of the emporia, which inevitably poses a major post-excavation and analytical challenge to the excavator. In publications to date the individual groups of evidence have been dealt with as wholes despite the long period of operation (Callmer 2001), and a static, orthogonal plot structure is proposed although one of the few published plans from the site appears to show that there appear to have been several different lines of alignment for the SFBs (Fig. 183) and thus also, conceivably, for the street plan of the town.

On the basis of the published evidence it is not possible to judge whether, or to what extent, Åhus II developed during its life time, while the position of the excavations in combination with the uneven levels of preservation caused by the millstream do not create a strong basis for assessing the internal topography of the town. However the distribution of the SFBs over a large area implies a major town zone consisting of blocks connected by a network of streets. Whether or not this was something that had appeared already in the 8th century or only in the course of the 9th century cannot be determined from the evidence that has been published.

In the case of Åhus, a topographical and hydrographical analysis directed at integrating the site into the surrounding cultural landscape and its communication networks is badly wanted. Such an initiative could also identify possible locations of the cemetery or cemeteries which presumably lie along one or more of the land routes into the town.

6.1.3 Summary: the first emporia

As the archaeological situation stands at the moment, three emporia of the 8th century are known within the area of southern Scandinavia: Ribe, Reric and Åhus (Fig. 184), alongside a large number of smaller, coastal sites of varying sizes. Altogether these formed the network of trading and landing sites that the exchange of goods by ship requires. While, presumably, more of the smaller sites will gradually be discovered, for reasons that are examined below there is little reason to anticipate that more true emporia will appear within the historical area of Denmark.

Ribe, Reric and Åhus all lie in the immediate neighbourhood of a later medieval town. Only in the case of Reric was there a significant chronological gap between the emporium and the Hanseatic town, which

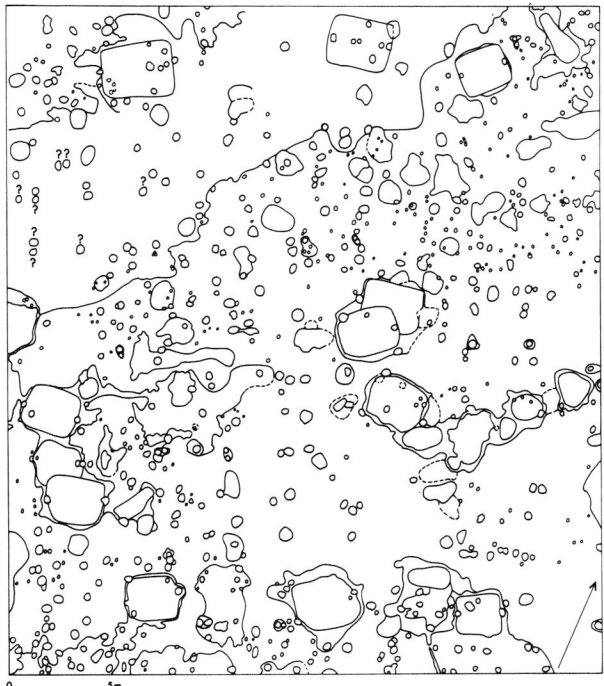

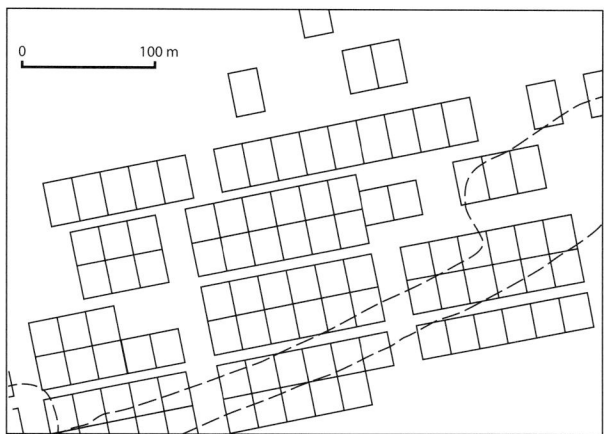

Fig. 183. Top: excavation plan from Åhus II, including sunken feature buildings on varying aligments. Below: Callmer's proposed plot structure. After Callmer 1991 and 2002.

is explicable through the political history of that site. In the case of historical Denmark, one should expect a hypothetically unknown emporium to be located in the close vicinity of an early town. This locational connexion probably shows that both emporia and medieval towns were sited at the centre of local resource areas upon natural nodes between land- and waterborne transport.

The numismatic evidence from Ribe shows that the town was or came to be under royal control at the latest in the year 725 (section 5.8.7), while the Frankish Royal Annals report that that was the situation with Reric around the year 800 and possibly earlier. The

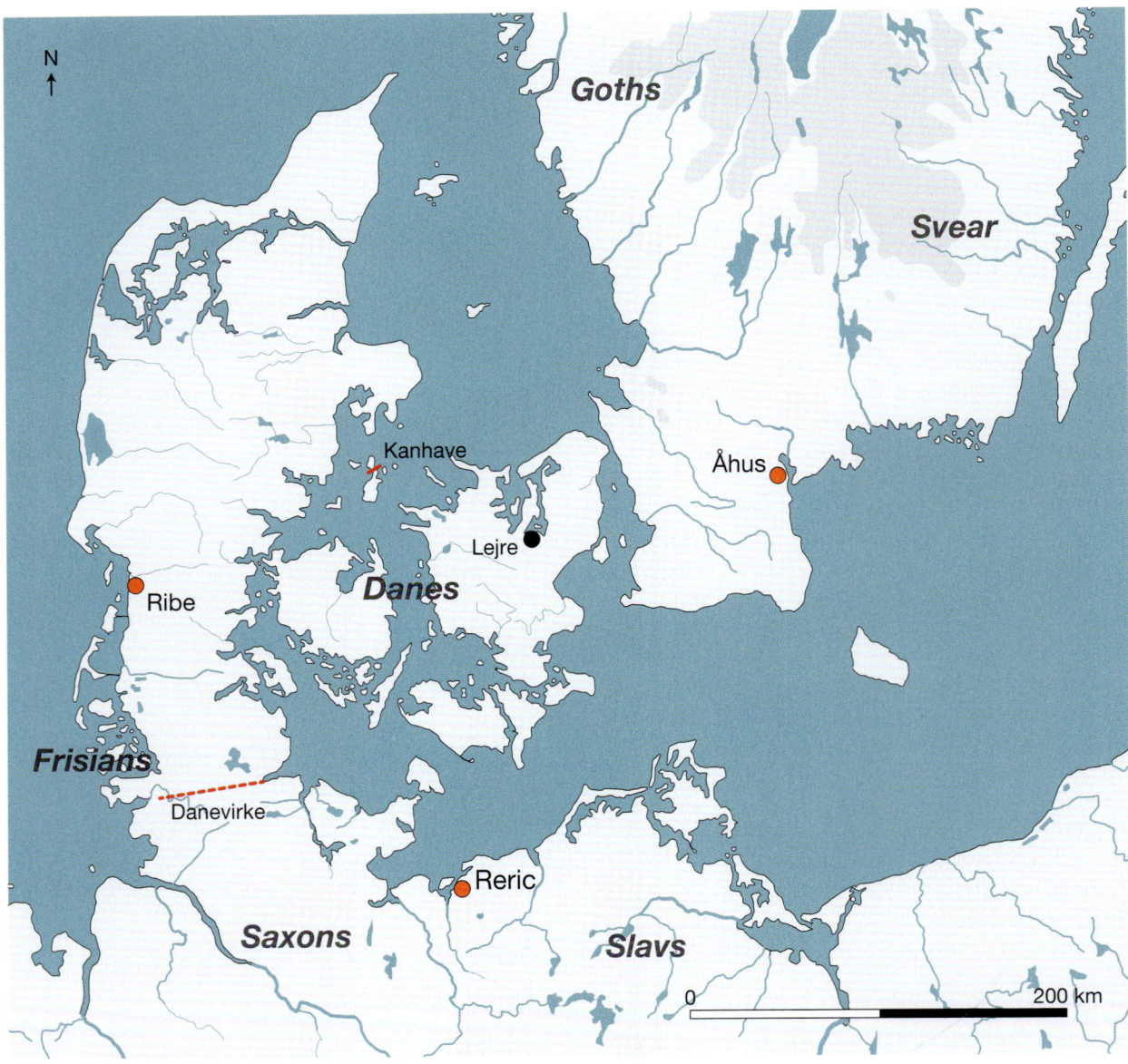

Fig. 184. The 8th-century emporia are sited within the ethnic and cultural limits of the Danish kingdom. The centre of this kingdom appears to have been Lejre. The Danevirke and the Kanhave canal are also marked.

new finds of Wodan/monster sceattas in Reric support this supposition. Ribe, Reric and Åhus are the three leading find places for sceattas in Scandinavia.

The emergence of Ribe around 700, the Kanhave canal on Samsø from AD 726 and the major development of the Danevirke in AD 737 are well known as evidence used to argue for the existence of a unified Danish kingdom as early as the 8th century (Sawyer 1988; Wickham 2005, 364ff; Näsman 2006; Gelting 2007; Roesdahl 2008), but the large-scale structures found in western Denmark have lacked counterparts in the east, and could appear to contradict the accounts in the Lejre Chronicle and other sources about Lejre as the seat of the Danish royal power at that time. If we add in to the picture the two emporia of

Reric and Åhus discussed above, it becomes clear that all three sites are situated in the known border zones of the later Danish kingdom: Ribe on the border with the Frisian zone; Reric on the border with the Saxon and Slavic zones; and Åhus on the border with Blekinge (Fig. 184). The Anglo-Saxon traveller Wulfstan reported at the end of the 9th century that Skåne belonged to Denmark while Blekinge was considered to belong to the Svear.

The location of the three southern Scandinavian emporia agrees with the pattern of location of other emporia in relation to the structuration of power around the North Sea in the 8th century (Hodges 1982; 2000; 2012). This indicates that the southern Scandinavian emporia were the product of a deliberate trade policy on the part of a Danish king, presumably with his seat at Lejre, where Thietmar of Merseburg spoke of heathen sacrificial feasts and the role of the site as *Caput*, 'the head' or capital (*Kilder til vikingetidens historie*, 53f). It is indeed at Lejre that the largest hall of this period in Scandinavia has been found (see below, section 6.3.3) (T. Christensen 2015, 59ff). The sequence of halls and the other known ancient monuments at Lejre have clear parallels at Gamla Uppsala, the ancient royal seat of the Svear, where Adam of Bremen could tell of former heathen sacrificial feasts.

The emporia and their single coinage, together with the rebuilding of the Danevirke in 737, must be the earliest unambiguous indications that in the 8th century the kingdom of the Danes had already grown to an extent which corresponded more or less to the situation later in the Middle Ages. In this light it is no surprise that it was within the power of this king to construct the Kanhave canal in the year 726; while, since the halls at Lejre exceed all other known examples, they form palpable components of a pattern that outlines a unified kingdom of Denmark in the 8th century with its cult centre and royal seat there. How much further back in time this Danish kingdom might be traced is another question, and one which is not to be pursued in any detail here, although Gudme appears to have been greater in wealth than Lejre in the period before AD 600 (Østergaard Sørsensen 2010).

From congruence of names, it has been suggested from several quarters that the Danish kings, who are referred to in the Frankish Royal Annals, were members of a family dynasty down to the end of the 9th century. Throughout the period they must have considered Lejre, with its halls, cult activities, monumental burial structures and ship-settings, as the dynasty's royal seat (A.E. Christensen 1969, 28ff; Sawyer 1991). The archaeology of Lejre corroborates that inference, and altogether there are grounds to argue that down to the end of the 9th century the Danish royal kindred had its homestead here, even if, inevitably, it must be presumed to have spent the greater part of any period of office on the move, and often in conflict with other pretenders to the throne, just as in the case of the medieval peripatetic kingships.

Were one to point out one particular site at which one might eventually find an as yet unknown emporium of the 8th century it would be on the Swedish west coast north of Halland, which at the end of the 9th century the Norwegian voyager Ohthere (Óttar) considered to be Danish, but therefore in a cultural border zone between Danish, Swedish (Västergötland) and Norwegian spheres of influence: a regional predecessor of Kaupang.

One could write many books about the inhabitants of the emporia – their social and ethnic backgrounds, internal organization, relationships with other emporia, those in power, the artefactual finds and more – but those are all beyond the scope of the current work.

As Chapter 4, *Topography*, helped to show, Iron-age society in southern Scandinavia was formed with a differentiated aristocracy which, from greater or minor elite farmsteads presided over the celebratory and sacrificial rituals that were central to the practice of the heathen religion (L. Jørgensen 2014). These elite farmstead complexes or central places lay at crossing points of land routes, often with extended continuity both back and forwards in time. The central-place system was well established around the year 700, and the emergence of the emporia formed a maritime *add-on* to this model that spread north and east from Ribe and brought in its train a network of subordinate landing places and anchorages of diverse character. Whether, or by whom, Ribe was actually founded is not known, but it is argued in this book that at the latest from around the year 725 Ribe was under royal control, and both Reric and Åhus must surely have been royal trading sites too. The emporia would scarcely have been able to exist without the compliance and/or involvement of the local elite, and supervision was probably delegated to these royal lieutenants, the *comites* of the Frankish sources (e.g. Gelting 2007, 77). The geographical range of the emporia is impressive, and even as early as the 8th century awareness of their existence as a market for special categories of goods seems to have diffused throughout the Scandinavian peninsula (Sindbæk 2011).

The 8th-century Danish emporia are characterized by the following features:

- They are part of a maritime network

- Their liminal position on the borders of the kingdom

- Their central position in the immediate resource area

- Extended settlement close to a shore or bank

- Local constructional traditions

- Local material culture with a marked input of imported or transported material

- Specialized craft dependent upon the supply of raw materials

- A monetized economy based upon the Wodan/monster sceatt

- Ethnically and culturally diverse cemeteries

6.2 Danish emporia in the 9th and 10th centuries

As the above shows, the 8th-century Danish emporia share many common features. In the course of the 9th century a gradual differentiation took place that concentrated trade to an increasing degree at Hedeby. The emporia of the North Sea suffered from the many Viking raids of the period while new markets opened up to the east via the Russian rivers and through the flow of Arabian silver which came that way, reaching Scandinavia in small quantities from the end of the 8th century but increasing greatly from c. AD 860 (Steuer 2002; Williams 2011; Hodges 2012, 113ff).

6.2.1 Hedeby/Schleswig

The Frankish Royal Annals record under the year 808 that King Godfred moved the merchants from Reric to a new site which in Norse was called Hedeby and in Saxon/Slavonic *Sliesthorp*, which later became *Slieswich* (Kalmring 2010, 41). Is it possible that the choice of names, Hedeby/Schleswig, was dependent upon whether one travelled there over land or sea? The two names remained in use until the town moved to its current location in the 11th century, when the Norse name went out of use. The removal of the traders from Reric proved successful. The favourable site at the neck of Jutland opened up a routeway for goods between the North Sea and the Baltic, and Hedeby had probably grown to be the largest and most important emporium in Scandinavia in the early 9th century – a position which the town held on to into the 11th century. All of the activity there has left behind an ancient monument which

despite the lack of later settlement and a long anti-quarian tradition still poses a lot of questions (von Carnap-Bornheim et al. 2007).

After it had been identified as the Hedeby of the historical sources by Sophus Müller in 1897, the first excavations took place in 1900, since when a variety of campaigns have excavated around 1.3 ha, corresponding to 5% of the 25.5 ha within the semicircular rampart, and around 0.2 ha of the 11 ha harbour basin inside the harbour palisade. In addition, 1.4 ha of the cemetery and the settlement south of the semicircular rampart have been dug. In 2002, comprehensive geophysical survey was launched, and from 2003 systematic metal-detecting. Both campaigns have produced critical new information. At the same time it has been possible to carry out a series of projects, the objective of which was to publish and make accessible a number of the earlier excavations (Arents & Eisenschmidt 2010; Kalmring 2010). Thus what one badly lacks in the case of Åhus has been done for Hedeby.

Hedeby was not founded on a greenfield site. South of the stream which flows through the area enclosed by the semicircular rampart, metal-detecting has produced a number of finds from the Germanic Iron Age. Cremation graves on what is known as Hochburg to the north have recently been dated to the Late Germanic Iron Age,[39] and what is known as the *Südsiedlung* ('south settlement') is of the 8th century (Steuer 1974; von Carnap-Bornheim et al. 2007). The evidence also shows that the earlier settlement was a limited one and can reasonably be classified as a landing place. This must be the existing settlement which the Frankish Royal Annals called Sliesthorp in 804 in connexion with a visit by King Godfred's army and fleet.

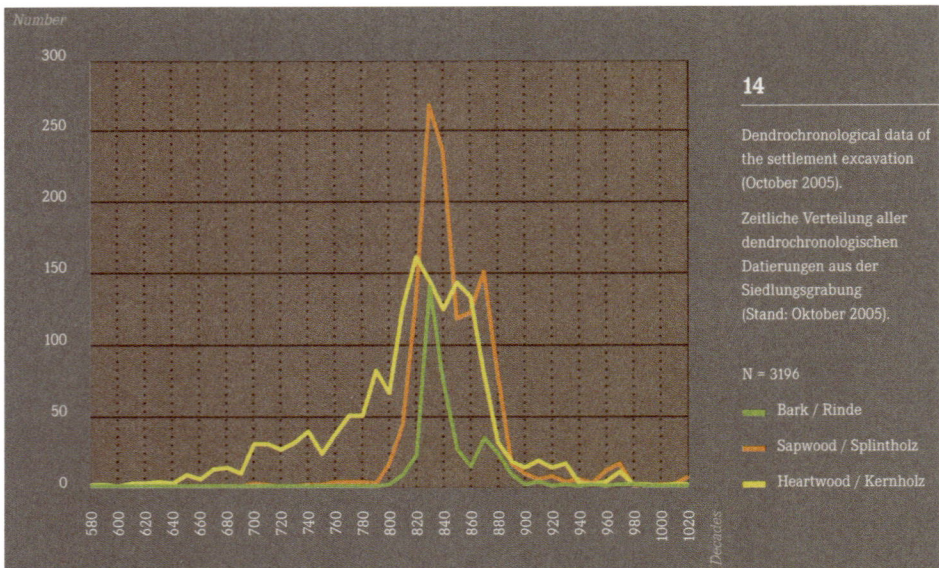

14

Dendrochronological data of the settlement excavation (October 2005).

Zeitliche Verteilung aller dendrochronologischen Datierungen aus der Siedlungsgrabung (Stand: Oktober 2005).

N = 3196

— Bark / Rinde
— Sapwood / Splintholz
— Heartwood / Kernholz

Fig. 185. The more than 3,000 dendro-dates from Hedeby have a sharp peak in the 9th century. After von Carnap-Bornheim et al. 2007.

The next reference is, as noted, under the year 808, providing an account of the destruction of Reric and the removal to Sliesthorp. From the excavations in Hedeby we have more than 3,000 dendrochronological dates from excavations both on the land and in the former harbour (Fig. 185). The earliest dating from a structure on land is to AD 811, and this is followed by a series of datings within the first half of the 9th century with a major increase in the second half of the century (Müller-Wille 2002, 321). The comparatively few datings from the first half of the 9th century may be due to the fact that the excavated area with the best conditions for preservation around the stream was first occupied at a later stage. As is also the case at Reric, there is a very tidy agreement between the information in the Frankish Royal Annals and the dendrochronological evidence.

The key structuring element of the emporium from the beginning appears to have been a N.-S. street along the cove (*Noor*: Fig. 186), where the earlier burials both to the north and the south show that there was some trackway on the site earlier too. On

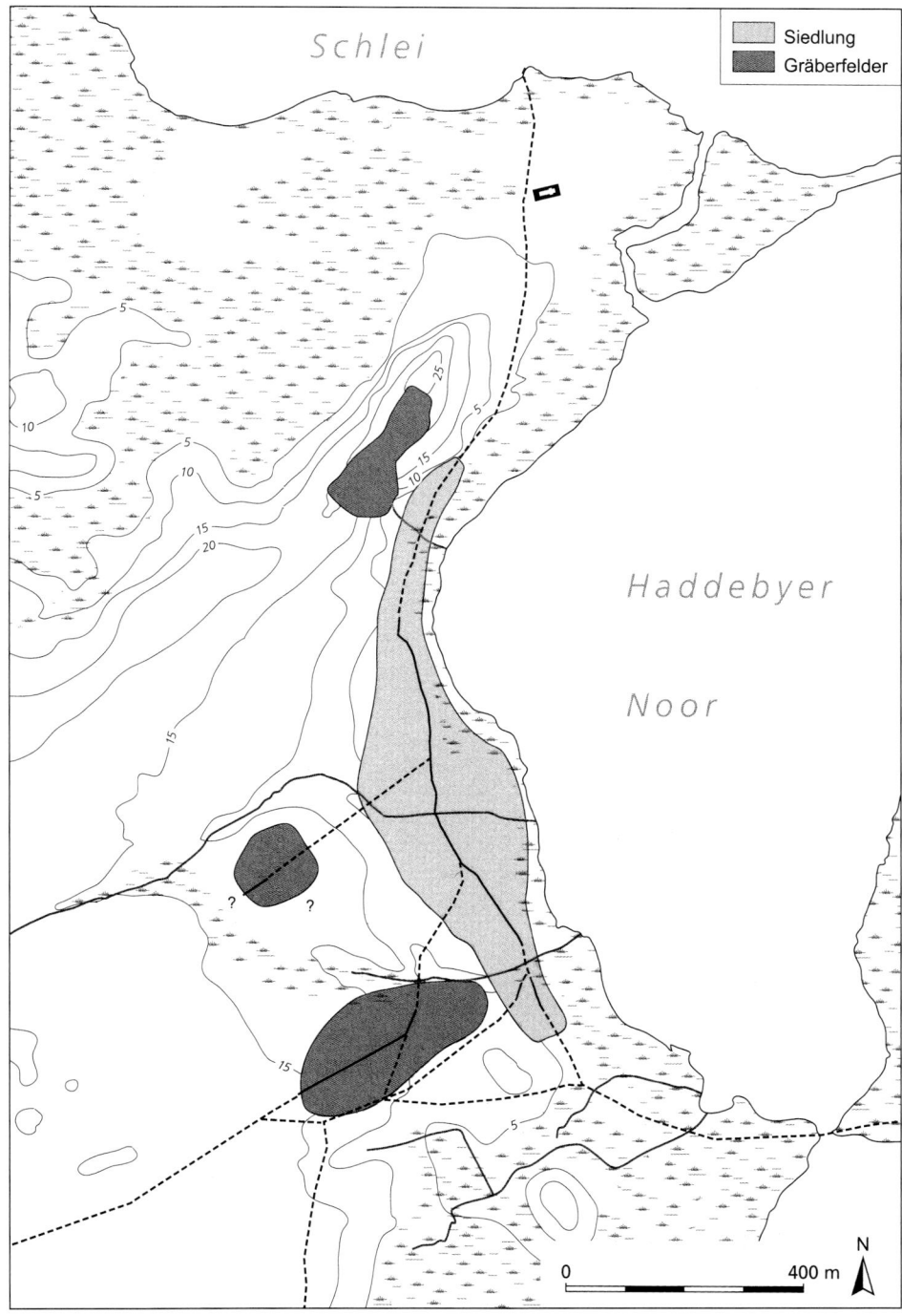

Fig. 186. Hedeby in the 9th century. The northern burial ground, Hochburg, *does not really continue into the 9th century. The other two burial grounds are the* Flachgräberfeld *and the large heathen* Südgräberfeld. *After Arents and Eisenschmidt 2010, vol. 1, p. 313.*

Fig. 187. Coins were minted in Hedeby from early in the 9th century. The earliest were of type combination group (KG) 3, which was then followed by types KG 7-9 in the late 9th century. The coins were modelled upon Charlemagne's Dorestad issues. After Malmer 1966. Left KG 3, pl. 6;1/16;6. Middle KG 7, pl. 7;1/17;3. Right KG 9b, pl. 11;1/20;21. Scale 2:1.

both sides of this main street not only geophysical surveys but also excavation show that plots were laid out; the excavations have revealed exceptionally dense settlement around this main thoroughfare.

In the wetter areas around the stream with the best conditions for preservation the buildings were overwhelmingly of very slight construction, standing on the ground, while the higher, drier areas also appear to have had a very large number of SFBs. In the harbour area the first small jetties were constructed early in the history of the town, and major extensions were introduced with the second half of the 9th century (Kalmring 2010, 239ff).

Early in the 9th century, Hedeby also obtained its own monopoly coinage in the form of imitations of Dorestad coins: what is labelled the KG 3 penny (Fig. 187) (Hillberg 2011). In the late 9th century this was superseded by other variants of the same coin-type, the KG 7-9 pennies, which remained in use down to the second half of the 10th century. The monopoly coinage must signify that the traders there were subject to compulsory exchange at a rate dictated by the king, and this appears to be parallel to the monetary system of the emporia in the 8th century.

Graves have been found in several places at Hedeby although the dominant, heathen burial area lay to the south; this is divided in the literature into a chamber-grave cemetery (*Kammergräberfeld*), and the comprehensive south cemetery (*Südgräberfeld*) (Arents & Eisenschmidt 2010) which contained the most strik-

ing of all of the graves of the town, the *boat chamber grave*. Beneath a ship around 20 m long that had been covered with a barrow three men were buried with weaponry in a central chamber. The higher status of one of these individuals was marked both by the organization of the burial chamber and the grave goods with him. In a pit beneath the prow of the ship were buried three fully harnessed horses. The date and interpretation of this magnificent burial are matters of debate. The primary publication assigned it to the decades around 900 but a dating to the period of 830-50 has since been proposed (Müller-Wille 1976; Wamers 1994). Irrespective of the dating, the grave expresses a high aristocratic or royal individual's desire to identify himself with and legitimize his right to this position (Carver 2001; Pedersen 2014, vol. 1, 258f).

The dating problem renders it relatively difficult to reach any secure interpretation, but two principal explanations can be put forward. If the early dating to 830-50 is correct, those interred must be understood to include a representative of the Lejre dynasty already referred to, who, apparently against the traditions of that family, was buried in a ship. According to that hypothesis, Harald Klak may be noted as a possible candidate.

If the later dating to the decades around 900 is held to, the grave should rather be interpreted as one of several examples of the fluid power structure in Denmark at that time, and so as a challenger to the Lejre dynasty (Müller-Wille 1976, 141f). The

234

presence of three weapon-bearing males and thus the high-status individual in the grave could possibly indicate that they had not died in their beds but were all victims of one of the 9th century's many conflicts around the royal family (Sawyer 1988, 37ff). It is interesting, in any case, that the grave was never robbed, unlike the majority of Viking-period ship graves, where the intrusions have in many cases proved to be datable or assignable to the reign of Harald Bluetooth (Bill & Daly 2012).

In the southern burial ground, but inside the later semicircular rampart, in 1930-1 H. Jankuhn excavated a small area which included, amongst other things, nine chamber graves which from their grave goods could securely be dated to the 9th and the early 10th centuries. These are the earliest known examples of this strikingly elite burial practice which would come to set its mark on the burials in Mid- and North Jutland in the 10th century (Arents & Eisenschmidt 2010, 228f).

After missionary journeys throughout the 820s, the Life of Ansgar reports that, around 850, the Danish king Haarik gave Ansgar permission for a church to be built in Hedeby, dedicated to Our Lady (Skovgaard-Petersen 1981, 37). A few years later permission was

granted for bellringing. Scholars have inevitably been intrigued by the question where exactly this first church in Denmark was sited, and one of several suggestions is underneath the present parish church of St Andreas in Haddeby, even though excavations on the site have produced no results to corroborate that (Arents & Eisenschmidt 2010, 298 and refs).

With the results from the excavations at Ribe Cathedral in mind, the question of the location of the first church in Hedeby should briefly be reviewed. Amongst the various burial grounds of Hedeby only the early excavated Flachgräberfeld displays unambiguously Christian characteristics in the form of a number of graves furnished with crosses and some examples of crosses made of riveted iron plates that decorated the coffins (Fig. 188). The functioning period of this cemetery was from the middle of the 9th century to the end of the 10th (Arents & Eisenschmidt 2010, 226).

The dating, the density of the burials, the burial practice and the types of coffin are reminiscent of the situation alongside the cathedral in Ribe, and for this reason it is proposed here that the flat-grave cemetery is part of the churchyard of Ansgar's church, which

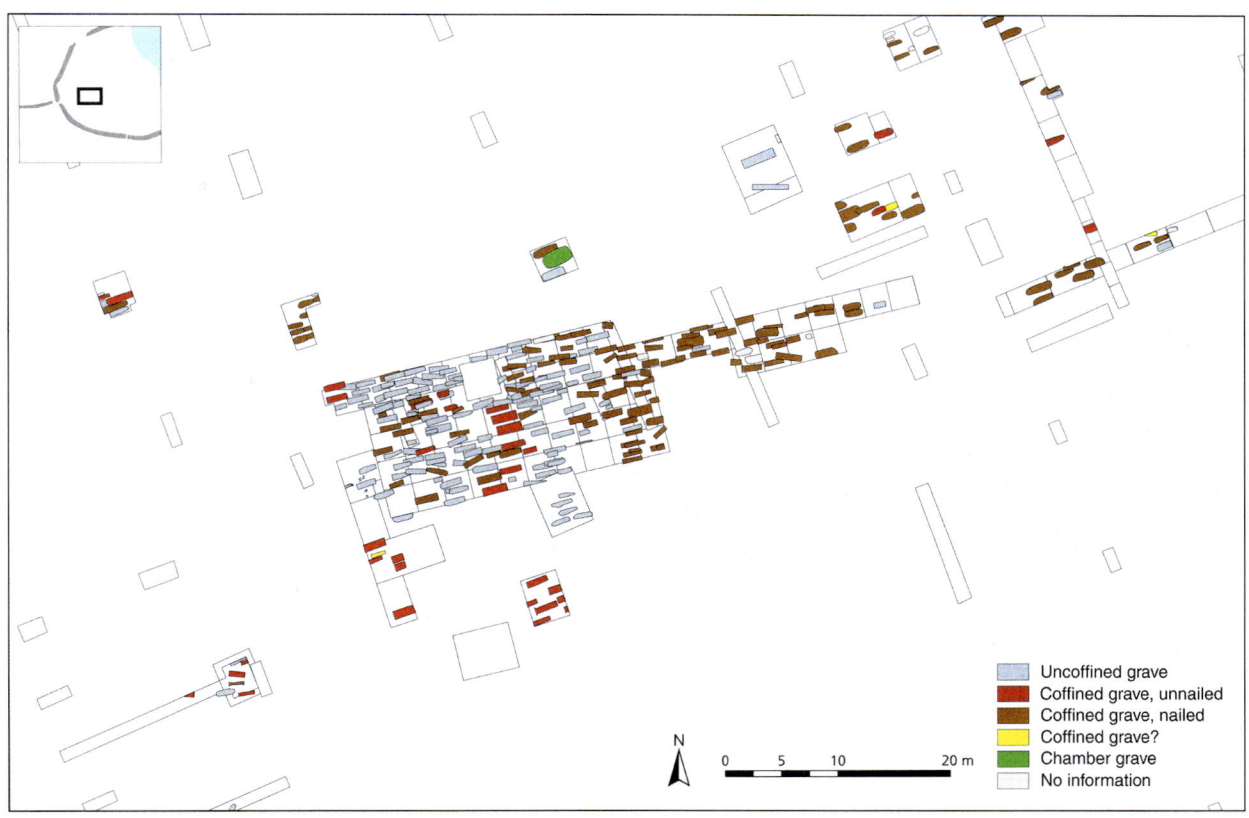

Fig. 188. The flat-grave cemetery showing the distribution of forms of coffin. The position of the burial ground is shown in the inset upper left. The cemetery is highly reminiscent in appearance to the Viking-period churchyard alongside Ribe Cathedral, and this location is considered to be the most likely one for Ansgar's church in Hedeby. After Arents & Eisenschmidt 2010, vol. 1, 221.

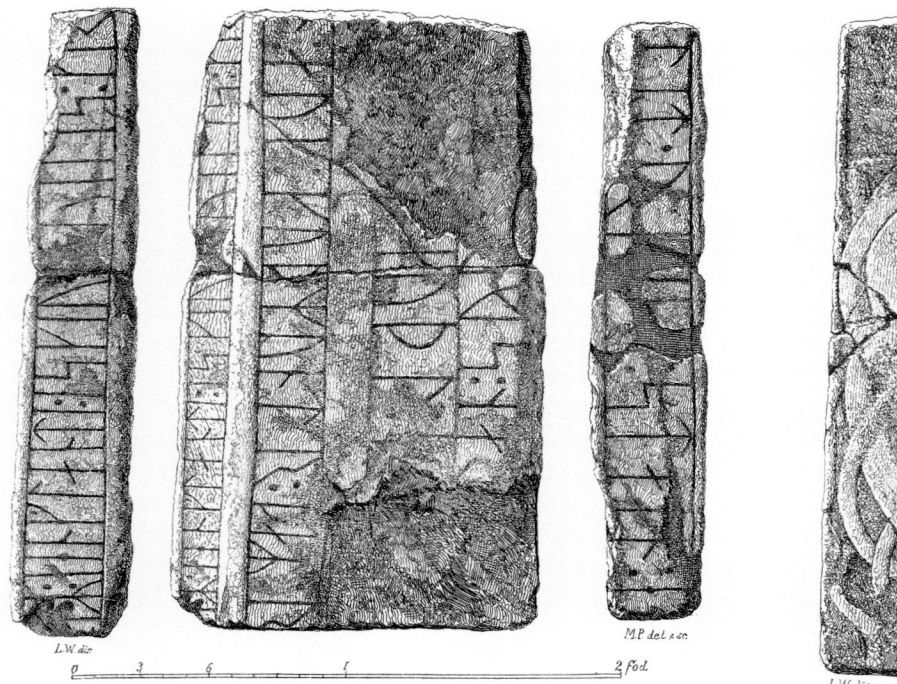

Fig. 189. Fragment of a runestone datable to 1025-50, carved in limestone, which is unusual for this type of monument. Found in 1897 built into the wall of Schleswig Cathedral. Drawn by J. Magnus Petersen. After Wimmer.

must therefore have been sited in the immediate vicinity of both the settlement and the large heathen burial area further south. The proximity to the town helps to explain Rimbert's information about the permission later obtained by Ansgar for bellringing and may also explain the finding of a church bell in the harbour in 1978 at a depth of only 2.7 m (Kalmring 2010, 440). The bell of 24.3 kg belongs typologically between the 8th/9th and mid-11th centuries, and it was furnished not only with a clapper but also with a wooden suspension structure and can therefore be inferred to have been used locally. One can only speculate on the circumstances which led to it ending up on the bottom of the cove and – every bit as remarkable – not being retrieved from this shallow water, but the scanty documentary evidence could support the view that even the church at Hedeby was laid waste as a result of one or more of the military conflicts that came about there at the end of the 10th century: a period which coincides with the abandonment of the flat-grave cemetery (Gelting 2004; 2007).

After Svein Forkbeard expelled the German bishops around the year 987 there is no definite evidence of a church at Hedeby/Schleswig before the reformation of the Danish dioceses under Svein Estridsen around 1059 (Gelting 2004). This does not, however, rule out that there might have been one there during the first half of the 11th century, although no traces

of any such church are known, and its location would presumably have been beneath the current cathedral in the old town of Schleswig, where the discovery of a decorated runestone dated to the period 1025-50 (Fig. 189) may indicate that the history of the church on this site goes back into that period, even though the stone itself could have been moved (Arents & Eisenschmidt 2010, 66).

It is difficult to express a view over whether the growth of Hedeby in the 9th century was abrupt and dramatic or more steady, but it does appear to be certain that activity there in the second half of the 9th century was at a very high level, as is reflected, for instance, by the dendro-dates from both the town and the harbour. In what is conventionally the period of the collapse of the emporia (Hodges 1982; Skre 2007c), then, there is no sign of any decline at Hedeby; on the contrary, there was growth, probably partly boosted by the demise of Dorestad and by the easterly trading links that brought large quantities of Islamic dirhams and other trade goods to Hedeby from the 860s onwards. From this date at the latest Hedeby seems to have been operating on a distinct and greater scale than when compared with the other Danish emporia at Ribe, Åhus and Kaupang.

The image of the 10th century in the archaeological evidence is more diffuse, to be explained to a great extent by the generally poorer state of survival in the

236

upper culture layers. It seems certain, though, that in the 10th century at the latest Hedeby developed a more dispersed pattern of settlement with the town, having formerly been focussed around a main street along the edge of the cove, spreading inland to the west. In the course of the century the impressive rampart around the town, up to 11 m in height, was added, the construction of which and its gradual development are regrettably little understood even though the Connecting Bank dated to AD 968 must have been built before it (Arents & Eisenschmidt 2010, 315ff). The extent of these defences is also in a class of its own compared with the other emporia, reflecting the key role of the town in the military conflicts not only between rivals for the Danish throne but also the kingdoms of Denmark and Germany. The most recent re-assessment of the numismatic evidence shows that there was an active monetized economy within the town throughout both the 9th and the 10th centuries, and that there is little reason to infer that Hedeby was subject to Swedish or German rule at any point in the second half of the 10th century as has formerly been suggested (Hilberg 2011; Moesgaard 2015).

Why the urban area enclosed by the semicircular rampart was abandoned in favour of the peninsula on the north side of the Schlei, where the old town of Schleswig is now located, is a question in itself. The latest dendro-dates from the settlement within the semicircular rampart are from a well constructed in AD 1020 while wreck 3 from the harbour is dated to c. AD 1023. Metal-detecting has also added a number of coins from the 1040s and one coin struck in the period 1060-86 as the latest so far. Altogether this indicates that the old urban area was abandoned around 1050, but whether that was a single event, such as destruction by fire during warfare, or a gradual relocation with some possible chronological overlap between the old urban area and the new, is unknown.

The earliest dendro-date from the old town peninsula is at present AD 1070, but the oldest culture layers lie up to 7 m deep under the current ground surface and in the central zone of the peninsula these are only poorly known through old excavations. By relocating, a well-defended urban area of 25.5 ha with an extensive and well-developed infrastructure plus a harbour that was a integral part of the comprehensive street plan was given up. Before reclamation the peninsula to the north was only half the size, around 12 ha, and had poorer links to the surrounding routeways. A lack of space was very rapidly apparent, and from 1087 at the latest large-scale land reclamation was set in train by building up deposits of material in the Schlei (Müller, Rösch & Schimmer 2014; Rösch 2018).

It has been proposed that the reason for the abandonment of the old Hedeby could have been the increasing draught of the ever larger ships, which made it difficult for them to enter the harbour. However neither the finding of wreck 3 from c. 1023 in the harbour with a draught of 1.5 m nor the most recent reconstruction of the depth of water in the Viking-period Schlei appear to suggest that conditions within the cove were worse than those around the peninsula to the north (Kalmring 2010, 289ff and 305).

It remains the case that it is not possible to identify convincing functional reasons for the relocation of the town, so that instead one may speculate on what the motives may have been for leaving the largest and best protected emporium of Scandinavia for an undefended urban site only half the size with poorer access. I suggest that some pre-existing structure at that site drew the town to it, the remains of which probably lie hidden under the thick culture layers in the centre of the peninsula. Two possibilities suggest themselves – a royal manor or a church, if not both of those. In research concerning Schleswig, royal power has played a key role as an explanatory factor (Müller, Rösch & Schimmer 2014 with refs), but with the discoveries at Ribe in mind the motive may also have had a religious dimension in that 11th-century towns gathered around a central church building. The old Hedeby was, concurrently, a markedly heathen landscape with extensive cemeteries distinguished by barrows, as well, perhaps, as other sites linked to the pre-Christian traditional cult which the now-Christian kings may have wished to distance themselves from. Similar motives could have been factors in the case of Lund and at several other towns of the same period (see below).

6.2.1.2 Havsmarken

As an appendix to Hedeby, the relatively newly discovered detector site of Havsmarken on the south-eastern coast of the island of Ærø must be briefly noted. It was found in 2008 and has subsequently produced a surprisingly large amount of finds from the period of c. 750-950 – western European coins, dirhams, hacksilver, weights, jewellery and more – which show that there was a trading site of some significance here (Fig. 190). In particular the finding of more than 40 Carolingian coins, typically deniers of Louis the Pious, is quite exceptional, while amongst the items of jewellery there are also many cross-decorated items, including a copper-alloy mould for a cross-decorated circular pendant. What may be hidden underground we do not know. As of yet, only a very limited trial excavation has been conducted.

Havsmarken has to be regarded as a purely maritime-oriented trading site located on the key sailing route to Hedeby. Its more precise character will have to be revealed by future investigations but it needs to be considered whether or not the site might have

Fig. 190. Finds from Havsmarken. Christiana Religio *deniers, Arabic dirhams, weights and hacksilver. Not to scale. Photography: Steen Agersø from web-site* http://www.historieinfo.dk/Fundhavsmarkn.html *(23 December 2016).*

been controlled by the chieftainly dynasty at Gudme and thus be a replacement for the site at Lundeborg? From this hypothesis it would thus belong to a group of smaller, elite-governed trading sites, as is also proposed for Henne and Sebbersund above in this book (see section 4.3). The temple deniers with their ostentatiously Christian iconography, together with the other cross-decorated artefacts, could cautiously be suggested to be signs of one of the visits from Frankish missionaries in the 820s (Knibbs 2011).

6.2.2 Aarhus

The remains of Viking-period Aarhus now lie hidden beneath a major town in which a great deal of digging and disturbance, especially in connexion with the growth of the town from the 19th century onwards, have to a significant extent destroyed traces of the initial stages of urbanization there but also given rise to a considerable number of archaeological excavations. Our archaeological information about Aarhus is based on a large number of investigations, although regrettably only a few have been published in a thorough manner (Andersen, Crabb & Madsen 1971; for an overview, see Jantzen 2013).

Along the northern bank of the Aarhus River east of the fording point at Immervad, which is one of the few really convenient crossing points of the river and forms a natural node of land and water traffic, a trading site appeared around the year 800 (H. Skov 2005; 2008). Traces of this site are few and small, and limited to an area of 2-3 ha (Fig. 191). The best preserved remains were excavated below the later rampart, consisting of closely spaced, post-built building foundations and SFBs on narrow lots which probably fronted on to a lane running parallel to the river for at most 300 m. Compared with the true emporia, the quantities of finds from Aarhus are low, although characterized by both trade and specialist craftwork. It is far from clear whether or not Aarhus was at all different at this date from other minor trading sites of the Early Viking Period such as Henne and Sebbersund, and the finds reveal nothing about whether this trading site was under royal or some other form of aristocratic control. Aarhus must have functioned throughout the 9th century as a minor trading site of this character.

When the town was subsequently defensively enclosed the rampart was placed, against normal practice, along the river bank too, so that it completely disrupted the existing settlement pattern and cut off the connexion with the river quayside (Fig. 192). This forceful and abnormal procedure contrasts markedly with the defensive works at Hedeby and Ribe, and it destroyed the trading street of Aarhus. To date, research into Aarhus has noted that the first defences must have been constructed as a royal initiative shortly

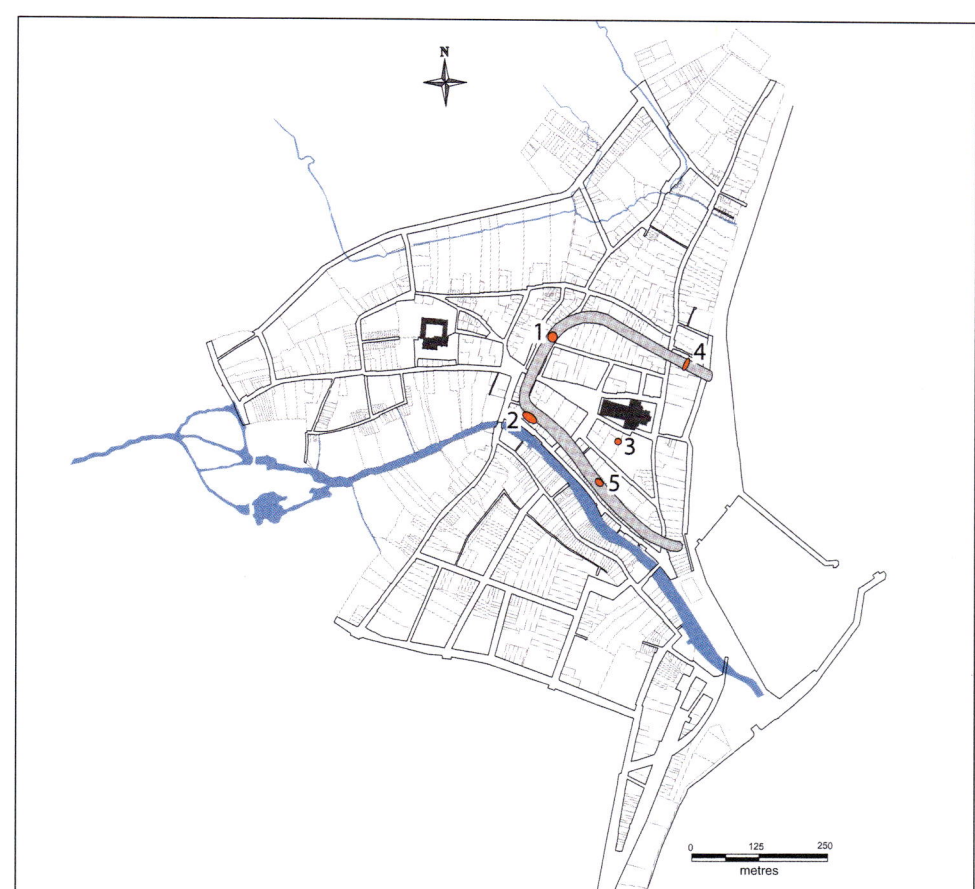

Fig. 191. The remains of 9th-century Aarhus have in almost all cases been discovered beneath the later rampart. After Jantzen 2013.

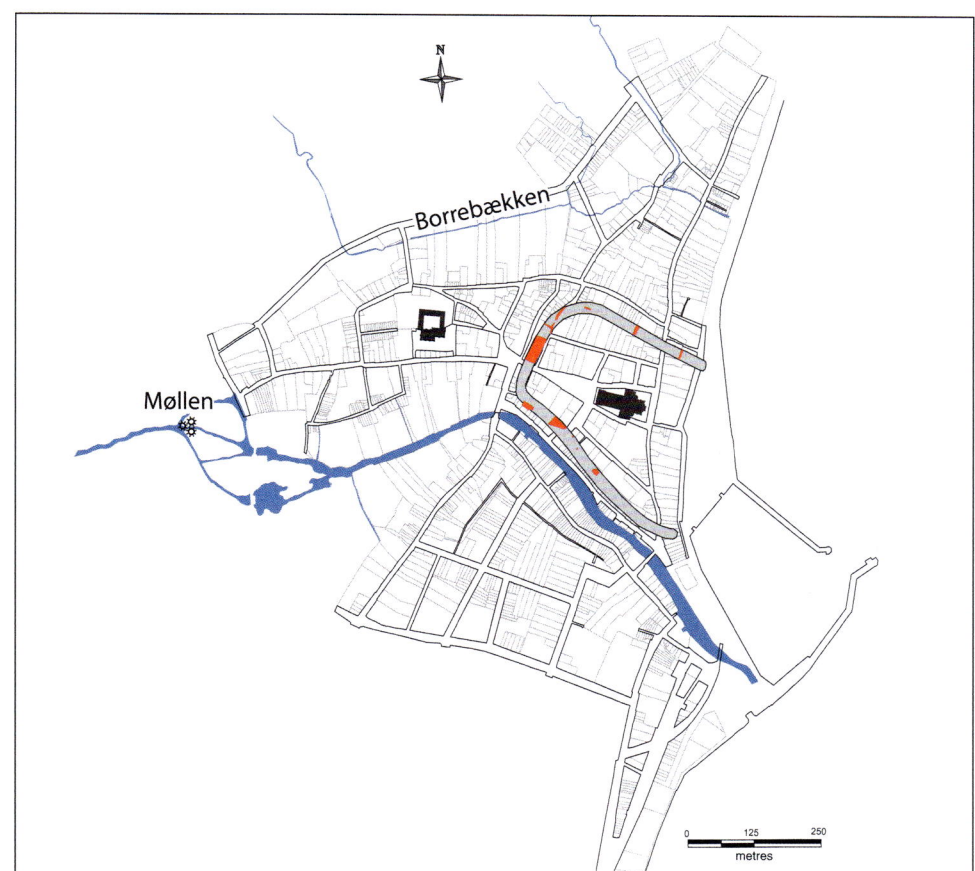

Fig. 192. Shown in red are the demonstrated stretches of the Viking-period defence work enclosing Aarhus. Coastal erosion has removed the Viking-period coastline, and it is not known whether or not the rampart defended the town where it faced the bay. After Jantzen 2013.

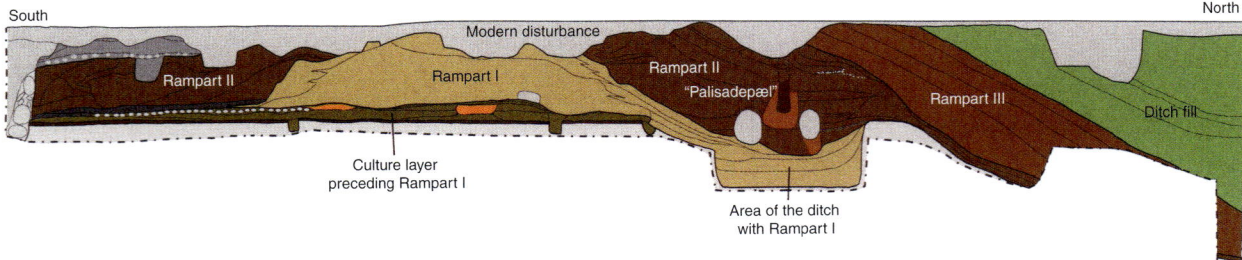

South · North · Modern disturbance · Rampart II · Rampart I · Rampart II · "Palisadepæl" · Rampart III · Ditch fill · Culture layer preceding Rampart I · Area of the ditch with Rampart I

Fig. 193. Section of the rampart enclosing Aarhus from the excavation at Mejlgade 8 (no. 4 on Fig. 191). The two earliest phases of the rampart, Ramparts I and II, belong to the Viking Period. After Jantzen 2013.

after Henry the Fowler's assumed expedition up into Jutland of 934 (H. Skov 2008) – in other words, they are explained as protection against external enemies. But it must also be possible that the defensive work expresses the fact that it was only then that Aarhus came under royal control with the new Jelling dynasty, and thus sprang from conflicts internal to Denmark.

The earliest defences, Rampart I, took the form of a relatively slight earth rampart around 2 m high, constructed of grass turf and upcast from the ditch which lay in front of it (Fig. 193). The enclosed area can be estimated at 6 ha. In size and construction the rampart is reminiscent of the first town ramparts of Hedeby and Ribe, which could be taken as evidence of royal initiative, but none of the wooden structures is securely dated.[40] The most reliable evidence is still the indirect dating of Hedeby's rampart to before AD 968 (see above). The rampart at Aarhus was subsequently massively developed as Rampart II, with a wide and deep moat. This substantial extension is not precisely dated either, although again it is reminiscent of the situation at Hedeby, and here too one must presume some royal initiative, probably based upon either a feared or an actual military threat from either land or sea.

Remains of a heathen cemetery at Aarhus are at best slight, coming from the area below Aarhus Theatre where during digging in connexion with the building of the theatre in 1898 fine drinking-horn mounts in the Ringerike Style were found which are suggested to have come from a disturbed grave. They cannot, however, pre-date the year 1000, too late a date for an elite heathen burial, especially if one also takes into account the possible age of the mounts when deposited (Fuglesang 1980, 55; Roesdahl 2006). One would expect considerably more grave goods in a burial with such fine artefacts, while the location in the middle of the small, strongly defended town, and away from the principal routeway down to Immervad, is untypical.

In AD 948 a Bishop Reginbrand of Aarhus was present at the Synod of Ingelheim, and by this date at the latest we must suppose there was a church in

Aarhus, the dedication of which is unknown. The most likely location in which to look for this church has to be under the later cathedral of St Nikolaj (now the Church of Our Lady) but this is not certain. St Nikolaj's Church lay outside the rampart, out by the western approach road, but there is no evidence concerning its chronological relationship with the earliest defences. The church may have been earlier than the defensive work and therefore not originally have been located outside of the town. It can be taken as certain that the cathedral of St Nikolaj dates back to the diocesan division of c. 1059 but only archaeological investigations would be able to clarify the earlier situation. The distance between the church and the town is approximately the same as that between the flat-grave cemetery and the main street in Hedeby.

The disruption of the settlement structure in Aarhus by the defensive works has not attracted research interest, and even though a number of Viking-period buildings have gradually come to light through excavations within the town it is for the most part remains of buildings underneath the rampart which have produced the best information. How the defences affected the topography and street plan of the town remains an unanswered question, and in many cases it has not been possible to determine whether a particular building foundation inside the rampart belongs to the period before the raising of the rampart or afterwards. It is to be considered doubtful that the settlement was a densely packed as has been suggested (H. Skov 2005, 17).

Like Hedeby but unlike Ribe, however, the 10th century is quite conspicuous in the archaeological evidence, in the form of both SFBs and artefactual finds. A number of strongly built SFBs with corner hearths of Slavonic/Saxon type in particular, together with a considerable quantity of Slavonic pottery, indicate that people from these regions were resident and working in the town. Not only the comprehensive development of the defences but also a number of finds of weaponry from the town bear witness to warfare. Several of the six runestones known from the town so far are aristocratic memorials to dramatic events which must have taken place either in or around the town in the period around the change of millennium (Roesdahl & Wilson 2006; Imer 2014).

Only three Viking-period coins are known from Aarhus, all cross coins of Harald Bluetooth. Coins were also struck in Aarhus under Kings Harthacanute (1035-42) and Magnus the Good (1042-7), but again none of these has been found in the town. The signs of a monetized economy in Viking-period Aarhus are thus extremely slight.

South-west of Aarhus, at Viby, there was a royal manor in the Middle Ages which, on the basis of a dubious application of place-names from the vicinity, has been suggested as the location of a Viking-period royal manor too (H. Skov 2005; 2008). This cannot be ruled out, but the hypothesis is as yet unsupported. North of Aarhus, around the northern exit route, beneath and around Lisbjerg church, remains of an elite farmstead consisting of a central hall standing within a palisaded courtyard of some 2 ha have been found. The earliest phase of this farmstead appears not to go any further back than the second half of the 10th century (Jeppesen & Madsen 1997; Jeppesen 2004).

On the basis of the above, it is proposed that the defences of Aarhus and the disruption of the existing settlement pattern that followed were reflections of a royal expropriation and/or military take-over of the town. From the structural similarities with the earliest defensive works at Hedeby and Ribe and their dating, weak as it is, the work is suggested to have been started by the new Jelling dynasty some time before the year 968.

6.2.3 Kaupang

Around the same time as King Godfred removed the merchants from Reric to Hedeby in the year 808, he is believed to have founded the trading site of Kaupang in Vestfold, a region which, according to the Frankish Royal Annals, fell subject to the Danish king about the same time (Skre 2007a; 2007b). Thanks to the recent major excavation and research project, this site and its finds have been published in wonderful detail. The structure of the site corresponds very closely with the other emporia: an extended settlement, close to the shore, divided into small tenement plots. The area of the plots is estimated at around 2 ha. On these plots fugitive traces of buildings have been found which, from a holistic interpretation of the archaeological remains, are understood to have been permanently occupied, following a short preliminary phase of more seasonal activities. The town remained functional down to around the middle of the 10th century but is thought to have fallen beyond the influence of the Danish king no later than around the year 900 (Skre 2007b, 466ff; Pilø & Skre 2011).

In the landscape around Kaupang there are several large cemeteries containing both cremation and inhumation graves. The original number of burials is estimated at around a thousand, 204 of which have been excavated from 1867 onwards.

Altogether, a little less than 5,000 sq m of the urban area has been excavated: 1,350 sq m during Charlotte Blindheim's excavations of 1959-74, and 3,150 sq m through slit trenches and open area excavations in 1999-2003. During the most recent excavations both the culture layers and some of the plough layer were sieved. The other accessible areas were also searched both by fieldwalking and metal-detecting. The thorough and comprehensive fieldwork has meant that a relatively large proportion of the total assemblage of finds from the town must have been retrieved for the archaeologists. The evidence shows that, in contrast to Hedeby and Ribe, there was no monetized economy at Kaupang. Rather, hacksilver was used for at least some transactions, although in light of the relatively small quantities of silver barter has to be considered to have been dominant form of exchange.

In comparison with the great extent of the archaeological investment the quantities of finds appear small, and even though direct comparisons are invalid, it is striking that the site of Havsmarken introduced above has, from a few years' metal-detecting, apparently produced an assemblage of silver and copper-alloy artefacts which is not inferior to the whole assemblage from Kaupang. There are 101 coins known from Kaupang, including clipped dirhams. The material from Havsmarken has not been published, but on the website *http://www.historieinfo.dk/Fundhavsmarken.html* (21 September 2016) more than 40 Carolingian coins are reported and many dirhams, weights, pieces of jewellery and more illustrated.

The archaeological material from the town leaves no room for doubt that Kaupang was a royal emporium, albeit of limited size and of a lower rank than Ribe in the 9th century and far below the supreme trading centre of the period, Hedeby.

6.2.4 Summary: Danish emporia in the 9th and 10th centuries

In international scholarship on the emporia, the period from the 830s onwards is described as a period of collapse which ended with the demise of Dorestad and the division of the Frankish Empire, to some extent caused by but also followed by series of Viking attacks and Scandinavian expansion over the whole of the North Sea area (Hodges 1982; 1989; Skre 2007b; Coupland 2010). Throughout the 9th century Vikings were raiding in northern Europe, and in Britain and Ireland and on the Continent alike several groups

Fig. 194. Danish emporia in the 9th and 10th centuries. With the foundation of Hedeby, trading activities became concentrated to a greater extent at a single site while the other emporia developed in different directions. Kaupang, and probably Åhus too, had only small parts to play in the 10th century. Since 810 the Limes Saxoniae defined the border between Saxons and Obotrites.

settled and established an immigrant warrior class whose wealth appears only to have returned to its homelands to a limited extent. Western European coin finds of the 9th or the beginning of the 10th centuries, for instance, are still uncommon in Danish hoards or amongst detector finds (Sawyer 1988, 153ff; Hilberg 2011).

In the history of the towns this period is a puzzling interval between the growth of the emporia in the 8th and 9th centuries and the classic medieval towns of the 11th century onwards. Turbulent political circumstances severely affected the towns both at home and abroad, but Hedeby in Denmark grew to the point of being the dominant node of long-distance trade in northern Europe which linked the western European trade network with the flow of goods and silver from the east (Fig. 194).

Since the emporia were royal, their development was closely linked to events of political and military history and is difficult to understand without an eye on those developments. The Frankish Royal Annals show that the Danish kingship was strong in the decades around the year 800 and it has been sug-

gested above (section 6.1.3) that this royal dynasty including kings such as Ongendus, Sigfred, Godfred and Hemming (Sawyer 1991; Gelting 2007) had a base at Lejre (see also section 6.3.3, below). The scant sources indicate that in the 870s this dynasty lost its grip on power, after which events remain largely in the dark until the age of Gorm the Old, corresponding with the situation which Adam of Bremen called *mutatio regnorum* (A.E. Christensen 1969, 197ff; Sawyer 1988, 215ff).

The flourishing of Hedeby ran in parallel with the decline of Dorestad, and can be interpreted as the outcome of a successful trade war, or rather war over trade, waged by the Danish kingship. The earliest coins from Hedeby were indeed copies of Dorestad issues: manifest evidence of the prototypes used by the issuing authority. Irrespective of what the background may have been, the result was that Dorestad failed while Hedeby took over the role of the leading emporium of northern Europe and the profits from the site must have been one of the most important sources of income for the kings. The harbour at Hedeby was expanded substantially in the 880s and 890s.

Hedeby's first Dorestad imitation coins, KG 3, remained in circulation until sometime post-867; however, probably as early as the 880s, this coinage was replaced by a new Dorestad imitation KG 7-9 (Hilberg 2011). The coins and the expansion of the harbour both indicate that the town was subject to some ruling authority all this time, which continued to issue coins rooted in the same design tradition through to Harald Bluetooth's cross coinage of the 970s (Moesgaard 2015).

The archaeology of Hedeby involves very clear military elements, be that the town's eventually massive defences, stray finds of weaponry, equestrian or warrior graves from the cemeteries of the town or its hinterland, or documentary reports of warfare. The majority of these activities are datable to the 10th century, and they testify to the huge economic importance of the town and to repeated attempts to secure access to and control of the profits.

In the 9th century, Ribe was still an important emporium with its own coins, and it was in these two towns that the first churches in Denmark were raised with royal agreement some time in the 850s. For the see of Hamburg-Bremen missionizing was the most important objective, while the Danish king's motive was not necessarily anything other than to create favourable conditions for trade by offering religious services to Christian merchants who came to the royal towns too.

Competition from the growing and relatively close Hedeby must be one of the key reasons why Ribe declined (see section 5.9.9), but the extent of that reversal is not easily assessed. Artefactual finds are few, but, like Hedeby, the town was enclosed with a semicircular rampart and burials continued alongside the church throughout the late 9th and the 10th centuries.

Aarhus remained quite a small trading site in this period, but the scale of the defences there and the large number of runestones could show that this town played some important political and military role for the royal power. The zenith of Kaupang as a smaller emporium was in the 9th century, concurrent with the dominance of the Danish royal power in Vestfold.

Danish emporia of the 9th and 10th centuries were characterized by the following developments:

- A high level of differentiation. The activities came to be concentrated increasingly at Hedeby.

- A monetized economy, although also a weight-based economy to a lesser extent.

- The foundation of churches in Hedeby (c. AD 850), Ribe (c. AD 855) and Aarhus (AD 948).

- Defensive enclosure within semicircular ramparts in the 10th century.

6.3 Towns as centres of the Christian kingship from around the year 1000: the *civitas* model

With the conversion of Harald Bluetooth, reinforced by Svein Forkbeard's subsequent conquest of England, the Danish royalty and the aristocratic circles around the king gained direct access to a sophisticated ecclesiastical organization, literacy and more. In the period that followed, the strongest cultural impulses which came to Denmark were from across the North Sea (Gelting 2004; 2010). Svein and Cnut struck coins using Anglo-Saxon prototypes, and in 1020 the Danish Church's ties to the metropolitan see of Hamburg-Bremen were dissolved and it was subjected instead to the archbishopric of Canterbury. Harald's idea of Jelling as the dynastic centre of the kingdom was dropped. Svein and Cnut appear to have preferred Lund, and the economic and political centre of the kingdom was moved back to the east, where it has remained. A series of new towns grew up, strategically located all around the kingdom. Their central positions in various regions with restricted access to the sea indicates that their intended role was to serve as local centres for the royal power and the growing Church, while the archaeological evidence shows very clearly that the earlier emporia still took care of trade. It is no wonder that where the new towns were planned and placed there were pre-existing earlier central sites in the form of elite manors or central places. As is suggested in the following survey, however, the pattern seems to have been one of the older centres being quashed and the new town sited in their vicinity rather than directly on top of where they had been, even though that was often a better location and perfectly integrated into the existing infrastructure. The motive for this non-functional approach is suggested to have been a religious one: that the Christian king and the Church wished to distance themselves from the heathen cult centres.

6.3.1 Viborg

The inland town of Viborg lies in the centre of North Jutland and is at the junction of land routes from all directions (Krongaard Kristensen 1987, 29ff.). The two components of the name mean 'shrine' (*vi*) and 'hill' (*bjerg*) but do not show whether the shrine in question lay upon or beside the hill.[41] Whichever the case, the name refers back to a pre-Christian religious central role for this site which was subsequently to house both the Jutlandic provincial assembly (*landsting*) and an episcopal see.

The precise character and location of the shrine are not known, but a variety of scattered pieces of evidence

Fig. 195. Map of Viborg with sites referred to in the text. The locations of Borgvold and Asmildkloster are marked with red squares. The excavations in Store Sct. Pedersstræde, alongside Søndersø and the find spot of the silver hoard of the 9th century at Overlund are marked with red dots. The base map is the Chief Survey sheet. © Geodata Agency, with additions by the author.

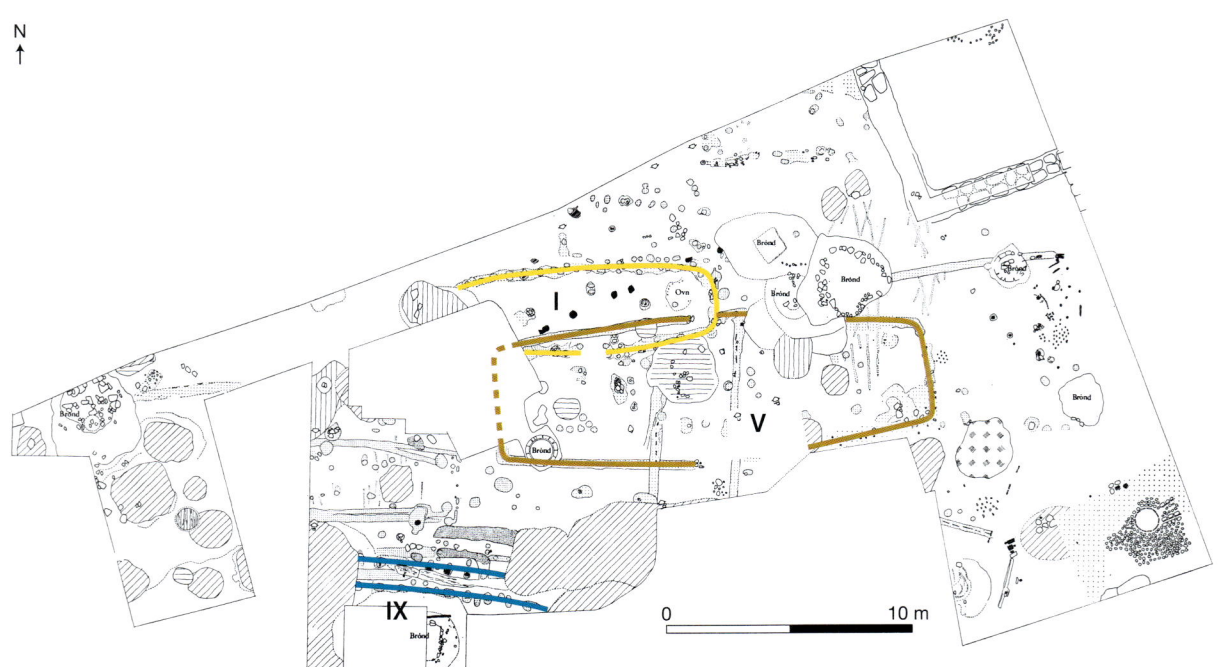

Fig. 196. The excavation in Store Sct. Pedersstræde of 1966-7 revealed, as the earliest phase, a number of building foundations which were understood by the excavator to be components of an agrarian farmstead of the Viking Period. The construction of these slight buildings implies rather that they are urban buildings of the first half of the 11th century. The largest of them, Building V, is 17 m long. After E.L. Nielsen 1969 with additions by the author.

establish a range of possibilities (Fig. 195). From the later urban area on the crest of the hill, an excavation in Store Sct. Pedersstræde of 1966-7 has produced the best information (Levin Nielsen 1969). From a dendrochronological dating subsequently produced, it could be determined that this area was re-organized out and built upon with houses facing on to a street around 1050, but that there had been buildings there before then (Krongaard Kristensen & Poulsen 2016, 105).

The earlier remains comprised a series of Viking-period building foundations which have been laid out as various phases of an agrarian farmstead (Fig. 196). These were rather slight buildings which had few comparanda at the date they were excavated. Viewed in the light of the many more recently excavated Viking-period farmsteads in Jutland, however, the buildings from Store Sct. Pedersstræde do not appear to fit with the image of an agrarian farmstead but rather to correspond more closely to the slight urban houses which are known from Hedeby and other sites. The architecture of the buildings has its closest parallels in the 11th century, indicating that the origins of this settlement can hardly lie much before the year 1000 if at all. The best preserved building foundation, Building V, at 17 x 6 m, is a wall-trench building with bowed long sides and no internal roof-bearing posts, corresponding to the fence-buildings at Lisbjerg and the so-called 'cross-over type building' excavated at Gammel Hviding close to Ribe. Both are dated to the first half of the 11th century (S. Jensen 1987; Jeppesen & Madsen 1997). The earlier Building I, at only 3.5 m wide, has close parallels in structures from the beginning of the 11th century excavated at Viborg Søndersø. A large amount of slags from iron-preparation were also found associated with this phase, and large quantities of scorched stone: probably evidence of extensive smithing work.

From the area of the town on the cathedral hill there are otherwise relatively few individual finds from the Viking Period in the form of single items of jewellery which are no different from what one would find in any village of the age. If the shrine was located on the crest of the hill one might have expected more stray finds of the Viking Period produced by the large amount of digging that has taken place in the town of Viborg over time. This absence has been noted before (Iversen et al. eds. 2005, 559). As the case stands at present, the earliest definite settlement evidence from the top of the hill appears to date back to around the year 1000, perhaps a little earlier, and the traces that have been found do not suggest that the shrine was located here.

The two banks of the Great and Small Borgvold (Castle Rampart) on the edge of the lake have alternatively been suggested as a location (Iversen et al. eds. 2005, 558), but there are no finds to corroborate

this hypothesis either – neither stray finds datable before the 11th century from the western shore nor discoveries of any form from the extensive excavations of the Borgvold in 1889. Through later excavations, rather, timbers have been retrieved from Borgvold which are dated to AD 1314 and demonstrate the role of the bank as part of Erik Menved's castle in the town (Krongaard Kristensen 1987, 35).

Cult activity in the Late Iron Age and Viking Period appears to have been performed at elite farmsteads (L. Jørgensen 2014). These farmsteads were often impressively large and could, like the site at Tissø for example, be located alongside a lake. On the eastern shore of Viborg Søndersø in the Middle Ages stood Asmild Nunnery, which was founded in the earlier Middle Ages and transformed into a manorial centre in the post-medieval period. The topographical preconditions for a major farmstead were thus found here, in contrast to the situation on the western side of the lake. The nuns of the Augustinian Order took over an extant three-aisled basilica in the Romanesque west end of which, from around the year 1100, a runestone was built into the wall in a conspicuous place. It bears an inscription which is translated as:

Thorgun(d), daughter of Thorgot, sone of Thjodulv, raised this stone after her spouse Bose, a man of news {muaR H ... daughter}[42]

The runestone is dated between 970 and 1020 and refers to two earlier generations of the family. Its position indicates that the patron of the church also wished to preserve and display this memorial, and suggests that at or near Asmild in the Viking Period there had been an elite farmstead. The family at this farmstead gained close links to the see in Viborg. Close to Asmild is the potentially religious place-name Overlund, and in these village lands in 2013 a major silver hoard was found that had been deposited in the period AD 850-950 and contained, inter alia, silver armrings (Fig. 195). The weight of the hoard was around 1.5 kg.[43]

These circumstances point towards an elite presence at Asmild in the Viking Period, so that altogether there is more to suggest that it is in this area one should look for the roots of Viborg in a pre-Christian religious centre, within the confines of an aristocratic farmstead complex. Such a complex must have been similar to the farmstead at Toftum Næs, 18 km west of Viborg (Fiedler Therkildsen 2014; 2015). There appear to be no military features in the earliest archaeological evidence from Viborg, and there was apparently no need either for a ringfort in the area. The position of Viborg as a central node of routeways must be the basis for the subsequent role of the site as the location of the Jutish regional assembly and the associated markets which are referred to for the first time by Ælnoth in the 1120s. The core N.-S. Hærvej ran along the western edge of the lake and was met by the land route to the east and west approximately where the modern roads also join. From the perspective of a traffic network the central junction of the town appears to have been by the western shore, and at this crossroads a number of excavations have shown that, from the year 1000, there was an urban settlement characterized by trade and craftwork and with clear indications of only intermittent use (Hjermind et al eds. 1998; Iversen et al eds. 2005). The settlement is located on natural peat formations since no drier areas were available on the sloping terrain between the cathedral plateau and the lake shore. Even though the water-level in the lakes was artificially raised in the Middle Ages, this does not alter the fact that the settlement on the peat flats alongside Søndersø would still have been a very damp place in the winter, and possibly only suitable for occasional occupation. The most reasonable way of interpreting the settlement on the western side of the lake has to be that it appeared

in connexion with the markets of the regional assembly and so indirectly dates the development of the assembly to the period around AD 1000, when also a non-agrarian settlement appeared on the cathedral plateau.

This settlement around the land routes and on the cathedral plateau from around the year 1000 can be regarded as urban, and as the embryonic town of Viborg. From this date at the latest, the urban area west of the lakes must have been royal property.

Jelling was not a town, and does not fall within the scope of this book. At present, the results of recent years' excavations are being studied as part of a major research project and it would go too far to enter in detail into that wide-ranging discussion (Holst et al. 2012). That the site is nevertheless referred to in the present context is due to the fact that Viborg was the seat of the Jutish provincial assembly and a similar role as thing-site may have been intended for Jelling (Roesdahl 2011). The decision subsequently to select Viborg should then be due to a later king, probably Svein Forkbeard (Krongaard Kristensen & Poulsen 2016, 55ff).

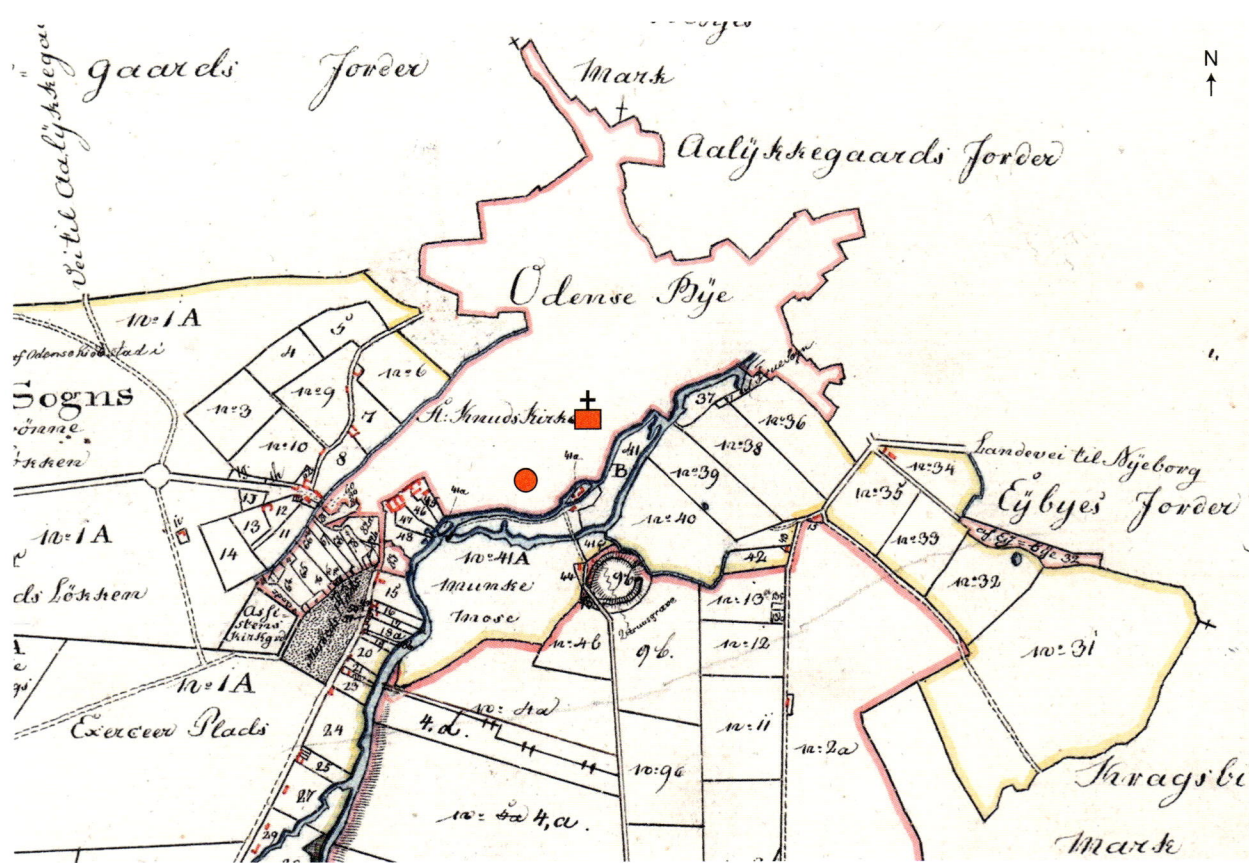

Fig. 197. Reduced parish map of the first half of the 19th century showing a segment of St Knud's parish in Odense. Nonnebakken south of the river is clearly visible, lying alongside a roadway that crosses the river. The red dot marks the location where sunken feature buildings of the Viking Period have been found and the cross the position of the first church of Odense, St Albani, which when founded was apparently dedicated to Our Lady. Additions by the author.

The presence of the king in Viborg also came to be expressed in the numismatic evidence. Coins were struck in the town from the reign of Cnut the Great, to start with only on a small scale although under Svein Estridsen the town mint became the most important one in Jutland. It is not known where the royal manor was sited but the most likely suggestion has still to be west of the cathedral (Krongaard Kristensen 1987, 88).

It is also unknown when the first church in Viborg was raised, but if the relocation of a Jutish thing-site to Viborg was due to Svein Forkbeard one should suppose that this Christian king also had a church built here. Through Svein Estridsen's diocesan reform of c. 1059 a diocese with its see at Viborg was created, and the first cathedral can be assumed to have been located at the same place as the current cathedral of Our Lady. Like the state of affairs in Lund and Roskilde, a profusion of churches were built in Viborg. Later on some 12-13 parish churches are known, the majority of which apparently go back to the 11th century (Krongaard Kristensen 1987). The aristrocratic stone church at Asmild was transferred to the cathedral chapter of Viborg in 1166 and therefore cannot have been the first cathedral but rather have been built by the elite family at that site.

The available archaeological data are able to support the suggestion that the emergence of Viborg as a town was due to Svein Forkbeard's abandonment of Jelling as a thing-site and selection, by preference, of Viborg for Jutland's provincial assembly. The extent of activities before the reign of Cnut the Great is imperfectly known, but the dendro-dates from the shore of Søndersø and the excavations in Store Sct. Pedersstræde show unambiguously that there was urban activity before 1018 too, even if its degree of seasonality can be discussed (Krongaard Kristensen & Poulsen 2016, 55ff). Like Odense, Roskilde and Lund, which are discussed below, Viborg can be classified as a religious and administrative centre of the Christian kingship, the role of which in the overall trading network was of lesser significance. All four towns were successors to pre-Christian central places that were apparently under local aristocratic control.

6.3.2 Odense

Odense is located centrally on the island of Fyn, and land routes from several directions meet in the town. From the Odense River it is possible to sail out into Odense Fjord, but not conveniently, and neither in the Middle Ages nor earlier does the town appear to have been focused on the sea. The place-name means 'Odin's shrine' and testifies to an originally religious role and a history which must extend back into the pre-Christian period. Probably in the period 975-80

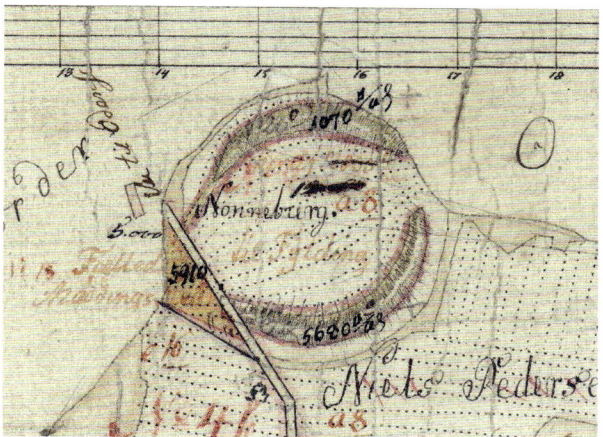

Fig. 198. Nonnebierg *(Nuns' Hill) as it appeared on the earliest cadastral map of 1785. From the original with the Geodata Agency.*

King Harald Bluetooth founded a ringfort on the southern side of the Odense River at a site which from topographical criteria must have offered a practical crossing of the river and so have been an important traffic artery (Fig. 197) (Roesdahl & Sindbæk 2014; Runge & Henriksen 2018). The ringfort was sited on a natural plateau, bounded to the north, east and west by terrain falling down to the Odense River (Fig. 198). Over the ringfort a nunnery for the Benedictine Order was founded in the 12th century but it removed to Dalum around the middle of the 13th century (*DK*, Odense amt, 1749ff).

The area was built upon in the 19th and 20th centuries with no associated archaeological recording, but digging in the ringfort area in 1889 and 1909 produced two small hoards consisting of jewellery, hacksilver and 9 coins in one case and 25/26 coins in the other. Both hoards are dated from the latest re-assessment of the coins to the period 960-80 (Moesgaard 2015, 156ff) and must be assumed to derive from the period of the ringfort although they could in fact be a little earlier. Outstanding hoards are known from this area (Fig. 199) (Skovmand 1942, Cat. 28-30; Roesdahl 1977, 167f).

In 2015, Odense Town Museums conducted excavations at Nonnebakken and revealed part of the rampart of the ringfort and the rampart road within it which is absolutely characteristic of this class of site (Hansen & Runge 2016). A detector find in addition was a Valkyrie brooch of the first half of the 9th century. Subsequently, a series of datings of carbonized material found in the features excavated has been obtained. These proved to represent a wide range of dates in the Late Germanic Iron Age and Viking Period which, together with the range of finds, help to show that there had been activity at this site during this period (Runge 2017b).

Fig. 199. Two of the three fine silver filigree brooches of different sizes and design amongst the finds from Nonnebakken. The brooch on the left, of 62 mm diameter, was found in 1889 in a hoard while the brooch to the right, of 77 mm diameter, was in the possession of the owner of Nonnebakken prior to 1900. NM C6271 and Fyns Stiftsmuseum mus. Nr. 7021. Photographs: NM; OBM.

It is not possible to draw concrete conclusions on this insubstantial basis, but one possible outline model could be that the ringfort, as a demonstration of both Christian and political power on behalf of Harald Bluetooth, was located over the earlier shrine.

In 988, Odense is recorded for the first time as an episcopal see (Gelting 2004) and at this date at the latest there must have been a church in the town. It is highly probable that the church was the now-demolished St Albani Church, where Knud the (eventual) Saint was assassinated in front of the high altar in 1086 (*DK*, Odense amt, 1729ff), and where archaeological excavations have identified a number of timber structural phases preceding the stone church that was pulled down during the Reformation. When Knud was killed the church was dedicated both to Our Lady and St Alban, and it was located on the northern side of the Odense River (*DK*, Odense amt, 66). Excavations on that side of the river have revealed that in the area of west of St Albani Church there is a settlement of SFBs of the Viking Period (Henriksen 2013) which appears to be datable to the 9th and 10th centuries (Runge 2017a).

A plausible model of the early development of Odense could be that, towards the centre of Fyn, where land routes crossed, there was an important religious centre of the Late Germanic and Viking Period, Odin's shrine, at the place which is now called Nonnebakken. That was brought to an end by Harald Bluetooth's ringfort, and at a short distance from the heathen holy place on the other side of the river between 965 and 988 Harald had the first church built on Fyn, probably dedicated to Our Lady, and probably through Cnut the Great's diocesan reform of 1020 with the addition of another tutelary saint, the proto-martyr in Britain St Alban. Whether or not the settlement of SFBs west of St Albani Church was associated with the shrine in the same way as the SFBs around Aggersborg or the Tissø complex, or was rather the beginnings of urbanization north of the river, we do not yet know (Runge 2017a, 51f). As in Viborg, a nunnery was founded on the site at which the heathen shrine is suggested to have been located. If this was not a coincidence, could there perhaps have been a religiously inspired desire to fight against the memory of the old sanctuary?

Coins were first struck in the town under Cnut the Great but so far no archaeological remains from the town of Odense representing this period have been found. The royal manor may, from Ælnoth's accounts, be presumed to have stood in the vicinity of St Albani Church. Real urban activity in Odense in the form of street paving, culture layers, and evidence of trade and specialized craft apparently emerge from around 1100, albeit then over a larger area with the churches of St Alban and St Knud as the physical and religious centre of the town.

From this interpretation of the archaeological data, the development of Odense is suggested to have been parallel to that of Viborg – a religious and administrative centre for the Christian kingship located at a central point of the landscape but with no essential role in the trans-regional trading network.

6.3.3 Lejre and Roskilde

Earlier on this chapter (section 6.1.3) it was argued that Lejre was the seat of the Danish royal dynasty in the Late Germanic Iron Age and Early Viking Period. The excavations at Lejre and the distribution of hoards in the area could indicate that this centre of wealth goes far back in time. In 2012, at Mannerup, 7 km south of Lejre, a hacksilver hoard of the 5th century was found which, with a total weight exceeding 7 kg, is far and away the largest hoard of this period. In 2015 yet another hoard was unearthed at Lille Karleby, 10 km north of Lejre. In this case it was a large collection of complete artefacts in the form of jewellery and two drinking vessels. Several of the objects were of extremely high quality. The Karleby hoard was deposited in the second half of the 10th century and testifies to continued wealth in the area five hundred years later. We can add to these the famous hoard from

Gammel Lejre found in 1850 and buried around the year 1000 and a second hoard from Gammel Lejre which was buried in the 6th century and found in 2011. What the relationship between Lejre and Gudme was in the period up to the year 600 we shall not enter into, but whatever the case Lejre can be regarded as having been the seat of an outstanding family from the Early Germanic Iron Age onwards (T. Christensen 2015, 263ff).

If we add to this also the fact that the excavations at Lejre have uncovered the largest known halls connected to fenced-off zones with special (cult?) buildings dated to the Late Iron Age and the Viking Period (Fig. 200), within a landscape of monumental funerary features, ship settings and a mass of other archaeological finds and features, in my view there is good reason to give credence to the Lejre Chronicle and other medieval sources when they locate the royal Skjoldung dynasty at Lejre. Both the hoards and the excavations show that the building of the

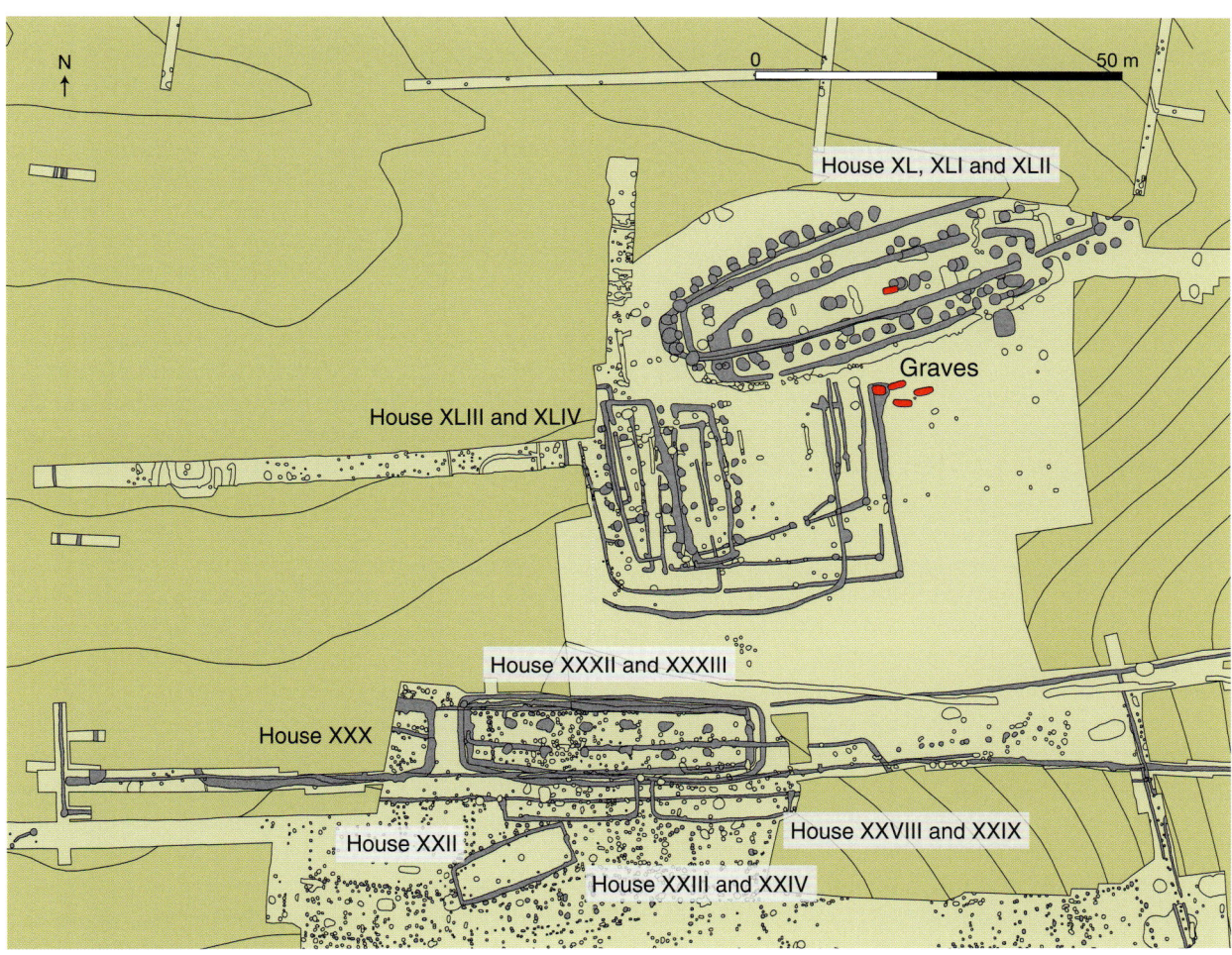

Fig. 200. From the excavations at Lejre. The building sequence XL, XLI and XLII, dated to the 8th century, is a series of halls up to 61 m in length with enclosed zones with special buildings that are characteristic of the elite farmsteads. The halls at Lejre are regarded as the most plausible location for the seat of the king who harvested the profits from the emporia of Ribe, Reric and Åhus. After Christensen 2015.

halls and the accumulation of wealth continued at this place through to around the year 1000 and even later (T. Christensen 2015, 275ff), so that, even though the dynasty may have lost its grip on parts of the Danish kingdom around the year 870, other elements of the economic system behind Lejre must have survived.

10 km north-east of Lejre is the town of Roskilde. The second element of the name refers to one of the many extraordinarily powerful springs within the area of the town while the first element was already early in the Middle Ages explained as a reference to the legendary king Ro (Hrothgar) who is associable with Lejre (Ulriksen, Krause & Jensen 2014). Earlier names with heathen echoes do not seem to have posed a problem for the newly founded towns of that period, which as Lund, Viborg and Odense probably retained their local appellations.

In the earlier Middle Ages, Roskilde was the largest town on Sjælland, from around 1020 the see of the Bishop of Roskilde. According to Adam of Bremen the town grew up around a church dedicated to the Holy Trinity that had been founded by Harald Bluetooth, and where the latter was also buried after his death at Jomsborg (Wolin) around AD 987. Unfortunately, the not-entirely reliable Adam is the only source for this story, which has much in common with Harald's successor Svein's better recorded death in England and subsequent translation home to Denmark in 1014 (Lund 1998). It has to be considered a real risk that Adam's information about the death of Harald imitates Svein Forkbeard, who in Adam's account was a scoundrel because he broke the links with the metropolitan see of Hamburg-Bremen in favour of the Anglo-Saxon Church (Gelting 2004). Adam's claim was included in the local Roskilde Chronicle and has to be the reason why a funerary monument was installed for Harald in the present choir of the cathedral. In contrast to the other tombs over Bishop Vilhelm, Svein Estridsen and a Margrathe, however, Harald's cenotaph has never contained a bone chest as it has never been possible to identify a grave; there is only the information in the Roskilde Chronicle (*DK*, Københavns amt, 1757ff).

What is most likely, then, is that we simply do not know where Harald Bluetooth died or was buried, and it may make perfect sense that the memory of his grave was not carefully preserved since the same fate befell his other great projects. Ælnoth mentions that the church in Roskilde was dedicated to Drotten (the Lord)/Trinity and the papal saint Lucius. It is inferred that receipt of the latter's skull took place during the episcopacy of Bishop Svein Norman, so we can assume that the first tutelary saints of the church of Roskilde were the St Drotten/the Trinity (*DK*, Københavns amt, 1267ff). Such a double dedi-

cation was a distinctly English phenomemon, which points rather in the direction of Svein as the founder (Krongaard Kristensen & Poulsen 2016, 84 with refs).

The town is located upon a massive moraine plateau with a wide viewshed over the Roskilde Fjord and with the cathedral as its centre. There appears to be no reason to doubt that the first wooden church was at the same spot. This building became the cathedral of Roskilde diocese around the year 1020 and in it Earl Ulf was assassinated in 1026 on the orders of Cnut the Great, after which the widow of the deceased, Estrid, had a stone church built from the compensation paid (*DK*, Københavns amt, 1267ff). There is a steep slope down from the church to the fjord which lies practically a kilometre to the north. Once again, the potential for maritime trade appears to have been quite subordinate to other considerations, and Roskilde did not come to play a major role in anything other than a local trading system. Copenhagen, which was in the possession of the Bishops of Roskilde, probably took care of the maritime interests of Roskilde to a greater degree.

Thorough studies of the archaeological finds from the town and the original topography of the urban area have shown that these finds run back to around the year 1000 but with no evidence for earlier use of the area in the form of either elite or more common settlement (Ulriksen, Krause & Jensen 2014). The locality appears rather to have been very wet and unsuitable for occupation.

One may well ask why the town did not come to be sited at the fine location of Lejre, which all of the land routes ran to. Once again, I would suggest that the decisive principles behind the founding of towns at this period were inspired by religion: not only a desire to distance oneself from the earlier heathen centre at Lejre but also consideration of a monumental site for the church which, when it was founded, formed a small Christian island in an otherwise heathen landscape steeped in the concepts, funerary monuments and cult sites of its predecessor religion. Later on in Roskilde, churches were founded in profusion. A high proportion of the 14 known parish churches probably go back to the 11th century.

The royal manorial centre of the later Middle Ages was situated west of the cathedral, and this relationship may go back to the foundation of the town although so far no archaeological excavations have been carried out in this area (Ulriksen, Krause & Jensen 2014). Cnut the Great had the first coinage struck in Roskilde which, after Lund, was the most important mint place in Denmark.

Christian Roskilde became the largest town on Sjælland and thus carried Lejre's role as the preeminent centre of the island forward at a similar level. As will be seen in the case of Lund and Uppåkra below, there was therefore a clear connexion between the size and importance of the heathen central place and its Christian urban successor. This relationship must be founded upon a complete or at least partial maintenance of the system for the distribution of the agricultural surplus that was the economic basis of the central place.

6.3.4 Uppåkra and Lund

Lund became the largest town in Denmark in the earlier Middle Ages. It was successor to the nearby central place at Uppåkra which had been 40 ha in area and possibly the largest central place of southern Scandinavia, with an unbroken history going to back the Early Iron Age. The economic foundation of both sites was the fertile Plain of Lund, agriculturally one of the most productive regions in southern Scandinavia, and both sites operated as the primary centre of the area. The unexpressive name Uppåkra (Up-field) can hardly have been the name of the site when it was functional. It should rather have been the religious place-name Lund, which was transferred to the town just as at Viborg and Odense. The finds from Uppåkra are extraordinary, including, amongst many other things, a temple building with rich sacrificial deposits and numerous other signs of cult activity as well as craft and other practices which led to the formation of culture layers up to 2 m thick on the site. For the same reason the overall arrangement of the site has not yet been determined (Helgesson 2002; L. Larsson 2002; L. Larsson & Lenntorp 2004).

The earliest traces of the town of Lund, 5 km north of Uppåkra, are dendro-datings to c. AD 990 from coffins buried in the churchyard around a stave church, the later stone-built successor to which was consecrated to St Drotten (the Holy Lord) (Johansson Hervén 2008). In 2016 earlier evidence still was produced in the form of as yet unpublished dates from log coffins found north of the cathedral of St Laurentius, the earliest of which is from AD 979/80. Lund must therefore be the first Danish town where two churchyards have been identified from before the year 1000.

Major excavations around St Drotten's stave church have shown that the area of the churchyard may be estimated at around 7,000 sq m. It has been suggested that this may be identifiable with the church that, according to the Roskilde Chronicle, Svein Forkbeard had raised in Skåne, and is interpreted as a *minster* or mother church for the whole newly Christianized Scanian territory (Carelli 2001a). Contemporary evidence of urban activity in the form of trade and craft are virtually absent from the area of the town. The earliest occupation seems to have comprised larger plots with comparatively large buildings that are pri-

marily reminiscent of agrarian farmsteads and thus again do not appear to have been intended for trade or craft (Mårtensson 1976). From the reign of Cnut the Great onwards the archaeological source material grows in quantity, and from the middle of the 11th century at Lund one can again see a change in the settlement pattern to smaller, narrower plots aligned upon the principal streets (Carelli 2001b, 106ff; Johansson Hervén 2008) – a topographical development like those recorded in Ribe and Viborg.

Before the end of the 11th century the boundaries of the town appear to have reached the limits known later on: a massive elliptical urban area of 84 ha. Lund's growth in the 11th century was thus unparalleled, and it was undoubtedly the largest town in Scandinavia when it became the location of the archiepiscopal see in 1104.

Coins were struck following a clear Anglo-Saxon prototype as early as under Svein Forkbeard, while Lund became the most important mint site in Denmark under Cnut. It is possible to hypothesize that the mint was located in the royal manor that was sited west of the cathedral – in an area where no archaeological excavations have been carried out however.

The terrain in which the earliest church of Lund was placed lay alongside the central, N.-S. routeway but was badly affected by dampness and there is no sign of earlier building on the site, just like the situations in Roskilde and Viborg. In the course of the 11th century a wide range of churches were founded in Lund, and the majority of the town's later 22 known parish churches were probably founded as private aristocratic churches that were subsequently linked to parishes. As in the other two towns with a profusion of churches, Roskilde and Viborg, the process for the raising of a church does not appear to have been tightly controlled.

Lund is rightly famed for the urban archaeological activity here, and for an exemplary tradition of publication (Blomqvist & Mårtensson 1963; Mårtensson 1976; 1980). Unfortunately, however, a number of very extensive excavations of the 1980s around the first church of the town, St Drotten, are as yet only summarily published (e.g. Andrén 2000; Carelli 2001a; M. Cinthio 2002), so that access to the basic archaeological data for this utterly core zone is wanting.

As was also the case in Roskilde, Lund took over and continued the role as religious and political centre of its predecessor, the central place of Uppåkra, albeit in a new Christian context. In Lund too there is a clear correspondence between the size and importance of the heathen central place and the following Christian town which must again be based upon either complete or partial continuity of the economic basis of the central place.

6.3.5 Summary: towns as centres of the Christian royal power from around the year 1000 – the *civitas* model

The above review of the towns from around the year 1000 onwards has shown that, down to c. 1050, trade was still focussed upon the old emporia, and that Hedeby/Schleswig was, as previously, the principal node for long-distance trade and luxury goods. This town must still have been a crucial source of income for the monarchy. In the other towns the evidence of trade and craft up to 1050 are relatively slight, except in the case of Viborg where the finds by Søndersø can be explained through the market activity which was associated with the function of the town as the provincial assembly site. The other central towns of Odense, Roskilde and Lund seem to have been characterized up to the year 1050 entirely by ecclesiastical and royal activities.

It is suggested above that the important towns of Viborg, Odense, Roskilde and Lund all succeeded to heathen cult and/or central places. At Roskilde and Lund the earlier centres are well known while in the cases of Viborg and Odense this can be proposed on the basis of place-name evidence and to some extent on the re-interpretation of archaeological data. The conversion of the kingdom is seen as a process which began in the first church foundations in Hedeby and Ribe around the middle of the 9th century, after which missionary efforts seem to have been modest in energy over the next hundred years with a possible concentration of efforts in the area of southern and western Jutland (Feveile 2011; Søvsø 2014).

After Harald Bluetooth's conversion, c. 963, there was royal might behind the words, and before the millennium the heathen burial practice of the aristocracy appears to have been discontinued right across Denmark while churches were raised in the vicinity

Fig. 201. Early churches of Denmark and their tutelary saints. Some of the foundation dates and the dedications are not entirely certain but there appears to have been a clear tendency for church foundations to have spread out from a point of origin in South Jutland, first northwards and then to the east. The tutelary dedications at Roskilde and Lund may been inspired from Anglo-Saxon England and imply that Svein Forkbeard was the founder.

of the most important heathen centres in eastern Denmark too (Roesdahl 2006). A range of observations indicate that Harald Bluetooth's ringforts were sited upon elite farmsteads and/or heathen cult centres. This has been proved archaeologically in the case of Aggersborg and Trelleborg (L. Jørgensen 2014). Fyrkat is in Nørre Onsild parish in Onsild district, a name meaning 'Odin's shelf'. This indicates an as yet unexplained religious central role in the pre-Christian era, as has also been suggested for Odense, above. To the selection of previously proposed interpretations of the ringforts, then (Roesdahl 2014), one can add an active role in suppressing heathen cult sites, which would be an appropriate objective for a Christian king and could perhaps explain the short functioning lives of the ringforts. Harald's cross coinage of the same period also provided unmistakable Christian propaganda (Moesgaard 2015).

Following the conversion, churches were raised at central locations in the landscape, but it appears to be significant that the new churches were never sited in the previously heathen centres but rather at a short distance (Fig. 201). This was the case in Roskilde and Lund, and may have been the case at Odense and Viborg. In many cases the location of the churches in the landscape and the infrastructure at the site seem clearly to be less favourable than those of the naturally evolved earlier centres, and the motive for this impractical relocation is suggested to a Christian-based desire quite literally to distance themselves from paganism.

The earliest churches in Hedeby/Schleswig, Ribe, Aarhus and Odense were founded from Hamburg-Bremen or Cologne, and all four were episcopal seats. It is striking that all four of those towns continued to have relatively few churches despite the great economic importance of Schleswig, Ribe and Odense in the earlier Middle Ages. The relatively few urban parishes, apparently nine in Schleswig, three to five in Aarhus and three or four in Odense (Kristensen & Poulsen 2016, 114f) match the pattern in the German kingdom and contrast with the profusion of churches in the Anglo-Saxon style of towns at Viborg, Roskilde and Lund, with their 12-13, 14 and 22 parish churches respectively. The number of parish churches in the Danish episcopal towns thus was no direct reflection of the size or importance of the town but apparently rather the result of specific ecclesiastical links and traditions.

Palpable traces of the towns of the first half of the 11th century are sparse, and neither royal manors nor mint sites have yet been identified for certain. On the other hand there is much better information about the ecclesiastical arrangements within the towns in the form of churches and churchyards, and this is where, plausibly, the effective reality lies: that the most important role of the central towns in the first half of the 11th century was to provide spiritual service for a wide hinterland which may not have been provided with its own local churches until after 1050 (Thaastrup-Leth 2004). To put it another way, the king's church was in archaeological terms a highly visible agent in the early 11th-century towns.

The emporia were provided with defences in the turbulent 10th century but the civitates of the following period remained undefended in the 11th century. Hedeby and Ribe both moved out of defended urban sites while in the cases of Viborg, Odense, Roskilde and Lund there is no sign of urban defences earlier than the 12th century. The following features characterize the central towns down to the middle of the 11th century:

- A central location in the landscape

- Churches on central sites

- Earlier heathen centres in the vicinity

- A royal mansion

- A mint

- No maritime role

- Few signs of trade or craft

- No defences

6.4 Conclusion: From emporium to civitas in Southern Scandinavia

In this chapter I have attempted to broaden the perspective and to compare the results from Ribe with the other towns of that period in the area of Denmark. What transpires is that the towns do follow the same overall course of development. Looked at as a whole, a distinction may be drawn between two different urban concepts: the emporium model, which covers the whole of the period in question, c. AD 700-1050, and the civitas model, which is closely connected with the emergence of the Christian kingdom of Denmark from the late 10th century.

The archaeological evidence from Ribe, Reric and Åhus shows clearly in the case of the former two and less certainly in the case of the latter that the emporia of the 8th century were royal trading sites organized to one and the same end. Their systems of coinage and location in the border areas of the subsequently defined Danish territory indicates a unified Danish kingdom with a dynastic centre at Lejre as early as the 8th century. The emporia had no known religious or administrative central functions and also appear to have been undefended, religiously and politically neutral zones, with large, ethnically and culturally mixed cemeteries. Their topographical structure seems in every essential respect to recall that of Dorestad and can be summarized as *Uferparallelle Einstraßenanlagen*: single-street settlements parallel to the river bank or shore. The three sites form a distinct group, the archaeological material from which clearly differentiates them from the many other known landing and trading sites of the period.

The emergence and/or foundation of the Danish emporia added new buds to a pre-existing network of emporia subject to other political systems around the southern North Sea, and their existence shows that they must have been crucial sources of income for those in power and probably also for other agents involved throughout the period. Both Ribe and Reric appear from c. AD 725 to have had a monetized economy based upon a royal monopoly coinage, the Wodan/monster sceatt, similar to later known systems in Hedeby. The three Danish emporia appear to have had much in common and to have produced a wide range of common goods which were not aimed at the high aristocracy but rather at a very much broader stratum of society which, on the evidence of recent years' metal-detecting in Denmark, was present in practically every single later parish of Denmark, and presumably similarly in the rest of Scandinavia (see Ch. 4).

The emporia attracted both sea- and land-based traffic of traders, raw materials and products, and in the wake of their emergence a system of subordinate stopping places evolved which, according to local topographical conditions and ambitions, could come to be either smaller landing sites or genuine trading sites that can be assumed to have been subject to local elites.

As today, trade was regulated both by social mechanisms and market mechanisms, and thus was neither *embedded* nor *disembedded* (see Ch. 2.4) but rather a blend of the two, the precise character of which it is difficult to assess. It can be regarded as certain that the trade of the emporia was of crucial economic significance to the king, while their role as national and international meeting places for the exchange of ideas and concepts between people of diverse cultural backgrounds should not be dismissed either. The emporia are thus the strongest exponent of *the trade model*, a belief in trade and exchange as economic and political driving forces (McCormick 2007; Sindbæk 2011, 44f).

The three, possibly more or less equal-sized emporia of the 8th century developed in the course of the 9th century into a more differentiated configuration, in which Hedeby grew and successfully appropriated

the role of Dorestad, which was overrun by the Vikings, as the largest emporium in northern Europe – possibly, indeed, as the outcome of deliberate efforts on the part of the Danish king. In the following period Hedeby must have been of indispensible economic importance to the kingship. Despite the political and military turmoil of the end of the 9th century and into the 10th century it is striking that the trade and coinage of Hedeby were not just maintained but apparently grew markedly within the period.

From the second half of the 9th century onwards Hedeby stood out as the overwhelmingly dominant *hypermarket* of the age while the activities in Ribe, Kaupang and probably Åhus too were at a much lower level. The structure of the emporia in the 9th century appears to change from having been concentrated upon the zone adjacent to the river banks or shore to spread over a wider area with more open settlement. They were still undefended and there do not appear to have been any military threats. In Hedeby and Ribe churches were established even though the overwhelming majority of the residents of and visitors to the towns were heathen. The foundation of the churches can be interpreted as reflecting the organization of the trading site in accordance with the needs of the market's traders – in this case the Christian ones – rather than from any desire on behalf of the king for evangelization in the hinterland of the emporia.

There is little available information about the period of turmoil from c. AD 870 through to the emergence of the Jelling dynasty around the middle of the 10th century, but the troubled political context came to be reflected in the defensive enclosure of Hedeby, Ribe and Aarhus within semicircular ramparts. The establishment of episcopal sees in the same three towns by 948 must reflect renewed interest in missionary activity on the part of Hamburg-Bremen, and indicates that there were functioning churches in all three towns, which in form can be grouped as *D-shaped enclosures*.

After the death of King Gorm and his heathen burial in the North Mound of Jelling in 958/9, his successor, Harald Bluetooth, was baptized c. AD 963 by the missionary Poppo from Cologne. It was suggested above that Harald was not only motivated by aspects of *Realpolitik* but also took the new faith seriously at a personal level, so that his later well-known building projects can be interpreted as demonstrations of Christianity. The ringforts are suggested to have been located upon heathen focal points, which they put an end to. The church in Odense, which emerged in the period 965-88 and thus was probably raised by Harald, was consecrated to Our Lady just like the cathedrals in Ribe and Viborg, while unfortunately we do not know the dedication of the earliest church in Aarhus.

Under Svein Forkbeard, probably, the possible thing-site at Jelling was relocated to Viborg, and in the decades either side of the year 1000 a new type of town emerged which was fundamentally different from the earlier emporia. The new civitas towns were Christian islands in an otherwise in many ways still heathen landscape and were arranged around a centrally sited church. They appear principally to have been religious and administrative centres for the Christian kingship and provided a home for early *minster churches* which served a wide hinterland. The success of the Christian monarchy was visible both in the German kingdom and in England, but it was apparently inspired first and foremost by the close links across the North Sea at that time.

The new urban archetype, *the civitas model*, thus came to be of decisive influence upon the earlier emporia, all of which were relocated or changed in structure in the 11th century. The clearest example is Hedeby, which abandoned a massive, defended, urban area for an impractical peninsula only half the size, while the defences around Viking-period Ribe were pulled down at the same time and the town shifted over to the other side of the river. In Aarhus the earlier ecclesiastical situation is obscure, but the town expanded in the course of the earlier Middle Ages far beyond the Viking-period enclosure on all sides of the centrally sited cathedral of St Nikolaj which was undoubtedly the cathedral following the diocesan reform of c. AD 1059 while the previous situation is unknown.

The civitas model represents structural contuinity from the earlier central places, albeit within the constraints of a new religious framework. Both the new towns and the earlier central places were directly or indirectly financed by the agrarian surplus of the surrounding territory, and thus were exponents of the *production model* (Wickham 2005; Sindbæk 2011, 43f). The capacity of the new towns to survive had to be based upon an underlying situation in which the royal power was able to channel and divert some of the working capital of the central places away to the new civitas model. This seems to have been successful everywhere in the Danish kingdom except for Vendsyssel, which had no such town at the diocesan reform of c. AD 1059.

With Svein Estridsen the Danish towns appear for the first time to have received legislation which, highly symptomatically, was awarded first to the most important trade town of Schleswig and then is suggested to have been extended to the other towns (Gelting 2016): a clear indication that this town was still at that date the commercial heart of the kingdom. With this formalization of the town in conceptual terms we approach the better known medieval situation.

In Ribe, Hedeby, Viborg and Lund alike, at more or less the same time around AD 1050, there were major topographical changes under which the areas around the principal streets were laid out in smaller plots which appear to have been well suited to trade and craftwork, and which thus represent a merging of the town's religio-administrative functions with those of trade and production: a fusion of the emporium and civitas models which would be definitive of the following period.

The towns came increasingly to be centres of trade and craft; market trade and monetization became established; and a large number of new towns were founded at the natural junctions of transport by land and sea: a location which emphasized the importance of maritime trade as well (Carelli 2001b). Around the year 1200 the familiar dense network of High-medieval market towns had formed which was to survive largely unchanged right through to the 19th century. At many of the towns, investigations of recent years have been able to show that they are situated close to an adjacent central place of the Iron Age, and thus have roots not only in the Middle Ages but far back into the 1st millennium AD.

7. Summary

Ribe AD 700-1050
– from Emporium to Civitas in southern Scandinavia

What can Ribe tell us about the early history of towns in Denmark? Were the first towns the planned products of decisions made amongst the powerful men of the day or was the real driver of change the supply and demand of market forces? What did the earliest towns look like? Who and how many were the towns' residents, and what did they do? How did the towns change over time? Was change initiated by those in charge, as in the case of the introduction of coinage or the installment of fortifications? Was it a result of large-scale political turmoil such as the splitting up of the Frankish Empire following the Treaty of Verdun of 843? Was it caused by structural changes in the flow of goods and commodities through the trade networks, such as the opening up of the trade routes via the Russian rivers connecting the Caliphate with Scandinavia and western Europe?

This series of major questions is essential to the study of Early-medieval urbanism and constitutes the framework of this book, with Ribe as its primary case study.

The topic is the earliest towns in southern Scandinavia, from their first appearance in the archaeological record until the establishment of the classic medieval town in the 11th century. The first Scandinavian towns did not appear in a vacuum but were dendritic buds on an expanding trade network interlinking northern Europe: a network whose major hubs, the emporia, literally grew from the ruins of the Roman civilization in the course of the 7th century. In areas where elements of Roman urban culture survived such as the Upper Rhine area there is continuity from Roman to Early-medieval (c. AD 500-1000) urbanism (Ellmers 1984), while other regions show no or only weak connections between the Roman towns and the new towns. This is the case in the Lower Rhine area and on the North Sea coasts (Hodges 1989). In Scandinavia, there were no towns, and the arrival of the emporia marks the introduction of the urban phenomenon per se.

The focus of attention is the earliest phase of urbanism in Scandinavia, a phenomenon which different researchers have looked at in different ways. There has been general agreement that trade and crafts dominated Early-medieval towns and that they lacked the religious and administrative centres known in later towns. These differences have been used to set them apart from the classic medieval town, and they have instead been called *ports of trade* (Polanyi 1963), *proto-towns* (Clarke & Simms 1985, Näsman 2000), *emporia* or *wics* (Hodges 1989), or given the more general term *Seehandelsplatz* or just *trading site*.

To complicate things furhter, the term *central place* has also been attributed to the Viking-period towns, albeit in two different senses. The first derives from the geographic tradition of Walter Christaller; the other is a label describing a Scandinavian elite residence (Hodges 1989, 16f, Skre 2007b, 335ff).

This book favours continuity over discontinuity and uses the term *town* as a label for the Early-medieval emporia and the later sites.

The early towns have been the subject of complex theoretical discussion in which the rich material from Ribe has regrettably only played a minor role ever since Richard Hodges's book *Dark Age Economics* (1982, 2nd ed. 1989) came out. Ribe has primarily been discussed within Danish national borders. The town was included in *Projekt Middelalderbyen*, which was not theoretical at all, and in the project focused upon state formation *Fra stamme til stat* which drew inspiration from processual archaeology. *Projekt Middelalderbyen* was based in the Department of *Middelalderarkæologi* (Medieval Archaeology) at Aarhus University and focused on the High- and Late-medieval towns (c. AD 1000-1500) while *Fra stamme til stat* was based in *Forhistorisk Arkæologi* (Prehistoric Archaeology) at Aarhus University and urbanism played only a minor role. Thus for structural reasons, early urbanism fell between two stools, a problem well-known from other parts of Scandinavia (Skre 2007a, 47). The Kaupang project of 2000-2002, the publication of *Ribe Studier I. Det ældste Ribe* (Feveile ed. 2006), and a new generation of internationally oriented researchers have revitalised the field in recent decades (Sindbæk 2007, Kalmring 2010, Arents & Eisenschmidt 2010).

The theoretical component of this book is in Chapter 2, *Træk af den teoretiske diskussion om byer og byernes opståen i Nordeuropa* (Aspects of the theoretical discussion of towns and their origins in northern Europe). It sets out to describe the author's own epistemological standpoint, followed by a discussion focusing on the emporia. The social structure of Early-medieval Jutland is reconstructed using finds from metal-detecting combined with historical sources from the Medieval and Early Modern Periods. The metal finds show that in what seems to be every parish in Jutland (and the rest of southern Scandinavia) there were social groups who wore gilt copper-alloy brooches. They constitute a significant group of "free" or well-off peasants more likely to resemble a "middle class" rather than a high aristocracy, who are in fact virtually absent in the archaeological record of the 8th century. This group of brooch-wearing, more or less free peasants were the dominant customer group in the emporia.

To highlight the topic of the book, the focus lies upon the abundant archaeological material from excavations in and around Ribe. The town's archaeology covers a wider time-span than any other urban site in Scandinavia, and for most periods is of a character that affords one a detailed insight into the shifting topography and economy of the emporium.

The antiquarian tradition in Ribe has a long history, and over time it has produced a significant mass of literature structured around different sets of ideas and theories about the town itself and urbanism per se. Some ideas have now been abandoned while others remain current issues. Despite the long tradition, no earlier research history has so far been compiled. To sort out the changing agendas and questions over time a thorough research history makes up chapter 3, *Ribes forskningshistorie* (History of research into Ribe).

The book aims at answering three overall questions:

Why and how did Ribe begin to exist?

One first step towards answering this question must be to look into the society in which Ribe appeared around AD 700. This period, in Danish chronology the 'Late [or 'Younger'] Germanic Iron Age' (c. AD 550-800) has traditionally been seen as an archaeological vacuum between rich finds from the preceding periods – graves, settlements, weapon offerings and more – stretching in time down to the middle of the 6th century, and similarly rich finds from the Viking Period from around AD 800, then also associable with a few written sources (Näsman 1991; 2006).

Metal-detecting in recent decades has, however, greatly improved the number of finds from the Late Germanic Iron Age. This material, used in combination with the study of older maps, palaeo-climatic models, and written sources in the form of the so-called Church List of c. 1325 from the diocese of Ribe (O. Nielsen 1869), constitutes the ingredients of a topographic study of society and settlement in Wes Jutland in the 1st millennium. This makes up chapter 4, *Topografi – den vestjyske kystzone i jernalder, vikingetid og middelalder* (Topography – the coastal zone of West Jutland in the Iron Age, the Viking Period and the Middle Ages).

How did Ribe evolve between AD 700 and 1050 – both in terms of topography and economy?

Archaeological excavation is the only source for 8th-century Ribe north of the minor Ribe River. The existence of an overlying modern town has always been a challenge to excavators. South of the river, the cathedral is the oldest surviving structure, with direct continuity from the 9th century, while the surrounding network of streets was laid out in the 11th century and has largely survived to the present day despite a massive accumulation of up to 5 m of medieval organic layers in the area. The stratigraphic sequence is in some parts well preserved, and offers excellent opportunities for highlighting this part of the town's history through archaeology. However, the Viking-period landscape is well hidden below the thick layers and has had to be reconstructed through a large number of dispersed excavations

North of the river, there are no surviving Viking-period or medieval structures. The area was suburban and used in different ways. Some areas were intensely cultivated, destroying the underlying stratigraphy, while other parts were sealed underneath medieval layers, which has resulted in very good preservation. For better or for worse the closeness of the existing town means that the survival of 8th-century Ribe varies greatly. This is very different from other Scandinavian emporia and the understanding of Ribe's taphonomy is vital for the assessment of the archaeological record.

The entire site of Ribe is extremely complex and holds an enormous amount of information affording the town's archaeologists insight into the development of the emporium and its inhabitants. The most recent publication of the archaeological material is from 2006 but since then many new excavations have been conducted with very interesting results. As a part of this book, the entire Ribe material has been re-analysed. This large dataset forms the backbone of the book's centre-piece, Chapter 5, *Ribe 700-1050 e. Kr.* (Ribe AD 700-1050). This chapter documents Ribe's development from an 8th-century *Uferparallelle Einstrassenanlage* to a 10th-century *D-shaped enclosure* and on to an 11th-century *Civitas*.

Whether or not Ribe was founded by a king around AD 700 we do not know, but from the numismatic evidence and its distribution in the stratigraphy it is suggested that no later than c. 725 Ribe came under royal Danish control and until the later 9th century had a monetized economy based upon a monopoly coinage. Between c. AD 725 and 800 the Wodan/monster sceatt was in use after which it was succeeded by a denier- or penny-type coin, Malmer's Combination Group 4-6.

The archaeological material from Ribe covers the entire time-span from c. AD 700 onwards. The town was changed in radical ways on several occasions and a church was founded in the mid-9th century. This offers a so far unique opportunity to trace how a Scandinavian and predominantly heathen emporium reacted to the presence of Christianity. It appears that the town remained in its place until the mid-11th century and was even fortified at a time when the church had already long been standing on the other side of the river. However, around 1050 the town moved over to the church, left its former fortified site, and created a Civitas-type town with a centrally placed church building.

Is the model of Ribe's development applicable to other early towns in southern Scandinavia?

In Chapter 6, The urbanization of southern Scandinavia, AD 700-1050, the other early towns in southern Scandinavia are brought into the discussion. The towns seem to fall within two overall groups drawing on different urban concepts: the *emporia* and the *civitates*.

The emporia are the older, and constituted the major hubs in the maritime trading networks. They came under royal control in the 8th century. Along the sailing routes used by the merchants there were many smaller coastal sites, landing places of different sizes and types, amongst which the larger were regular trading places, probably under local aristocratic control. The emporia form one rootstock of what later became the medieval town and are represented by the sites Ribe, Reric/Hedeby/Schleswig, Åhus, Kaupang and Aarhus. Being royal sites the emporia also reflect political history, and the nature and development of the urban sites are considered in connection with the dynamic history of Denmark between AD 700 and 1050.

The so-called central places of the Iron Age make up another rootstock of the medieval towns. Shortly after the conversion of Denmark in the second half of the 10th century a new group of royal urban sites was founded across the country. They functioned as administrative and religious centres for the Christian king and are collected under the term *civitates*, a Christian urban concept that would go on to transform the emporia in the mid-11th century.

The heathen central places were situated at natural meeting places for land-borne traffic and seem to have been elite residences for the local aristocracy and the scene of cultic activities and feasting – conduct rooted in the pre-Christian religion. They vary greatly in size, reflecting the differing wealth and power of the aristocratic/royal families controlling them. Gudme, Lejre, Uppåkra and Sorte Muld are the largest known in Denmark. Towns like Viborg, Odense, Roskilde and Lund are seen as representatives of the central place-civitates pattern. Towns of this type show no or few signs of trade or crafts in the first half of the 11th century. From c. 1050, however, the emporia model and the civitas model seem to merge into a common urban concept, around the time when the most important emporium of the time, Schleswig, was supposedly given its first town law by the King Svein Estridsen.

8. Bibliography

Agerskov Madsen, H. 2012: *Antropologisk beretning, ASR 13 II, Lindegården.* Unpubl. report, Sydvestjyske Museer

Agersnap Larsen, L. 2015: Muldfjælsplovens tidlige historie. Fra yngre romersk jernalder til middelalder. *kuml* 2015, 165-200.

Alrø Jensen, M. 2013: Udgravningerne i Sct. Nikolajgade – Nyt om Ribes markedsplads i det 9. og 10. årh. *By, marsk og geest* 25, 9-27.

Andersen, H.H., P.J. Crabb & H.J. Madsen 1971: Århus Søndervold – en byarkæologisk undersøgelse. Højbjerg: Jysk Arkæologisk Selskab.

Andersen, K.H. 2017: *Da danerne blev danske. Dansk etnicitet og identitet til ca. år 1000.* Unpubl. PhD thesis. Aarhus University.

Andersen, L. 1997: Dæmningen over Ribe Å. *By, marsk og geest* 9, 32-38.

- 1999: Udgravningen under den gamle bakelitfabrik i Slotsgade. *By, marsk og geest* 11, 29-38.

- 2003: Ribe gråbrødrekloster – det sidste kapitel. *Mark og Montre* 2003, 23-40.

Andersen, Aa. 1998: Ribeegnens bebyggelsesnavne. In: S. Jensen ed. *Marsk, land og bebyggelse. Ribeegnen gennem 10.000 år,* vol. 1, Højbjerg: Jysk Arkæologisk Selskab, 65-67.

Andrén A. 1985: *Den urbana scenen. Städer och samhälle i det medeltida Danmark.* Lund: CWK Gleerups Forlag.

- 2000: Ad sanctos – de dödas plats under medeltiden. *hikuin* 27, 7-26.

Andresen, J., R.B. Iversen & P. Jensen 2008: On the War-path: Terrestrial Military Organisation in Prehistoric Denmark. In: A. Posluschny et al. eds. *Computer Applications and Quantitative Methods in Archaeology: Layers of perception. Advanced technological means to illuminate our past.* Bonn: Dr. Rudolf Habelt, 1-8.

Arbman, H. 1940: *Birka I, Die Gräber.* Tafeln. Uppsala: Almqvist & Wiksell.

- 1943: *Birka I, Die Gräber.* Text. Uppsala: Almqvist & Wiksell.

Arents, U. & S. Eisenschmidt 2010. *Die Gräber von Haithabu.* Vol. 1-2. Neumünster: Wachholtz.

Ashby, S.P., A.N. Coutu & S.M. Sindbæk 2015: Urban networks and Arctic outlands: Craft specialists and reindeer antler in Viking towns. *European Journal of Archaeology,* vol. 18(4), 679-704.

Augé, M. 1998: *A Sense for the Other: The Timeliness and Relevance of Anthropology.* Stanford: Stanford University Press.

Axboe, M. 2001: Amulet Pendants and a Darkened Sun. In: B. Magnus ed. *Roman Gold and the Development of the Early Germanic Kingdoms: Aspects of Technical, Sociopolitical, Socio-economic, Artistic and Intellectual Development, A.D. 1-500,* Stockholm: Almqvist & Wiksell, 51.

Bang, J. 2013: The Route to a History of the Cultural Landscape: A Danish Record of Prehistoric and Historic Roads, Tracks and related Structures. In: S. Bergerbrant & S. Sabatini eds. *Counterpoint: Essays in Archaeology and Heritage Studies in Honour of Professor Kristian Kristiansen.* Oxford: Oxford University Press, 703-715.

Behre, K. 2008: *Landschaftsgeschichte Norddeutschlands.* Neumünster: Wachholtz.

Bencard, M. 1969: Grubehuse i Okholm. *Mark og Montre* 1969, 26-36.

- 1972: Om anvendelsen af runepind 2 fra Ribe. *Mark og Montre* 1972, 38-42.

- 1973: *Ribes vikingetid. En foreløbig redegørelse fra udgravningerne 1972-73. Mark og Montre* 1973, 28-48.

- 1974: Ribes ældste udvikling. *Mark og Montre* 1974, 20-27.

- 1979a: Et middelalderligt bebyggelsesmønster. In: N. Bech et al. eds. *Arkitektur Studier tilegnede Hans Henrik Engqvist,* København: Arkitektens forlag, 35-45.

- 1979b: Jernankeret fra Ribe. *Nationalmuseets Arbejdsmark* 1979, 156-57.

- 1981: Introduction/Indledning. In: M. Bencard ed. *Ribe Excavations 1970-76,* vol. 1, Esbjerg: Sydjysk Universitetsforlag, 9-19.

- 1990: The Stratigraphy and Dating of 8th Century Ribe. *Journal of Danish Archaeology,* vol. 7, 1988 (1990), 225-228.

- 2004: Introduction. In: M. Bencard, A. Kann Rasmussen & H. Brinch Madsen eds. *Ribe Excavations 1970-76,* vol. 5, Højbjerg: Jysk Arkæologisk Selskab, 7-18.

- 2010: Introduction. In: M. Bencard & H. Brinch Madsen eds. *Ribe Excavations 1970-76,* vol. 6, Højbjerg: Jysk Arkæologisk Selskab, 7-16.

Bencard, M., K. Ambrosiani, L. Bender Jørgensen, H. Brinch Madsen, I. Nielsen & U. Näsman 1979: Wikingerzeitliches Handwerk in Ribe. Eine Übersicht. *Acta Archaeologica,* vol. 49, 1978 (1979), 113-138.

Bencard, M. & L. Bender Jørgensen 1990: Excavation and Stratigraphy. In: M. Bencard, L. Bender Jørgensen og H. Brinch Madsen eds. *Ribe Excavations 1970-76,* vol. 4, Esbjerg: Sydjysk Universitetsforlag, 15-167.

Bendixen, K. 1972: Mønterne fra Dankirke. *Nationalmuseets Arbejdsmark* 1972, 61-66.

- 1985: Skandinaviske fund af Sceattas. *hikuin* 11. Festskrift til Brita Malmer, s. 33-40.

Bentsen, L. 2008: Udgravningerne ved Gl. Sct. Jacobi Skole. *Opdatering. Museet for Varde By og Omegn årbog 2008,* 32-46.

Biddle, M., D. Hudson & C. Heighway 1973: *The Future of London's Past.* Worcester: Rescue: a trust for British archaeology.

Bill, J. & A. Daly 2012: The plundering of the ship graves from Oseberg and Gokstad – an example of power politics? *Antiquity* 86, 808-824.

Bischop, D. 2014: Der Bistumssitz Bremen im späten 8. und 9. Jahrhundert. In: R-M. Weiss & A. Klammt eds. *Mythos Hammaburg. Archäologische Entdeckungen zu den Anfängen Hamburgs.* Hamburg: Archäologisches Museum Hamburg, 417-433.

Bjerg, Line 2007: *Romerske denarfund fra jyske jernalderbopladser.* Aarhus: Aarhus Uninversity Press.

Blomqvist, R. & A.W. Mårtensson 1963: *Thulegrävningen 1961 – En berättelse om vad grävningarna för Thulehuset i Lund avslöjade.* Archaeologica Lundensia II. Lund: Kulturhistoriska Museet Lund.

Bork-Pedersen, K. 2011: *Stammebåde.* Højbjerg: Middelalderarkæologisk Nyhedsbrev.

Braun & Hogenberg 1572-1617: *Civitates orbis terrarum/Cities of the World.* New Edition 2015. Taschen Verlag.

Breuning-Madsen, H. et al. 2013: Jordbunden som landskabsdannende faktor. *Geoviden* 4:2013, 6-8.

Brinch Madsen, H. 1984: Metal-casting. Techniques, Production and Workshops. In: M. Bencard ed. *Ribe Excavations 1970-76,* vol. 2. Esbjerg: Sydjysk Universitetsforlag, 15-189.

- 2004: Absolute Dating of a Bronze Casting Workshop. In: M. Bencard, A. Kann Rasmussen & H. Brinch Madsen eds. *Ribe Excavations 1970-76,* vol. 5. Højbjerg: Jysk Arkæologisk Selskab, 19-26.

Brink, S. 2008: Christianisation and the emergence of the early Church in Scandinavia. In: S. Brink & N. Price eds. *The Viking World.* London: Routledge, 621-628.

Büntgen, U. et al. 2016: Cooling and societal change during the Late Antique Little Ice Age from 536 to around 660. *Nature Geoscience* 9, 231-236.

Busk Laursen, B. 1981: Den antikvariske Samlings stiftere og støtter. *hikuin* 7, 275-280.

Baastrup, M.P. 2007: Vikingetidens og den tidlige middelalders emaljefibler fra Sydvestjylland. *By, marsk og geest* 19, 5-16.

Baastrup, M. P. 2009: Småfibler af karolingiske og ottonske typer i Danmark. *Aarbøger for Nordisk Oldkyndighed og Historie* 2005 (2009), 209-255.

Callmer, J. 1991: Platser med anknytning til handel og hantverk i yngre jernalder. In: P. Mortensen & B.M. Rasmussen eds. *Fra Stamme til Stat i Danmark 2.* Højbjerg: Jysk Arkæologisk Selskab, 29-47.

- 2002: North-European trading centres and the Early Medieval craftsman. Craftsmen at Åhus, north-eastern Scania, Sweden ca. AD 750-850+. In: B. Hårdh & L. Larsson eds. *Central Places in the Migration and the Merovingian Periods. Papers from the 52nd Sachsensymposiu*m. Uppåkrastudier 6, 125-157.

- 2007: Urbanisation in Northern and Eastern Europe ca. AD 700-1100. In: J. Henning ed. *Post Roman Towns, Trade and Settlement in Europe and Byz-*

antium, vol. 1, The Heirs of the Roman West. Berlin: Walter de Gryuter, 233-270.

Carelli, P. 2001a: Lunds äldsta kyrkogård – och förekomsten av ett senvikingtida parochialsystem. *Aarbøger for Nordisk Oldkyndighed og Historie* 2000 (2001), 55-90.

- 2001b: *En kapitalistisk anda. Kulturella forändringar i 1100-tallets Danmark.* Stockholm: Almqvist & Wiksell.

von Carnap-Bornheim, Claus, V. Hilberg, S. Kalmring & J. Schultze 2007: Hedeby's settlement and harbor: recent research in a Viking age trading center. Amsterdam: Erfgoed Nederland.

Carver, M. 2001: Why that? Why there? Why then? The Politics of Early Medieval Monumentality. In: H. Hamerow ed. *Image and Power in the Archaeology of Early Medieval Britain: Essays in honour of Rosemary Cramp*, 1-22.

Christensen, A.E. 1969: *Vikingetidens Danmark.* København: Gyldendal.

Christensen, E.F., J. Hjermind, J. Simonsen & P.B. Vegger 1984: Posthusudgravningen i Skive 1982. *MIV – Museerne i Viborg Amt* 12, 1984, 16-31.

Christensen, K. 1990: Wood-anatomical and Dendrochronological Studies. In: M. Bencard, L. Bender Jørgensen og H. Brinch Madsen eds. *Ribe Excavations 1970-76*, vol. 4, Esbjerg: Sydjysk Universitetsforlag, s. 169-181.

Christensen, P.M. 2009: Erritsø. *Skalk* 4:2009, 9-15.

Christensen, T. 2015: *Lejre bag myten.* Højbjerg: Jysk Arkæologisk Selskab.

Christensen, T. & N. Lynnerup 2004: Kirkegården i Kongemarken, med et appendix af Jan Heinemeier. In: N. Lund ed. *Kristendommen i Danmark før 1050.* Roskilde: Roskilde Museums Forlag, 142-152.

Christiansen, T.T. & T. Sarauw 2010: Vognfaddinggraven fra Sønder Tranders. Årsberetning 2009. Nordjyllands Historiske Museum, 71-76.

Cinthio, E. 1973: Variationsmuster in dem mittelalterlichen Städtewesen Schones. In: H. Hinz ed. *Frühe Städte im westlichen Ostseeraum. Kiel Papers 1972 (1973).* Neumünster: Wachholtz, 57-64.

Cinthio, M. 2002: *De första Stadsborna.* Stockholm: Symposion.

Clarke, H.& A. Simms 1985: Towards a comparative history of urban origin. In: H. Clarke & A. Simms eds. *The comparative history of urban origins in non-roman Europe.* Oxford: BAR international Series vol. 255/1-2, 669-714.

Clemmensen, L. 2005: Sandflugt ved Jyllands vestkyst gennem årtusinder. *Geoviden* 3:2005, 10-15.

Coupland, S. 2010: Boom and Bust at 9th C. Dorestad. In: A. Willemsen & H. Kirk eds. *Dorestad in an International Framework.* Turnhout: Brepols, 95-103.

Croix, S. 2015: Permanency in Early Medieval Emporia: Reassessing Ribe. *European Journal of Archaeology,* vol. 18, s. 497-523.

Dalsgaard, Kristian 2006: Fygesandsaflejringer ved Ribe. In: C. Feveile ed. *Det ældste Ribe,* Ribe Studier vol. 1.1, 93-105.

Dalsgaard, K. et al. 2000: Bakkeølandskabet, hede og fygesand. In: K. Dalsgaard et al. eds. *Mellem hav og hede.* Aarhus: Aarhus University Press, 59-86.

Daly, A. 2007: *Timber, Trade and Tree-rings. A dendrochronological analysis of structural oak timber in Northern Europe, c. AD 1000 to c. AD 1650.* PhD thesis. University of Southern Denmark.

- 2017: Timber – regionality and temporality in Northern Europe's shipbuilding resource. In: J. Gawronski, A. van Holk & J. Schokkenbroek eds. *Ships and Maritime Landscapes: Proceedings of the Thirteenth International Symposium on Boat and Ship Archaeology, Amsterdam 2012.* Eelde: Barkhuis Publishing, 334.

Dangvard Pedersen, D. 2009: *Antropologisk Rapport, ASR 13 Lindegården Fase 1.* Unpublished report. Sydvestjyske Museer.

Danmarks Kirker (Udgivet af Nationalmuseet) 1933ff.

Dansk Biografisk Leksikon. 3rd ed. København: Gyldendal.

Degn, O. 1983: *Scandinavian Atlas of historic Towns No. 3. Denmark. Ribe 1500-1950.* Odense: Odense University Press.

- 1985: Indledning. In: J. Kinch: *Ribe Bys Historie og Beskrivelse. 1. Indtil Reformationen.* Reissued by Jysk Selskab for Historie. Aarhus: Aarhus University Press, 5-15.

Eckstein, D. 1978. Dendrochronologisch onderzoek naar ouderdom en herkomst van het hout uit waterputten. In: R.J. Demarée et al. eds. *Dorestad Supplement, Spiegel Historiael* 13-4, 308-312.

Edelberg, L. & M. Bencard 1962: Ribes lod. *Skalk* 3:1962, 20-29.

Egeberg, T. 1990: Værktøjsfundet fra Dejbjerg. En vikingetidshåndværkers redskaber. *kuml* 1989-90 (1990), 311-324.

- 1996: Et jernalderhus med drikkeglas i Dejbjerg, Vestjylland. *kuml* 1993-94 (1996), 211-236.

- 2004: Høje og hjulspor i tusindvis – færdsel i det vestjyske landskab. *FRAM – Fra Ringkøbing Amts Museer* 2004, 44-51.

Eisenschmidt, S. 2004a: *Grabfunde des 8. bis 11. Jahrhunderts zwischen Kongeå und Eider. Studien zur Siedlungsgeschichte and Archäologie der Ostseegebiete*, vol. 5.1 & 5.2. Neumünster: Wachholtz.

- 2004b: Kristendommens indtrængen i Syddanmark. In: N. Lund ed. *Kristendommen i Danmark før 1050*. Roskilde: Roskilde Museums Forlag, 123-141.

Ellmers, D. 1984: *Frümittelalterliche Handelsschifffahrt in Mittel- und Nordeuropa*. Offa Bücher 28, 2. ed. Neumünster: Wachholtz.

Engberg, N. & J. Kieffer-Olsen 1992: Kirkegårdens grøft. *Nationalmuseets Arbejdsmark* 1992, 168-177.

Engqvist, H.H. 1969: *Bevaringsplan Ribe.*

Eriksen, C. 1727: *Viborg byes beskrivelse.*

Eriksen, P., T. Egeberg, L.H. Olesen & H. Rostholm 2009: *Vikinger i vest. Vikingetiden i Vestjylland.* Højbjerg: Jysk Arkæologisk Selskab.

van Es, W. A. & J. H. Verwers 1980: *Excavations at Dorestad 1. The Harbour: Hoogstraat I.* Amersfort: Rijksdienst voor het Oudheidkundig Bodemonderzoek, ROB.

Ethelberg, P. 2003: Gården og landsbyen i jernalder og vikingetid (500 f.Kr.-1000 e.Kr.). In: L.S. Madsen & O. Madsen eds. *Det Sønderjyske Landbrugs Historie. Jernalder, Vikingetid og Middelalder.* Haderslev: Historisk Samfund for Sønderjylland, 123-374.

- 2014: Early state formation in southern Scandinavia in the 1st-4th century AD. In: E. Stidsing, K. Høilund Nielsen & R. Fiedel eds. *Wealth and Complexity. Economically specialized sites in Late Iron Age Denmark.* Aarhus: Aarhus University Press, 157-178.

Etting, V. 2010a: Riberhus. In: S. Bitsch Christensen ed. *Ribe Bys Historie 1*, 710-1520. Esbjerg: Dansk Center for Byhistorie/Esbjerg Kommune, 82-90.

Etting, Vivian 2010b: Riberhus. In: S. Bitsch Christensen ed. *Ribe Bys Historie 2*, 1520-1850. Esbjerg: Dansk Center for Byhistorie/Esbjerg Kommune, 72-78.

Fabech, C. 1991: Samfundsorganisation, religiøse ceremonier, og regional variation. In: C. Fabech & J. Ringtved eds. *Samfundsorganisation og regional variation*, Højbjerg: Jysk Arkæologisk Selskab, 283-303.

Feveile, C. 2001: Okholm – en plads med håndværksspor og grubehuse fra 8.-9. århundrede. *By, marsk og geest* 13, 5-32.

- 2006a. Ribe på nordsiden af åen, 8.-12. århundrede. In: C. Feveile ed. *Det ældste Ribe.* Ribe Studier vol. 1.1. Højbjerg: Jysk Arkæologisk Selskab/Den antikvariske Samling, 13-63.

- 2006b: Mønterne fra det ældste Ribe. In: C. Feveile ed. *Det ældste Ribe.* Ribe Studier vol. 1.1. Højbjerg: Jysk Arkæologisk Selskab/Den antikvariske Samling, 279-312.

-2006c: ASR 863 Seminarievej 4-8. In: C. Feveile ed. *Det ældste Ribe.* Ribe Studier vol. 1.2. Højbjerg: Jysk Arkæologisk Selskab/Den antikvariske Samling, 195-201.

-2006d: ASR 926 Ribelund I. In: C. Feveile ed. *Det ældste Ribe.* Ribe Studier vol. 1.2. Højbjerg: Jysk Arkæologisk Selskab/Den antikvariske Samling, 211-238.

- 2006e: ASR 937 DSB Øst/Dronning Dagmars Vej 5a. In: C. Feveile ed. *Det ældste Ribe.* Ribe Studier vol. 1.2. Højbjerg: Jysk Arkæologisk Selskab/Den antikvariske Samling, 239-247.

- 2006f: ASR 951 Plejehjemmet Riberhus. In: C. Feveile ed. *Det ældste Ribe.* Ribe Studier vol. 1.2. Højbjerg: Jysk Arkæologisk Selskab/Den antikvariske Samling, 249-254.

-2006g: ASR 985 Tvedgade 13-17. In: C. Feveile ed. *Det ældste Ribe.* Ribe Studier vol. 1.2. Højbjerg: Jysk Arkæologisk Selskab/Den antikvariske Samling, 257-265.

- 2006h: ASR 1000 Ribelund II. In: C. Feveile ed. *Det ældste Ribe.* Ribe Studier vol. 1.2. Højbjerg: Jysk Arkæologisk Selskab/Den antikvariske Samling, 267-287.

- 2006i: ASR 1085 Gasværksgrunden. In: C. Feveile ed. *Det ældste Ribe.* Ribe Studier vol. 1.2. Højbjerg: Jysk Arkæologisk Selskab/Den antikvariske Samling, 313-329.

-2006j: ASR 1357 Giørtzvej. In: C. Feveile ed. *Det ældste Ribe.* Ribe Studier vol. 1.2. Højbjerg: Jysk Arkæologisk Selskab/Den antikvariske Samling, 353-380.

- 2006k: Sceattaerne fra Dankirke. *Nordisk Numismatisk Unions Medlemsblad* 1:2006, 3-9.

- ed. 2006: *Det ældste Ribe.* Ribe Studier vol. 1.1 & 1.2. Højbjerg: Jysk Arkæologisk Selskab/Den antikvariske Samling.

- 2008: Series X and Coin Circulation in Ribe. In: T. Abramson ed. *Studies in Early Medieval Coinage, vol. 1. Two Decades of Discovery.* Woodbridge: Boydell, 53-67.

- 2010: Mayen Lava Quern Stones from Ribe Excavations 1970-76. In: M. Bencard & H. Brinch Madsen eds. *Ribe Excavations 1970-76*, vol. 6. Højbjerg: Jysk Arkæologisk Selskab, 133-156.

- 2011: Korsfibler af Råhedetypen – En upåagtet fibeltype fra ældre vikingetid. *Kuml* 2011, 143-160.

- 2014: At the geestland edge southwest of Ribe: On the track of a centre of wealth during the 1st millenium AD. In: E. Stidsing, K. Høilund Nielsen & R. Fiedel eds. *Wealth and Complexity. Economically specialized sites in Late Iron Age Denmark*. Aarhus: Aarhus University Press, 73-89.

- 2019: Sceattas i Sydskandinavien – fra ekspanderende frisere til kontrollerende kongemagt. *By, marsk og geest* 31, 21-43.

Feveile, C., L.B. Frandsen & I. Stoumann 2006: Magnetisk kortlægning af grubehuslokaliteter i Ribe Amt. *Mark og Montre* 2006, 5-17.

Feveile, C. & S. Jensen 2000: Ribe in the 8th and 9th Century. A Contribution to the Chronology of North Western Europe. *Acta Archaeologica* 71, 9-24.

Feveile, C. & S. Jensen 2006a. ASR 8 Rosenallé. In: C. Feveile ed. *Det ældste Ribe*. Ribe Studier vol. 1.2. Højbjerg: Jysk Arkæologisk Selskab/Den antikvariske Samling, 65-118.

Feveile, C. & S. Jensen 2006b. ASR 9 Posthuset. In: C. Feveile ed. *Det ældste Ribe*. Ribe Studier vol. 1.2. Højbjerg: Jysk Arkæologisk Selskab/Den antikvariske Samling, 119-189.

Feveile, C. & J.C. Moesgaard 2018: Appendiks: *Damhusskatten – et fantastisk indspark til den tidlige møisthistorie*. By, marsk og geest 30, 28-30.

Feveile, C. & M.H. Søvsø 2009: Vikingetidsgravpladsen ved Hunderup – 15 jordfæstegrave omkring en storstensgrav fra stenalderen. *By, marsk og geest* 21, 33-48.

Feveile, L. 2006: Hulglasskår fra markedspladsen. In: C. Feveile ed. *Det ældste Ribe*. Ribe Studier vol. 1.1. Højbjerg: Jysk Arkæologisk Selskab/Den antikvariske Samling, 195-256.

Fiedler Therkildsen, K. 2014: Høvdingen på Toftum Næs. *Viborg Bogen* 2014, 51-62.

-2015: Høvdingen på Toftum Næs – en fortsat fortælling. *Viborg Bogen* 2015, 17-31.

Foucault, M. 1966: *Ordene og tingene. En arkæologisk undersøgelse af videnskaberne om mennesket*. Danish edition 2002, København: Spektrum.

Frandsen, L. B. 2001: De stenrige grave i Billum – jordfæstegrave fra ældre romersk jernalder. *Mark og Montre* 2001, 19-32.

Frandsen, L.B., P.K. Madsen & H. Mikkelsen 1990: Byudgravninger og byarkæologiske undersøgelser i Ribe 1983-89. *By, marsk og geest* 1, 1989 (1990), 2-27.

- 1991: Ausgrabungen in Ribe in den Jahren 1983-89. *Offa* 47, 1990 (1991), 177-207.

Frandsen, L.B. & S. Jensen 1988: Pre-Viking and Early Viking Age Ribe. *Journal of Danish Archaeology*, vol. 6, 1987 (1988), 175-189.

- 1990: The Dating of Ribe's earliest Culture Layers. *Journal of Danish Archaeology*, vol. 7, 1988 (1990), 228-231.

- 2006: ASR 7 Sct. Nicolajgade 8. In: C. Feveile ed. *Det ældste Ribe*. Ribe Studier vol. 1.2. Højbjerg: Jysk Arkæologisk Selskab/Den antikvariske Samling, 9-64.

Fruergaard, M. et al. 2013: Superstormen i 1634. *Geoviden* 3:2013, 2-5.

Fuglesang, S.H. 1980: *Some Aspects of the Ringerike Style. A phase of 11th century Scandinavian art*. Odense: Odense University Press.

Galthen, M. 1792: *Beskrivelse over Kiøbstæden Ribe fra sin Begyndelse indtil nærværende tid*. Odense: Lauritz Nicolai Faber.

Gammeltoft, P. 2005: Drivvejen gennem Ribe amt – set fra stednavnene. *Mark og Montre* 2005, 15-34.

Gannon, A. 2003: *The Iconography of Early Anglo-Saxon Coinage. Sixth to Eighth Centuries*. Oxford: Oxford University Press.

Gelting, M.H. 2004: Elusive Bishops: Remembering, Forgetting, and Remaking the History of the Early Danish Church. In: S. Gilsdorf ed. *The Bishop: Power and Piety at the First Millennium*. Neue Aspekte der europäischen Mittelalterforschung, 4, Münster: LIT-Verlag, 169-200.

- 2007: The Kingdom of Denmark. In: Nora Berend ed. *Christianization and the Rise of Christian Monarchy*. Cambridge: Cambridge University Press, 73-120.

- 2010. Poppo's Ordeal: Courtier Bishops and the Success of Christianization at the Turn of the First Millennium. *Viking and Medieval Scandinavia*, vol 6, 101-133.

- 2016: Kong Svend, Slesvig Stadsret og arvekøbet i de jyske købstæder: Spor af Danmarks ældste købstadsprivilegier. In: L.C.A. Sonne & S. Croix eds. *Svend Estridsen*. Odense: Syddansk Universitetsforlag, 195-216.

Gerds, M. 2015: *Das Gräberfeld des frühmittelalterlichen Seehandelsplatzes von Groß Strömkendorf, Lkr. Nord-*

westmecklenburg. Forschungen zu Groß Strömkendorf V, 1. Wiesbaden: Reichert Verlag.

Goethe, J. W. von, 1821: *Wilhelm Meisters Wanderjahre*, Stuttgart und Tübingen: Cotta.

Gräslund, B. 2007: Ragnarök och klimatkrisen år 536-537 e.Kr. *Saga och Sed*, 93-123.

Haarnagel, W. 1979: *Die Grabung Feddersen Wierde. Methode, Hausbau, Siedlungs- und Wirtschaftsformen sowie Sozialstruktur*. Wiesbaden: Franz Steiner Verlag.

Hansen, J. 2015: *Landsbydannelse og bebyggelsesstruktur i det 1. årtusinde – et bebyggelseshistorisk regionalstudie*. PhD thesis, Syddansk Universitet.

Hansen, J. & M. Runge 2016: Nonnebakken. *Skalk* 6:2016, 3-9.

Hanssen, P.T. 1831: *Efterretninger angaaende Byen Ribe udgivne som Indbydelsesskrift til den offentlige Examen i Ribe Cathedralskole 1831. Første Samling*. Ribe: N.S. Hyphoff.

Harris, E.C. 1989: *Principles of Archaeological Stratigraphy*. 2nd ed. London: Academic Press.

Hartley, L.P. 1953: *The Go-Between*. London: Hamish Hamilton.

Hauberg. P. 1900: *Myntforhold og Udmyntninger i Danmark indtil 1146*. Det Kongelige Danske Videnskabernes Selskab Skrifter, 6. Række, vol. V, 1. København: B. Luno.

Helgesson, B. 2002: Central places and regions in Scania during the Iron Age. In: L. Larsson & B. Hårdh eds. *Centrality – Regionality. The Social Structure of Southern Sweden during the Iron Age. Uppåkrastudier 7*, 323-335.

Helles Olesen, L. & E. Schlosser Mouritsen 2015: *Luftfotoarkæologi i Danmark*. Holstebro: Holstebro Museum.

Helms, J. 1870: *Ribe Domkirke*. København: E.M. Bærentzen & Co.

Henriksen, M.B. 2013: Odenses forgænger – eller: én af mange. In: L. Bisgaard, M. Bruus & P. Gammeltoft eds. *Beretning fra toogtredivte tværfaglige vikingesymposium*, Højbjerg: Forlaget Wormianum, 68-83.

Hermansen, V. 1959: Antikvarer i det gamle Ribe. *Fra Ribe Amt* 1959, vol. XIV, 593-650.

Herschend, F. 1995: Hus på Helgö. *Fornvännen* vol. 90, 1995/4, 221-228.

Hilberg, V. 2011: Silver economies of the Ninth and Tenth Centuries AD in Hedeby. In: J. Graham-

Campbell, S.M. Sindbæk & G. Williams eds. *Silver Economies, Monetisation and Society in Scandinavia AD 800-1100*. Aarhus: Aarhus University Press, 203-225.

Hilberg, V. & T. Lemm eds. 2018: Viele Funde – grosse Bedeutung? Potenzial und Aussagewert von Metalldetektorfunden für die siedlungsarchäologische Forschung der Wikingerzeit. Bericht des 33. Tværfaglige Vikingesymposiums. Kiel: Ludwig.

Hjermind, J., M. Iversen & H. Krongaard Kristensen eds. 1998: *Viborg Søndersø 1000-1300. Byarkæologiske undersøgelser 1981 og 1984-85*. Højbjerg: Jysk Arkæologisk Selskab.

Hodges, R. 1982: *Dark Age Economics*. London: Duckworth.

- 1989: *Dark Age Economics*. 2nd edition. London: Duckworth.

- 2000: *Towns and Trade in the Age of Charlemagne*. London: Duckworth.

- 2012: *Dark Age Economics. A new Audit*. London: Bristol Classical Press.

Hodges, R. & D. Whitehouse 1983: *Mohammed, Charlemagne & the origins of Europe*. London: Duckworth.

Hoffmann, G, T. Lund & H.C. Hansen 1833-35: *Domkirken i Roeskilde tegnet og stukket i Omrids for Kunstforeningen i København*.

Hohenberg, P.M. & L.H. Lees 1995: *The Making of Urban Europe 1000-1994*. London: Harvard University Press.

Holst, M.K. 2010: Inconstancy and stability – large and small farmsteads in the village of Nørre Snede (Central Jutland) in the first millennium AD. In: H. Jöns et al eds. *Herrenhöfe und die hierarchie der Macht im Raum südlich und östlich der Nordsee von der Vorrömischen Eisenzeit bis zum frühen Mittelalter und zur Wikingerzeit*. Siedlungs- und Küstenforschung im südlichen Nordseegebiet, vol. 33, Rahden: Verlag Marie Leidorf, 155-179.

- 2014: Warrior aristocracy and village community. In: E. Stidsing, K. Høilund Nielsen & R. Fiedel eds. *Wealth and Complexity. Economically specialized sites in Late Iron Age Denmark*. Aarhus: Aarhus University Press, 179-197.

Holst, M.K., M.D. Jessen, S.W. Andersen & A. Pedersen 2012: The Late Viking-Age Royal Constructions at Jelling, central Jutland, Denmark. *Praehistorische Zeitschrift* 2012, vol.87(2), 474-504.

Hvass, S. 1988: Jernalderens bebyggelse. In: P. Mortensen & B.M. Rasmussen eds. *Fra Stamme til Stat i Danmark 1*. Højbjerg: Jysk Arkæologisk Selskab, 53-92.

Høilund Nielsen, K. 1998: En gravplads i Okholm – lokal eller fremmed befolkning? *By, marsk og geest* 10, 7-21.

- 2014: Key issues concerning 'central places'. In: E. Stidsing, K. Høilund Nielsen & R. Fiedel eds. *Wealth and Complexity. Economically specialized sites in Late Iron Age Denmark.* Aarhus: Aarhus University Press, 11-50.

Imer, L.M. 2014: The Danish runestones – when and where? *Danish Journal of Archaeology* 2014, 164-174.

Imer, L., M. Knudsen & M. Søvsø 2012: Runestenen fra Ribe. *Skalk* 2:2012, 24-30.

Imer, L., M. Knudsen & M. Søvsø 2013: Ribe-stenen. *By, marsk og geest* 25, 29-39.

Iversen, M., D. Robinson, J. Hjermind & C. Christensen eds. 2005: *Viborg Søndersø 1018-1030. Arkæologi og naturvidenskab i et værkstedsområde fra vikingetid.* Højbjerg: Jysk Arkæologisk Selskab.

Jantzen, C. 2013: *Middelalderbyen Aarhus.* Aarhus: Den Gamle By.

Jantzen, C., J. Kieffer-Olsen & P.K. Madsen 1994: De små brødres hus i Ribe. *Mark og Montre* 1994, 26-36.

Jarl Hansen, H. 1985: Fragmenter af en bronzebeslået pragtvogn fra Dankirke. *Aarbøger for Nordisk Oldkyndighed og Historie* 1984 (1985), 217-43.

- 1990: Dankirke. Jernalderboplads og rigdomscenter. Oversigt over udgravningerne 1965-70. *Kuml* 1988-89 (1990), 201-247.

Jensen, C.A. 1942: *Riberhus Slotsbanke.* Nationalmuseets blaa Bøger. København: Nationalmuseet.

Jensen, C.V. & C. Klinge 2016: Algade 9 i Aalborg. *Kuml* 2016, 195-253.

Jensen, J.Aa. 1988: "Marie, Marie, du skal sgu' møæ te æ haw!" – med arkæologen på Holmsland Klit. *FRAM, Fra Ringkøbing amts museer* 1988, 7-35.

Jensen, S. 1984: Ribeegnen gennem 10.000 år. *Mark og Montre* 1984, 5-29.

-1985: Et grubehus fra Darum. Bidrag til keramikudviklingen gennem 6. årh. e.Kr. *kuml* 1985, 111-121.

- 1987: Overgangshuset. *Skalk* 6:1987, 3-8.

- 1990: Ribes befæstning i vikingetiden. *Mark og Montre* 1990, 69-73.

- 1991a: Dankirke-Ribe. Fra handelsgård til handelsplads. In: P. Mortensen & B.M. Rasmussen eds.

Fra Stamme til Stat i Danmark 2. Højbjerg: Jysk Arkæologisk Selskab, 73-88.

- 1991b: *Ribes Vikinger.* Ribe: Den antikvariske Samling.

- ed. 1998: *Marsk, land og bebyggelse. Ribeegnen gennem 10.000 år.* Højbjerg: Jysk Arkæologisk Selskab.

- 2006: ASR 1030 Seminarievej. In: C. Feveile ed. *Det ældste Ribe.* Ribe Studier vol. 1.2. Højbjerg: Jysk Arkæologisk Selskab/Den antikvariske Samling, 289-291.

Jensen, S., P.K. Madsen & O. Schiørring 1982: Udgravninger i Ribe 1979-81. *Mark og Montre* 1982, 50-65.

- 1983: Excavations in Ribe 1979-82. *Journal of Danish Archaeology,* vol. 2, 1983, 156-70.

Jensen, T.B. 2011: Fiskergade i Ribe – arkæologiske undersøgelser i forbindelse med gaderenoveringen i 2009. *By, marsk og geest* 23, 34-45.

- 2018: Degnestien. In: P. Eriksen & P.O. Rindel eds. *Lange linjer i landskabet. Hulbælter fra jernalderen.* Højbjerg: Jysk Arkæologisk Selskab, 238-44.

Jeppesen, J. 2004: Stormandsgården ved Lisbjerg kirke. Nye undersøgelser. *kuml* 2004, 161-180.

Jeppesen, J. & H.J. Madsen 1997: Trækirke og stormandshal i Lisbjerg. *kuml* 1995-96 (1997), 149-171.

Johansen K.L., S.T. Laursen & M.K. Holst 2004: Spatial patterns of social organization in the early bronze age of South Scandinavia. *Journal of Anthropological Archaeology* 23, 33-55.

Johansson Hervén, C. 2008: Den tidiga medeltidens Lund – vems var egentlig staden? In: H. Andersson, G. Hansen & I. Øye eds. *De første 200 årene – nyt blikk på 27 skandinaviske middelalderbyer.* Bergen: Universitetet i Bergen, 259-275.

Jonsson, K. & B. Malmer 1986: Sceatttas och den äldsta nordiske myntningen. *Nordisk Numismatisk Unions Medlemsblad,* 1:1986, 66-71.

Jørgensen, L. 2014: Norse Religion and Ritual Sites in Scandinavia in the 6th-11th century. In: H.C. Gulløv ed. *Northern Worlds – Landscapes, Interaction and Dynamics – Proceedings of the the Northern Worlds Conference, Copenhagen 28-30 November 2012,* 129-150.

Jørgensen, M.S. 1988: Vej, vejstrøg og vejspærring. Jernalderens landfærdsel. In: P. Mortensen & B.M. Rasmussen eds. *Fra Stamme til Stat i Danmark 1.* Højbjerg: Jysk Arkæologisk Selskab, 101-116.

Kalmring, S. 2010: *Der Hafen von Haithabu.* Neumünster: Wachholtz Verlag.

Kalmring, S., J. Runer & A. Viberg 2017: At Home with Herigar: A Magnate's Residence from the Vendel- to Viking Period at Korshamn, Birka (Uppland/S): *Archäologisches Korrespondenzblatt* 47/2017, 1-24.

Kann, O. 2001: Ribe Å – dens historie og betydning for Ribe by og omegn. *By, marsk og geest* 13, 62-94.

Kann Rasmussen, A. 1971: Sct. Nicolaj i Ribe – og en grav fra yngre germansk jernalder. *Mark og Montre* 1971, 13-15.

Kieffer-Olsen, J. 2008: Ribe – de første par hundrede år. In: H. Andersson, G. Hansen & I. Øye eds. *De første 200 årene – nyt blikk på 27 skandinaviske middelalderbyer.* Bergen: Universitetet i Bergen, 155-164.

Kilder til vikingetidens historie. Published by J. Bjernum, 1965. København: Gyldendal.

Kilger, C. 2008: Wholeness and Holiness: Counting, Weighing and Valuing Silver in the Early Viking Period. In: D. Skre ed. *Means of Exchange.* Kaupang Excavation Project Publication Series, vol. 2. Oslo: University of Oslo, 253-325.

Kinch, J.F. 1869: *Ribe Bys Historie og Beskrivelse indtil Reformationen.* Ribe: C.E.C. Gad.

- 1884: *Ribe Bys Historie og Beskrivelse 2den Del. Fra reformationen indtil Enevoldsmagtens Indførelse* (1536-1660). Odder: C.E.C. Gad.

Kiær, J.J. 1888: Kjøbstaden Ribe. Jordbunds-, Grundvands-, og Brøndforhold. – Sygdomsforhold før Vandværket – Vandværket. *Ugeskrift for Læger,* 4. Rk. XVIII, Følgeblad til Nr. 4-5, July 21st, 1888.

Kleingärtner, S. 2014: *Die frühe Phase der Urbanisierung an der südlichen Ostseeküste im ersten nachchristlichen Jahrtausend.* Neumünster: Wachholtz.

Klemensen, M.F. 1996: Arkæologisk undersøgelse af Torvet 9 i Ribe. *By, marsk og geest* 8, 17-22.

- 2000: Et middelalderligt benværksted – arkæologiske undersøgelser på Vægtergade 2 i Ribe. *By, marsk og geest* 12, 29-46.

Klæsøe, I.S. 2005: Et sælsomt spænde fra Ribe-egnen. *By, marsk og geest* 17, 5-13.

Knibbs, E. 2011: *Ansgar, Rimbert and the Forged Foundations of Hamburg-Bremen.* Farnham: Ashgate.

Krants Larsen, L. 2010: Udgravningerne af forborgen til Tønderhus. In: L.S. Madsen ed. *Tønderhus – en købstadsborg i hertugdømmet Slesvig,* Haderslev: Museum Sønderjylland, 18-79.

Krogh, K.J. 1965: Det grønne æg. *Skalk* 4:1965, 13-15.

Krongaard Kristensen, H. 1987: *Middelalderbyen Viborg.* Viby: Centrum.

Krongaard Kristensen, H. & B. Poulsen 2016: *Danmarks byer i middelalderen.* Aarhus: Aarhus Universitetsforlag.

Larsen, M. 2010: *Romanske vesttårne i det nuværende Danmark.* Højbjerg: Middelalderarkæologisk nyhedsbrev.

Larsson, L. 2002: Uppåkra – Research on a Central Place. Recent Excavations and Results. In: B. Hårdh & L. Larsson eds. *Central Places in the Migration and the Merovingian Periods. Papers from the 52nd Sachsensymposiu*m. Uppåkrastudier 6, 19-30.

Larsson, L. & K.M. Lenntorp 2004: The Enigmatic House. In: L. Larsson ed. *Continuity for Centuries. A ceremonial building and its context at Uppåkra, southern Sweden.* Uppåkrastudier 10, 3-48.

Larsson, S. 2000: *Stadens dolda Kulturskikt. Lundaarkeologins förutsättningar och förståelsehorisonter uttryckt genom praxis för källmaterialsproduktion 1890-1990.* Archaeologica Lundensia IX. Lund: Kulturhistoriska Museet Lund.

Lassen, Thomas W. 1981: Omkring billedmaterialet i Ripæ Cimbricæ. *hikuin* 7, 265-274.

Latour, B. 1991: *Vi har aldrig været moderne.* Danish edition, 2006. København: Hans Reitzels forlag.

Lauridsen, J.G. 2014: The metal detector site of Sig Syd. In: E. Stidsing, K. Høilund Nielsen & R. Fiedel eds. *Wealth and Complexity. Economically specialized sites in Late Iron Age Denmark.* Aarhus: Aarhus University Press, 91-98.

Lebecq, S. 1992: The Frisian trade in the Dark Ages; a Frisian or a Frankish/Frisian trade? *Rotterdam Papers* VII, 7-15.

Lerche Nielsen, M. 2001: Runestenen i Horne og spørgsmålet om stenens oprindelige placering. *Fra Ribe Amt* 2001, 441-448.

Levin Nielsen, E. 1969: Pedersstræde i Viborg. Købstadsarkæologiske undersøgelser i 1966/67. *Kuml* 1968 (1969), 23-81.

Liebgott, N.K. 1989: *Dansk Middelalderarkæologi.* København: Gads forlag.

Lobbedey, U. 2014: Die frühen Bistumsitze Sachsens – Einsichten aus der aktuellen Forschung. In: R-M. Weiss & A. Klammt eds. *Mythos Hammaburg. Archäologische Entdeckungen zu den Anfängen Hamburgs.* Hamburg: Archäologisches Museum Hamburg, 391-406.

Lund, J. 2006: Vikingetidens værktøjskister i landskab og mytologi. *Fornvännen* vol. 101, 2006/5, 323-341.

Lund, N. 1998: *Harald Blåtands død og hans begravelse i Roskilde?* Roskilde: Roskilde Musems forlag.

- 2004: Mission i Danmark før Harald Blåtands dåb. In: N. Lund ed. *Kristendommen i Danmark før 1050.* Roskilde: Roskilde Museums Forlag, 20-27.

Løffler, J.B. 1897: En Kirkegaard fra den ældre Middelalder. *Aarbøger for Nordisk Oldkyndighed og Historie* 1897, 225-246.

Madsen, L.S. 2000: Undersøgelse af værfter i den danske marsk. In: T. Rejnholt Kristensen, S. Eisenschmidt & L. Christensen eds. *Archäologie in Schleswig/Arkæologi i Slesvig 6:1998* (2000). Haderslev: Haderslev Museum, 84-89.

Madsen, P.K. 1978: Puggaardsgade i Ribe – en arkæologisk undersøgelse. *Mark og Montre* 1978, 27-35.

- 1991a: Handelskeramik fra middelalderens Grønnegade. *By, marsk og geest* 2, 3-33.

- 1991b: Theophilus Hansens tegning fra 1836 af Nørreport i Ribe. *Mark og Montre* 1991, 52-57.

- ed. 1999: *Middelalderkeramik fra Ribe. Byarkæologiske undersøgelser 1980-87.* Højbjerg: Jysk Arkæologisk Selskab.

Madsen, P.K. & O. Schiørring 1981: En udgravning i Ribes "nye grav" og et fund af keramik fra 1500- og 1600-årene. *hikuin* 7, 209-254.

Madsen, P.K., J. Balslev Jørgensen & S.G. Petersen 1984: Udgravninger på Sct. Catharinæ kloster i Ribe. *Mark og Montre* 1984, 59-69.

Malmer, B. 1966: *Nordiska mynt före år 1000.* Lund: CWK Gleerups Forlag.

- 2002: Münzprägung und frühe Stadtbildung in Nordeuropa. In: K. Brandt, M. Müller-Wille & C. Radtke eds. *Haithabu und die frühe Stadtentwicklung im Nördlichem Europa.* Neumünster: Wachholtz, 117-132.

Matthiessen, H. 1927: *Middelalderlige byer.* København: Gyldendal.

- 1930: *Hærvejen.* København: Gyldendal.

Matthiessen, H., O. Smith & V. Hermansen 1929: *Ribe Bys Historie 1660-1730.* København: Nyt Nordisk Forlag.

McCormick, M. 2001: *Origins of the European Economy.* Cambridge: Cambridge University Press.

- 2007: Where do trading towns come from? Early medieval Venice and the northern Emporia. In: J. Henning ed. *Post Roman Towns, Trade and Settlement in Europe and Byzantium, vol. 1, The Heirs of the Roman West.* Berling: Walter de Gryuter, 41-68.

Mertz, E.L. 1977: *Ribe og omegns jordbundsforhold.* En ingeniør-geologisk beskrivelse. Danmarks Geologiske Undersøgelse/Rapport nr. 11. Bygeologi nr. 8 – Ribe.

Messal, S., M. Karle, A.B. Kowalska & F. Lüth 2020: Frühmittelalterliche Häfen zwischen Wismar Bucht und Danziger Bucht – Abschlussbericht des Forschungsvorhabens. *Siedlungs- und Küstenforschung im südlichen Nordseegebiet* vol. 43, Rahden: Verlag Marie Leidorf, 143-182.

Metcalf, D. M. 1986: Nyt om sceattas af typen wodan/ monster. *Nordisk Numismatisk Unions Medlemsblad,* 6:1986, 110-120.

-1993: *Thrymsas and Sceattas in the Ashmolean Museum Oxford,* Vol. 1. London: Royal Numismatic Society and Ashmolean Museum Oxford.

- 2014: Thrymsas and Sceattas and the Balance of Payments. In: R. Naismith & M Allen eds. *Early Medieval Monetary History. Studies in Memory of Mark Blackburn.* Farnham: Ashgate, 243-256.

Middleton, N. 2005: Early medieval port customs, tolls and control on foreign trade. *Early Medieval Europe* 13(4), 313-358.

Moesgaard, J.C. 2007: Møntskatten fra Danelund og møntvæsenet i Sydvestjylland i vikingetid og tidlig middelalder. Årbøger for *Nordisk Oldkyndighed og Historie* 2004 (2007), 107-156.

- 2015: *King Harold's Cross Coinage.* Publications from the National Museum vol 20:2. Copenhagen: National Museum of Denmark.

- 2018: Den fremadskuende hjort – en hidtil uerkendt fase i Ribes udmøntning i 800-tallet? *By, marsk og geest* 30, 17-27.

Moltke, E. 1960: Runepindene fra Ribe. En lyf-stav og et håndtag. *Nationalmuseets Arbejdsmark* 1960, 122-136.

Mortensen, P & B.M. Rasmussen eds.: *Fra Stamme til Stat i Danmark,* vol. 1 (1988) & vol. 2, (1991).

Mulvad, S. & M. Søvsø 2011: Skallebæk Mølle i Seem sogn. *By, marsk og geest* 23, 21-33.

Müller, S. 1884: Mindre Bidrag til den forhistoriske Archæologis Methode II. Den archæologiske Sammenligning som Grundlag for Slutning og Hypothese. *Aarbøger for Nordisk Oldkyndighed og Historie* 1884, 183-203.

Müller, U., F. Rösch & M. Schimmer 2014: Von Haithabu nach Schleswig. Aktuelle Forschungen zur Gründung einer Metropole zwischen Wikinger- und Hansezeit. *Mitteilungen der Deutschen Gesellschaft für Archäologie des Mittelalters und der Neuzeit* 27, 25-36.

Müller-Wille, M. 1976: *Das Bootkammergrab von Haithabu.* Berichte über die Ausgrabungen in Haithabu 8, Neumünster: Wachholtz.

- 1995: Boat-Graves, Old and New Views. In: O. Crumlin-Pedersen & M. Thye eds. *The Ship as Symbol in Prehistoric and Medieval Scandinavia.* Papers from an International Research Seminar at the Danish National Museum, Copenhagen, 5th-7th May 1994. Copenhagen: National Museum of Denmark, 101-110.

- 2002: Ribe-Reric-Haithabu. Zur frühen Urbanisierung im südskandinavischen und westslawischen Gebiet. In: K. Brandt, M. Müller-Wille & C. Radtke eds. *Haithabu und die frühe Stadtentwicklung im Nördlichem Europa.* Neumünster: Wachholtz, 321-337.

- 2003: The Cross goes North: Carolingian Times between Rhine and Elbe. In: M. Carver ed. *The Cross goes North. Processes of Conversion in Northern Europe AD 300-1300.* York: The Boydell Press, 443-462.

- 2014: Ansgar und seine Mission im Norden. In: R-M. Weiss & A. Klammt eds. *Mythos Hammaburg. Archäologische Entdeckungen zu den Anfängen Hamburgs.* Hamburg: Archäologisches Museum Hamburg, 236-244.

Munch Kristiansen, S., S. Croix, O.E. Gundersen, J. Olsen, S. Sindbæk & M. Søvsø 2019: Dating earthwork fortifications: Integrating five dating methods in Viking-age Ribe, Denmark. *Journal of Archaeological Science: Reports* 26:101906.

Møller, E. 1971: Ribe domkirkes nordre tårn. *Nationalmuseets Arbejdsmark* 1971, 204-5.

Møller, J.T. 2000: Engang en del af havet: Fjorde og søer i Ulfborg herred. In: K. Dalsgaard et al. eds. *Mellem hav og hede.* Aarhus: Aarhus University Press, 36-58.

Møller-Jensen, E. 2010: The "princely" estate at Tjørring on Jutland. In: H. Jöns et al eds. *Herrenhöfe und die hierarchie der Macht im Raum südlich og östlich der Nordsee von der Vorrömischen Eisenzeit bis zum frühen Mittelalter und zur Wikingerzeit.* Siedlungs- und Küstenforschung im südlichen Nordseegebiet, vol. 33, Rahden: Verlag Marie Leidorf s. 197-223.

Mårtensson, A. W. 1976: *Uppgrävt förflutet för PKbanken i Lund. En investering i arkeologi.* Archaeologica Lundensia VII. Lund: Kulturhistoriska Museet Lund.

- 1980: *S:t Stefan i Lund. Ett monument ur tiden.* Lund: Föreningen Gamla Lund.

Naumann, H. 1922: *Grundzüge der deutschen Volkskunde,* Leipzig: Quelle & Meyer.

Nielsen, I. 1979: Paypyt i Ribe. Introduktion og skriftlige kilder. *Mark og Montre* 1979, 52-55.

- 1985: *Middelalderbyen Ribe.* Viby: Centrum.

Nielsen, J.N. 2004: Sebbersund – tidlige kirker ved Limfjorden. In: N. Lund ed. *Kristendommen i Danmark før 1050.* Roskilde: Roskilde Museums Forlag, 103-122.

Nielsen, L.C. 1979: Omgaard. A Settlement from the Late Iron Age and the Viking Period in West Jutland. *Acta Archaeologica,* vol. 50, 173-208.

-1998: Ekskurs 3. Okholm, Vester Vedsted sogn. In: S. Jensen ed. *Marsk, land og bebyggelse. Ribeegnen gennem 10.000 år,* vol. 2, Højbjerg: Jysk Arkæologisk Selskab ,173-184.

Nielsen, O. 1868: *Historiske Efterretninger om Slavs Herred.* Kjøbenhavn: Wibes Bogtrykkeri.

Nielsen, O. 1869: *Samling af Adkomster, Indtægtsangivelser og kirkelige Vedtægter for Ribe Domkapitel og Bispestol nedskrevet 1290-1518 kaldet "Oldemoder" (Avia Ripensis).* Kjøbenhavn: Thiele.

Nyborg, E. 2004: Kirke og sogn i højmiddelalderens by. In: S. Bitsch Christensen ed. *Middelalderbyen.* Aarhus: Aarhus University Press, 113-190.

Näsman, U. 1991: Det syvende århundrede – et mørkt tidsrum i ny belysning. In: P. Mortensen & B.M. Rasmussen eds. *Fra Stamme til Stat i Danmark 2.* Højbjerg: Jysk Arkæologisk Selskab, 165-176.

- 2000: Exchange and politics: the eighth-early ninth century in Denmark. In: I. Lyse Hansen & C. Wickham eds. *The long Eighth Century.* Leiden: Brill, 35-68.

- 2006: Danerne og det danske riges opkomst. *kuml* 2006, 205-241.

Nørnberg, P. 1979: Paypyt i Ribe. Geologiske vidnesbyrd. *Mark og Montre* 1979, 56-63.

Odgaard, B. 2000: Fra skov til hede: Vegetationens historie i Ulfborg herred. In: K. Dalsgaard et al. eds. *Mellem hav og hede.* Aarhus: Aarhus University Press, 28-35.

Odgaard, B. & K. Dalsgaard 2014: Sedimenter. In: A. Bøgh, H. Henningsen & K. Dalsgaard eds. *Nørre Vosborg i tid og rum. Borg og herresæde,* vol. 1. Aarhus: Aarhus University Press, 31-33.

Olsen, O. 1975: Nogle tanker i anledning af Ribes uventet høje alder. *Fra Ribe Amt* 1975, 225-258.

- 1981: Mogens Bencards femogtyve år i Ribe. *hikuin* 7, 11-14.

Ottosen, K. 2004: Liturgi og ritualer i middelalderen. In: N. Lund ed. *Kristendommen i Danmark før 1050.* Roskilde: Roskilde Museums Forlag, 13-19.

Pedersen, A. 2014: *Dead Warriors in Living Memory. A Study of Weapon and Equestrian Burials in Viking-Age Denmark, AD 800-1000.* Publications from the National Museum vol 20:1. Copenhagen: National Museum of Denmark.

Pejrup, M. m.fl. 2009: Vadehavet: Dannelse, historie og processer. *Geoviden* 1:2009, 2-7.

Petersen, H. 1888: *Vognfundene i Dejbjærg Præstegaardsmose ved Ringkjøbing.* København: C.A. Reitzel.

Petersen, J.E. 1985: To somre i Ribes kloakker. Arkæologiske undersøgelser under et anlægsarbejde. *Mark og Montre* 1985, 99-108.

Petersen, P.V. 1991: Nye fund af metalsager fra yngre germansk jernalder. In: P. Mortensen & B.M. Rasmussen eds. *Fra Stamme til Stat i Danmark 2.* Højbjerg: Jysk Arkæologisk Selskab, 49-66.

Pilgaard, M. 2009: Grænzezoner og transportkorridorer i Slesvig. *Sønderjyske Aarbøger 2009*, 99-128.

Pilø, L. & D. Skre 2011: Introduction to the site. In: D. Skre ed. *Things from the town.* Kaupang Excavation Project Publication Series, vol. 3. Oslo: University of Oslo, 17-26.

Pirenne, H. 1939: *Mohammed and Charlemagne.* London: G. Allen & Unwin.

Ploug, M, P.U. Jepsen & L.B. Frandsen 2012: *Henne.* Varde: Museet for Varde By og Omegn.

Pol, A. 2010: Madelinus and the disappearing of gold. In: A. Willemsen & H. Kirk eds. *Dorestad in an International Framework.* Turnhout: Brepols, 91-94.

Polanyi, K. 1944: *The great Transformation: the political and economic origins of our time.* New York: Rinehart.

Polanyi, K. 1963: Ports of Trade in Early Societies. *The Journal of Economic History*, vol. 23, 30-45.

Porskrog Rasmussen, C. 2013: *Det Sønderjyske Landbrugs Historie 1544-1830.* Aabenraa: Historisk Samfund for Sønderjylland.

Porsmose, E. 1987: *De fynske landsbyers historie – i dyrkningsfællesskabets tid.* Odense: Odense Universitetsforlag.

Post, C. 2011: Nye undersøgelser i Ribes vestby. *By, marsk og geest* 23, 46-62.

Poulsen, B. 2003: Pest, krig, skat og stormflod – tiden 1340-1430. In: L.S. Madsen & O. Madsen eds. *Det Sønderjyske Landbrugs Historie. Jernalder, Vikingetid og Middelalder.* Haderslev: Historisk Samfund for Sønderjylland, 493-537.

- 2008: Hertugdømmets dannelse 700-1544. In: H. Schultz Hansen, L.N. Henningsen & C. Porsk-rog Rasmussen eds. *Sønderjyllands Historie I. Indtil 1815.* Aabenraa: Historisk Samfund for Sønderjylland, 41-186.

Pöche, A. 2005: *Perlen, Trichtergläser, Tesserae. Spuren des Glashandels und Glashandwerks auf dem frühgeschichtlichen Handelsplatz von Groß Strömkendorf, Landkreis Nordwestmecklenburg.* Forschungen zu Groß Strömkendorf II. Schwerin: Archäologisches Landesmuseum und Landesamt für Bodendenkmalpflege Mecklenburg-Vorpommern.

Price, N. 2008: Dying and the dead: Viking Age mortuary behaviour. In: S. Brink & N. Price eds. *The Viking World.* London: Routledge, 257-273.

Qvistgaard, S. & M. Søvsø 2018: Nye hedenske grave fra det ældste Ribe. *By, marsk og geest* 30, 5-16.

Randsborg, K. 1980: *The Viking Age in Denmark. The Formation of a State.* London: Duckworth.

Rasmussen, B.M. 1995: Brokær: ein Reichtumszentrum der römischen Kaiserzeit in Südwestjütland. *Acta Archaeologica* vol. 66, 39-109.

Ravn, M. 1999: Nybro. En trævej fra Kong Godfreds tid. *kuml* 1999, 227-257.

Refskou, N. 2004: Ottonernes missionsvirksomhed. In: N. Lund ed. *Kristendommen i Danmark før 1050.* Roskilde: Roskilde Museums Forlag, 28-42.

Resen, P. H. 1682: *Haffnia antiqva et moderna.* København.

Resi, H. G. 2011: Whetstones, Grindstones, Touchstones and Smoothers. In: D. Skre ed. *Things from the Town.* Kaupang Excavation Project Publication Series, vol. 3. Oslo: University of Oslo, 373-393.

Rieck, F. 2004: The Anchor from Sct. Nicolaigade in Ribe. In: M. Bencard, A. Kann Rasmussen & H. Brinch Madsen eds. *Ribe Excavations 1970-76*, vol. 5. Højbjerg: Jysk Arkæologisk Selskab, 173-182.

Riismøller P. 1960: Nålemageren i Strandstien. *Kuml* 1960, 117-131.

Rindel, P.O. & P. Eriksen 2018: Lange linjer i jernalderens landskab. In: P. Eriksen & P.O. Rindel eds. *Lange linjer i landskabet – hulbælter fra jernalderen.* Højbjerg: Jysk Arkæologisk Selskab, 421-428.

Roesdahl, E. 1977: *Fyrkat. En jysk vikingeborg. II Oldsagerne og gravpladsen.* Nordiske Fortidsminder Serie B in quarto, vol. 4. København: Det kgl. nordiske Oldskriftselskab.

- 1978: Otte vikingetidsgrave fra Sdr. Onsild. *Aarbøger for Nordisk Oldkyndighed og Historie* 1976, 22-49.

- 2006: Aristocratic Burial in Late Viking Age Denmark. Custom, Regionality, Conversion. In: C. von Carnap-Bornheim, D. Krausse, A. Wesse eds. *Herrschaft, Tod, Bestattung. zu den vor- und frühgeschichtlichen Prunkgräbern als archäologisch-historische Quelle; Internationale Fachkonferenz Kiel 16.-19. Oktober 2003.* Bonn: Dr. Rudoph Habelt, 169-183.

- 2008: The Emergence of Denmark and the Reign of Harold Bluetooth. In: S. Brink & N. Price eds. *The Viking World.* London: Routledge, 652-664.

- 2011: Scandinavia in the Melting-pot, 950-1000. In: S. Sigmundsson ed. *Viking Settlements and Viking Society. Papers from the Proceedings of the Sixteenth Viking Congress, Reykjavík and Reykholt, 16th-23rd August 2009.* Reykjavik: University of Iceland Press, 347-374.

- 2014: Forskningshistorie. In: E. Roesdahl, S.M. Sindbæk & A. Pedersen eds. *Aggersborg i vikingetiden. Bebyggelsen og borgen.* Højbjerg: Jysk Arkæologisk Selskab, 58-63.

Roesdahl, E. & S.M. Sindbæk 2014: Borgens formål. In: E. Roesdahl, S.M. Sindbæk & A. Pedersen eds. *Aggersborg i vikingetiden. Bebyggelsen og borgen.* Højbjerg: Jysk Arkæologisk Selskab, 435-464.

Roesdahl, E. & D. Wilson 2006: The Århus runestones. In: P. Gammeltoft & B. Jørgensen eds. *Names through the Looking-glass: Festschrift in Honour of Gillian Fellows-Jensen.* København: Museum Tusculanum Press, 208-229.

Runge, M. 2017a: Det tidligste Odense. In: J. Hansen & M. Runge eds. *Knuds Odense – vikingernes by.* Odense: Odense Bys Museer, 43-55.

- 2017b: Nonnebakken – Odenses skjulte vikingeborg og dens potentiale som verdensarv. In: J. Hansen & M. Runge eds. *Knuds Odense – vikingernes by.* Odense: Odense Bys Museer, 56-63

Runge, M. & M.B. Henriksen 2018: The origins of Odense – new aspects of early urbanisation in southern Scandinavia. *Danish Journal of Archaeology,* vol. 7:1, 2-68.

Rösch, F. 2018: *Das Schleswiger Hafenviertel im Hochmittelalter. Entstehung – Entwicklung – Topographie.* Bonn: Dr. Rudolph Habelt.

Saunders, T. 2001: Early mediaeval *emporia* and the tributary social function. In: D. Hill & R. Cowie eds. *Wics: The Early Mediaeval Trading Centres of Northern Europe.* Sheffield: Sheffield Academic Press, 7-13.

Sawyer, P. 1988: *Da Danmark blev Danmark* (700-1050). Gyldendals og Politikens Danmarkshistorie, bd. 3. København: Gyldendal.

- 1991: Konger og kongemagt. In: P. Mortensen & B.M. Rasmussen eds. *Fra Stamme til Stat i Danmark 2.* Højbjerg: Jysk Arkæologisk Selskab, 277-288.

Schietzel, K. 2014: *Spurensuche Haithabu.* Neumünster: Wachholtz.

Schovsbo, P.O. 1987: *Oldtidens vogne i Norden.* Frederikshavn: Bangsbomuseets forlag.

Segschneider, M. 2014: Centrality and trade on the North Frisian Islands during the Migration period. In: E. Stidsing, K. Høilund Nielsen & R. Fiedel eds. *Wealth and Complexity. Economically specialized sites in Late Iron Age Denmark.* Aarhus: Aarhus University Press, 65-71.

Severinsen, P. 1921: Oldemoders Kirkeliste. *Fortid og Nutid,* vol. 3, 154-157.

Siegmüller, A. 2010: *Die Ausgrabungen auf der frühmittelalterlichen Wurt Hessens in Wilhelmshaven.* Studien zur Landschafts- und Siedlungsgeschichte im südlichen Nordseegebiet, vol. 1. Rahden: Verlag Marie Leidorf.

Siemen, P. & I. Stoumann 1996: Grave og samfund. In: V. Bruhn et al. eds. *Esbjerg Bys Historie 1,* Esbjerg: Rosendahls forlag, 103-158.

Sindbæk, S.M. 2007: Networks and nodal points: the emergence of towns in early Viking Age Scandinavia. *Antiquity* 81, 119-132.

- 2011: Silver Economies and Social Ties: Long Distance Interaction, Long-term Investments – and why the Viking Age happened. In: J. Graham-Campbell, S.M. Sindbæk & G. Williams eds. *Silver Economies, Monetisation and Society in Scandinavia AD 800-1100.* Aarhus: Aarhus University Press, 41-65.

- 2014a: Udgravningernes forløb og strategier. In: E. Roesdahl, S.M. Sindbæk & A. Pedersen eds. *Aggersborg i vikingetiden. Bebyggelsen og borgen.* Højbjerg: Jysk Arkæologisk Selskab, 76-95.

- 2014b: Aggersborg og andre borge. In: E. Roesdahl, S.M. Sindbæk & A. Pedersen eds. *Aggersborg i vikingetiden. Bebyggelsen og borgen.* Højbjerg: Jysk Arkæologisk Selskab, 233-250.

- ed. in prep: *Northern Emporium I,* Højbjerg: Jysk Arkæologisk Selskab.

Sindbæk, S.M. & S. Croix 2016: Helhest og Himmelhund: Dyrebegravelser på Ribes ældste gravplads. *Skalk* 4:2106, 3-9.

Skov, E. 1959: Næstved gråbrødrekloster. *Nationalmuseets arbejdsmark* 1959, 57-68.

Skov, H. 1992: De arkæologiske undersøgelser af Sortebrødregade i Ribe i 1991. *By, marsk og geest 4*, 1991 (1992), 25-30.

- 1993: Arkæologiens vej gennem Bispegade i Ribe. *By, marsk og geest 5*, 1992 (1993), 15-22.

- 1995: Dæmning, møllestrøm og byport – en arkæologisk undersøgelse af Nederdammen og Nørreport i Ribe. *By, marsk og geest 7*, 1994 (1995), 31-40.

- 2005: Aros 700-1100. In: A. Damm ed. *Vikingernes Aros*. Højbjerg: Moesgaard Museum, 15-39.

- 2008: Det ældste Aarhus 770-1200. In: H. Andersson, G. Hansen & I. Øye eds. *De første 200 årene – nyt blikk på 27 skandinaviske middelalderbyer*. Bergen: Universitetet i Bergen, 215-226.

Skov, S.P. 1937: Anders Sørensen Vedels Ribebeskrivelse. *Fra Ribe Amt* 1937, 98-109.

Skovgaard-Petersen, I. 1981: The Written Sources. In: M. Bencard ed. *Ribe Excavations 1970-76*, vol. 1, Esbjerg: Sydjysk Universitetsforlag, 21-62.

Skovmand, R. 1942. De danske Skattefund fra Vikingetiden og den ældste Middelalder indtil omkring 1150. *Aarbøger for Nordisk Oldkyndighed og Historie* 1942.

Skre, D. 2007a: Introduction. In: D. Skre ed. *Kaupang in Skiringssal*. Kaupang Excavation Project Publication Series, vol. 1. Oslo: University of Oslo, 13-24.

- 2007b: Towns and Markets, Kings and Central Places in South-Western Scandinavia c. AD 800-950. In: D. Skre ed. *Kaupang in Skiringssal*. Kaupang Excavation Project Publication Series, vol. 1. Oslo: University of Oslo, 445-469.

- 2007c: Post-substantivist Towns and Trade. In: D. Skre ed. *Means of Exchange*. Kaupang Excavation Project Publication Series, vol. 2. Oslo: University of Oslo, 327-341.

Skyum-Nielsen, N.: 1949: Haandskriftet 'Ribe Oldemoder', En kritisk Studie. *Scandia* XIX, 1948-49, 127-156.

Smith, O. & V. Hermansen 1929: *Ribe Bys Historie 1730-1820*. København: Nyt Nordisk Forlag.

Sode, T. & C. Feveile 2002: Segmenterede og metalfolierede glasperler og blæste hule glasperler med metalbelægning fra markedspladsen i Ribe. *By, marsk og geest* 14, 5-14.

Staecker, J. 1999: *Rex regum et dominus dominorum. die wikingerzeitlichen Kreuz- und Kruzifixanhänger als Ausdruck der Mission in Altdänemark und Schweden*. Stockholm: Almqvist & Wiksell.

Steuer, H. 1974: *Die Südsiedlung von Haithabu. Studien zur frühmittelalterlichen Keramik im Nordseeküstenbereich*. Ausgrabungen in Haithabu 6. Neumünster: Wachholtz.

- 2002: Der Wechsel von der Münzgeld- zur Gewichtsgeldwirtschaft in Haithabu um 900 und die Herkunft des Münzsilbers im 9. und 10. Jahrhundert. In: K. Brandt, M. Müller-Wille & C. Radtke eds. *Haithabu und die frühe Stadtentwicklung im Nördlichem Europa*. Neumünster: Wachholtz, 133-167.

Stidsing, E., K. Høilund Nielsen & R. Fiedel ed. 2014: *Wealth and Complexity. Economically specialized sites in Late Iron Age Denmark*. Aarhus: Aarhus University Press.

Stiesdal, H. 1957: Et par bemærkninger om Ribeudgravningen. *Skalk* 1:1957, 16-17.

- 1968: An excavation in the town of Ribe, Denmark. A Preliminary Report. *Rotterdam Papers: A Contribution to Medieval Archaeology* 1968, 155-160.

Stoklund, M. 2004: The Runic Inscription on the Ribe Skull Fragment. In: M. Bencard, A. Kann Rasmussen & H. Brinch Madsen eds. *Ribe Excavations 1970-76*, vol. 5. Højbjerg: Jysk Arkæologisk Selskab, 27-42.

Stoumann, I. 2009: *Ryttergraven fra Grimstrup og andre vikingetidsgrave ved Esbjerg*. Esbjerg: Sydvestjyske Museer.

Søgaard, H. 1973: Ribe bispekrønike: *Fra Ribe Amt* 1973, vol. XVIII-II, 260-273.

Sørensen, A.B. 2002: Østergård – undersøgelserne 1998-99. In: L. Christensen, S. Eisenschmidt & T. Rejnholt Kristensen eds. *Archäologie in Schleswig/ Arkæologi i Slesvig 8:2000* (2002), Haderslev: Haderslev Museum, 137-148.

- 2011: Østergaard. Vikingetid & middelalder. Haderslev: Museum Sønderjylland – Arkæologi Haderslev.

Søvsø, M.H. & C.V. Jensen 2020: Workshop production of brooches with religious symbolism around the year 1100 in Denmark. *Danish Journal of Archaeology 2020*, vol. 9, 1-31.

Søvsø, M. 2006: Arkæologiske undersøgelser i Sønderportsgade – Ribes hovedgade gennem 900 år. *By, marsk og geest* 18, 5-33.

- 2007a. Arkæologiske undersøgelser i Ribes Dagmarsgade – topografi og bebyggelsesstruktur i de ånære områder. *By, marsk og geest* 19, 17-48.

- 2007b: Et møntstempel fra Ribe. *Nordisk Numismatisk Unions Medlemsblad* 3:2007, 117-123.

- 2009: I hjertet af Ribe. *Skalk* 4:2009, 3-8.

- 2010a: Tidligkristne begravelser ved Ribe Dom-kirke – Ansgars kirkegård? In: S. Kleingärtner, S. Lützau Pedersen, L. Matthes eds. *Arkæologi i Slesvig/Archäologie in Schleswig 13:2010.* Neumünster: Wachholtz, 147-164.

- 2010b: Byens Befæstning. In: S. Bitsch Christensen ed. *Ribe Bys Historie 1,* 710-1520. Esbjerg: Dansk Center for Byhistorie/Esbjerg Kommune, 77-82.

- 2010c: Et udsnit af en landsby fra omkring 500 e.Kr. udgravet i St. Darum ved Ribe. *By, marsk og geest* 22, 5-20.

- 2011a: High Medieval Magnate Farms in Jutland with Particular Focus on the Region of Ribe. In: B. Poulsen & S.M. Sindbæk eds. *Settlement and lord-ship in Viking and early medieval Scandinavia.* Turn-hout: Brepols, 119-135.

- 2011b: Tidligkristne begravelser ved Ribe Dom-kirke – Ansgars kirkegård? In: S. Kleingärtner et al. eds. *Arkæologi i Slesvig/Archäologie in Schleswig 13:2010 (2011).* Neumünster: Wachholtz, 147-164.

- 2013: Enkeltgården syd for Kalvslund Kirke – dens historie og udvikling gennem yngre germansk jernalder og vikingetid. In: L. Matthes et al. eds. *Arkæologi i Slesvig/Archäologie in Schleswig 14:2012 (2013).* Neumünster: Wachholtz, 131-147.

-. 2014: Ansgars Kirche in Ribe. In: R-M. Weiss & A. Klammt eds. *Mythos Hammaburg. Archäologische Ent-deckungen zu den Anfängen Hamburgs.* Hamburg: Archäologisches Museum Hamburg, 245-254.

- 2016a: Ribes ældste gravpladser, ca. 700-1050. In: J. Ulriksen & H. Lyngstrøm eds *Død og begravet – i vikingetiden.* København: Forhistorisk Arkæologi v. Saxo-instituttet, 154-164.

- 2018: Detektorfund og bebyggelsesarkæologi – på markerne vest for Gl. Hviding kirke ved Ribe. In: V. Hilberg & T. Lemm eds. 2018: *Viele Funde – grosse Bedeutung? Potenzial und Aussagewert von Metalldetektorfunden für die siedlungsarchäologische Forschung der Wikingerzeit.* Bericht des 33. Tværfa-glige Vikingesymposiums. Kiel: Ludwig, 67-80.

- 2018b: Emporia, sceattas and kingship in 8th C. "Denmark". In: J. Hansen & M. Bruus eds. 2018: *The Fortified Viking Age. 36th Interdisciplinary Viking Symposium.* Odense: University Press of Southern Denmark, 75-86.

- 2020: Frie og ufrie bønder. *Landsbyer, gårde og social-struktur på den jyske vestkyst i la longue durée.* kuml 2020, 109-168.

Termansen, C.N. 1905: St. Klemens Kirke i Ribe. *Fra Ribe Amt* 1905, 1-14.

Terpager, P. 1702: *Inscriptiones Ripenses.* Hafniæ: Just Hög.

Terpager, P. 1736: *Ripæ Cimbricæ seu urbis Ripensis in Cimbria sitæ descriptio.* Flensburg: David Korte.

Thamdrup, K. 1998: Landskabet. In: S. Jensen ed. *Marsk, land og bebyggelse. Ribeegnen gennem 10.000 år,* vol. 1, Højbjerg: Jysk Arkæologisk Selskab, 33-42.

The Oxford Companion to Philosophy, 1995. Oxford: Oxford University Press.

Theuws 2004: Exchange, religion, identity and cen-tral places in the early Middle Ages. *Archaeological Dialogues,* vol. 10:2, 2004, 121-38.

Thomsen, T. 2005: Udgravningen – en kronolo-gisk gennemgang af de fysiske spor. In: Iversen, M., D. Robinson, J. Hjermind & C. Christensen eds. 2005: *Viborg Søndersø 1018-1030. Arkæologi og naturvidenskab i et værkstedsområde fra vikingetid.* Højbjerg: Jysk Arkæologisk Selskab, 61-82.

Thorup, P.N. 1833: *Efterretninger angaaende Byen Ribe.* Anden Samling. Udgivne som Indbydelsesskrift til den offentlige Examen i Ribe Cathedralskole 1833. Ribe: N.S. Hyphoff.

- 1835: *Efterretninger angaaende Byen Ribe.* Fjerde Sam-ling. Udgivne son Indbydelsesskrift til den offent-lige Examen i Ribe Cathedralskole 1835. Ribe: Chr. sal. Hyphoff

- 1839: *Efterretninger angaaende Byen Ribe.* Syvende Samling. Udgivne som Indbydelsesskrift til den offentlige Examen i Ribe Cathedralskole 1839. Ribe: Chr. sal. Hyphoff.

Thorvildsen, E. 1972: Dankirke. *Nationalmuseets Ar-bejdsmark* 1972, 47-60.

Ti byer. Diskussionsoplæg til mødet på Skarrildhus maj 1980. Stencil, Projekt Middelalderbyen.

Thaastrup-Leth, A. K. 2004: Trækirker i det mid-delalderlige Danmark indtil ca. 1100. Hvornår blev de bygget? In: N. Lund ed. *Kristendommen i Danmark før 1050.* Roskilde: Roskilde Museums Forlag, 207-214.

Trap, J.P. 1858-60: *Statistisk-topographisk Beskrivelse af Danmark.* København: C.E.C. Gad.

Trotzig, G. 2004: Trons försvarare i Birka. I: *Fornvän-nen* vol. 99, 2004/3, 197-208.

Tummuscheit. A. 2010: *Die Baubefunde des frühmitte-lalterlichen Seehandelsplatzes von Groß Strömkendorf, Lkr. Nordwestmecklenburg.* Forschungen zu Groß Strömkendorf IV. Wiesbaden: Reichert Verlag.

Ulriksen, J. 1998: *Anløbspladser. Besejling og bebyggelse i Danmark mellem 200 og 1100 e.Kr.:* en studie af søfartens pladser på baggrund af undersøgelser i Roskilde Fjord. Roskilde: Vikingeskibshallen.

- 2014: Find-rich settlements from the Late Iron Age and the Viking Age and their external contacts. In: E. Stidsing, K. Høilund Nielsen & R. Fiedel eds. *Wealth and Complexity. Economically specialized sites in Late Iron Age Denmark.* Aarhus: Aarhus University Press, 199-211.

Ulriksen, J., C. Krause & N.H. Jensen 2014: Roskilde – en bygrundlæggelse i vanskeligt terræn. *kuml* 2014, 145-185.

Varenius, B. 1994: The Hedeby Coinage. *Current Swedish Archaeology,* vol. 2, 1994, 185-193.

Vensild, H. 2004: *Bondegårde i Skast Herred 1636-1760.* Kerteminde; Brørup: Landbohistorisk Selskab; Historisk Samfund for Ribe Amt.

Villadsen, V. 1974: *Ribe Domkirke. Et motiv i dansk guldalderkunst.* Esbjerg: Historisk Samfund for Ribe Amt.

Vikingerne i Franken. Skriftlige kilder fra det 9. århundrede. Translated by Erling Albrechtsen. Odense: Odense University Press.

Vogel, Volker 1989: *Schleswig im Mittelalter. Archäologie einer Stadt.* Neumünster: Wachholtz.

Wamers, E. 1992: Ribes Gral. *By, marsk og geest* 4, 1991 (1992), 2-13.

- 1994: König im Grenzland. Neue Analyse der Bootkammergrab von Haithaby. *Acta Archaeologica* vol. 65, 1-56.

- 2007: Some remarks on the topography of Franconofurd. In: J. Henning ed. *Post Roman Towns, Trade and Settlement in Europe and Byzantium, vol. 1, The Heirs of the Roman West.* Berlin: Walter de Gryuter, 341-51.

Wickham, C. 2005: *Framing the Early Middle Ages.* Oxford: Oxford University Press.

Williams, G. 2007: Kingship, Christianity and Coinage. Monetary and Political Perspectives on Silver Economy in the Viking Age. In: J. Graham-Campbell & G. Williams eds. *Silver Economy in the Viking Age,* Walnut Creek, CA: Left Coast Press, 177-214.

- 2010: The Influence of Dorestad Coinage on Coin Design in England and Scandinavia. In: A. Willemsen & H. Kirk eds. *Dorestad in an International Framework.* Turnhout: Brepols, 105-111.

- 2011: Silver Economies, Monetisation and Society: An Overview. In: J. Graham-Campbell, S.M. Sindbæk & G. Williams eds. *Silver Economies, Monetisation and Society in Scandinavia AD 800-1100.* Aarhus: Aarhus University Press, 337-372.

Wilschewski, F. 1998: Die Befestigung des Bremer Bischofsitzes. Ein Rekonstruktionsvorschlag. *Bremer Archäologische Blätter* '96/97 (1998), 88-98.

Wimmer, L.F.A. 1897-1908: *De danske Runemindesmærker.* København: Gyldendal.

Wood, R. 2014: The pictures on the greater Jelling stone. *Danish Journal of Archaeology,* vol. 3 issue 1, 19-32.

Ørsnes, M. 1966: *Form og stil i Sydskandinaviens yngre germanske jernalder.* København: Nationalmuseet.

Østergaard Sørensen, P. 2010: The Political and religious Centre at Gudme on Funen in the late Roman and Germanic Iron Ages – Settlements and central halls. In: H. Jöns et al eds. *Herrenhöfe und die hierarchie der Macht im Raum südlich og östlich der Nordsee von der Vorrömischen Eisenzeit bis zum frühen Mittelalter und zur Wikingerzeit.* Siedlungs- und Küstenforschung im südlichen Nordseegebiet, vol. 33, Rahden: Verlag Marie Leidorf, 186-198.

Aaby, B. 1993: Pollenanalyser af de ældste kulturlag i Ribe. *By, marsk og geest* 5, 1992 (1993), 23-32.

Aakjær, S. 1952: Korntiende og kornareal i det 14. årh. *Historisk tidsskrift,* vol. 11:3 (1950-52), 176-209.

Notes

1. The Oxford Companion to Philosophy (1995), p. 637.
2. Biddle et al. 1983. Personal communication, Per Kristian Madsen.
3. A worker with this telling name was operative in the town and is known through a preserved bill of 1538. *Danmarks Kirker, Ribe amt,* p. 828 with references.
4. The pit was later dendro-dated to the period 1146-91 and the timber dendro-provenanced to France (Champagne/Burgundy), presumably from a wine cask. See Appendix 1, Dendrochronological dates from Ribe.
5. Personal communication, Per Kristian Madsen.
6. Taken from a letter of 16 July 1979 addressed to the State Museum Committee (translated). In the Museum of South-West Jutland archive.
7. When the ASR acronym was phased out in 2012 and replaced by an SJM acronym, ASR 15 was the last of the reserved numbers to have been used, while the ordinary series ran to ASR 2441.
8. Feveile and Jensen 2006a, p. 65. The removal of soil is implied indirectly by the distribution of both the modern disturbances (fig. 8.2) and the medieval structures (fig. 8.27).
9. It is strange, however, that Phase B is not subdivided in keeping with the distinctions seen in ASR 7. Phase B covers both the first phase, with irregular ditches, and the first regular plot-division.
10. Personal communication to Jakob Kieffer-Olsen from the Minister of Culture at the time, Brian Mikkelsen from the Conservative Party.
11. Personal communication, Museum Inspector Peter Vang Petersen, National Museum.
12. Personal communication from Lecturer Peder Gammeltoft, Department of Name Research, Copenhagen University.
13. Information in the Danmarks Stednavne ('Denmark's Place-names') database: *http://danmarksstednavne.navneforskning.ku.dk/*
14. Information in the Danmarks Stednavne database: *http://danmarksstednavne.navneforskning.ku.dk/*
15. Personal communication, Lecturer Peder Gammeltoft, Department of Name Research, Copenhagen Univeristy.
16. Personal communication, Niels Christian Nielsen, former owner of Roager Kloakservice.
17. Personal communication, former Museum Inspector Palle Siemen.
18. With annual level of sediment movement put at 12.5 cu m per sq km of the area of drainage. The Ribe River drains c. 940 sq km: 12.5x940x1000 = 11,750,000 cu m.
19. Mouldboard ploughmarks dated to the Viking Period or the earlier Middle Ages are, however, known from ASR 926 Ribelund I and at the base of moat B, ASR 8/SJM 348.
20. The street-facing part of an entire plot was excavated for the first time in 2017-18, as part of the Northern Emporium-project. On this plot, houses were present from the early 8th C. (Sindbæk ed. in prep).
21. Apart from a single dendro-date for a well, originally dated to *post-AD 770* but subsequently redated to *post-AD 1165*: Feveile 2006d; Daly 2007.
22. Feveile 2006j does not note this possibility; however the postulated course of the routeway is consistent with the area of destruction with no preserved pale sand.
23. This section is based to some extent upon Søvsø 2016.
24. From SJM 348 there are three sceattas, including one from a grave. A single coin was found in Dagmarsgade on the opposite side of the river in 2006, but in soil that had been moved from the north side of the river (ASR 2087x1). For the sake of completeness, it should also be recorded that the earliest coins from Ribe are three Roman bronze coins which were antiquities when they were brought to the town, and presumably were imported as scrap metal.

25. Except for a Maastricht sceatt from ASR 7, which was considerably older than the layer in which it was found (Bendixen 1994, p. 44 no. 7).

26. Pers. comm. from Dr Ralf Wiechmann, who is preparing a publication of the coin finds.

27. The heathen cemetery of Ribe is being studied and published by Sarah Croix as part of the project 'The Town of the Dead' (*Den Dødes By*) funded by the Research Committee of the Culture Ministry.

28. http://d.lib.rochester.edu/camelot/text/gerald-of-wales-arthurs-tomb (accessed 27 October 2017).

29. The figures are derived from physical anthropological reports produced by cand. scient. Dorthe Dangvard Pedersen and cand. scient. Helene Agerskov Madsen (Dangvard Pedersen 2009; Agerskov Madsen 2012).

30. 83 graves in 408 sq m = 0.2 per square metre.

31. Charcoal burials and graves with lime at the base that are known principally from eastern Danish contexts were not found in this excavation and apparently reflect Anglo-Saxon influence (M. Cinthio 2002, 52).

32. Strontium isotope studies carried out by Karin M. Frei.

33. Excluded from the table are clearly intrusive finds from the uppermost spits and the categories of fired clay, daub, two small pieces of copper alloy, and samples of charcoal and burnt bone. These categories of find have no analytical value in the immediate context.

34. The datings were carried out by Nationalmuseets Naturvideskabelige Undersøgelser, NNU. The reports can be accessed at *www.nnu.dk* .

35. ASR 13x434. Hermann (Billunger), Emden c. AD 1059-86, (Dannenberg 773).

36. Personal communication, Dr Ralf Wiechmann, Hamburg.

37. Personal communication, Lecturer Peder Gammeltoft, Department of Name Research, Copenhagen University. It is astonishing that the excavator, Johan Callmer, has not paid more attention to the place-name *Ripa*, but rather proposes *Transval* as the name of the Åhus II site. *Transval* measn 'on the other side of the moat' and refers to the medieval defences; certainly a later name than the site itself (Callmer 2002, 127).

38. Personal communication, PhD student Gitte Tarnow Ingvardson, on the basis of an extract from LUHM's coin database.

39. Radiocarbon dates from Hochburg, pers. comm. Dr Sven Kalmring.

40. H. Skov describes the first rampart around Aarhus as being provided with a timber-built, vertical face, but the archaeological evidence for this is not completely convincing (H. Skov 2008, 221). The dendro-dating to 'shortly after 957' does not stand up to required statistical probability and does not include any sapwood.

41. Pers. comm., Lecturer Peder Gammeltoft, Copenhagen University.

42. A man of news is suggested to mean 'a herald' or 'a messenger'. Quoted from the database *Danmarks Runeindskrifter*.

43. SB no. 130801-211.

Appendix
Dendrochronology in Ribe until 2015

Museum case no.	Site	Year	Lab.	Lab. Case no.	Sample name	Heart-wood	Sapwood	Wald-kante	Dating	"Secure dating"
ASR 33/63	Telefonhuset, Præstegade	1963	NNU	NNU j. nr. A7577	D1216	106	0	no	after c. 1145	yes
ASR 33/63	Telefonhuset, Præstegade	1963	NNU	NNU j. nr. A7577	D1216	132	0	no	after 1158	yes
ASR 33/63	Telefonhuset, Præstegade	1963	NNU	NNU j. nr. A7577	D1216	182	0	no	after 1153	yes
ASR 33/63	Telefonhuset, Præstegade	1963	NNU	NNU j. nr. A7577	D1216	136	0	no	after 1152	yes
ASR 33/63	Telefonhuset, Præstegade	1963	NNU	NNU j. nr. A7577	D1217	130	0	no	after 1143	yes
ASR 33/63	Telefonhuset, Præstegade	1963	NNU	NNU j. nr. A7577	D1217	176	0	no	after 1149	yes
ASR 33/63	Telefonhuset, Præstegade	1963	NNU	NNU j. nr. A7577	D1218	113	0	no	after 1151	yes
ASR 33/63	Telefonhuset, Præstegade	1963	NNU	NNU j. nr. A7577	D1218	147	0	no	after 1148	yes
ASR 33/63	Telefonhuset, Præstegade	1963	NNU	NNU j. nr. A7577	D1219	160	6	no	1146-1191	yes
ASR 7M70D	Dagmarsgade	1969	NNU	NM nat.vid. A5539	D305	107	15	no	c. 1186	?
ASR 7M70D	Dagmarsgade	1969	NNU	NM nat.vid. A5539	D308	87	40	yes?	1189	?
ASR 7M70D	Dagmarsgade	1969	NNU	NM nat.vid. A5539	D312	106	15	no	after 1123	?
ASR 7M70D	Dagmarsgade	1969	NNU	NM nat.vid. A5539	D313	152	0	no	after 1105	?
ASR 7M70D	Dagmarsgade	1969	NNU	NM nat.vid. A5539	D314	226	3	no	after 1158	?
ASR 7M70D	Dagmarsgade	1969	NNU	NM nat.vid. A5539	D315	195	0	no	after 1147	?
ASR 7M70D	Dagmarsgade	1969	NNU	NM nat.vid. A5539	D316	110	0	no	after 1134	?
ASR 7M70D	Dagmarsgade	1969	NNU	NM nat.vid. A5539	D317	100	0	no	after 1132	?
ASR 7M70D	Dagmarsgade	1969	NNU	NM nat.vid. A5539	D318	149	26	yes?	1167	?
ASR 7M70D	Dagmarsgade	1969	NNU	NM nat.vid. A5539	D319	103	21	yes?	1164	?
ASR 7M70D	Dagmarsgade	1969	NNU	NM nat.vid. A5539	D320	105	0	no	after 1133	?
ASR 7M70D	Dagmarsgade	1969	NNU	NM nat.vid. A5539	D321	83	15	no	c. 1168	?
ASR 6M73 Area 5	Kunstmuseets kælder	1973	NM	NM nat.vid. A5539	FØ, Mag. No. D566	93	0	no	after 658	yes
ASR 6M73 Area 5	Kunstmuseets kælder	1973	NM	NM nat.vid. A5539	DY, mag. No. D567	64	0	no		yes
ASR 6M73 Area 5	Kunstmuseets kælder	1973	NM	NM nat.vid. A5539	BZ, Mag. No. D568	112	17	no	c. 719	yes
ASR 6M73 Area 5	Kunstmuseets kælder	1973	NM	NM nat.vid. A5539	GC, Mag. no. D955	74	0	no	after 645	yes
ASR 6M73 Area 5	Kunstmuseets kælder	1973	NM	NM nat.vid. A5539	AB129, Mag. No. D565	84	0	no	after 759	yes
ASR 6M73 Area 5	Kunstmuseets kælder	1973	NM	NM nat.vid. A5539	AB183, Mag. No. D569	102	0	no	after 730	yes
ASR 5M74	Dommerhaven	1974	NM	NM nat.vid. A5820	PN, Mag. No. D715	182	0	no	after 688	yes
ASR 5M74	Dommerhaven	1974	NM	NM nat.vid. A5820	PP, Mag. No. D716	138	14	no	c. 704	yes
ASR 5M74	Dommerhaven	1974	NM	NM nat.vid. A5820	PR, mag. No. D717	c. 33	18-19	no	c. 696	yes
ASR 5M74	Dommerhaven	1974	NM	NM nat.vid. A5820	PS, mag. No. D718	39	16	no	c. 696	yes
ASR 5M74	Dommerhaven	1974	NM	NM nat.vid. A5820	PØ, mag. No. D719	175	0	no	after c. 707	yes
ASR 5M74	Dommerhaven	1974	NM	NM nat.vid. A5820	QH, Mag. No. D720	178	0	no	after 688	yes
ASR 5M74	Dommerhaven	1974	NM	NM nat.vid. A5820	OC, mag. No. D1038	149	0	no	after c. 707	yes
ASR 5M74	Dommerhaven	1974	NNU	NM nat.vid. A5820	D721	174	0	no	after 1175	?
ASR 4M75	Kunstmuseets have	1975	NM	NM nat.vid. A5820	KA, Mag. No. D767	58	11	no	not dated	
ASR 4M75	Kunstmuseets have	1975	NM	NM nat.vid. A5820	JÅ, Mag. No. D768	16	10-11	no	not dated	
ASR 8M75	Ribe Katedralskole	1977	Wormianum	Case no. 109	ASR8M75D	74	25	yes	1257	yes
ASR 8M79D	Gravsgade	1979	Wormianum	Case no. 47	AN 16				after 1502	?
ASR 8M79D	Gravsgade	1979	Wormianum	Case no. 47	AE 2	147	0	no	after 1604	yes
ASR 8M79D	Gravsgade	1979	Wormianum	Case no. 47	AE 6	68	9	no	after 1608	yes
ASR 8M79D	Gravsgade	1979	Wormianum	Case no. 47	AE 10		yes	no	after 1605	yes
ASR 8M79D	Gravsgade	1979	Wormianum	Case no. 47	AE 12		yes	no	after 1609	yes
ASR 2M80	Saltgade	1980	Wormianum	Case no. 80	2M80D Well A	116	0	no	after 1272	yes
ASDR16M80	Stampemøllen	1981	NNU	J. nr. A6461	Post from Stamping Mill	86	?	?	after 1614	
ASR1	Riberhus	1980	NNU	J. nr. A6461	From Riberhus	150	?	?	after 1175	
ASR 160	Tingslippe	1981	Wormianum	Case no. 109	ASR160	246	0	no	after 1233	yes
ASR 346	Grønnegade	1983	Wormianum	Case no. 151	ASR346x5	121	0	no	after 1196	yes
ASR 420	Badstuegade	1984	Wormianum	Case no. 168	A4	121	0	no	after 1159	yes
ASR 420	Badstuegade	1984	Wormianum	Case no. 168	A72	172	0	no	after 1097	yes

Museum case no.	Site	Year	Lab.	Lab. Case no.	Sample name	Heart-wood	Sapwood	Wald-kante	Dating	"Secure dating"
ASR 420	Badstuegade	1984	Wormianum	Case no. 168	A52	117	0	no	after 1160	yes
ASR 420	Badstuegade	1984	Wormianum	Case no. 168	A57	129	0	no	after 1149	yes
ASR 420	Badstuegade	1984	Wormianum	Case no. 168	A114	204	0	no	after 1170	yes
ASR 420	Badstuegade	1984	Wormianum	Case no. 168	A80	120	36	yes	1179	yes
ASR 420	Badstuegade	1984	Wormianum	Case no. 168	A113	164	0	no	after 1108	yes
ASR 420	Badstuegade	1984	Wormianum	Case no. 168	A61	153	0	no	after 1123	yes
ASR 420	Badstuegade	1984	Wormianum	Case no. 168	A140	236	0	no	after 1144	yes
ASR 233	Grønnegade 12	1985	Wormianum	Case no. 189	P1	168	0	no	after 1523	no
ASR 233	Grønnegade 12	1985	Wormianum	Case no. 189	P2	118	0	no	after 1495	no
ASR 503	Nederdammen 31	1987	Wormianum	Case no. 247	P4	98	16	no	c. 1489	yes
ASR 503	Nederdammen 31	1987	Wormianum	Case no. 247	P3	55	12	no	c. 1489	yes
ASR 503	Nederdammen 31	1987	Wormianum	Case no. 247	P2	45	22	no	c. 1486	yes
ASR 503	Nederdammen 31	1987	Wormianum	Case no. 247	P1	40	0	no	after 1455	yes
ASR 503	Nederdammen 31	1987	Wormianum	Case no. 247	P6	79	0	no	after 1452	yes
ASR 503	Nederdammen 31	1987	Wormianum	Case no. 247	P7	97	17	no	c. 1487	yes
ASR 548	Mellemdammen 18	1987	Wormianum	Case no. 247	p1	77	0	no	after 1454	yes
ASR 572	Badstuegade	1987	Wormianum	Case no. 294	ASR 572x1	87	49	yes	1137	yes
ASR 572	Badstuegade	1987	Wormianum	Case no. 294	ASR 572x2	90	0	no	after 1272	yes
ASR 572	Badstuegade	1987	Wormianum	Case no. 294	ASR 572x3	55	7	no	c. 1325	yes
ASR 778	Puggaardsgade	1989	Wormianum	Case no. 393	ASR478:1	76	15	no	c. 1190	yes
ASR 778	Puggaardsgade	1989	Wormianum	Case no. 393	ASR478:46	176	9	no	c. 1200	yes
ASR 778	Puggaardsgade	1989	Wormianum	Case no. 393	ASR478:20	59	30	yes	1196	yes
ASR 8	Rosen Allé	1989	Wormianum	Case no. 402	ASR8A351	123	15	no	c. 1359	yes
ASR 8	Rosen Allé	1989	Wormianum	Case no. 402	ASR8A513	151	0	no	after 1140	yes
ASR 8	Rosen Allé	1989	Wormianum	Case no. 402	ASR8A420	173	0	no	after 1163	yes
ASR 8	Rosen Allé	1989	Wormianum	Case no. 402	ASR8A357	161	0	no	after 1140	yes
ASR 8	Rosen Allé	1989	Wormianum	Case no. 402	ASR8A420	136	9	no	after 1144	yes
ASR 858	Riberhus	1990	Wormianum	Case no. 371	ASR 8637a	152	0	no	after 1115	yes
ASR 858	Riberhus	1990	Wormianum	Case no. 372	ASR 8637b	62	0	no	after 1127	yes
ASR 859	Sønderportsgade 21a	1990	Wormianum	Case no. 385	ASR 859b	151	16	no	c. 1574	yes
ASR 859	Sønderportsgade 21a	1990	Wormianum	Case no. 385	ASR 859c	51	26	yes	1579	yes
ASR 863	Seminarievej 4	1990	Wormianum	Case no. 425	ASR 863a	121	0	no	after 751	yes
ASR 863	Seminarievej 4	1990	Wormianum	Case no. 425	ASR 863b	107	0	no	after 749	yes
ASR 863	Seminarievej 4	1990	Wormianum	Case no. 425	ASR 863c	98	0	no	after 729	yes
ASR 863	Seminarievej 4	1990	Wormianum	Case no. 425	ASR 863d	101	0	no	after 731	yes
ASR 863	Seminarievej 4	1990	Wormianum	Case no. 425	ASR 863e	67	0	no	after 712	yes
ASR 926	Ribelund I	1990	Wormianum	Case no. 426	ASR 926x164	97	0	no	after 1157	yes
ASR 926	Ribelund I	1990	Wormianum	Case no. 426	ASR 926x164	101	0	no	after 1158	yes
ASR 926	Ribelund I	1990	Wormianum	Case no. 426	ASR 926x164	99	0	no	after 1159	yes
ASR 926	Ribelund I	1990	Wormianum	Case no. 426	ASR 926x164	89	0	no	after 1154	yes
ASR 926	Ribelund I	1990	Wormianum	Case no. 426	ASR 926x164	86	0	no	after 1159	yes
ASR 926	Ribelund I	1990	Wormianum	Case no. 426	ASR 926x164	69	0	no	after 1156	yes
ASR 926	Ribelund I	1990	Wormianum	Case no. 426	ASR 926x164	101	0	no	after 1148	yes
ASR 926	Ribelund I	1990	Wormianum	Case no. 426	ASR 926x164	98	0	no	after 1138	yes
ASR 926	Ribelund I	1990	Wormianum	Case no. 426	ASR 926x164	84	0	no	after 1154	yes
ASR 926	Ribelund I	1990	Wormianum	Case no. 426	ASR 926x164	84	0	no	after 1160	yes
ASR 926	Ribelund I	1990	Wormianum	Case no. 426	ASR 926x164	69	0	no	after 1162	yes
ASR 926	Ribelund I	1990	Wormianum	Case no. 426	ASR 926x164	58	0	no	after 1158	yes
ASR 926	Ribelund I	1990	Wormianum	Case no. 426	ASR 926x164	48	0	no	after 1163	yes
ASR 926	Ribelund I	1990	Wormianum	Case no. 426	ASR 926x164	62	0	no	after 1159	yes
ASR 941	Smalleslippe	1990	Wormianum	Case no. 431	ASR 941	218	4	no	c. 1180	yes
ASR 941	Smalleslippe	1990	Wormianum	Case no. 431	ASR 941	213	0	no	after 1169	yes
ASR 941	Smalleslippe	1990	Wormianum	Case no. 431	ASR 941	166	25	yes	1212	yes
ASR 9	Posthuset	1990-91	Wormianum	Case no. 432	ASR9P73	109	0	no	after 710	yes
ASR 9	Posthuset	1990-91	Wormianum	Case no. 432	ASR9P74	86	0	no	after 711	yes
ASR 9	Posthuset	1990-91	Wormianum	Case no. 432	ASR9P101	135	0	no	after 709	yes
ASR 9	Posthuset	1990-91	Wormianum	Case no. 432	ASR9P57	107	6	no	c. 730	yes
ASR 9	Posthuset	1990-91	Wormianum	Case no. 432	ASR9P63	84	12	no	c. 737	yes
ASR 9	Posthuset	1990-91	Wormianum	Case no. 432	ASR9P94	123	0	no	after 718	yes
ASR 9	Posthuset	1990-91	Wormianum	Case no. 432	ASR9P2	85	1	no	c. 708	yes
ASR 9	Posthuset	1990-91	Wormianum	Case no. 432	ASR9P4	155	22	?	c. 730	yes
ASR 9	Posthuset	1990-91	Wormianum	Case no. 432	ASR9P8	44	0	no	after 734	yes
ASR 9	Posthuset	1990-91	Wormianum	Case no. 432	ASR9P9	166	19	no	c. 728	no
ASR 9	Posthuset	1990-91	Wormianum	Case no. 432	ASR9P10	53	23	no	c. 710	yes
ASR 9	Posthuset	1990-91	Wormianum	Case no. 432	ASR9P13	150	23	yes	729/30	yes
ASR 9	Posthuset	1990-91	Wormianum	Case no. 432	ASR9P18	62	9	no	c. 722	yes
ASR 9	Posthuset	1990-91	Wormianum	Case no. 432	ASR9P24	74	0	no	after 704	yes
ASR 9	Posthuset	1990-91	Wormianum	Case no. 432	ASR9P25	164	5	no	c. 729	yes
ASR 9	Posthuset	1990-91	Wormianum	Case no. 432	ASR9P26	140	0	no	after 690	yes
ASR 9	Posthuset	1990-91	Wormianum	Case no. 432	ASR9P30	97	0	no	after 707	yes
ASR 9	Posthuset	1990-91	Wormianum	Case no. 432	ASR9P36	72	0	no	after 708	yes
ASR 9	Posthuset	1990-91	Wormianum	Case no. 432	ASR9P46	176	5	no	c. 741	yes
ASR 9	Posthuset	1990-91	Wormianum	Case no. 432	ASR9P47	101	0	no	after 729	yes
ASR 9	Posthuset	1990-91	Wormianum	Case no. 432	ASR9P80	136	0	no	after 712	yes

Museum case no.	Site	Year	Lab.	Lab. Case no.	Sample name	Heart-wood	Sapwood	Wald-kante	Dating	"Secure dating"
ASR 9	Posthuset	1990-91	Wormianum	Case no. 432	ASR9P81	123	0	no	after 694	yes
ASR 9	Posthuset	1990-91	Wormianum	Case no. 432	ASR9P33	131	16	no	c. 727	yes
ASR 9	Posthuset	1990-91	Wormianum	Case no. 432	ASR9P35	78	0	no	after 719	yes
ASR 9	Posthuset	1990-91	Wormianum	Case no. 432	ASR9P52	83	3	no	c. 726	yes
ASR 9	Posthuset	1990-91	Wormianum	Case no. 432	ASR9P53	155	0	no	after 719	yes
ASR 9	Posthuset	1990-91	Wormianum	Case no. 432	ASR9P54	170	0	no	after 607	yes
ASR 9	Posthuset	1990-91	Wormianum	Case no. 432	ASR9P40	69	0	no	after 708	yes
ASR 9	Posthuset	1990-91	Wormianum	Case no. 432	ASR9P95	71	17	no	c. 712	no
ASR 9	Posthuset	1990-91	Wormianum	Case no. 432	ASR9P98.1	154	0	no	after 695	yes
ASR 9	Posthuset	1990-91	Wormianum	Case no. 432	ASR9P98.2	63	0	no	after 695	yes
ASR 9	Posthuset	1990-91	Wormianum	Case no. 432	ASR9P102	64	15	no	c. 736	yes
ASR 949	Frislusen, Toldboden	1991	Wormianum	Case no. 433	nr 1	26	0	no	after 1396	no
ASR 949	Frislusen, Toldboden	1991	Wormianum	Case no. 433	nr 2	54	0	no	after 1426	no
ASR 949	Frislusen, Toldboden	1991	Wormianum	Case no. 433	nr 3	37	6	no	c. 1383	no
ASR 949	Frislusen, Toldboden	1991	Wormianum	Case no. 433	nr 8	142	0	no	after 1502	yes
ASR 949	Frislusen, Toldboden	1991	Wormianum	Case no. 433	nr 9	212	0	no	after 1582	yes
ASR 949	Frislusen, Toldboden	1991	Wormianum	Case no. 433	nr 6	75	4	no	c. 1524	yes
ASR 949	Frislusen, Toldboden	1991	Wormianum	Case no. 433	nr 4	142	14	no	c. 1340	yes
ASR 949	Frislusen, Toldboden	1991	Wormianum	Case no. 433	nr 7	42	0	no	after 1562	no
ASR 949	Frislusen, Toldboden	1991	Wormianum	Case no. 433	nr 10	79	0	no	after 1453	no
ASR 974	Sortebrødregade	1991	Wormianum	Case no. 534	ASR974P24	105	26	yes	1483?	no
ASR 990	Giørtzvej	1991	Wormianum	Case no. 398	ASR 990x4,1	264	0	no	after 716	yes
ASR 990	Giørtzvej	1991	Wormianum	Case no. 398	ASR 990x4,2	219	0	no	after 695	yes
ASR 990	Giørtzvej	1991	Wormianum	Case no. 398	ASR 990x6,1	246	0	no	after 701	yes
ASR 990	Giørtzvej	1991	Wormianum	Case no. 398	ASR 990x6,2	231	0	no	after 716	yes
ASR 990	Giørtzvej	1991	Wormianum	Case no. 398	ASR 990 fyld A7	75	0	no	after 854	?
ASR 1000	Ribelund II	1992	Wormianum	Case no. 531	ASR1000x68	213	20	no	c. 1229	yes
ASR 1015	Dagmargården	1993	Wormianum	Case no. 498	ASR1015x1556	159	0	no	after 1178	yes
ASR 1015	Dagmargården	1993	Wormianum	Case no. 575	x1268/8	199	0	no	after 1126	yes
ASR 1015	Dagmargården	1993	Wormianum	Case no. 575	X1268/11	177	0	no	after 1141	yes
ASR 1015	Dagmargården	1993	Wormianum	Case no. 575	x1268/10	242	0	no	after 1136	yes
ASR 1015	Dagmargården	1993	Wormianum	Case no. 575	x1268/2	94	0	no	after 1134	no
ASR 1015	Dagmargården	1993	Wormianum	Case no. 575	x1268/20	88	0	no	after 1133	no
ASR 1015	Dagmargården	1993	Wormianum	Case no. 575	x1268/1	71	0	no	after 1148	no
ASR 1025	Bispegade	1992	Wormianum	Case no. 501	ASR1025P15	178	24	no	c. 1208	yes
ASR 1025	Bispegade	1992	Wormianum	Case no. 501	ASR1025P14	101	30	?	c. 1238	yes
ASR 1070	Grønnegade	1993	Wormianum	Case no. 497	ASR1070P3	300	20	yes	1221/22	yes
ASR 1074	Korsbrødregade	1993	Wormianum	Case no. 499	ASR1074P1	136	28	yes	1177	yes
ASR 1108	Nederdammen	1994	Wormianum	Case no. 529	ASR1108P15	35	31	yes	1278/79	no
ASR 1108	Nederdammen	1994	Wormianum	Case no. 535	ASR1108P9	60	25	yes	1271/72	yes
ASR 1108	Nederdammen	1994	Wormianum	Case no. 535	ASR1108P11	167	0	no	after 1182	yes
ASR 1123	Vægtergade	1994	Wormianum	Case no. 534	ASR1123P1	163	29	no	c. 1238	yes
ASR 1124	Fiskergade 5	1994	Wormianum	Case no. 536	ASR1124p1	167	0	no	after 1512	yes
ASR 1124	Fiskergade 5	1994	Wormianum	Case no. 536	ASR1124p5	143	0	no	after 1528	yes
ASR 1124	Fiskergade 5	1994	Wormianum	Case no. 536	ASR1124p6	128	0	no	after 1510	yes
ASR 1150	Peppers	1995	Wormianum	Case no. 547	ASR1150A23	158	0	no	after 1098	yes
ASR 1152	Gråbrødregade	1995	Wormianum	Case no. 540	ASR1152A27	103	27	yes	1181	yes
ASR 1152	Gråbrødregade	1995	Wormianum	Case no. 540	ASR1152A11	110	17	yes	1223	yes
ASR 1152	Gråbrødregade	1995	Wormianum	Case no. 540	ASR1152A22	55	15	yes	1192	no
ASR 1158	Bispegade Skole	1996	Wormianum	Case nc. 555	ASR1158x49	41	12	yes	1490	no
ASR 1174	Over- og Mellemdammen	1996	Wormianum	Case nc. 552	ASR1174x34	123	0	no	after 1156	yes
ASR 1174	Over- og Mellemdammen	1996	Wormianum	Case no. 552	ASR1174x45	198	0	no	after 1185	yes
ASR 1174	Over- og Mellemdammen	1996	Wormianum	Case no. 552	ASR1174x55	119	0	no	after 1049	yes
ASR 1174	Over- og Mellemdammen	1996	Wormianum	Case no. 552	ASR1174x37	77	44	yes	1208	yes
ASR 1174	Over- og Mellemdammen	1996	Wormianum	Case no. 552	ASR1174x41	158	15	no	c. 1214	yes
ASR 1174	Over- og Mellemdammen	1996	Wormianum	Case no. 552	ASR1174x56	130	0	no	after 1088	yes
ASR 1174	Over- og Mellemdammen	1996	Wormianum	Case no. 552	ASR1174x30	39	15	yes	1223	yes
ASR 1174	Over- og Mellemdammen	1996	Wormianum	Case no. 552	ASR1174x33	207	0	no	after 1166	yes
ASR 1174	Over- og Mellemdammen	1996	Wormianum	Case no. 552	ASR1174x13	93	0	no	after 1326	yes
ASR 1174	Over- og Mellemdammen	1996	Wormianum	Case no. 552	ASR1174x20	193	0	no	after 1229	yes
ASR 1174	Over- og Mellemdammen	1996	Wormianum	Case no. 552	ASR1174x21	20	13	yes	1268	yes
ASR 1174	Over- og Mellemdammen	1996	Wormianum	Case no. 552	ASR1174x47	107	0	no	after 1459	no
ASR 1174	Over- og Mellemdammen	1996	Wormianum	Case no. 552	ASR1174x49	64	18	yes	1165	no
ASR 1174	Over- og Mellemdammen	1996	Wormianum	Case no. 552	ASR1174x14	45	10	no	c. 1317	no
ASR 1174	Over- og Mellemdammen	1996	Wormianum	Case no. 552	ASR1174x24	37	11	yes	1183	no
ASR 1174	Over- og Mellemdammen	1996	Wormianum	Case no. 552	ASR1174x26	30	17	yes	1079	no
ASR 1174	Over- og Mellemdammen	1996	Wormianum	Case no. 552	ASR1174x8	48	6	no	c. 1351	no
ASR 1174	Over- og Mellemdammen	1996	Wormianum	Case no. 552	ASR1174x12	67	12	yes	1301	no
ASR 1174	Over- og Mellemdammen	1996	Wormianum	Case no. 552	ASR1174x16	67	11	no	c. 1326	no
ASR 1165	Danielsen I, Nygade	1996	Wormianum	Case no. 571	ASR1165x170A264	120	22	yes	1141	yes
ASR 1188	Torvet 20	1996	Wormianum	Case no. 551	ASR1188x1	127	0	no	after 767	no
ASR 1200	Bakelitten, Slotsgade	1998	Wormianum	Case no. 570	ASR1200A3074	85	9	no	c. 1265	yes
ASR 1200	Bakelitten, Slotsgade	1998	Wormianum	Case no. 570	ASR1200A3074	127	2	no	c. 1273	yes
ASR 1200	Bakelitten, Slotsgade	1998	Wormianum	Case no. 570	ASR1200A3074	113	13	no	c. 1270	yes

Museum case no.	Site	Year	Lab.	Lab. Case no.	Sample name	Heart-wood	Sapwood	Wald-kante	Dating	"Secure dating"
ASR 1200	Bakelitten, Slotsgade	1998	Wormianum	Case no. 570	ASR1200A3074	75	15	no	c. 1272	yes
ASR 1200	Bakelitten, Slotsgade	1998	Wormianum	Case no. 570	ASR1200A3074	133	0	no	after 1256	yes
ASR 1200	Bakelitten, Slotsgade	1998	Wormianum	Case no. 570	ASR1200A3074	114	0	no	after 1258	yes
ASR 1200	Bakelitten, Slotsgade	1998	Wormianum	Case no. 570	ASR1200A1855	95	25	yes	1077	yes
ASR 1200	Bakelitten, Slotsgade	1998	Wormianum	Case no. 570	ASR1200A1855	77	22	yes	1077	yes
ASR 1200	Bakelitten, Slotsgade	1998	Wormianum	Case no. 570	ASR1200A1855	60	23	yes	1077	yes
ASR 1275	Præstegade	1998	Wormianum	Case no. 590	ASR1275A149	189	0	no	after 1163	
ASR 1275	Præstegade	1998	Wormianum	Case no. 590	ASR1275A153	114	0	no	after 1111	
ASR 1275	Præstegade	1998	Wormianum	Case no. 590	ASR1275A152	153	0	no	after 1114	
ASR 1275	Præstegade	1998	Wormianum	Case no. 590	ASR1275A150	133	0	no	after 1107	
ASR 1275	Præstegade	1998	Wormianum	Case no. 590	ASR1275A18	150	0	no	after 993	?
ASR 1275	Præstegade	1998	Wormianum	Case no. 590	ASR1275A8	108	25	yes	292	!!!
ASR 1275	Præstegade	1998	Wormianum	Case no. 590	ASR1275A14	129	0	no	after 1095	
ASR 1275	Præstegade	1998	Wormianum	Case no. 590	ASR1275A7	66	15	no	1164	
ASR 1275	Præstegade	1998	Wormianum	Case no. 590	ASR1275løsfund	126	0	no	after 1100	
ASR 1275	Præstegade	1998	Wormianum	Case no. 590	ASR1275A63	98	0	no	after 1053	
ASR 1275	Præstegade	1998	Wormianum	Case no. 590	ASR1275A85	231	5	no	1239-1263	
ASR 1289	Sct. Catharinæ Plads	1998	Wormianum	Case no. 578	ASR1289k3	113	20	yes	1194	yes
ASR 11	Danielsen II, Nygade	1999-2000	NNU	NNU A8135	ASR11A15244	61	51	yes	1207	yes
ASR 11	Danielsen II, Nygade	1999-2000	NNU	NNU A8135	ASR11A1394	63	21	yes	1175/76	yes
ASR 11	Danielsen II, Nygade	1999-2000	NNU	NNU A8135	ASR11A1711	43	24	no	c. 1134	yes
ASR 11	Danielsen II, Nygade	1999-2000	NNU	NNU A8135	ASR11A4159	174	51	yes	1314	yes
ASR 11	Danielsen II, Nygade	1999-2000	Wormianum	WM2241	ASR11A6215	102	0	no	after 1640	yes
ASR 11	Danielsen II, Nygade	1999-2000	Wormianum	WM2241	ASR11A7333	150	35	no	c. 1543	yes
ASR 11	Danielsen II, Nygade	1999-2000	Dendro.dk	G001	ASR	?	yes	no	1210-30	
ASR 11	Danielsen II, Nygade	1999-2000	Dendro.dk	G002	ASR	59	?	no	1210-30	yes
ASR 1357	Giørtzvej	2000	NNU	NNU A8135	ASR 1357A159	174	0	no	c. 712	yes
ASR 1357	Giørtzvej	2000	NNU	NNU A8135	ASR 1357A159	165	2	no	c. 712	yes
ASR 1357	Giørtzvej	2000	NNU	NNU A8135	ASR 1357A159	139	0	no	after 654	yes
ASR 1357	Giørtzvej	2000	NNU	NNU A8135	ASR1357A52b	106	0	no	after 1335	yes
ASR 1445	Sviegade, Katedralskolen	2002	Wormianum	Case no. 020718/2005	ASR1445A153X158	101	5	no	c. 1318	?
ASR 1445	Sviegade, Katedralskolen	2002	Wormianum	Case no. 020718/2005	ASR1445A153x158	111	9	no	c. 1325	
ASR 1445	Sviegade, Katedralskolen	2002	Wormianum	Case no. 020718/2005	ASR1445A152x157	52	10	no	c. 1287	
ASR 1843	Sønderportsgade	2004	Wormianum	Case no. 2072	ASR1843A34x9	212	15	no	c. 1168	yes
ASR 1843	Sønderportsgade	2004	Wormianum	Case no. 2072	ASR1843A25x21	100	3	no	c. 1122	yes
ASR 1843	Sønderportsgade	2004	Wormianum	Case no. 2072	ASR1843A26x1	32	19	yes	1182	yes
ASR 1843	Sønderportsgade	2004	Wormianum	Case no. 2072	ASR1843A125x105	36	10	no	c. 1106	no
ASR 1843	Sønderportsgade	2004	Wormianum	Case no. 2072	ASR1843A89x37	89	17	yes	1165	yes
ASR 1843	Sønderportsgade	2004	Wormianum	Case no. 2072	ASR1843A145x75	133	25	yes	1184	yes
ASR 1843	Sønderportsgade	2004	Wormianum	Case no. 2072	ASR1843A111xX134	168	51	yes	1186	yes
ASR 1843	Sønderportsgade	2004	Wormianum	Case no. 2072	ASR1843A69x32	36	23	yes	1252	no
ASR 1843	Sønderportsgade	2004	Wormianum	Case no. 2072	ASR1843A70X28	129	34	yes	1186	yes
ASR 1843	Sønderportsgade	2004	Wormianum	Case no. 2072	ASR1843A77x27	80	36	yes	1231	yes
ASR 1843	Sønderportsgade	2004	Wormianum	Case no. 2072	ASR1843A200x241	135	c. 66	yes	1184-86	yes
ASR 1843	Sønderportsgade	2004	Wormianum	Case no. 2072	ASR1843A146x74	163	15	no	c. 1163	yes
ASR 1843	Sønderportsgade	2004	Wormianum	Case no. 2072	ASR1843A125x106	88	0	no	after 1081	yes
ASR 1843	Sønderportsgade	2004	Wormianum	Case no. 2072	ASR1843A111x140	83	0	no	after 1116	no
ASR 1843	Sønderportsgade	2004	Wormianum	Case no. 2072	ASR1843A191x219	125	0	no	after 1168	yes
ASR 1843	Sønderportsgade	2004	Wormianum	Case no. 2072	ASR1843A156x139	38	23	yes	1186	yes
ASR 1843	Sønderportsgade	2004	Wormianum	Case no. 2072	ASR1843A111x138	197	25	yes	1188	yes
ASR 1843	Sønderportsgade	2004	Wormianum	Case no. 2072	ASR1843x220	82	13	yes	1194	yes
ASR 1843	Sønderportsgade	2004	Wormianum	Case no. 2072	ASR1843A114x135	45	13	yes	1253?	no
ASR 1843	Sønderportsgade	2004	Wormianum	Case no. 2072	ASR1843A87x137	41	29	yes	1232	yes
ASR 1843	Sønderportsgade	2004	Wormianum	Case no. 2072	ASR1843A29x8	127	0	no	after 1107	yes
ASR 1843	Sønderportsgade	2004	Wormianum	Case no. 2072	ASR1843A111x132	118	29	yes	1192	yes
ASR 1843	Sønderportsgade	2004	Wormianum	Case no. 2072	ASR1843A155x136	70	46	yes	1232	yes
ASR 1843	Sønderportsgade	2004	Wormianum	Case no. 2072	ASR1843A65x22	58	20	yes	1229	yes
ASR 2088	Sct. Catharinæ Plads	2005	Wormianum	Case no. 2188	ASR2088P1	180	1		1208-1233	yes
ASR 2088	Sct. Catharinæ Plads	2005	Wormianum	Case no. 2188	ASR2088P7	78	0		after 1093	yes
ASR 2088	Sct. Catharinæ Plads	2005	Wormianum	Case no. 2188	ASR2088P4	118	1		1140-1158	yes
ASR 2088	Sct. Catharinæ Plads	2005	Wormianum	Case no. 2188	ASR2088P5a	115	0		after 1082	yes
ASR 2088	Sct. Catharinæ Plads	2005	Wormianum	Case no. 2188	ASR2088P5b	81	0		after 1140	yes
ASR 2088	Sct. Catharinæ Plads	2005	Wormianum	Case no. 2188	ASR2088P6	140	1		1176-1200	yes
ASR 2088	Sct. Catharinæ Plads	2005	Wormianum	Case no. 2188	ASR2088P3	153	7		1166-1187	yes

Museum case no.	Site	Year	Lab.	Lab. Case no.	Sample name	Heart-wood	Sapwood	Wald-kante	Dating	"Secure dating"
ASR 2088	Sct. Catharinæ Plads	2005	Wormianum	Case no. 2188	ASR2088P2	219	3		1164-1179	yes
ASR 2089	Dagmarsgade	2005	Wormianum	Case no. 2118	ASR2089P1	158	0	no	after 1079	yes
ASR 2089	Dagmarsgade	2005	Wormianum	Case no. 2118	ASR2089P2	95	16	?	c. 1150	yes
ASR 2089	Dagmarsgade	2005	Wormianum	Case no. 2118	ASR2089P4	131	0	no	after 1086	yes
ASR 2089	Dagmarsgade	2005	Wormianum	Case no. 2118	ASR2089P6	172	9	no	c. 1127	yes
ASR 2089	Dagmarsgade	2005	Wormianum	Case no. 2118	ASR2089P7	109	0	no	after 1094	yes
ASR 2089	Dagmarsgade	2005	Wormianum	Case no. 2118	ASR2089P8	95	14	no	c. 1140	yes
ASR 2089	Dagmarsgade	2005	Wormianum	Case no. 2118	ASR2089P9	120	0	no	after 1106	yes
ASR 2089	Dagmarsgade	2005	Wormianum	Case no. 2118	ASR2089P11a	110	0	no	after 1175	no
ASR 2089	Dagmarsgade	2005	Wormianum	Case no. 2118	ASR2089P11b	69	0	no	after 1103?	no
ASR 2090	von Støckens Plads	2005	Wormianum	Case no. 2188	ASR2090P4	92	1		1116-1135	yes
ASR 2090	von Støckens Plads	2005	Wormianum	Case no. 2188	ASR2090P3	132	1		1089-1110	yes
ASR 2090	von Støckens Plads	2005	Wormianum	Case no. 2188	ASR2090P2	125	1		1104-24	yes
ASR 2090	von Støckens Plads	2005	Wormianum	Case no. 2188	ASR2090P6	181	0		after 1153	no
ASR 2090	von Støckens Plads	2005	Wormianum	Case no. 2188	ASR2090P10	111	0		after 1143	yes
ASR 2090	von Støckens Plads	2005	Wormianum	Case no. 2188	ASR2090P7	137	0		after 1105	yes
ASR 2090	von Støckens Plads	2005	Wormianum	Case no. 2188	ASR2090P8	86	10		1079-1101	yes
ASR 2090	von Støckens Plads	2005	Wormianum	Case no. 2188	ADR2090P1	73	9		1075-1089	yes
ASR 2090	von Støckens Plads	2005	Wormianum	Case no. 2188	ASR2090P9	122	0		after 1087	yes
ASR 2090	von Støckens Plads	2005	Wormianum	Case no. 2188	ASR2090P11	84	0		after 1066	yes
ASR 2090	von Støckens Plads	2005	Wormianum	Case no. 2188	ASR2090P5	235	10		1243-1269	yes
ASR 2162	Hundegade	2006	Wormianum	Case no. 2169	ASR2162P2	124	0	no	after 1142	yes
ASR 2360	Sct. Nicolaj Gade	2011	NNU	J. nr. A5820	ASR2360P7	121	16	no	c. 775	yes
SJM 126	Riberhus' tilløbskanal	2012	NNU	J. nr. A6461	SJM126P1	89	18	no	c. 1260	yes
SJM 126	Riberhus' tilløbskanal	2012	NNU	J. nr. A6461	SJM126P2	88	20	yes	1268/69	yes
SJM 126	Riberhus' tilløbskanal	2012	NNU	J. nr. A6461	SJM126P3	79	30	yes	1268/69	yes
ASR13	Lindegården	2008-12	NNU	J. nr. A8820	ASR13P14	109	0	no	after 1037	yes
ASR13	Lindegården	2008-12	NNU	J. nr. A8820	ASR13P16	122	20	yes?	1077?	yes
ASR13	Lindegården	2008-12	NNU	J. nr. A8820	ASR13P17	45	0	no	after 1039	yes
ASR13	Lindegården	2008-12	NNU	J. nr. A8820	ASR13P19	58	0	no	after 1048	yes
ASR13	Lindegården	2008-12	NNU	J. nr. A8820	ASR13P20	110	18	no	1077-89	yes
ASR13	Lindegården	2008-12	NNU	J. nr. A8820	ASR13P32	86	0	no	after 1593	
ASR13	Lindegården	2008-12	NNU	J. nr. A8820	ASR13P35	75	22	no	1248-55	yes
ASR13	Lindegården	2008-12	NNU	J. nr. A8820	ASR13P58	171	0	no	after 1298	yes
ASR13	Lindegården	2008-12	NNU	J. nr. A8820	ASR13P61	163	0	no	after 1112	yes
ASR 13 II	Lindegården	2012	NNU	J. nr. A8820	ASR13P79	98	0	no	after c. 1187	yes
ASR 13 II	Lindegården	2012	NNU	J. Nr. A8820	ASR13P81	110	0	no	after c. 1097	yes
ASR 13 II	Lindegården	2012	NNU	J. Nr. A8820	ASR13P82	107	0	no	after c. 1094	yes
ASR 13 II	Lindegården	2012	NNU	J. Nr. A8820	ASR13P86	92	0	no	after c. 1101	yes
ASR 13 II	Lindegården	2012	NNU	J. Nr. A8820	ASR13P87	151	0	no	after c. 1150	yes
ASR 13 II	Lindegården	2012	NNU	J. Nr. A8820	ASR13P80	95	0	no	after c. 1168	yes
ASR 13 II	Lindegården	2012	NNU	J. Nr. A8820	ASR13P89	70	0	no	after c. 1077	yes
ASR 13 II	Lindegården	2012	NNU	J. Nr. A8820	ASR13P111a	57	10	no	c. 1399	yes
ASR 13 II	Lindegården	2012	NNU	J. Nr. A8820	1323-1390	57	11	no	c. 1399	yes
ASR 13 II	Lindegården	2012	NNU	J. Nr. A8820	ASR13P122a	45	0	no	after c. 1045	yes
ASR 13 II	Lindegården	2012	NNU	J. Nr. A8820	ASR13P122b	53	0	no	after c. 1041	yes
ASR 13 II	Lindegården	2012	NNU	J. Nr. A8820	ASR13P122b	36	0	no	after c. 1026	yes
ASR 13 II	Lindegården	2012	NNU	J. Nr. A8820	ASR13P127	59	0	no	after c. 1106	yes
ASR 13 II	Lindegården	2012	NNU	J. Nr. A8820	ASR13P128	320	3	no	c. 1174	yes
ASR 13 II	Lindegården	2012	NNU	J. Nr. A8820	ASR13P130	159	0	no	after c. 1185	yes
ASR 13 II	Lindegården	2012	NNU	J. Nr. A8820	ASR13P131	94	0	no	after c. 1122	yes
ASR 13 II	Lindegården	2012	NNU	J. Nr. A8820	ASR13P133	111	0	no	after 1080	yes
ASR 13 II	Lindegården	2012	NNU	J. Nr. A8820	ASR13P134	138	0	no	after 1080	yes
ASR 13 II	Lindegården	2012	NNU	J. Nr. A8820	ASR13P135	99	7	no	c. 1611	yes
ASR 13 II	Lindegården	2012	NNU	J. Nr. A8820	ASR13P138	95	7	no	c. 1168	yes
ASR 13 II	Lindegården	2012	NNU	J. Nr. A8820	ASR13P149	115	25	no	1354/55	yes
ASR 13 II	Lindegården	2012	NNU	J. Nr. A8820	ASR13P150	46	23	no	1354/55	yes
ASR 13 II	Lindegården	2012	NNU	J. Nr. A8820	ASR13P151	76	23	no	1354/55	yes
ASR 2391	Ribe Domkirkeplads	2012	NNU	NNU J. nr 9130	ASR2391P 1	42	19	yes	1255/56	
ASR 2391	Ribe Domkirkeplads	2012	NNU	NNU J. nr 9130	ASR2391P 2	159	36	yes	1180	
ASR 2391	Ribe Domkirkeplads	2012	NNU	NNU J. nr 9130	ASR2391P 3	130	26	yes	1149	
ASR 2391	Ribe Domkirkeplads	2012	NNU	NNU J. nr 9130	ASR2391P 4	138	23	yes	1243	
ASR 2391	Ribe Domkirkeplads	2012	NNU	NNU J. nr 9130	ASR2391P 11	260	2		c. 1205	
ASR 2391	Ribe Domkirkeplads	2012	NNU	NNU J. nr 9130	ASR2391P 18	32	14	yes	1255/56	
ASR 2391	Ribe Domkirkeplads	2012	NNU	NNU J. nr 9130	ASR2391P 19	213	28	yes	1249/50	
ASR 2391	Ribe Domkirkeplads	2012	NNU	NNU J. nr 9130	ASR2391P 21	50	18	yes	1255/56	
ASR 2391	Ribe Domkirkeplads	2012	NNU	NNU J. nr 9130	ASR2391P 22	62	23	yes	1255/56	
ASR 2391	Ribe Domkirkeplads	2012	NNU	NNU J. nr 9130	ASR2391P 23	60	24		c. 1255	
ASR 2391	Ribe Domkirkeplads	2012	NNU	NNU J. nr 9130	ASR2391P 24	64	18	yes	1255/56	
ASR 2391	Ribe Domkirkeplads	2012	NNU	NNU J. nr 9130	ASR2391P 25	78	20	yes	1255/56	
ASR 2391	Ribe Domkirkeplads	2012	NNU	NNU J. nr 9130	ASR2391P 26	85	17	yes	1255/56	
ASR 2391	Ribe Domkirkeplads	2012	NNU	NNU J. nr 9130	ASR2391P 27	75	17	yes	1255/56	
ASR 2391	Ribe Domkirkeplads	2012	NNU	NNU J. nr 9130	ASR2391P 28	23	16	yes	1255/56	
ASR 2391	Ribe Domkirkeplads	2012	NNU	NNU J. nr 9130	ASR2391P 29	50	34	yes	1255/56	

Museum case no.	Site	Year	Lab.	Lab. Case no.	Sample name	Heart-wood	Sapwood	Wald-kante	Dating	"Secure dating"
ASR 2391	Ribe Domkirkeplads	2012	NNU	NNU J. nr 9130	ASR2391P 30	45	35	yes	1255/56	
ASR 2391	Ribe Domkirkeplads	2012	NNU	NNU J. nr 9130	ASR2391P 31	59	23	yes	1255/56	
ASR 2391	Ribe Domkirkeplads	2012	NNU	NNU J. nr 9130	ASR2391P 32	87	15	yes	1255/56	
ASR 2391	Ribe Domkirkeplads	2012	NNU	NNU J. nr 9130	ASR2391P 33	42	18	yes	1255/56	
ASR 2391	Ribe Domkirkeplads	2012	NNU	NNU J. nr 9130	ASR2391P 35	94	13		c. 1261	
ASR 2391	Ribe Domkirkeplads	2012	NNU	NNU J. nr 9130	ASR2391P 36	75	1		c. 1259	
ASR 2391	Ribe Domkirkeplads	2012	NNU	NNU J. nr 9130	ASR2391P 37	39	7		c. 1264	
ASR 2391	Ribe Domkirkeplads	2012	NNU	NNU J. nr 9130	ASR2391P 39	149	0		after c. 1224	
ASR 2391	Ribe Domkirkeplads	2012	NNU	NNU J. nr 9130	ASR2391P 40	146	0		after c. 1164	
ASR 2391	Ribe Domkirkeplads	2012	NNU	NNU J. nr 9130	ASR2391P 41	50	0		after c. 1212	
ASR 2391	Ribe Domkirkeplads	2012	NNU	NNU J. nr 9130	ASR2391P 42	27	15	yes	1255/56	
ASR 2391	Ribe Domkirkeplads	2012	NNU	NNU J. nr 9130	ASR2391P 43	173	18	yes	1251/52	
ASR 2391	Ribe Domkirkeplads	2012	NNU	NNU J. nr 9130	ASR2391P 44	32	11	yes	1255/56	
ASR 2391	Ribe Domkirkeplads	2012	NNU	NNU J. nr 9130	ASR2391P 45	26	8		c. 1265	
ASR 2391	Ribe Domkirkeplads	2012	NNU	NNU J. nr 9130	ASR2391P 46	38	13	yes	1255/56	
ASR 2391	Ribe Domkirkeplads	2012	NNU	NNU J. nr 9130	ASR2391P 47	101	20	yes	1246/47	
ASR 2391	Ribe Domkirkeplads	2012	NNU	NNU J. nr 9130	ASR2391P 48	195	0		after c. 1134	
ASR 2391	Ribe Domkirkeplads	2012	NNU	NNU J. nr 9130	ASR2391P 49	110	17		c. 1253	
ASR 2391	Ribe Domkirkeplads	2012	NNU	NNU J. nr 9130	ASR2391P 51	57	24	yes	1243/44	
ASR 2391	Ribe Domkirkeplads	2012	NNU	NNU J. nr 9130	ASR2391P 52	201	5		c. 1111	
ASR 2391	Ribe Domkirkeplads	2012	NNU	NNU J. nr 9130	ASR2391P 53	110	0		after c. 1135	
ASR 2391	Ribe Domkirkeplads	2012	NNU	NNU J. nr 9130	ASR2391P 58	120	0		after c. 1107	
ASR 2391	Ribe Domkirkeplads	2012	NNU	NNU J. nr 9130	ASR2391P 59	129	6		c. 1147	
ASR 2391	Ribe Domkirkeplads	2012	NNU	NNU J. nr 9130	ASR2391P 60	170	0		after c. 1150	
ASR 2391	Ribe Domkirkeplads	2012	NNU	NNU J. nr 9130	ASR2391P 62	75	0		after c. 1114	
ASR 2391	Ribe Domkirkeplads	2012	NNU	NNU J. nr 9130	ASR2391P 64	60	0		after c. 1043	
ASR 2391	Ribe Domkirkeplads	2012	NNU	NNU J. nr 9130	ASR2391P 65	46	0		after c. 1028	
ASR 2391	Ribe Domkirkeplads	2012	NNU	NNU J. nr 9130	ASR2391P 66	230	0		after c. 1189	
ASR 2391	Ribe Domkirkeplads	2012	NNU	NNU J. nr 9130	ASR2391P 67	125	0		after c. 1135	
ASR 2391	Ribe Domkirkeplads	2012	NNU	NNU J. nr 9130	ASR2391P 68	168	0		after c. 1160	
ASR 2391	Ribe Domkirkeplads	2014	NNU	J. nr. A9130	ASR2391P54	142	3	no	1100-15	yes
ASR 2391	Ribe Domkirkeplads	2014	NNU	J. nr. A9130	ASR2391P56	70	0	no	after 1029	yes
ASR 2391	Ribe Domkirkeplads	2014	NNU	J. nr. A9130	ASR2391P70	105	0	no	after 1118	yes
ASR 2391	Ribe Domkirkeplads	2014	NNU	J. nr. A9130	ASR2391P71	141	1	no	1154-69	yes
ASR 2391	Ribe Domkirkeplads	2014	NNU	J. nr. A9130	ASR2391P72	46	16	yes	1037	yes
ASR 2391	Ribe Domkirkeplads	2014	NNU	J. nr. A9130	ASR2391P73	160	14	yes	1195	yes
ASR 2391	Ribe Domkirkeplads	2014	NNU	J. nr. A9130	ASR2391P74	236	15	yes?	1188	yes
ASR 2391	Ribe Domkirkeplads	2014	NNU	J. nr. A9130	ASR2391P75	112	36	yes?	1184	yes
ASR 2391	Ribe Domkirkeplads	2014	NNU	J. nr. A9130	ASR2391P77	76	11	yes	1318	yes
ASR 2391	Ribe Domkirkeplads	2014	NNU	J. nr. A9130	ASR2391P78	57	16	yes	1326	yes
ASR 2391	Ribe Domkirkeplads	2014	NNU	J. nr. A9130	ASR2391P79	76	0	no	after 1090	yes
ASR 2391	Ribe Domkirkeplads	2014	NNU	J. nr. A9130	ASR2391P80	75	0	no	after 1110	yes
ASR 2391	Ribe Domkirkeplads	2014	NNU	J. nr. A9130	ASR2391P82	27	15	yes	1227	yes
ASR 2391	Ribe Domkirkeplads	2014	NNU	J. nr. A9130	ASR2391P85	213	0	no	after 1157	yes
ASR 2391	Ribe Domkirkeplads	2014	NNU	J. nr. A9130	ASR2391P86	128	34	yes	1197	yes
ASR 2391	Ribe Domkirkeplads	2014	NNU	J. nr. A9130	ASR2391P88	174	11	no	1171-86	yes
ASR 2391	Ribe Domkirkeplads	2014	NNU	J. nr. A9130	ASR2391P89	87	1?	no	1033-48?	yes
ASR 2391	Ribe Domkirkeplads	2014	NNU	J. nr. A9130	ASR2391P90	89	1?	no	1041-56?	yes
ASR 2391	Ribe Domkirkeplads	2014	NNU	J. nr. A9130	ASR2391P91	63	18	yes	1196	yes
ASR 2391	Ribe Domkirkeplads	2014	NNU	J. nr. A9130	ASR2391P97	81	14	yes	1066	yes
ASR 2391	Ribe Domkirkeplads	2014	NNU	J. nr. A9130	ASR2391P110	163	1?	no	1095-1110?	yes
ASR 2391	Ribe Domkirkeplads	2014	NNU	J. nr. A9130	ASR2391P114	232	0	no	after 1111	yes
ASR 2391	Ribe Domkirkeplads	2014	NNU	J. nr. A9130	ASR2391P115	173	0	no	after 1186	yes
ASR 2391	Ribe Domkirkeplads	2014	NNU	J. nr. A9130	ASR2391P116	186	1?	no	1203-18?	yes
ASR 2391	Ribe Domkirkeplads	2014	NNU	J. nr. A9130	ASR2391P117	67	16	no	1076-90	yes
ASR 2391	Ribe Domkirkeplads	2014	NNU	J. nr. A9130	ASR2391P118	155	0	no	after 12??	yes
ASR 2391	Ribe Domkirkeplads	2014	NNU	J. nr. A9130	ASR2391P119	170	9	no	1128-43	yes
ASR 2391	Ribe Domkirkeplads	2014	NNU	J. nr. A9130	ASR2391P120	186	1	no	1184-99	yes
ASR 2391	Ribe Domkirkeplads	2014	NNU	J. nr. A9130	ASR2391P121	207	1	no	1185-1200	yes
ASR 2391	Ribe Domkirkeplads	2014	NNU	J. nr. A9130	ASR2391P122	135	0	no	after 1105	yes
ASR 2391	Ribe Domkirkeplads	2014	NNU	J. nr. A9130	ASR2391P124	168	16	yes	1196	yes
ASR 2391	Ribe Domkirkeplads	2014	NNU	J. nr. A9130	ASR2391P125	134	0	no	after 1154	yes
ASR 2391	Ribe Domkirkeplads	2014	NNU	J. nr. A9130	ASR2391P126	182	0	yes?	1205?	yes
ASR 2391	Ribe Domkirkeplads	2014	NNU	J. nr. A9130	ASR2391P127	180	0	yes?	1234?	yes
ASR 2391	Ribe Domkirkeplads	2014	NNU	J. nr. A9130	ASR2391P128	102	0	no	after 1111	yes
ASR 2391	Ribe Domkirkeplads	2014	NNU	J. nr. A9130	ASR2391P130	169	0	no	after 1224	yes
ASR 2391	Ribe Domkirkeplads	2014	NNU	J. nr. A9130	ASR2391P132	161	0	yes	1235	yes
ASR 2391	Ribe Domkirkeplads	2014	NNU	J. nr. A9130	ASR2391P101	211	10	no	1350-65	yes
SJM 348	Rosen Allé	2014	NNU						1175-85	yes
SJM 501	Tvedgade	2015	NNU	A9380	SJM501P1	75	10	no	c. 1840	yes

Plate 1

Riberhus

ASR 1

Hovedengen

ASR

Sct. Pede

Erik Menveds vej

Ribe Vesterå

Skibbroen

Slotsgade

Sct. Clemens Gade

ASR 1200

Grønnegade

Fiskergade

Ne

Kongensgade

Sct. Laurentii Gade

Korsbrødregade

Præstegade

ASR 52/64

Overdammen

Mellemdammen

NM 1911

ASR 1015

Grydergade

ASR 2391

Stenbogade

Sortebrødregade

Albert Skeels Gade

Nygade

Gråbrødregade

ASR 13

Badstuega

Skovgade

ASR 11

Sønderportsgade

Hundegade

Klostergade

Stampemøllestrømmen

Sviegade

Puggaardsgade

Bispegade

Gravsgade

0   200 m